T0180107

IFIP Advances in Information and Communication Technology 386

IFIP – The International Federation for Information Processing

IFIP was founded in 1960 under the auspices of UNESCO, following the First World Computer Congress held in Paris the previous year. An umbrella organization for societies working in information processing, IFIP's aim is two-fold: to support information processing within its member countries and to encourage technology transfer to developing nations. As its mission statement clearly states,

> *IFIP's mission is to be the leading, truly international, apolitical organization which encourages and assists in the development, exploitation and application of information technology for the benefit of all people.*

IFIP is a non-profitmaking organization, run almost solely by 2500 volunteers. It operates through a number of technical committees, which organize events and publications. IFIP's events range from an international congress to local seminars, but the most important are:

- The IFIP World Computer Congress, held every second year;
- Open conferences;
- Working conferences.

The flagship event is the IFIP World Computer Congress, at which both invited and contributed papers are presented. Contributed papers are rigorously refereed and the rejection rate is high.

As with the Congress, participation in the open conferences is open to all and papers may be invited or submitted. Again, submitted papers are stringently refereed.

The working conferences are structured differently. They are usually run by a working group and attendance is small and by invitation only. Their purpose is to create an atmosphere conducive to innovation and development. Refereeing is also rigorous and papers are subjected to extensive group discussion.

Publications arising from IFIP events vary. The papers presented at the IFIP World Computer Congress and at open conferences are published as conference proceedings, while the results of the working conferences are often published as collections of selected and edited papers.

Any national society whose primary activity is about information processing may apply to become a full member of IFIP, although full membership is restricted to one society per country. Full members are entitled to vote at the annual General Assembly, National societies preferring a less committed involvement may apply for associate or corresponding membership. Associate members enjoy the same benefits as full members, but without voting rights. Corresponding members are not represented in IFIP bodies. Affiliated membership is open to non-national societies, and individual and honorary membership schemes are also offered.

Magda David Hercheui   Diane Whitehouse
William McIver Jr.   Jackie Phahlamohlaka (Eds.)

ICT
Critical Infrastructures
and Society

10th IFIP TC 9 International Conference
on Human Choice and Computers, HCC10 2012
Amsterdam, The Netherlands, September 27-28, 2012
Proceedings

 Springer

Volume Editors

Magda David Hercheui
Westminster Business School
35 Marylebone Road, London, NW1 5LS, UK
E-mail: m.hercheui@westminster.ac.uk

Diane Whitehouse
The Castlegate Consultancy
27 Castlegate, Malton, YO17 7DP, UK
E-mail: diane.whitehouse@thecastlegateconsultancy.com

William McIver Jr.
University of New Brunswick, Faculty of Computer Science
Fredericton, NB, E3B 5A3, Canada
E-mail: wmciver@acm.org

Jackie Phahlamohlaka
Council for Scientific and Industrial Research (CSIR)
P.O. Box 395, Pretoria, 0001, South Africa
E-mail: jphahlamohlaka@csir.co.za

ISSN 1868-4238   e-ISSN 1868-422X
ISBN 978-3-642-44600-9   ISBN 978-3-642-33332-3 (eBook)
DOI 10.1007/978-3-642-33332-3
Springer Heidelberg Dordrecht London New York

CR Subject Classification (1998): K.4.1, K.4.3-4, K.6.5, J.1, H.4.1-3, H.3.4-5, H.5.3

Typesetting: Camera-ready by author, data conversion by Scientific Publishing Services, Chennai, India

Printed on acid-free paper

Springer is part of Springer Science+Business Media (www.springer.com)

Preface

The present book contains the proceedings of the international conference on Human Choice and Computers (HCC10), held in Amsterdam, The Netherlands, September 27–28, 2012. The conference was organised by the International Federation for Information Processing (IFIP), Technical Committee 9 – ICT and Society.

The proceedings have been subdivided into four sections: National and International Policies; Sustainable and Responsible Innovation; ICT for Peace and War; and Citizens' Involvement, Citizens' Rights and ICT. The proceedings are introduced by the editors, in Chapter 1, with an overall view of the whole book and the HCC10 conference.

The papers selected for this book cover a variety of relevant subjects, drawing upon high-quality research and experience from professionals working in various parts of the world. It is our intention that academics, practitioners, governments and international organisations alike will benefit from these contributions. We hope readers will engage in the debate, pushing forward the collective work we present here.

July 2012

Magda David Hercheui
Diane Whitehouse
William McIver, Jr.
Jackie Phahlamohlaka

HCC10 – 2012
Chairs and Programme Committee

HCC10 Chairs

Magda David Hercheui   Westminster Business School, UK
Diane Whitehouse   The Castlegate Consultancy, UK

HCC10 Programme Committee

Anna Vartapetiance   Surrey University, UK
Diane Whitehouse   The Castlegate Consultancy, UK
Gunilla Bradley   Royal Institute of Technology, Sweden
Jackie Phahlamohlaka   Council for Scientific and Industrial Research,
    South Africa
Lorenz M. Hilty   University of Zurich, Switzerland, and Empa,
    Swiss Federal Laboratories for Materials Science
    and Technology, Switzerland
Louise Leenen   Council for Scientific and Industrial Research,
    South Africa
Magda David Hercheui   Westminster Business School, UK
Martin Warnke   Computer Science & Culture, Leuphana University,
    Germany
Norberto Patrignani   Politecnico di Torino, Italy
Oliver Burmeister   University of Wollongong, Australia
Penny Duquenoy   Middlesex University, UK
William McIver Jr.   National Research Council, Canada

Acknowledgements

We would like to express our thanks for additional support also to:

Marc Griffiths   The Castlegate Consultancy, UK
Therese Cory   Analyst, Report and Newsletter Writer in IT
    and Telecoms, UK
Mick Phythian   De Montfort University and formerly Ryedale
    District Council, UK
Richard Taylor   International Baccalaureate, UK

Table of Contents

Human Choice and Computers International Conference (HCC10)

ICT Critical Infrastructures and Society: Introduction to the HCC10
Conference Proceedings 1
   Magda David Hercheui, Diane Whitehouse,
   William J. McIver Jr., and Jackie Phahlamohlaka

Section 1: National and International Policies

Formatting the Public Sector with ICTs: Exploring Institutional
Sources and Processes 11
   Noora H. Alghatam

Building ICT Critical Infrastructures for Trade Regulations:
Implications from a National Initiative in Mexico 22
   Carla M. Bonina

Getting It Right: The Importance of Targeting Structural Causes
of Failure in E-Government 34
   Silvia Masiero

National Identity Infrastructures: Lessons from the United Kingdom 44
   Aaron K. Martin

International Norms and Socio-technical Systems: Connecting
Institutional and Technological Infrastructures in Governance
Processes 56
   Claudia Padovani and Elena Pavan

Section 2: Sustainable and Responsible Innovation

ICT and Environmental Sustainability: A Case Study of a Grassroots
Initiative 69
   Ana Cardoso and João Carvalho

Green IT for Innovation and Innovation for Green IT: The Virtuous
Circle 79
   Christina Herzog, Laurent Lefèvre, and Jean-Marc Pierson

The Role of ICT in Sustainable and Responsible Development:
E-Skilling 90
   Hossana Twinomurinzi

Sustainable and Responsible ICT Innovation in Healthcare: A Long
View and Continuous Ethical Watch Required   100
    Tony Cornford and Valentina Lichtner

Impact of ICT on Home Healthcare   111
    Sokratis Vavilis, Milan Petković, and Nicola Zannone

Technology and Care for Patients with Chronic Conditions: The
Chronic Care Model as a Framework for the Integration of ICT   123
    Nick Guldemond and Magda David Hercheui

Information Waste, the Environment and Human Action: Concepts and
Research   134
    Fons Wijnhoven, Pim Dietz, and Chintan Amrit

Towards a Sustainable Governance of Information Systems: Devising
a Maturity Assessment Tool of Eco-Responsibility Inspired by the
Balanced Scorecard   143
    Amélie Bohas and Laïd Bouzidi

Building Human Infrastructure for the Digital Economy: Ryerson's
Digital Media Zone   156
    Wendy Cukier, Valerie Fox, and Hossein Rahnama

Sustainable Communications and Innovation: Different Types of Effects
from Collaborative Research Including University and Companies in
the ICT-Sector   170
    Mattias Höjer, Katarina Larsen, and Helene Wintzell

Is the Post-Turing ICT Sustainable?   183
    Norberto Patrignani and Iordanis Kavathatzopoulos

ITGS – A Blueprint for a Social Informatics Course in Pre-university
Education   192
    Richard Taylor

Governance, Risk and Compliance: A Strategic Alignment Perspective
Applied to Two Case Studies   202
    Abbas Shahim, Ronald Batenburg, and Geert Vermunt

Section 3: ICT for Peace and War

Implementation of a Cyber Security Policy in South Africa: Reflection
on Progress and the Way Forward   215
    Marthie Grobler, Joey Jansen van Vuuren, and Louise Leenen

Mapping the Most Significant Computer Hacking Events to a Temporal
Computer Attack Model   226
    Renier van Heerden, Heloise Pieterse, and Barry Irwin

The Dark Side of Web 2.0 237
    Aubrey Labuschagne, Mariki Eloff, and Namosha Veerasamy

Towards a Social Media-Based Model of Trust and Its Application 250
    Erik Boertjes, Bas Gerrits, Robert Kooij, Peter-Paul van Maanen,
    Stephan Raaijmakers, and Joost de Wit

Video Games and the Militarisation of Society: Towards a Theoretical
and Conceptual Framework 264
    John Martino

Challenges to Peace in the 21st Century: Working towards a Good
Information and Communication Society 274
    Gunilla Bradley and Diane Whitehouse

Section 4: Citizens' Involvement, Citizens' Rights and ICT

Implementing Ethics in Information Systems, Presuppositions and
Consequences in Ethics and Information Systems 287
    Laurence Masclet and Philippe Goujon

Redesigning the Relationship between Government and Civil Society:
An Investigation of Emerging Models of Networked Democracy
in Brazil 299
    Eduardo Henrique Diniz and Manuella Maia Ribeiro

Cyberactivism and Collective Agency: Cases from China 310
    Yingqin Zheng and Cheng Zhang

Information Inadequacy: The Lack of Needed Information in Human,
Social and Industrial Affairs 320
    Miranda Kajtazi

Social Games: Privacy and Security 330
    Mathias Fuchs

Is Privacy Dead? – An Inquiry into GPS-Based Geolocation and Facial
Recognition Systems 338
    Jens-Martin Loebel

Theorising Open Development through an Institutional Lens: A Study
of Iranian Online Interactions 349
    Magda David Hercheui, Brian Nicholson, and Aghil Ameripour

Packet Inspection — Shifting the Paradigm of Fundamental Rights 360
    Agata Królikowski

Civic Intelligence and CSCW 369
    Douglas Schuler

Informed Strategies of Political Action in IP-Based Social Media 376
    Andrea Knaut

Corporate Social Media Use Policy: Meeting Business and Ethical
Responsibilities 387
    Don Gotterbarn

Author Index 399

ICT Critical Infrastructures and Society: Introduction to the HCC10 Conference Proceedings

Magda David Hercheui[1], Diane Whitehouse[2]
William J. McIver, Jr.[3], and Jackie Phahlamohlaka[4]

[1] Westminster Business School, London, United Kingdom
m.hercheui@westminster.ac.uk
[2] The Castlegate Consultancy, Malton, United Kingdom
diane.whitehouse@thecastlegateconsultancy.com
[3] University of New Brunswick, Fredericton, Canada
wmciver@acm.org
[4] CSIR, Pretoria, South Africa
jphahlamohlaka@csir.co.za

Abstract. For 40 years, the academics and business executives who have attended the Human Choice and Computers international conference series have discussed human choices and social responsibility in relation to information and communication technology (ICT). At this 2012 conference, the focus is on ICT critical infrastructures, and the challenges they pose to governments, businesses and people. Several topics have emerged as relevant in this conference: ICT developments at international and national levels; sustainable and responsible innovation; dilemmas involving ICT, peace and war; and the implications of ICT and social media for citizens' involvement and citizens' rights. What should national computing associations be doing to explore these serious issues? How should the International Federation for Information Processing (IFIP) itself respond? Responses are needed that are flexible and durable enough to face the challenges of the coming four decades.

Keywords: citizens, computing, democracy, human choice and computers, information and communication technology (ICT), infrastructure, innovation, involvement, peace, policy, responsibility, rights, social media, sustainability, war.

1   Introduction

The Human Choice and Computers (HCC) conferences have been organised by the Technical Committee 9 (TC9)[1] of the International Federation for Information Processing (IFIP) ever since 1974. This series of conferences has offered an important setting in which to discuss the impact of information and communication technology (ICT) on society. The conference subjects have ranged from the ways in which ICT

---

[1] The IFIP Technical Committee 9 (TC9) is dedicated to the study of the relationship of ICT and Society http://www.ifiptc9.org/

M.D. Hercheui et al. (Eds.): HCC10 2012, IFIP AICT 386, pp. 1–7, 2012.
© IFIP International Federation for Information Processing 2012

affects people's lives at home and in the workplace, to the impact that they have had on communities and institutions. The gatherings have offered fora where academics and practitioners have been able to discuss technology from a social, and even societal, perspective [3].

TC9 concentrates on developing an understanding of how ICT innovation is associated with change in society, and having an influence on the shaping of socially responsible and ethical policies and professional practices. By holding its meetings in international locations, it acts globally. In particular, its last two conferences in 2008 and 2010 in South Africa and Australia reconfirmed this international reach. They stretched TC9's panorama geographically and thematically. Issues such as social dimensions of ICT policy [1] and ethical and governance dimensions of privacy, surveillance, sustainable development, and virtuality [3] were tackled. HCC10, which takes place in the Netherlands on 27-28 September 2012, is the tenth in this conference series. Some forty contributions bring a wealth of output and range to this conference. The attendees, and the countries they come from, cover cases and investigations from as far afield as Africa, Australasia, Europe, the Far East and Middle East, Latin America, and North America.

2   Overview of HCC10[2]

Today, ICT critical infrastructures provide a basic foundation to society, increasingly regardless of location. Governments, businesses and individuals are more and more dependent on these pervasive ICT infrastructures that underpin diverse methods of governing, controlling and assuring security and safety in all spheres of human life. How people produce, trade and consume goods and services, and how people communicate, interact and collaborate in their political, professional and private lives are all affected by these technologies and infrastructures.

The Internet, mobile networks, and even social media, have become new critical infrastructures. Many documents of long-term importance are stored on ephemeral media and in digital formats. Major key data and communication centres exist in a limited number of locations around the globe. Human dependence on these infrastructures extends from business and commerce, finance, healthcare and public health, to the provision of services – public or private, and the organisation of communities. It also includes the continuous provision of such basic utilities as electricity, gas and water.

This reliance poses immense challenges in terms of sustainability, long-term provision, societal organisation, innovation, democracy, and the competences and resilience of human beings. New methods, tools and techniques, and ways of thinking, and particularly acting, will be needed to tackle these challenges. They may be required at many levels of society from policy-making to interactions occurring in people's local communities. ICT may facilitate new democratic activities of engagement [6],[9], but dependency or over-dependency on these technologies may also be problematic [2],[5].

---

[2] This overview is based on two sets of ideas: the first expressed in the description of this conference and the second in a call for a workshop held by IFIP's working group 9.2 at Middlesex University, United Kingdom, on 4 February 2012.

3   HCC10's Conference Themes

HCC10 discusses the impact that these ICT critical infrastructures are having on society as well as the ways in which members of various social groups are responding to them. The conference reflects on the main challenges that governments, organisations and individuals are already facing, and are likely to face in the decades to come. The focus is dual: it is both on strategic directions, and on the effects on people's everyday and routine activities – reactions that can be very different in the various parts of the globe. The conference also explores how to mitigate risks and reduce some of the potentially more negative outcomes of these developments.

A number of specific topics are covered. They include: national and international policies; sustainable and responsible innovation; ICT for peace and war; and citizens' involvement, rights, and the implications of social media. Each of these HCC10 conference themes is explained below in more detail.

3.1   National and International Policies

The Organisation for Economic Co-operation and Development and the European Union (EU) and its countries, international organisations such as the International Telecommunications Union, United Nations and World Bank, individual nations, and regional and municipal authorities, are all coming together to shape the character and foundations of ICT critical infrastructures. They are attempting to manage the development and deployment of more efficient, inclusive, resilient, and secure ICT critical infrastructures. As society is increasingly recognising, it can be hugely beneficial to explore the implications of successes as well as errors and failures in this field. Different perspectives on policies are emerging in both general and detailed forms as a result of these conference proceedings.

These HCC10 conference papers describe applications introduced in a range of countries worldwide (e.g., Dubai, India, Mexico and the United Kingdom), several of which are developing countries and/or emerging economies. The focus is on governance-related issues, and the domains covered are in government and the public sector. The types of applications involve eGovernment generally, identity mechanisms, a portal for foreign trade, and ration cards. While some of the initiatives have been applied in practice in the countries concerned, others are either in transition or on hold. The final paper in this section [8] reminds us that – while it is always important to examine the grassroots and immediate implications of any development – it is wise to keep an eye on the bigger picture: hence, a multi-dimensional analytical framework is presented.

3.2   Sustainable and Responsible Innovation

Globalisation and competition have rendered the topic of ICT innovation a major concern for any local, regional or national economy. Governments around the world are proposing policies to foster innovation in their digital industries and spread the successful adoption of these technologies. Not only national needs, but also the implications that innovations have for different countries, must be borne in mind at the international level. More in-depth discussion is also needed on the societal, social and ethical values underpinning the innovations that societies aim to pursue.

HCC10 considers the innovations on which governments, organisations and society should focus, and which criteria should drive research and investment in innovation. HCC10's perspective is that technology is not neutral. Thus, it is important to discuss the explicit and implicit social and ethical aims, together with the real outcomes of innovation policies. The debate focuses on how economic, societal and environmental sustainability are to be taken into consideration in all investments in ICT critical infrastructures. The more specific subjects covered include environmentalism, green ICT and sustainability; the role of innovation in the economics of communities; healthcare; future post-Turing era challenges; and the role that can be played by education, training and skills development to forge sustainability and responsible innovation.

It is important to bear in mind a general overview of Green IT, and its argument that it is closely associated with innovation. New directions in ICT, especially in distributed computing are important, with a focus on what this means for e-waste management. Two corporate-related examples of energy management are introduced: one based on data mining and the other on a balanced scorecard. There are also community-based environmental concerns and innovative approaches to handling energy management through ICT.

How to encourage and attract responsible innovation is one of today's major societal and economic challenges. Three examples, two from Canadian cities and one from a European country's national research network, offer ideas for innovators that could be transferable to other social and geographical settings.

Responsible innovation is particularly vital in the field of healthcare. Three illustrations are introduced from different clinical areas: healthcare generally, home healthcare and chronic care. A range of ethical concerns is covered.

Various aspects of responsible innovation in the educational, research and corporate worlds emerge. The emphasis is very much on ethics and how they can be taught, researched, introduced and implemented in various educational, employment and social settings. Ultimately, the solutions range from some more technical and technological approaches to infrastructures, to law, philosophy and behavioural change.[3] The stakeholders concerned involve policy-makers at international or national levels as well as local inhabitants. They include people of all ages, from the eldest in our societies to young high school attendees.

3.3   ICT for Peace and War

Information is a vital element of post-modern society, and its safety and security is crucial. ICT critical infrastructures are fundamental to human beings' attempts to live

---

[3] This section of the conference has an affinity with the 2012 IFIP WG9.2 Namur Award ceremony. This international award for an outstanding contribution with international impact to the awareness of social implications of information technology is to be given in 2012 to Prof. Stefano Rodotà of Italy.

in peace. On the one hand, cyber security is a key factor in the maintenance of international and national security, and in guarding many of the interests of citizens. On the other hand, cyber warfare can refer to politically – or otherwise – motivated hacking to conduct sabotage and espionage against specific nation states. Countering the latter is important; but questioning undue interference by states is also an important exercise. There are many implications of ICT critical infrastructures for people's current understanding and experiences of building peace in a world that is coping with many separate, yet often interlinked, wars and numerous other forms of violence and aggression.

HCC10 introduces these themes in a section on ICT for peace and war. This section of the conference proceedings explores how social media are used for a number of different purposes. Initially, three applications are introduced from two countries: one that is used for social engineering, another for measuring consumer trust, and another for modelling crowd control. Later, questions are raised about the relationship between war, violence and video or ICT-based games and the need for more in-depth investigation of the effects these can have on the young (and not so young) people who play them. The section ends with a proposal for agendas for research, discussion and action that cover all of these areas of concern.

3.4   Citizens' Involvement, Citizens Rights' and ICT

The Internet can enable citizens' participation in democratic social structures and governments. ICT critical infrastructures, such as eGovernment and social media platforms, can foster public debate and people's emancipation. Some countries have been successful in implementing social media interfaces so as to be more attentive to the views of their citizens. Events, in particular in 2011 during the so-called Arab Spring, have reinforced a positive belief that people can use ICT critical infrastructures to defend their rights and interests, and even to organise themselves against oppressive regimes. However, it is also known that governments have used these very same tools to monitor and control their citizens [6],[9].

The extensive diffusion of social media environments that has taken place over the last five years in particular, warrants greater attention and is receiving it in many academic and broadcasting circles. Social media tools, especially social networks, are disrupting the way people interact in society, in both their private and professional lives. The boundaries between private and public are blurring, with consequences for people's identity, privacy and security.

HCC10 discusses numerous aspects of this debate. The conference covers the necessary interrelationship between the technological and institutional infrastructures that are required to understand the outcomes of citizen participation mediated by ICT. This section of the book deepens the discussion on the implications of social media for society. It explores several instances of citizens' social media use in a number of countries including Brazil, China, Iran, and South Africa. Examples of social media use in crisis situations, and what kinds of approaches are needed to support people in these circumstances, are highlighted. This section also investigates how virtual relationships affect the social tissue of societies. It questions the ethics of organisations that use social media to investigate the personal lives of their employees, and profiling techniques to increase their sales and improve their brands. It discusses how society may be organised to defend citizen privacy and security. It also covers citizens' relationship with upskilling and decision-making.

4   Implications for International Computing Associations

This HCC10 conference topic stimulated the desire to bring together a number of TC9 representatives to take part in a panel discussion on how ICT infrastructures are perceived by their national computing societies. The aim is to debate ICT-related critical infrastructures, and various possible ways of handling their challenges. Prospective panellists represent computing associations in Canada, Japan, and South Africa. From Europe, the Dutch, German, Finnish, and Hungarian computing associations will offer their views. A representative of the international computing association, the Association for Computing Machinery (ACM) will also make a contribution. Participants have been invited to submit a short description of the problems posed by ICT critical infrastructures from the perspective of either their own country or computing society. As a result, TC9 members will be able to share their perceptions of a range of different infrastructural problems, face these concerns together, and search for solutions. These stakeholders will add their voice to those of policy-makers, industrialists, and civic society.

5   Current and Future Reflections

This book of HCC10 conference proceedings will be published in time for the conference. The proceedings are not, however, intended to pre-empt the conference's discussions and outcomes. These conversations will extend far wider than the book's contents. Indeed, the conference is intended to be a dynamic, fluid and interactive forum for debate. It is organised so as to place the emphasis on brainstorming, ideas exchange, discussion and dialogue.

These conference proceedings record the contributions delivered to the HCC10 programme committee as of July 2012. They offer a picture of the current state of thinking on ICT critical infrastructures from a number of stakeholders in terms of assumptions, attitudes, empirical evidence, and policies. The conference will highlight the main similarities and differences between the contributors' opinions. However, the conference will not privilege or prioritise specific methods or methodologies. Indeed, the techniques used by the authors of papers in this volume are diverse. Many of the papers are case study-based and delve into the experiences of countries, societies, and communities. Others are based on literature searches, questionnaire surveys, or assessments of software applications. Other papers are either position papers or reflection papers.

Among the outcomes of the conference is likely to be a growing awareness of new directions for international non-governmental organisations, such as IFIP and its technical committees and working groups, in relation to ICT infrastructures and society. New ideas and perceptions could also arise for civic society. These may affect how policy-makers, business executives, researchers and teachers interact in the future. Such collaborative approaches will help them in various ways: to analyse historical circumstances and contexts that have affected ICT infrastructures, to overcome any persistent barriers, to prepare for new challenges, and to promote improved foresight into future developments.

Such envisioning is particularly necessary to face not only the challenges of this second decade of the twenty-first century but also at least several further decades to come. Flexible yet durable, resilient, responses are needed.

References

1. Social Dimensions of Information and Communication Technology Policy. In: Avgerou, C., Smith, M.L., Besselaar, P.v.d. (eds.) Proceedings of the 8th International Conference on Human Choice and Computers (HCC 2008), IFIP TC 9, Pretoria, South Africa, September 25-26, Springer, New York (2008)
2. Facing the Challenge of Risk and Vulnerability in an Information Society. In: Berleur, J., Beardon, C., Laufer, R. (eds.) Proceedings of the IFIP WG9.2 Working Conference on Facing the Challenge of Risk and Vulnerability in an Information Society, Namur, Belgium, May 20-22 (1993)
3. Berleur, J., Hercheui, M.D., Hilty, L.M.: What Kind of Information Society? Introduction to the HCC9 Conference Proceedings. In: Berleur, J., Hercheui, M.D., Hilty, L.M. (eds.) HCC9 2010. IFIP AICT, vol. 328, pp. 3–9. Springer, Heidelberg (2010)
4. Bradley, G., Whitehouse, D.: Challenges to Peace in the 21st Century: Working towards a Good Information and Communication Society. In: [7] (2012)
5. Cameron, J.: A Survival Kit for Resilient Citizens in the Information Society. Presentation made at the IFIP WG9.2 & WG 9.9 Joint Workshop, Milan, Social Accountability & Sustainability in the Information Society: Perspectives on Long-Term Responsibility, June 4-5 (2011)
6. Castells, M.: Communication Power. Oxford University Press, Oxford (2009)
7. Hercheui, M.D., Whitehouse, D., McIver Jr., W.J., Phahlamohlaka, J.: ICT Critical Infrastructures and Society: HCC10 Conference Proceedings. In: Hercheui, M.D., et al. (eds.) HCC10 2012. IFIP AICT, vol. 386, pp. 1–7. Springer, Heidelberg (2012)
8. Padovani, C., Pavan, E.: International Norms and Socio-Technical Systems: Connecting Institutional and Technological Infrastructures in Governance Processes. In: [7] (2012)
9. Shirky, C.: The Political Power of Social Media; Technology, the Public Sphere, and Political Change. Foreign Affairs 90(1), 28–41 (2011)

Section 1
National and International Policies

Formatting the Public Sector with ICTs: Exploring Institutional Sources and Processes

Noora H. Alghatam

Information Systems and Innovation Group,
London School of Economics and Political Sciences, London, United Kingdom
n.h.alghatam@lse.ac.uk

Abstract. This paper discusses the process in which e-government projects are initiated and locally negotiated within the public sector organizations. The issue is explored by employing the theoretical concept of global formats. The concept of formats is employed to explore two interlinked themes: the institutional sources for e-government projects and the processes of locally appropriating these projects within the organizational setting. This paper focuses on an e-government project that was successfully implemented in one of Dubai's public sector organizations.

Keywords: e-government, global formats, institutions, information systems implementation.

1   Introduction

E-government projects have been adopted in both developed and developing countries as a means to reform the public sector, and as part of a broader objective of achieving social and economic sustainability goals [1], [4], [7], [9], [13], [26]. This paper does not focus in particular on the implications of e-government in contributing to development; rather the aim is to explore how the projects that are part of these national initiatives are locally understood, encountered and appropriated by people who work in the public sector.

Institutional arrangements play a role in shaping how the planning, design and use of ICTs in the public sector is enacted [11], [16]. Similarly, some academics discuss e-government in terms of the historical developments in the public sector and policies of New Public Management (NPM) [10], [15], [16], [19]. For instance, e-government is conceptualized as an extension to a history of NPM initiatives in the west [19]. These initiatives are also considered to be the mark of the digital era governance where information and communication technologies (ICTs) can resolve the problems associated with NPM initiatives of the past [15]. Adopting an institutional lens explains why there are challenges in adopting standardized systems and models, and why there is diversity in the outcomes [3]. For example, we often find in the case of developing countries that the ICTs adopted are inscribed with values and assumptions that originate from other contexts, which Heeks refers to as the design-actuality gap

M.D. Hercheui et al. (Eds.): HCC10 2012, IFIP AICT 386, pp. 11–21, 2012.

[20]. Such mismatches between e-government systems and contexts are also depicted in the work of Cordella and Iannacci who present the case of an e-government project in the justice department in the United Kingdom and Wales. The authors employ institutional theory to explain how implementation involved building on an existing system that was inscribed with concepts from past NPM initiatives and notions of decentralization [10].

Studies that examine e-government projects from an institutional lens often focus on whether e-government systems have become institutionalized or not [6], [25]. There is not enough work that explores the nature of institutional interplay and how it conditions the micro-level process of implementation [6]. There are a few studies that have adopted Actor Network Theory and concepts of improvisations to explore this process [5], [21]. In this paper, the theoretical concept of formats [27] is employed to explain how semi-configured packages arrive with e-government projects, and how local actors in the public sector work on appropriating them to fit within existing institutional arrangements.

The research question addressed here is: how are e-government projects experienced, negotiated and localized in the context of the public sector organization? The main argument presented is that e-government projects are shaped by interplay between historical developments and the semi-configuration of formats. This combination sets in motion (and conditions) a series of interactions within the organization that localizes e-government.

The paper consists of seven sections. The paper began with an overview of e-government studies and the research question. The second section introduces the theoretical concept of formats. The third section is the methodology. The fourth section presents an overview of the case study of Dubai's e-government initiative. The fifth section presents the findings, and the sixth a discussion of the key themes that are guided by the theoretical concept of formats. The paper concludes with a summary and key findings.

2   Theoretical Framework: Global Formats

The concept of formats refers to a semi-configured arrangement of institutional norms, modes of organizing and technology that are (in part) designed by powerful institutional actors and the discourses they engage in. Sassen [29] identifies these three elements when she states that a format "... is precisely at the intersection of the technology and the organizational forms and norms".

Technology is at the heart of these formats, because artifacts bring relevant institutional norms and modes of organizing. It is through this technological component that formats arrive into the organizations and gain legitimacy for adoption and use, mainly because ICTs are associated with transformation, modernization and efficiency gains. As noted by Sassen [28], formats require the invention of tools to support their activities and, in the case of e-government, this can be the code, the infrastructure, the work supporting software, or the web portal. The technology component is enacted within organizations and is shaped through use: "...technology is mutant and indeterminate and its potential is performative if other variety of variables are there" [27].

In relation to mode(s) of organizing, international, regional and national institutional actors influence most organizations when they plan, develop and use ICTs. Latham and Sassen describe this in the context of CSO as "...a variety of non-state actors and forms of cross-border cooperation and conflict – global business networks, the new cosmopolitanism, NGOs, Diaspora networks, and trans-boundary public spheres" [23, p. 22, 23]. As the authors explain, the involvement of these actors is understood to be an established hierarchy of scale. For example, in the case of e-government projects, there are various international organizations or management consultancies that play a role in the practices adopted. The new modes of organizing include working in ways that conform to the best practices such as the stages of growth models and implementation strategies that these institutional actors promote in presentations and publications on e-government.

Finally, the concept of formats incorporates new institutional norms surrounding the development and use of technology. For example, most e-government projects respond to the institution of NPM, which is strongly associated with e-government. Such an institution sets expectations on how the public sector staff perform, specifies the roles of the staff members as they work on e-government, and frames what is deemed to be a successful implementation. For example, it is common in such projects to consider clients who interact with the public sector as 'customers'.

3   Methodology

The empirical part of this study focuses on the e-government project in one of Dubai's largest public sector organizations for the period of 2000-2008. The empirical research began with a preparatory study in October 2006 that included five interviews to learn more about the e-government initiative and the kind of projects that were being implemented. During this time, interviews were conducted with IT managers from various government departments, the central government organization for e-government and a researcher from a research institution in Dubai. This provided insight into the developments of the project since year 2000 that included the institutional structures of the state that were set up to plan and manage the e-government initiative. Shortly after that, from October 2006 to May 2007, several visits were made to the main research site, each visit lasting up to one week. The author mainly focused on the e-government section, which is part of the IT department and where the IT managers, system analysts, developers and support officers worked on the e-government systems.

The research design was a single case study and the data collection methods were mainly based on semi-structured interviews and on-site observations [33], [34]. Following the interpretivist approach to research, the fieldwork was shaped by the interpretations of the researcher in the field as she attempted to capture the actors' perspectives [8], [31], [32]. The interviews were based on the themes of: the history of the project; the nature of the planning and development activities; the ICT staff's early expectations of e-government; challenges encountered during the project and finally any changes to the nature of operations in the public sector. The interviews were based on a list of questions that guided the interview process to a large extent. However, the nature of qualitative research enabled the researcher to follow up certain themes with questions and shift focus [8]. The interviews were in Arabic or English depending on the interviewee's nationality or preference. The researcher took notes and sometimes tape recorded the interviews.

In addition to interviews, other data collection methods were employed. For example, there were notes taken about the overall work environment, which included the office spaces and work activities of the ICT staff. Secondary data were collected and reviewed during fieldwork to inform the interview process. The researcher reviewed technical specification documents for the systems, job descriptions of the ICT staff and presentations by management consultants. The researcher also read articles published by the central government agency Dubai eGovernment Department (DeG) about the e-government initiative.

4   Case Description

The e-government project that is the focus of this paper was in one of Dubai's largest public sector organizations, which we will refer to in the paper as The Public Office, abbreviated as TPO. The project is part of a large national e-government initiative to modernize and transform the public sector through the employment of ICTs, and specifically the Internet, in the provision of public services. The initiative was officially announced in the state media in the year 2000 and this set a clear deadline for public organizations to set up 70% of their services over the Internet within a timeframe of a year-and-a-half. The target later changed to 90%. There were two main objectives specified: creating convenience and positioning Dubai as an economic hub for the region. During that year a contract was signed with an international consultancy to assist in the initiative. The consultancy provided guidance in a pilot project to develop four systems and that involved a number of public organizations. Later the consultancy was involved in the design of three institutional structures for the state to plan and manage the e-government initiative, which are: the executive office, Dubai eGovernment and the Government Information Resource Planning Department. Table 1 presents an overview of the role and some of the activities of these institutional structures. Over time these institutional structures took over the planning role off the management consultancy.

TPO was faced with the dilemma of limited experience and expertise in web-based technologies and a strict deadline. There was not enough time to learn and work independently on the project, so a contract was signed with an IT and management consultancy that had international expertise in e-government projects. The focus of the study is on the development of the online applications for public services that were to be provided on the web portal, and not the development of back-end systems. One of the first actions taken by the management consultants was to conduct an assessment study of the organization's 'readiness' to embark on the project. Later, they provided a conceptualization on how the project would progress towards the state's deadline. The plan was based on the service prioritization model, which suggests beginning with the simple services first and then gradually progressing to the more complex ones.

The later stage of the model refers to services that require the development of inter-organizational systems to integrate work processes with other public sector organizations. The plan was that the systems were implemented over four phases. The project conformed to the best practice model and plan, and an IT service provider team was hired to work in the IT department to conduct most of the development of applications. The internal team in TPO was expected to work on the support of these services, later taking up a bigger role in the development of applications. It was only a matter of time until bugs were found in the systems that disrupted their operation. The internal team was worried about the situation and in response developed a coding template and checklist to improve the coding process and documentation. A pilot of the new template was developed and presented to IT managers in the department who agreed on introducing it to improve the development process. There were fewer bugs in the systems reported after the new template was adopted in phases three and four. The internal IT team worked on recoding the older applications that were problematic. TPO's system met and even surpassed the state deadline. During phase four, a new project to develop a new infrastructure was introduced to allow flexibility in design. This required additional work in coding the online applications.

Table 1. An Overview of Institutional Structures for E-government in Dubai

Institutional Structures	Objectives
The Executive Office	Responsible for formulating the strategy for e-government, and the vision and mission for DeG
Dubai eGovernment (DeG)	Promote e-government to the public to reduce physical visits to public sector organizations.
	Assist in the simplification of business processes for the development of online services.
	Assist the public sector organizations in transitioning towards the integration of databases across different organizations.
	Ensure there is a single access point for government services.
Government Information Resource and Planning Department	Responsible for the set up and management of the technical infrastructure for the e-government initiative.

Source: Interview with a former manager at DeG in December 2006 [14], [30]

5   Findings

5.1   The Context: History, City Development and ICTs

Revisiting the early phases of setting up of the public administration in Dubai, and the United Arab Emirates (UAE) as a whole in the early 1970s, reveals a series of efforts to build and modernize public systems. It was also apparent that ICTs acquired a significant role in these initiatives in later years. There were numerous investments made in human and financial resources to set up an operable public administrative system in the early 1970s upon attaining independence and the formation of the federation [12], [35]. Dubai's economic activities at the time coincided with one of the earliest efforts in the region to set up a system to support the development of the state and its operations. As the region's social and economic activities expanded, particularly with the exports of oil and industrialization, there was a need to improve the public administrative systems to support this [12], [17], [18].

In the 1980s there were programs set up with international organizations such as the United Nations Development Programme (UNDP) to provide guidance and consultation to improve the operations of the public administrative systems. The outcome of the UNDP study was mainly in relation to human resource recruitment and training [22]. Following on this pattern, there were computerization initiatives for data storage and improving levels of efficiency. The significance of employing ICTs in improving the functioning of the public sector is still present today. The main difference with e-government in Dubai is the stronger emphasis on the transformation of operations and the creation of a relationship between the public and the public sector that is more customer-oriented [2].

5.2   The Arrival and the Acceptance of the E-government Format

The e-government format, which was in part shaped by global discourses and semi-configuration, was introduced into TPO through three institutional actors. One of the most significant events was the initial announcement of the electronic government initiative in Dubai in 2000. The state mandate for e-government specified objectives for the public sector. They were expected to set up 70% of public services over the Internet within a time frame of 18 months. Moreover, the e-government initiative was framed as a means to make it more convenient for all those who interact with the public sector. Another objective of the initiative was to support Dubai in positioning itself as an economic hub for the region. The emphasis on creating convenience in the public sector is linked to a history of managerial ideas and practices in the UAE. There were various efforts over the years to improve and modernize the public sector since the 1980s by focusing on quality and initiating privatization projects.

Second, the e-government initiative established three institutional structures to plan and manage the e-government initiative across the public sector, which were outlined in Table 1. The central agency DeG played a pivotal role in managing the way these systems were developed by providing key performance indicators and evaluating progress based on quarterly reports that were sent to them. DeG was also involved in communicating objectives about the project to various actors in the public sector through presentations. These presentations often included framing expected progress in the e-government initiative in terms of criteria in the stages of growth models.

Third, the e-government project involved working in collaboration with the private sector. The management consultants provided guidance and a plan and the IT service provider worked with them in the development of online applications for the web portal. The involvement of the private sector instantiated and supported the managerial approaches and concepts introduced into the public sector. One of the most significant was the service prioritization model that in essence was based on international best practices.

5.3   Localizing E-government

At this point we focus on the process of localizing these systems, which resulted from the actions of the ICT staff in TPO, and which were conditioned by interplay between old and new institutional elements. This section presents three examples of such actions taken by the ICT staff and how they link to institutional elements of the public sector or the new format.

The first example is when the ICT manager registered the e-government project in one of the online competitions offered by an international organization. The action was driven by a sense of ambiguity and the relative newness of these projects, as well as an aspiration to find guidelines on how these projects are developed and evaluated according to global criteria. The act of signing up to the competition shows the influence of international best practices and managerial models in the public sector.

However, there are also examples of the e-government format not fitting with institutionalized dimensions of the public sector. For instance, the emphasis of using standardized models during the planning of the project does not account for local pragmatic concerns of the public sector staff. This was evident when the service prioritization model, which suggests working on simple services first, was not conformed to during the planning of the systems. Instead the managers who were working on e-government took the decision to go ahead with developing a complex inter-organizational system early on. This was because the manual system was a problem that the public and the business community were facing and it needed to be resolved quickly. Another example was the new work arrangements that involved cooperation with the IT service provider that had international expertise and the situation of finding bugs in the system. The internal ICT team in TPO introduced a coding template and checklist to improve the quality of the coding. The semi-configured nature of the format is expected to generate standardized outcomes, and to shape the understanding of e-government implementation. The two examples presented here illustrate that local actors appropriate elements of these formats in ways that come to shape how the systems are developed.

6   Discussion

The earlier section described key events that took place during the implementation of the e-government project that involved improvisation and innovation during work. This section elaborates on two themes: institutional sources of e-government and the design and shaping of formats. These themes discuss the process of localizing the e-government systems.

6.1   Institutional Sources of E-government

Revisiting e-government formats that arrive in the public sector consists of understanding elements from early generations of e-government as well as NPM. NPM in the west has been influential since the 1970s in the adoption of ICTs in the public sector with the aim of improving efficiency and creating a client culture. Similar trends were present in the UAE, which has initiated programmes to modernize the public administrative system since the 1970s and 1980s that included computerization programmes. As such, e-government initiatives are seen as an extension to the history of automation of work processes to the current initiative to set up web-based systems and the provision of services to create convenience for the public. Yet, there are features to e-government that make it distinct from the previous initiatives. E-government emphasizes the theme of transformation of the public sector when it comes to service delivery and relationships with the public. Also, unlike ICT use within NPM initiatives, e-government positions ICT as a central component of change, and not at the periphery. This emphasis on the significance of ICTs introduces with e-government a package of standardized models and approaches to plan, develop and evaluate these systems.

As noted in the previous section, e-government formats that arrive are supported by disembodied institutions that include international organizations and IT and management consultancies [3]. These institutions provide legitimacy to the e-government project since it is associated with organizational change and socio-economic objectives. In addition to this, local institutions in Dubai's public sector conditioned local actors to accept e-government and took actions that localized the systems. As noted earlier, the ICT staff adapted the service prioritization model and developed a coding template and checklist to meet pragmatic concerns in the public sector. These actions also conformed to the institutionalized role of the public sector as a contributor to development. Thus, the e-government format (the semi-configured package) is intertwined with the historical developments in Dubai's public sector. It came to inform the actions of the ICT staff to localize the system.

6.2   Between the Design and Shaping of Formats

E-government projects introduce common objectives and practices to develop and use these systems. Even perceptions of success and failure are defined in similar ways that are guided by best practice models. This is partly from the influence of the private sector and international organizations, which promote similar managerial approaches to ICT projects. These formats for e-government are semi-configured at both the global and national level and thus there is room for locally determining their content to meet local needs and priorities. For example, there are state policies that determine the objectives of these projects, and which element (technology, modes of organizing or new norms) is the central one through which these initiatives are introduced, supported and granted legitimacy. This is illustrated when state policies determine how the systems are to be developed: a new system that is developed from scratch or a system that is built on an existing legacy system, built in-house or outsourced.

As this paper has discussed, e-government formats are also constantly shaped as people in organizations engage with their elements. For instance, some elements are accepted such as the concept of considering the client as 'the customer'. There are other elements of the format that compete with institutionalized dimensions of the public sector and create puzzles that need to be resolved. As the case study has shown, the ICT team adapted elements of the format when they encountered these puzzles and drew upon the historical role of the public sector in development.

7   Conclusion

This paper focuses on how an e-government project in Dubai was negotiated and localized through the actions of the people working on planning and developing the systems. The paper consists of seven sections. The paper begins with an overview of e-government studies and presented the research question addressed here, which is: how are e-government projects locally experienced, negotiated and localized within the context of the public sector organization? The second section presented the theoretical framework of formats and described its main constructs. The following two sections were the methodology and case study sections that described fieldwork activities and an overview of the public sector in Dubai and the e-government initiative.

The findings section presents a narrative of the developments over the course of the project including an overview of the historical context of the public sector in Dubai and the role of ICTs in city development. The section following this discusses the arrival of the e-government format and its acceptance in the public sector. Finally, the section presents findings within the context of TPO, where local staff encountered the e-government format and took action to localize the e-government systems.

The paper then discusses why actions were taken to localize the systems by drawing on some themes from the theoretical concept of formats. It begins by discussing the institutional sources of e-government in the UAE and then the institutional dynamics that come to inform actions in e-government project. On the one hand, there is the design of formats. On the other, there is ongoing negotiation and shaping of these formats as people encounter new ideas, concepts and artifacts that compete with institutionalized dimensions of the public sector.

In summary, this paper has shown that the e-government format introduced new institutional elements of NPM, and early generations of e-government, into the public sector organization TPO. The public sector employees encountered and appropriated these elements into their daily work activities. In the organizational context, the ICT staff's acceptance of the e-government project, and the efforts to make it work through localization, reflects an ongoing interplay between the historical dimensions of the public sector in Dubai and the new e-government format. As illustrated in this paper, these dynamics are most evident during subtle breakdowns in the project and contradictions that required the ICT staff to resolve them.

References

1. Andersen, K., Henriksen, H.: E-government Maturity Models: extension of the Layne and Lee model. Government Information Quarterly 23(2), 236–248 (2006)
2. Arif, M.: Customer Orientation in e-Government Project Management: a case study. The Electronic Journal of e-Government 6(1), 1–10 (2008)
3. Avgerou, C.: Information Systems and Global Diversity, 1st edn. Oxford Univer-sity Press Inc., New York (2002)
4. Avgerou, C., et al.: Interpreting the Trustworthiness of Government Mediated by In-formation and Communication Technology: lessons from electronic voting in Brazil. Information Technology for Development 15(2), 133–148 (2009)
5. Azad, B., Faraj, S.: Making E-Government Systems Workable: Exploring the evolution of frames. The Journal of Strategic Information Systems 17(2), 75–98 (2008)
6. Azad, B., Faraj, S.: E-Government Institutionalizing Practices of a Land registration map-ping system. Government Information Quarterly 26(1), 5–14 (2009)
7. Baum, C., Di Maio, A.: Gartner's Four Phases of E-government Model. Stamford, Ct., Gartner Group 21, 12–6113 (2000)
8. Bryman, A.: The Debate about Quantitative and Qualitative Research: a question of me-thod or epistemology? British Journal of Sociology 35(1), 75–92 (1984)
9. Ciborra, C., Navarra, D.: Good Governance, Development Theory, and Aid Policy: risks and challenges of e-government in Jordan. Information Technology for Develop-ment 11(2), 141–159 (2005)
10. Cordella, A., Iannacci, F.: Information Systems in the Public Sector: the e-Government enactment framework. The Journal of Strategic Information Systems 19(1), 52–66 (2010)
11. Coursey, D., Norris, D.F.: Models of E-government are they Correct? an empirical as-sessment. Public Administration Review 68(3), 523–536 (2008)
12. Davidson, C.: The United Arab Emirates: A Study in Survival. Lynne Rienner Publishers, Boulder (2005)
13. Davison, R.M., Wagner, C., Ma, L.: From Government to E-government: a transition model. Information Technology and People 18(3), 280–299 (2005)
14. Dubai eGovernment: Dubai e-Government: Achievements and Lessons Learnt. UNDP Presentation (2005)
15. Dunleavy, P., et al.: New Public Management Is Dead-Long Live Digital-Era Governance. Journal of Public Administration Research and Theory 16(3), 467–494 (2006)
16. Fountain, J.: Building the Virtual State: Information Technology and Institutional Change. Brookings Institution Press, Washington, DC (2001)
17. Fox, J., Mourtada-Sabbah, N., Mutawa, M.: The Arab Gulf region: traditionalism glob-alized or globalization traditionalized? In: Fox, J., Mourtada-Sabbah, N., Mutawa, M. (eds.) Globalization and the Gulf, pp. 3–60. Routledge, New York (2006)
18. Heard-Bey, F.: The United Arab Emirates: statehood and nation building in a tradi-tional society. The Middle East Journal 59(3), 357–375 (2005)

19. Heeks, R.: Reinventing Government in the Information Age: International practice in IT-enabled public sector reform. Routledge, London (1999)
20. Heeks, R.: E-Government as a Carrier of Context. Journal of Public Policy 25(1), 51–74 (2005)
21. Heeks, R., Stanforth, C.: Understanding e-Government project trajectories from an ac-tor-network perspective. European Journal of Information Systems 16(2), 165–177 (2007)
22. Jakka, A.: Client-Quality Dimensions: empirical evidence from the public sector of the United Arab Emirates. Public Organization Review 4(3), 239–257 (2004)
23. Latham, R., Sassen, S.: Digital formations: constructing an object of study. In: Lat-ham, R., Sassen, S. (eds.) Digital Formations: IT and New Architectures in the Global Realm, pp. 1–33. Princeton University Press, New Jersey (2005)
24. Layne, K., Lee, J.: Developing fully functional E-government: a four stage model. Government Information Quarterly 18(2), 122–136 (2001)
25. Luna-Reyes, L.F., et al.: Information Systems Development as Emergent Socio-technical Change: a practice approach. European Journal of Information Systems 14(1), 93–105 (2005)
26. Okot-Uma, R.W., London, C.S.: Electronic Governance: re-inventing good governance. Commonwealth Secretariat, London (2000)
27. Sassen, S.: Constructing the Digital Object of Study. In: The 6th Social Study of IT workshop at the LSE in Celebration of Claudio Ciborra, London School of Economics and Political Science, London (2006a)
28. Sassen, S.: Forward. In: Dean, J., Anderson, J., Lovink, G. (eds.) Reformatting Poli-tics: Information Technology and Global Civil Society. Routledge, New York (2006b)
29. Sassen, S.: Personal communication with author via email (2006c)
30. Sethi, N., Sethi, V.: E-government Implementation: a case study of Dubai e-government. E-governance in Practice, pp. 185–195 (2009) (online), http://www.csi-sigegov.org/egovernance_pdf/22
31. Van Maanen, J.: Qualitative Studies of Organizations. Sage Publications, Thousand Oaks (1998)
32. Walsham, G.: Interpreting Information Systems in Organizations. John Wiley & Sons, New York (1993)
33. Yin, R.: The Case Study Crisis: some answers. Administrative Science Quarterly 26(1), 58–65 (1981)
34. Yin, R.: Case Study Research: Design and methods. Sage, Thousand Oaks (1994)
35. Zahlan, R.S.: The Origins of the United Arab Emirates. St. Martin's Press, New York (1978)

Building ICT Critical Infrastructures for Trade Regulations: Implications from a National Initiative in Mexico

Carla M. Bonina

London School of Economics and Political Science, Department of Management, Information Systems and Innovation Group, London, United Kingdom
c.m.bonina@lse.ac.uk

Abstract. New information and communication technologies (ICT) promise an era of remarkable changes for society. In this paper, I propose to reflect on the processes underlying a national ICT initiative in Mexico aimed at improving foreign trade regulation – the Single Window for Foreign Trade. The case offers an example of the complexities of building ICT critical infrastructures in a given context. Using a narrative approach, I address the challenges and potential strategic lessons that can be learned from the case. Overall, the study offers implications that can serve as a point for comparison to similar projects.

Keywords: e-government, ICT infrastructures, modernisation reforms, trade, Mexico.

1   Introduction

The use of the internet and new information and communication technologies (ICT) promises an era of remarkable changes for society, particularly in terms of opening up new channels of connectivity and organisation among business, governments, individuals and civil society groups. Governments around the world have been investing large amounts of money in public information systems. The main rationale for these investments relies on the strategic potential of these new ICT to reorganize tasks, routines and internal processes [10, pp.10–12], as well as them being a low-cost medium to interact with citizens more broadly [12]. Yet ICT adoption in the public sector (otherwise known as e-government) is a complex undertaking. Research in the field suggests that there have been over-optimistic and highly descriptive claims of the actual benefits that the internet has delivered to governments [9], [15], [30].

My research focuses broadly on technology-motivated programmes (e-government) within the process of public sector reforms that has been dominated by the global discourse relating to new public management, economic individualism and neoliberalism [5], [11]. Although there is a vast literature on e-government, the process of organising technology within the public sector in the context of broader modernisation reforms remains understudied.

M.D. Hercheui et al. (Eds.): HCC10 2012, IFIP AICT 386, pp. 22–33, 2012.

In this paper, I propose to reflect on the processes underlying a national ICT initiative in Mexico aimed at foreign trade facilitation. More precisely, the case focuses on the trajectory of events to build a digital single window (hereafter single window) for foreign trade. It represents an enormous effort of coordination between government agencies, the private sector and business associations. The aim of the paper is to address the potential strategic directions that can be drawn from the case, and to reflect on the main challenges that are presented when developing an ICT critical infrastructure for foreign trade.[1]

Deconstructing a large-scale and longitudinal case such the one described here is by no means straightforward. I reflect on the role of national governments in shaping the e-government strategy. Thus, my focus will remain on the organisational aspects of the case, its negotiating tensions and the potential effects on society as identified by looking at the various discourses of the champions involved in the project. To do so, I employ a narrative strategy to present the main events of the longitudinal case. This entailed a mixture of different collection methods: 38 in-depth interviews, direct observation, and extensive archival research. Employing a narrative approach seems fruitful to account for the particular design features, and process contextual factors and their interactions that underlie the case under study [2].

Theory on studies of e-government is not well developed (i.e. [15], [30]). To overcome this limitation, this work studies networked technologies in government not only as information processing tools and communicating technologies but also as elements of socio-technical systems composed of humans, technologies, politics, values, knowledge and tensions [12], and does so in context. The usefulness of this approach relies on the distinctive characterisation of technology within social contexts [1]. This distinction between technologies and their social context is of importance, because it rejects the common tool view of technology, which generally assumes that technology is neutral, unproblematic, or can be treated as a black box [23].

2   E-government and Modernisation Reforms

During the last two decades the diffusion of affordable networked technologies appeared as a useful tool to reinforce a powerful wave of reforms in many countries. Usually referred as New Public Management, these reforms were initiated in the 1980s in the developed economies (i.e. Canada, New Zealand, United Kingdom and the United States of America) and then spread globally. The reforms' motto, of a government that 'works better and costs less', led to a growing interest in adopting CT to support the reform of public administrations [13], [16], [17] and to reinvent citizen-government relations, giving growing attention to the term e-government. In many countries, most research on e-government is understood as a tool to reinforce the objectives of public administration reforms [21], [22], although the connection

---

[1] I use the term 'ICT critical infrastructure' in a rather loose way to refer to a technology-based information infrastructure that have a vital importance for the country, which its destruction or disruption can have negative impacts on the national economy, national security or the efficient operation of government.

between broader institutional reforms and e-government is less explicit. E-government has been studied from many perspectives, from a means to achieve something else (i.e. administrative reforms) or as an end in itself [30]. Yet the most common view understands e-government as the generalised use of new ICT to provide better public services, to improve public administration performance and to broaden citizen participation and democratic processes [4], [8], [12], [14], [30].

From a normative perspective, there have been many claims that new ICT will make citizen-government transactions easier, cheaper and faster. These claims have been mainly supported by models that build on stages of development and different levels of e-government maturity that were originally developed for e-business processes [18]. Usually, the models depict a transaction-oriented view in which electronic government development occurs in three general maturity phases: the early, middle, and later stages. The more mature the stages, the levels of interaction, collaboration and management increase in complexity both, in terms of government's back office functionality and the interactions with citizens. These models imply a sequence towards more e-government, assuming that more e-government is better. However, they usually remain limited as they cannot account for processes, contextual factors, and triggers that make some strategies more successful than others.

Research in the area of ICT and development has provided valuable insights into the multiple social, political, economic and technical dimensions that shape, and are shaped during, modernization reforms that include building technological platforms (see for example [1] and [19]). The fact that political forces together with other multiple socio-technical factors shape the design, implementation or use of ICT in government does not remain an exclusive domain of research on development. Studies in the particular area of e-government that have been conducted in other settings such as Europe and the United States of America have already demonstrated that political influences shape the outcomes of public information systems [12], [10].

Mexico presents hybrid characteristics that make it hard to classify the country simply as a developing economy. For example, Mexico has been a member of the Organisation for Economic Co-operation and Development OECD since 1995, and has been recently classified as a newly industrialised countries (NICs) suggests a more complex scenario. Yet it is not the purpose of this article to enter into a classification debate. Rather, the aim is to suggest that a contextualist approach is crucial to understand not only the local dynamics embedded in the case but also those particular features that shape the organisation, its actors and the technology employed [1]. The narrative approach will thus be used to highlight these processes.

3   A Brief Context of Mexican Reforms and Foreign Trade

Mexico is the 13th largest economy in the world, the second largest in Latin America after Brazil, and the third major merchant of the emerging economies, after China and Russia. Mexico's international trade is crucial for its economy, representing about

60% of the total gross domestic product (GDP).[2] For the last 30 years, Mexico has implemented strong economic and political reforms, ending its welfare state model, and embarking on drastic economic liberalisation based on neoliberal ideals. In economic terms, the country is one of the most open in the world, and has stable and strong macroeconomic indicators. Liberalisation of trade was undoubtedly achieved in 1994 when Canada, Mexico, and the United States launched the North America Free Trade Agreement (NAFTA), the largest free trade agreement in the world.

Yet, social inequalities and distribution of income remain unresolved. Gradual modernisation reforms were started in the public administration, partly because of the economic, market-driven reforms, and partly because of f political democratisation. As a result, the Mexican public administration has also been transformed from a clientelistic and highly political bureaucracy towards a more professionalised and impartial one. In sum, these broader institutional changes that Mexico has started in the mid-1980s have persisted as the contextual features of this case[3].

My entrance point in this case is the regulatory activities of Mexican foreign trade. In Mexico, the administrative procedures related to foreign trade activities involve the issue of around 37,000 export licenses, 1 million import licenses and 10 million importation requests per year. There are more than 55 thousand foreign trade users and around 30 main actors from several sectors, including government agencies, exporters, importers, logistics and trade associations. The regulatory requirements and normativity of trade procedures are complex: a common operation of foreign trade entails the presentation of at least 40 different documents that include between seven and 14 paper sheets. The government estimates that at least 65% of single data points are captured on more than one occasion (i.e. the identification of a given enterprise).

The events I will introduce correspond to several developments that the central offices of the government in Mexico put in place to build a single window for foreign trade procedures from 2008 to 2012 (*"Ventanilla Digital de Comercio Exterior"*). The initiative aims to simplify, and make more efficient and transparent the trade regulation. The case entails an enormous back-office integration effort –that is still ongoing– intended to support the facilitation of international trade, based on efforts that can be traced back to mid-1990s. Given the fact that Mexico faces important challenges related to economic growth, income distribution and social policies, gains from international trade are considered key for improving the country's welfare.

4   The Mexican ICT Infrastructure for Foreign Trade

The case description is structured into three chronological periods. Period 1 (SICEX phase I) goes back to the mid-1990s and covers the award-winning technological platform to support international trade procedures, called SICEX (Integral System for

---

[2] Data for the year 2010; based on a nominal GDP list of countries. Source: International Monetary Fund, World Economic Outlook Database, April 2011: Nominal GDP list of countries.

[3] For reasons of space, I have been very brief on the Mexican reforms. For a review of the economic and social policy aftermath in Mexico see [20]. For changes in the bureaucratic structure and Mexico's steps towards democratisation, see [6] and [24].

Foreign Trade). I pay particular attention to this phase's initial problems and what problems the platform came to resolve as well as its main achievements. Period 2 (SICEX phases II and III) presents very briefly the main actions, developments and results from 2000 until 2008. From 2008 to 2012 (period 3), I review more extensively the recent developments and advances towards the design and pre-implementation of "the Mexican Digital Window for Foreign Trade". The phases, main events and contextual factors are summarised in the figure 1 below. The entry point is the Ministry of Economy which has been the agency leading the initiative.

4.1   Period 1: Building an ICT Platform for Trade Procedures from Scratch (1995-2000)

Back in 1995, the Mexican government started its first steps to build a new technological platform to support administrative simplification [27]. The initial motivation behind the project was the need to have clear rules and procedures to eliminate the disparate variations in decision-making, performance, and results of foreign trade regulation in an increasing competitive environment created by NAFTA. The absence of a clear system of rules co-existed with disparate and precarious technological platforms, each operating according to its own logic. Moreover, there was at best a weak communication infrastructure to connect databases in different locations. This means that the diverse offices of the Ministry of Economy (i.e. the central office and the 52 federal delegations) analysed procedures that drew on different information standards. Security was not robust and, together with the different interpretations of decision standards, there were notable differences between offices when issuing administrative decisions.

   With the help of its own "clients" (foreign trade companies), the government started several actions in parallel: a process redesign, a rationalisation of procedures, and the design of a unified, central database that would enable the decentralisation of the administrative operations. By the end of 2000, trade procedures were standardised, responded to newly created rules, and were broadly incorporated into a single and integrated database. By 2000 it was also possible to comply with certain regulations over the internet, mainly those that were informative such as annual reports from the beneficiaries of special export programs. [4] The implementation of the technological platform meant that foreign trade procedures (i.e. rules of origin certificate approvals, authorisation and management of import quotas and licenses) became integrated under a single and unique database, registered and standardised into one information system that could be accessed from decentralised points across the country.

---

[4] The capabilities of the system, by 2000, where mainly reduced to streamlining the processes of reception, authorisation and resolution inside the ME. Submission or collection of procedures was vastly done face to face.

Overall, average response times were reduced, and also allowed the first steps towards collaboration with other government agencies. In particular, the connectivity with Customs became a salient feature.

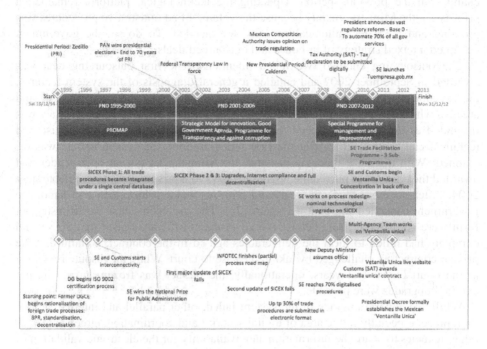

Fig. 1. Case timeline: from SICEX to digital-window for foreign trade. Source: own data[5]

These initial efforts may seem modest compared to the progress that other countries were making at the same time (i.e. International Trade database in the United States of America) or in terms of scope. After all, one may argue that the case was simply all a matter of putting things in order, and streamlining processes with the help of a single database. Yet, the system represented a milestone for the Mexican public administration and set a precedent for other e-government programmes. In 1999, the National Institute of Public Administration awarded the Ministry of Economy with the most prestigious national prize in public administration for its innovative achievements and possibilities of replication. [6]

---

[5] SE stands for Ministry of Economy; SICEX stands for Integral System for foreign trade; PND stands for National Development Plan.

[6] In Spanish, the Prize is called *"Premio Nacional de Administracion Publica"*, and it is the only one granted to the Ministry of Economy and to an e-government programme in Mexico.

4.2   Period 2: Turning into a Slower Pace (2000-208)

During the next phase (2000-2006 and 2006-2008) the project was strengthened in terms of continuity, although but with modest achievements in comparison to the changes in the previous period. Updating the technological platform remained a priority for the Ministry, mainly because the volume of administrative procedures was growing and more technological capacity was needed. To do so, the government occupied a mixed strategy of in-house and outsourced deals.

The outsourcing entailed two failed intentions. The first outsourcing deal was awarded in September 2002 and entailed a general diagnosis of the system features, the revision of procedures (a classic business process re-engineering exercise) and areas in which SICEX should be upgraded. [7] Only three months later, the contract was rescinded as the Ministry alleged that the company lacked sufficient expertise and technical capabilities [26]. After the first failed attempt, the system update was re-planned. With a clearer roadmap in hand, the Ministry set out an open tender and awarded the contract to pursue the upgrading tasks to a private company in September 2004. After no more than one year, and with no major achievements in hand, the government cancelled the contract again [26]. The arguments that the Ministry set forth were no different from before; the government officials argued that the second company had failed to meet the deliverables agreed in the contract, a claim that the private contractors challenged by taking the case to court. While the dispute remained in the court for several years, operationally, the budget was frozen and no further external upgrades were possible.

While the general upgrade of the system failed, other parallel and internal actions took place, especially in the area of digital security and coordination agreements with other agencies to share the information and availability for the electronic validation of a growing number of formalities. By 2008, most of the results concentrated on updating and maintaining the technological capabilities internally (both the platform and the digital connectivity with Customs), continuing the efforts towards simplification and elimination of red tape (such as unnecessary trade regulations), and building the basis for international collaborations with other countries. In technological terms, there were neither major changes in the ways in which the system worked or was operated nor was there a notable change in the main features the system could support.

4.3   Period 3: From SICEX to the Digital Single Window for Foreign Trade (2008-2012)

In August 2008, a new Minister of Economy was appointed, and with him, new leaders in trade regulations took office. [8] From then onwards, SICEX's fate was to be

---

[7] The whole contract included the revision of 18 modules that were on SICEX. The total length of the contract was about three months.

[8] In Mexico is common that, one a new Minister is appointed, he or she will pick new undersecretaries and eventually, new General Directors. In terms of the project, a new Deputy Secretary of Industry and a new General Director of foreign trade were appointed accordingly.

converted radically: the idea of 'seriously' building a single window for foreign trade was born.

A number of institutional forces contributed to this new idea. The first came from a technical opinion that the Mexican Competition Authority (Comisión Federal de Competencia, (CFC)) produced in May 2008 regarding issues affecting Mexico's performance in foreign trade. In the opinion, which was grounded in economic terms and international statistics, the CFC identified that Mexico could achieve a significantly better performance in economic growth and competitiveness by investing in foreign trade facilitation policies [7]. The CFC recommended the reduction in the levels and dispersion of tariff regulations, to simplify and deregulate customs clearance procedures and to build institutional capabilities for government agencies that regulate foreign trade. The use of new ICT to support the processes of simplification of trade procedures, especially for customs clearance, was also highlighted. The opinion was timely with regard to Mexico's concerns concerning its relative worsening position against China as a main export supplier for the United States of America (the main market for Mexico's exports). The Ministry of Economy adopted this opinion – in conjunction with others coming from international bodies (i.e. World Bank, OECD) – so as to support an ambitious trade reform that included a massive reduction in tariffs, and a more strategic use of networked technologies, to support the trade facilitation process. The policy was grouped under the label "Programme for Trade Facilitation" and was initiated in 2008 with clear goals to achieve before the end of the Presidential period (December 2012).

A further fact, also related to the CFC's opinion, had to do with Mexico's poor performance in world's competitiveness and trade facilitation indexes. The World Bank's [29] report entitled Doing Business positioned Mexico number 41 across 183 economies for doing business in 2010. Yet, in terms of trading across borders (a sub-category on which the total score is built), Mexico scored as number 69. Given the complexity of the current system of trade procedures, according to government data, Mexico could advance at least 40 positions with the single window [28]. Not surprisingly, escalating positions in a world ranking such as the World Bank Doing Business or the World Economic Forum Competitiveness Report, translates into a strong political incentive, given the publicity and visibility of the two reports both nationally and in global trade forums.

Within this context, after a series of informal meetings between Customs, the Ministry of Economy and other members of the Foreign Trade Commission, the initiative was formally founded within a working group for the simplification of trade procedures that was set up in July 2009. The people participating in the sub-group knew each other well – at least in their majority. In some cases, they had worked together in setting up the first steps towards coordination mechanisms between Customs and the Ministry of Economy back in the 1900s. In other words, there was a history of collaboration or coordination that had started several years before. Yet, it was not until 2009 that this sub-group gained a rather more formal status.

The two following figures can offer a clearer illustration of the main policy ideas behind the single window. The left hand side of figure 2 depicts the complexity of foreign trade procedures in the year 2010. The right-side figure portrays the Ministry of Economy and Customs' view on how the trading across borders would (or should) look like once the project is put in place.

Current Scenario   2012: One-Stop-Shop

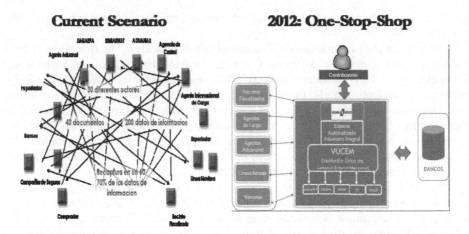

Fig. 2. Current versus planned scenario of foreign trade procedures. Source: [28]

In June 2010, Customs set forth an open tender to outsource the project, which was awarded later in October of the same year. The contract includes an exhaustive revision of procedures, the design and implementation of the web-based platform, the digitalisation of five years of paper-based procedures (archival information of Customs daily operations), and the mobile operation of the entire system. The contract was awarded for five years, had tough deadlines, and stipulated achievable results within the current presidential administration.

With the contract awarded, one of the major milestones of the project was the passage of the Presidential Decree on January 2011. In order to avoid relying on the "good will" of the governmental agencies, the passage of a decree gave a strong political and legal support to the single window for foreign trade. The legal tool, entitled "Decree that establishes the Mexican Digital Window of Foreign Trade", put firm deadlines for interagency integration and required that each authority should facilitate the necessary infrastructure required. In addition, it established three phases for the project implementation (article III) on a progressive calendar of integration which was due to be finished by the end of 2012[9]. The decree also gave legal support to the above-mentioned working group for trade facilitation, by setting up officially an Inter-Secretariat Commission for the Single Window. The Commission has provided the basis for negotiating, debating and coordinating the tight deadlines that the project set forth. The Ministry of Economy retained the lead role in the project, even though the funds for building the single window come from the Customs budget.

In parallel, there were two important institutional changes in the area of digital policy agenda in Mexico that contributed towards the trajectory of the project. The

---

[9] The phases of implementation were described according to the actors that should be operating in different points in time. Thus, phase I establishes that the Ministry of Economy and Customs start operating no later than 30 September 2011; and all the other ten Ministries with inference in trade (i.e. the Ministries of Agriculture, Health, Environment) should be included on the platform no later than 30 June 2012).

first one was the approval for the use of the advanced electronic signature (FIEL) in Mexico. In June 2009, the Mexican Tax Authority implemented a federal resolution that made the electronic submission of patrimonial tax declaration mandatory for all public servants. That was the starting point for making the use of FIEL a reality, and was also an example of the public sector relying on the monopoly of the use of authority [3]. In the context of the case, it meant a strategic step: from 2009, the rollout of authorised digital signatures among public servants became pervasive. A second institutional change entailed a tough agenda for digital electronic procedures. In 2010 the President announced a big step towards regulatory clearance, which set forth to automate 70% of all government services by 2012. Together with other measures, such as the raising importance of the Digital Government Agenda and the Austerity Decree, it gave even more support to the Ministry of Economy-Customs single window initiative.

In January 2012, the President formally inaugurated the Single Window for Foreign Trade, which is still operating within a trial period and limited to some locations and only 21 trade procedures. In March 2012, more than 24,000 companies have registered as potential users of the single window (half of the entire universe of users). There have been around 25,000 digital invoices, even when they are as yet optional until June 1st, 2012. The process of digitalisation of the paper-based archive of trade procedures has reached around 70% of completion, while the website has had more than 280,000 visits since its opening in October 2011. From June 2012, the use of the single window will be mandatory for every foreign trade operations with Customs.

5   Concluding Remarks

While at first glance the progress and results that the project achieved between 2008 and 2012 look impressive, a more detailed understanding of the case shows that the single window project has been immersed in a strong, longer history of broader institutional dynamics. On the one side, for example, the constant work towards simplifying and eliminating unnecessary regulation has been supported by broader modernisation reforms in the public administration in Mexico. On the other side, economic reforms and the opening to trade, particularly after the enforcement of NAFTA in 1995, changed remarkably the scenario of trade in Mexico. As a senior Mexican official in foreign affairs put it: "the changes that NAFTA brought into the economy of Mexico were impressive... You could not explain Mexico's trade today (2012) without considering NAFTA and all the concomitant regulatory changes that it meant for trade operations".

There were lots of tensions and negotiations that happened during the years and, particularly, within the latest three. A salient and visible feature is the strong political support that the project achieved, especially with the passage of the Presidential Decree in 2010. But many other less 'visible' factors contributed to what in a first sight could be seen as an easily replicable experience. A remarkable characteristic is the longstanding process of building state capacity in the agencies involved (Customs and Economy) and the level of expertise and collaboration that the members of the project achieved throughout a process of more than 10 years. Another characteristic is the personal capabilities of senior government officials to drive the project to the highest levels of support possible. And a third characteristic involves the broader institutional dynamics that push for more use of technology in government, red tape elimination, and the space that foreign trade policies occupy in the national agenda. In addition, the presence of international bodies, whether providing technical support (i.e. OECD and the World Bank) or opening up platforms for sharing knowledge (Latin American and Caribbean Economic System (SELA), Inter-American development Bank (IADB), has also helped to shape the trajectory of the project. This is not to say that the international bodies imposed their own views and agendas. Rather, Mexico enacted some of them to achieve its own policy on trade.

The conclusions of the 3rd Latin American and Caribbean Regional Meeting on International Trade Single Windows held in November 2011 summarised what the Mexican project has seemed to have achieved so far: "The plans to establish International Trade Single Windows form an integral part of the structure of public services and promotion of competitiveness... Such projects should take due account of fundamental variables, such as: support from governments, formulation of public policies on the matter, the consolidation of a legal and regulatory framework, the linkage of the agencies involved with trade processes, and the establishment of the Single Windows architecture, based on an all-encompassing vision of the institutional framework for foreign trade and its stakeholders" [25, pp.3].

Although the implementation effects on trade flows, transparency and control mechanisms are yet to be seen, the steps that the Mexican federal government has taken are remarkable. The focus of the narrative has been to reflect on the government role and the processes underlying the construction of an ICT critical infrastructure such as that on trade in Mexico.

References

1. Avgerou, C.: The significance of context in information systems and organizational change. Information Systems Journal 11(1), 43–63 (2001)
2. Barzelay, M.: Learning from Second-Hand Experience: Methodology for Extrapolation-Oriented Case Research. Governance 20(3), 521–543 (2007)
3. Benington, J., Moore, M.H.: Public value in Complex and Changing Times. In: Benington, J., Moore, M.H. (eds.) Public Value: Theory and Practice, pp. 1–30. Palgrave Macmillan, Basingstoke (2011)
4. Bhatnagar, S.C.: E-government: from vision to implementation: a practical guide with case studies. Sage Publications, New Delhi (2004)
5. Bozeman, B.: Public values and public interest: Counterbalancing economic individualism. Georgetown University Press, Washington, DC (2007)
6. Cejudo, G.: Explaining Change in the Mexican Public Sector: The Limits of New Public Management. International Review of Administrative Sciences 74(1), 111–127 (2007)
7. Comisión Federal de Competencia: Opinión con el fin de promover la aplicación de los principios de competencia y libre concurrencia en el diseño y aplicación de políticas y regulaciones del comercio exterior de mercancías. Presidencia, Mexico City (2008)

8. Cordella, A.: E-government: towards the e-bureaucratic form? Journal of Information Technology 22(3), 265–274 (2007)
9. Coursey, D., Norris, D.F.: Models of E-Government: Are They Correct? An Empirical Assessment. Public Administration Review 68(3), 523–536 (2008)
10. Dunleavy, P., Margetts, H., et al.: Digital-era governance. IT Corporations, The State, and E-Government. Oxford University Press, Oxford (2006)
11. Fairclough, N.: Critical discourse analysis: the critical study of language, 2nd edn. Longman, Harlow (2010)
12. Fountain, J.: Building the virtual state: information technology and institutional change. Brookings Institution Press, Washington, DC (2001)
13. Gruening, G.: Origins and theoretical basis of New public Management. International Public Management Journal 4(1), 1–25 (2001)
14. Heeks, R.: Reinventing Government in the Information Age. In: Heeks, R. (ed.) Reinventing Government in the Information Age - International Practice in IT-enabled Public Sector Reform, pp. 9–21. Routeledge, London (2002)
15. Heeks, R., Bailur, S.: Analyzing e-government research: Perspective, philosophies, theories, methods, and practice. Government Information Quarterly 24(2), 243–265 (2007)
16. Hood, C.: A Public Management for All Seasons? Public Administration 69(1), 3–19 (1991)
17. Kettl, D.F.: The global public management revolution. Brookings Institution Press, Washington, D.C. (2005)
18. Layne, K., Lee, J.W.: Developing fully functional E-government: A four stage model. Government Information Quarterly 18(2), 122–136 (2001)
19. Madon, S., Sahay, S., Sudan, R.: E-Government Policy and Health Information Systems Implementation in Andhra Pradesh, India: Need for Articulation of Linkages Between the Macro and the Micro. The Information Society 23(5), 327–345 (2007)
20. Moreno-Brid, J.C., Pardinas Carpizo, J.E., Ros Bosch, J.: Economic Development and Social Policies in Mexico. Economy and Society 38(1), 154–176 (2009)
21. OECD: E-government for better government. OECD, Paris, France (2005)
22. OECD: The e-Government imperative. OECD, Paris (2003)
23. Orlikowski, W., Iacono, S.: Research Commentary: Desperately Seeking the "IT" in IT Research–A Call to Theorizing the IT Artifact. Information Systems Research 12(2), 121–134 (2001)
24. Panizza, F., Philip, G.: Second Generation Reform in Latin America: Reforming the Public Sector in Uruguay and Mexico. Journal of Latin American Studies 37(4), 667–691 (2005)
25. SELA: Conclusions and Recommendations: III Latin American and Caribbean Regional Meeting on International Trade Single Windows, Caracas, Venezuela: Latin American and Caribbean Economic System, SELA (2011)
26. Secretaría de Economía: Memoria Documental Hacia la Administración Sin Papeles/SICEX (2006)
27. Secretaría de Economía: Sistema Integral de Comercio Exterior. Un caso de éxito en la administración de autorizaciones de comercio exterior (1999)
28. Secretaría de Economía: Ventanilla Única de Comercio Exterior Mexicana (2010)
29. World Bank: Doing Business 2010: Reforming Through Difficult Times. Doing Business. The World Bank, Washington D.C. (2010)
30. Yildiz, M.: E-government research: Reviewing the literature, limitations, and ways forward. Government Information Quarterly 24(3), 646–665 (2007)

Getting It Right: The Importance of Targeting Structural Causes of Failure in E-Government

Silvia Masiero

Information Systems and Innovation Group,
London School of Economics and Political Sciences, London, United Kingdom
s.masiero@lse.ac.uk

Abstract. In this paper we look at the application of ICTs to the improvement of state-citizen relations in developing countries. Our argument is that, to maximize responsiveness of the government, ICTs need to "get it right," by targeting exactly those problems from which unresponsiveness of the state to citizens emerges. Failure arises from the fact that ICTs, rather than being used for targetting issues in government responsiveness, are utilized for other purposes, primarily as a means to obtaining and preserving political support. This argument is illustrated through a case study of computerization of the ration card procedure in Kerala, southern India. Here, while the structural problems of the ration card process lie at the back-end level of application processing, the technology devised by the government addresses predominantly the front-end, politically appealing node of application performance by the citizens. This strategy does not "get it right," as it leaves untouched the crucial reason of state unresponsiveness, and indeed, it produces long-run dissatisfaction in citizens. Implications are both theoretical, as a cause for expectation failure in IS is identified and deconstructed, and practical, as an orientation to structural problems is recommended to ICT designers and policymakers.

Keywords: e-government, failure, ration cards, Public Distribution System, Kerala.

1 Introduction

ICTs have been applied to a plethora of objectives, among which the construction of a better government that maximizes the state's capacity of serving its citizens. The logic behind the onset of e-government practices lies in the idea that by automating the interaction between public officers and recipients ICTs remove the discretional power of street-level bureaucrats, and are, therefore, instrumental in eliminating the inefficiencies derived by human management of this relation [3]. This idea, over the last decades, has been largely applied to the domain of less-developed countries (LDCs), generally characterized by institutional frailty and flawed accountability of the state.

In this paper we look at the application of ICTs to the improvement of state-citizen relations in a developing country context. Our argument is that, to maximize responsiveness of the government, ICTs need to "get it right," which means that they must

M.D. Hercheui et al. (Eds.): HCC10 2012, IFIP AICT 386, pp. 34–43, 2012.

target exactly those structural problems from which unresponsiveness of the state to citizens is generated. Failure arises from the fact that the solution to structural problems, affecting interaction between the state and citizens, is not necessarily a politically appealing objective, whereas ICTs tend to be conceived primarily as a means to achieving and maintaining political support. Mistargeting of ICT policies, towards politically popular objectives and away from structural problems, lies at the root of perpetuated interaction problems and citizen dissatisfaction.

To illustrate this proposition, we focus on an information system devised by the government of Kerala, southern India, to deliver ration cards to citizens. A ration card is the document needed, in all India, to access subsidized food and supplies under the Public Distribution System (PDS), the biggest national anti-poverty programme. The government of Kerala has invested on automating front-end procedures for application performance; though, it emerged from our work that structural problems with ration card delivery lie at the level of application processing, because procedures for managing citizen requests are uncertain and largely unknown by bureaucrats. Failure emerges from the fact that the government, instead of using ICTs for addressing structural problems in the application procedure, has focused on a politically appealing objective, namely amelioration of a single, front-end component of the process.

This paper is structured as follows. First, we outline our theoretical perspective, as a context-oriented vision inscribed in the field of ICT for development (ICT4D). Then, we look at the Keralite experience with the Ration Card Management System (RCMS), an information system which arises as a paradigm of technology usage for maximizing responsiveness of the state to disadvantaged citizens. In our discussion of the case, we deconstruct the procedure behind ration card delivery, and the role of technology at each stage of the process. It emerges that, while application performance has been fully computerized in Kerala, RCMS has not targeted the structural node of the process (i.e., application processing by government bureaucrats). We conclude by discussing the contribution of this case to theory, as a cause for failure is identified and de-constructed in the domains of ICT4D and practice, as an orientation to structural problems is recommended for ICT designers and policymakers.

2   Theoretical Perspective: Context Orientation in ICT4D

The field of ICT4D, in which digital technologies are conceptualized as potential or actual agents of human development, is the focus of a burgeoning amount of literature. Our reading of ICT4D draws on the domain of Information Systems (IS), and is therefore concerned with IS research conducted with respect to developing countries. In spite of the proliferation of research, the field still lacks a stable conceptualization of the causes of e-government failure [5]: anecdotal evidence prevails, and reflection on the etiological roots of negative experiences is ultimately overlooked. Here, we concentrate on the level of causal linkages between actors' decisions and failure, in order to foster reflection on this scarcely analyzed component of ICT4D.

Our point of departure is that of Avgerou [1], according to whom it is fundamental for IS research to associate technology innovation with the context in which it is embedded. The key implication of this approach for our research is that the idea of "good government," should be defined with specific respect to the context of analysis provided in our work by a state in southern India. To unpack the idea of "good government", we rely on the work of Corbridge et al. [4] whose account identifies good government with the possibility for citizens to "see the state" in a better way, which means accessing governmental provisions in an equal and frequent manner.

The idea of "seeing the state," elaborated with specific reference to India, relies on a system of institutional characteristics that are specifically proper for this nation. In the heavy fabric of Indian bureaucracy, interaction between citizens and the central government is problematic [2], [4], [6]. Lacking capacity to access government arises perhaps as the main problem of contemporary India, perpetuating the issues of a poor quality of life. Encounters with the state systematically turn into frustrating experiences, especially for the poor and disadvantaged. People can be left for hours waiting outside a public office, just to be attended to by time-pressed and unwilling bureaucrats, or not to be attended to at all. As we engage with observing ICTs for state-citizen relations in the Indian context, we need to keep these specificities into account. As a result, we postulate that in our case a better government is a government that maximizes its responsiveness to the citizens. That is, a better government responds to its citizens' requests in a prompt and timely manner, without hidden costs.

This leads us to deconstruct the idea of governmental technologies [9] on which the vision of government by Corbridge et al. [4] is grounded. Technologies of rule comprise all the government-led instruments that enable spaces of encounter between citizens and the bureaucracy. ICTs, the logic goes, are able to make these encounters more fruitful, as they can infuse effectiveness and accountability through automation. In our context of analysis, constituted by the frailty and complexity of Indian institutions, a good technology of rule is one that allows citizens to better "see the state" in that it maximizes responsiveness of the government to the citizens. Therefore, it is important to illuminate the mechanisms that flow from ICT adoption to better governmental technologies.

Hence, our work is grounded on a context-oriented approach, according to which concepts are to be analyzed with specific reference to the space of action in which they are embedded. Thus our idea of "good government" is conceptualized with specific reference to India, whose core problem is identified as lacking capacity of citizens to "see the state" in equal terms. As a result, our idea of "good government" coincides with a government that can maximize responsiveness of the state to its citizens, especially the poor and disadvantaged. As noted above, ICTs arise as potential actors in the improvement of this responsiveness, due to capacity of automating state-citizen relationships. The system at the centre of our case study, implemented in a state in southern India, has been conceived exactly for this purpose.

3   Methodology

Our case study is part of a broader research project, namely a Ph.D. in Information Systems, which focuses on a modular set of computerized applications at the

Government of Kerala, known as the Targeted Efficient Transparent Rationing and Allocation Public Distribution System (TETRAPDS). The software at the centre of this paper, namely the Ration Card Management System (RCMS), constitutes just one of the several modules of the TETRAPDS fabric. The study of the actor network centred on RCMS has involved three months in the field. While based in Trivandrum, the capital city of Kerala, we engaged in diverse forms of investigation of the actor network, more specifically:

- Interaction with software developers has consisted of three demonstration sessions on the diverse components of TETRAPDS-RCMS, each of which lasted between 30 and 90 minutes, followed by questions from the researcher. Demonstration sessions have been complemented by in-depth interviews with software designers and decision-makers.
- Government officials have been approached at two levels: firstly, at the level of the Department of Food and Civil Supplies, where the central applications of TETRAPDS-RCMS are located and managed; secondly, at the level of Taluk Supply Offices (TSOs), which constitute the interface between the Department of Food and Civil Supplies and citizens. Out of seventy Taluk Supply Offices in Kerala, seven have been the object of participant observation, which was complemented by in-depth interviews at both levels.
- Citizens – the final users of the programme – were studied in two aspects of their relation with TETRAPDS-RCMS: firstly, in the telecentres where application for a ration card is performed; and secondly, in the ration shops where PDS goods are supplied. Participant observation has been carried out in both settings, encompassing 3 cities and 5 rural villages. This has been also complemented by in-depth interviews, which were, except in a few cases, mediated by a translator.

Furthermore, primary research has been complemented by encyclopedic insights on anti-poverty programmes, especially as far as the peculiarities implicit in the Indian context are concerned, and on the usage of digital technologies in these toolkits for poverty reduction. The purpose of this research design was to gain a full understanding the network of actors around TETRAPDS-RCMS. Adoption of this perspective results in the researcher's capability of overcoming dichotomy in the juxtaposition of the technical domain and the social domain [1]. Instead, the focus is on mechanisms that link technicality to socially-oriented outcomes, in this case conceptualized in terms of change of the relations between the state and citizens.

4   Case Study: The Ration Card Management System (RCMS)

Our case study can be viewed as a typical one, as its content is paradigmatic in two different respects: in terms of the problem, which qualifies a typical situation of non-responsiveness of the state to its citizens; and in terms of the solution, in which ICTs are used to tackle the problem of unresponsiveness. The context for the case is provided by the state of Kerala, where access to subsidized PDS goods is conditional to ownership of a document known as ration card. Unresponsiveness of the state is mirrored by its inaction, in front of a huge amount of unattended ration card applications: the solution devised by the government relies on RCMS, an information system that has computerized the procedure for obtaining a ration card. Digitalization aimed at achieving prompt and timely delivery of this crucial document.

The PDS is the biggest anti-poverty programme ever implemented in India, in terms of both coverage and public expenditure. The purpose of this programme is that of maximizing food security for poor people, by subsidizing the price of primary necessity items, mainly rice, wheat, sugar and kerosene. Originally, the PDS was universal, which means that the subsidy was intended to reach all citizens without discrimination: so designed, the programme accounted for an unsustainable level of expenditure for the central government [10]. As a result, in 1997 the programme has been re-designed as the Targeted Public Distribution System (TPDS) in which the central government, on the basis of a standard income-based poverty line, determines the number of Below Poverty Line (BPL) people in each state, and allocates PDS goods among the states on the basis of relative poverty incidence.

Before the changes occurred in 1997, Kerala boasted one of the best state-level PDS systems in India as a whole. Yet, with the introduction of targeting policies, the PDS in Kerala has been put under severe strain: indeed, given that only 25% of the Kerala population has been termed BPL by the Government of India, allocation of food grains to the state has been reduced to only 10% of the previous supply. In this complicated situation, the Government has decided to revitalize the PDS through computerization: hence, it has relied on the National Informatics Centre (NIC) for development of a suite of software for PDS implementation, known as TETRAPDS. The system at the centre of our study, RCMS, is the part of TETRAPDS that digitalizes the procedure for ration card applications. The ration card is the document on which access to PDS goods crucially depends. Indeed, purchase of subsidized commodities happens exclusively upon presentation of the ration card to the authorized ration dealer (ARD), in the dedicated fair-price shops.

This document is household-based, and displays, on its first page, the poverty status of the family, from which the entitlement to PDS goods depends: as a result of targeting policies, poorer families are entitled to a higher amount of PDS goods per month, at a lower price resulting from greater subsidy. The rationale behind this document is twofold: firstly, by assigning a unique identification to each household, ration cards should enforce targeting policies and minimize leakage of the programme to non-poor families, a problem for which the universal system was severely criticized. Second, as a stamp is put by the ARD on the card at the moment of purchase of PDS commodities, this document should guarantee that households refrain from getting subsidized goods beyond their ration.

As a result of its strong tradition in terms of public action, and of the deep level of decentralization that has followed Panchayati Raj reforms, Kerala is by far one of the best-administered states in the Indian federation as a whole. In such a well-managed state, the governmental procedure for obtaining a ration card should flow smoothly. Instead, perhaps paradoxically in the "good government" landscape that characterizes Kerala, the procedure is ridden with serious problems. A key symptom of which is the disastrous result, registered in August 2010, constituted by 600,000 unprocessed ration card applications. This means that as a result of government inaction, 600,000 families were unable to benefit from an anti-poverty net of crucial importance.

The government of Kerala, whose reliance on e-governance is very high, has decided to resort to the computerized RCMS to solve the problem. The purpose of this system is that of computerizing the entire procedure for ration card release, from application to final delivery of the document required. This system is based on the digitalization of data for all the PDS recipients in Kerala (i.e., 6.4 million households). The functioning of RCMS is organized as follows. Firstly, citizens present their application for a ration card. Applications, which were previously processed at the TSOs, are now submitted on the Internet through telecentres operated across the entire state. Secondly, applications and of the documents supporting them are verified by bureaucrats at the office of the Rationing Inspector. In the case of a positive outcome, the new document is produced electronically and delivered by the local TSO.

So devised, the system should ensure delivery (or a clear motivation, in case of document denial) along three dimensions: actual performance, as applications made on the Internet should not be lost or deleted; time, as a specific time frame is ensured by the technology; and cost, as malpractice and corruption are to be avoided by computerized enforcement of the queue discipline. Hence, RCMS aims to ensure that a request of the citizen is matched by a prompt and timely response by the government, with respect to a document – the ration card – which is of paramount importance in the life of Keralite citizens. Is the programme actually able to do so?

5   Discussion

The encounter between state and citizens, related to delivery of a ration card, is articulated in two phases. The first phase concerns application for a new document by citizens through telecentres. The second phase focuses on application processing by government bureaucrats, which should precede the actual delivery of the document. The functioning of this twofold procedure will be examined here, with particular regard to the role of technology in the pursuit of each of the two phases.

5.1   Application Performance

Upon access to the website of the Kerala Department of Food and Civil Supplies (http://civilsupplieskerala.gov.in), at the moment of writing, users are faced with a captivating, bright-red message: "Online ration card applications can be submitted by citizens through Akshaya centres". Akshaya centres are the telecentres – government-sponsored spaces, where computers and the Internet are made available to the public – located across Kerala.

Trust-building around Akshaya, one of the key objectives of this telecentre project, has been proactively sustained by two combined factors. Firstly, Keralites rely heavily on government institutions [7], which have been transferred to the Akshaya project as a governmental brand, but the actual management of e-kiosks is left with private entrepreneurs. Second, there is strong leverage in the Akshaya project for the construction of human relations between e-kiosk entrepreneurs and citizens. These entrepreneurs were selected among socially influential people in their communities, and as revealed by a previous round of fieldwork in Kerala [8], they were constructed as the "human link" between people and the novelty of ICTs. The combination of these two elements -- the governmental versus the personal one -- accounts for major reliance of citizens on the Akshaya brand, and makes telecentres a highly used environment – in which the Internet-based devices for ration card applications have been installed.

The RCMS toolkit for online applications, after a pilot-project launch in Kannur district (northern Kerala) in late 2009, was rolled out to the entire state of Kerala in September 2010. Online applications for ration cards are submitted as follows: citizens approach the local Akshaya centre, fill in the application form available on the website of the Department of Food and Civil Supplies, provide the documents required (which are scanned by the telecentre staff, or in a private shop before application), pay a fee of Rs.15 ($0.34), and get an acknowledgement receipt that displays the date when the new ration card will be available for collection from the closest TSO. It should be noted here that the ration card is a composite document, which needs to be updated in correspondence to several changes in household composition, including the creation of a new family unit or addition of new names. Therefore, occasions in which a new ration card is requested by citizens are numerous.

In this discourse, it is important to point out the strength of political appeal exercised by the Akshaya brand on the Keralite population. In the perception of people, Akshaya constitutes the dominant technology for interfacing with the government, and its good reputation and experience made it a synonym for computer accessibility and reliance. Uncertainty that normally surrounds a new Internet-based application tends to be drastically minimized when the application is subsumed under the Akshaya brand. As a result, the bright-red message on the website of the Department of Food and Civil Supplies does not surprise us, because bringing something under the umbrella of Akshaya is almost a guarantee for success. As a result, this part of the ration card procedure seems to work well and its user-friendliness is positively appraised.

5.2   Application Processing

Before the launch of RCMS, Keralite citizens requesting new ration cards or modifications to existing cards needed to go physically to a TSO. There they would spend long hours in a queue, after which they would be provided with an acknowledgement receipt reporting the expected day of availability of the requested document. Processing time reported on the receipt would be calculated by work-pressed Taluk officers who were informed in terms of the time required by the Government for giving clearance. Now, time frames are provided automatically by the system set up by RCMS. Online application has translated this part of the process into a system-level bureaucracy [3], where the discretion previously exerted by street-level officials has been removed. Yet, after submission of applications, what role is left for technology in document processing and delivery?

Application processing at the Government of Kerala works as follows. Online applications are submitted along with the required documents to the office of the Rationing Inspector, located at the Department of Food and Civil Supplies. Bureaucrats at the office of the Rationing Inspector perform field-level verification and prepare a report that is then sent to the TSO for reference. The report specifies whether application was accepted, in which case a new ration card is to be printed; or whether it was rejected, in which case the reasons for rejection are clearly stated. This process should occur within 7-15 working days. As a result, on the date established for collection, citizens should go physically to the TSO and receive either the new card or a clear explanation for the rejection of their application.

Before the rollout of RCMS, 600,000 ration card applications on average were pending at any one time. Where was the problem then? Our research revealed that the bottleneck existed at the heart of application processing: verification of applications by bureaucrats at the office of the Rationing Inspector. In the dominant perception of citizens, this phase is encapsulated in an aura of confusion and discretion. Citizens, when asked about the mechanics and objects of verification, displayed high uncertainty in terms of the parameters being verified and their meaning. Even more strikingly, interviews conducted at the office of the Rationing Inspector itself shed little light on these dynamics. Bureaucrats interviewed uniformly spoke about "regularity of documentation," but attempts to gain more precise insights -- which documents, how is "regularity" measured, what is actually verified -- were unsuccessful. As a result, there is significant uncertainty surrounding state-level verification of ration card applications, which is affected by systematic and severe delays.

Here is where the problem emerges. The phase of processing that is structurally causing delays in ration card releases is one in which computerization has not at all being achieved. Digitalization, as devised by RCMS, is limited to what happens before this stage -- submission of applications from Akshaya telecentres to the office of the Rationing Inspector -- and after it -- printing of the new ration card by the TSO. Still, the principal node of the problem (i.e., processing itself) remains paper-based and surrounded by uncertain criteria, which is why the process turns out, ultimately, to perpetuate existing failure. Indeed, even after full implementation of RCMS, citizens report with frustration major delays in ration card delivery.

It is to be noted that had we used a different etiological lens on the same case tracing the reason of an outcome to the conscious agency of those involved – our interpretation of data would help illuminate the human factors of the failure in RCMS and their meaning. However, this goes beyond the scope of this paper, whose purpose is limited to proposing a rational explanation for failure in e-government, and using it for grounding a suggestion in terms on how to act to prevent this type of failure. Still, etiological analysis would constitute an important complementary lens for re-interpreting our data. Indeed, reading them in terms of "who gains" and "who loses" from the anatomy of failure observed – concerning essentially the mid-part of the RCMS process – would help us having a clear picture of what is really at stake in the minute texture of the ICT dynamics behind RCMS. A viable route for further research would, therefore, include the usage of this type of analysis, which would also help us devise informed case-specific policy recommendations.

5.3   Getting It Right: Targeting versus Political Appeal

As it emerges from our discussion, digitalization of ration card releases revolves primarily around application performance, whereas the crucial node constituted by application processing is left entirely untouched by computerization. This key phase, with which the technology of RCMS does not deal, has two characteristics. Firstly, it is the one structural node in the process, as it is crucial for the requests of citizens to be properly met. Secondly, it lacks political attractiveness, as application processing happens entirely "behind the scenes." It is, indeed, performed exclusively by government bureaucrats and it leaves no room for citizen sighting or participation.

Conversely, computerization induced by RCMS has been targeted in order to match a politically appealing node, namely that of applications submitted directly by citizens through Akshaya centres. The political payoff has a twofold origin. First, citizens directly participate in the system, which allows them to take an active role as they interface with the government. Second, the consolidated trust of Keralite citizens in Akshaya, collectively conceived as the primary digital interface with the government, tends to be transferred to the application, which is what usually happens when a new digital tool is subsumed under the well-established, trusted Akshaya brand.

As a result, the maximization of responsiveness of the state to citizens, as originally aimed, remains by and large unfulfilled by this application. Responsiveness, in the process of ration card releases, is predicated on a structural node that due to its lack of political attractiveness has been dismissed by the new technology, while digitalization has been tailored specifically for pursuing political support. To use the formulation of Bovens and Zouridis [3], application processing remains firmly in the hands of street-level bureaucrats, and automation does not affect this part of the process. With an information system organized like this, the government does not "get it right." As a result, state responsiveness continues to be low because the prevalence of political considerations leaves the causal roots of the problem un-touched.

Our suggestion is that for information systems to optimize state-citizen relations, ICTs need to "get it right" by targeting exactly those problems from which the problem of unresponsiveness emerges. Failure arises, instead, from the governmental misdirection of ICTs towards generation of political support, which while gaining short-term approval from citizens leave unattended the issues that lie at the core of unresponsiveness. The case of RCMS makes a paradigmatic illustration of this argument.

6   Conclusion

Our proposition, as illustrated throughout the case study, is that to effect responsiveness of the government in state-citizen relations, ICTs need to target the structural problems from which unresponsiveness is generated, rather than use e-government as a toolkit for political propaganda. Indeed, while the latter usage is devised to generate returns on the short run, it is highly unlikely that a strategy that ignores the structural nodes of the problem might pay off on the longer run, even as the permanence of existing problems generates widespread frustration in the citizenry.

In theoretical terms, this observation should be set against the background of ICT4D, a field that while highly preoccupied with unsuccessful project outcomes generally fails to lay out the causal foundations on which failure is predicated. In our work, a cause for failure is identified in the mismatch between targeting of ICT-based intervention towards structural problems and its political appeal. Reflection, as we suggest it for those engaging in analysis of ICT4D projects, should be on (1) the existence or not of a clear identification of the problems to be targeted and (2) adequacy of information system design for finding a solution to these problems. This implication, we maintain, is instrumental in shedding some light on the largely obscure field of causes of failure in ICT4D.

In practical terms, implications of our argument are translated into operational suggestions, for those that engage in ICT-based policymaking and information system design. The core recommendation, if long-term improvements in state-citizen relations are to be effected through ICTs, is that of prioritizing structural problems, rather than using e-government as a tool for obtaining and preserving political support. Indeed, the short-term payoff earned by propaganda is not likely to generate long-term returns, as demonstrated by dissatisfaction of the Keralite citizens with RCMS. Identifying the structural nodes of the existing problems and addressing them by the design of specific ICT-based toolkits constitutes the one way for linking ICTs to "good government" in terms of state responsiveness.

References

1. Avgerou, C.: The Significance of Context in Information Systems and Organizational Change. Information Systems Journal 11(1), 43–63 (2001)
2. Bardhan, P., Mookherjee, D.: Poverty Alleviation Efforts of Panchayats in West Bengal. Economic and Political Weekly 39(9), 965–974 (2004)
3. Bovens, M., Zouridis, S.: From Street-Level to System-Level Bureaucracies: How Information and Communication Technology is Transforming Administrative Discretion and Constitutional Control. Public Administration Review 62(2), 174–184 (2002)
4. Corbridge, S., Williams, G., Srivastava, M., Veron, R.: Seeing the State: Governance and Governmentality in India. Cambridge University Press, London (2005)
5. Heeks, R.: Health Information Systems: Failure, Success, and Improvisation. International Journal of Medical Informatics 75(2), 125–137 (2006)
6. Kochar, A.: The Effectiveness of India's Anti-Poverty Programmes. Journal of Development Studies 44(9), 1289–1308 (2008)
7. Madon, S.: Governance Lessons from the Experience of Telecentres in Kerala. European Journal of Information Systems 14(4), 401–417 (2005)
8. Masiero, S.: Financial vs. Social Sustainability of Telecentres: Mutual Exclusion or Mutual Reinforcement? Electronic Journal of Information Systems in Developing Countries 45(3), 1–23 (2011)
9. Rose, N.: Powers of Freedom. Routledge, London (2009)
10. Umali-Deininger, D.L., Deininger, K.W.: Towards Greater Food Security for India's Poor: Balancing Government Intervention and Private Competition. Agricultural Economies 25(2-3), 321–335 (2001)

National Identity Infrastructures:
Lessons from the United Kingdom

Aaron K. Martin

Information Systems and Innovation Group
London School of Economics and Political Science, United Kingdom
a.k.martin@lse.ac.uk

Abstract. Despite growing interest in the technologies of biometrics such as fingerprinting, facial recognition and iris scanning, there are too few in-depth case studies exploring their deployment on a national scale. This paper offers a qualitative analysis of biometric technologies by examining the National Identity Scheme – a recently abandoned United Kingdom government-sponsored program for a national identity card infrastructure. Leveraging organizing visions theory, it focuses in particular on government discourses about implementing a national infrastructure for biometrics. The discussion reflects on how the vision for implementing biometrics in the Scheme unravelled and tries to explain the course of these discourses in the political context of the UK.

Keywords: biometrics, case study research, e-government, failure, identification technology, organizing visions, surveillance.

1   Introduction

Governments around the world are establishing new identity policies to apply new technologies to their civil registration and citizen identity systems [32]. Long-established forms of paper-based documentation such as identity cards, visas and passports are being upgraded with machine-readable zones, computer chips and radio frequency identification (RFID). These new 'smart' artefacts are promoted as being more reliable and secure than traditional paper documents. The latest trend is to include 'biometrics' in these documents in order to further secure identity infrastructures.

Biometrics are physiological or behavioural measurements, generally performed by computers, to identify someone or verify an identity. Examples of biometrics include facial recognition, fingerprinting, hand geometry, vein pattering, iris patterning, DNA profiling, signature recognition, keystroke dynamics recognition, gait recognition and speech or voice recognition, among other emerging and prospective techniques. Unlike conventional methods of secure authentication that rely on what you know (such as passwords, personal identification numbers (PINs) or cryptographic keys) or what you possess (e.g., identity tokens or access cards), biometrics depend on facets of the human body – specifically what you are or what you do [21]. They are assumed to be a stronger means of identification because they cannot be forgotten or misplaced.

M.D. Hercheui et al. (Eds.): HCC10 2012, IFIP AICT 386, pp. 44–55, 2012.

Following the terrorist attacks of September 2001, the Labour Government in the UK proposed a new identity policy that would take the form of a biometric-based identity card. What was originally uncontested later became politically controversial, taking four years to pass into law as the *Identity Cards Act 2006*. It then took a number of years to make progress in deploying the National Identity Scheme ("the Scheme") because of the unprecedented size and complexity of the proposals, including a centralized National Identity Register (the database on which the population's identity data would be held) and the recording of extensive amounts of personal information from individuals, including iris, fingerprint and facial biometrics. The government's plan for real-time, online biometric identification against a centralized, government-managed database was also a major innovation. In part because of the slow deployment of the Scheme, following a national election, the new Coalition Government repealed the law in December 2010, thereby cancelling the programme.

It is therefore important to study the discourses around a complex technology policy like identity policy, particularly when technologies like biometrics are introduced. A government-sponsored scheme for biometrics may bring with it a political dimension, often because of its compulsory nature, which is also an interesting source of data. This case study focuses on both the public and political discourses in the UK, as both were rich sources of data.

Motivated by theories on the role of discourse in organizing visions for new IT innovation, this paper seeks answers to the following question: To what extent were government spokespeople able to organize efforts and mobilize actors to innovate a national infrastructure for biometrics in the UK?

The remainder of the paper is structured as follows. First, I review the extant information systems literature on biometrics, exposing a dearth of in-depth case studies on the deployment of these technologies. Then I summarize the analytical framework, based on Swanson and Ramiller's organizing visions theory. Afterwards, I present the critical analysis of government discourses on the planned implementation of biometrics in the Scheme. The discussion offers an explanation for the course of the visions for biometrics in the case and the conclusion reflects on the paper's limitations and suggests areas for future research.

2   Critical Literature Review

While the technical literature on biometrics focuses on the details of trials and tests of various biometric techniques, the information systems literature is largely captivated by modelling user acceptance and surveying public perceptions of the technologies, with some exceptions (see, for example, [4] and [22]). Many consider the acceptance of biometric systems by user groups an important requirement for success. It is believed that without user acceptance, perfectly functioning systems are doomed to fail.

These studies focus on what Chau, Stephens and Jamieson [1] call the "people" side of biometrics. Some of this literature is inspired by the technology acceptance model (see, for example, [1], [11], [16-17]). Much of it lacks a theoretical grounding (e.g., [2], [5], [8-10], [20], [23]). Virtually all of this work is survey-based and hypothetical in nature. Respondents are asked to opine about biometrics without an understanding of the context of use or substantial engagement with the technologies in question.

One of the principal aims of these analyses of biometrics acceptance is to understand user resistance in order to overcome it, often through "better" marketing and information campaigns to "educate" uninformed consumers about the benefits of biometrics [1]. In many of these studies resistance to biometrics is viewed as a problem or as somehow irrational – the result of misunderstandings about the technology which ought to be corrected.

One grapples to make sense of the sometimes-contradictory findings of these studies. While some conclude that most users are ready to accept and use biometrics [24], others note on-going reluctance and potential resistance [20]. Some try to confront the unclear and contradictory nature of public opinion regarding these issues [10], [20], noting that understanding context and how exactly biometrics will be used by organizations is important. However, the literature lacks comprehensive studies on the real-world implementation of biometrics.

There is a good explanation for this: biometric systems are often spoken about, but rarely seen. This is partly to do with their novelty as well as the difficult political and technological environments in which they are pursued. While politicians speak with excitement about the possibilities of biometrics in achieving varying policy objectives, and deployment teams try to build the perfect environments for their solutions, few systems actually see the light of day in large-scale, real-world implementations. Biometrics are complex technologies that require vast technological, organizational and operational resources to operate seamlessly. As a result, there are insufficient cases of biometrics being used 'in the wild' and therefore the research investigations that typically study such systems once they are up and running have failed to materialize in substantial numbers. When biometrics are actually implemented for civilian purposes, typically in immigration applications, there is a void of objective information about their effectiveness and impacts. Border systems are often opaque and are not subjected to accountability measures applied to other government systems with which citizens interact. Similarly, to date many large-scale deployments of modern biometrics have been in non-democratic countries (e.g., UAE, Malaysia) where access to data is more challenging.

How then can we study such technologies? One way is to focus on the discourses around the proposals themselves, rather than waiting for the systems to appear. This case study therefore examines the organizational discourses that motivated the implementation of biometrics in the UK.

3   Theoretical Framework

The main theoretical construct that motivates this study is the 'organizing vision' in innovation projects [26-27], which provides a useful concept to help to explain the discursive emergence and development of IT innovation such as the government's pursuit of multiple biometrics in a national identity card programme.

Swanson and Ramiller aim to understand better the institutional processes that facilitate the adoption and use of new technology. In contrast to the traditional view that the early decision to adopt a given innovation happens as the result of local, rational organizational processes, which are subsequently institutionalized with the increased update of the technology, they argue that a better way of explaining innovation is as a collective process of creating and propagating an organizing vision that helps to coordinate decisions and actions related to the technology's materialization and diffusion. The organization vision can, thus, be understood as a sense-making device [30].

Organizations are frequently confronted with novel technologies that they perceive as demanding their attention: "New technology often arrives on the marketplace in an immature state, puzzling as to its benefits, future prospects, and long-term form" [27, p. 459]. Defined as "a focal community idea for the application of information technology in organizations" [27, p. 460], an organizing vision is thus intended to reduce, in broad strokes, the uncertainty that accompanies these new technologies. The organizing vision provides a conceptual framework that permits simplified understandings about novel and, as yet unsettled, technologies.

Swanson and Ramiller identify three main functions of an organizing vision:

- **Interpretation:** When a new technology arrives on the scene its meaning and implications are not well understood by organizational actors. It is in this space that organizing visions are generated to give some interpretive coherence to the innovation. They provide a focus for the innovation's interpretation [28, p. 556].
- **Legitimation:** These visions also give organizations reasons and justifications for pursing an innovation. They provide an answer to the question, 'why do it?' This legitimation process is facilitated through the reputations and authority of those promulgating the vision. To adapt an example from Swanson and Ramiller's paper to fit the case at hand, this process might be initiated as follows: "Why aren't we doing [biometrics] yet?" the [Home Secretary] might ask his or her [civil servant], having just read about it (and all the good things that come to leading [countries] doing it) for the first time in Business Week [27, p. 461].
- **Mobilization:** The organizing vision is a "creative force" that sparks and energizes market interest and activity to support the realization of the innovation. "Would be adopters look to the market for needed resources, including hardware, software, and skills, following clues and guidelines embedded in the organizing vision" [27, p. 461].

Organizing visions are produced and sustained discursively, by a community with a common interest, which may agree or disagree about the content of the vision [27, p. 462]. The potential for disagreement means that there is an on-going contest of interpretations over the meaning of the technology. For Swanson and Ramiller, the depiction of the vision as an appropriate response to a certain business problematic will determine its currency and perceived relevance. Furthermore, the vision's perceived distinctiveness, intelligibility, informativeness and plausibility will also affect its compellingness and eventual success (or failure) [27, p. 469]. Importantly, there must be some new or emerging technology accompanying the vision that can be exploited by, but which also constrains, the vision. Often buzzwords (such as 'customer relationship management' [7] or 'enterprise resource planning' [29], or as in this present case, 'biometrics') play an important discursive role in signalling and strengthening the vision. However, there are risks to the overuse and overextension of such terms.

The organizing vision concept provides us with a core analytical tool to study imaginative discourse in innovation. Its emphasis on the early stages of discursive development, when understandings and outcomes about new technology are most uncertain, is especially apposite to the current case.

4   Research Methods

The analysis presented in this paper is the result of a multi-year case study of identity policy in the UK, focussing on the government discourses on biometrics. It is based on an exhaustive review of relevant government communications around the Scheme. The final corpus included every known public government document relating to the National Identity Scheme, published between July 2002 and December 2008. In total, there were 129 documents in this corpus, including:

- Legislative, parliamentary, research, and corporate publications
- Speeches and PowerPoint presentations by civil servants and ministers
- Interviews and interactive web chats
- Monthly newsletters (which were published by the Identity and Passport Service)
- Leaked government documents (which were made available to No2ID, the anti-ID card campaign group, and subsequently published on-line)
- Publicly-available responses to Freedom of Information requests

The analysis of documents is well established in social research [25]. To cope with the "attractive nuisance" of these qualitative data [19], the corpus was indexed in its entirety in the ATLAS.ti software for analysis, and then coded in accordance with principles and techniques from critical discourse analysis [6].

5   Analysis

This analysis encompasses official discourses on how the Home Office, the UK government ministry responsible for the Scheme, and the Identity and Passport Service, the department responsible for its deployment, would establish, run and manage a nationwide network of equipment for recording and reading biometrics. These discourses concern the organizations' knowledge, expectations and experiences of the design, development and installation of a new technology. These concerns are rife with future expectations about an implementation that, in the end, never happened.

5.1   Implementing Infrastructures

In practice, doing biometrics involves two major steps: the initial enrolment of biometrics from a person and the subsequent comparison of his or her biometrics against the previously enrolled data, during either an identification or verification mode.

From the beginning of proposals for the Scheme, the government paid considerable attention to how it might enrol the nation's biometrics. For example, noting the significant "learning curve" associated with implementing biometrics [12, p. 64], it sought opinions on this issue during the very first consultation exercise.

The Government would like to hear the views of potential partners on how a nation-wide network of easily accessible biometric recording devices could be established and operated, how people who are not mobile or who live in sparsely populated areas could be served and what other value added services potential partners might offer. [12, p.110]

Such discourses explained the importance of providing biometric enrolment facilities in locations across the UK, and where that proved impractical the use of mobile recording devices.

As well as local centres there will also be mobile centres for sparsely populated areas. [13, p.4]

However, much less attention was paid to how these enrolled biometrics would then be used in practice, particularly in ways that benefited the citizen whose data were being used. That is, the government's priority seemed to be figuring ways of collecting and storing everyone's biometrics in the first instance, and not how they would be subsequently used. Indeed, as a focus group interviewee from one of the early government's consultation exercises complained:

For [biometrics] to be beneficial all these places would have to have finger scanning and eye scanning facilities. Otherwise it's pointless. [3, p.55]

One could argue that the government was especially focused on enrolment-related aspects because it is a necessary first step in the practice of biometrics and that other concerns would be addressed later on. Indeed, the government admitted in the beginning that, in the initial stages of the Scheme, the use of biometrics would likely be limited, with the focus being on checking that people were not enrolling more than once.

The use of any of the above types of biometric information (or a combination of these) would probably be limited in the early stages of an entitlement card scheme to ensuring that a person could not establish multiple, false identities. [12, p.105]

A further argument is that it was up to the organizations that would eventually use the Scheme to decide when and how they would make use of people's biometrics. That is, that it was the government's job only to provide the basic infrastructure for an identity scheme and that the eventual use of biometrics by public and private sector organizations should be demand-led and not dictated by the government.

However, the government's marketing activities for biometrics in the Scheme never extended beyond enrolment issues, with various attempts at forging relationships with organizations capable of enrolling large volumes of biometrics, without a clear explanation of how these would be used afterward. This further fuelled speculation amongst critics that the Scheme was one massive government data collection exercise, with little eventual benefit to the citizen. These suspicions were partly responsible for the Scheme's demise.

Another aspect of implementing an identity infrastructure based on biometrics has to do with the human resources required for such an undertaking, including both specialist training for facilitating and overseeing the enrolment process but also identifying and acquiring the expertise necessary for dealing with system errors and other anomalies as they emerge during biometric checking [cf. 4].

A major concern in government discourses was whether the public sector had suitable human resources to conduct large-scale biometric enrolment. At first, the need for trained specialists was downplayed by the Home Office.

> The Government envisages a much simpler scanning system than that used by the police or the Immigration Service, which would probably involve just the scanning of four fingers. The prints would not be scanned to a legal standard of proof of identity. *The staff taking the fingerprints therefore would not need to be as highly trained as those working for police forces of the Immigration Service and there would be no need for trained fingerprint officers to interpret the results of any potential matches detected by the computer.* [12, pp. 115-116, emphasis added]

Government discourses would shift in later documents, with revised claims that while expertise was needed, there were sufficient human resources already in the civil service on which to found an expert base. For example in the *Strategic Action Plan* the government stated:

> We will put in place the skills and expertise to support large-scale use of biometric matching. Biometric technology identifies small percentages of what are known as 'false matches' or 'false non-matches'. These need expert human assessment to ensure that matches are being made correctly. For this, *we will build on resources which currently exist within government.* [14, p. 15, emphasis added]

Soon thereafter the discourses about biometrics training and expertise began to shift again, with the emphasis being placed on the need for 'support services'. As was admitted in the *Strategic Supplier Framework Prospectus*:

> With the use of probabilistic biometric matching technologies, there may also be associated biometric support services within this package (i.e. those services requiring expert human intervention). [15, p. 34]

The question, of course, was where this expertise would come from. While the government claimed that the UK Borders Agency was developing the relevant human resources through its programmes for collecting asylum seekers' biometrics and issuing biometric visas to foreigners, the size of these programs was dwarfed by the potential scale of a national identity programme. Concurrently, the government began articulating the need for "biometric enrolment services" for the Scheme, to be developed and provided by the market.

The capacity to handle these enrolments – in terms of high street estates, personnel and technology – does not exist today. The Biometric Enrolment Service would need to deploy a nationwide capacity capable of handling five million+ enrolments a year, in a way that is convenient for customers, efficient and of high integrity. [15, p. 39]

Yet again, in these discourses the focus was on the human resources needed for the initial enrolment of biometrics for second-generation biometric passports (with fingerprint data) and identity cards, and not the human resources required for biometrics in various identification and authentication contexts. As previously noted, had the plans for biometrics matured and a significant number of people's biometrics been enrolled in the Scheme, this likely would have enhanced consideration of how biometrics would be used – including consideration of the attendant human resource implications. However, the Scheme was scrapped prior to the completion of contracting processes and these issues were never fully explored.

6   Discussion

The 'organizing vision' concept provides a means to understand how organizations seeking to develop and implement new technologies deal with their inherent uncertainties and ambiguities. By unifying and co-ordinating discourses and activities, organizing visions help to reduce doubts or unknowns about the future adoption and use of technology. With a single vision and a single goal, it becomes easier to implement new technologies, all the more so if potential defects and imperfections are discursively diminished. These discourses draw on a pool of conceptual resources that exist beyond the organization, and which are shared by a larger community that is also interested in the technological innovation. When an organization brings together these cognitive and discursive resources in a cohesive manner, the organizing vision is said to be more stable, and thus sustainable. However, problems may arise – "where the innovation entails novel technology, this task can appear especially speculative and problematic" [27, p. 459]. In such cases, sustaining an unproblematic vision may prove difficult.

Organizing visions function to mobilize actors for the purposes of materializing an innovation. There were at three main groups of actors that the government aimed to mobilize in the case: the companies engaged to help the Home Office build the National Identity Scheme – including systems procurement and the outsourcing of biometric enrolment; a wide range of other public sector departments (which were expected to adopt the technologies and contribute to their diffusion); and the public, who were supposed to be the eventual end users of the system.

We will never know for certain whether the vision for biometrics would have successfully mobilized industry to develop and implement the biometric systems and services required for the Scheme had the Labour Party won the 2010 general election.

By 2008, several firms had been engaged through the *Strategic Supplier Framework*, and certain contracts had even been agreed, but the programme for biometric identity cards was ended well before large-scale procurement and system design were completed. Before, during and after the election, we witnessed the demise of the Scheme, not because there were not any commercial actors willing to work with the Home Office, or because the technology failed to live up to expectations, but rather due to the course of political change. In brief, mobilization efforts were cut short by politics and in the process the debates about the technology's readiness, reliability and practicability were never entirely resolved.

As of 2010, none of the government departments that were expected to take up the biometric systems being developed for the Scheme had committed to using them (with the possible exception of the UK Border Agency, which was already collecting biometrics from foreigners). Champions of the Scheme had failed to mobilize these important organizational actors. But as before, this was arguably a matter of timing. The Home Office had cautioned that uptake by government departments would only begin once its identity infrastructure was in place. The election disrupted the original time frames for this project.

Finally, the third set of actors to be mobilized in the Scheme was the public. Suffice it to say, this was an enormous and diverse group of people, whose bodies were intended to be read, recorded and repeatedly validated by biometric devices. Their mobilization was especially critical to the Scheme's success but the government's programme for identity cards and new (fingerprint) biometric passports was terminated before the public were to begin enrolling their biometrics *en masse*. The systems required for mass enrolment were never implemented. Critics such as No2ID had argued that it was at the point of mass enrolment that public resistance would mount, but this is a hypothesis that remains untested. What is known is that by the time the Scheme was finally abandoned, only 14,670 Britons had volunteered for an identity card. A significant fraction of these – nearly 3,000 airside workers from select airports – received their identity cards for free. In addition, an unknown number of the enrollees were civil servants who were privately encouraged to apply for an identity card before the election [18].

What can we learn from this episode? The project for a national identity infrastructure based on biometrics was unsuccessful for a number of reasons:

- **Organizational complexity:** The Scheme was a Labour Party policy, which the Home Office and Identity and Passport Service were responsible for implementing. The presence of multiple actors from such varied organizations (including both politicians and civil servants in this case), who are responsible for articulating and co-ordinating a coherent vision for new technology is something that the organizing visions theory (as articulated in Swanson and Ramiller's original article) does not easily accommodate. Historically, organizing visions theory has focused on the institutionalization of an innovation within a single organization, rather than looking at visions spanning multiple organizations, and which voyage into 'society at large'.
- **Scale:** The Scheme was a huge undertaking, encompassing not just the Home Office, but also eventually the entirety of government and certain private sector

organizations (such as banks). Moreover, a successful Scheme would require some degree of participation from national public and certain classes of foreign citizens. It is highly debatable whether such top-down visioning and innovating is possible on this scale, especially considering the range of organizations, people and bodies involved.

- **Politics:** A vision for the implementation of an enterprise resource planning system in a business organization, for example, may encounter resistance, which may even be political in nature; however it is unlikely to be tightly bound to notions of citizenship, freedom and identity. The government's proposals for biometric identity cards, by contrast, elicited considerable political distrust, fears of government tracking 'innocent' citizens and worries about privacy intrusions, as was represented in the political opposition's discourses as well as media reports on the Scheme [31]. There is therefore a qualitative difference between visions for a corporate accounting system, for instance, and a nationwide, government-sponsored identity system. The former is a solution to a problem. The latter is a political choice about how society should look and be organized, where the search for a solution may precede the event of a problem. Where the 'need' for such a large communal effort seems the stuff of choice and not necessity, political opposition is always difficult to surmount. Not surprisingly then, the proposals became highly politicized over time as the urgency which supposedly underpinned them grew more and more elusive. These politics affected the content of the vision for biometrics, with the government reworking its messages to focus on themes of 'empowerment' and 'inclusion' as the Scheme's fate grew more and more uncertain.

7   Conclusion

The widespread introduction of biometrics has proven to be controversial in the UK, but this is not an inevitable outcome. Some argue that a national infrastructure for biometrics would represent a sea change in identification practices. Others argue that in a modern world the collection of this information is inevitable and no longer sinister. These debates are ongoing.

This chapter focused its analysis on publicly available discourses, as one must surely do with such a topical matter of public security provision where classification and industrial secrecy loom large. I would have liked to get inside the organizations responsible for delivering the Scheme in order to gain access to those individuals responsible for overseeing its creation, design and implementation. These include civil servants in the Home Office and Identity and Passport Service, whom I believe would have provided an interesting source of data. However, this was not possible for various reasons, the most obvious of which was the sensitivity of the project and institutional concerns about protecting what was said to be 'commercially confidential' and 'security sensitive' information regarding the programme.

Finally, this research project was a single case study. Future research should aim for comparative analyses. Two other national programmes for biometrics (namely, Mexico and India, both of which aim to enrol multiple biometrics including irises) have been recently launched and would make interesting comparative cases.

References

1. Chau, A., Stephens, G., Jamieson, R.: Biometrics Acceptance – Perceptions of Use of Biometrics. In: Proceedings of the 15th Australasian Conference on Information Systems, Hobart, Tasmania, Australia, pp. 1–6 (2004)
2. Clarke, N.L., Furnell, S.M., Rodwell, P.M., Reynolds, P.L.: Acceptance of Subscriber Authentication Methods For Mobile Telephony Devices. Computers & Security 21(3), 220–228 (2002)
3. Cragg Ross Dawson: Identity cards – People with special issues: Response to the proposed customer experience report (2004)
4. Davis, C.J., Hufnagel, E.M.: Through the Eyes of Experts: A Socio-Cognitive Perspective on the Automation of Fingerprint Work. Management Information Systems Quarterly 31, 681–704 (2007)
5. Deane, F., Barrelle, K., Henderson, R., Mahar, D.: Perceived acceptability of biometric security systems. Computers and Security 14(3), 225–231 (1995)
6. Fairclough, N.: Critical Discourse Analysis: The Critical Study of Language. Longman, New York (2010)
7. Firth, D.: The Organizing Vision for Customer Relationship Management. In: Proceedings of the 7th Americas Conference on Information Systems, Boston, Massachusetts, USA (2001)
8. Furnell, S.M., Dowland, P.S., Illingworth, H.M., Reynolds, P.L.: Authentication and Supervision: A Survey of User Attitudes. Computers & Security 19(6), 529–539 (2000)
9. Furnell, S., Evangelatos, K.: Public awareness and perceptions of biometrics. Computer Fraud & Security 2007(1), 8–13 (2007)
10. Heckle, R.R., Patrick, A.S., Ozok, A.: Perception and acceptance of fingerprint biometric technology. In: Proceedings of the 3rd Symposium on Usable Privacy and Security, pp. 153–154. ACM, Pittsburgh (2007)
11. Ho, G., Stephens, G., Jamieson, R.: Biometric Authentication Adoption Issues. In: Proceedings of the 14th Australasian Conference on Information Systems, Perth, Western Australia (2003)
12. Home Office: Entitlement Cards and Identity Fraud: A Consultation Paper. Stationery Office, London (2002)
13. Home Office: Identity Cards Briefing (2005)
14. Identity & Passport Service: Strategic Action Plan for the National Identity Scheme: Safeguarding Your Identity. Home Office, London (2006)
15. Identity & Passport Service: National Identity Scheme Strategic Supplier Framework Prospectus. Home Office, London (2007)
16. James, T., Pirim, T., Boswell, K., Reithel, B., Barkhi, R.: Determining the Intention to Use Biometric Devices: An Application and Extension of the Technology Acceptance Model. Journal of Organizational and End User Computing 18(3), 1–24 (2006)
17. Jones, L.A., Antón, A.I., Earp, J.B.: Towards Understanding User Perceptions of Authentication Technologies. In: Proceedings of the 2007 ACM Workshop on Privacy in Electronic Society, pp. 91–98. ACM, Alexandria (2007)
18. Lettice, J.: ID card astroturf - No2ID beats the truth out of IPS. The Register (2010)
19. Miles, M.B.: Qualitative Data as an Attractive Nuisance: The Problem of Analysis. Administrative Science Quarterly 24(4), 590–601 (1979)
20. Moody, J.: Public Perceptions of Biometric Devices: The Effect of Misinformation on Acceptance and Use. In: Issues in Informing Science and Information Technology, Rockhampton, Australia, pp. 753–761 (2004)

21. O'Gorman, L.: Comparing Passwords, Tokens, and Biometrics for User Authentication. Proceedings of the IEEE 91(12), 2021–2040 (2003)
22. Otjacques, B., Hitzelberger, P., Feltz, F.: Interoperability of E-Government Information Systems: Issues of Identification and Data Sharing. Journal of Management Information Systems 23(4), 29–52 (2007)
23. Perakslis, C., Wolk, R.: Social Acceptance of RFID as a Biometric Security Method. IEEE Technology and Society Magazine 25, 34–42 (2006)
24. Ponemon Institute: Global Study on the Public's Perceptions about Identity Management. Unisys Corporation, USA (2006)
25. Prior, L.: Using Documents in Social Research. Sage, London (2003)
26. Swanson, E.B.: Talking the IS Innovation Walk. In: Wynn, E.H., Whitley, E.A., Myers, M.D., DeGross, J.I. (eds.) Global and Organisational Discourse about Information Technology, pp. 15–32. Kluwer, Boston (2003)
27. Swanson, E.B., Ramiller, N.: The Organizing Vision in Information Systems Innovation. Organization Science 8(5), 458–474 (1997)
28. Swanson, E.B., Ramiller, N.C.: Innovating Mindfully with Information Technology. MIS Quarterly 28(4), 553–583 (2004)
29. Wang, P.: Popular Concepts beyond Organizations: Exploring New Dimensions of Information Technology Innovations. Journal of the Association for Information Systems 10(1), 1–30 (2009)
30. Weick, K.E.: Sensemaking in Organizations. Sage, Thousand Oaks (1995)
31. Whitley, E.A.: Perceptions of Government Technology, Surveillance and Privacy: the UK Identity Cards Scheme. In: Neyland, D., Goold, B. (eds.) New Directions in Privacy and Surveillance, Willan, Cullompton, UK, pp. 133–156 (2009)
32. Whitley, E.A., Hosein, G.: Global Identity Policies and Technology: Do We Understand the Question? Global Policy 1(2), 209–215 (2010)

International Norms and Socio-technical Systems: Connecting Institutional and Technological Infrastructures in Governance Processes[*]

Claudia Padovani[1] and Elena Pavan[2]

[1] Dipartimento di Scienze Politiche, Giuridiche e Studi Internazionali, Uni. of Padova, Italy
claudia.padovani@unipd.it
[2] Dipartimento di Sociologia e Ricerca Sociale, University of Trento, Italy
elena.pavan@unitn.it

Abstract. This paper looks at the challenges posed by ICT critical infrastructures in their interaction with governance processes. The authors argue that, in order to develop better understanding of how (global) governing arrangements are made in a highly mediatised environment, adequate frameworks should be elaborated to study the interrelation between institutional and technological infrastructures. In this context, institutions are conceived as collections of norms - including a mix of rules and practices - while technological infrastructures are seen as instruments that transform governance processes, also enabling different actors' participation. Adopting a constructivist approach, combined with a focus on governance networks, the authors introduce a multi-dimensional analytical framework to investigate governance processes where institutions and technologies converge to create socio-technical systems.

Keywords: international norms, socio-technical systems, institutional and technological infrastructures, communication governance, analytic framework.

1   Introduction

There are at least three ways in which we can read the 'non-neutrality' of technology – and of ICT in particular. First, from a broad social perspective, ICT inform and reform the dynamics of con-temporary societies constituting one of the primary elements for globalizing processes [5], [12]: they transform societal interactions, respond to and solicit needs, create expectations. Hence, in a first sense, ICT are not neutral because they are mediating infrastructures that contribute to change both societal perceptions of the world and of the role of human agency in it.

---

[*] The authors share responsibility for the contents of this article and jointly realized the Introduction and sections §2.3, §3 and §4. However, they contributed to the realization of specific sections. In particular, §2.1 was drafted by Claudia Padovani; §2.2 was drafted by Elena Pavan in conjunction with the project REACtION, funded by the Provincia Autonoma di Trento (PAT) and carried on at the University of Trento, Department of Sociology and Social Research (www.reactionproject.info).

M.D. Hercheui et al. (Eds.): HCC10 2012, IFIP AICT 386, pp. 56–65, 2012.
© IFIP International Federation for Information Processing 2012

Secondly, from a political perspective, ICT have progressively emerged as a policy relevant domain [22]. In the last 50 years or so, from the national to the global level, policy actors have been called to respond to challenges posed by technological transformations. Moreover, the consolidation of the ICT policy field has been accompanied by the evolution of a number of different governing arrangements – self-governance, public-private partnership, multi-stakeholder interventions – aimed at meeting the challenges brought by technological development to regulatory practices. Hence, in a second way, technology is not neutral because it constitutes a domain wherein different political interests and agendas are played out and because it has fostered change in (especially supra-national) governance practices.

Thirdly, at the junction of the social and the political perspectives, ICT evolution (and particularly of the Internet) and their capillary penetration into our daily lives do multiply the possibility for individuals, groups, communities to act politically and become 'part of the process.' As ICT contribute to the structuring of network societies, they also challenge traditional political processes by enabling political participation of non-conventional and non-governmental actors. This also favours the diffusion of ideas, knowledge, and cultural practices that characterize such diverse sets of actors. Hence, in a third way, ICT are not neutral because they become enabling factors for citizens' involvement, both as individuals and in their associational forms.

While social transformations brought about by ICT developments and diffusion have received increased scholarly attention, we are still in need of adequate conceptual tools and analytical frameworks to investigate the dynamics that develop when transformed policy arrangements meet the opportunity and claims for citizens' enhanced participation. This includes frameworks to investigate both the basic principles that guide the development of technological infrastructures, but also the principles those very technologies may contribute to shape and consolidate, including in other domains beside and beyond technology governance. Adequate frameworks should then be elaborated to study the interrelation between institutional and technological infrastructures. Institutions are to be understood here as collections of norms, including a mix of rules and practices [8]; while technological infrastructures are seen simultaneously as instruments for global interaction, means for transforming (global) governance processes, and enabling factors for participation in political processes.

In our attempt to address this challenge, we believe a constructivist approach to world politics, provides a fruitful theoretical framework within which to position our reflections. Such an approach is grounded in the conviction that actors' interpretations of the material world depends on dynamic epistemic and normative understandings [19]: the world is not a given, but rather the outcome of interactions and interpretations based on actors' experience, knowledge, and preferences. In this context, ideational forces – ideas, values, knowledge – become central and imbue communicative exchanges [14] that sometimes consolidate into discourses, understood as "shared sets of ideas that provide frameworks that allow us to make sense of situations, embody judgments, and foster capabilities" [7].

Starting from these premises, we argue that a focus on the ideational components of policy processes – and particularly norms – is crucial in studying the interrelationships between institutional and technological infrastructures. Indeed, norms emerge at the intersection between actors' discursive interactions, through which they may redefine their identities and interests. As "shared standards of behaviour for actors with a given identity," [8] norms represent the consolidation of principled discourses into defined frameworks. Hence, agreed upon normative frameworks inform and orientate the outcome of political processes; consequently, they can be understood as one of the core 'infrastructural' elements (beside formal rules and provisions) that support governance processes and subsequent policy decisions.

Moreover, the emergence and consolidation of norms presupposes the interplay of cognitive and relational components upon which the current development and diffusion of ICT has a dramatic impact. In fact, the unprecedented levels at which ICT are embedded into every domain of human action fosters what we label socio-technical breakthrough: a unique situation where the social and the technical infrastructures overlap and create a hybrid social space where the circulation of ideas and principles, and the construction of social relations, cross the boundary between 'the virtual' and 'the real' thus making the distinction between the online and the offline obsolete. This breakthrough poses new challenges to the study of normative developments, and invites us to expand our perspective to include in the analysis all those practices – framing, agenda setting – that inform norms' consolidation beyond the translation into official provisions, as well as the technical infrastructures that accompany and support such practices.

This paper acknowledges this centrality of norms and outlines an analytical approach to the study of the relationship between institutional and technological infrastructures. Our approach aims at meeting the conceptual and methodological challenges posed by the current socio-technical context to the study of normative frameworks emergence and consolidation, in particular that of overcoming the separation between the online and the offline. Also, our approach translates into an analytic framework whose components can be flexibly adapted to different governance domains.

The paper is organized as follows. First, we outline the two core conceptual elements of our proposal: the study of norms as 'infrastructures' in world politics and the broader context in which they evolve, which we understand as a set of 'socio-technical systems.' We conclude this first section outlining the methodological challenges to be addressed. Afterwards, we introduce and illustrate an analytical framework elaborated to meet the identified methodological and theoretical challenges. We conclude by discussing research perspectives in the application of the framework and we outline the deriving implications by referring to an ongoing research project.

2   Core Elements and Methodological Challenges

2.1   Norms as 'Infrastructures' of Governing Arrangements

Global governance can be understood as the multiplicity of networks of interdependent, but operationally autonomous actors, that produce relevant knowledge and cultural practices and/or develop frames that imbue public discourse and orientate policy

agendas and/or articulate principles, norms and rules while engaging in political negotiation with a view to orientate policy-relevant outcomes [22], [20].

As a specific ideational element in the dynamics we observe, norms set standards
of behaviour for actors; for instance, contributing to the definition of limits to state-
actors' agency in fostering national interests and committing states and other actors to
respect agreed upon principles and fundamental rights. Norms emergence and evolution on the supra-national scene are, therefore, central to governance processes, as
they open up spaces for change in actors' preferences and provide reference to appropriate behaviour, sometimes contributing to "restructuring world politics" [15].

We, therefore, argue that norms should not be conceived of as 'soft' components of
political processes, in comparison to the 'hard' nature of regulation and decision-
making. Rather, norms can be considered as 'infrastructures' that enable and structure
such processes. Norms contribute to the definition and transformation of actors' identities and perceptions, and to orientate their behaviour. Norms also provide cognitive-
normative spaces for the formulation of new policies [23]. As a consequence, their
definition may become a site of struggle for actors who strategically engage in 'struggles over meaning'; thus, norms - as agreed upon standards of behaviour - can also be
understood as a reflection of the (structure of) strategic interactions and power struggles that occur in political processes[1].

Several authors remind us that norms are "difficult to see" (when do we recognize
a norm when we see one?); and yet "leave an extensive trail of communication among
actors that we can study" [8]. For example, we can investigate statements and policy
inputs as well as less formalized discursive practices amongst actors. In doing so, it is
possible to trace their "life-cycle" of "emergence" in the policy context, including the
following processes: '"cascade" occurs when their adoption by a wide number of
relevant actors turns them into "standards of behaviour"; while "internalization" occurs when they become "a given" and are perceived as natural frameworks to orientate actors' behaviour [8], [9].

More recent literature on norms suggests a more articulated view of such a 'life-
cycle' [15], [23], [17], according to which norms are always contested because, even
after adoption by a broad number of actors, struggles may emerge between alternative
perspectives. Furthermore, norms do not automatically imply change; rather, they
provide opportunities for actors' behaviour and, as such, they are always 'works in
progress' in that they are constructed and re-constructed in practice, according to
actors' adoption in their actual activities and political interventions. Therefore, looking at international norms calls for a specific attention to the multi-level 'game' of
interaction between norms adoption and application at the local/national and at the
global levels [4]. Finally, norms are always exposed to 'shocks': changes in the envi-

---

[1] As a consequence, norms and normative frameworks can also be investigated in relation to the
different forms of power that intervene in their very elaboration and adoption: the productive
power of issue framing, the institutional power of agenda setting, the coercive power of
norms definition and application, as well as the network power of actors engaging in norm-
oriented interactions. Limited space here does not allow an adequate elaboration on the challenges of adopting a multi-dimensional approach to power in world politics and global
governance; we refer to the relevant literature [1], [3], [6].

ronment where norms are debated, applied, and contested can certainly interfere with their consolidation and eventually lead to further redefinition of these normative infrastructures. This has been the case, in the context of norms pertaining to global communications and its governance, with the explosion, evolution and diffusion of information technologies in the past two decades: a situation that has originated what can now be conceived as 'socio-technical systems.'

2.2   Socio-technical Systems

It is widely acknowledged that developments in the ICT domain have been one of the driving forces of globalization processes. Hence, the network society we live in is first and foremost a society of communication networks: "patterns of contact that are created by the flow of messages among communicators through time and space" [18]. The fact that ICT are now ubiquitous [11] makes communication networks global in a twofold way: they potentially expand along telecommunication infrastructures to reach all corners of the globe; and, with the diffusion of computers and portable devices, they innervate all fields of public and private action.

Together with Hall [11], we support a vision for which changes in ICT are shaped by and, at the same time, shape society in a fluid and very dynamic way. In this sense, we believe that changes in ICT influence and, at the same time, are influenced by the structure of communication networks that innervate our society. Consistent with this perspective, we also argue that the integration of Internet communication into mobile and portable devices together with the transition to Web 2.0, are by-products of and an influencing factors in relation to the structure and the dynamics of global communication networks. Indeed, the ubiquitous presence of Internet has progressively led to a situation of seamless adaptation of social relations to the Internet infrastructure [10]. As a consequence, the online and the offline dimensions merge together, thus blurring the boundaries between the virtual and the real, and technology becomes the means through which we make sense of our social reality more and more [2].

In such a context, global communication networks resulting from the interconnection of individuals and groups and events and data are better seen in terms of socio-technical systems that result from the intertwinement of two 'infrastructure': one given by the maze of social relations, the other by the maze of physical networks on top of which they are built [24]. The social space within socio-technical systems is hybrid, as it results from the merging of the online and the offline, while social relations become cross-dimensional because they are nurtured by both mediated and unmediated interactions and are defined recursively across the two spaces [2].

Also, the transition from Web 1.0 to Web 2.0 technologies changes the logic through which connections within socio-technical systems are structured. From a 'culture of publicity' pursued through websites in the Web 1.0 era, we switch now to a 'culture of participation' pursued through social media tools [13]. The key element is the possibility for users to create and share their own information and content in real time through social media platforms, which reduces the need for specific technical knowledge for content creation, meaningfully augmenting the possibilities to enter global communication networks [11].

2.3 The Challenge of Investigating Norms in Socio-technical Environments

According to what has been exposed, the study of norms evolution within dynamic socio-technical systems can prove to be a useful entry point to a better understanding of the interrelation between institutional and technological infrastructures (in our case in relation to the global governance of communication). If we see norms as 'institutional infrastructures' and socio-technical systems as a revised version of 'technological infrastructure,' we are left with the challenge of developing adequate analytical frameworks to study processes that take place at the junction of policy arrangements and citizens' involvement.

Norms as institutional infrastructures reflect the richness of the ideational components that enter governance processes and embody the interplay of power positions, thus inviting due consideration of how such processes are deployed. We argue that it is often in networked interactions that governing arrangements are being shaped: ideas shared, issues framed and put on the agenda, priorities defined, alternative solutions discussed, and norms agreed upon [20], [21]. And yet, as they operate within socio-technical systems, these networks are constantly at risk of being transformed by available technological infrastructures at least at two levels:

- Ideational/Communicative: The articulation of policy issues and decisions happens on the basis of discursive practices for which both the social interaction amongst actors and the semantics around which interactions evolve are relevant. ICT impact the creation of both social and semantic relations as they increase the relational potential of every actor (individual, organizational, governmental and non-governmental nature) and fosters the circulation, the blending and the clash of ideas, agendas and perspectives.
- Spatial: The dynamics of social and semantic construction of governance practices are recursive between the off-line (within expert committees, on the occasion of high level summits or less formal gatherings) and the on-line (through on-line consultations and mailing list exchange, but also through the structuring of thematic and issue networks in the web space). ICT embeddedness in daily social and political practices fosters the merging of the two dimensions and the hybridization of practices.

The challenge to be faced in investigating norms in their socio-technical context is to find adequate ways of dealing with the complexities deriving from actors' interactions across diverse ideational as well as spatial levels/spaces. We contend that a focus on actors' characteristics and attributes – such as the human, financial, and symbolic resources they can play out in a policy negotiations – does not suffice in addressing the complexities deriving from multi-level interactions.

3 Connecting Institutional and Technological Framework

To investigate the interplay between institutional and technological infrastructures, we propose a multidimensional analytical framework based on the concept of networks, which we consider as a suitable metaphor but also as a powerful analytic tool. The framework has been developed for the study of global communication governance but it is proposed here as a resource to investigate other policy domains. In order to address the challenges outlined above, a focus on relational dynamics involving both actors and concepts allows us to trace the 'trails of communication' that underpin the evolution of normative frameworks in governing processes. Acknowledging the "dynamics, diversity, and complexity" of such processes [16], different types of networks provide entry points for investigating meaningful aspects: semantic networks are useful to "map similarities amongst [actors' perceptions and] interpretations" [18], while social networks help unveiling patterns of collaborative and/or conflicting interaction. Moreover, in the context of widely diffused information technologies, semantic as well as social network develop across the online/offline boundary. In response to this, the explicit acknowledgement of both online and offline interactions interactions in our framework provides the means to acknowledge and investigate the hybrid feature of social space within socio-technical structures.

Table 1. Analytic framework to study networks and interactions in governance processes

		Spatial Dimension	
		Offline	Online
Ideational/Communicative Dimension	Social	Offline Collaboration/ Conflicting Networks	Online Networks of Interaction
	Semantic	Offline Semantic Networks	Online Thematic Networks

Although each network type included in Table 1 helps us to understand a specific aspect of normative framework evolution, only by analyzing and interpreting the combination and interplay of the different network structures we can reach a more comprehensive understanding of how policy domains are structured, where their boundaries are set, and what kinds of power are distributed along network ties and among actors. We have elaborated elsewhere on the heuristic potential of a network approach to communication governance [20]; here we provide a brief description of what each network allows us to look at and investigate.

Offline collaboration/conflicting networks gather social actors – whether they are individuals or organizations – operating in a certain policy domain. They can be read in terms of how relational patterns are being developed in a multi-actor environment; thus clarifying what logics inform political interactions, such as long term solidarity and instrumental coalition-building. Indeed, ties between actors exist if a particular kind of relationship is established amongst nodes, such as cooperation, opposition, or sponsorship; and relationships can be characterized by presence, absence, and strength, such as quantifying the number of joint initiatives two organizations have realized. Furthermore, the specific positions of nodes can be evaluated in terms of their prestige, whether they involve a brokerage role, or the facilitation or control of communication flows within the network.

Offline semantic networks trace conversational patterns along which different themes are brought into the policy agenda and, in this way, provide a useful entry point from which to assess how discursive practices actually inform political processes, possibly influencing policy outcomes. They depict the collective construction of meanings and are particularly relevant when it comes to analyzing governance structures that may not aim at producing formal policy outputs, such as high-level summits as occasions for multi-stakeholder debates. Nodes are concepts and the presence of ties can be understood as a positive association among issues; while the absence of ties signals a disconnection in conversational dynamics. Also, the strength of a tie can be conceived in terms of 'semantic proximity' between different themes: the stronger the tie, the greater the association between two issues. Also, more central themes indicate priorities emerging in a field, while clusters can be read in terms of subfields catalyzing the attention of specific actors.

Online networks of interaction represent conversational dynamics deployed online that often, but not necessarily, accompany more formal governance processes. Analyzing this type of network can help uncover dynamics that may create the conditions for an enlargement or refinement of the policy agenda when physical presence is not possible. These networks can be structured by more participative settings, such as conversations involving several actors; less shared exchanges, such as conversations between only two actors; and information sharing, such as messages sent where no response is required. Nodes can be actors entering a specific discursive space, such as a forum, a mailing list; but they can also be web pages, web portals, or news services relevant to the issues being addressed. Ties can be traced to investigate actors' participation and this would allow for the identification of 'hot-spots' of online discussions. Also, ties could be traced to indicate participation in the same conversational thread, thus contributing to the identification of 'hot-topics' in the same discussions.

Online thematic networks show how different web-based resources, such as websites, online documents, and blogs, deal with policy areas that are related to one another through hypertext links. Thus online thematic networks may provide insights on how multi-actor conversations pushed offline by a relevant governance process are translated into web-based conversational fluxes that are accessible to all Internet users. Thematic networks can also help in mapping out the online spaces of discourse that parallel social mobilization around specific issue areas or topics. These networks can be made up of very heterogeneous nodes connected by a relation of recognition, which are not necessarily mutual; and their analysis contributes to assessing how a diversified articulation of relevant discourses may take place in the web-sphere.

4   Research Perspectives and Framework Application

In this paper, we have discussed the interrelationships between institutional and techno-logical infrastructures. Our discussion started from the centrality of international norms as ideational elements that are crucial for governing arrangements; and we considered the challenges posed by growingly mediatised social contexts in which norms emerge and evolve that we label 'socio-technical systems.' We then proposed a multidimensional analytical framework to investigate such complex dynamics and address the challenges posed by the consolidation of socio-technical systems. By explicitly including social and semantic as well as online and offline dimensions, the proposed approach allows us to account for the dispersion and multiplication of cognitive and relational elements that characterize the 'life-cycle' of normative frameworks within socio-technical systems. Furthermore, by looking at networked interactions, the approach moves from a predominant focus on the formal diversity of the actors involved in governance dynamics to a better understanding of how different constituencies relate to one another and how such patterns of interaction might change over time, thus providing the grounds for norms evolution.

We are currently testing this approach by applying the framework to the case study of 'gender-oriented communication governance,' understood as that area of global communication governance that pertains to the nexus between media and gender[2]. The ongoing project maps all four types of networks, investigates the position of nodes, and interprets links amongst them in order to trace the evolution of normative frameworks that have over time informed governing arrangements in this domain, from the local to the global. The final aim is to reach a comprehensive understanding of how institutional and technological infrastructures interact and contribute to the transformation of power relations in the domain under investigation.

The actual conduct of the project and preliminary results seem to confirm the validity of the approach, pointing to the necessity for a joint reading of results obtained from the exploration of the different types of networks. Furthermore, it provides elements to critically reflect on the implications of translating the theoretical framework into empirical fieldwork. Certainly, research in different domains will be needed to further assess the heuristic potential of the proposed perspective and methodological approach.

References

1. Barnett, M., Duvall, R.: Power in International Politics. International Organization 59(1), 39–75 (2005)
2. Beer, D.: Social Network(ing) Sites/Dots Revisiting the Story so far: A Response to Danah boyd & Nicole Ellison. Journal of Computer-Mediated Communication 13, 516–529 (2008)
3. Berenskoetter, F., Williams, M.J.: Power in World Politics. Routledge, London (2007)
4. Brown Thompson, K.: Women's Rights are Human Rights. In: Khagram, S., Riker, J.V., Sikkink, K. (eds.) Restructuring World Politics: Transnational Social Movements, Networks and Norms, pp. 96–122. University of Minnesota Press, Minneapolis (2002)

---

[2] Funded by the University of Padova, the project titled 'Networks and Power in Gender-oriented Communication Governance,' adopts the theoretical approach and analytical framework outlined in this contribution. The case study has been chosen because it presents most of the features that characterize global governing arrangements, and because, due the long 'history' of supra-national interventions in this area, it allows to trace and compare stages of norms formation that have been characterized by different types of infrastructures, only recently coming to reflect what we have identified as 'socio-technical systems.'

5. Castells, M.: The Rise of Network Society. Blackwell Publishers, Oxford (1996)
6. Castells, M.: A Network Theory of Power. International Journal of Communication 5, 773–787 (2011)
7. Dryzek, J.S.: Deliberative Democracy in Divided Societies: Alternatives to Agonism and Analgesia. Political Theory 33(2), 218–242 (2005)
8. Finnemore, M., Sikkink, K.: International Norm Dynamic and Political Change. International Organization 52(4), 887–917 (1998)
9. Florini, A.: The Evolution of International Norms. International Studies Quarterly 40(3), 363–389 (1996)
10. Giunchiglia, F., Robertson, D.: The Social Computer: Combining machine and human computation. DISI, University of Trento, Tech. Rep. 10-036 (2010), http://eprints.biblio.unitn.it/archive/00001851/01/036.pdf
11. Hall, W.: The Ever Evolving Web: The Power of Networks. International Journal of Communication 5, 651–664 (2011)
12. Held, D., McGrew, A., Goldblatt, D., Perraton, J.: Global Transformations: Politics, Economics, and Culture. Polity Press, Cambridge (1999)
13. Kaplan, A.M., Haenlein, M.: Users of the World, Unite! The Challenges and Opportunities of Social Media. Business Horizion 53, 59–68 (2010)
14. Keck, M.E., Sikkink, K.: Activists Beyond Borders: Advocacy Networks in International Politics. Cornell University Press, New York (1998)
15. Khagram, S., Riker, J.V., Sikkink, K. (eds.): Restructuring World Politics. Transnational Social Movements, Networks and Norms. University of Minnesota Press, Minneapolis (2002)
16. Kooiman, J.: Governing as Governance. Sage Publications, London (2003)
17. Krook, M.L., True, J.: Rethinking the Life Cycles of International Norms: The United Nations and the global promotion of gender equality. European Journal of International Relations XX(X), 1–25 (2010)
18. Monge, P.R., Contractor, N.S.: Theories of Communication Networks. Oxford University Press, Oxford (2003)
19. Onuf, N.: World of Our Making: Rules and Rule in Social Theory and International Relations. University of South Carolina Press, Columbia (1989)
20. Padovani, C., Pavan, E.: Actors and Interactions in Global Communication Governance: The Heuristic Potential of a Network Approach. In: Mansell, R., Raboy, M. (eds.) The Handbook of Global Media and Communication Policy, pp. 543–563. Blackwell, Oxford (2011)
21. Pavan, E.: Frames and Connections in the Governance of Global Communications. A Network Study of the Internet Governance Forum. Lexington Books, Laham (2012)
22. Raboy, M., Padovani, C.: Mapping Global Media Policy: Concepts, Frameworks, Methods. Communication, Culture and Critique 3(2), 150–169 (2010)
23. Sending, O.J.: Norms, Knowledge and Constitutive Relations. Paper presented at the ISA Annual Convention, San Diego, March 22-25 (2006)
24. Vespignani, A.: Predicting the Behavior of Techno-Social Systems. Science 325, 425–430 (2009)

Section 2
Sustainable and Responsible Innovation

ICT and Environmental Sustainability: A Case Study of a Grassroots Initiative

Ana Cardoso and João Carvalho

Department of Information Systems, University of Minho
Campus de Azúrem, Guimarães, Portugal
id2629@alunos.uminho.pt, jac@dsi.uminho.pt

Abstract. Increasingly, local communities develop projects and grassroots initiatives that address climate change and environmental sustainability issues. These projects often commence informally and adopt web-based free information and communication technologies (ICT) applications to support their functioning. ICT applications are used to promote the goals of the project, to recruit more supporters and to facilitate debate among citizens sympathetic to the cause of environmental stewardship. However, as some of these projects evolve they become more complex. Struggling with lack of funding, the solution is to imaginatively combine free web-based ICT applications, to adapt existing open source applications, and even to develop customized solutions. We present the results of an exploratory case study of a grassroots initiative with environmental sustainability goals. The study shows some evidence of innovative practices in the appropriation of ICTs and in the communication campaign. Implications of this research for online communities and society are also discussed.

Keywords: Community-based projects, grassroots initiative, case study, ICT applications, innovation, and environmental sustainability.

1   Introduction

Lately, more attention has been dedicated to the issues of sustainable development and impact of human activities in the environment. As developing nations became more industrialized and the competition for natural resources increased, concern has shifted from how to induce and sustain economic growth to whether planet Earth can resist the pressing for more natural resources, specially energy, if developing countries achieve the living standards of most people in Europe and North America.

The immediate answer to this concern has been a top-down approach. Indeed, these issues have been discussed in conferences at an international level, for example the United Nations Climate Change Conference, but consensus has been difficult to achieve and progress has been minimal. The foreseeable solution of more taxation based on CO2 emissions and more state interventionism is controversial and its possible benefits are not unequivocally recognized.

The discussion of solutions at an international level has not hampered the initiative of resolute groups of citizens that have developed community-based projects to

---

The original version of this chapter was revised, a wrong link has been removed from reference 2.

M.D. Hercheui et al. (Eds.): HCC10 2012, IFIP AICT 386, pp. 69–78, 2012.
© IFIP International Federation for Information Processing 2012

address environmental sustainability concerns and related problems, as for example Let's Do It World [1], Carbon Rally [2], or Transition Network [3]. These grassroots initiatives have gathered a significant support base and are demonstrating that bottom-up approaches can effectively complement top-down solutions. This complementarity of top-down and bottom up approaches to address a complex and wicked problem such as climate change has been suggested in the field of information systems [4].

Our working definition of community-based projects with environmental sustainability goals regards these initiatives as organized expressions of voluntary work initiated by citizens in order to benefit the natural environment. In other words, these informal nonprofit projects gather citizens from all societal quadrants that voluntarily contribute with their resources to a joint enterprise that will positively impact the natural environment, as for example cleaning up illegal dumpsites, reforestation of burned areas, monitoring of forests in order to prevent fires, and lifestyle change to reduce individual carbon emissions in ordinary activities.

Sometimes these projects commence after in-person encounters, where the discussion of ideas that will benefit the community and its environment take place, but that is not always the rule. While it is necessary that a founding group of people agree on the merits of an idea for it to materialize into a project, the discussion of ideas can happen in online discussion forums or through exchange of e-mails. Besides, since these projects aim to involve the largest possible number of citizens, the creation of an online community facilitates the engagement of a large number of supporters.

Online communities or virtual communities have been studied in the past for different reasons. For example, in the information systems (IS) area some of the first studies about online communities focused on collaboration in the context of virtual teams, that is teams of people located in different geographical locations, working collaboratively [5], [6]. A review of the literature about virtual community informatics attempted at clarifying the definition of virtual community, and identified commonalities among different definitions, namely the use of computer-mediated spaces and computer-based technology, the focus on communication and interaction, and the building of relationships among its members [7].

Another issue of concern has been the sustainability of online communities in terms of their ability to survive and to hold a steady or increasing number of members. It has been found that membership size is contingent on the availability of resources and on the communication activity provided by the online community [8]. Research in this topic has also explored the motivation of members to contribute knowledge to an online community and the governance of these communities.

More recently, the issue of influence of institutions on online communities has also drawn the attention of researchers [9]. It was found that even though online communities present themselves as open channels for free speech, there are constrained to pure democratic debates because of institutional influences. Moreover, this often results in these communities becoming channels for reproducing institutionalized perspectives instead of facilitating the emergence of democratic debates in social movements [10].

Despite some research on online communities, basic issues as the success or failure of online communities and even agreement on the basic definition of online community remain open. Moreover, a panel of IS experts recently identified the need to investigate the management and evolution of community boundaries, "the evolution of community affordances as online communities enact a variety of technological solutions in support of their evolving needs," and also the opportunities and threats resulting from the new relational capabilities enacted by social media software [11].

In this article we describe a case that shows how a community-based project adopted ICTs to support its functioning and discuss the project's results from the point of view of innovation. The rest of the article has the following structure. In Section 2 we explain the research approach and describe the case. Section 3 reports on the results, and we conclude with a discussion of findings and limitations in Section 4.

2   Methods

2.1   Research Approach

We adopted an exploratory research design because of our interest in the topics of ICT for sustainable development and online communities, which are relatively new and under-investigated phenomena. An exploratory case study design is appropriate for describing and analyzing a new or relatively unstudied phenomenon and it is not required that such an approach tests propositions based on established theory [12], or inductively generates new theory [13]. However, exploratory case studies need to "state their purpose, as well as the criteria by which an exploration will be judged successful" [12]. Thus, we conducted an exploratory case study with the goal of better understanding how community-based projects with pro-environmental goals adopt ICT applications to support their operations and achieve their goals and also to understand how these ICTs contribute to the success of the project.

The purpose of this exploration is to provide insights about these issues and also to refine our future data collection plans for an in-depth case study. Since we already identified some themes for an in-depth analysis, namely the leadership of community-based projects, the process of evolving an online community into a formal institution, and the creation of intellectual capital within an online community, we will follow this exploratory study with an in-depth interpretive case study.

The selection of cases for our exploratory study was based on the following criteria: we were looking at community-based projects or initiatives with environmental sustainability goals that used web-based ICTs to organize groups of citizens doing volunteer-based work. Moreover, we also applied the criteria of opportunity, that is, we looked first into cases where access could be more easily negotiated. Multiple cases were selected based on these criteria, but the fact that the case we present here was quite unique and could yield richer insights, made its selection more interesting.

Data collection was done from March to November 2011. As this case happened in 2010, was widely promoted online and through mass media, a rich collection of archival data was available. We collected archival data such as minutes of meetings, forms and tutorials, pictures, project documentation, news reports about the project, newspaper articles, and also transcribed four interviews (about 12.800 words). The interviews consisted primarily of open-ended questions, were audio recorded and transcribed. The archival data includes image, text, video and audio files amounting to

142 files. We acknowledge the limitation in terms of number of interviews and argue that the rich and varied archival sources partially compensate for this.

2.2   Case Description: Let's Do It Portugal!

In March 2010, more than 100.000 persons went voluntarily to the Portuguese forests on a rainy day to clean up illegal dumpsites. The preparation of this event started 9 months before, when a group of 3 friends learned about a grassroots initiative that organized a clean-up of Estonia's forests in 2008. This group was inspired by the Estonian project and decided to lead an identical project in Portugal. The project's vision was not the cleaning up itself but, instead, to raise awareness of the problem of illegal dumping of forests and broadcast the message that illegal dumping is not acceptable.

A chain of e-mail messages, inviting people to join a social network website created in the Ning platform triggered an impressive number of 4.000 registrations after only two weeks, and this number grew to more than 30.000 people. Ning (www.ning.com) is a platform to create and host micro social network websites that allow users to interact in similar ways as other popular social sites.

This project involved only donated and lent resources of different types: tools, bags and gloves for collecting trash, use of technical equipment, trucks and tractors, free public transportation for volunteers, and volunteer workforce - from cleaning to coordination and management tasks. In fact, one of the guidelines of the project specifically stated that no monetary donations could be accepted, only donations of goods and services.

The organization of the project was decentralized across districts and municipalities. A leading group took the national coordination. It included the founders, plus 20 district coordinators together with 3 coordinators for the environmental, legal and technological areas. District coordinators were volunteers that lead the project in their districts with the help of municipal teams of volunteers and municipal authorities. Technical coordinators offered their expertise in key areas for the smooth progress of the project.

All volunteers were invited to in-person monthly meetings. The purpose of these meetings was to engage a large number of possible volunteers, to promote the project and to explain to volunteers what needed to be done and how. In order to create a coordinated and integrated effort, the national coordination issued broad guidelines about how to proceed and published them in the projects' website.

Each coordination unit decided how to enact those guidelines and autonomously identified their cleaning needs and defined their goals. This involved locating and characterizing the illegal dumpsites in each municipality, finding sponsors to provide the necessary material resources, recruiting volunteers for the cleaning day, signing protocols with environmental services companies that received the collected trash, and rehearsing the logistics of a one-day cleaning event with a small group of volunteers, usually children, that cleaned up a public space.

The national coordination sought collaboration and support of various online communities related with outdoors activities in forests, namely the forum of all-terrain vehicle owners and drivers, cyclists, and the growing online communities of geocachers - a modern form of treasure hunt for recreational purposes. They also involved public and private schools, Scouts groups, and signed protocols with the military, the civil protection, private companies, municipalities and parishes.

The project developed a bottom-up communication strategy with chains of e-mails and social networking websites. Later, local media such as radio and newspapers helped promote it, and it grew steadily during six months. In the final three months, it drew attention of national television channels and newspapers, especially because the president of the Portuguese Republic was appointed as the honorary sponsor of the project.

For the discovery and characterization of the dumpsites, the project adopted an open approach for both the way of doing it and the technology to support it. Following a crowd source procedure, any volunteer could report the existence of a dumpsite and its characteristics (e.g. size, composition). The report of a dumpsite included its GPS coordinates, a textual description of the type of trash (e.g. furniture, tires, domestic appliances, etc) and pictures. These data were inserted in a web-based platform, thus enabling the creation of a map of illegal dumpsites and facilitating the estimation of the necessary material resources for the clean-up.

Hence, in the cleaning day there were 11.000 illegal dumpsites inserted in the database of this web-based platform. Local coordination teams retrieved information about the dumpsites in their municipalities and assigned cleaning tasks to teams of volunteers that showed up at previously defined meeting points. At the end of the day, more than 50 tons of illegal wastes were removed from the forests. Both the volunteers and the general public were surprised with the results of the project, especially with the high figures of volunteer participation and impressive quantity of waste removed.

3   Results

This project was very ambitious in terms of its goals: cleaning all the country's forests in one single day. To obtain the necessary resources and to mobilize a very large number of volunteer citizens was a great challenge. In fact, their dependency on donated resources and voluntary workers posed threats to the project's success. To cope with their self-imposed limitations, they used several free web-based ICT applications to broadcast the project's goal and to gather a supporting base of volunteers. This was a fundamental first step for the development of working teams that prepared the cleaning day locally.

The initial broadcasting strategy also reached mass media and facilitated access to inexpensive promotion time and space on mass media through interviews with project members, news pieces, and sponsorship of free advertising time. This made possible the connection of the online world with the offline world, and thus increased the supporting base of volunteers and sponsors.

In Table 1 we summarize the different ICTs adopted by the project and relate them to the project needs. The data for drawing this table was gathered from the project documentation. In the following sections, we discuss how the adoption of ICT was phased throughout the project.

Table 1. Project needs and ICTs adopted by the project

Project Needs	ICTs adopted	Category
Have a webpage where all relevant information about the project is available	Joomla	Communication
Report the progress of local teams	Wordpress, Blogger	Communication
Advertize and broadcast information about the events of the project at national level	E-mail chains Facebook; Twitter	Communication
Extend social circles of the project	Facebook page; Hi5; LinkedIn Group	Communication
Organize working teams across the country	Ning	Team management
Manage mailing lists for coordination units	Google groups	Team management
Collaborative writing of project documentation	Google Docs Dropbox	Operations
Registration of volunteers	Google Docs (forms)	Operations
Map the location and characterize illegal dump-sites	3rd Block; LimparPt Wikiloc; Wikimapia	Operations

3.1   Improvisation Stage: July to November 2009

The project's kick-off happened in July 2009, nine months before the cleaning day, which was 20 March 2010. At the time, the likely date for the cleaning day was the end of October, which was three months after the project's inception. However, in September, when the first meeting of national coordination took place, the date of 20 March was chosen instead because it overlapped with public school vacations, allowed more time for the preparative work of mapping the trash across the country, had a higher likelihood of good weather, and was also symbolic in terms of transition from Winter to Spring time.

In these first months, the set up of supporting ICTs and platforms involved some improvisation, based on the experience and knowledge of project members, as the following quotation of a project member shows:

> *"We need a site that describes the project. There, we can insert information about the project and link it to other project-related sites, as for example Ning and Wikiloc. I do not know how to build a website from scratch but have some experience with Joomla, a content management system, and can give it a try."*

Another example is the communication and promotion strategy. In a first stage of the project, national coordinators contacted friends and acquaintances via email. Then, they sought the cooperation of online communities related with outdoor activities such as drivers of all terrain vehicles, mountain bikers, hikers, geocachers, hunters and fishers. As one project member explained about emailing a standard message about the project:

> "In this phase the important [task] is to spread the word. I know some-
> one from the community X and you know someone from the community
> Y, that in turn also knows someone from [the community] B, and so
> on... In a month, if all goes well, [our message] will reach the whole
> country."

Social networking websites were also explored as communication tools. They created a group in LinkedIn, a page and a profile in Facebook, a Twitter account, a profile and a page in Hi5. These groups and pages were used to convey information about the project but also enabled the creation of a web presence, which was important for the project to connect with volunteers. Some local groups also created their Facebook groups and pages. It is interesting to notice that the web presence through groups and pages had different impacts. For example, the Facebook page of the project has more than 4.000 fans and continues to be active to date. On the other hand, the LinkedIn group of only 122 members had little activity before the cleaning event and is not active anymore.

We can also recognize improvisation in the choice of ICTs to support the task of creating a map of the trash existent in the Portuguese forests. In the first months, the project leaders explored free web-based ICT applications that allowed the creation of points of interest in Google Maps or Google Earth. As one project member explains:

> "I think it should be possible to create a database and then insert [the
> data] in Google Earth. Or even better, we can create the waypoints di-
> rectly in Google Earth and assign a code to describe them. (...) The
> possibility of using Wikiloc also seems viable especially because
> [another member] is very experienced with it. Linked with the waypoint
> there should also be a photo so that we can see the quantity and type of
> trash to be removed."

They also tried Wikimapia, another free web-based ICT application, as a project member explains:

> "Following the suggestion of a friend from Ning (...), I created an ac-
> count in Wikimapia. Wikimapia is more interesting for this project than
> Wikiloc because we can visualize an entire area with the registered
> waypoints. I think it facilitates the mapping [of dumpsites] because
> there are many persons who know where the dumpsites are but who do
> not have a GPS. Thus, they can locate the place in Google Earth and
> send an e-mail with the coordinates or with a print screen to the project
> team."

However, none of these solutions were satisfactory and were abandoned when the developers of 3rd Block, a geo-referencing web-based platform with some social features, approached the national coordinators and suggested the use of their software.

3.2 ICT Customization and Innovation: November 2009 to March 2010

After some time improvising with Wikiloc and Wikimapia, it was becoming clearer that these web-based ICT applications did not address the project needs. Wikiloc is a web-based ICT application that allows users to upload and share trails based on their GPS tracks. On the other hand, the goal of Wikimapia is to "create and maintain a free, complete, multilingual, up-to-date map of the whole world." Wikimapia combines Google Maps with a wiki system and allows users to add information, in the form of a note, to any location on Earth. Therefore, it is more flexible than Wikiloc in terms of how it can be utilized, but the GPS capabilities are not as good as Wikiloc, as this functionality only works in Windows systems and it cannot articulate fully with GPS devices.

When the developers of 3rd Block learned about the project, they had already developed a web-based platform that allowed users to locate places of interest in a map. This platform was very flexible and could be used in different ways, as for example to build an ICT application for selling properties without the need of intermediaries. At the time, 3rd Block team noticed the project had problems in terms of management of dumpsites' locations and they wanted to test their prototype, as they explain:

> "We noticed that the project had some problems at the level of management of trash locations and we had a platform ready to be tested that could be used for that. So, we needed users to test our software and they needed a software tool but, given the national scale of the project, they had much more to do [than build a software tool]. So, we presented them what we had done and explained what could be done on top of that, and from that moment on we worked together for the success of the project."

An innovative feature of 3rd Block is the crowd sourcing of information. In other words, any person can register as a user and insert information about a particular site. For this reason, 3rd Block was appropriate for the task of mapping and characterizing dumpsites, which was done by volunteers.

The platform 3rd Block had been designed to support the work of a "manager of geographical areas", as for example the team of a city council who is responsible for the management of public spaces in the municipality. As such, 3rd Block allowed the citizens of a council to report positive and negative aspects found in these public areas so that the manager of that area could quickly identify problems, resolve them and provide feedback about them.

Hence, developers of 3rd Block platform built a web-based ICT application that likened the role of the manager of geographical areas to the national and district coordinators, and the role of the citizens to the volunteers that located dumpsites in the forests. The mapping of trash points required a GPS device and, if possible, a digital camera. Equipped with these devices and with a paper form, the volunteers went to the forests and collected data to insert later in 3rd Block.

In order to automate the process of data collection about dumpsites, an independent programmer later developed an ICT application that allowed volunteers to collect data with the GPS and the camera incorporated in their smart phones and to send it automatically to 3rd Block. This made data collection easier and also minimized user created data mistakes.

4   Discussion

In this article we report on a case study of a nationwide project of cleaning up illegal dumpsites in Portuguese forests on a single day. This case is exemplary in terms of how ICT is appropriated as a tool for civic participation and demonstrates that citizens are ever more capable of using ICT devices and applications to organize grassroots initiatives that have impact. However, this case study has its limitations. First, even though this project is a replication of the original one-day clean up of Estonian forests, the findings are idiosyncratic to the Portuguese context and thus are not generalizable. Second, we reiterate that data collection focused mostly on archival data and that a following in-depth study will therefore capitalize on interviews of volunteers having different roles in this project.

We identify two innovative outcomes of this project. The first is the development of ICT applications, both for smart phone and web-based, to collect data about dumpsites and to create a map of existing trash in the forests. Even though the quick development of software had benefited from the existence of a generic platform (3rd Block) for geo-mapping locations of interest, it was this nationwide project that made possible the testing and improvement of that platform. Indeed, incremental changes of 3rd Block were made after suggestions of project's members and detection of software errors.

Another innovation is the communication strategy. This project demonstrates that a communication campaign can be done with no prior funding and no monetary donations. In fact, it was possible to mobilize about 100.000 people that voluntarily removed 50 tons of trash from the forests on a single day with only donated or borrowed resources (material goods and services). The communication campaign commenced with e-mail chains and word of mouth, evolved to social networks, and then interested local mass media, who provided free advertising time and space (e.g. one-minute radio spots, reports and interviews in local radios and local newspapers). Finally, it reached national mass media, where it had some prime time in the daily news.

Additionally, we recognize implications of ICTs and social media for society in this case. ICTs can build a "big picture", as for example the map of dumpsites in the country and, on the other hand, social media fosters the adoption of a collaborative paradigm because it facilitates connectedness, communication and coordination. Thus, citizens are nowadays more empowered to actively participate in their community and to co-create projects and grassroots initiatives because they understand that small efforts, if coordinated, can have large impact.

In terms of online communities, there are insights on how an online community commences and evolves. Three factors played an important role in growing this online community: the creation of web presence from an early stage, the involvement of other online communities with common interests, and the conspicuous communication of a very simple and consistent message. Although the Ning website had been deactivated last year due to lack of activity after the clean-up day, there remains a group of more than 5.000 persons in Facebook that follows the updates of this project.

Acknowledgments. We acknowledge support of FCT via Bolsa de Doutoramento SFRH/BD/60838/2009 and support of Fundos Feder – COMPETE and FCT via FCOMP-01-0124-FEDER022674. We are grateful to the informants of the case discussed in this paper for providing the information upon which this case is based.

References

1. Let's Do It: Let's Do It World!, http://www.letsdoitworld.org/
2. Carbon Rally: Carbon Rally
3. Transition Network: Transition Network, http://www.transitionnetwork.org/
4. Hasan, H., Dwyer, C.: Was the Copenhagen Summit doomed from the start? Some insights from green IS research. In: Proceedings of Americas Conference on Information Systems 2010, Lima, paper 67 (2010)
5. Jarvenpaa, S., Leidner, D.: Communication and trust in global virtual teams. Organization Science 10, 791–815 (1999)
6. Jarvenpaa, S., Knoll, K., Leidner, D.: Is anybody out there? Antecedents of trust in global virtual teams. Journal of Management Information Systems 14, 29–62 (1998)
7. Lee, F.S.L., Vogel, D., Limayen, M.: Virtual community informatics: a review and research agenda. Journal of Information Technology Theory and Application (JITTA) 5, 47–61 (2003)
8. Butler, B.S.: Membership size, communication activity, and sustainability: a resource-based model of online social structures. Information Systems Research 12, 346–362 (2001)
9. Hercheui, M.D.: A literature review of virtual communities. Information, Communication and Society 14, 1–23 (2011)
10. Hercheui, M.D.: Virtual communities and democratic debates: a case study on institutional influences. In: ICIS 2009 Proceedings, paper 118 (2009)
11. Johnson, S.L., Butler, B., Faraj, S., Jarvenpaa, S., Kane, G.: New directions in online community research. In: ICIS 2010 Proceedings, paper 173 (2010)
12. Yin, R.K.: Case Study Research: Design and Methods. Sage, Thousand Oaks (2009)
13. Eisenhardt, K.M.: Building theory from case study research. The Academy of Management Review 14, 532–550 (1989)

Green IT for Innovation and Innovation for Green IT:
The Virtuous Circle

Christina Herzog[1], Laurent Lefèvre[2], and Jean-Marc Pierson[1]

[1] IRIT, University of Toulouse, France
{Herzog,Pierson}@irit.fr
[2] INRIA, Ecole Normale Supérieure de Lyon, Université de Lyon, France
{Laurent.Lefevre}@ens-lyon.fr

Abstract. Green IT has recently appeared as a mandatory approach to take into account energy efficiency in information technology. This article investigates the Green IT area and its opportunities for innovation. This chapter analyses the main motivations for Green IT, and proposes a definition of Green IT including social, environmental and economic concerns. Beyond simply listing areas of possible innovation, this paper studies the virtuous circle that appears in Green IT: while Green IT has its own motivations, the resulting research feeds into other research fields. Innovation in this particular sector paves the way for further innovation by means of original research not foreseen initially.

Keywords: cooling, energy efficiency, green IT definition, innovation, virtualization.

1 Introduction

Until recently the ecological impact of the usage of IT was not a subject of discussion compared to reliability, performance or quality of service. Since some alarming studies were conducted around the world [1], [19], [20], governments, funding agencies and industries saw the tremendous impact of IT in both economic and ecological terms and started funding efforts to push innovation in the sector of Green IT. Researchers in the public and private sectors, driven by sustainable consciousness (i.e. partly economic, ecological, political, and societal incentives) have proposed a number of technological solutions to cope with the problem, and have actually managed to reduce effectively part of the IT impact on the Earth.

In this paper, after analyzing the definitions of Green IT and the motivations for going green, we study the virtuous circle between innovation and Green IT. We argue that Green IT is nowadays a motor for innovation which is by itself preparing the ground for Green IT research for the next decades. The paper is organized as follows. Section 2 presents definitions of Green IT. Section 3 focuses on the motivations for Green IT. Section 4 proposes a final definition of Green IT. Section 5 analyzes two sources of Green IT innovation: server virtualization and hardware cooling. Section 6 concludes this paper and presents some perspectives.

M.D. Hercheui et al. (Eds.): HCC10 2012, IFIP AICT 386, pp. 79–89, 2012.

2   Defining Green IT

Numerous definitions of Green IT have been proposed in the scientific and public press for the past five years, taking into account several aspects. Without enumerating all the definitions, we propose in this section to analyze their main differences and approaches; this will help us to propose our definition within the scope of this paper.

IT Wissen [9] defines Green IT as "a movement coping with the increasing ecological awareness and representing the development of environment-sparing hard- and software and for energy saving technology". This definition reflects that about 75% of German companies have some Green IT regulations, but mainly takes into account ecological aspects and neglects economic effects. In this definition, costs for servers and laptops, for instance, do not appear, while in reality these are important investments which appear in the financial statements of a company. It is quite striking that only hardware and software are covered.

TecChannel [7] gives the following definition: Green IT is "[e]nergy saving in server rooms due to an optimum of energy management". TecChannel confines Green IT in its definition to electricity saving in server rooms. This point of view is quite remarkable. Firstly, electricity saving in server rooms is only one – and not even a very precise – description of several environmentally-friendly actions. Another such action would be to manage the load of the servers in order to maintain the same service for the consumers, users, besides saving energy. Secondly, IT cannot be only reduced to server rooms as it is in this definition. For example, personal computers in almost every private household are neglected. Looking to statistics [13], over 80% of private households own a computer. Also notable is that the ecological motives of TecChannel are not explicitly mentioned.

But IT is more than this. Lorenz Hilty [8] gives a definition of the life cycle: there is the use phase, the production phase, and the end-of-life treatment. Green IT can be employed in each stage to reduce the ecological damage. In this definition of Green IT, the costs of production are not mentioned – the real costs but also the "costs" for the environment, which we all have to pay-in reality only the producing countries, on a closer examination the people producing the servers or components and living in these areas, have to "pay" for the erroneous trend.

Green computing or Green IT refers to environmentally sustainable computing or IT. In [5], San Murugesan defines the field of green computing as "the study and practice of designing, manufacturing, using, and disposing of computers, servers, and associated subsystems – such as monitors, printers, storage devices, and networking and communications systems – efficiently and effectively with minimal or no impact on the environment".

The Wikipedia [6] definition of the term is worth a mention: "The keyword Green IT (rarely Green ICT) is understood as an effort to create the usage of information technology alternatively information- and communication technology through the whole life cycle in an environmental friendly and resource conserving way; starting from the design and ending up with the disposal and recycling of the device". This definition is, in comparison with the previous definition, rather general and global. It takes into account the whole life cycle of information technology, starting with the construction until the disposal, and is not only limited to the usage. It is positive that the resources are mentioned, although a list of resources would be desirable. However, the incentives for the efforts of Green IT are not listed in this definition.

These definitions show there are various ideas about Green IT. One reason might be that the whole IT area is quite a young topic of research and usage. Fifty years ago, the number of information technologies was so low that the impact on the environment was insignificant. However, in 2008, 95% of the companies in Germany and 75% of the private households had Internet access. In other words, there is a clear trend of a continuous rising in the use of information technologies [4]. Consequently, the greater the number of IT devices, the more they become an essential part of our lives. The interests of users and companies are therefore dynamic and are changing accordingly. As an example there are the rising costs of electricity in companies for additional equipment. This aspect was understood by companies and they started setting up some measures – mainly under the financial focus.

These measures, not only with the same effectiveness, addressed mainly energy reduction in order to reduce costs. Later, they were summarized under the definition Green IT. It has to be noticed that these thoughts were concretized principally during the last years and, during this time, even more companies were considering Green IT measures. This is making it difficult to find and to maintain a single, definitive definition of Green IT under such changing influences.

3   Motivations for Green IT

3.1   Ecological Reasons

Mainly because of the title "green", the first associated reason for the usage of Green IT is ecological. The following reasons do not only apply to IT but also to other areas such as the car industry. The following reasons do lead the end users and producer to an ecological awareness.

It is common knowledge that carbon dioxide (CO_2) emission caused by humans is boosting the natural greenhouse effect and is thus causing global warming. IT is participating in CO_2 emissions. Worldwide, the carbon dioxide emission attributable to IT is an estimated 600 millions tons, still growing up to 60% more by 2020. This fact is explainable by the high consumption of energy during the life-time of IT. The lower power requirements of Green IT could reduce energy consumption, which would lead to the decrease of CO_2 emission of the production of energy.

The environment is mainly polluted during the production of information technologies. Many computers are as an example produced in China under inadequate ecological conditions. According to Hilty [8], the ecological damage that occurs through the production of a computer in China is almost the same as the ecological damage of the use of a computer during six years in Switzerland.

Figure 1 illustrates this statement. There are three stages of the life cycle in IT. It is remarkable that the ecological pollution during production has the highest impact. The production marks the ecological damage for the environment, but additionally for the worker, as well as for the residents around the production centers. For the production of information technologies, rare metals, such as indium, are used for the production of flat screens. Not to reuse these metals, nowadays means that the resources will soon be exhausted and none will be available for future generations and for future technologies which will be developed. A Green IT policy could ensure that resources are used efficiently, and that there will be no shortage in the future. It could also reduce the damage to the environment during the production of information technologies [3].

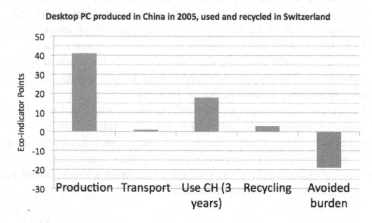

Fig. 1. Comparing production, transport, usage, recycling and loss for a typical Desktop PC, modified from [26]

Interestingly, the usage itself is limited to a few percent of the ecological impact. It must be noted that this study concerns the usage in Switzerland where most of the electricity comes from hydroelectric (50%) and nuclear plants (35%). The International Energy Agency (IEA) [2] publishes regular statistics about the energy production and usage in the world, aggregating them by countries or regions in the world. Thus, depending on the area of production of the electricity, the ecological impact can be drastically different. For example, France is generating electricity altogether about 85% from nuclear plants, and about 10% of this is hydroelectricity, while Austria is 60% hydroelectricity and 10% gas, and China is 85% coal and 10% hydroelectricity. These numbers reflect directly on CO_2 emissions. While at the global level the CO_2/kWh is averaged at 500g per kWh, in Iceland it is roughly 0, in France about 90g and as much as 1 kg more in China.

Often undervalued is the e-waste, which appears after the usage. The United States' (U.S.) Environmental Protection Agency (EPA) declared that Americans throw out more than two million tons of consumer electronics annually, making electronic waste one of the fastest growing components of the municipal waste stream. In the European Commission (EC) the disposal of e-waste is regulated by guidance such as the Waste Electrical and Electronic Equipment (WEEE) guideline. This guideline has the aim to reduce e-waste and to ensure environmental-friendly cleaning. Unfortunately, this rule is bypassed because of financial reasons. E-waste is transported to the developing world, where the waste is recycled in a very primitive way leading to a contamination of human beings and the environment. Green IT should point out these aspects and should insist that recycling is done in a "green way".

3.2   Economic and Social Reasons

Besides ecological reasons, there are multiple economic reasons that make Green IT interesting for industry. IT in industry needs energy in the form of electricity and is therefore an expense factor, especially considering the increasing costs of electric energy in the last decades.

Green IT could reduce the consumption of electricity used for IT in companies, thereby decreasing the electricity bills. Actions could take place to assure "green production", using renewable energy relative to the actual needs of the IT infrastructure.

Companies invest annually a huge amount in information technologies. Mainly high performance technologies are bought, but their memories, storage and computing power and capacity are not well-utilized. Often such investments are too high for the current needs, given that in the course of replacement investments and expansion investments technologies are renewed while it would not be necessary. Green IT could provide a more efficient usage of older equipment and a higher workload of new technologies. Hence, a better utilization of existing resources and the need of new hardware could be reduced. High costs for new acquisitions could be minimized.

Green IT is not only important for industry but is also in the interest of governments. Public administration aims to preserve the environment and to serve the country and its inhabitants. For instance, Germany offers governmental support for companies that reduce environmental contamination. Hence, Green IT can bring governmental funding and tax advantages. Green IT is useful for a government since it aims at conserving the environment while taking a long-term view.

Industry may use Green IT intentions also for marketing aims. Therefore their internal processes or own products may be labeled as green. The company is creating a positive image in a sensitized society [22]. The prime example of this is the "Big Green" project of IBM. IBM promoted the reduction of up to 80% of energy consumption. For several years now, IBM has been promoting energy-efficient solutions and promising that these solutions help to improve the image of clients [23].

First introduced long ago by Jevons in 1865 [17], and re-emerging in the 1990s [18] with the climate change question, the rebound effect cannot be ignored in the context of Green IT. The idea behind it is that the greater the energy reductions that are possible thanks to technological means, the more the global energy consumption will increase due to the resulting increased access to technologies.

4   Final Definition of Green IT

Based on the above definitions and motivations, a definition of Green IT is stated, which is for now the basis for the work described in this paper. *"Green IT is the environmental and resource saving effort in the IT. The reason for using Green IT may arise from economic or ecological interests. Actions can affect on the whole lifecycle of information technology – meaning from the construction via utilization through to disposal."*

Green IT should be understood from the tendency to the movement (effort) towards sustainability. In general, as shown in figure 2, sustainability is the area where ecological, economical and social aspects overlap.

Ecological sustainability is oriented closely to the definition that relates to forestry, meaning trees should not be chopped down before others have reached the same height [24]. Ecological and social sustainability represents a visionary world order where the lifestyle of today's society incurs a penalty for future generations, and gives access to this lifestyle to all the society. It is more important to understand the effects of choosing a sustainable course of action than to categorize the action according to its motivation [25]. As already mentioned, there are different motivations for Green IT efforts but the result is more important than the original kind of motivation. It does not matter to the environment why I am saving electricity – to reduce my electricity bill or to have a pure conscience – but the environment benefits regardless.

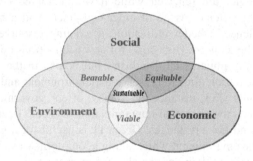

Fig. 2. The place for sustainability (picture from Wikipedia, built from [21])

In the best cases, Green IT is sustainable. In figure 2, Green IT is in the central "sustainable" area and stays there whatever the operations on the system. For instance, buying less expensive hardware will lead to a movement away from sustainability that can be compensated for when this new hardware consumes less electricity. It should be noted that making no effort at all will lead the IT to move away from this sustainability area due to the obsolescence of the equipment.

In the common case, Green IT can be represented in figure 2 as a movement towards the optimal area (i.e., the sustainable area). For instance, calculating the price of the products including the financial costs for the e-waste (for example, people working in this sector need health protection) before renewing some equipment will move within the social point of view towards sustainability.

In the worst case, Green IT is unfortunately a movement away from the sustainable area to a border area, and it is not important towards which field this point is moving. For instance, a company can buy new hardware that consumes more electricity than the older hardware (the business of the company is growing and needs more IT infrastructure), but still consuming the minimum maximum (instead of minimum) electricity from the market for the computing power needed. In that example, the movements in the environment and the economic domains are clearly not towards sustainability. But the company can still advertise some Green IT efforts.

Green IT is always moving, there is always a development in one of the regions shown in the graph. Depending in which direction it is moving, how far it is moving towards the sustainable area or far away from it, you can say that there is still a part of Green IT in these changes. Maybe this new development is only Green IT but it will lead to difficulties in the economic region of the chart. This graph allows us to give a first label to Green IT. All known components will be filled, and the result indicates whether it can still be considered Green IT or not. After developing some standards/limits for Green IT, for the economic, environmental and social aspects, a special innovation, meaning a movement within the Green IT, can be categorized, perhaps even assigning them a value according to their usefulness to Green IT.

5   Analysis of Two Green IT innovation Sources

This section discusses the links between Green IT and innovation. We choose two well-known mature mechanisms for Green IT: server virtualization and hardware cooling. This allows us to describe enough background of the field in order to anticipate in the next section some forthcoming potential innovations.

5.1   Server Virtualization

Server virtualization technologies allow the embedding of services in virtual machines and to group several such virtual machines on physical hosts. This mechanism decreases the number of servers needed to handle users' requests to services. Several studies show that the companies are using server virtualization mainly from an economic point of view: fewer servers mean lower maintenance costs in terms of human resources and hardware changes. This technology serves as a basis for cloud computing, which may not be as green as expected [27], [28]. A recent study from TNS for CSC [10] on 3,645 companies from eight countries shows that companies adopt cloud computing for data everywhere for accessibility and performance reasons as first incentives before economic reasons, while reducing the energy footprint of the company comes after. Green IT is therefore only a side effect of server virtualization.

Interestingly, it must be noted that the server virtualization technology has been developed after the monitoring of standard enterprise services found that only a fraction of the servers were actually used to handle the hosted services. Typically, only 15% to 20% of the servers' resources were consumed to perform useful business over peak load. This over provisioning is actually inefficient but comes with an ignorance of the actual needs of the systems.

Green IT has not been the main reason for the development of innovation in terms of server virtualization. But Green IT benefits obviously from these advances: fewer servers require less electricity to run and less energy (hence materials) to produce, maintain, replace and finally dispose of.

Conversely, Green IT is also a motor for innovation in server virtualization. For instance, to propose innovative Green IT solutions in server virtualization to consolidate the virtual machines in the best configurations (in terms of Quality of Service and energy issues), classical solutions are based on the monitoring of the usage of the servers [11]. Hence the monitoring of the applications on the servers has to be extended to monitor virtual machines. It is not sufficient to know how a server is using its resources; it is also necessary to be precise in the amount each virtual machine is using of the host server in order to optimize the placement of virtual machines on the set of physical hosts. When this monitoring improves, the server virtualization will be more efficient since this precise monitoring will allow for a better consolidation on even fewer servers. Unfortunately this monitoring is not directly possible and mathematical models must be developed. This field is under development and the accuracy of current models are either too low (10% [29]) or too specialized for one benchmark field (3% accuracy, [30]).

This example shows how server consolidation fed Green IT, and vice versa.

5.2   Hardware Cooling

For a long time, computer rooms were small enough in size that their electricity consumption was not an issue. The need to cool the machines made companies deploy air conditioning solutions in the early days. While computer rooms evolved to become data centers hosting thousands of machines to cool, the air was soon seen to be inefficient in terms of heat transfer despite the development of innovative software to arrange and manage computer rooms in the best way. To measure the efficiency of data centers, the IT community developed several metrics like the Power Use Efficiency (PUE) that measures the amount of electricity put into the data center compared to the electricity actually used by the computers. It does not say anything about the actual amount of power needed, and nothing about the impact on the environment (CO_2, waste). Indeed, there are several ways to optimize the PUE: to use alternative cooling such as water cooling, free cooling with ambient air, hot/cold aisles in the computer rooms, or better/newer computing equipment While these techniques should actually reduce electricity costs, it is unclear whether this is actually the case, since this may increase the amount of IT infrastructure actually deployed (see the previously mentioned rebound effect). It must be noted that new usage such as social networks, advanced search tools and the like would not exist without innovative solutions to cool data centers for operational reasons.

The side-effect of these developments is a better energy efficiency of individual data centers building up the clouds. But the long-term global impact has not been measured, in particular from an environment-friendly perspective taking also into account Life Cycle Assessment (LCA) and the overall resource usage or CO_2 emissions. It then appeared not to be sufficient and new metrics were developed, some of them by large consortia such as the GreenGrid [14], standardization bodies or within research projects like CoolEmAll [15]. For instance the CUE (Carbon Usage

Effectiveness) accounts for the total CO2 Emissions/ caused by the total datacenter energy per kWh, and the WUE (Water Usage Effectiveness) measures the number of liters of water per kWh.To go further Green IT needed to travel in new directions in the field of cloud computing: to take into account the usage of the infrastructure (in terms of business value), the distribution of the tasks in the infrastructure according to heat and production means to favor greener energy, the energy markets, the energy usage, the full life cycle of equipment. For instance, Moore et al. [12] showed the airflow in the rooms, and proposed scheduling algorithms of the tasks in the computer rooms according to the actual heat of the system to avoid hot spots and finally to reduce CO2 emissions.

In [16], the authors exhibit the "Follow the Sun Follow the Wind" (FTSFTW) approach that migrates tasks according to the availability of renewable energy supply to the data centers. While this idea is not new in the industry (service companies with offices spread over the world allow a 24/7 service), its realization is limited to companies with data centers distributed worldwide. However, the advances in cloud computing make this paradigm interesting again nowadays.

These examples show that the need for better and larger IT (optimizing the efficiency of data centers in terms of electricity needs) opened up a number of questions in Green IT (new metrics) and how, conversely, these innovations fed the IT sector with new solutions (such as FTSFTW) improving the overall usage of the infrastructure.

6   Conclusion and Perspective: The Virtuous Circle

The research in Green IT has shown some merits thanks to innovations such as those analyzed in the previous section. Several other options have been developed by industries and researchers that altogether reduced the ecological impact of IT. A virtuous circle can be seen between innovation that drives Green IT, and Green IT that drives innovation. Giving a fine analysis of these bilateral links is necessary to understand how to accelerate the course of industrial transfer.

To analyze this virtuous circle and to propose analytical methodologies to speed up the process is our goal. We aim to pursue this goal in the future, in particular in the light of coming innovations to be accepted by industry players. We believe that the development of Green IT in all its dimensions (including the full life cycle of IT equipment) towards sustainability will enlarge the opportunities for innovation.

A few promising innovations, chosen to be complementary and addressing several aspects of the problem, include:

- Software development toolkits to optimize energy usage of the IT infrastructures. Nowadays software development toolkits do not include any indication of the application's ecological impact on the infrastructure. These toolkits aim at helping developers in writing efficient code in terms of performance (with integrated monitoring/code analyzer), or they aim at hiding the complexity of the runtime infrastructure. Choosing for a developer between two concurrent libraries doing the same work, based on their respective energy impact, is not possible today. Much effort has to be followed to include energy awareness and efficiency at the software level. This can only be achieved with the help of informed development toolkits.

- Developing global knowledge about energy production and markets. Large-scale infrastructure such as that used for cloud computing could benefit from a detailed knowledge of the production means, in real time. Indeed this could help for instance to migrate tasks and divert network traffic to hosts and routes where the ecological impact is minimum. We believe that SmartGrids have to be tightly coupled with IT infrastructure to provide the necessary information on a large scale.
- Usage, production and optimization of (renewable) energy means direct links with the IT infrastructure. Nowadays too much energy is wasted by inefficient transport and transformation of electricity between their production points and their utilization places. We foresee the developments of renewable energy such that its source can be located closer to its usage, limiting the transport costs and allowing for the direct provisioning of current to computer rooms, with on-site innovative batteries.
- Changing the production of IT hardware by exploring some alternatives for replacing rare metals which have to be used with care, both from an ecological point of view and also from a political point of view. This research on rare metals might be post-disruptive since all the production flows have to be rethought.

Acknowledgement. The ideas presented in this paper are partially funded by the European Commission under contract 288701 through the project CoolEmAll.

References

1. U.S. Environmental Protection Agency ENERGY STAR Program. Report to congress on server and data center energy efficiency (August 2007) (online),
2. http://www.energystar.gov/ia/partners/prod_development/downloads/epa_datacenterre-port_congress_final1.pdf
   http://www.iea.org
3. Butollo, F., Kusch, J., Laufer, T.: Buy IT Fair, Procure IT Fair, Berlin (2009)
4. http://www.destatis.de/jetspeed/portal/cms/Sites/destatis/Internet/DE/Content/Statistiken/Informationsgesellschaft/InformationsgesellschaftDeutschland,property=file.pdf
   (in German)
5. Murugesan, S.: Harnessing Green IT: Principles and Practices. IT Professional 10(1), 24–33 (2008)
6. Wikipedia,
   http://de.wikipedia.org/wiki/Green_business
   (accessed on June 23, 2009)
7. TecChannel (2008),
   http://www.tecchannel.de/server/hardware/1760738/green_it_strom_sparen-in_serverraeumen_durch_optimales_energiemanagement/index.html
8. Hilty, L.M.: Information Technology and Sustainability. Essays on the Relationship between ICT and Sustainable Development. Books on demand (2008) ISBN: 9783837019704
9. IT Wissen 2009 Green IT online, DATACOM Buchverlag GmbH (June 23, 2009),
   http://itwissen.info/definition/lexikon/FreenIT-green-IT.html

10. SCS Cloud Usage Index, http://assets1.csc.com/newsroom/downloads/ CSC_Cloud_Usage_Index_Report.pdf (retrieved on February 2012)
11. Da Costa, G., Dias de Assunção, M., Gelas, J.P., Georgiou, Y., Lefèvre, L., Orgerie, A.-C., Pierson, J.M., Richard, O., Sayah, A.: Multi-facet approach to reduce energy consumption in clouds and grids: The green-net framework. In: e-Energy 2010: First International Conference on Energy-Efficient Computing and Networking, Passau, Germany, pp. 95–104 (April 2010)
12. Moore, J., Chase, J., Ranganathan, P., Sharma, R.: Making Scheduling "Cool": Temperature-Aware Workload Placement in Data Centers. Science, pp. 61–74. USENIX Association (2005)
13. http://www.statista.com
14. The GreenGrid, http://www.thegreengrid.org
15. CoolEmAll Project, http://www.coolemall.eu
16. http://gigaom.com/cleantech/data-centers-will-follow-the-sun-and-chase-the-wind/ (July 2008) (retrieved February 2012)
17. Jevons, J.S.: The Coal Question: Can Britain Survive? First published 1865. Republished Macmillan, London (1906)
18. Grubb, M.J.: Communication energy efficiency and economic fallacies. Energy Policy 18(8), 783–785 (1990)
19. Bertoldi, P., Atanasiu, B.: Electricity consumption and efficiency trends in the enlarged European Union (2006), http://www.re.jrc.ec.europa.eu/energyefficiency/ pdf/eneff_report_2006.pdf
20. Pickavet, M., Vereecken, W., Demeyer, S., Audenaert, P., Vermeulen, B., Develder, C., Colle, D., Dhoedt, B., Demeester, P.: Worldwide energy needs for ICT: The rise of power-aware networking. In: ANTS 2008. 2nd International Symposium on Advanced Networks and Telecommunication System, pp. 1–3 (December 2008)
21. Adams, W.M.: The Future of Sustainability: Re-thinking Environment and Development in the Twenty-first Century. Report of the IUCN Renowned Thinkers Meeting, January 29-31 (2006)
22. IBM Deutschland, Greenbook Energieeffizienz: Trend und Lösungen, Zürich (2008) (in German)
23. IBM Deutschland GmbH - Presseinformation: IBM Projekt "Big Green" konsolidiert 3900 Server auf 30 Linux-Großrechner, Stuttgart (2007) (in German)
24. Buhl, H.U., Laartz, J., Löffler, M., Röglinger, M.: Green IT reicht nicht aus! WuM, Ausgabe 01 (2009) (in German)
25. Hilty, L.: FachPress online interview, http://fachpresse.a.customer.sylon.net/ index.php?id=1600 (in German)
26. Eugster, M., Hischier, R., Huabo, D.: Key Environmental Impacts of the Chinese EEE-Industry – A Life Cycle Study. Empa and Tsinghua University, St. Gallen and Bejing (2007)
27. Cook, G., Van Horn, J.: How Dirty is your data: A look at the Energy choices that Power Cloud Computing, Greenpeace (April 2011)
28. Cook, G.: How Clean is Your Cloud? GreenPeace (April 2012)
29. Rivoire, S., Ranganathan, P., Kozyrakis, C.: A comparison of high-level full-system power models. In: Zhao, F. (ed.) HotPower, USENIX Association (2008)
30. Da Costa, G., Hlavacs, H.: Methodology of Measurement for Energy Consumption of Applica-tions. Energy Efficient Grids, Clouds and Clusters Workshop (co-located with Grid) (E2GC2 2010), Brussels (October 25-29). IEEE (2010)

The Role of ICT in Sustainable and Responsible Development: E-Skilling

Hossana Twinomurinzi

Department of Informatics, University of Pretoria, South Africa
twinoh@up.ac.za

Abstract. Skilling unquestionably plays the most practical role in creating innovations which will be financially, socially and economically sustainable in developing countries (DCs). And because we now live in an economic age dependent on knowledge and driven by the rapid and global advances in Information and Communication Technologies (ICT), skilling in ICT is even more important. Key to participating in the knowledge-based economy is the ability to creatively and productively apply whatever ICT is within reach to be e-skilled. While ICT has become an important national strategy in all DCs, e-skilling has not. The emphasis has primarily been on education to produce more ICT and science graduates. The irony in DCs is that more ICT graduates do not necessarily result in greater productive participation in the knowledge-based economy. The result is often unemployed ICT graduates or the increased brain-drain of ICT and science graduates to developed countries. E-skilling is clearly a new strategic problem in DCs. The productivity paradox points to the unique need for DCs to re-think e-skilling so as to create financially, socially and economically sustainable local innovations driven by ICT. While many articles appear on how DCs may participate in the knowledge-based economy, very few offer practical suggestions that are locally relevant in DC contexts. Developing a DC e-skills agenda is clearly of interest. In this chapter, we draw on early efforts being undertaken in South Africa to present progressive perspectives on e-skilling in DCs based on four important provisions; a national budget for e-skills development, an environment that fosters creativity and innovation, a collaborative platform that recognizes the collectivist nature of DCs, and a national support structure that in inclined to e-skills brain-circulation.

Keywords: capabilities approach, developing countries, development, e-skills, ICT, innovation, knowledge-based economy, sustainability.

1   Introduction

We live in an economic age dependent on knowledge and driven by the rapid and global advances in Information and Communication Technologies (ICT) in what has been referred to as the knowledge-based economy [1]. For example, the emphasis on knowledge can be seen from the increased investment in research and development, education and software which stand at 9% of the Gross Domestic Product in OECD (Organisation for Economic Co-operation and Development) countries [2]. The

M.D. Hercheui et al. (Eds.): HCC10 2012, IFIP AICT 386, pp. 90–99, 2012.
© IFIP International Federation for Information Processing 2012

convergence of media (text, video, telephony and images) and the constant advancement in the power of technology and communications infrastructure to generate, transmit and distribute information at faster speeds and yet at a lower cost amplifies the necessity to have a different labour market. This is a labour market that has the ability to innovate the readily and easily available scientific and technological knowledge for sustainable gain [3].

In this paper, we adopt a view of knowledge as the intangible sum of – what is known and what one has become familiar with – fact, truth, principles acquired with education and experience. Knowledge is however not sufficient for sustainable growth and economic development. While it remains a good starting point, creativity and innovation are required to turn knowledge into a product, idea or artefact that will add value to an individual, group, organization and society. We refer to the productive end point of knowledge as a skill. A skill goes beyond knowledge to the capacity to achieve desirable results with minimal effort within a context [4].

Dreyfus and Dreyfus' [4] model of skills acquisition suggests that knowledge is transformed into a skill through formal instruction and practice in several stages: novice, competence, proficiency, expertise, and mastery. At the novice stage rules about a field are followed without consideration of how they can be applied in context. The person will often need to be guided on the rules. At the competence stage the person is now able to apply the rules within the context and make trade-offs although in a limited way. At the proficient stage, a person is able to make decisions within the context and even make rules to guide later decisions. A person who has acquired expertise is able to prioritize what is important within the context, and even innovate within the situation at hand. The mastery stage is where the person has embedded a deep knowledge such that he or she can now develop visions of the future and guide others towards achieving those visions.

A simple example could be when at the novice stage an entrepreneur could learn to use a mobile app to send information about his or her products to clients. Then as the entrepreneur becomes comfortable with the app, he or she could create client groups within the mobile app which could send preferential information to different types of clients. Based on physical client feedback, the entrepreneur could later modify the groupings to decide on better management of the information sent to the clients. Beyond this, the entrepreneur could request customized modifications from the mobile app that would allow for supply chain type inter-communication with clients. The entrepreneur would have mastery of the mobile app by creating new channels which would apply to similar entrepreneurs, train employees on its use, and project modifications that are needed for future business.

The model by Dreyfus and Dreyfus is however insufficient in not being prescriptive enough on the process required in moving from one stage to the next, nor allowing for the place of creativity and innovation [5].

We posit that e-skilling, applying creativity and innovative processes using ICT as a tool, plays the most practical role in creating new artefacts which are financially, socially and economically sustainable in the knowledge-based economy in developing countries (DCs). Next, we consider the complex issue of development and show the special attention needed to stimulate e-skilling in DCs.

2   The Nature of Development

The nature of development is a subject of continuing theoretical debate [6] ranging from something that happens in the third world [7] to a structured and linearly staged process of enabling DCs to catch up with developed countries [8]. The issues that stand out in the debates on development generally arise from two areas; how development is defined and for whom development is aimed. These issues include the measurement of development, the economics of development, the contribution of international aid, political and civil development, the globalization influences on development, gender, development such as modernization, regional variation, underdevelopment, the environment, and community development [9], [10].

The current discourse appreciates that development does not occur in a vacuum but requires harmonious collaboration between governments, the private sector, civil society and citizens. Policies that are aimed at development need to consider at least five important DC aspects: they should support local institutional structures such as the collectivist culture, play a role in the implementation of other pro-development policies, ride on democratic freedoms to foster creativity and innovation, take caution to increase self-reliance, and play a unifying role in the country [11].

The ideas on development by Amartya Sen [12], which have significantly influenced the United Nations approach to development, take a more sustainable approach to development by centring on individual choice and the freedoms to make the choices. Sen's [12] Capabilities Approach (CA) is a broad framework that assesses individual well-being and social arrangements based on what individuals are able to do and to be. The basic premise is to enlarge the choices available to individuals so they can live the life they choose [12]. Sen contends that the assessment of well-being should be concerned with an individual's capability to function, "what a person can do or can be", and the real opportunities that the person has especially compared with others. Robeyns [13] proposed a schematic representation to visualize the CA (Fig. 1).

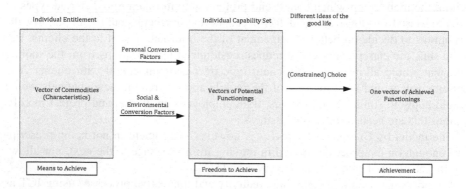

Fig. 1. Schema of the Capabilities Approach [14]

The figure can be summarized as follows, beginning from the left. An individual may have the means to achieve such as access to a mobile phone or a computer. The means to achieve are expected to assist to emancipate the person from conditions of deprivation. However, the person's psyche needs to be transformed in order to exercise control of the available commodities for his or her benefit. The transformation of the person requires social and environmental factors, such as training. The trained person will then have obtained the freedom to achieve. Then, based on the person's perspective of what is considered good and beneficial, what Sen refers to as a constrained choice, the freedom to achieve is drawn on to actually do something. For example, a person can create a website to advertise products. By doing this, the person will have made an achievement based on what he or she desires.

Sen's humane way of thinking is a fundamental shift away from the linear and structured development norms which measure well-being based on financial estimates such as Gross Domestic Product and Gross National Product. In CA it is not enough to only remove obstacles that inhibit individuals from living the life they value; individuals should be provided with the means to achieve such a life [12], [14].

Nonetheless, Sen's developmental approach is limited for many DCs in especially two areas; it is overly individualistic because it ignores the strong collectiveness nature of DC cultures [15], and it is non-prescriptive. The CA is strong on values but weak on prescriptions in contrast to the traditional approaches to development [16]. For example, Sen's framework accounts only for knowledge but leaves open the constrained factors that will move a group, organization or a society from knowledge to exercising a skill to mastery. Creativity and innovation are required for a person, group, organization or society to take the acquired knowledge through to implementation. And in the knowledge-based economy, a creative and innovative manipulation of ICT tools needs to be emphasized as a significant part of the constrained choice.

3   Examples of E-Skilling as Means of Sustainable Development

There are a number of countries that have already adopted a creative and innovative ICT approach to the knowledge-based economy such as Australia, China, Hong Kong, New Zealand, Singapore, Sweden, as well as the EU. For example, Malaysia and India moved the focus from foreign direct investments in ICT to investments in indigenous companies. Malaysia intentionally forces multinational corporations to employ local resources in the ICT sector which has resulted in a brain-circulation where skills eventually remain in Malaysia. South Korea invests in its human capital by upgrading the quality of higher education and the employment opportunities available to indigenous high-tech labour. South Korea purposefully created industries that could lure back critical ICT skills. South Korea's decision to offshore some ICT skills has additionally been a factor that has caused a change in the economic paradigm from looking for low-wage labour to perform low-wage work to low-wage labour to perform high-skilled work [17]. It is clear from these examples that government has played a significant role in creating and enforcing an amiable environment for the creative and innovative sustenance of ICT skills [17]. With the exception of India, these are all developed countries. We present below a budding e-skilling agenda in a DC, using South Africa as an example.

3.1   The National E-Skills Plan of Action, South Africa

South Africa recently developed an e-skills agenda in the National e-Skills Plan of Action 2010 (NeSPA). The agenda aims to stimulate the creative and innovative use of ICT among citizens, communities, and organizations so they can favourably participate in the knowledge-based economy [18]. NeSPA was the climax of two years' consultation across business, government, education and civil society in South Africa and with international donor agencies, international IT corporations and research co-ordinators. The five areas identified for focused effort are:

- The alignment of an e-skilling agenda within existing developmental policy – national and international, budgeted for and linked with human capacity development
- The cultivation of cross-collaborative research on e-skills across the main four sectors of government, business, education and civil society
- The creation of a cascading hub-and-spoke type of collaborative administrative structure which places universities at the centre of bringing together the sectors
- Improving economic access to Internet and telecommunications
- The formation of a high-level advisory council that takes care of the interests of the different sectors.

In the context of South Africa, seven e-skills were identified:

- e-Literacy Skills: the basic use of ICT, for example, the Internet and email
- e-Participation and e-Democracy Skills: focusing on enhancing participative citizen-government engagement
- e-Government/Governance Skills: to increase a more efficient and productive use of ICT within government
- e-Business Skills: aimed at increasing organizational efficiency and productivity
- e-User Skills: focusing on enhancing efficiency of people for any task at hand
- e-Practitioner Skills: for the more traditional mainstream ICT professional
- e-Community Skills: aimed at communities for building social cohesion within local contexts, for example, to deal with crime, health and education.

The e-skills agenda sees impact as being measured based on the degree of:

- Employment readiness: a higher ability to become employed
- Effective e-governance and service delivery: using ICT to improve government services
- Business development: leveraging ICT to enhance business productivity
- Socio-economic development: an increase in national productiveness
- Research and development: to guide policy and curriculum development.

4   Towards a DC E-Skilling Agenda

The local context of DCs differs from developed countries in at least five ways: the history and culture, technical staff, infrastructure, citizens and government officers

(Chen et al., 2006). The recent democracy of most DCs, relative to other developing countries, is particularly distinctive. In terms of culture, Western societies are highly individualistic while DC cultures are more collectivist [19]. DCs also typically suffer from e-skills shortages, unlike developed countries where, on the one hand, most government officials use and may in fact depend on ICT. On the other hand, government officers in DCs are often vaguely familiar with ICT and will in most instances prefer not to dedicate the already few human capital resources to a notion that is vague.

The contextual differences highlight the need to create an e-skilling agenda that suits the development needs of DCs.

In summary, we see an opportunity for an e-skilling agenda that takes into account the following key principles:

1. An increased national budget for research and development in e-skills development
2. An environment that fosters creativity and innovation, and further enables people, groups, organizations and societies to progress from knowledge through to a mastery of e-skills in creating and innovating artefacts that suit their specific contexts
3. A collaborative platform to share ideas, and one that recognizes the collectivist nature of DC communities
4. A national support structure that in many respects enforces and is inclined towards brain-circulation.

In the next section, we offer a fuller discussion on the points presented above and later use the discussion to evaluate the e-skilling agenda of South Africa.

5   Discussion

The following discussion is primarily guided by Dreyfus and Dreyfus' [4] model of skills acquisition presented in the introduction section. The model throws light on how basic/novice knowledge of ICT could be transformed into a mastered e-skill through formal instruction and practice following the stages of novice, competence, proficiency, expertise, and mastery. The model will also assist as a lens through which to evaluate the e-skilling programme of South Africa and glean conceptual ideas for an e-skilling agenda for DCs taking into account Sen's ideas on humane development [12].

5.1   A Necessary Stimulant Budgetary Provision for an E-Skills Programme

A key ingredient for development of any kind is for there to exist a range of commodities which people or groups of people can draw on to emancipate themselves. One of the most important of these commodities in DCs is finances. These countries are DCs because the greater majority of the populations do not have sufficient economic capabilities. Therefore, for an e-skilling agenda, commodities such as economic access to ICT and the Internet would be the vital starting point. Sen [12] is quick to caution that having access of whatever kind to a commodity does not necessary mean the commodity will be productively utilized. There are personal and social factors where a person needs to be trained on how to use the ICT. In South Africa, like many other countries, there are multi-purpose community centres which have computers with an Internet capability. However, access to the computers is constrained by the inability of the people in the community to pay for the relatively high cost to learn how to use the computers or access the Internet by using the computers. The second constraint is that where training is done, it is often focused on creating the novice knowledge of ICT, and no path is provided to reach mastery levels such that the few people who gain such novice knowledge are not able to do much with their new knowledge except to have a certificate. The above two constraints have been the main reasons why many of the multi-purpose community centres have not added much value in terms of getting people to use ICT.

The lessons that can be learnt from multi-purpose community centres shows that DC governments need to go beyond providing access to ICT and the Internet, to providing economic access to ICT/Internet up to mastery level by either making access to the ICT/Internet free, and/or by providing economic incentives for people in the community to learn to use the ICT/Internet in their vicinity up to the level of mastery.

Nonetheless, making the provision is still not enough. While a person may have a mastery of how to use a commodity, it does not necessarily mean that the person will take advantage of the commodity to do something productive. Sen [12] describes the necessary step as a constrained choice which is often tapered by personal and social notions of what is beneficial. For example, a person who has mastered how to use ICT may prefer to only use the ICT to send emails to relatives and friends or apply for jobs online. Another person could take the same opportunity through self-taught free Internet education to create a free-website and advertise products for sale. Another may not even use the mastery of e-skills.

Although the responsibility for a productive use of an e-skill eventually lies with an individual, and not with government, government can provide an environment whereby people will be stimulated or encouraged to make an attempt at trying out their new e-skills. We posit the answer to lie in creating an environment that encourages innovation.

5.2   An Environment that Fosters Creativity and Innovation

Creativity is the creation of a valuable artefact, procedure, or process often by people who work in collaboration [20]. Innovation carries the same essence as creativity except the end-result is from an improvement of something that already existed. Creativity is a part of innovation which in turn is part of organizational change. For groups to be creative, the leadership should be democratic and collaborative, the structure should be organic rather than mechanistic, and the groups preferably "composed of individuals drawn from diverse fields or functional backgrounds." [20]. The key to innovating with ICT is therefore individuals with a mastery of e-skills.

An example of a needed innovation in DCs is the advent of the mobile. The uptake of mobile technology in the form of basic cell phones, smartphones and tablets has already outpaced the traditional personal computer (PC) and fixed-line telephones, creating with it an opportunity for innovation. For example, South Africa has a 101% mobile phone penetration, which means that each and every person has access to a mobile phone. This means that innovations in e-skilling should pay close attention to mastering e-skills in developing mobile applications. Although there are some successful models such as Kenya's M-PESA and u-Shahidi, it is unpromising that most mobile apps are created in developed countries and are not relevant to DCs. This creates an opportunity for the creation of valuable mobile apps which are locally relevant to DCs.

In addition, in 2007 South Africa made provision in its income tax law for a 150% tax incentive to organizations that invest in research and development in areas such as software development. Coupled with the 150% tax incentive, the South African e-skills agenda has a number of qualities that encourage an environment which fosters creativity and innovation. The cascaded hub-and-spoke system is fluid and allows a degree of autonomy to each of the hubs to participate in advancing the agenda and developing funded research programmes. The individuals participating in the hubs are from a broad range of functional and organizational areas beyond information systems, such as, for example, chemical engineering, mathematics, physics, management, computer science, government, education, business and civil society.

It is too early to tell whether the environment of creativity in the South African e-skills agenda will pay off and what, if any, were the factors that may previously have inhibited creativity and innovation.

5.3 A Collaborative Platform to Share Ideas that Acknowledge Collectivist Culture

The collectivist nature of people in DCs means that people without sufficient economic means often group together not only to leverage scarce economic resources but also because it is a fundamental part of their social fabric. For a DC e-skilling agenda, cognizance must be taken of the fact that people prefer to work in groups and will not suddenly prefer the individualistic modes of ICT training often offered by traditional institutions where each person sits alone on a computer [15]. There are a number of education models that allow for group learning which ICT training could borrow from such as the jigsaw classroom cooperative learning technique.

If the individuals in a collective all had mastery of special e-skills and a mastery of their different functional areas, this could create even greater opportunities for innovation. The collaborative nature of South Africa's e-skills agenda at the high-level offers an ideal platform to share ideas. It will be important for the curricula developed by the e-skills agenda to incorporate such cooperative learning techniques.

5.4 A National Support Structure Inclined towards Brain-Circulation

It is advantageous to upskill people to a mastery of e-skills, yet two global problems constantly hover on the economic horizon; the brain-drain of the best e-skills from DCs to developed countries, and the globalization of ICT skills to lower labour markets such as China, Eastern Europe and India. Developed countries have the economic muscle to target and offer "heavenly salaries" to highly e-skilled people from DCs who, without good employment, are understandably forced to repatriate. The few e-skilled people who stay are not able to compete favourably against the cheaper rates offered in low labour markets. The two problems create an even greater need for governments to create environments where e-skilled people have an opportunity to reap a comfortable economic benefit where the best e-skills prefer to stay and are accessible within the country at a competitive rate.

In South Africa's e-skills agenda, an intentional effort has been placed on making the organizational structure a cross-cutting one that includes partners from all spheres in government, business, education and civil society in an attempt to address the national issues that affect every sector of South African society. There are also other collaborative partnerships beyond South Africa to other countries such as Kenya, Rwanda, Mexico and Australia.

6   Conclusions

With the advancement of ICT in society, business and government, the dependence on knowledge has become more complex and pronounced, and presents new challenges for participation in the knowledge-based economy [21]. In this paper, we have seen that while access to ICT is on the increase in DCs, it remains a challenge to productively find sufficient means, economic and skilling, of using it for sustainable development. The problem is not that there is not enough knowledge about ICT, there is not enough skilling to a level of mastery in ICT. There is insufficient economic access to ICT such that the ICT which is available is not being put to productive use. The paper posits that there is a great need for economic access to e-skilling to a mastery level. Dreyfus and Dreyfus' [4] model of skilling showed that skilling goes beyond knowledge to mastering the capacity to achieve desirable results with minimal effort in a given context.

This paper contributes to knowledge in identifying that the needed change is the creation of interactive spaces that will allow more innovation and creativity among adopters of ICT. The change from producing more knowledge to producing more skills at a mastery level will require a great deal of innovation and creativity to create an e-skills agenda that meets the dynamic needs of DCs. The new e-skills agenda calls for a collaborative partnership between government as a stimulator, the business sector as a consumer of ICT, civil society to ensure that common interests are advanced without negatively affecting other interests and from citizens who will be using ICT. The e-skills efforts of South Africa appear to be on the right track to create such an interactive space that allows for creativity and innovation.

A limitation of this paper is the focus on the e-skilling agenda from South Africa without taking into account the e-skilling agendas of other DC countries, thereby making generalizations about the contribution to knowledge to a wider DC context problematic. The reason is that, because while many DCs are investing in national ICT strategies and in improving ICT skills, South Africa has established a clear national e-skilling agenda which does not only focus mainly on ICT skills but also on training the entire country in e-skills.

References

1. Drucker, P.F.: The Age of Discontinuity: Guidelines to our Changing Society. Harper and Row, New York (1978)
2. Quah, D.: Introduction: The Knowledge Economy and ICTs. In: Mansell, R., Avgerou, C., Quah, D., Silverstone, R. (eds.) The Oxford Handbook of Information and Communication Technologies, xxi, 620 p. Oxford University Press, Oxford (2009)
3. Hearn, G., Rooney, D.: Knowledge Policy: Challenges for the 21st Century. Edward Elgar, Cheltenham (2008)
4. Dreyfus, S.E., Dreyfus, H.L.: A five-stage model of the mental activities involved in directed skill acquisition. DTIC Document (1980)
5. Flyvbjerg, B.: Sustaining nonrationalized Practices: BodyMind, Power and Situational Ethics. Praxis International 92 (1991)
6. Avgerou, C.: Discourses on Innovation and Development in Information Systems in Developing Countries' Research. In: Conference Discourses on Innovation and Development in Information Systems in Developing Countries' Research, p. 510. Dubai School of Government, International Federation for Information Processing (2009)
7. Chari, S., Corbridge, S.: The Development Reader. Routledge, London (2008)
8. Cypher, J.M., Dietz, J.L.: The Process of Economic Development. Routledge, London (2009)
9. Kingsbury, D.: Introduction. In: Kingsbury, D., McKay, J., Hunt, J., McGillivray, M., Clarke, M. (eds.) International Development: Issues and Challenges, viii, 375 p. Palgrave Macmillan, Basingstoke (2008)
10. Nederveen Pieterse, J.: Development Theory: Deconstructions/Reconstructions. Sage, London (2009)
11. Twinomurinzi, H.: Facilitating Policy Implementation using ICT in a Development Context: A South African Ubuntu Approach. Department of Informatics, Faculty of Engineering, Built Environment and Information Technology, vol. PhD thesis, p. 185. University of Pretoria, Pretoria (2010)
12. Sen, A.K.: Commodities and Capabilities. Oxford University Press, Delhi (1999)
13. Technology Republic, http://www.ingridrobeyns.nl/Ac_publ_list.html
14. Robeyns, I.: The capability approach and welfare policies. In: Conference on Gender Auditing and Gender Budgeting, Bologna, Italy (2005)
15. Twinomurinzi, H., Phahlamohlaka, J., Byrne, E.: The small group subtlety of using ICT for participatory governance: A South African experience. Government Information Quarterly (2012)
16. Fukuda-Parr, S.: The Human Development Paradigm: Operationalizing Sen's Ideas on Capabilities. Feminist Economics 9, 301–317 (2003)
17. Lazonick, W.: Globalization of the ICT Labour Force. In: Mansell, R., Avgerou, C., Quah, D., Silverstone, R. (eds.) The Oxford Handbook of Information and Communication Technologies, xxi, 620 p. Oxford University Press, Oxford (2009)
18. NeSPA: National e-Skills Plan of Action: e-Skilling the Nation for Equitable Prosperity and Global Competitiveness. In: Department of Communications, The e-Skills Institute (2010)
19. Hofstede, G.: Culture's Consequences. Sage, Beverly Hills (1980)
20. Woodman, R.W., Sawyer, J.E., Griffin, R.W.: Toward a theory of organizational creativity. Academy of Management Review 18, 293–321 (1993)
21. Hearn, G., Rooney, D.: Introduction. In: Hearn, G., Rooney, D. (eds.) Knowledge Policy: Challenges for the 21st Century, xv, 277 p. Edward Elgar, Cheltenham (2008)

Sustainable and Responsible ICT Innovation in Healthcare: A Long View and Continuous Ethical Watch Required

Tony Cornford and Valentina Lichtner

Information Systems and Innovation Group,
London School of Economics and Political Sciences, London, United Kingdom
{t.cornford,v.lichtner}@lse.ac.uk

Abstract. Healthcare is of central importance to all communities and generally has a high political profile. Access and availability of care, rising costs, and emerging new relationships between experts (doctors and nurses) and users (patients, citizens) pose new challenges. ICT-based innovation is often proposed as a solution, accompanied by optimistic accounts of its transformative potential, both for the developing world and the developed. These ambitions also implicitly endorse new social agreements and business models. In this respect, as in others, technology is not neutral or simple in the service of modernization; it has its own politics. This paper discusses ICT innovation in healthcare in these terms focused on issues of sustainability and responsibility adapting two economic concepts: redistribution and externalities. The analysis reveals ICT innovation in health care as essentially raising 'trans-scientific' questions – matters of policy and intergenerational ethics rather than narrow science.

Keywords: healthcare, ICT, technological innovation, sustainability, ethics, redistribution, externalities.

1   Introduction

Today's healthcare challenges and their potential technological 'solutions' are well known. They appear as an often-repeated 'mantra' in the opening paragraph of publications on health policy and information technology (e.g. [1]). The basic themes are low-growth and aging western economies facing a future with an increasingly expensive and less affordable healthcare system. Important drivers of the growing burden placed on these systems, and on public health and economic life in general, comes from the complex mixture of an aging population with multiple care and medical needs, and the availability of expensive new treatments. These themes are combined in the rising numbers of people with chronic but increasingly treatable conditions such as diabetes or COPD which are life-style related and require treatments 'for life'. As a consequence, the mission of healthcare is increasingly directed towards assisting people to live well, a matter of prevention and quality of life rather than narrowly medical concerns of diagnosis and treatment, or matters of 'life or death'.

M.D. Hercheui et al. (Eds.): HCC10 2012, IFIP AICT 386, pp. 100–110, 2012.
© IFIP International Federation for Information Processing 2012

These pressures are compounded in a globalised world by movement of people across borders, which leads to concern over faster and wider spread of diseases and epidemics (e.g. [2], [3]). London, for example, has now a substantial programme to combat TB [4], a disease that was considered exceptional a generation ago. We also see migration among healthcare professionals, with many developed countries dependent on doctors and nurses recruited away from countries with greater health needs.

Against this background it is perhaps unsurprising that information and communication technologies (ICT), ubiquitous access to networks and data , and the rapid growth of mobile and distributed computing, offers enticing opportunities for reducing costs of service provision, raising effectiveness of interventions and improving access to healthcare [5], [6]. In this paper we discuss some of the consequences of increased reliance on ICT innovations in healthcare systems – the socio-technical consequences across time and space. We thus consider the sustainability of the deepening engagement of healthcare systems with digital technologies and consider the ethical questions posed. In presenting this analysis we develop our argument around the twin themes of redistribution and externalities.

2   ICT Innovation in Healthcare

The penetration of healthcare by digital technologies occurs at many levels and in many places. Here we highlight three contemporary and contrasting examples.

Digital Imaging. There has been in the last decade a move from film based x-rays to digital imaging technologies. There is reasonable evidence of immediate clinical benefit arising from networked sharing of this information, credible expectation of cost saving over time, and real environmental benefits from the use of fewer chemicals in film processing [7]. Digital images and scans also are available to become part of an electronic patient record, which can serve clinical decisions making that draws upon more complete patient information.

Telemedicine ('Consultation at a Distance'). Telecommunications and networks can obviate patient travel (e.g. to hospital), and optimize access to and sharing of medical expertise. Telemedicine has found successful implementations in geographically remote regions, improving access to care and expertise, but also in reorganization of emergency services such as stroke care (e.g. [8]) or more generally interlinking primary and secondary care. We may also extend the definition to technologies for assisted living (telecare), with technologies serving to allow people to remain in their homes longer thus avoiding hospitalization costs and improving quality of life. Telecare, in its various forms, has been reported in England to generate potential savings such as "45% reduction in mortality rates, 20% reduction in emergency admissions, 15% reduction in A&E visits, 14% reduction in elective admissions, 14% reduction in bed days, 8% reduction in tariff costs" [9].

Patient Centered Care. Patient accessed and managed health services are now provided digitally. While telemedicine and telecare maintain broadly the traditional service model (doctor – nurse – patient), there are a set of technological innovations applied in healthcare, often delivered on the Internet or by mobile phones, that embody greater patient/citizen participation and ownership of health matters. This can lead to a rebalanced (we might even say more equal) doctor-patient relationship, with greater responsibility taken by patient-citizens and their families for their own health and care, or allowing them to by-pass healthcare professionals and healthcare institutions altogether [10]. Online citizen participation can also be a driver of new public health strategies such as online smoking cessation initiatives, the monitoring of epidemics by crowd-sourcing (see http://healthmap.org) or the use of two-way SMS phone messaging to monitor emergencies [11]. Finally, a new form of participatory health research is emerging, with crowd-sourced health research studies complementing, if not yet replacing, more traditional clinical trials [12].

The three broad examples of contemporary technological innovations sketched above suggest distinct aspects of the move to digitalize. First, the gains that derives from new ways to carry out or extend the range of existing types of task (e.g. x-ray imaging) within an established institutional setting. Second, the redistribution of resources across space so as to reconfigure and improve services and support equality of access, and finally a (potential) systemic change as healthcare takes a turn towards the patient-consumer and is less about a 'do to' or 'do for' model and more 'do with' [13] - even 'do alone'.

The most innovative but also potentially disruptive aspects of ICT in healthcare derive from the inherent characteristics of digital innovations to generate, store and share large amounts of data (sometimes described as 'big data') and connect and serve multiple people in both tight or loose social structures. In all these examples we see digital data being generated and changing or rebalancing the way healthcare is delivered, experienced and how and by who control is exercised. Digital data is drawn upon and influences decisions, at large scale as in healthcare planning, pharmaceutical research or population surveillance, clinically as in a clinical decision support systems (DSS), or less formally as in a patient group based discussion forums.

In this sense digital innovation in healthcare is founded on both technical and social networking – sometimes known as web 2.0 (and hence health 2.0) – and embraces in some mix data aggregation and analysis, user-generated content and new business models (open innovation, social networking and the economy of 'free' [14]).

3   Sustainability and Responsibility: Redistribution and Externalities

It is certainly not foolish to believe in the potential of digital technologies for changing the nature of service provision across all economic and administrative sectors. In our own lives we see pertinent examples in business (e.g. travel, music) and in the public realm (e-government, e-petitions). And ICT may well offer entirely new 'solutions' to both the old and the new healthcare and public health problems.

No technology is, however, politically or ethically neutral [15]. All innovation embodies certain interests and neglects others, and there is a risk that digitally innovated systems may not be, in the long term, sustainable whatever specific improvements in aspects of healthcare they deliver. We should apply to digital development within healthcare the spirit of the United Nations definition for sustainable development – "[S]ustainable development is development that meets the needs of the *present* without compromising the ability of *future* generations to meet their own needs" ([16], emphasis added).

Developmental interventions in society or the economy have effects on the distribution of income or access to resources both within, and given globalisation, beyond national borders, as well as across time. By distributional effects we mean the "modifications of the holdings of particular persons, collective agents, or groups [...] with respect to a 'baseline'" [17]. What is redistributed may not be only access to resources but roles, risks, and responsibilities. Barry goes on to suggest that redistribution should be understood relative to some defined set of subjects. In healthcare these groups may be, for instance: types of clinicians (e.g. nurses versus doctors), clinical staff versus other healthcare employees (e.g. administrative staff), clinicians versus patients, or in a more macro dimension, healthcare providers (e.g. hospitals versus community care or self-care). It may also be, indeed should be, seen in terms of citizens and generations (e.g. the old versus the young, or the healthy versus the ill).

Some distributional effects are expected from most policies or initiatives, not just those 'purposively' launched for redistributive goals, such as national welfare policies. All of the types of digital interventions in healthcare introduced above have distributional effects across many domains; on access to care, on labour and workload, on professional roles and autonomy, on who bears risk and takes responsibilities, and on doctor-patient relationships [18-21]. Berg [22] for example speaks of the unpredictable and unknown redistribution of responsibilities in future systems built to support a patient-centric workflow and notes that this would probably, "ensure a conflict-rife implementation process; yet it could be an important part of a more patient-oriented care process." [22]

Redistributive effects of ICT use may be expected and desired, others may occur as 'unexpected consequences' [23] or what economists would call externalities. The term 'externalities' refers not simply to effects beyond the intended but to "situations when the effect of production or consumption of goods and services imposes costs or benefits on others which are not reflected in the prices charged for the goods and services being provided" [24]. The concept originates from Pigou [25] who identified that the actions of economic agents can and will influence the utility of others without mechanisms for compensation [26] and were later known as external (dis)economies or externalities [27].

Externalities may be negative – e.g. social costs that counterbalance private benefits – or positive – e.g. social benefits that counterbalance private costs. The motorcar is a well-understood example of externalities of the first kind. The technological invention of the combustion engine brought, in the last century in Western countries, freedom of movement to the masses and contributed to women's emancipation. Yet new problems emerged – from accidents, to traffic jams and air and noise pollution.

Thus the cost for the individual of driving a car does not take adequately into account society's costs – the externalities. Similarly it can be argued that the unfettered use of insurance markets in healthcare cause externalities in the social cost of the uninsured. When private cars were the luxury of a few, their impact on the environment did not present the sustainability challenges that emerge when it becomes a technology for the masses. An example of positive externalities might be the inoculation of children for diseases such as mumps, measles or chicken pox. This has a private cost and benefit for the child or family, but also strong social benefit in the 'herd immunity' it helps to create.

As in the case of the motorcar, also in healthcare, when a technology reaches a significant scale of implementation, the related negative externalities may have long-term consequences for sustainability. By sustainability we refer to both the capacity of the services (and associated technology) to be sustained economically through time (e.g. [28]) as well as the impact on the sustainability of the wider context (social, economical, and environmental) and hence on the ethical worth.

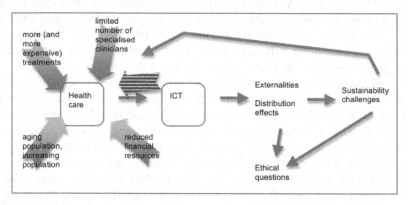

Fig. 1. ICT innovations have a life of their own – what 'can be built' often gets built. But pressures on healthcare lead to ICT innovations intended as a solution to some of these pressure. ICT investments can also constitute one of the pressures on healthcare, e.g. in terms of financial resources. ICT have consequences in terms of externalities and redistributive effects, with ethical implications, and in the long term, sustainability repercussions on other aspects of life (e.g. environment, or social agreements) as well as health itself.

Here we apply this analytical lens of redistribution and externalities to the digitalization of healthcare. We accept that these technologies will deliver individual and current benefits, but also assume that they will present their own distributional effects and externalities – leaving a legacy. Furthermore, the effects of today's technological choice will last through future phases of innovation constraining what is possible (what has been referred to as the 'durability of the present' [29]).

For example, the benefits of telemedicine for patients and carers may be seen in terms of access, convenience and efficiency of clinical services. However, telemedicine will also involve a redistribution of clinical tasks and roles (for example nurses taking over some medical tasks from doctors); a greater social and physical distance between doctor and patient (transforming the doctor-patient relationship); a redistribution of associated responsibilities and changes in risks [30]. In telecare the increased efficiency of service provision through a central location – for example a central monitoring station or call centre - potentially produces negative externalities at the periphery as patients lose human contact. In the longer term telecare may bear the risk of exacerbating the medical 'brain drain' and promoting imbalances in distribution of the health workforce [10], [31], with sustainability and ethical repercussions for healthcare global (in)equity.

Reliance on digital 'solutions' may also negatively influence the development of other services – driving out basic health provision. As Rao and Lombardi [32] note, while "telemedicine [projects] have demonstrated positive effects in countries in need, they have not substantially reduced or compensated for a fundamental lack of healthcare". Investments in forms other than face-to-face healthcare provision, may drive healthcare away from holistic care and patient intimacy with the doctor or nurse [33], and leave an unsustainable legacy of fragmentation of care and remoteness of relationships. This is at the very least a very different form of healthcare provision and one that may in time become dislodged from the central place in social and political life that healthcare now enjoys.

Social networks and other web 2.0 technologies show potential as a support structure for patients with chronic conditions and may offer valuable information sources for patients and health professionals [34]. Furthermore, crowd-sourcing is starting to show potential in healthcare as a means to collect and share patient narratives and ratings, used as 'evidence' "for product development, quality improvement, or policy reform" [35]. Though, as the scale of this increases, the 'option' of participating in the social network may be transforming into an 'obligation' – "an obligatory activity" for patients as good citizens [36]. This reminds us that online participation "involves work" [35]– specifically work that is redistributed ("shifted") from healthcare providers and government to patients and carers. This redistribution of work and new areas of responsibility/obligation is not in general financially recognized and suggests that we need to ask if crowd-sourcing is always economically fair?

Online participation also has evident consequences (i.e. externalities) for anonymity and privacy of individuals [37] and presents challenging implications in terms of surveillance. Today the law is still inadequate in most jurisdictions to protect individuals from (possibly incorrect, incomplete, or misleading) information posted online by individuals or companies [38]. Thus the world of social media and online marketing may create new challenges to public health policies, such as undermining stop smoking initiatives [39] or influencing negatively suicide or eating disorders [40].

Data protection laws are also often seen as inadequate for protecting individual's privacy, particularly so when policy is to integrate health data across organizations (within and outside healthcare) and patients are given little choice in the matter. In the United States this concern is a major element of resistance to President Obama's healthcare reforms and one that suggests legitimate ethical concern [41].

Aggregate data collected through the ubiquity of online devices and social media can usefully inform public health debate and support surveillance, providing early warning of emergencies, serving clinical research, tracking progress of interventions or informing strategies. However, data aggregation and surveillance evoke easily the image of 'big brother', or the fear that those who are monitoring gain power over people, "including the power to reprimand or punish" [42]. Privacy and associated issues of trust have become central to many health information systems initiatives and are tackled in a number of ways and to various degrees in different jurisdictions. It is unclear today if this concern is or can be adequately addressed by the various professional codes, data protection laws and technical measures available – adequately in the sense of gaining and sustaining public acceptance, minimizing harm, releasing the beneficial potential of digital technologies and retaining choice as to future development. Beyond the many 'solutions' available for aspects of health care practice, there remains a more fundamental set of questions as to the appropriate tests for legitimacy of the use of big data, for example in research, service management, for subpopulation monitoring or for public or private benefits beyond healthcare.

4   Concluding Remark – Science and Trans-Scientific Questions

Robert Oppenheimer, discussing the ethical dilemmas of the Manhattan Project says: "when you see something that is technically sweet, you go ahead and do it and you argue what to do about it only after you have had your technical success. That is the way it was with the atomic bomb" (cited in [43]). So too we suspect with health information systems. If it can be built, it will be built, and they will come, not least because there is often a persuasive short-term case to justify the investment and motivate use. But there is or should be more.

Sustainable digital investments in healthcare, a category we introduce here, do need to respond to the immediate needs of citizens for appropriate healthcare provision and the wider concerns of public health, as well as governments' concern for efficiency and value-for-money. But it must do so taking into account distributional effects, externalities, and the technical and societal legacy left to future generations. This is a legacy that will then constrain or promote further innovation.

Taking account of distribution and externalities implies making ethical choices, and hence raise matters of values. The burgeoning investments in ICT and implementation projects in healthcare are matters of politics and ethics, ultimately becoming trans-scientific questions [44] that cannot be answered by science alone. Enid Mumford makes a similar point, quoting Vickers as saying "technology always make ethical demands in what it requires people to expect of each other and therefore of themselves" [45], citing [46] and she goes on to note that "Ethical principles are particularly hard to develop and apply when times are hard, as economic pressures tend to overcome others" [45].

Thus, while policy makers and healthcare organizations keep solving today's problems and looking for 'scientific evidence' (on efficiency and effectiveness) to guide their investments in digital health, they face similar issues to those encountered by NASA on their Challenger missions:

"Observational data, backed by an intuitive argument, were unacceptable in NASA's science-based, positivistic, rule-bound system. Arguments that could not be supported by data did not meet engineering standards and would not pass the adversarial challenges of the FRR process. [so the hunch on the effect of cold weather on the o-ring was not reported]... Phillip Thompkins ... observed that 'only the easy decisions at Marshall were made by scientific evidence or demonstration. The difficult decisions created a rhetorical problem because the solution could not be demonstrated scientifically'" [47].

Charles Perrow expresses this as a more overtly political concern. Writing about risk in civil nuclear technologies he says: "...where body counting replaces social and cultural values and excludes us from participating in decisions about the risks that a few have decided the many cannot do without. The issue is not risk, but power" [48]

Change cannot stop, indeed probably should not. So accommodations and intelligent reflection and response to these issues (but we would argue not 'solutions'!) will have to be found, pragmatically, while and during the time that digital innovations are introduced into healthcare systems – rather than solving them *ex-ante* as *a priori* conditions for technological innovation. The incessant, perhaps even deterministic, pace of technological innovation in any case does not wait for society's considered ethical answers. Indeed, these are old and enduring questions that have been applied to technological innovations of the past, in a variety of fields, and for which, in the past society has had to struggle to find appropriate accommodations. The industrial revolution in Britain and its societal and political consequences are written across at least a century in intense reflection found in literature, natural and political science and the arts.

The new types of ICT innovations we are encountering today – especially the 'free' and participatory models mentioned above – are changing structurally and fundamentally these questions, in their nature and in their possible answers. Even the most straightforward and traditional computer implementations in healthcare require complex judgments [49]. How do we develop the ethical apparatus to deal with them?

Walsham [50] offers some modest ideas as to how we might move in this direction when he asks of the IS community, "Are we making a better world with ICTs?". He goes on suggest that we do not have very convincing answers to this question and thus argues for "a strong ethical agenda" and "...a sharper critical agenda towards existing approaches and power structures...". Interestingly he makes these comments while contrasting the wider IS field with the firmer ethical underpinning of architects who want to build better buildings, or doctors who want people to live longer and healthier lives.

Thus we suggest here a simple research agenda for sustainability in digital healthcare. This is based on addressing three core ideas:

- Redistribution of risk and responsibility across social actors including the patient-citizen, healthcare professions and the state
- Accounting for externalities in design of systems and in operational practices
- Application of an intergenerational model that can account for constraints placed on possible futures.

References

1. Jha, A.K., Doolan, D., Grandt, D., Scott, T., Bates, D.W.: The use of health information technology in seven nations. Int. J. Med. Inform. 77, 848–854 (2008)
2. Suk, J.E., Semenza, J.C.: Future Infectious Disease Threats to Europe. American Journal of Public Health 101, 2068–2079 (2011)
3. Hanvoravongchai, P., Coker, R.: Early reporting of pandemic flu and the challenge of global surveillance: a lesson for Southeast Asia. Southeast Asian J. Trop. Med. Public Health 42, 1093–1099 (2011)
4. NHS: London Health Programmes: Tuberculosis (2012),
   http://www.londonhp.nhs.uk/services/tuberculosis/
   (last accessed March 17, 2012)
5. Bates, D.W., Gawande, A.A.: Improving Safety with Information Technology. New England Journal of Medicine 348, 2526–2534 (2003),
   http://www.nejm.org/doi/full/10.1056/NEJMsa020847
   (last accessed April 30, 2012)
6. Jackson, G., Krein, S., Alverson, D., Darkins, A., Gunnar, W., Harada, N., Helfrich, C., Houston, T., Klobucar, T., Nazi, K., Poropatich, R., Ralston, J., Bosworth, H.: Defining Core Issues in Utilizing Information Technology to Improve Access: Evaluation and Research Agenda. Journal of General Internal Medicine 26, 623–627 (2011)
7. Joint Services, DLA and USCD: Digital Imaging Systems. In: P2 Opportunity Handbook, Joint Service Pollution Prevention and Sustainability Technical Library, A Website Supported by the Joint Services, the Defense Logistics Agency, and the U.S. Coast Guard, (2008),
   http://205.153.241.230/P2_Opportunity_Handbook/12_11.html
   (last accessed March 26, 2012)
8. Mathieson, S.A.: Videoconference consultants boost emergency stroke care. The Guardian (February 16, 2011),
   http://www.guardian.co.uk/healthcare-
   network/2011/feb/16/informatics-hospitals-and-acute-care
   (last accessed March 17, 2012)
9. DoH: '3 million lives' initiative. Department of Health, UK,
   http://www.3millionlives.co.uk/About-Telecare-and-
   Telehealth.html (last accessed March 17, 2012)
10. Nuffield Council on Bioethics: Medical profiling and online medicine: the ethics of personalised healthcare in a consumer age. The Nuffield Council on Bioethics (2010),
    http://www.nuffieldbioethics.org/personalised-healthcare-0
    (last accessed April 30, 2012)
11. Magee, M., Isakov, A., Paradise, H.T., Sullivan, P.: Mobile phones and short message service texts to collect situational awareness data during simulated public health critical events. Am. J. Disaster Med. 6, 379–385 (2011)
12. Swan, M.: Crowdsourced Health Research Studies: An Important Emerging Complement to Clinical Trials in the Public Health Research Ecosystem. J. Med. Internet. Res. 14, e46 (2012), http://www.jmir.org/2012/2/e46/ (last accessed April 30, 2012)
13. Leadbeater, C.: We-Think: Mass innovation, not mass production: The Power of Mass Creativity. Profile Books (2008)
14. Anderson, C.: Free: how today's smartest businesses profit by giving something for nothing. Hyperion, New York (2010)
15. Winner, L.: Do Artifacts Have Politics? In: The Whale and the Reactor: A Search for Limits in an Age of High Technology, pp. 19–39. University of Chicago Press, Chicago (1986)

16. UN General Assembly: Our Common Future, Report of the World Commission on Environment and Development, World Commission on Environment and Development. In: Published as Annex to General Assembly document A/42/427, Development and International Co-operation: Environment (1987), http://www.un-documents.net/ocf-02.htm (last accessed March 17, 2012)
17. Barry, C.: Redistribution. In: Zalta, E.N. (ed.) The Stanford Encyclopedia of Philosophy (2011), http://plato.stanford.edu/archives/fall2011/entries/redistribution/ (last accessed March 17, 2012)
18. Vikkelsø, S.: Subtle Redistribution of Work, Attention and Risks: Electronic Patient Records and Organisational Consequences. Scandinavian Journal of Information Systems 17, 3–29 (2005)
19. Ash, J., Sittig, D., Campbell, E., Guappone, K., Dykstra, R.: An unintended consequence of CPOE implementation: shifts in power, control, and autonomy. In: AMIA Annu. Symp. Proc., pp. 11–15 (2006)
20. McAlearney, A.S., Chisolm, D.J., Schweikhart, S., Medow, M.A., Kelleher, K.: The story behind the story: Physician skepticism about relying on clinical information technologies to reduce medical errors. Int. J. Med. Inform. 76, 836–842 (2007)
21. Motulsky, A., Sicotte, C., Lamothe, L., Winslade, N., Tamblyn, R.: Electronic prescriptions and disruptions to the jurisdiction of community pharmacists. Social Science & Medicine 73, 121–128 (2011)
22. Berg, M.: Lessons from a Dinosaur: Mediating IS Research Through an Analysis of the Medical Record. In: Proceedings of the IFIP TC9 WG8.2 International Conference on Home Oriented Informatics and Telematics,: Information, Technology and Society, pp. 487–506. Kluwer, B.V. (2000)
23. Ash, J.S., Sittig, D.F., Poon, E.G., Guappone, K., Campbell, E., Dykstra, R.H.: The Extent and Importance of Unintended Consequences Related to Computerized Provider Order Entry. Journal of the American Medical Informatics Association 14, 415–423 (2007)
24. OECD: Externalities. In: Glossary of statistical terms (2012), http://stats.oecd.org/glossary/detail.asp?ID=3215, (last accessed March 17, 2012)
25. Pigou, A.C.: The Economics of Welfare. Macmillan (1946)
26. Cornes, R., Sandler, T.: The theory of externalities, public goods, and club goods. Cambridge University Press, Cambridge (1996)
27. Samuelson, P.A.: Foundations of economic analysis. Harvard University Press, Cambridge Mass. (1948)
28. NORC: Health Information Exchange Economic Sustainability Panel: Final Report. Prepared for the U.S. Department of Health and Human Services Office of the National Coordinator for Health Information Technology, NORC at the University of Chicago (2009)
29. Aanestad, M.: Information Systems Innovation Research: Between Novel Futures and Durable Presents. In: Chiasson, M., Henfridsson, O., Karsten, H., DeGross, J.I. (eds.) Researching the Future in Information Systems. IFIP AICT, vol. 356, pp. 27–41. Springer, Heidelberg (2011)
30. Mort, M., May, C.R., Williams, T.: Remote Doctors and Absent Patients: Acting at a Distance in Telemedicine? Science, Technology, & Human Values 28, 274–295 (2003)
31. Dussault, G., Franceschini, M.C.: Not enough there, too many here: understanding geographical imbalances in the distribution of the health workforce. Human Resources for Health 4, Published online (2006), http://www.ncbi.nlm.nih.gov/pmc/articles/PMC1481612/ (last accessed April 30, 2012)

32. Rao, B., Lombardi, A.: Telemedicine: current status in developed and developing countries. J. Drugs Dermatol. 8, 371–375 (2009)
33. Mort, M., Smith, A.: Beyond Information: Intimate Relations in Sociotechnical Practice. Sociology 43, 215–231 (2009)
34. Sarasohn-Kahn, J.: The wisdom of patients: Health care meets online social media. California Healthcare Foundation (2008),
    http://www.chcf.org/publications/2008/04/the-wisdom-of-
    patients-health-care-meets-online-social-media
    (last accessed April 30, 2012)
35. Adams, S.A.: Sourcing the crowd for health services improvement: The reflexive patient and "share-your-experience" websites. Social Science & Medicine 72, 1069–1076 (2011)
36. Adams, S.A.: "Letting the people speak" or obliging voice through choice? In: Harris, R., Wyatt, S., Wathen, N. (eds.) Configuring Health Consumers. Palgrave Macmillan, Houndmills (2010)
37. Zimmer, M.: The Externalities of Search 2.0: The Emerging Privacy Threats when the Drive for the Perfect Search Engine meets Web 2.0. First Monday 13 (2008),
    http://firstmonday.org/htbin/cgiwrap/bin/ojs/index.php/fm/
    article/viewArticle/2136 (last accessed April 30, 2012)
38. Edwards, L.: Privacy and data protection online: The laws don't work? In: Edwards, E., Waelde, C. (eds.) Law and the Internet, pp. 472–473. Hart Publishing, Oxford and Portland, Oregon (2009)
39. Ribisl, K.M., Jo, C.: Tobacco control is losing ground in the Web 2.0 era: invited commentary. Tobacco Control 21, 145–146 (2012)
40. Luxton, D.D., June, J.D., Fairall, J.M.: Social Media and Suicide: A Public Health Perspective. American Journal of Public Health 102, S195–S200 (2012)
41. Trotter, G.: The Moral Basis for Healthcare Reform in the United States. Cambridge Quarterly of Healthcare Ethics 20, 102–107 (2011)
42. Dobson, J.E.: Big Brother has evolved. Nature (2009),
    http://www.nature.com/nature/journal/v458/n7241/full/
    458968a.html (last accessed March 23, 2012)
43. Sennett, R.: The craftsman. Yale University Press, New Haven (2008)
44. Weinberg, A.M.: Science and trans-science. Minerva, 209–222 (1972)
45. Mumford, E.: Systems design: ethical tools for ethical change. Macmillan, Basingstoke (1996)
46. Vickers, G.: Making Institutions Work. Associated Business Programmes (1973)
47. Vaughan, D.: The Challenger launch decision: risky technology, culture, and deviance at NASA. University of Chicago Press, Chicago (1996)
48. Perrow, C.: Normal accidents: living with high-risk technologies. Basic Books, New York (1984)
49. Cornford, T., Klecun-Dabrowska, E.: Ethical Perspectives in Evaluation of Telehealth. Cambridge Quarterly of Healthcare Ethics 10, 161–169 (2001)
50. Walsham, G.: Are we making a better world with ICTs? Reflections on a future agenda for the IS field. Journal of Information Technology advance online publication (2012),
    http://www.palgrave-journals.com/jit/
    journal/vaop/ncurrent/abs/jit20124a.html
    (last accessed April 30, 2012)

Impact of ICT on Home Healthcare

Sokratis Vavilis[1], Milan Petković[1,2], and Nicola Zannone[1]

[1] Eindhoven University of Technology, Netherlands
{s.vavilis,n.zannone}@tue.nl
[2] Philips Research Eindhoven, Netherlands
milan.petkovic@philips.com

Abstract. Innovation in information and communication technology has a great potential to create large impact on modern healthcare. However, for the new technologies to be adopted, the innovations have to be meaningful and timely, taking into account user needs and addressing societal and ethical concerns. This paper focuses on ICT innovations related to the home healthcare domain. To ensure the adoption of new healthcare services, the new innovative technologies need to be complemented with new methods that can help patients to establish trust in healthcare service providers in terms of privacy, reliability, integrity of the data chain and techniques that help service providers to assess the reliability of information and data contributed by patients. This paper sketches various lines of research for the development of trusted healthcare services namely, patient compliance, reliability of information in healthcare, and user-friendly access control.

Keywords: healthcare security, home healthcare, trust management.

1 Introduction

The high bandwidth connectivity provided by the Internet enables new services to support citizens in their daily lives. An important category of these services is healthcare services. The first examples of these services already exist today, and soon new services will emerge offering increased sophistication and improved but cheaper healthcare. An exponential growth of these services is expected, due to two tendencies. First, demand for care and cures will increase over the next decades caused by the ageing population (within 40 years, one in every four people will be over 60). Secondly, the number of healthcare workers is expected to diminish relative to the total population (without changes to the healthcare system, 25% of the working population would be needed to provide today's level of care by 2040 in a typical western country). New ICT supported healthcare services can overcome this problem by allowing people not to rely only on traditional care. However, to ensure the adoption of new healthcare services, the new innovative technologies need to be complemented with new methods that can address related ethical and societal issues.

A good example is home healthcare. Current home healthcare services are rudimentary in nature. Often they rely on call centers or nurses visiting the patient while

M.D. Hercheui et al. (Eds.): HCC10 2012, IFIP AICT 386, pp. 111–122, 2012.

new propositions are based on the Internet. One of the important impediments for the use of the Internet is the lack of trust. Trust is a requirement for the widespread adoption of healthcare services by clients (patients), by caregivers and by the parties that are financially responsible.

Existing techniques address part of the trust and security requirements, for example tools for identity management and for encryption of connections. Missing are techniques that help end-users to establish trust in a healthcare service in terms of privacy, reliability, integrity of the data chain, as well as techniques that help physicians to assess the reliability of information and data contributed by patients. There is a need for an integrated and easy to understand approach to trust in terms of security, privacy, and transparency, where users can make informed decisions whether to trust a service and can control the usage of their personal information.

In this paper, we present the research lines for trust management in home healthcare services. Home healthcare services aim to support people who are chronically ill or who are rehabilitating. These services gather patient's sensitive information that is then interpreted by medical professionals to manage their diseases. The adoption of such services, however, hardly relies on the patients' trust in a healthcare service provider in terms of privacy of the data chain and physicians' trust in the reliability of information and data contributed by patients. In particular, a number of questions should be addressed:

- How can compliance with a treatment be reliably measured?
- Can a physician trust data measured by a patient at home?
- How can patients use home healthcare services while ensuring their privacy and controlling the use of information in a simple intuitive way?

Answers to these questions require investigating different research lines including patient compliance, reliability of information in healthcare, and user-friendly access control. The paper discusses the existing proposals in these areas and describes a research plan for enhancing the state-of the-art.

The structure of the paper is as follows. The next section presents the impact of ICT innovation on healthcare. Section 3 discusses the problem of trust towards healthcare services. Section 4 discusses trust management for home healthcare services. Finally, Section 5 concludes the paper providing directions for future work.

2   ICT Innovation in Healthcare

The advance of ICT technologies is leading to the design of novel electronic healthcare services that improve people's health and well-being but also extend beyond the individual towards sustainability of our society. Consequently, many countries created policies to foster innovation and spread the successful adoption of these technologies in their healthcare sector. In this process of innovation creation it is crucial to focus on meaningful innovations, sustainability, and societal and ethical values underpinning the innovations. Meaningful innovation means new ideas, new approaches, new solutions that make lives healthier, more enjoyable, and more productive. It also means that they should be driven by user needs (not by technology), taking into consideration economic, societal and environmental sustainability. They should be well timed and introduced when they really make sense.

In healthcare, we witness many examples of such innovations ranging from electronic health records (EHRs), clinical decision support systems, via medical apps for mobile devices to next generation gene sequencing. The creation of national/regional EHR infrastructures such as RHIO's in the US, the NHS Spine project in the United Kingdom and NICTIZ in the Netherlands, is complemented with efforts on creating commercial Web-based personal health record (PHR) systems such as Microsoft HealthVault. These applications process, store, and exchange patient's medical information and allow for harnessing big data to improve healthcare.

Clinical decision systems assist healthcare providers with decision making tasks. They allow clinicians to take into account all important clinical observations and up-to-date clinical knowledge when diagnosing and treating patients.

Advances in mobile Health (mHealth) allow healthcare providers and patients to take part in a revolution in the way healthcare information is accessed and delivered. Healthcare providers and patients can access the most up to date medical resources anytime anywhere on their mobile devices.

New technologies for genome sequencing will make possible that everyone's genome is sequenced quickly for an affordable price, which is expected to decrease to one thousand dollars very soon. This will allow not only quick and cheap sequencing, but it will allow for the use of genomics in diagnostics and treatment enabling personalized medicine.

Finally, there are an increasing number of extramural telemedicine applications in the home healthcare domain such as remote patient monitoring (RPM). RPM systems combine consumer electronics and the Internet to connect patients and their care providers, thus enabling new care models. They allow patients to stay at home attached to monitoring devices/sensors that are getting smaller and wireless. In this way, patient's physiological and other contextual data can be collected and transmitted to remote care providers for review or intervention. Typically, RPM systems comprise several measurement devices (such as a blood pressure meter, weighing scale or glucose meter) a medical hub device that collects the data from measurement devices and sends them to a backend service. Furthermore, a hospital EHR or PHR systems are also considered as part of this eco system (the measurement data are sent from the medical hub to a PHR system, but in certain cases they are sent from the medical hub to a backend service which forwards them to an EHR or PHR system). A typical architecture of an RPM system as defined by the biggest standardization initiative in the domain of personal healthcare, called Continua Health Alliance[1] is shown in figure 1.

In this paper we will focus on home healthcare technologies, as they are very controversial. On one hand, these technologies improve the quality of patient life (he can stay at home), and provide faster and cheaper healthcare services. On the other hand, they are exposed to different security and safety threats as the patient is far from healthcare providers, and it becomes simpler to collect, store, and search electronic health data, thereby endangering people's privacy.

---

[1] http://www.continuaalliance.org

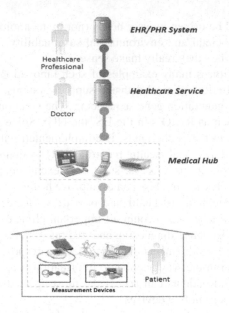

Fig. 1. Architecture of an RPM system

3   Trusted Healthcare Services

Electronic healthcare services offer important economic and social benefits for our society. Patients rely on these services for their safety and care and for improving their quality of life. For physicians, electronic health and wellness services offer support for providing more effective and continuous care. For insurers and governments, these services bring a reduction of costs, and for commercial service providers, this is a new business opportunity. However, electronic healthcare services cannot be exploited until the trust question has been addressed in a fundamentally correct way.

Indeed, trust is a pre-requisite for the acceptance of these services by end users. Trust establishment is crucial for physicians and service providers as they will use healthcare services to implement and extent (medical) treatments. In particular, healthcare providers need to trust the patient data they obtain remotely from the measurement devices deployed in patient's home. It is crucial for them to know that a vital sign of a registered user is measured (not of his friends/children), that the measurement was taken with a certified device, under standardized conditions (e.g., with the blood pressure cuff on the arm at the heart level) and that it is not obtained as a result of device malfunctioning.

In a healthcare setting, trust is also of special relevance because healthcare services deal with very personal and private information. Home healthcare services monitor patients and gather data that are interpreted by medical professionals. Health and wellness services support people in need in many ways on the basis of personal and health related information. People in health communities share health and well-being information which then becomes potentially available to the whole community and beyond.

Privacy is a major concern of many citizens and the government has an important role in protecting the privacy of the citizen [1]. Therefore, the government has developed legislation to protect its citizens, who may make use of the legal facilities provided. For example, on December 17, 2008, 2% of the Dutch population (330.000 people) had submitted objection forms to the Dutch Ministry of Health, stating that their electronic health records cannot be shared electronically.[2]

To facilitate the acceptance of electronic healthcare services, it is necessary to develop the technology that help end users to establish trust in healthcare service providers in terms of privacy, reliability, integrity of the data. Standard Internet security techniques provide authentication and encryption of the communication with a service provider. However, they do not provide the user with means to control or even know how a service provider will actually use their personal information. It is important to have mechanisms in place that allow users to make an informed decision to trust a service provider on the basis of facts, such as reputation and security attributes.

The THeCS project addresses the very important trust questions (transparency, privacy and security) for healthcare services. THeCS is a Dutch national project in the COMMIT program with 11 partners including representatives from industry, Dutch research institutes, Dutch universities and hospitals. The project addresses trust as one of the key issues for new electronic healthcare services. It will create measurable and enforceable trust. This notion is new for electronic healthcare services (and for Internet services in general), and it is fundamental for their success. The objective of THeCS is to create new techniques for measuring and controlling the reliability and use of (healthcare) information. These techniques allow users and service providers to trust each other and to benefit from these new services.

The concrete goal of the THeCS project is to create and define:

- Ethical, legal, sociological and psychological requirements for trust in healthcare services. The spectrum of healthcare services is very wide, ranging from formal medical services to pure commercial services that support every day activities. Often these services share information. It is this integration of services from different domains and information sharing that is of particular interest.
- A technical protocol to reliably assess the quality of medical data (e.g., blood pressure) measured by patients at home, including the identification of the patient, compliance with the specified measurement protocol, and certification of the measurement device.
- A cryptographic technology that enables health service providers to process encrypted medical information so that only intended operations are possible and that information is not disclosed otherwise. A specific example is categorization of a community into groups of patients with similar (according to a definition relevant for healthcare) characteristics, without disclosing the characteristics of individual patients.

---

[2] See www.minvws.nl/kamerstukken/meva/2008/
bezwaarprocedure-epd.asp

- A cryptographic technology for privacy preserving data mining of patient health data to support clinical research and knowledge creation for clinical decision support systems.

In the remainder of this paper, we will focus on trust management for home healthcare services.

4   Trust Management for Home Healthcare Services

Home healthcare services have been proposed to decrease the cost of healthcare while making it more comfortable for the patient. These services aim to support people who are chronically ill (e.g., post-stroke, diabetes, Chronic Obstructive Pulmonary Disease (COPD)) or people who are being rehabilitated. They monitor the health and well-being of people, enabling tailored assistance where and when needed. In particular, they gather sensitive personal information that is then interpreted by medical professionals in order to provide treatment. The adoption of such services, however, hardly relies on the trust that both patients and medical professionals have in the provided healthcare services. In particular, a number of questions should be addressed:

- How can compliance with a treatment be reliably measured? Patients' adherence to medication and to the treatment in general (e.g., activities, exercises, dietary guidelines) is a fundamental factor for the success of a treatment. However, treating a certain disease usually requires a variety of different medication schemes and treatment plans, making the compliance checking a complex task.
- Can a physician trust data measured by a patient at home? Home healthcare patients measure physiological parameters at home and a physician uses the data to make treatment and diagnosis decisions. It is very important that the measurements are accurate and that a physician can accept them as medical information.
- Patients and consumers want the possibility to control their personal health information. How can patients use home healthcare services while ensuring their privacy and controlling the use of information in a simple intuitive way?

Answering these questions requires developing the technology for physicians and other users of measured home healthcare information to easily determine the trustworthiness of the information and patient compliance. Moreover, there is the need of user-friendly technologies which will allow patients to control the processing and sharing of their information. In the remainder of the section, we discuss various research lines to address these challenges.

4.1   Patient Compliance

In home healthcare services, patients do not receive treatment (e.g., medication, rehabilitation) directly at the hospital; rather, healthcare service providers prescribe treatment to their patients who should follow such a treatment at home. This, however, leads to a question on how to assess patient compliance with the prescribed treatment.

Compliance with a medication regimen or a treatment is generally defined as the extent to which patients take medications and follow the treatment as indicated by their healthcare providers [2]. The adherence to a treatment by the patient is crucial both for the treatment evaluation and for the patients' recovery. However, given the large range of existing treatments, patient compliance is difficult to assess.

Several solutions for patient compliance have been proposed in the literature. A number of proposals focus on medication adherence. Here, compliance measurement methods can be classified in direct and indirect methods [2]. Direct methods measure, for instance, concentration of a drug or its metabolite in some biologic factor such as blood. Indirect, methods are based on the assessment of clinical responses by medical professionals, patient questionnaires about adherence, patient diaries, and pill counting. Other types of adherence measurements [3-6] include medication possession ratio and related measures of medication availability, discontinuation/continuation, switching, medication gaps, refill compliance, and retentiveness/turbulence. A comprehensive list of existing methods is presented in [7].

An example of an indirect method is proposed in [8]. This work aims to identify hypertensive patients who do not adhere to prescribed medication using an ontology based approach. In particular, patient information such as patient prescription details, medication possession ratios and blood pressure measurements are specified in an ontology. Adherence of patients to medication is then determined by querying the ontology using non-adherence criteria (e.g., patient who have lapsed in taking their medication while having a low medication possession ratio).

Recently, advances in patient monitoring systems have made possible to remotely monitor the patient to keep track of his health status, as well as providing limited abilities to monitor compliance. Such solutions include, for instance, the application of body sensors [9-11], smart device integration for patient monitoring [12, 13] and event-based methods [14], which aim to capture the patient's activities and vital metrics. In addition, some preliminary work on patient compliance prediction has been done by applying statistical methods and text mining techniques [15].

In summary, several efforts have been devoted to the definition of methods for treatment adherence. However, existing solutions only concentrate on a specific type of treatment such as medication adherence or monitoring of patients' activities. These efforts are insufficient in practice as the treatment for certain diseases often consists of different types of treatments. The effectiveness of the treatment can be assessed only by assessing and combining the adherence to the single treatments.

Providing a solution for patient compliance to the treatment still remains a challenge. In particular, we need comprehensive solutions for measuring patient compliance for home healthcare services. The development of such solutions requires investigating and integrating existing measurement mechanisms for patient compliance. The study should not be limited to existing solutions specific for healthcare, but it should consider compliance checking techniques proposed in other domains like privacy and business process [16,17].

4.2   Reliability of Information in Healthcare

To assess patient health status, healthcare providers have to rely on measurements which may have been taken directly by the patients. Thus, trust and reliability of the measurements is a necessary condition for the acceptance of the service by healthcare providers. Next to ensuring proper patient/device authentication, data authenticity and integrity, it is important to capture the correctness of the authentication process too. An overall solution that can capture all these aspects is the application of reputation systems, where providers build a level of trust in the patient based on his ability to take measurements [18].

Reputation systems have been studied in the literature for different domains, such as auction websites and peer-to-peer sharing networks [19]. Lately, reputation systems have been proposed for healthcare. Most existing approaches, however, focus on the patient perspective, where patients rate the services of doctors and healthcare providers via a web portal or a health oriented network [20, 21]. Conversely, very few studies address patients' trustworthiness from the perspective of healthcare providers and in particular the reliability of measurements taken by patients. Existing proposals [18, 22] mainly focus on the reliability of the data maintained in the form of electronic and personal health records.

Additional problems appeared with the use of web portals rating healthcare services. Patients often subscribe to expert websites and search information regarding their illness on the Internet. Although this practice may have advantages, the major drawback concerns the trustworthiness of information. For instance, in Revolution Health[3] and other similar online community reputation systems, the trustworthiness of information is assessed only by considering the information source. To assure information trustworthiness we also need to consider the information itself [23, 24].

Summarizing, there are no comprehensive studies on assessing the trustworthiness of patients' measurement and on addressing the problem of trust in home healthcare services. Moreover, to reassure patient safety, a method for measuring the trustworthiness of information originating from the Internet should be integrated. An interesting research challenge is, thus, the design of solutions for measuring information trustworthiness for home healthcare that also address the trust issues related to Internet data. We believe that a reputation-based solution can ensure the reliability of home healthcare data needed by physicians. To this end, it is necessary to investigate the issue of data trustworthiness from both healthcare providers and patients' perspectives and elicit the requirements for reputation systems to be deployed in healthcare systems. To get such systems accept by end-users, information on data reliability should be easily accessible and understandable. Therefore, methods for assessing data reliability should be coupled with methods and tools that visualize indicators for data reliability in a way that is understandable by end-users.

---

[3] http://www.revolutionhealth.com/

4.3   User Friendly Advanced Access Control

Healthcare services deal with very personal and sensitive information. The protection of sensitive information is usually enforced using access control. Several access control models have been proposed in the literature (see [25] for a survey). In particular, access control for the healthcare domain has been intensively studied in [26-28]. The challenge in designing an access control system for healthcare is that, while posing strict constraints on the access to sensitive information, the system has to cope with the dynamic environment of healthcare and the potential exceptions that are raised in emergency cases. Furthermore, medical data can also be formed as arbitrary text, such as a patient report made by healthcare practitioners, leading to the need for policies based on content. In this trend, content-based access control [29, 30] and tag-based access control [31] methods have been proposed. For instance, content-based approaches have been used for the protection of medical images [32]. Although these access control models are very expressive and allow the specification of a wide range of authorization policies, they are usually difficult to use by end users.

The last years have seen an increasing interest in the development of user friendly privacy management and access control systems. For instance, various enterprises designed platforms which allow users to set their privacy and access control policies. One example is Google dashboard privacy tool, which through a web interface displays to users what information about them is stored and who can access it. Similarly, social networks such as Facebook let users restrict or grant access to other users or groups on their data (e.g., wall posts, photos). Although these proposals provide a simple and straightforward solution, they neither allow users to understand the effect of the specified policies nor ensure secure access control.

Therefore, a need for more flexible yet friendly privacy management exists. Efforts such as privacy dashboard[4], PrivacyOS project[5], Primelife project[6]) and privacy room [33] provide tools (e.g., browser add-ons, mobile applications) for regulating the exposure of user data to the network. Pearson et al. [34] propose a client privacy management scheme based on data obfuscation (not necessarily using encryption) and user "personas." Although these proposals increase usability and flexibility, they do not provide users with the overview of the effect of the specified policy.

In conclusion, although several studies on access control have been carried out, no comprehensive studies on user-friendly access control for healthcare exist. The challenge is to define a novel access control model that guarantees an appropriate level of security and allows users to specify the policies regulating the exposure of their information to others. In addition, the model should be easy to use by end users. Ideally, the access control system should not only allow users to define access rules to their data but also to support them in "visualizing" the effect of the defined access control policy and therefore in ensuring that the created policy reflects users' intentions. The lack of such an overview might result in a loss of sensitive information. As an example, a patient affected by HIV might want to prevent the disclosure of information

---

[4] http://code.w3.org/privacy-dashboard/wiki
[5] https://www.privacyos.eu/
[6] http://www.primelife.eu

regarding his medical condition, restricting access to information regarding his disease (e.g., HIV status, HIV antibodies). However, the patient might not restrict access to other fields (e.g., white blood cell count, CD4 T-cells count) from which, although they do not contain his HIV status, his disease may be inferred.

The design of a user-friendly access control model requires that we divide the access control model conceptually into two layers: a high-level layer, in which end users can specify privacy preferences, and a low-level layer, which consists of machine-readable policies eventually enforced by the system. The refinement and mapping of high-level policies (specified by users) into enforceable policies can be achieved, for instance, by enabling semantic interoperability between high-level descriptions of information to be protected and the data objects in which such information is stored. The aim of this semantic alignment is to support the automatic generation of enforceable policies from the high-level policies specified by users. As a result, enforceable policies can be dynamically customizable with respect to user preferences.

5   Conclusions

The growth of the Internet and ICT technologies had a large impact on modern healthcare. A fundamental need is to design novel electronic healthcare services that improve people's health and well-being but also extend beyond the individual towards sustainability of our society. However, although the use of ICT in healthcare can offer several benefits to society, the adoption of electronic healthcare services relies also on ethical and societal aspects such as the trust that end users (e.g., patients and physicians) have towards such services. This paper discussed the challenges for developing trusted home healthcare services. The THeCS project addresses the issue of trust in healthcare services. In particular, the project aims to define the technology necessary to deploy trusted healthcare services. We presented various lines of research that will be also investigated within the project to address such challenges, namely patient compliance, reliability of information in healthcare, and user-friendly access control.

Acknowledgements. This work has been done in the context of the THeCS project which is supported by the Dutch national program COMMIT.

References

1. Guarda, P., Zannone, N.: Towards the development of privacy-aware systems. Inf. Softw. Technol. 51(2), 337–350 (2009)
2. Osterberg, L., Blaschke, T.: Adherence to medication. New England Journal of Medicine 353(5), 487–497 (2005)
3. Hess, L., Raebel, M., Conner, D., Malone, D.: Measurement of adherence in pharmacy administrative databases: a proposal for standard definitions and preferred measures. The Annals of Pharmacotherapy 40(7/8), 1280–1288 (2006)

4. Steiner, J., Prochazka, A.: The assessment of refill compliance using pharmacy records: methods, validity, and applications. Journal of Clinical Epidemiology 50(1), 105–116 (1997)
5. Halpern, M., Khan, Z., Schmier, J., Burnier, M., Caro, J., Cramer, J., Daley, W., Gurwitz, J., Hollenberg, N.: Recommendations for evaluating compliance and persistence with hypertension therapy using retrospective data. Hypertension 47(6), 1039–1048 (2006)
6. Leslie, S., Gwadry-Sridhar, F., Thiebaud, P., Patel, B.: Calculating medication compliance, adherence and persistence in administrative pharmacy claims databases. Pharmaceutical Programming 1(1), 13–19 (2008)
7. Andrade, S., Kahler, K., Frech, F., Chan, K.: Methods for evaluation of medication adherence and persistence using automated databases. Pharmacoepidemiology and Drug Safety 15(8), 565–574 (2006)
8. Mabotuwana, T., Warren, J.: A Semantic Web Technology Based Approach to Identify Hypertensive Patients for Follow-Up/Recall. In: Proceedings of the 21st IEEE International Symposium on Computer-Based Medical Systems, pp. 318–323. IEEE Press, New York (2008)
9. Reiter, H., Maglaveras, N.: HeartCycle: Compliance and effectiveness in HF and CAD closed-loop management. In: Proceedings of Annual International Conference of the IEEE Engineering in Medicine and Biology Society, pp. 299–302. IEEE Press, New York (2009)
10. Otto, C., Milenković, A., Sanders, C., Jovanov, E.: System architecture of a wireless body area sensor network for ubiquitous health monitoring. J. Mob. Multimed. 1(4), 307–326 (2005)
11. Alemdar, H., Ersoy, C.: Wireless sensor networks for healthcare: A survey. Comput. Netw. 54(15), 2688–2710 (2010)
12. Schmidt, S., Sheikzadeh, S., Beil, B., Patten, M., Stettin, J.: Acceptance of telemonitoring to enhance medication compliance in patients with chronic heart failure. Telemedicine and e-Health 14(5), 426–433 (2008)
13. Pang, Z., Chen, Q., Zheng, L.: A pervasive and preventive healthcare solution for medication noncompliance and daily monitoring. In: Proceedings of the 2nd International Symposium on Applied Sciences in Biomedical and Communication Technologies, pp. 1–6. IEEE Press, New York (2009)
14. Mouttham, A., Peyton, L., Eze, B., Saddik, A.: Event-driven data integration for personal health monitoring. Journal of Emerging Technologies in Web Intelligence 1(2), 110–118 (2009)
15. Petrou, C.: Use of text mining to predict patient compliance. SAS Global Forum, ProQuest (2008)
16. Banescu, S., Zannone, N.: Measuring privacy compliance with process specifications. In: Proceedings of the 7th International Workshop on Security Measurements and Metrics, pp. 41–50. IEEE Press, New York (2011)
17. Petković, M., Prandi, D., Zannone, N.: Purpose Control: Did You Process the Data for the Intended Purpose? In: Jonker, W., Petković, M. (eds.) SDM 2011. LNCS, vol. 6933, pp. 145–168. Springer, Heidelberg (2011)
18. van Deursen, T., Koster, P., Petković, M.: Hedaquin: A Reputation-based Health Data Quality Indicator. Electron. Notes Theor. Comput. Sci. 197(2), 159–167 (2008)
19. Jøsang, A., Ismail, R., Boyd, C.: A survey of trust and reputation systems for online service provision. Decis. Support Syst. 43(2), 618–644 (2007)
20. Jøsang, A.: Online reputation systems for the health sector. Electronic Journal of Health Informatics 3(1), e8 (2008)

21. Ebner, W., Leimeister, J.M., Krcmar, H.: Trust in Virtual Healthcare Communities: Design and Implementation of Trust-Enabling Functionalities. In: Proceedings of the 37th Annual Hawaii International Conference on System Sciences, p. 70182a. IEEE Press, New York (2004)
22. Alhaqbani, B., Jøsang, A., Fidge, C.: A medical data reliability assessment model. J. Theor. Appl. Electron. Commer. Res. 4(2), 64–78 (2009)
23. Bertino, E., Dai, C., Kantarcioglu, M.: The Challenge of Assuring Data Trustworthiness. In: Zhou, X., Yokota, H., Deng, K., Liu, Q. (eds.) DASFAA 2009. LNCS, vol. 5463, pp. 22–33. Springer, Heidelberg (2009)
24. Moturu, S.T., Liu, H., Johnson, W.G.: Trust evaluation in health information on the World Wide Web. In: Proceedings of the 30th Annual International Conference of the IEEE Engineering in Medicine and Biology Society, pp. 1525–1528. IEEE Press, New York (2008)
25. Samarati, P., de Capitani di Vimercati, S.: Access Control: Policies, Models, and Mechanisms. In: Focardi, R., Gorrieri, R. (eds.) FOSAD 2000. LNCS, vol. 2171, pp. 137–196. Springer, Heidelberg (2001)
26. Zhang, L., Ahn, G.J., Chu, B.T.: A role-based delegation framework for healthcare information systems. In: Proceedings of the 7th ACM Symposium on Access Control Models and Technologies, pp. 125–134. ACM, New York (2002)
27. Becker, M.Y., Sewell, P.: Cassandra: Flexible Trust Management Applied to Electronic Health Records. In: Proceedings of the 17th IEEE Workshop on Computer Security Foundations, pp. 139–154. IEEE Press, New York (2004)
28. Røstad, L.: Access control in healthcare information systems. PhD thesis, Norwegian University of Science and Technology (2008)
29. Hart, M., Johnson, R., Stent, A.: More Content - Less Control: Access Control in the Web 2.0. In: Proceedings of Web 2.0 Security and Privacy Workshop, W2SP 2007 (2007)
30. Giuri, L., Iglio, P.: Role templates for content-based access control. In: Proceedings of the 2nd ACM Workshop on Role-Based Access Control, pp. 153–159. ACM, New York (1997)
31. Hinrichs, T.L., Garrison III, W.C., Lee, A.J., Saunders, S., Mitchell, J.C.: TBA: A Hybrid of Logic and Extensional Access Control Systems. In: Barthe, G., Datta, A., Etalle, S. (eds.) FAST 2011. LNCS, vol. 7140, pp. 198–213. Springer, Heidelberg (2012)
32. Tzelepi, S.K., Koukopoulos, D.K., Pangalos, G.: A flexible content and context-based access control model for multimedia medical image database systems. In: Proceedings of the 2001 Workshop on Multimedia and Security: New Challenges, pp. 52–55. ACM, New York (2001)
33. Kahl, C., Böttcher, K., Tschersich, M., Heim, S., Rannenberg, K.: How to Enhance Privacy and Identity Management for Mobile Communities: Approach and User Driven Concepts of the PICOS Project. In: Rannenberg, K., Varadharajan, V., Weber, C. (eds.) SEC 2010. IFIP AICT, vol. 330, pp. 277–288. Springer, Heidelberg (2010)
34. Pearson, S., Shen, Y., Mowbray, M.: A Privacy Manager for Cloud Computing. In: Jaatun, M.G., Zhao, G., Rong, C. (eds.) Cloud Computing. LNCS, vol. 5931, pp. 90–106. Springer, Heidelberg (2009)

Technology and Care for Patients with Chronic Conditions: The Chronic Care Model as a Framework for the Integration of ICT

Nick Guldemond[1] and Magda David Hercheui[2]

[1] Delft University of Technology, Faculty of Electrical Engineering,
Mathematics & Computer Science, Dept. Interactive Intelligence, Netherlands
N.A.Guldemond@tudelft.nl
[2] Westminster Business School, London, United Kingdom
m.hercheui@westminster.ac.uk

Abstract. Worldwide, healthcare systems are considered unsustainable due to an increase in demand for care and an associated rise in healthcare costs. Ageing of societies and the growth of populations with chronic conditions are making a paradigm shift in western healthcare systems necessary. The Chronic Care Model (CCM) provides a framework for healthcare change, including a prominent role for the community and patients' self-management. Information and communication technology (ICT) is indispensable to accomplish the model's objectives. The role of ICT in the provision of care is discussed as an opportunity to facilitate the application of the CCM and improve healthcare in general.

Keywords: healthcare, ICT, innovation, integrated care, technology.

1 Introduction

The ageing of society is a key societal challenge for many countries worldwide. The prevalence of chronic diseases is rising globally due to the ageing of societies in combination with the effects of a sedentary life style. This trend results in a rise of healthcare costs an enormous pressure on the resources in society [31]. Implementation of healthcare services where medical and social aspects are integrated is imperative as well as the use of technology to facilitate self-management and cost-effective service delivery. When they grow older, people are more prone to multiple and chronic ailments. Chronic diseases such as cardiovascular disease, diabetes, arthritis and dementia are among the most common, costly, and preventable of all health problems in the world and are leading causes of death and disability. Currently the working population is shrinking. Projections show a growing imbalance between the number of elderly citizens in need of care and the actual supply of formal care services[1]. This is indicated by the age dependency ratio[2], which shows an increasing pressure on the

---

[1] http://europa.eu.int/comm/economy_finance/
epc/epc_publications_en.htm
[2] http://esa.un.org/wpp/Sorting-Tables/tab-sorting_ageing.htm

M.D. Hercheui et al. (Eds.): HCC10 2012, IFIP AICT 386, pp. 123–133, 2012.
© IFIP International Federation for Information Processing 2012

productive population of many countries[3]. In 2007, the age dependency ratio of the European Union (EU) was on average one retired citizen to four working people. Without anticipatory action, the average in 2050 will be an estimated 1:2. In the Netherlands, there will be an average ratio of 1:3 and in Italy and Spain an average ratio of 1:1.5, while in China this age dependency ratio will be less than 1. By 2025 the EU will lose an average of one million workers a year, while an increasing number of people has to be employed in healthcare. By then, about 25% of the working population should be employed in healthcare in the Netherlands, while optimistic scenarios for Greece, Italy and Spain will approach 50% [43]. The consequence of this growth in both chronic diseases and ageing is an increasing demand on healthcare while financial and human resources are decreasing. Current western healthcare systems are considered to be unsustainable, since the institutional care provision maintains a focus on curing diseases rather than preventing them. We can no longer expect that formal carers and professional institutions will provide the services for the support of an increasing number of people with a chronic condition.

In a complex health system, the management of chronic illness requires the coordination of care. Historically, there has been little coordination across the multiple settings, providers and treatments of chronic illness care. Integrated care may be seen as a response to the fragmented delivery of health and social services. The proposed paradigm shift in healthcare systems comprises a transition: 1) from mainly a monodisciplinary to a multi-disciplinary form of care provision, 2) from a curative approach to preventive medicine and public health, 3) from institutional care to community care, and 4) from professional care to informal care.

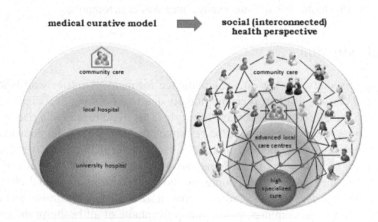

Fig. 1. Paradigm shift in healthcare systems

The concept of healthcare practice and healthcare change is based on frameworks or models. Healthcare models are a set of policies and organizational arrangements for meeting the three basic goals of a healthcare system: keeping people healthy, treating people who are sick, and protecting citizens against the financial burden as a

---

[3] http://www.euphix.org/object_document/o5117n27112.html

result of the amount of care that is consumed. Hence, these models provide the framework that should guarantee accessibility, quality and affordability of healthcare and ensure that patients get the optimal care, at the right time, by the right people and in the right place.

2   The Chronic Care Model and Integrated Care

In the search for effective strategies to prevent and manage chronic diseases, different models and programs have been proposed such as the Disease Management Program [22], Shared Care Program [23], [39], Chronic Care Model [2], [46], and Guided Care Model [6], [33]. In spite of their differences, all these models or programs aimed at a less fragmented, more integrated provision of patient-centered care.

The Chronic Care Model (CCM) by Wagner and colleagues [46] is currently central to European and United States' healthcare policy, and includes important elements of self-management, social support organizations, informal carers and the community. The CCM was intended to be a framework for innovation and improvement of care for chronic conditions. The CCM was later refined by Barr and colleagues [2], so that it became i.e. "the expanded CCM" that accentuated prevention and health promotion. The CCM assumes that good health outcomes require productive interactions between a multi-disciplinary team of professionals and an active patient and his or her proxies, such as families and informal caregivers. This interaction is the result of a form of coordinated care that is composed of six distinctive elements along with its relevant aspects, as laid out in the CCM (figure 2). There are two contextual elements: 1) the community and 2) the healthcare system. Within the healthcare system there are four focus areas for innovation: 3) the delivery system, 4) information systems, 5) decision support and 6) self-management. In the community element, Barr and colleagues emphasized the necessary community resources and policies that facilitate concrete actions, as well as the importance of public health and a supportive environment [2]. While technology is mentioned in most healthcare models, further elaboration on the required functionalities remain absent, as well as the implications of future information and communication technology (ICT) developments.

In this paper, the role of ICT and future developments are discussed from the perspective of CCM and its related components (figure 2), as follows. *Health System:* program planning (including measureable goals for better care of chronic illness) to meet the health needs of target populations. *Community:* mobilizing people to engage in informal care and developing partnerships with community organizations that meet the needs of patients with chronic conditions. *Delivery system:* the process of re-orientation of health services with a focus on multidisciplinary teamwork drawing on individuals and skills from the health and social care sectors. *Information system:* smart information systems based on patient populations to provide all the relevant client data (medical, health and social). *Decision support:* integration of evidence-based medicine, protocols and guidelines into a holistic approach. *Self-management:* interventions, training, and skills by which patients with a chronic condition can effectively take care of themselves. Note: health system and community are dealt with in two separate sections below, where the section on "health system" explores the notions of information systems, decision support, delivery system and self-management. The text on the health system is treated purely as background and is not explored in detail.

Fig. 2. Expanded Chronic Care Model: adopted from Barr et al. [2]

3   Health System

The health system is the operational body that translates healthcare policy into practice through programs that subsume and support the management, define the performance indicators in relation to the standard of healthcare quality, and formulate the related business plan. The health system comprises information systems, decision support, the delivery system and self-management.

3.1   Information Systems

Health information systems provide a means of making the information about an entire patient population (a registry) available to the patient and provider [30]. Over the last decades, the digital revolution has made an enormous change in the availability of clinical information. This accounts for traditional information sources such as patient records, daily practice data (e.g. laboratory results and radiographs) as well as protocols, guidelines and science-related information. Clinicians also have increasingly more access to animated information on patients' physiology, anatomy and pathology.

Besides these developments in bio-medical based practice, there is a current trend of collecting personal health or life style data. This is made possible through common devices such as weight scales, blood pressure and glucose monitors that communicate through the Internet and through a variety of innovative diagnostic tools for home care. Portable devices and smartphones also enable monitoring of activity, sleep and food consumption. Millions of individuals are storing streams of personal data through their websites, cell phones, laptops and other digital devices, which might be used to predict and anticipate conditions, behaviors and events relevant to their health.

For adequate healthcare management, an integration of bio-medical, health and social care data is needed, including community data [2]. In chronic care management, relevant users of information systems are also patients, informal carers, advocacy groups, municipalities and everyone who is indispensable in the provision of care. This requires data integration of various sources, data analysis and data stewardship with which intelligent agent software can help [28], [38], [40]. Software agents that incorporate learning, context-sensitivity, personalization, collaboration and proactivity will enable a support system that provides tailored medical information for practice teams [4]. For patients and informal carers, agent-based technology could offer personalized information with alerts, recalls and instructions for health promotion. Agent technology is also useful for population data-mining to identify subgroups that need proactive care, and to see whether preventive policy measures have an effect on primary medical, life style and social indicators [44]. Data technologies are becoming so important in providing solutions for societal challenges that government and citizens have to address urgently questions about protection from the misuse or abuse of large databases in a wide number of areas that also include health and healthcare. Besides the technological solutions for data protection and privacy, new regulations and legislation are needed. Data privacy should be seen in a wider context than just secure data transfer and information sharing among healthcare professionals.

3.2   Decision Support

Decision support provides healthcare professionals with instructions, guidelines and protocols to ensure that best evidence-based care is delivered. Decision support is strongly dependent on the expertise of the clinician, clinical information systems and evidence from medical research. As described in section 3.1, most important information needed for decision support is digitally available, but it is fragmented and only partially used. The overwhelming amount of clinical information generally available has made it much more difficult to extract useful information, and keep up with the progress in particular medical disciplines [35]. Considering the limited time for consultation by a clinician, it is unrealistic that all information regarding a specific patient can be part of the clinical reasoning process. To translate data into practice, clinicians typically have to: 1) formulate questions that are answerable from the information sources, 2) search for and identify evidence to answer the clinical questions and 3) appraise the evidence identified for quality, reliability, accuracy and relevance [36]. A clinician or a practice team would be greatly supported by an automated clinical reasoning support tool in which available evidence from the literature is selected, deliberated on, summarized, and attuned with guidelines and treatment protocols [16]. A patient's profile, derived from both medical and social data, could form a basis for personalization through which the available evidence could be tailored into relevant instructions for each person involved in the care process. Automated decision support is an important facilitating tool for integrated care.

3.3   Delivery System

The delivery system of healthcare addresses the overall workflow coordination. High-quality healthcare requires certain elements for adequate performance. The most vital elements in the delivery system dedicated to integrated care are well-trained and motivated people, accurate information, and technologies that enable providers to use resources effectively. This involves cross-sectorial primary, secondary and social care work flow planning, communication and quality control.

Planning in a delivery system deals with 1) who should be on a care team, 2) what kind of interaction each member of the team should have with the patient, 3) how team members should interact with each other, and 4) how patients communicate with caregivers. Efficient planning and harmonizing tasks of formal and informal carers is crucial for effective care [8]. Software tools for care management can help with the scheduling of appointments and services such as case management.

Communication in the delivery system is indispensable for the collaboration between stakeholders. Chronic care needs collaboration between primary and informal care (in the community) as well as secondary care (in an institution). The organizational structure of distinctive primary and secondary care sectors hampers the provision of integrated care [9], [14]. Due to the existence of so many unique specialisms and disciplines, horizontal communication among different medical specialists in secondary care and vertical communication between primary and secondary care is problematic [19].

Computerized health information systems could overcome most cross-sectorial communication issues. However, the implementation of shared information systems is far behind that seen in other sectors and industries. Despite the overwhelming evidence of the cost-effectiveness of multi-disciplinary use of electronic medical records, email, text-messages, social media and video communication services such as Skype [37], [51]. Many technology-related reasons have been mentioned as obstacles to the use of health information systems, including security, privacy, incompatibility between systems, maintenance, upgrades, ease of use and lack of integration with other applications [17]. Web-based applications and solutions provided by cloud computing as an alternative to local hosted software and storage concepts could overcome many of these issues.

Quality control and transparency of data about clinical effectiveness and cost-effectiveness of procedures, diagnostic and therapeutic devices and drugs is an increasing societal need. Healthcare consumers might be involved in providing feedback on performance indicators. Patients and their proxies could rate their carers, consumed services and hospitals visited [21]. Accordingly, competitiveness among healthcare providers can be stimulated. With shared information systems and social media it is possible to link healthcare services to patient satisfaction, quality indicators, cost and, ultimately, regional or national benchmarks.

3.4   Self-management

Patient engagement is increasingly important as a solution to lowering costs and improving population health. Self-management aims to enable people to remain independent and active and to support them to live in their own homes as long as possible. Self-management support involves empowering patients and their caregivers through education, training, skills acquisition, and help with integrating problem-solving and goal-setting into everyday care [1], [2], [5], [32]. Many aspects of self-management could be supported by solutions enabled by technologies. There is evidence of improvement of patients' self-management through web-based applications and social media [45]. Most research is focused on technologies for self-monitoring and self-education, where changes in patient adherence and levels of knowledge showed significant improvements [10], [24]. Hence, opportunities for further improvement lie in supporting patients to manage their health by finding information about their condition on the web and participating in social networks through which they can exchange information and provide support to each other [3]. This could be supported by intelligent systems that provide personalized assistance by remembering past interactions, and inferring the user's preferences through his or her actions [20].

4   Community

Community resources and policies are essential to facilitate the implementation of technology supported integrated care [27]. To implement integrated care according to CCM, new partnerships in the community with citizens, medical and social professionals have to be established. Communication and sharing of information, and alignment of objectives, resources and actions are also essential. Prevention of illness and readmission requires community actions, while informal carers play an important role in maintaining the health and wellbeing of people with chronic conditions. Health is predominantly influenced by the community factors, including the quality of housing, safety, social interaction, and transport. Supportive environments could help dependent and vulnerable people keep actively involved, people who would be otherwise be at risk of losing their independence. Outreach to outlying and underserved communities is being supported through a number of technological approaches [42].

4.1   Public Health

The objective of public health is to improve health and quality of life through the prevention and treatment of disease. Public health comprises a multidisciplinary approach, where health promotion is dedicated to enable people to manage their health by education and social marketing focused on changing behavioral risk factors such as a sedentary lifestyle, unhealthy food consumption, mental stress and smoking [7]. Social marketing applies commercial marketing strategies to promote public health in mass communication. The combination of market strategies and social media could influence the attitudes, beliefs and behaviors of communities and individuals [41]. Social media stimulate active participation of the patient, which is an element of successful behavioral change [47]. Healthcare providers can contribute to the effectiveness of patient involvement during their direct and indirect contacts with patients [11].

4.2   Supportive Environment

Supportive environments provide support for daily life activities and facilitates patients to stay active and independent, including solutions that support people in the work environment, and incorporate home automation through sensor technology and service robots [13], [34]. Smartphones and tablets can enable empowerment, wellness and the provision of social care services to the homes of dependent elderly persons and patients [26], [29]. Interactive multimedia allows a two-way communication for family, friends and caregivers. Agent-based software could enable more sophisticated communication and problem-solving between professional and non-professional carers. Integration of social networking and serious gaming elements into communication services could engage people in sharing community care. Mobilizing local communities for the support of care-dependent people is a great societal need and will have a major positive impact on social cohesion and the economy [15], [18].

4.3   Community Action

Informal caregivers are individuals who provide on-going assistance, without pay, for family members and friends in need of support. Informal care is a resource that is under both demographic and economic pressure [25]. Projections show that less informal care will be available within households as a result of trends in family size and scarcity on the labor market (in combination with an increase in the participation of women in the labor market[4]). The only solution to these limited resources for the support of vulnerable and dependent people is to organize informal support systems more efficiently. We need mobilization within our communities, thus it is imperative that we "engage all": technologies such as social media could help to achieve this [12].

5   Conclusion

The ageing of western society is a great challenge that is having a major impact on healthcare costs and community resources. Overcoming the problems of ageing and chronic conditions can only be achieved by transforming the current healthcare system with an integrated approach where multidisciplinary care teams, self-management and community involvement all play a central role. Technology is essential to this transition. The CCM provides essential health system and community elements into which technology could be integrated purposefully.

---

[4] http://ec.europa.eu/economy_finance/publications/
archive/special_reports_en.htm

Medical and social information has to be merged into a shared and personalized record, for patients as well as for both professional and informal carers. Decision support could be improved by an integration of evidence-based medicine, clinical expertise and patient values (based on social, medical and cultural profiles) into an automated clinical reasoning system. A cross-sectorial resource management and communication system would overcome the problems of the current siloed structure of social, primary and secondary care sectors. Patients' self-management would benefit from cloud-based computing and mobile technologies. Smart web-based management tools with automated personalized support would be a solution desired by many patients and carers: the most recent data and support tools could be instantly available to provide the most optimal care. Current developments in ICT are the ultimate facilitators for integrated care and the CCM.

References

1. Barlow, J., Wright, C., Sheasby, J., Turner, A., Hainsworth, J.: Self-management approaches for people with chronic conditions: a review. Patient Education and Counseling 48(2), 177–187 (2002)
2. Barr, V.J., Robinson, S., Marin-Link, B., Underhill, L., Dotts, A., Ravensdale, D., Salivaras, S.: The expanded Chronic Care Model: an integration of concepts and strategies from population health promotion and the Chronic Care Model. Hospital Quarterly 7(1), 73–82 (2003)
3. Bickmore, T., Schulman, D., Yin, L.: Maintaining Engagement in Long-term Interventions with Relational Agents. Engineering Applications of Artificial Intelligence 24(6), 648–666 (2010)
4. Bickmore, T.W., Mauer, D., Brown, T.: Context Awareness in a Handheld Exercise Agent. Pervasive and Mobile Computing 5(3), 226–235 (2009)
5. Bickmore, T.W., Pfeifer, L.M., Byron, D., Forsythe, S., Henault, L.E., Jack, B.W., Silliman, R., Paasche-Orlow, M.K.: Usability of conversational agents by patients with inadequate health literacy: evidence from two clinical trials. Journal of Health Communication 15(suppl. 2), 197–210 (2010)
6. Boult, C., Karm, L., Groves, C.: Improving chronic care: the "guided care" model. The Permanente Journal 12(1), 50–54 (2008)
7. Bunton, R., Macdonald, G.: Health promotion: disciplines, diversity, and developments. Routledge, London & New York (2002)
8. Butt, G., Markle-Reid, M., Browne, G.: Interprofessional partnerships in chronic illness care: a conceptual model for measuring partnership effectiveness. International Journal of Integrated Care 8, e08 (2008)
9. Castillo, V.H., Martinez-Garcia, A.I., Pulido, J.R.: A knowledge-based taxonomy of critical factors for adopting electronic health record systems by physicians: a systematic literature review. BMC Medical Informatics and Decision Making 10, 60 (2010)
10. Dorr, D.A., Wilcox, A., Burns, L., Brunker, C.P., Narus, S.P., Clayton, P.D.: Implementing a multidisease chronic care model in primary care using people and technology. Disease Management 9(1), 1–15 (2006)
11. Evans, W.D.: How social marketing works in health care. British Medical Journal 332(7551), 1207–1210 (2006)

12. Fyrand, L.: Reciprocity: A Predictor of Mental Health and Continuity in Elderly People's Relationships? A Review. Current Gerontology and Geriatrics Research (2010)
13. Graf, B., Jacobs, T.: Robots in the nursing home. It gives the impression of something pleasantly service-like. Zeitschrift für die Gesundheits- und Krankenpflege 64(11), 646–649 (2011)
14. Granlien, M.F., Simonsen, J.: Challenges for IT-supported shared care: a qualitative analyses of two shared care initiatives for diabetes treatment in Denmark "I'll never use it" (GP5). International Journal of Integrated Care 7, e19 (2007)
15. Harley, D., Kurniawan, S.H., Fitzpatrick, G., Vetere, F.: Age matters: bridging the generation gap through technology-mediated interaction. Extended Abstracts on Human Factors in Computing Systems (2009)
16. Hatzakis, M.J., Allen Jr., C., Haselkorn, M., Anderson, S.M., Nichol, P., Lai, C., Haselkorn, J.K.: Use of medical informatics for management of multiple sclerosis using a chronic-care model. Journal of Rehabilitation Research and Development 43(1), 1–16 (2006)
17. Hayrinen, K., Saranto, K., Nykanen, P.: Definition, structure, content, use and impacts of electronic health records: a review of the research literature. International Journal of Medical Informatics 77(5), 291–304 (2008)
18. Hennessey, B., Suter, P., Harrison, G.: The home-based chronic care model: a platform for partnership for the provision of a patient-centered medical home. Caring 29(2), 18–24 (2010)
19. Hicks, J.M.: Leader communication styles and organizational health. Health Care Management (Frederick) 30(1), 86–91 (2011)
20. Hsu, W., Taira, R.K., El-Saden, S., Kangarloo, H., Bui, A.A.: Context-based electronic health record: toward patient specific healthcare. IEEE Transactions on Information Technology in Biomedicine 16(2), 228–234 (2012)
21. Hvenegaard, A., Arendt, J.N., Street, A., Gyrd-Hansen, D.: Exploring the relationship between costs and quality: does the joint evaluation of costs and quality alter the ranking of Danish hospital departments? European Journal of Health Economics 12(6), 541–551 (2011)
22. Jonker, A.A., Comijs, H.C., Knipscheer, K.C., Deeg, D.J.: Promotion of self-management in vulnerable older people: a narrative literature review of outcomes of the Chronic Disease Self-Management Program (CDSMP). European Journal of Ageing 6(4), 303–314 (2009)
23. Kahan, M., Wilson, L., Midmer, D., Ordean, A., Lim, H.: Short-term outcomes in patients attending a primary care-based addiction shared care program. Canadian Family Physician 55(11), 1108–1109, e1105 (2009)
24. Kaufman, N.: Internet and information technology use in treatment of diabetes. International Journal of Clinical Practice (166), 41–46 (2010)
25. Keefe, J., Legare, J., Carriere, Y.: Developing New Strategies to Support Future Caregivers of the Aged in Canada: Projections of Need and their Policy Implications. Social and Economic Dimensions of an Aging Population (SEDAP). Hamilton, Ontario. RP no. 140 (2005)
26. Lenert, L.: Transforming healthcare through patient empowerment. Studies in Health Technology and Informatics 153, 159–175 (2010)
27. Leykum, L.K., Palmer, R., Lanham, H., Jordan, M., McDaniel, R.R., Noel, P.H., Parchman, M.: Reciprocal learning and chronic care model implementation in primary care: results from a new scale of learning in primary care. BMC Health Services Research 11, 44 (2011)

28. Lieberman, H., Mason, C.: Intelligent agent software for medicine. Studies in Health Technology and Informatics 80, 99–109 (2002)
29. Lynch, C.P., Egede, L.E.: Optimizing diabetes self-care in low literacy and minority populations–problem-solving, empowerment, peer support and technology-based approaches. Journal of General Internal Medicine 26(9), 953–955 (2011)
30. McEvoy, P., Laxade, S.: Patient registries: a central component of the chronic care model. British Journal of Community Nursing 13(3), 127–128, 130-123 (2008)
31. McPherson, B., Wister, A.V.: Aging as a social process: Canadian perspectives. Oxford University Press, Oxford (2008)
32. Miller, W., Rollnick, S.: Motivational interviewing: preparing people for change. Guilford Press, New York (2002)
33. Mitchell, G.J., Bournes, D.A., Hollett, J.: Human becoming-guided patient-centered care: A new model transforms nursing practice. Nursing Science Quarterly 19(3), 218–224 (2006)
34. Oborn, E., Barrett, M., Darzi, A.: Robots and service innovation in health care. Journal of Health Services Research & Policy 16(1), 46–50 (2011)
35. Olkin, I.: Meta-analysis: reconciling the results of independent studies. Statistics in Medicine 14(5-7), 457–472 (1995)
36. Oxman, A.D., Sackett, D.L., Guyatt, G.H.: Users' guides to the medical literature. I. How to get started. The Evidence-Based Medicine Working Group. Journal of the American Medical Association 270(17), 2093–2095 (1993)
37. Piette, J.D., Mendoza-Avelares, M.O., Ganser, M., Mohamed, M., Marinec, N., Krishnan, S.: A preliminary study of a cloud-computing model for chronic illness self-care support in an underdeveloped country. American Journal of Preventive Medicine 40(6), 629–632 (2011)
38. Rialle, V., Lamy, J.B., Noury, N., Bajolle, L.: Telemonitoring of patients at home: a software agent approach. Computer Methods and Programs in Biomedicine 72(3), 257–268 (2003)
39. Sanchez, I.: Implementation of a diabetes self-management education program in primary care for adults using shared medical appointments. Diabetes Educator 37(3), 381–391 (2011)
40. Sayyad Shirabad, J., Wilk, S., Michalowski, W., Farion, K.: Implementing an integrative multi-agent clinical decision support system with open source software. Journal of Medical Systems 36(1), 123–137 (2012)
41. Segbers, R.: Go where the customers are. Marketing (and managing) your patient experience with social media. Marketing Health Services 30(1), 22–25 (2010)
42. Siminerio, L.M.: The role of technology and the chronic care model. Journal of Diabetes Science and Technology 4(2), 470–475 (2010)
43. SPB: Actualisatie en aanpassing ramingsmodel verpleging en verzorging 2009-2030. Den Haag, Sociaal en Cultureel Planbureau (2012)
44. Szalma, S., Koka, V., Khasanova, T., Perakslis, E.: Effective knowledge management in translational medicine. Journal of Translational Medicine 8(1), 68 (2010)
45. Thielst, C.B.: Social media: ubiquitous community and patient engagement. Frontiers of Health Services Management 28(2), 3–14 (2011)
46. Wagner, E.H., Austin, B.T., Von Korff, M.: Improving outcomes in chronic illness. Managed Care Quarterly 4(2), 12–25 (1996)
47. Watson, A., Bickmore, T., Cange, A., Kulshreshtha, A., Kvedar, J.: An internet-based virtual coach to promote physical activity adherence in overweight adults: randomized controlled trial. Journal of Medical Internet Research 14(1), e1 (2012)

Information Waste, the Environment and Human Action: Concepts and Research

Fons Wijnhoven, Pim Dietz, and Chintan Amrit

University of Twente, AE Enschede, Netherlands
fons.wijnhoven@utwente.nl

Abstract. Information technology is powered by electricity. Although its impact on Green House Gasses (GHG) is still rather limited, the next decade will show an explosion of its impact because technological innovations on data communication, information retrieval and datacenter operation will not compensate the increased need for energy of information technology. This paper approaches the problem not from a technical perspective, but from the perspective of information value and the opportunities to detect and remove information waste. For this we identify several indicators of information waste and we then propose some key ideas for researching the topic.

Keywords: information value, information waste, file retention, web site quality.

1 Introduction

This essay is part of a more general interest in e-waste: the consequences of the information industry on hazardous waste. Ruth [20] states (p. 74) that "Seventy percent of all hazardous waste is e-waste, which is bulky, complicated to recycle, and sometimes contains unsafe levels of heavy metal and other dangerous chemicals." E-waste may have several causes:

1. PCs, monitors, workstations and other hardware: According to the US agency for the environmental protection (EPA): "...over 25 billion computers, televisions, cell phones, printers, gaming systems, and other devices have been sold since 1980, generating 2 million tons of unwanted electronic devices in 2005 alone, with only 15 to 20 percent being recycled" [20].
2. Software: Software can be designed and developed to improve the efficiency of energy consumption of electronic devices and computers. Microsoft claimed that its Windows Vista product saves roughly $50 per year in electricity costs per PC and thus also causes reduced GHG emissions. McAfee estimates the number of spam messages in 2008 to be about 62 trillion, which causes 33 billion KWh of unnecessary use (which is equivalent to the annual use of 2.4 million homes in the US).

M.D. Hercheui et al. (Eds.): HCC10 2012, IFIP AICT 386, pp. 134–142, 2012.

3. Data centers and servers: In 2005, the power and cooling costs of servers world-wide is estimated to be US\$26 billion. Greenpeace[1] reports that many of the large data centers in the USA use electricity produced by coal, i.e. the largest GHG emission creator during electricity production.

This paper focuses on a specific under-researched aspect of e-waste, namely, information waste. Information waste are data which are unnecessary (e.g. redundant) and unusable (e.g. not understandable) and which are the consequence of human limitations of knowing which data are of no use and could thus be removed or stored on a non-direct access medium. Detecting information waste will help in reducing the energy needs of information technology and related GHG emissions. Information waste can still be regarded as a minor influencer of e-energy waste, but in the next decades we may be confronted with an explosion of it. For example, IDC expects the digital universe to grow from 0.8 ZB (one ZB is 1 trillion gigabyte) in 2009 to 35 ZB in 2020; which is factor of 44 in 10 years [25]. Thus research in this area is needed in order to be prepared for this future. It is likely that the percentage of the total amount of information that is considered as waste will grow substantially as a consequence of the increased complexity of finding information in larger databases and in the Internet. Thus a major question is how we can detect information waste?

2   The Concept of Information Waste

Information is meaningful data or meaningful representations [5], [32]. Information is a key resource for organizations, and information technology is able to hugely reduce information collection, storage, manipulation, and distribution costs. In fact, the marginal reproduction and distribution costs of digital information are nearly zero [23]. The real costs are the creation of the first copy. On a world scale, though, the energy costs are very substantial, and often information technology is run on not-green electricity[2]. With more than 200 million internet searches estimated globally daily, the electricity consumption and greenhouse gas emissions caused by computers and the internet is provoking concern. A recent report by Gartner said that the global IT industry generated as much greenhouse gas as the world's airlines - about 2% of global CO2 emissions [6]. Data centers are among the most energy-intensive facilities imaginable. Servers storing billions of web pages require power. Mobile devices and smartphones also consume internet resources and substantial energy for data communication. We are not saying here that any internet use or information service use (for business or personal needs) should be avoided, but we say that it has "carbon costs." We have to be aware of these facts, and next start using information technology most intelligently. Information services should be there to help on this matter, but we lack

---

[1] http://www.greenpeace.org/international/en/
publications/reports/How-dirty-is-your-data/

[2] http://www.greenpeace.org/international/Global/international/
publications/climate/2011/Cool%20IT/dirty-data-report-greenpeace.pdf

tools for detecting information waste and thus remove it. Thus this paper poses a key question: How can we detect information waste?

This description of information waste indicates that information waste can be found on different media (on the disks in proprietary environments of persons and organizations and on the internet) and information waste can have information use and knowledge dimensions. This implies that at least four areas of information waste can be identified, as presented in Table 1, which we discuss in the following subsections.

Table 1. Types of information waste

		Information waste media	
		Proprietary disks	**Web**
Information waste dimensions	Information use indicators	Section 3.1	Section 3.3
	Knowledge value indicators	Section 3.2	Section 3.3

3   Identifying Information Waste

3.1   Use Indicators of Information Waste in Existing File Retention Methods

Determining the value, or the lack of value of information, i.e.: information waste, is complex. We can, for instance, easily calculate the number of data available on a hard disk by looking how many kilo-, mega- or gigabytes are occupied by our documents. But this does not say much about its value, as sometimes less is better. Most current information waste research is file retention research and focusses on the analysis of statistical patterns of files.

The key assumption of file retention research is that throughout its lifecycle, the value of a file in general grows after the first stage and declines in the final stage [27]. In the final stage, the intensity of usage mostly decreases and the accessibility of the files becomes less important. But, not all types of files have the same value and the file value may evolve differently depending on the file type. Consequently, one of the most important functions of a file valuation method is the ability to differentiate files by its value and non-value in an unbiased manner so that decisions can be made on the appropriate storage medium or possible deletion of these files [2]. Hence, what is required is a method to relatively easily measure the use value of files by which a file retention (or deletion) policy can be determined. We found ten data retention policy formation methods in the literature. Table 2 gives an overview of these methods.

A number of criteria for a file retention policy method are present in the literature:

1. The retention policy determination method has to function with little to no human intervention [2], [28]. The execution of file valuation as a manual rating of individual is mostly too costly. A simple directory can easily contain 6,000 files; evaluating them piece for piece will take many hours if not days.

2. The method should be based on the subjective use value of files over time in their different life stages [2], [28]. It is obvious that value is a subjective and often individual characteristic.
3. The method has to use multiple file attributes for the valuation process [28]. One file attribute will not be able to cover all value determining variables.

Table 2. File Policy Retention Determination Methods

Author	Goal of data retention policy	Important file attributes
[2]	Capture the changing file value throughout the lifecycle and present value differences of files	Frequency of use; Recency of use
[28]	Determine the probability of future use of files for deciding on the most cost-effective storage medium	Time since last access; Age of file; Number of access; File type
[1]	Lay out storage system mechanisms that can ensure high performance and availability	Frequency of use
[30]	Optimize storage allocation based on policies	Frequency of use; File type
[14]	Classify automatically the properties of files to predict their value	Frequency of use; File type; Access mode
[34]	Select files that can be compressed to reduce the rate of storage consumption	Directory; File name; User; Application
[26]	Optimize storage in a hierarchal storage management (HSM) solution	Least recently used
[7]	Reduce storage consumption on primary storage location	Time since last Access
[22]	Design a cost efficient data placement plan while allowing efficient access to all important data	Metadata; User input; Policies
[10]	Determine file value based on supply and demand	Frequency of use (by different users)

All the file retention policy determination methods of table 2 can be automated, and thus fulfill the first criterion. They all classify files by file attributes in order to make retention decisions. In some way these methods must be able to represent file value (criterion 2) and some combination of these file attributes must be able to identify waste. File value, however, is a subjective dimension and consequently must be measured and cannot be derived from file behavior alone.

3.2 Knowledge Value

Five paradigms to the knowledge value have been codified by epistemological (i.e., knowledge theory) traditions [3]. These paradigms are:

- The empirical paradigm based on John Locke (1632-1704) [15], [29] evaluates information value by its correctness in representing facts and events in reality.
- The rationalist paradigm founded by Gottfried Wilhelm Leibniz (1646-1716) [9], [13] evaluates information by its opportunity to causally explain, predict and reason about problems and reality.
- The transcendental idealist paradigm, founded by Immanuel Kant (1724-1804) [8] evaluates information by both empiricist and rationalist criteria, but on top of that it analyzes the key a priori of the views taken and from there aims at further integrating different perspectives in a larger coherent view of a subject.
- The Hegelian paradigm developed by Georg Wilhelm Friedrich Hegel (1770-1831) [18], [24] evaluates information by its historical context and sees information as representation of conflicting interests that can be synthesized by dialect logic. As such Hegelian dialects gives concepts for interpreting human behavior and critically looking at the status quo, and as such is a foundation for interpretive [11] and critical [31] explanatory insights.
- The Lockean, Leibnizian, and Kantian paradigms of knowledge all aim at finding an ultimate truth. The Hegelian approach regards truth as part of historical and social reality, and as arguments in favor of certain ideals. The pragmatist paradigm, as described by Churchman [3] on the basis of Edgar Singer's (1873-1954) work, in contrast proposes that the continuous search for new and improved insights is important, but only valuable as far as it results in human progress, which implies the practical solving of human problems. For the measurement of the pragmatic value of information, Sajko et al. [21] developed an information value questionnaire (IVQ) that allows information workers to value the information they use. The IVQ has five dimensions (1) Files Lost, (2) Costs of File (Re)building; (3) Market Value; (4) Legislative, and (5) Time as an indicator of obsolescence. The "Lost" dimension measures the impact of information loss on the business operations. This can be anything from "nothing special" to "making wrong decisions with major consequences". "(Re)building" measures the cost of replacing the lost information (from "negligibly small" to "intolerably high costs"). "Market value" measures the consequences if competitors obtain the information (from "nothing" to "competitor gets competitive advantage"). "Legislative" identifies the obligation to keep the information and the legal consequences if the information is lost (from "no obligation" to "keeping information is obligatory and sanctions are strict"). The "Time" dimension measures the rate at which the information depreciates in value (from "very quickly" to "does not depreciate at all").

These approaches to knowledge give different indications to information waste, as summarized in Table 3.

3.3   Web Information Waste

For internet information, a number of behavioral indicators can be found and several scales for the knowledge value of sites exist. Several web analytics companies (like Google, Alexa and URLSpy) deliver behavioral data on the intensity of use of sites.

Alexa.com also publishes a top million list every day. These web data collectors produce the following behavioral site attributes as possible waste indicators:

Table 3. Knowledge value criteria for information waste

Paradigm	Information waste criteria
Lockean	No correspondence with reality; incorrect representations; not interpretable in natural language
Leibnizian	Inconsistency, wrong or obsolete parameters and fomulas, over-complex models
Kantian	Statements or content not related to an ontology.
Hegelian	Information serving no one's interest
Singerian	Irrelevant and un-usable information

- Access speed. More access speed has been indicated as poor maintenance or less professional support to the sites quality [4], [16], [33].
- One of the most important behavioral metric is the number of incoming links. If a website has a lot of incoming links, it is expected to contain good information.
- The number of broken links on a website is an indicator of maintenance problems.
- Currency can be easily measured by the last update or modification time of a site.
- Frequency of Access can be measured by the number of unique (monthly) visitors to a site. If a site has a lot of visitors it most likely is valuable information.
- Time on a site. If a user stays at a site for a long time, it most likely is good information. Precautions need to be taken with this metric because if a user keeps his browser open at a certain page while he is away, it will give a false positive.
- Bounce percentage. Bounce percentage gives the percentage of unique users which visited only one page on a certain website. Therefore this might give an indication of poor information quality.

For the knowledge value of sites, a lot of research has already been done in the area of website quality [4], [16], [33]. The research realized various metrics, both objective and subjective, to classify the value of websites. Although these metrics are relatively old for the fast changing internet, they are still used in relative new researches, for example [12], [17], [18]. At the time these studies were performed most of the current content of websites was already present. The following scales for information value have been developed:

- Content quality and correctness [4], [16] determines information on a site is correct. This is necessary to determine the information quality of a website since a low content quality means a low information quality and vice versa.
- Information relevancy [33] determines whether a site delivers relevant or irrelevant information.
- Information comprehensiveness [4], [33] indicates the completeness and understandability if a site's content.

4   Researching Information Waste

Returning to our question how information waste can be detected, we have stated that the individual rating of files or sites is too laborious for estimating the knowledge value of the content of these media. Consequently, an measurement of value on basis of behavioral indicators using analytics or file system tools can be tried, because it is much more efficient, but it is unclear until now how reliably behavioral indicators can estimate (subjective) knowledge value. If in ad random selected files and sites a high correlation can be found between some behavioral indicators and knowledge value of files, these behavioral indicators can be used as proxies for information waste.

For Internet information waste estimation, the following set of assumptions and hypotheses can be used for further research:

- Assumption 1: The higher the processing costs of servers, the higher the server's GHG footprint.
- Assumption 2: The higher the search and access costs of information, the higher the Internet users GHG footprint.
- Hypothesis 1: The higher the information waste (=% of unnecessary data on the Internet), the higher unnecessary amount of the processing costs of servers.
- Hypothesis 2: The higher the information waste, the higher the avoidable search and access costs of useful information.
- Hypothesis 3: The availability of an effective information detector will result in a reduction of information waste by increased information waste awareness of information service customers.

Figure 1 summarizes this in a causal research model.

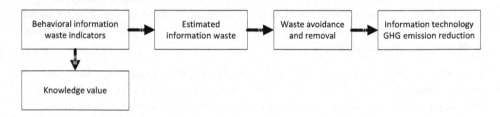

Fig. 1. An information waste design science research model

References

1. Bhagwan, R., Douglis, F., Hildrum, K., Kephart, J.O., Walsh, W.E.: Time Varying Management of Data Storage. In: Workshop on Hot Topics in System Dependability, Yokohama, pp. 222–232 (2005)
2. Chen, Y.: Information Valuation for Information Lifecycle Management. In: Proceedings of Second International Conference on Automatic Computing, Seattle, Washington, pp. 135–146 (2005)
3. Churchman, C.W.: The design of inquiring systems: basic concepts of systems and organization. Basic Books, New York (1971)

4. Eppler, M., Muenzenmayer, P.: Measuring information quality in the web context: a survey of state-of-the-art instruments and an application methodology. In: Proceedings of the Seventh International Conference on Information Quality (2002), http://mitiq.mit.edu/iciq/iqpapers.aspx?iciqyear=2002

5. Floridi, L.: Is semantic information meaningful data? Philosophy and Phenomenological Research 70, 351–370 (2005)

6. Gartner: Gartner Says Data Centres Account for 23 Per Cent of Global ICT CO_2 Emissions (2007)

7. Gibson, T., Miller, E.: An Improved Long-Term File-Usage Prediction Algorithm. In: Annual International Conference on Computer Measurement and Performance (CMG 1999), Reno, NV, pp. 639–648 (1999)

8. Hartnack, J.: Kant's theory of knowledge. Harcourt, Brace & World, New York (1967)

9. Huenemann, C.: Understanding rationalism. Acumen, Chesham (2008)

10. Jin, H., Xiong, M., Wu, S.: Information value evaluation model for ILM. In: 9th ACIS International Conference on Software Engineering, Artificial Intelligence, Networking and Parallel/Distributed Computing, SNPD. IEEE (2008)

11. Klein, H.K., Myers, M.D.: A set of principles for conducting and evaluating interpretive field studies in information systems. MIS Quarterly 23, 67–94 (1999)

12. Kuo, Y.F., Wu, C.M., Deng, W.J.: The relationships among service quality, perceived value, customer satisfaction, and post-purchase intention in mobile value-added services. Computers in Human Behavior 25, 887–896 (2009)

13. Look, B.C.: Gottfried Wilhelm Leibniz. Stanford Encyclopedia of Philosophy (2007), http://plato.stanford.edu/archives/spr2009/entries/leibniz/

14. Mesnier, M., Thereska, E., Ganger, G.R., Ellard, D.: File Classification in Self-* Storage Systems. In: Proceedings of the First International Conference on Autonomic Computing. IEEE Computer Society Press (2004)

15. Meyers, R.G.: Understanding empiricism. Acumen Publishing, Chesham (2006)

16. Palmer, J.W.: Web site usability, design, and performance metrics. Information Systems Research 13, 151–167 (2002)

17. Petter, S., Delone, W., Mclean, E.: Measuring information systems success: models, dimensions, measures, and interrelationships. European Journal of Information Systems 17, 236–263 (2008)

18. Popovič, A., Coelho, P., Jaklič, J.: The impact of business intelligence system maturity on information quality. Information Research 14, 4 (2010)

19. Redding, P.: Georg Wilhelm Friedrich Hegel. The Stanford Encyclopedia of Philosophy (1997), http://plato.stanford.edu/archives/sum2002/entries/hegel

20. Ruth, S.: Green it more than a three percent solution? IEEE Internet Computing 13, 74–78 (2009)

21. Sajko, M., Rabuzin, K., Baca, M.: How to calculate information value for effective security risk assessment. Journal of Information and Organizational Sciences 30, 263–278 (2006)

22. Shah, G., Voruganti, K., Shivam, P., Alvarez, M.: ACE: Classification for Information Lifecycle Management. Computer Science IBM Research Report, RJ10372, (A0602-044) (2006)

23. Shapiro, C., Varian, H.: Information rules: a strategic guide to the network economy. Harvard Business School Press, Boston (1999)

24. Sinnerbrink, R.: Understanding Hegelianism. Acumen Pub. Ltd. (2007)

25. Slawsky, D.: Teaching digital asset management in a higher education setting. Journal of Digital Asset Management 6, 349–356 (2010)
26. Strange, S.: Analysis of Long-Term UNIX File Access Patterns for Application to Automatic File Migration Strategies. University of California, Berkeley (1992)
27. Tallon, P.P., Scannell, R.: Information Lifecycle Management. Communications of the ACM 50, 65–70 (2007)
28. Turczyk, L., Frei, C., Liebau, N., Steinmetz, R.: Eine Methode zur Wertzuweisung von Dateien in ILM. In: Bichler, M., et al. (eds.) Multikonferenz Wirtschaftsinformatik. Gito Verlag, Berlin (2008)
29. Uzgalis, W.: John Locke. The Stanford Encyclopedia of Philosophy. Stanford University, Stanford (2010),
   http://plato.stanford.edu/archives/fall2008/entries/locke/
30. Verma, A., Pease, D., Sharma, U., Kaplan, M., Rubas, J., Jain, R., Devarakonda, M., Beigi, M.: An Architecture for Lifecycle Management in Very Large File Systems. In: 22nd IEEE / 13th NASA Goddard Conference on Mass Storage Systems and Technologies, pp. 160–168 (2005)
31. Walsham, G., Sahay, S.: GIS for District-Level Administration in India: Problems and Opportunities. MIS Quarterly 23, 39–66 (1999)
32. Wijnhoven, F.: Information services design: A design science approach for sustainable knowledge. Routledge, New York (2012)
33. Yang, Z., Cai, S., Zhou, Z., Zhou, N.: Development and validation of an instrument to measure user perceived service quality of information presenting web portals. Information & Management 42, 575–589 (2005)
34. Zadok, E., Osborn, J., Shater, A., Wright, C., Muniswamy-Reddy, K., Nieh, J.: Reducing Storage Management Costs via Informed User-Based Policies. In: IEEE Conference on Mass Storage Systems and Technologies, Maryland, pp. 101–105 (2004)

Towards a Sustainable Governance of Information Systems: Devising a Maturity Assessment Tool of Eco-Responsibility Inspired by the Balanced Scorecard

Amélie Bohas and Laïd Bouzidi

Team Magellan, Group SICOMOR, University Jean Moulin Lyon 3, France
{amelie.bohas,laid.bouzidi}@univ-lyon3.fr

Abstract. The assessment of the maturity of Information System (IS) regarding its contribution to corporate social responsibility policy is considered as a stake for organizations. However, few research efforts have been dedicated to this evaluation and even less to the elaboration of a management tool. This paper adopts an engineering perspective to develop a performance assessment approach in this field. Theoretically, this communication (1) mobilizes the methodology of engineering research to build a measurement system of the IS maturity in relation to the economic, social and environmental performance, (2) extends the researches about the sustainable balanced scorecard (SBSC) to the field of IS governance. Practically, this study provides organizations with a global approach to this complex phenomenon as well as a guide to assess it. The originality of this research lies in the application of the conceptual framework of the SBSC to a new research domain.

Keywords: information system governance, CSR policy, sustainable balanced scorecard, maturity measure, engineering research.

1   Introduction

In a context of global warming and depletion of resources, practitioners and researchers tend to worry in an increasing way about the role of ICTs (Information and Communication Technologies) towards the environment. Indeed, if the technologies had remained exempt up to now from a reflection on their environmental impacts because of their "immaterial" presupposed character, they entered recently into the heart of the political debate and the professional concerns [1], [2], including professional associations (ADEME, CIGREF, SYNTEC, etc.) and websites (GreenIT.fr, ecoinfo.cnrs.fr...) which are dedicated to it. On the academic level, there are a growing number of publications proposed on this topic every year [3-6] that give evidence of the scientific interest in this emergent problem.

In October 2009, the CIGREF (Professional association of French companies and organizations from all sectors using information systems) published a report on "Eco-responsible information systems" and especially "the use of ICT in the service of sustainable business." In this document, it identified three key issues for the future:

M.D. Hercheui et al. (Eds.): HCC10 2012, IFIP AICT 386, pp. 143–155, 2012.
© IFIP International Federation for Information Processing 2012

- "To ensure the accompanying change of users through awareness, training and education, in thinking about the ways to consume less and work differently;
- To optimize the ICT sector, by developing technical and organizational innovation and eco-design, and creating eco-labels covering hardware, software and services benefits;
- To exploit the potential of the ICT sector to help other sectors to develop sustainably, by rethinking their processes and their trades, and reduce their carbon footprint." [7, p. 2]

These last two issues invite a dialectical reflection on one hand on the liability of the information system (IS) in the environmental problems [4], [8], [9] that organizations and society as a whole are currently facing and conversely on the possible contribution of the IS to the sustainability of ecosystems on the other hand [5], [10-14].

To reduce the impact of IT on the environment and put their IS in the service of the CSR policy, organizations should implement practices that contribute to the reduction of their energy consumption, extending the life cycle of their hardware (only real solution to limit the volume of WEEE), limiting the consumables (paper, ink cartridges, etc.), and creating new economic and ecologic opportunities (eco-innovation, smart building, supply chain optimization, among others) as shown in Table 1.

Table 1. Sample of actions to reduce the environmental impact of IS organization

ICT life cycle phase	Issues for organizations
Production	Responsible procurement policy: eco-labels Lobbying computer manufacturers Lengthening of the frequency of renewal of computer parks
Use	Measures to reduce energy consumption and the volume of consumables Education and training of employees to consume less and work differently
End of life	Regulation compliance Extension of the life cycle of materials Reduction of the amount of e-waste

So, as regards IS, the stake for every organization is to work towards "a responsible attitude, to question its way of functioning, its mode of consumption, and its relation to the computer object" [13, p.2]. To this end, it has to define new goals for action, new mechanisms of government and integrate new designs of IS. Also, it appears that governance is a key issue in the implementation of actions related to sustainable development (SD). Then the question arises to business executives, chief information officers (CIOs) and IT managers in particular, is "how to assess the eco-responsibility of IS and its alignment with CSR policy?" Indeed, although there is a growing concern about this thematic in organizations, it still lacks, for the majority of them, a system of evaluation of the performances [15].

In this context, the objectives of this paper are twofold. Firstly, to expose the theoretical framework of the eco-responsible maturity of IS and of its governance. Secondly, and this is the main contribution of this paper, to propose an approach, based on an adaptation of the model of the Balanced Scorecard, which will enable companies to assess the eco-responsible maturity of IS and its governance. Derived steering model result of an engineering research approach led since October 2011 in partnership with a consulting firm specialized in "eco-responsible IS."

2   Theoretical Framework

2.1   Emergence of Responsible IS

The transformations engendered by the new ICT were numerous since their advent, which were of social, economic or systemic order. In particular, digital uses allowed abolishing the boundaries of space and time of action – individual or collective – thanks to the immediacy of the flows they generate contributing to the emergence of a network society [16]. Also, they gave rise to their subject to much speculation. So as underlined it Crozier and Friedberg [17, p.36], "we believed to see in the computer the technical instrument making possible self-management" before noticing that "without new organizational capacities, [it] is only an additional instrument of routinisation." Even of constraint if we refer to certain structurationist works in IS. Recently other "bad" assumptions were raised by Rodhain and Fallery [13] on the subject this time of their role in the environment.

But this awareness is not limited to the environmental dimension of ICT, it corresponds to a more global reflection which questions the connection between IS and SD as evidenced by works as "ICTs and sustainable development" [18] and "Information system and sustainable development" [19] If the concept of SD is present in numerous works in strategic management [20], [21], its link with works in IS may seem surprising so much practices implemented in IS remain deeply antithetical, and at the very least antagonistic, with the principles of sustainability [13], [22-24].

Ethical reflection is however not new in IS since following the works of Foucault (in what is called the "last Foucault" under the three phases of reflection which we can identify as the philosopher's), authors such as Zuboff [25] were able to blame the technologies for their panoptic effect as far as they enable surveillance of people and even a certain control with regard to their "informing" effect. The words of the latter besides never had much echo than at time of unbridled development of the systems of video surveillance but also "smartphones" and all the applications and techniques of geo-localization they integrate.

However never until now has this reflection been pursued as far as this analysis by questioning simultaneously the economic, social and environmental dimensions. These three concerns corresponds to the "three pillars of sustainable development" that organizations have to manage to reconcile in their activities.

The connection of the concept of CSR with that of SD was concretized through the recent publication of the standard ISO 26000 that gives the following definition of CSR: the corporate social responsibility is the contribution of organizations to sustainable development [26]. Each organization must answer for its acts and in particular its environmental or social impacts and behave in full transparency by reporting its activities with its stakeholders and more broadly with the society.

"The organizational IS (or this part of the IS) dedicated to the data capture, collection, processing and dissemination of information related to CSR can be described as IS Responsible." [3, p.3] These new functions assigned to IS are not the only ones. Thus, Faucheux and al. [18] identified at least three typologies of ICT with regard to their contribution to SD, as shown in Table 2.

Table 2. Typologies of ICT with regard to their contribution roles to sustainability

Typology according to...	Role of ICT
...their use function	• Observation and analysis for assistance to the decision
	• Management and protection of the Environment
	• Education and dissemination of knowledge
... the objectives achievable in the short term	• Role of catalyst
	• Role of quantifier
... the degree of innovation	• Standardisation, control and management
	• Adaptation /substitution
	• Radical Innovation

2.2   The Balanced Scorecard as a Suitable Sustainable Performance Measurement Approach

"The balanced scorecard is a strategic management system that links performance measurement to strategy using a multidimensional set of financial and nonfinancial performance metrics." [27, p.2] This new approach was devised at the beginning of the 90s by Kaplan and Norton [28-30] in response to the hegemony of the financial indicators for the measurement of performance. It articulates in a same scheme the strategic vision of the firm with corporate goals and specific measures of performance within a set of four perspectives related to the cores values of the company: financial, customer, internal business processes and organizational learning and growth.

This ability of BSC to interconnect several dimensions of performance and to integrate non-monetarized factors led some researchers and firms to view this strategic management system as a relevant approach to implement a sustainability strategy and to drive global performance. As Figge et al. [31, p.272] said, "such an approach to sustainability management aims at a simultaneous achievement of ecological, social and economic goals" and thus BSC makes it possible to overcome the traditional conflicts that can exist between these three performance dimensions.

In this perspective, several authors have studied "the process and steps of formulating a Sustainability Balanced Scorecard" [31, p.269]. Three main ways of implementation were identified:

1. The incorporation of social and environmental indicators in the existing set of measures of each perspective. These "sustainability key success factors" [27, p.7] deepen the performance measurement without changing the model structure.
2. The creation of a fifth sustainability perspective which seems to be suitable for firms who have identified this dimension as a strategic core aspect for its success. This introduction of a new perspective expands the model towards non markets aspects and communicates the importance of the sustainability strategy.
3. The "deduction of a derived environmental and social scorecard" [31, p.275]. This specific environmental and social scorecard represents an extension of the conventional BSC and aims to drive specifically the ecological and social metrics.

The various advantages of the BSC for the integration of sustainability management are listed in the Table 3.

Table 3. The BSC as a suitable framework to implement sustainability

Authors	Advantages
Epstein-Wisner, 2001 [27, p.9]	"It increases social and environmental accountability by explicitly including performance metrics related to social and environmental goals, and by recognizing their interconnection with a multidimensional set of corporate objectives."
Epstein-Wisner, 2001 [27, p.9-10]	"In addition, incorporating social and environmental metrics into the balanced scorecard can help senior managers reposition their organizations toward improved corporate responsibility."
Figge et al. 2002 [31, p.273]	"An SBSC fulfils the central requirement of the sustainability concept for a permanent improvement of the business' performance in economic, ecological and social terms."
Figge et al. 2002 [31, p.283]	"It helps significantly to overcome the short-comings of the often parallel approaches of environmental, social and economic management systems implemented in the past."

However, despite arguments in favour of the use of the BSC approach to manage a sustainability strategy, some authors have reservations about the real effectiveness of this model. Thus, for Quairel [32], SBSC can't be considered as a global performance management tool since it doesn't take into consideration the social and environmental performance not related to the economic performance. Moreover it seems that finally informed indicators are essentially monetary and conversely qualitative aspects are very weakly taken into account and the relations of cause and effects very little studied. Besides, Zingales and Hockerts [33] underlined the limits of the approach through the study of several case studies of companies integrating environmental and social issues in a BSC. In practice, they noticed a lack of alignment of environmental management with the BSC and a frequent misuse of the tool associated with measures rarely updated. They also suggested some hypothesis regarding the success factors of "the causal relationship between the Balanced Scorecard use and Sustainability" such as the presence of an "Environmental / Sustainability manager" [33, p.12].

At present, concerning the appropriateness of BSC for IS management, some authors have already used BSC methodology to measure IT project success [34], to "achieve IT-business strategic alignment" [35, p.173] or even more recently "to drive and check the performance of a green storage policy" [36, p.1].

3   Methodological Device

The assessment of the eco-responsible maturity of IS is an emergent phenomenon which is complex as it is "simultaneously multi-criteria, multi-actors, multi-rational, and evolutionary" [37, p.2]. In our knowledge, this academic study on the devising of an assessment tool of the eco-responsible maturity of IS is a first, at least in France. This favours the implementation of engineering research that comes within the scope of a constructivist epistemology.

Table 4. Main features of the engineering research: the devising of an assessment tool of the eco-responsible maturity of IS in a consulting firm

Dimensions	Organisation
Organizational structure	Consulting firm in eco-responsible IS – 5 employees
Period of study	October 2011 – June 2012
Object of study	Evaluation of the eco-responsible maturity of IS and its governance
Status of the researcher within the organization	Member of the team in charge of the development and scientific validation of the tool
Test of the tool with user companies	2 IS eco-responsible maturity diagnostic studies planned between January 2012 and June 2012
Use of additional information sources	Scientific and professional literature on the subject, internal documents, interview with experts and interview with the CIO of user companies

"Engineering research is similar in some ways to the action-research by the fact that it focuses on organizational change processes and that it involves the actors affected by the change in the approach of research. It differs however, in devising a new status of "scientist-engineer" that develops its research support tool, built it, and is both as organizer and appraiser of its implementation in organizations, contributing in doing so to the emergence of representations and new scientific knowledge. These scientific knowledge are procedural and not substantive in nature, and are intended to provide a guide to "organizational engineering", to build complex problems and drive processes." [37, p.1] Table 4 presents the main features of this engineering research.

3.1   The Elaboration of the Scorecard

We began the empirical study by modelling the actual knowledge of the consulting firm about the eco-responsible maturity of IS. They had already identified ten technical domains of assessment: data centre, waste, IT purchase, uses, CSR, governance, printing, tele-work and transport, work station and software, environmental management software. For each domain, they had defined several sub-domains, processes and sub-processes. This resulted in a complex system with an abundance of detailed information about many aspects but with no links between all these elements. As the various domains were not interconnected, we obtained a fragmented view of the maturity of IS towards sustainability. Consequently, there was a need to link performance measures and summarize these elements in global perspectives so "that managers be able to view performance in several areas simultaneously" [28, p.72].

So inspired by the BSC of Kaplan and Norton, we presented to the consulting firm a new approach to devise the tool, based on a vision by "perspective" instead of a division by "process" as they had previously proposed it. In the same logic, we assumed that behind the questions in the consulting firm's scorecard, it exists a vision of what is an IS eco-responsible and that this one could be translated into perspectives.

Thus, we defined four important perspectives and we classified the technical sub-domains and sub-processes previously defined by the firm according to their pertaining to one or other of these perspectives. Afterwards, for each of one, we formulated four global objectives in connection with the technical sub-domains and sub-processes.

Then we established a representation, under the shape of a map of the four perspectives, of the wished scorecard by limiting the number of measures used and agreeing on a certain number of clusters to be made to simplify the current model and avoid any redundancy.

Finally, we assigned for each question and indicator up to two objectives. In this way, the achievement of one objective is measured through several questions and indicators but this objective belongs to only one perspective. Figure 2 gives a representation of the structure of the scorecard.

In conclusion, as for the BSC, we operationalized the vision of the eco-responsible IS through four perspectives which were then translated into four general goals. Finally the latter were associated with specific measures.

In the process of assessment conducted by the consulting firm to its clients, the aim is to measure the good fit between the values of indicators and questions found within the company with the objectives defined previously according what we defined as a mature responsible IS.

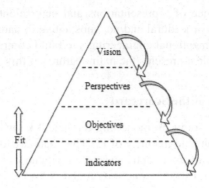

Fig. 1. The logic of the tool

4   Results

To define the four perspectives, we considered the ones existing in the BSC, those of the Skandia navigator and the three pillars of SD. These four dimensions are described below.

4.1   Economic Perspective: "What Is Necessary to Bring to Our Economic Stakeholders?"

The economic perspective gathers the imperatives of the "Financial" and "Customer" dimensions of the conventional BSC. Indeed, it takes into account, in the IS field, the economic issues as the search for a "competitive advantage (through factors such as corporate image, reputation and product differentiation)" [27, p.8] and the trade-offs between the conflicting interests of the different stakeholders.

On the financial aspect, the economic perspective incorporates indicators of costs savings, productivity gains, profitability and some key financial measures for the IT performance as the Return on Investment (ROI) or even the Total Cost of Ownership (TCO). It also comprised non-monetary performance indicators such as legitimacy or reputation.

On the customer dimension, the economic perspective is concerned with striving to meet their needs and with all the objectives of a commercial policy. It reflects how IS contributes to the customer value creation. It also questions the implication of the considered company in the civil society and the role played by IS in this perspective.

Finally, this dimension evaluates the management of IT purchases and particularly the regulatory compliance, the policy management of the suppliers and the integration of Eco-labels criteria in the requests for proposal.

4.2   Human Perspective: "How to Leverage the Human Capital?"

This perspective does not really exist as it is in the model of Kaplan and Norton, so we draw our inspiration both from the social pillar of SD and from the Skandia Navigator devised by Leif Edvinsson and Michael Malone in 1997 [38]. This scorecard differs from the BSC of Kaplan and Norton by adding a fifth Human perspective which is placed at the heart of the approach. It includes knowledge, experience, and competencies.

In this way, it is close to the "Learning and growth" perspective of the BSC which takes into account "qualification, motivation and goal orientation of employees" [31, p.271].

In our conception, the Human perspective integrates the human capital valorisation i.e. the consideration of the individual with its organizational knowledge.

The main areas considered in this dimension were the management of training, competences, work tools, work place and transport, uses, behaviours and eco-friendly gesture.

4.3   Environmental Perspective: "How to Preserve the Environment?"

The environmental Perspective includes all actions contributing to the preservation of the environment. These latter ones can be divided into three main categories which represent the main phases of IT life-cycle: conception, use and end-of-life.

We find in these areas preoccupations about the resources and raw material management, energy consumption, GHG emissions, WEEE management and consumable management.

There is another area in this perspective which does not concern the IT footprint on the environment but its potential of contribution to SD and particularly to the CSR policy of the firm.

4.4   Management System Perspective: "How to Drive Change and Continuous Improvement?"

The Management System Perspective covers some goals of the previous dimensions of "Internal Business Processes" and "Learning and growth" perspectives. It aims to evaluate "how well a company performs on key internal dimensions" [27, p.2]. It integrates measures on the three categories of performance simultaneously through evaluation areas which are Energy Consumption, Carbone Footprint, IT Purchases, Transport, Shareholders' Expectations, Compliance Regulatory, among others.

This perspective also "describes the infrastructure necessary for the achievement of the objectives of the other three perspectives" [31, p.271] and in particular it defines the organization and decision system. It is concerned with the elaboration of an IS eco-responsible charter which aims to disseminate values and good practices throughout the company. This perspective incorporates issues about support change and continuous improvement in the other three perspectives. It is therefore a transversal dimension.

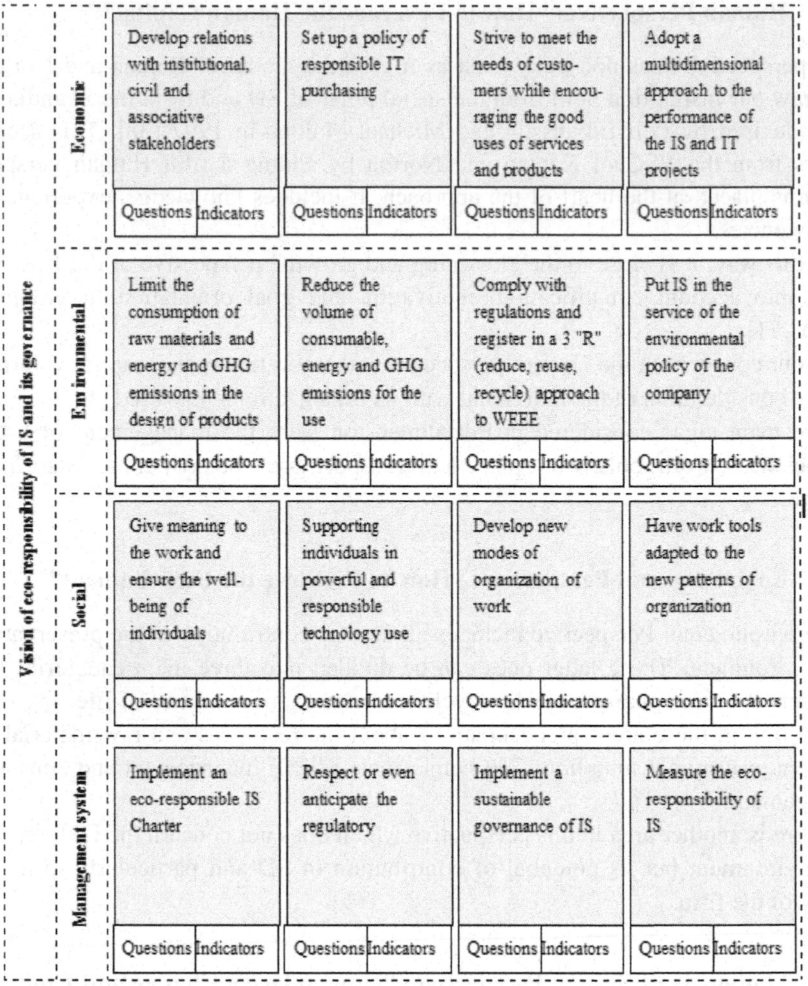

		Develop relations with institutional, civil and associative stakeholders	Set up a policy of responsible IT purchasing	Strive to meet the needs of customers while encouraging the good uses of services and products	Adopt a multidimensional approach to the performance of the IS and IT projects
	Economic	Questions Indicators	Questions Indicators	Questions Indicators	Questions Indicators
	Environmental	Limit the consumption of raw materials and energy and GHG emissions in the design of products	Reduce the volume of consumable, energy and GHG emissions for the use	Comply with regulations and register in a 3 "R" (reduce, reuse, recycle) approach to WEEE	Put IS in the service of the environmental policy of the company
Vision of eco-responsibility of IS and its governance		Questions Indicators	Questions Indicators	Questions Indicators	Questions Indicators
	Social	Give meaning to the work and ensure the well-being of individuals	Supporting individuals in powerful and responsible technology use	Develop new modes of organization of work	Have work tools adapted to the new patterns of organization
		Questions Indicators	Questions Indicators	Questions Indicators	Questions Indicators
	Management system	Implement an eco-responsible IS Charter	Respect or even anticipate the regulatory	Implement a sustainable governance of IS	Measure the eco-responsibility of IS
		Questions Indicators	Questions Indicators	Questions Indicators	Questions Indicators

Fig. 2. Proposal of a scorecard of the eco-responsible maturity of IS and its governance

5   Conclusion

The ICT are not the immaterial devices we imagine them to be. They consume resources and generate abundant e-waste. It is only with the massive distribution of these technologies - as an example, the number of computers should reach 2 billion before 2014 [39] - that we became aware of all the negative externalities engendered by the production, the uses and the end of life of these products [4], [8]. But conversely, ICT can reduce emissions and thus contribute to sustainability in others sectors. Within firms, IS can be put at the service of CSR policy. The assessment of the maturity of the eco-responsibility of IS makes it possible to measure how IS performs in the ecological, social and economic perspectives. Evaluate the impact of IS on the environment and its contribution to sustainability represents a major stake for CIO.

In this paper, we wanted to expose the theoretical framework of the measurement of the eco-responsible maturity of IS and shown that this thematic originates from the interconnection with the concepts of SD and CSR in the field of IS. We saw that although the ethical reflection is not new in IS, it has never encompassed such variety of subjects simultaneously. Then we demonstrated that the logic of the BSC methodology could be relevant to formulate a measurement system of sustainability strategy even if some limits and conditions of success can be identified.

As there was a need for a measurement system of the maturity of the eco-responsible IS, we devised a scorecard derived from the BSC in an engineering research approach.

The major interest of this tool is not to provide an exact measure of the eco-responsibility of IS but to give a sense of responsibility to actors and to lead them to reflect on this subject in order to change their practices in a conscious way. Kaplan and Norton also emphasize that "the balanced scorecard should be used as a communication, informing, and learning system, not as a controlling system." [29, p.25]

This scorecard enables one to give visibility to the actions carried out at the level of the IS and to provide consistency with the practices of CSR. Like this, it represents a tool for dialogue between DSI and Directions: "Through using a causal chain analysis to link performance metrics to business value and strategic objectives, managers have a tool to communicate the business value of sustainability actions to the CEO and CFO of the organization, to help justify resource allocations to EH&S initiatives, and to tell the story of sustainability in business language." [27, p.10]

This study could be extended using this model in different organizational contexts. Like this, we could analyze (1) the transformations of actors' representations with the implementation of the tool and (2) the efficiency of the tool in helping to identify actions plans to improve the maturity of the eco-responsibility of IS.

References

1. Breuil, H., Burette, D., Flüry-Hérard, B., Cueugniet, J., Vignolles, D.: Rapport TIC et Développement durable, Ministère de l'Ecologie, de l'Energie, du Développement Durable et de l'Aménagement du Territoire, Ministère de l'Economie, de l'Industrie et de l'Emploi, p. 96 (December 2008)
2. Petit, M., Breuil, H., Cueugniet, J.: Rapport Développement éco-responsable et TIC (Detic) CGIET, Conseil Général de l'Industrie, de l'Energie et des Technologies (2009)
3. Pensel, J.L.: Les systèmes d'information au service de la responsabilité sociale d'entreprise. In: 14th AIM Symposium, Marrakech, Morocco, June 10-12 (2009)
4. Ait-Daoud, S., Laqueche, J., Bourdon, I.: Ecologie & technologies de l'information de la communication: une étude exploratoire sur les éco-TIC. In: AIM Symposium, May 19-21, La Rochelle (2010)
5. Freeman, I., Hasnaoui, A.: Technologies de l'Information et de Communication: un outil pour implémenter et véhiculer la responsabilité sociale des entreprises (RSE). In: 15th AIM Symposium, May 19-21, La Rochelle (2010)

6. Mathieu, A.-L., Bohas, A.: Une typologie de pratiques de Système d'information durables. In: 16th AIM Symposium, May 25-27, La Réunion (2011)
7. CIGREF, Systèmes d'information éco-responsable: l'usage des TIC au service de l'entreprise durable (2009)
8. Berkhout, F., Hertin, J.: Impacts of Information and Communication Technologies on Environmental Sustainability: Speculations and Evidence, p. 21. Report to the OECD. University of Sussex, Brighton (2001)
9. Hilty, L.M.: Information Technology and Sustainability: Essays on the Relationship Between ICT and Sustainable Development. BOD, Norderstedt (2008)
10. Hilty, L.M., Arnfalk, P., Erdmann, L., Goodman, J., Lehman, M., Wäger, P.A.: The relevance of information and communication technologies for environmental sustainability – A prospective simulation study. Environment Modelling & Software 21, 1618–1629 (2006)
11. Fuchs, C.: Theoretical foundations of defining the participatory, co-operative, sustainable information society. Information, Communication & Society 13(1), 23–47 (2010)
12. Deltour, F.: Peut-on produire des TIC vertes? Equipementiers et parties prenantes dans le débat sur le caractère écologique des TIC. In: 15th AIM Symposium, May 19-21, pp. 19–21. La Rochelle (2010)
13. Rodhain, F., Fallery, B.: Après la prise de conscience écologique, les TIC en quête de responsabilité sociale. In: 15th AIM Symposium, May 19-21, pp. 19–21. La Rochelle (2010)
14. Pensel, J.L.: TIC et Parties Prenantes minoritaires: vers l'entreprise responsable. In: 15th AIM Symposium, May 19-21, pp. 19–21. La Rochelle (2010)
15. GARTNER: Green IT Initiatives Are Moving beyond Power and Cooling Efficiency, 8 February, n° G00173836 (2010)
16. Castells, M.: The Rise of the Network Society. Blackwell Publishing, New York (2000)
17. Crozier, M., Friedberg, E.: L'acteur et le Système. Le Seuil, Paris (1977)
18. Faucheux, S., Hue, C., Nicolaï, I.: TIC et développement durable – Les conditions du succès, p. 222. Editions De Boeck Université, Bruxelles (2010)
19. Tassin, P., Berhault, G., Berthoud, F., Bonnet, P., Bordage, F., Bordes, F., Delsol, E.: Systèmes d'information et développement durable – économie, société et environnement, p. 345. Publications Hermes Science, Editions Lavoisier, Paris (2010)
20. Martinet, A.-C., Reynaud, E.: Stratégies d'entreprise et écologie. Economica, Paris (2004)
21. Carroll, A.B.: A three dimensional conceptual model of corporate social performance. Academy of Management Review 4, 97–505 (1979)
22. Berthoud, F., Pons, J.-L., Drezet, E., Louvet, V.: Comment se diriger vers une informatique durable? In: Actes du JRES, Strasbourg, November 20-23 (2007)
23. Fuchs, C.: The implications of new information and communication technologies for sustainability. Environment, Development and Sustainability 10(3), 291–309 (2008)
24. Flipo, F., Gossart, C., Deltour, F., Gourvennec, B., Dobré, M., Michot, M., Berthet, L.: Technologies numériques et crise environnementale: peut-on croire aux TIC vertes? Rapport Ecotic (2009)
25. Zuboff, S.: In the Age of the Smart Machine. Basic Books, New York (1988)
26. AFNOR: PR NF ISO 26000: Lignes directrices relatives à la responsabilité sociétale (2010)
27. Epstein, M.J., Wisner, P.S.: Using a balanced scorecard to implement sustainability. Environmental Quality Management, 1–10 (Winter 2001)
28. Kaplan, R.S., Norton, D.P.: The Balanced Scorecard -Measures That Drive Performance. Harvard Business Review (January-February 1992)
29. Kaplan, R.S., Norton, D.P.: The Balanced Score-card: Translating Strategy into Action. Harvard Business School Press, Boston (1996)

30. Kaplan, R.S., Norton, D.P.: The Strategy-Focused Organization: How Balanced Scorecard Companies Thrive in the New Business Environment. Harvard Business School Press, Boston (2000)
31. Figge, F., Hahn, T., Schaltegger, S., Marcus, W.: The Sustainability Balanced Scorecard: Linking Sustainability Management to Business Strategy. Business Strategy and the Environment 11, 269–284 (2002)
32. Quairel, F.: Contrôle de la performance globale et responsabilité sociale de l'entreprise (RSE). Association Francophone de Comptabilité, Tunis (2006)
33. Zingales, F., Hockerts, K.: Balanced Scorecard and Sustainability: Examples from Literature and Practice. CMER, Working Paper no 30, Insead (2003)
34. Martinsons, M., Davison, R., Tse, D.: The balanced scorecard: A foundation for the strategic management of information systems. Decision Support Systems 25, 71–88 (1999)
35. Huang, C.D., Hu, Q.: Achieving IT-business strategic alignment via enterprise-wide implementation of balanced scorecards. Information Systems Management 24(2), 173–184 (2007)
36. Laura, F., Coelho, F., Delmond, M.H.: Gestion durable des données: point sur les enjeux et proposition d'une démarche de pilotage de la performance appuyée sur un balanced scorecard thématique. In: 15th AIM Symposium, May 19-21, pp. 19–21. La Rochelle (2010)
37. Chanal, V., Lesca, H., Martinet, A.-C.: Vers une ingénierie de la recherche en sciences de gestion. Revue Française de Gestion 116, 41–51 (1997)
38. Edvinsson, L., Malone, M.: Intellectual Capital: Realizing Your Company's True Value by Finding Its Hidden Brainpower. Harper Business, New York (1997)
39. Gartner: Gartner Says More than 1 Billion PC. In: Use Worldwide and Headed to 2 Billion Units by 2014. Gartner Newsroom (2008),
    http://www.gartner.com/it/page.jsp?id=703807
40. SMART 2020: Enabling the low carbon economy in the information age United States Report Addendum. Report Addendum in The Climate Group, London (2008),
    http://www.mendeley.com/research/smart-2020-enabling-low-carbon-economy-information-age-united-states-report-addendum/

Building Human Infrastructure for the Digital Economy: Ryerson's Digital Media Zone

Wendy Cukier, Valerie Fox, and Hossein Rahnama

Ryerson University, Toronto, Canada
{wcukier,vfox,hossein}@ryerson.ca

Abstract. Drawing upon the policy literature and empirical work, this paper proposes an ecological model in which entrepreneurial skills are a critical part of the human infrastructure needed to fuel national Digital Economy and Innovation strategies. While many countries around the world reference the importance of building a "culture of innovation" and some countries, such as Israel, are seen as having this deeply embedded, there are few definitions and fewer empirical studies assessing this. We suggest that the prevalence of individuals with entrepreneurial mindsets and a willingness to take risks will drive economic growth and development but that developing this is easier said than done, as complex factors shape values and aspirations. While University-based incubators have long been seen as important parts of the innovation ecosystem, we provide a case study of a unique incubator, Ryerson University's Digital Media Zone (Toronto, Canada), and suggest that it not only offers short term outcomes but also offers a model that is critical to fostering a culture of innovation. We conclude that more needs to be done in Canada to promote this culture of innovation and that it needs to begin long before students reach university.

Keywords: digital economy, digital skills, Canada, ecological model, entrepreneurs, innovation, innovators, incubators.

1   Digital Skills and the Culture of Innovation

Recent reports [36] lament Canada's lagging global performance on innovation and recommend a variety of interventions at the policy or macro level. At the same time, the evidence is clear that the challenges are complex, also demanding attention at sectoral, firm, and individual levels and their inter-relationships. For example, the availability of venture capital [35], the social acceptance of entrepreneurs, and formal-informal networks all influence the development of entrepreneurial culture [4]. Comparisons of countries have focused on differences in tax policies, investments in research and development (R&D), and regulations [61]. Less attention has been paid to cultural differences [24]. The characteristics of individual entrepreneurs have been the subject of much research [71], [28], [29], [53], [85]. However, less research exists on the effectiveness of specific interventions aimed at developing entrepreneurs and entrepreneurial culture. While globally there are broad discussions of the need to strengthen the "culture of innovation" [22], [27], [39], [49], [50], [51], [70], this is not well defined, nor has there been much attention to how it will be fostered.

M.D. Hercheui et al. (Eds.): HCC10 2012, IFIP AICT 386, pp. 156–169, 2012.

Canada's Digital Skills Strategy stresses the importance of a technological infrastructure, the need to strengthen ICT markets, the need to promote applications, and the importance of developing the human infrastructure. However, critical digital skills tend to be defined as basic digital literacy (to enable access and use of the internet for example) or on Science, Technology, Engineering and Mathematics (STEM) disciplines. Less attention has been paid to the importance of fostering entrepreneurial skills in order to grow digital companies [15].

Previous research [3], [19] [31], [67] has also explored social networks that constitute innovation ecosystems and the geographical clustering of technology company entrepreneurs in innovation hubs. Universities often play a critical role in these ecosystems and university-based technology transfer centres and incubators have been successful in effectively mobilizing research knowledge [52]. Stanford University in Silicon Valley and MIT in Cambridge, Massachusetts are key players in well-known hot spots for digital innovation and fostered many wildly successful high-tech companies [10]. University-based and other incubators have a long history in many nations in promoting local economic development and the creation of new businesses. Canada, for example, is home to more than 200 distinct technology incubators and accelerators, including at least ten specifically focused on digital media. In some countries, national networks of small business incubators are an explicit part of national innovation strategies [65]. Yet there are still numerous unanswered gaps in understanding the process of startup success and the role that incubators may play [59].

Our paper suggests that:

1. Entrepreneurial Skills and Entrepreneurship must be a critical part of national Digital Economy and Innovation strategies;
2. The prevalence of individuals with entrepreneurial mindsets and a willingness to take risks will drive economic growth and development, and are a critical aspect of a "Culture of Innovation";
3. University-based incubators can not only offer short term outcomes such as the creation of technologies, companies and jobs, but are also a critical element in developing the skills and mindset needed to foster a culture of innovation.

We will first review the relevant research on entrepreneurs and entrepreneurship, entrepreneurial culture, building entrepreneurial skills and the role of incubators. We will then describe the Canadian context broadly and provide a case study of a Canadian digital media incubator at Ryerson University in Toronto, Ontario.

2   Entrepreneurs and Entrepreneurship

The 'entrepreneurial mindset' includes the ability to sense, act, and mobilize under certain circumstances – characteristic of entrepreneurs and entrepreneurial behaviour [32]. But the question of how this is defined and measured and, more importantly, where it comes from, is the subject of much debate.

There have also been efforts to define entrepreneurship and identify the characteristics of entrepreneurs through profiles [9], [81] or psychographic testing and surveys

[8], [40], [73], [90]. Some scholars have focused on refining the measures and instruments used to assess entrepreneurial traits such as self-efficacy [55]. Various instruments purport to measure key entrepreneurial characteristics such as the need for achievement, a locus of control, and creative tendencies [13], [16], [63]. Non-psychological variables such as education, family, and life experience influence the tendency to behave entrepreneurially [17]. Donaldson [18] suggests that the single most important factor is an individual's belief that starting a business is a suitable course for them and this, in turn, is affected by many factors.

The prevalence of individuals with entrepreneurial mindsets and a willingness to take risks will drive economic growth and development [18], [88]. Entrepreneurial culture is defined as a set of "values, beliefs and attitudes commonly shared in a society which underpin the notion of an entrepreneurial 'way of life' as being desirable and in turn support the pursuit of 'effective' entrepreneurial behavior by individuals or groups" [25]. Social norms reflect the interplay of many variables including historical context, institutions [43], and political and economic systems [42], [47], which have a significant impact on the decisions to pursue entrepreneurial activities [30], [62]. Similarly, national culture, as reflected in institutions, laws, and policies, may also influence the propensity towards entrepreneurship [38], [41], [46], [66], [72].

Some studies attempt to measure the national culture of innovation [33] and entrepreneurship based on aggregate measures such as creation of new enterprises on a per capita basis or by national productivity [12], [37]. The Global Entrepreneurship Monitor (GEM) assesses country entrepreneurial attitudes and general societal attitudes towards entrepreneurship. Other studies consider the relationship between national culture and the characteristics of individual entrepreneurs, attempting to assess the values, beliefs, motivations, and cognitions of entrepreneurs across cultures [44], [87]. Building on Hofstede's [34] cultural indices, some scholars have attempted to link national culture with individual entrepreneurial characteristics. For example, Licht and Siegal [44] suggested that cultures that were ranked as more individualistic had a higher likelihood of an internal locus of control orientation, one characteristic often associated with an entrepreneurial orientation. This is also more likely in low uncertainty avoidance cultures. Rates of innovation are most closely associated with the cultural value of uncertainty acceptance, but a lack of power distance and individualism also are related to high rates of innovation. This research suggests that nations may differ in their rates of innovation because cultural and religious values [6], [11], [23], [56], [82].

There have also been a number of studies to assess whether or not, in addition to building knowledge and skills, entrepreneurial intentions are affected by education [83]. The findings make logical sense when one considers the relationship between knowledge, skill and self-efficacy, which are important traits of entrepreneurs. Although research has been specifically directed at developing entrepreneurial skills for engineers, scientists, and physicians [20], the impact of entrepreneurial training and education programs in promoting innovation is inconclusive [23], [78], [85].

3   Incubators

Specialized services and infrastructures (e.g., incubators, research centers, business parks, and technology transfer offices) can promote entrepreneurship and foster the commercialization of research and new ideas to stimulate scientific entrepreneurship [2], [14], [75], [77]. A business incubator is an organization designed to accelerate the growth and success of new entrepreneurial companies by nurturing them at their inception. Globally, there are high profile university-based incubators. For example, MIT in Cambridge, Massachusetts; Imperial College, London; University of Houston, Twente University; University of Monterrey and many others [5], [21]. Case studies which have documented the impact of individual incubators at universities including the University of Central Florida [69], the United States Market Access Center (USMAC) at San Jose State University [57], Northwestern and the University of North Carolina [58], in Sweden [68] and France [54], an Irish Dublin-based university campus incubator [1] as well as two in Canada [54].

Scholars have examined the evolution of incubators and research parks in the commercialization of research at universities [26], [58]. Many focus on their role in commercializing technology, nurturing firms and new products. However, incubators can also support broader objectives related to developing innovation ecosystems [60]. Among the benefits to client firms are access to student and faculty talent. Discussions of "entrepreneurial universities" in developing skills and attitudes have also emphasized their role in fostering technology entrepreneurs.

While the definitions of success vary, several studies have attempted to address performance issues [45], [74]. There are different ways to approach the question of effectiveness, the goal of the approach, the system resource approach, the stakeholder approach, and the internal processes approach [58]. The proposed University Technology Business Intelligence model included performance outcomes (program sustainability and growth, tenant survival and growth, contributions to the university mission, and community impacts). Management policies and their effectiveness particularly the effective use of resources (e.g. governance, finance and capitalization, operational policies, and target markets), services and their value added with a focus on the perceived value of the services provided (e.g. space, business assistance, human resources, and consulting) have also been studied. Sun et al. propose a framework of critical success factors [86] which includes environment-related, incubator-related and incubatee-related factors.

Bergek and Norma propose a model of incubator best practices that is contextual and goals-based [7]. They suggest that the incubator performs several functions 1) selection, 2) business support, and 3) mediation. In effect, the incubator is a mediator between the company and the external innovation system, acting as a bridge with the intention of leveraging talent and resources. Critical resources include knowledge and technology, capital, market-related resources, and human capital. Incubators may also engage in network mediation, matching incubatees with other actors, and institutional mediation by helping navigate and even shape laws, traditions, values, and norms.

One of the most important success factors to be considered for technology-based incubators is the selection of incubatees [84]. Support in the development of markets and products are also key factors. However, other determinants of success lie within the incubatees and in their relationship with the incubator [86]. A common thread in the literature is that the major functions of an incubator, apart from subsidizing early stage growth, is to provide access to social networks, which in combination with intellectual capital, increase the chances of an entrepreneur's success [48].

Some studies have suggested that incubators simply prolong the survival of companies that would normally fail sooner. Rigorous evaluation early in the process by experienced entrepreneurs is the most effective way of increasing success rates by producing a survivor bias. This then raises questions about the role of the incubation process. Consequently, some research has focused on case control assessments of incubated versus non-incubated startups. The results, however, are ambiguous [1], [79]. The evidence on the value of specialization in incubators is also mixed [80].

4   Ryerson's Digital Media Zone

In Canada, there are more than 200 incubators that are members of the Canadian Association of Business Incubation. These incubators serve a range of sectors and purposes from general small business support, to fostering social enterprises in small communities, to large scale commercialization. They also operate across and within specific sectors.

The Digital Media Zone (DMZ) was established in 2010, at Ryerson University, a former polytechnic based in Toronto, Ontario, with deep roots in experiential learning and applied research. With more than 30,000 undergraduate students, Ryerson has one of the largest undergraduate entrepreneurship programs in Canada's largest business school (with more than 8,000 students). A high percentage of faculty members bring business experience along with academic qualifications. The University also has active student entrepreneurship clubs and competitions including Students in Free Enterprise (SIFE), Advancing Canadian Entrepreneurship (ACE) Canada, and Students Advancing Global Entrepreneurship (SAGE), which involve a substantial proportion of students and promote entrepreneurial activity.

The Digital Media Zone (DMZ) was created by the President of Ryerson University, Sheldon Levy, in response to student requests. He invested in prime real estate and infrastructure with a clear focus on supporting students with ideas for new businesses. In April 2010, the University rented 6,400 sq. ft. at the busiest corner in Canada, Dundas Street East and Yonge Street. The location was then equipped with state of the art technology [76] and a rigorous application processes for students to qualify for entry was established. The goals of the DMZ evolved beyond meeting student needs, however. It aspires to become a critical part of the downtown Toronto ecosystem:

- To strengthen the collaborative community of entrepreneurs;
- To improve and promote commercialization of technology;
- To help build industry clusters (in areas such as context-aware computing, for example) that can compete globally; and
- To help keep intellectual property and talent in Canada.

In less than two years, the size of DMZ has more than doubled – it now consists of 16,450 sq. ft. with plans for further expansion. To date it has reported:

- 41 startups incubated and accelerated;
- More than 64 projects initiated;
- 382 jobs fostered and created through newly formed startups and market-driven research, plus 56 new jobs at Ryerson itself;
- Eight companies which have outgrown the space and since leased their own;
- One company has more than 50 employees, while one has failed; and
- Currently, the DMZ houses 161 innovators in 36 teams.

One of DMZ's principal differentiators is the focus on communications and outreach facilitated in part because of its location. In the past year, there have been approximately 430 tours to the DMZ including by government ministers and financiers as well as leading business people and industry associations. There has also been substantial press coverage, with over 600 instances of positive media coverage locally, nationally, and internationally. High profile presentations have been made at the Toronto Economic Club (a prominent business network) and at conferences and events around the world – including in India, Brazil, China and Russia.

4.1   The DMZ Approach

Like other incubators, the DMZ performs the three basic functions identified and proposed by [7]: 1) selection, 2) business support, and 3) mediation. Companies apply to enter the DMZ and must pass an initial evaluation, have a unique innovation in the prototype stage, and a strong business plan that demonstrates a clear market need. The selection committee consists of industry leaders, faculty experts, peers, and mentors. Prior to entering the DMZ, prospective entrepreneurs typically have some experience with a project as well as coaching on basic business planning, provided via SIFE.

The DMZ provides open, flexible workspace, equipment, utilities, and services such as business plan counseling, mentoring, and workshops. It also provides training. While the typical DMZ company has entered the Zone with strong training and technical skills in their discipline, they receive support with business plan development and have ongoing access to coaching and training. Increasingly, there is a focus on progress monitoring with mandatory check-in meetings scheduled every few months to provide guidance and advice, monitor progress, and ensure companies are receiving the help they need to achieve their set milestones. Companies must submit monthly reports to ensure the DMZ has current information. The DMZ also helps provide human resources to companies including funded internship and student employees. Finally, as noted above, the DMZ provides extensive marketing and communications support including key marketing and communications materials such as sell-sheets, website pages, news releases, video pitches, and photoshoots.

In terms of "mediation", the DMZ actively promotes networking through special events, networking sessions, workshops, etc. for incumbent entrepreneurs. This helps companies tap into resources which include experienced serial entrepreneurs or mentors, financing, customers, other incubators, and media (which fuels access to the others). The DMZ provides a directory of available mentors and profiles networking opportunities through a variety of events and tours. The DMZ identifies sources of funding and assists its companies with grant applications as well as with finding and securing other forms of financial support, such as Angel Investments. Given its high profile, the DMZ ensures a steady stream of prospective corporate customers. It also organizes joint events with other incubators as well as complimentary passes to start-up related events in Toronto. Finally, a dedicated Media Relations Officer pitches stories, fields calls, and helps Zone companies with media training and PR strategies in order to build profile and fuel traffic. Apart from the formal services, there is ample anecdotal evidence of peer-to-peer mentoring and collaboration across companies.

4.2   The Results

Although a formal evaluation is yet to be undertaken, the DMZ has produced tangible results in a short time frame. Table 1 (next page) provides a brief description of some of the DMZ companies and results that they have achieved.

Table 1. The DMZ company summary

Company	Outcomes (number of employees, sales etc.)
500px *DMZ Graduate* Founded in April 2011, 500px is a fast growing photography website.	• Their iPad app is one of the top free photography apps in iTunes. • Voted the number one startup in Toronto in January 2012 by Techvibes, Canada's leading technology media property. • Has 16 employees; left the DMZ in December 2011.
Bionik Labs *Currently Incubating* Founded in March 2011, Bionik Labs is a medical engineering research and development corporation with a focus on prosthetics and rehabilitation devices.	• Working with major hospitals in the United States and Canada on clinical trials related to assisted technology for paraplegics. • Has over 20 employees.
Finizi *Currently Incubating* Founded in February 2011, Finizi is a free online platform where financial institutions bid for the business of customers in live auctions.	• Recently completed a three month beta pilot for GICs during which it processed over \$Can 30M in auction requests and \$Can 2M in completed sales. • Finizi has been featured in the Financial Post, Investment Executive, Business News Network, Yahoo Finance, and several other online finance and technology publications.

Table 1. (*continued*)

Flybits
Currently Incubating
Founded in April 2010, Flybits is a
Canadian leader in mobile context-
aware computing.

- Developed Toronto's GO Transit's first official mobile application.
- The app was downloaded over 150,000 times
  in its first eight weeks.
- Their software solution running on Motorola
  Golden-I product, the world's first hands-free
  and wireless headset computer received Motorola's Golden-idea Award.
- Developed the first Connected Vehicle Mobile Solution as part of a research project for
  the Ontario Ministry of Transportation.
- Department of Foreign Affairs and the Ministry of Economic Development and Innovation selected it as a top 10 Canadian company
  to present at the Mobile World Congress in
  2012 and CTIA Wireless in New Orleans in
  the United States; has 17 staff.

HitSend
Currently Incubating
Founded in April 2010, HitSend is a
community crowdsourcing tool for
gathering, prioritizing, and executing
ideas. It integrates these into existing
online communities.

- Chapters/Indigo Canada's largest bookstore
  uses their technology as part of its recently
  launched *Indigo Ideas* campaign for improving customer service.
- Has five staff.

HugeMonster
Currently Incubating
Founded in April 2011, HugeMonster
builds casual social games that blend
traditional storylines with interactive
and viral elements.

- Approximately 3,000 players play their
  game, Code of War, daily.
- Has 12 staff.

Shape Collage
DMZ Graduate
Founded in September 2010, Shape
Collage is an online collage maker that
optimally arranges photos into collages
of different shapes.

- The product has been downloaded more than
  five million times since 2009 and has been
  translated into 22 different languages.
- Has five staff.

Sound Selecta
Currently Incubating
Founded in April 2010, Sound Selecta
makes ArtJam, a mobile platform that
blends music, art, and technology to
bring users new interactive media experiences.

- Apple named ArtJam's Nursery Jam as one
  of its Top 10 apps for toddlers.
- Has five staff.

Table 1. (*continued*)

Phosphorus Media *Currently Incubating* Founded in April 2010, Phosphorus Media specializes in high impact media systems and interactive displays.	• Select clients include: Sony, Ikea, Club Med, The Gap, Starbucks, Red Bull, L'Oreal, Adidas, and Pampers. • Has five staff.
Teamsave *DMZ Graduate* Founded in April 2010, Teamsave is a social buying website and platform.	• Partnered with Kijiji; both the Kijiji deal site and Daily Deals run on the TeamSave platform. • TeamSave operates in 20 cities in North America and has over 50 staff.
Viafoura *Currently Incubating* Founded in May 2011, Viafoura is a cloud-based plug-and-play commenting platform targeted to premium digital publishers.	• Currently partnered with 12 of the world's largest digital publishers. • Expanded from two employees to 17 in only six months.

5   Conclusions

Based on a cursory assessment of the data, Ryerson's DMZ appears to produce a high number of companies and jobs relative to similar initiatives. While longer term tracking is needed, along with additional empirical analysis, it seems that among the key factors affecting positive outcomes are the rigour of the original screening process and the heavy emphasis on outreach and communications which, in turn, ensure that the companies are exposed to a wide range of investors and customers. This is also facilitated by the central location of the incubator site.

However, beyond the specific results with respect to firm and job creation, the impact of the DMZ seems to be broader in terms of fuelling a culture of innovation. The importance of the educative effects of the experiential learning in the DMZ along with the influence of the DMZ in shaping entrepreneurial intentions among the broader Ryerson community (students and professors) should not be overlooked. Further research is needed to explore this in detail.

The research on entrepreneurship and a culture of innovation suggests that shaping entrepreneurial intention is a complex process. It is reasonable to assume that the publicity around the DMZ and its companies, as well as the competition to enter the DMZ, plays a critical role in building culture by shaping values and narratives of entrepreneurial successes (and failures). Culture is about stories and values and can, therefore, play an important role in broadening the aspirations of young people. We need to understand how this can be done earlier, as many students in the DMZ have self-selected themselves based on earlier experiences. More work is needed to push this experience upstream, so that young people are exposed to these opportunities earlier and see the full range of entrepreneurial opportunities. Exploring this will be the focus of further research.

References

1. Ahmad, A.J., Ingle, S.: Relationships matter: Case Study of a University Campus Incubator. International Journal of Entrepreneurial Behaviour & Research 17(6), 626–644 (2011)
2. Andersson, M., van der Sijde, P.C., Mateos, A.: New Strategies for Innovation Support. Signum, Salamanca (2006)
3. Arechavala-Vargas, R., Díaz-Pérez, C., Holbrook, J.A.: Globalization of Innovation & Dynamics of a Regional Innovation Network. In: Atlanta Conference on Science and Innovation Policy Proceedings, Georgia Institute of Technology, Atlanta (2009)
4. Audretsch, D.B., Keilbach, M.: Entrepreneurship Capital and Economic Performance. Regional Studies 38(8), 949–959 (2004)
5. Barrow, C.: Incubators: A Realists' Guide to the World's New Business Accelerators. John Wiley & Sons, London (2001)
6. Baum, J.R., Olian, J.D., Erez, M., Schnell, E.R., Smith, K.G., Sims, H.P., Scully, J.S., Smith, K.A.: Nationality and Work Role Interactions. Journal of Business Venturing 8(6), 499–512 (1993)
7. Bergek, A., Norma, C.: Incubator Best Practice: A Framework. Technovation 28(1-2), 20–28 (2008)
8. Borghans, L., Duckworth, A., Heckman, J., Ter Weel, B.: The Economics & Psychology of Personality Traits. Journal of Human Resources 43(3), 972–1059 (2008)
9. Brody, L., Cukier, W., Grant, K., Holland, M., Middleton, C., Shortt, D.: Innovation Nation: Canadian Leadership from Java to Jurassic Park. Wiley, Toronto (2002)
10. Bubela, T.M., Caulfield, T.: Role in Reality: Technology Transfer at Canadian Universities. Trends in Biotechnology 28(9), 447–451 (2010)
11. Buegelsdijk, S.: Entrepreneurial Culture, Regional Innovativeness and Economic Growth. Journal of Evolutionary Economics 17(2), 187–210 (2007)
12. Carree, M.A., van Stel, A.J., Thurik, A.R., Wennekers, A.R.M.: The Relationship Between Economic Development and Business Ownership Revisited. Entrepreneurship & Regional Development 19(3), 281–291 (2007)
13. Carsrud, A., Krueger, N.: Social Psychology: Behavioral Technology for Understanding the New Venture Initiation Processes. Advances in Entrepreneurship & Growth 2, 73–96 (1995)
14. Chiesa, V., Chiaroni, D.: Industrial Clusters in Biotechnology: Driving Forces, Development Processes and Management Practices. Imperial College Press, London (2005)
15. Cukier, W., Smarz, S., Baillargeon, A., Rylett, T., Munawar, M., Hsu, C., Hannan, C., Yap, M.: Improving Canada's Digital Advantage: Building the Digital Talent Pool and Skills for Tomorrow. Ryerson University, Toronto (2010)
16. Cromie, S.: Assessing Entrepreneurial Inclinations: Some Approaches and Empirical Evidence. European Journal of Work and Organizational Psychology 9(1), 7–30 (2000)
17. Cuervo García, Á., Ribeiro, D., Roig, S.: Entrepreneurship: Concepts, theory and perspective. Springer, Berlin (2007)
18. Davidsson, P.: Determinants of Entrepreneurial Intentions. In: RENT IX Workshop, pp. 1-31. Queensland University of Technology, Brisbane (1995),
   http://eprints.qut.edu.au/archive/00002076/
19. Davis, C.H., Creutzberg, T., Arthurs, D.: Applying an Innovation Cluster Framework to a Creative Industry. Innovation: Management, Policy & Practice 11(2), 201–214 (2009)
20. Elfenbein, D., Hamilton, B., Zenger, T.: The Small Firm Effect and the Entrepreneurial Spawning of Scientists and Engineers. Management Science 56(4), 659–681 (2010)

21. Estrin, J.: Closing the Innovation Gap: Reigniting the Spark of Creativity in a Global Economy. McGraw-Hill, New York (2009)
22. Federman, M.: Creating a Culture of Innovation: Keynote Address. Canadian School of Public Service, Cornwall, Ontario (2006),
    http://individual.utoronto.ca/markfederman/
    CultureOfInnovation.pdf
23. Foreman-Peck, J., Zhou, P.: The Strength and Persistence of Entrepreneurial Cultures. Journal of Evolutionary Economics (2011), doi:10.1007/s00191-011-0239-z
24. Freytag, A., Thurik, R. (eds.): Entrepreneurship and Culture. Springer, Berlin (2010)
25. Gibb, A.: Creating an Entrepreneurial Culture in Support of SMEs. Small Enterprise Development 10(4), 27–38 (1999)
26. Gibson, L.J.: Economic Development: The University and Commercialization of Research. Economic Development Review 6(2), 7–11 (1988)
27. Government of Canada: State of the Nation. Science, Technology, & Innovation Council (STIC), Ottawa (2010),
    http://www.stic-csti.ca/eic/site/stic-csti.nsf/eng/h_00038.html
28. Grilo, I., Irigoyen, J.M.: Entrepreneurship in the EU: To Wish and Not To Be. Small Business Economics 26(4), 305–318 (2006)
29. Grilo, I., Thurik, R.: Determinants of Entrepreneurial Engagement Levels in Europe and the US. Industrial and Corporate Change 17(6), 1113–1145 (2008)
30. Hansen, J.D., Dietz, G.D., Tokman, M., Marino, L.D., Weaver, K.M.: Cross-National Invariance of Entrepreneurial Orientation Scale. Journal of Business Venturing 26(1), 61–78 (2011)
31. Harrison, R.C., Cooper, S.Y., Mason, C.M.: Entrepreneurial Activity & the Dynamics of Technology-based Cluster Development. Urban Studies 41(5/6), 1045–1070 (2004)
32. Haynie, J.M., Shepherd, D., Mosakowski, E., Earley, P.C.: A Situated Metacognitive Model of the Entrepreneurial Mindset. Journal of Business Venturing 25(2), 217–229 (2008)
33. Hayton, J.C., George, G., Zahra, S.A.: National Culture and Entrepreneurship: A Review of Behavioral Research. Entrepreneurship: Theory & Practice 26(4), 33–52 (2002)
34. Hofstede, G.: Culture's Consequences: comparing values, behaviors, institutions, and organizations across nations, 2nd edn. Sage Publications, Thousand Oaks (2001)
35. Hsu, S.H.C.: Industry Technological Changes, Venture Capital Incubation, & Post-IPO Firm Innovation & Performance. European Finance Association, Bergen (2009)
36. Industry Canada: Innovation Canada. Industry Canada, Ottawa (2011)
37. Iversen, J., Jørgensen, R., Malchow-Moeller, N.: Defining and Measuring Entrepreneurship. Foundations & Trends in Entrepreneurship 4(1), 1–63 (2008)
38. Jones, G.K., Davis, H.J.: National Culture and Innovation: Implications for Locating Global R&D Operations. Management International Review 40(1), 11–39 (2000)
39. Kitagawa, K.: Building and Sustaining a Culture of Innovation/Entrepreneurialism in Canada for Competitiveness and Growth (Case study 40). In: Conference Board of Canada, Ottawa (2001),
    http://www.conferenceboard.ca/Libraries/
    EDUC_PUBLIC/case40.sflb
40. Koellingera, P., Minniti, M., Schaded, C.: I Think I Can, I Think I Can: Overconfidence and Entrepreneurial Behaviour. Journal of Economic Psychology 28(4), 502–527 (2003)

41. Kreiser, P.M., Marino, L.D., Dickson, P., Weaver, K.M.: Cultural Influences on Entrepreneurial Orientation: The Impact of National Culture on Risk Taking and Proactivness in SMEs. Entrepreneurship: Theory & Practice 34(5), 959–983 (2010)
42. Lee, S.M., Peterson, S.J.: Culture, Entrepreneurial Orientation and Global Competitiveness. Journal of World Business 35(4), 401–416 (2000)
43. Lee, J.H., Venkataraman, S.: Aspirations, Market Offerings, and the Pursuit of Entrepreneurial Opportunities. Journal of Business Venturing 21(1), 107–123 (2006)
44. Licht, A.N., Siegal, J.I.: The Social Dimensions of Entrepreneurship. In: Casson, M., Yeung, B. (eds.) Oxford Handbook of Entrepreneurship. Oxford University Press, Oxford (2006), http://www.cultivaturk.com/content/SSRN
45. Lictenstein, G.A.: The Significance of Relationships in Entrepreneurship: A Case Study of the Ecology of Enterprise in Two Business Incubators (Doctoral Dissertation). University of Pennsylvania, Philadelphia (1992), http://repository.upenn.edu/dissertations/AAI9227709
46. Liñán, F., Chen, Y.W.: Development and Cross-Culture Application of a Specific Instrument to Measure Entrepreneurial Intentions. Entrepreneurship: Theory and Practice 33(3), 593–617 (2009)
47. Lumpkin, G.T., Dess, G.G.: Clarifying the Entrepreneurial Orientation Construct and Linking it to Performance. The Academy of Management Review 21(1), 135–172 (1996)
48. Maalel, I., Mbarek, M.K.B.H.: Intervention of Incubator and Its Impact on Entrepreneur's Success. Through Social Capital View International Journal of Innovation & Learning 10(1), 1–21 (2011)
49. Macaulay, J., Ledwell, P., Mitchell, D.: Innovation Nation: Building a Culture and Practice of Innovation in Canada. Ottawa: Public Policy Forum (2009), http://www.govrelations.ualberta.ca/en/FederalGovernment/~/media/University%20of%20Alberta/Administration/External%20Relations/Government%20Relations/Documents/Federal/Final_Report_Science_Day.pdf
50. MacKay, N.: Entrepreneurial Talent: How to Create a Culture of Innovation. MacKay & Associates, North Vancouver (2011), http://www.mackayandassociates.ca/wp-content/uploads/2012/01/Creating-a-culture-of-innovation.pdf
51. Manley, J.: Creating Canada's Culture of Innovation: From Cradle to Career. The Empire Club of Canada Addresses, 303–312 (2000), http://speeches.empireclub.org/59855/data
52. Martinez-Gomez, V., Baviera-Puig, A., Mas-Verdú, F.: Innovation Policy, Services and Internationalisation: The Role of Technology Centres. The Service Industries Journal 30(1), 43–54 (2010)
53. Matthews, R.B., Stowe, C.R.B., Jenkins, G.K.: Entrepreneurs – Born or Made? Academy of Entrepreneurship Proceedings 17(1), 49–56 (2011)
54. Maxwell, A., Levesque, M.: Technology Incubators: Facilitating Technology Transfer or Creating Regional Wealth? International Journal of Entrepreneurship & Innovation Management 13(2), 122–143 (2011)
55. McGee, J.E., Peterson, M., Mueller, S.L., Sequira, J.M.: Entrepreneurial Self-Efficacy: Refining the Measure. Entrepreneurship: Theory & Practice 33(4), 965–998 (2009)
56. McGrath, R., Macmillan, I., Yang, E., Tsai, W.: Does Culture Endure or Is It Malleable? Issues for Entrepreneurial Economic Development. Journal of Business Venturing 7(6), 441–458 (1992)

57. Mencin, O., Erikson, C.: Case Study: Silicon Valley's US Market Access Center: The Incubator as a Soft Landing Zone. International Journal of Entrepreneurship & Innovation Management 10(3), 233–241 (2009)
58. Mian, S.A.: Assessing Value-Added Contributions of University Technology Business Incubators to Tenant Firms. Research Policy 25(3), 325–335 (1996)
59. Mian, S.A.: University's Involvement in Technology Business Incubation: What Theory and Practice Tell Us? International Journal of Entrepreneurship & Innovation Management 13(2), 113–121 (2011)
60. Mian, S.A., Hulsink, W.: Building Knowledge Ecosystems through Science & Technology Parks. In: 26th IASP World Conference on Science and Technology Parks, Research Triangle Park, NC (2009)
61. Minniti, M.: Entrepreneurship and Network Externalities. Journal of Economic Behavior & Organization 57, 1–27 (2005)
62. Mitchell, J.R., Shepherd, D.A.: To Thine Own Self Be True: Images of Self, Images of Opportunity, and Entrepreneurial Action. Journal of Business Venturing 25(1), 138–154 (2010)
63. Morrison, A.: Entrepreneurship: What Triggers It? International Journal of Entrepreneurial Behaviour & Research 6(2), 59–71 (2000)
64. Mustar, P.: Technology Management Education: Innovation and entrepreneurship at MINES Paris Tech., a Leading French Engineering School. Academy of Management Learning & Education 8(3), 418–425 (2009)
65. National Innovation Council (NIC). Report to the People. Government of India, New Delhi (2011),
    http://www.innovationcouncil.gov.in/images/stories/reportpeo
    ple/Report_To_The_People-2011.pdf
66. Newman, K.L., Nollen, S.D.: Culture and Congruence: The Fit Between Management Practices and National Culture. Journal of International Business Studies 27(4), 753–779 (1996)
67. Niosi, J., Bas, T.G.: The Competencies of Regions: Canada's Clusters in Biotechnology. Small Business Economics 17(1-2), 31–42 (2001)
68. Ollila, S., Williams-Middleton, K.: The Venture Creation Approach: Integrating Entrepreneurial Education and Incubation at the University. International Journal of Entrepreneurship & Innovation Management 13(2), 161–178 (2011)
69. O'Neal, T., Schoen, H.: The Co-Evolution of the University of Central Florida's Technology Incubator and the Entrepreneurial Infrastructure of the University of Central Florida. International Journal of Entrepreneurship & Innovation Management 13(2), 225–242 (2011)
70. Innovation: Opportunities without Frontiers. The OECD Observer, 284, 46-48 (2011),
    http://www.oecdobserver.org/m/fullstory.php/
71. Parker, S.C.: The Economics of Self-Employment and Entrepreneurship. Cambridge University Press, Cambridge (2004)
72. Perlitz, M., Seger, F.: European Cultures and Management Styles. International Journal of Asian Management 3(1), 1–26 (2004)
73. Petrof, J.V.: Entrepreneurial Profile: A Discriminant Analysis. Journal of Small Business Management 18(4), 100–123 (1980)
74. Rice, M.P., Abetti, P.A.: A Framework for Defining Levels of Intervention by Managers of Business Incubators in New Venture Creation and Development. In: Wetzel Jr., W.E. (ed.) Frontiers in Entrepreneurship Research, pp. 102–116. Babson College, Wellesley (1993)

75. Rosenfeld, S.A.: Over Achievers: Business Clusters That Work – Prospects for Regional Development. Regional Technology Strategies, Carrboro (1995), http://rtsinc.org/publications/pdf/OverAchievers.pdf
76. Ryerson University Opens Digital Media Zone, Student Centre for Innovation and Entrepreneurship. Canada NewsWire (2010), http://www.newswire.ca/en/story/603613/ryerson-university-opens-digital-media-zone-student-centre-for-innovation-and-entrepreneurship
77. Saublens, C., Bonas, G., Husso, K., Komárek, P., Koschatzky, K., Oughton, C., Santos Pereira, T., Thomas, B., Wathen, M.: Regional Research Intensive Clusters and Science Parks. Brussels, Belgium (2007), http://ec.europa.eu/research/regions/pdf/sc_park.pdf
78. Scherer, R.F., Adams, J.S., Carley, S.S., Wiebe, F.A.: Role Model Performance Effects on Development of Entrepreneurial Career Preference. Journal of Economic Psychology 28(4), 502–527 (1989)
79. Schwartz, M.: A Control Group Study of Incubators' Impact to Promote Firm Survival (IWH Discussion Papers 11). Halle Institute for Economic Research, Halle (2010), http://ideas.repec.org/p/iwh/dispap/11-10.html
80. Schwartz, M., Hornych, C.: Cooperation Patterns of Incubator Firms and the Impact of Incubator Specialization: Empirical Evidence from Germany. Technovation 30(9-10), 485–495 (2010)
81. Schweikart, L., Doti, L.P.: American Entrepreneur. Amacom, New York (2010)
82. Shane, S.C.: Cultural Influences on National Rates of Innovation. Journal of Business Venturing 8(1), 59–73 (1993)
83. Soiutaris, V., Zerbinati, S., Al-Laham, A.: Do Entrepreneurship Programmes Raise Entrepreneurial Intention of Science and Engineering Students? The Effect of Learning, Inspiration and Resources. Journal of Business Venturing 22(4), 556–591 (2007)
84. Somsuck, N., Teekasap, S.: Tenant Screening Evaluation for Business Incubator: The Application of an AHP Methodology. In: Proceedings from Advances in Management Science and Risk Assessment. ACTA Press, Phuket (2010), http://www.actapress.com/Abstract.aspx?paperId=42118
85. St. Jean, E., Audet, J.: The Role of Mentoring in the Learning Development of the Novice Entrepreneur. International Entrepreneurship & Management Journal (2009), doi:10.1007/s113 65-009-0130-7
86. Sun, H., Ni, W., Leung, J.: Critical Success Factors for Technological Incubation: Case Study of Hong Kong Science and Technology Parks. International Journal of Management 24(2), 346–363 (2007)
87. Thomas, A.S., Mueller, S.L.: A Case for Comparative Entrepreneurship: Assessing the Relevance of Culture. Journal of International Business Studies 31(2), 287–301 (2000)
88. Uhlaner, L.M., Thurik, A.R.: Postmaterialism Influencing Total Entrepreneurial Activity Across Nations. Journal of Evolutionary Economics 17(2), 161–185 (2007)
89. Vernon-Wortzel, H., Wortzel, L.: Strategic management in a global economy. John Wiley, New York (1997)
90. Welsh, J., White, J.F.: The Entrepreneur's Manual Master Planning Guide. Prentice-Hall, Englewood Cliffs (1983)

Sustainable Communications and Innovation: Different Types of Effects from Collaborative Research Including University and Companies in the ICT-Sector

Mattias Höjer[1], Katarina Larsen[2], and Helene Wintzell[3]

[1] Centre for Sustainable Communications, Royal Institute of Technology, Stockholm, Sweden
hojer@kth.se
[2] Div. History of Science, Technology and Environment,
Royal Institute of Technology, Stockholm, Sweden
katarina.larsen@abe.kth.se
[3] Helene Wintzell AB, Stockholm, Sweden
helene@helenewintzell.se

Abstract. This paper presents experiences from the Centre for Sustainable Communications (CESC) located at KTH – The Royal Institute of Technology in Stockholm. Since 2007, the centre has carried out research in collaboration with private firms in the information and communication technology (ICT) and media sectors as well as with public sector organizations in the city of Stockholm. The aim is to share experiences from how the partners of the centre describe benefits and effects from collaborative research. Since the centre is focusing on use of ICT and media technology, rather than technology development per se, this provides an account of a wide range of effects from university-industry collaborations and new insights into the innovation processes targeting sustainability in the ICT and media sectors. This is an important perspective of sustainable and responsible innovation that is not captured in traditional innovation surveys (counting the number of new products or patents). Areas examined here include: increased knowledge and competence, new contacts and networks, publications, methods and new technology as well as changes in business operations and behaviour targeting sustainable solutions. The results also confirm firm-level business value as a driver for sustainability and provide experiences from involving users in the quest for sustainable and responsible innovation.

Keywords: added value, benefit, collaboration, effects, environment, ICT.

1   Sustainable Communications: Collaboration with Public and Private

The Centre for Sustainable Communications (CESC) was established in 2007 as one of 18 so-called Vinnova Centres of Excellence in Sweden. Centres within the Vinnova Excellence Centre programme receive core funding from the Swedish Governmental Agency for Innovation Systems (Vinnova) complemented with contributions from the Universities and a group of partners. The programme aim is "… to create

M.D. Hercheui et al. (Eds.): HCC10 2012, IFIP AICT 386, pp. 170–182, 2012.

and develop vigorous academic research milieus in which industrial and/or public partners actively participate in order to derive long-term benefits for society. The programme is also a link in the governmental effort to develop university-industry interaction." [14]. The objective of the Vinnova Excellence Centre programme is to promote sustainable growth in Sweden. This is expected to happen through concentrating experts from different fields in interdisciplinary research centres, and developing products, processes and services [14].

It can be noted that the "long-term benefit for the society" that is mentioned as the aim of the programme is translated into a "development of products, processes and services" in the formulation of the objective. This slight change of words is interesting for centres working towards societal benefits, but not necessarily directly linked to products, processes and services, like CESC. Can societal benefits always be measured in products, processes and services? Is this always what industrial partners in university-industry partnerships demand?

This leads to a bigger question about the usefulness of university-based research, the third mission of universities and, more specifically, research and innovation processes that lead to other types of results than development of new technology or products that are close to market.

The excellence centres, such as CESC, that have been established have to find forms of interaction that will enable collaborative projects to address some of these major challenges ahead and create added value for both industry and academia. The user perspective is important in this work in order to face the challenges of new needs defined by different types of user groups, as well as for private actors' needs, so as to catalyse new innovation processes and create new products.

The areas of activity for CESC include information and communication technology (ICT), media and sustainable development where focus of the areas of activity is environmental issues linked to ICT and media, but also social effects. The research is carried out in collaboration between researchers based at the Royal Institute of Technology (KTH), private firms and regional authorities. This includes collaborative research with people from larger telecommunication firms (such as Ericsson and TeliaSonera), from the City of Stockholm and Stockholm county, as well as major organizations from the media sector (such as Bonnier, Stampen, SVT – Swedish public service TV, and the Swedish media publishers association).

Taking the objective of development of products, processes and services into consideration, it is likely that many partners join Vinnova Excellence centres with an ambition of getting rather direct benefits for business. With a centre like CESC focusing on environmental research, the link may not be as direct and, therefore, the partners might have other reasons for joining. Instead, they may be in the collaborative research venture in order to increase the understanding of ICT's potential environmental impacts and to increase knowledge about how it can be analysed. In that case, the focus is to get a better understanding of environmental impacts of ICT – rather than focusing on development of new short-term businesses and technology. This would go hand in hand with the fact that innovation processes aiming for more sustainable solutions naturally are informed by an increased understanding of environmental impacts and how these can be analysed to capture barriers for introducing more sustainable solutions as well as understanding behavioural change when new technology solutions are introduced. With this background, the management of CESC decided to examine how the partners looked upon benefits of being a part of CESC, and started an initiative in 2011 to analyse this.

The aim of this paper is to investigate what benefits partners see in industry-society-university collaborations on environmental research, and how this relates to long-term benefits for society. The case used here is the VinnEx Centre for Sustainable Communications, CESC. We are using the CESC internal study on partner benefit from 2011 as our main empirical material.

2   The Investigation of Effects from Collaboration with CESC

In this paper we report on an examination of how the research partners engaged in collaborative research in CESC have expressed different dimensions of "usefulness" or "effects" from the joint research activities. The immediate outcomes of CESC may not be products, processes or services. This enables an examination of other dimensions of expected and perceived benefits from collaborative research.

There may be many reasons for research partners to collaborate with universities – since there are many different domains of activity that they can refer to their own organization or their members. In order to find these reasons, CESC performed an interview study during 2011 with researchers in academia, and their collaborators in the private sector, about their views on different types of "usefulness" stemming from the collaborative projects at CESC.

One reason for raising these issues at CESC is the variety in the forms of collaboration that the centre has with different types of project partners including collaboration with larger companies in the traditional ICT industry, service companies (in media technology) and public sector organizations at the municipal and county level with an interest in developing new ICT solutions targeting more sustainable communication.

Partners are a crucial and indispensable part of any excellence centre, and there is an outspoken demand on excellence centres to create added-value and to be useful. The interview study at CESC in 2011 had several goals. They were to:

- Show what use and which results were the outcome of the collaboration.
- Describe how the collaboration is operating and suggest improvements.
- Describe partners' preferences on future activities.

The investigation was mainly undertaken through interviewing CESC participants, and using literature to analyse and interpret the interviews. The interview guide was developed during the period of interviews, and thus the responses are not directly comparable. It was an explicit aim of the study to get as much information from each interview as possible, and to do so by using experiences from previous interviews to improve the questionnaire. Moreover, in parallel with the interviews, some literature was used mainly as a help to navigate and structure the responses. When summarizing the results, a Canadian study [12] was important for structuring the results. This study, and other studies, were used when developing the interview guide, in order to find ways of identifying the partner benefits. Forty-four people were interviewed (see table 1), including representatives from virtually all partners. Most of the interviews were group interviews, so that several people from the same partner were interviewed at the same time. One of the authors of this paper (Wintzell) made all the interviews. She had deep knowledge regarding CESC and its partners, since she had been director of the centre 2008-2009 and is currently a member of the CESC board of managers. She continuously discussed the interviews with the other two authors of this paper. One of those authors (Höjer) is the current director of CESC, and the other is a researcher on innovation and environment.

Thus, the interview study should not be seen as an objective attempt to define the pros and cons of the partnership, but rather as a way of searching for reasons for the partners to take part in CESC. Each of them pays about 25,000 Euro per year and allocates 0.5-3 full-time employees to CESC activities. Since CESC does not produce so many direct products, processes and services, the rationale for the partnership must be another.

Table 1. Number of interviewees at each partner

Partner	Number of interviewees
Bonnier	4
Ericsson	7
Community hub Foundation	2
Institute for Futures studies	1
Stockholm County Council	2
Stampen	4
City of Stockholm	2
SVT	3
TeliaSonera	3
Swedish Media Publishers Association	3
KTH Holding	1
KTH heads of units	7
KTH project leaders	5
Sum	44

3   What Is Added Value and Usefulness?

A set of categories of "added value" was developed as a framework for analysis based on a review of literature on university-industry collaboration [4], an analysis of effects from collaborative research and channels for knowledge transfers [3] and a study about measuring societal impacts from participatory sustainability research [12]. The study about channels of knowledge transfer was carried out in three areas of technology innovation and was designed to reveal the variety and broad scope of areas of interaction between university-based researchers and industry in the United Kingdom (UK). The wide range of activities originating from a great variety of research partners is also relevant to take into consideration when analysing the added value that partners see from participating in projects hosted by CESC.

In summary, there are two take-home messages from the study on channels for knowledge transfer. Firstly, that the private sector collaborates with academia to get access to networks (that they would not have access to otherwise) and skills relating to methods and problem formulations in an academic setting. Secondly, that the types of interaction and, therefore, the perceived benefit from collaboration is highly specific to the type of company (and their customers, need for skills, and knowledge).

Another more recent initiative in UK is the "Pathways to impact" launched by the Research Councils of UK (RCUK) which describes different domains of effects from research carried out at universities and technical colleges. One of these domains is "interaction with companies" and another domain describes effects in terms of shaping public policy and services [11] for example, benefits of research contributing to UK policies on how to change peoples' travelling behaviour. Statements regarding this type of broader description of usefulness of research is requested from researchers' activities in governmentally funded projects and although it may be difficult to foresee what the impact is (or may be) from planned research collaboration, it raises questions about knowledge transfer and perceived usefulness by private and public sector from collaborative projects with researchers based at universities. This example from the UK can, with a broader view of different categories of impacts, be important as a step towards incorporating different types of users' views of benefits from engaging in collaborative research. This issue of capturing impacts in evaluation of social sciences has received renewed attention [13] and can benefit from incorporating the collaborative effects and benefits as they are articulated by different user groups engaging in collaborative research.

The discussion about effects of collaborative research also raises questions about the value of including users of services or products early in the innovation process. Studies of innovation and invention networks describe this in terms of "user-innovation" or "open innovation" [2]. These concepts can also be used to describe user-interaction in the area of climate change policy [8] and roles of users in the innovation process [1], [9]. Other methods for engaging users in the innovation process are developed in the field of environmental futures studies, where citizens can have a say in describing what new services and ICT solutions they consider to be important to solve the environmental challenges of tomorrow for transport and mobility [10]. Actively incorporating experiences from ICT companies themselves is another way of integrating the user perspective on how private firms are perceiving environmental challenges and what solutions they can see on the horizon from a business point of view [6], [7] in the area of ICT and new media for sustainable solutions in a future society.

The expectations of ICT as a "key enabling technology" that can solve many problems in future society is not new. From a Swedish and European perspective there is however a renewed attention to this issue. This can be seen in the reply by the Swedish Agency for Innovation System (Vinnova) to the European Union's Green paper about European research and innovation[1] where research is expected to respond to and solve several of the Europe's futures challenges. Among these Grand Societal Challenges are questions related to finding solutions to environmental problems by the increased use of ICT and other key enabling technologies to face challenges by industry [15]. These challenges are described in terms of finding energy efficient solutions, sustainable cities, and using the potential in the interaction achieved by partnerships between actors to enhance competitiveness.

One reason for studying innovation systems, from an environmental policy perspective, is to identify system weaknesses that require different kinds of policy interventions to balance the inertia for change and other barriers for new markets to evolve [5]. Some areas of policy interventions (that seek to reduce the system weaknesses) that are described aim to improve the framework conditions for development of new knowledge, create arenas for entrepreneurial experimentation, resources and incentives for actors in the innovation system develop new more environmentally efficient technology. This can, in turn, be an important part of the puzzle to facilitate the emergence of new markets for environmentally compatible technology solutions and to enhance the legitimacy for new sustainability-oriented innovations. For the innovation system as a whole, the knowledge that is generated in interaction between actors in certain domains of technology, in centres such as the CESC, can serve as a way to cater for the transfer of knowledge between actors in the system (between users, producers, universities, and firms etc.). In the case of the CESC, an operational and practical task is to explore the potential for interdisciplinary teams to understand processes of behavioural change in both citizens and firms (through ethnography, sociology, and business management), and how to integrate that knowledge with tools for environmental management in companies (Life Cycle Assessment, environmental strategies) with technical skills relating to ICT and new use of media technology in sustainable communication.

So in conclusion to the policy perspective on collaboration, this brief review indicates that research partnerships and collaborative projects in ICT carry expectations to solve some major challenges in industry and societal challenges relating to seeking more environmentally compatible ways of living, travelling and sustainable communication. The next question is how we can describe the dimensions of different types of benefit or "usefulness" that the different partners and consortiums see from examples of collaboration carried out by CESC?

The categories used for analysis of interaction benefitted from a framework developed in a study about measuring societal impacts from participatory sustainability research [12]. The categories are further described in the following section outlining the scope of the investigation carried out by CESC about different types of effects from collaborative research including university and companies in the ICT sector.

The literature study resulted in the conclusion that partner benefit can be classified into six categories:

---

[1] European Commission, From Challenges to Opportunities: Towards a Common Strategic Framework for EU Research and Innovation funding, Green Paper, COM(2011) 48.

1. Increased knowledge and competence.
2. New contacts and network.
3. Increased credibility.
4. New products in the form of publications, methods and technology.
5. Processual and behavioural changes towards more sustainability.
6. Business value/Operational value.

These were not formulated as six distinctive categories when the interviews started, but came out of a combination of the development of the interviews and the literature.

4   Results

When partners describe in what ways the CESC collaboration has been of use to them, the aspect given most importance is the increased knowledge and competence within the area of sustainability and ICT that they have gained. The second most important outcome that partners consider is the credibility of the value added to their internal sustainability work when meeting clients, chief executive officers and co-workers, and also the extended network between partners, KTH and the companies, and within KTH internally. Scientific articles that result from the collaborative research are considered important mainly by the industrial CESC partners. Processual and behavioural/routine changes are harder to link to the partnership, while the internal sustainability work is considered as strengthened. It is seen as being too early to evaluate business value, but the partners all agree that they see a lot of potential for this in the future. Two corporate partners note that they have made cost savings due to decreased travelling partly as a consequence of focusing more on mediated meetings and highlighting the environmental effects of travel. Another aspect mentioned by partners is that research is more efficient when done in collaboration rather than on their own. Partners also maintain that the primary outcome of the collaboration is not seen necessarily as new products per se, but rather learning new methods, technology and getting new knowledge, which then can lead to learning loops within the partners' internal organization. Below some of the different categories mentioned above are described more in-depth.

4.1   Increased Knowledge and Competence

Increased knowledge and competence is a key result area emphasised by the partners when discussing the outcome of the CESC partnership. Some of the outcomes brought up and estimated by the partners are, for instance, learning a new way of doing things, working long-term and having the possibility to become immersed in a topic or research area and learn the process of publishing articles. Other important aspects related to increased knowledge are getting wider and deeper approaches to the concept of sustainability that also includes areas as behaviour and other social aspects. Getting more knowledge concerning environmental issues with related quantifiable measures is yet another important factor raised by the partners. It is seen as something positive to gain knowledge about how large the environmental impacts of their specific activities and specific products are.

One company explained the value of the broad range of competence of the centre and the analytic approach applied in the collaboration with the KTH-based centre CESC:

"The way of thinking at KTH/CESC is different – another time perspective. There is an analytical capacity and you get time to think and re-consider different aspects and not just accept a number. Our data is more credible when including different aspects (of the problem). It is also good that the project teams are not just including engineers – but also sociologists, psychologists, behavioural scientists – which is competence that we do not have at the company."

4.2   New Contacts and Networks

Partners find being part of the CESC network as a great value. To be able to exchange ideas and experiences, and have a platform for discussing complicated issues with people that have a variety of backgrounds, knowledge, experiences and motives, is treasured. The CESC partnership has also led to many new contacts between the different corporate partners. New contacts have also been established between researchers and companies and internally within KTH. The new networks have also resulted in several new collaborations that have been set up around common issues. For example, companies express that they have gained "a natural collaboration with other companies" and, from the university perspective, the collaboration with firms also provides new research questions that would not have been formulated otherwise.

One company expressed a value from new contacts and networks in terms of exchange of experiences and sharing knowledge:

"There is a great value in being able to network with collaboration partners, interesting partners, some of which are competitors."

A public sector partner involved in traffic and infrastructure plans in the Stockholm region explained:

"The collaboration creates discussion and a dialogue that helps us to find arguments or new questions that will be interesting to respond to in the future".

4.3   Increased Credibility

Collaborating with CESC gives the partners (both corporate and internal to KTH) increased credibility, an increased legitimacy within the area of sustainable ICT, a better position on the market and good public relations. Quality assured data gives an increased credibility and a better image to the companies' sustainability work both internally towards management and co-workers, and externally towards clients and suppliers. One concrete example of how this works is quantified environmental assessments and Life Cycle Assessments. When working with technological issues, it is a major credibility factor to be involved in collaboration with KTH. Credible research results give the corporate partners a position on the market. CESC has also helped to position KTH in the areas of ICT and sustainability. To KTH partners, and CESC itself, the collaboration with established and well-known corporate partners gives increased status and legitimacy. The partnership with CESC is often mentioned in annual reports and in relation to lectures, something that has great public relation's value. CESC's partners express that it is important to review their own organization (environmental impact, etc.) if they want to maintain their credibility.

Credibility is also mentioned in terms of CESC becoming a recognized competence centre internationally through collaboration with some leading institutions. According to a KTH researcher:

"CESC now has a position as one of the world's most interesting centres in the area ...as shown by collaboration with Waterloo in Canada and MediaLab at MIT".

4.4   New Products in the Form of Publications, Methods and Technology

Several scientific articles, reports and dissertations have been produced as a result of the collaboration between CESC and the partners. The corporate partners have participated in the projects in all phases of the projects. The publications (i.e. reports, articles, and so on) are emphasized time and again in the interviews as one of the most important results of the collaboration. Another significant result is the development of a detailed Life Cycle Assessment, different methods for studying city climate goals, and how to measure quantitatively a climate neutral city.

Various partners point out that the aim of their CESC partnership lies beyond mere technological development. Instead they request a broader scope and an opportunity to grasp and understand the complex processes of ICT, media and sustainability and how this can be linked to behavioural changes, both ongoing and coming. Some partners state that it is too soon to show results yet, but they are looking forward to seeing what the results will be. One type of activity, also mentioned by partners is seminars arranged by CESC.

4.5   Processual and Behavioural Changes towards More Sustainability

It is quite difficult for partners to assess the extension of impact on internal processes (such as policies and routines) towards increased sustainability that is the outcome of the CESC collaboration, and to know what would have been gradual changes in a more sustainable direction anyway. It is, however, likely that the partnership has speeded up the process in the internal organization of some partners. KTH has certainly been influenced, particularly the division of environmental strategies research (fms). The central organization of KTH has also created several positions and added organizations in relation to increased sustainability.

Many project members state that they have experienced a personal growth as part of the collaboration, and it has been stressed that the work is meritorious on an individual level. The potential of cross-recruitment, i.e. recruiting of employees between partner organizations, is also something mentioned in the evaluation as well as implementation of ICT solutions in pilot projects.

"The collaboration with CESC has enabled us to start our digital conference system. There is a room and a pilot-project is launched. This has facilitated daily meetings between cities replacing daily travels within Sweden."

Other partners of CESC emphasize changing procurement of services where a travel agency was replaced to obtain feedback about environmental impact from travels and changes in travel patterns (favouring train options when possible) as a result of the travel policy.

4.6   Business Value/Operational Value

Several corporate partners think that there is potential business value in the collaboration with CESC because the clients are attracted by the fact that there is quantitative published data. Two corporate partners have noticed savings on travel, something that is related to impacts on company policy by the CESC collaboration.

However, some corporate partners say it is too soon to present commercial results, a fact referenced to short-term collaboration, but long-time corporate partners also state that it is too soon to see any economic results. The private sector partners also express the differences between their (daily) activities and the nature of the research process in relation to the expectations about "applicability" of research reports directly to their business activity, concluding that:

"The journey is more rewarding than the result, and maybe that is the way it has to be".

Other private sector partners of CESC describe that the collaboration with CESC in projects has also opened up other types of networks as a result of interest from other firms relating to collaborative research with CESC.

5   Conclusions

Some conclusions can be drawn from the experiences of the CESC at KTH in Stockholm. These conclusions both relate to different types of benefits that can be discerned from collaborative projects involving CESC and also from some practical lessons from collaborative projects between university-based researchers, firms and partners from public sector.

Some practical lessons from the work at CESC and reviewing effects from collaborative projects are:

- It takes time to develop collaborative projects, so any evaluation of results or expected outcomes needs to take that into consideration.
- Involving people with decision power in the organization is of key importance. Making changes in organizations is not done easily – even if it is motivated by sustainability objectives.

- The importance of tracking different dimensions of what are the expected benefits of collaboration rather than either a general "usefulness" or alternatively reliance on traditional indicators (patents, spin-offs) that may not capture the different domains of benefits that comes out from collaborative projects that involves such a diverse set of public-private actors.

Experiences from CESC about the benefits from the viewpoint of the private sector partners reveal a number of different effects that the collaborative projects generated:

- The collaboration with CESC also catalysed contacts with other firms.
- Access to a broad range of knowledge domains relevant to understand travel behaviour.
- An analytical 'mind set' about environmental impact of the firm.
- New routines for the firm's own travel plans to reduce environmental impact

These points indicate some benefits at the firm-level arising from collaborative projects, as described by the companies themselves, in terms of processes of change within the firm that are necessary for credibility towards customers and markets. In a wider policy context these results reflect some aspects of business value in sustainability as well as respond to grand societal challenges described by the European Union and at national level. This wider policy discussion about the potential of key enabling technologies, such as ICT, emphasizes the importance of involving users in the quest for sustainable and environmentally responsible innovation. The examples and experiences shown here from CESC offer a small step towards operationalizing these grand words into practices that can provide some guidance on how to describe, in a meaningful way, different types of effects from collaborative projects about environmental sustainability.

The broad range of different types of effects raised by the private CESC partners relates to the theme of partner benefit that is defined in the general goals for CESC; to be a resource when it comes to ICT and sustainability; that CESC activities lead to a continuous growth in importance when it comes to positive sustainability effects; and that CESC partners find the activities within CESC beneficial for long-term business. Other goals stated by CESC relate to societal impact and can be mirrored in the responses regarding, for example, visibility of CESC nationally and internationally (visible through collaboration with leading institutions). The use of results from CESC leads to sustainable practices in society. Examples of the latter are found both by responses by public sector partners (identifying new questions in travel and infrastructure planning) and private firms (procedural changes and individual travel choices) with benefits for sustainable communications.

There are some broader lessons from this case that can be valuable for other centres engaged in collaborative research and development that targets sustainable communications or planning when setting up collaborative projects aiming for integrating environmental sustainability with innovation. To catalyse some of the benefits from new networks (with universities, but also with firms and public sector partners) that we have discussed here, the centres can benefit from introducing regular seminar activities in addition to specific project collaboration in teams. This creates forums for interaction that facilitate spontaneous interaction and sharing the "odd idea" that may be an inspiration to a joint initiative in the future. Public-private collaboration involving university-based Centres of Excellence is targeting collaborative projects, but is also ultimately about meetings between people so that seminars can be an important arena for exploring areas of shared interest.

Another lesson is to encourage collaboration partners to express their expectations in greater detail rather than in general terms about "being useful" to the company. This will help the centre to identify and define process values in partner organizations and see where the centre can play a role – whether it is to reduce environmental impact, create pilots for ICT solutions; understand processes of behavioural change for travels; and how to make these aspects visible to the organization as a whole.

References

1. Bienkowska, D., Larsen, K., Sörlin, S.: Public-private innovation: Mediating roles and ICT niches of industrial research institutes. Innovation: Management Policy and Practice 12, 206–216 (2010)
2. Chesbrough, H.: Open Innovation: A New Paradigm for Understanding Industrial Innovation. In: Chesbrough, H., Vanhaverbeke, W., West, J. (eds.) Open Innovation: Researching a New Paradigm, pp. 1–12. Oxford University Press, Oxford (2006)
3. Faulkner, W., Senker, J.: Making sense of diversity: public-private sector research linkage in three technologies. Research Policy 23, 673–695 (1994)
4. Jacobsson, S.: Universities and industrial transformation: an interpretative and selective literature study with special emphasis on Sweden. Science and Public Policy 29(5), 345–365 (2002)
5. Jacobsson, S., Bergek, A.: Innovation system analysis and sustainability transitions. Environmental Innovation and Societal Transitions 1, 41–57 (2011)
6. Kramers, A., Gustafsson, G.M.: How telecom could save the planet. Ericsson Business Review 1, 17–21 (2009)
7. Larsen, K.: Science and technology parks and the integration of environmental policy. Innovation, Management, Policy and Practice 6(2), 294–305 (2004)
8. Larsen, K., Gunnarsson-Östling, U., Westholm, E.: Environmental scenarios and local-global level of community engagement – environmental justice, jams, institutions and innovation. Futures 43(4), 413–423 (2011)
9. Larsen, K., Gunnarsson-Östling, U.: Climate change scenarios and citizen-participation: Mitigation and adaptation perspectives in constructing sustainable futures, Habitat International. Special Issue on Climate Change and Human Settlements 33(3), 260–266 (2009)
10. Larsen, K., Höjer, M.: Technological innovation and transformation perspectives in environmental futures studies for transport and mobility. International Journal of Foresight and Innovation Policy (IJFIP) 3(1), 95–115 (2004)
11. RCUK Research Councils UK, Pathways to impacts (2011),
   http://www.rcuk.ac.uk/kei/impacts/Pages/home.aspx

12. Robinson, J.: Report from project: Measuring societal impacts from participatory sustainability research. Social Sciences and Humanities Research Council of Canada (2008)
13. SSHRC: What have we learned about 'capturing impacts' in Social Sciences and Humanities? Report by the Social Sciences and Humanities Research Council (2010)
14. Vinnova: Guidelines for the Second evaluation of VINN Excellence Centres, Stockholm (2011)
15. Vinnova: Vinnova position paper on the common strategic framework, Stockholm, May 5 (2011)

Is the Post-Turing ICT Sustainable?

Norberto Patrignani[1] and Iordanis Kavathatzopoulos[2]

[1] Politecnico of Torino, Italy and Uppsala University, Sweden
norberto.patrignani@polito.it
[2] Uppsala University, Sweden
iordanis@it.uu.se

Abstract. In this paper we introduce a definition of post-Turing ICT with an initial analysis of its sustainability. At the beginning of the history of computing the attention was concentrated on the single machine: a device able to read and write a memory and able to execute different actions depending on the internal state. It was only in the 1960's that the fifth function (after input, memory, processing and output) was introduced: the network, the capability of this single computational node to be connected and exchange data with similar machines. In the last fifty years the network has grown at an incredible speed, introducing us into the post-Turing ICT era: billions of electronic devices interconnected. ICT has now a significant environmental impact along all its lifetime phases: manufacturing (based on scarce minerals), application (based on growing power consumption) and e-waste management (with open cycles difficult to close). In this paper, we introduce relevant topics to understand whether the current ICT production and consumption paradigms are sustainable, and the social consequences and implications of such a problem for stakeholders.

Keywords: post-Turing, sustainability, material intensity, cloud computing, open hardware, smart software applications, e-waste management, stakeholders' network, social issues.

1 Introduction

When Alan Turing introduced the concept of a universal machine in 1937 in his historical article on "computable numbers," probably he never imagined the impact that such a machine would have had to our society. Indeed at those times the attention was concentrated on just one computational node: a machine able to read and write into a memory and to execute different actions depending on the symbols read and on the internal state [22].

In modern world we would say that the Turing Machine was able to perform the four basic functions of a computer: input, memory, processing and output. The fifth function, the capability to communicate with other computational nodes (networking) was introduced in 1969, with the "ancestor" of Internet, ARPANET, a vision of a global network: "... *a network of such computers, connected to one another by wideband communication lines*" [13].

M.D. Hercheui et al. (Eds.): HCC10 2012, IFIP AICT 386, pp. 183–191, 2012.
© IFIP International Federation for Information Processing 2012

This was the beginning of what we call the post-Turing ICT (Information and Communication Technology) era. It is based on a network of interconnected nodes, where the convergence of social networks (people interconnected, Web 2.0) and semantic web (knowledge interconnected, Web 3.0) will introduce humanity into a radically new ICT environment.

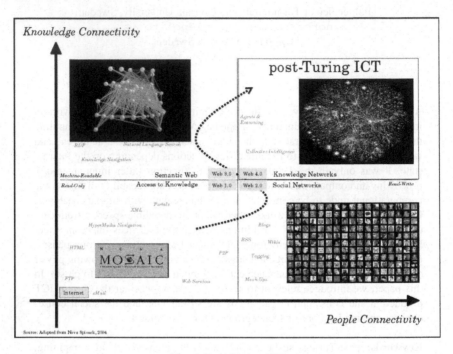

Fig. 1. Post-Turing ICT

Open and collaborative networks will take advantage of the huge amount of machine-readable knowledge, the linked open data. The last update of the Linked Open Data Project contains more than three billions of RDF (Resource Description Format) triples (subject, predicate and object) available on the Web [25].

In this new scenario it is no more the original computational node the core of our attention, but the network effect triggered by the immense power that social networks will have when they will access the global semantic web. It will empower humanity for facing many of the social and environmental challenges ahead of us: a collective intelligence using many knowledge networks. For the first time in our history, we will be able to access tools and knowledge that will enable us to face scientific challenges and to provide services like: e-accessibility for all, socio-cultural-geographical inclusion, e-ageing.

On the other side, the post-Turing ICT poses to us new questions related to its environmental, personal and social sustainability.

2   Environmental and Social Issues of Post-Turing ICT

In the last forty years we have witnessed the explosion of the global network: on January 2012 we had more than 888 Million of hosts, the entries in the DNS, the Domain Name System that enable us to use symbolic names on the Internet and the Web [7]. In 2011, the Internet traffic reached more than 500 Exabytes (10^{18} bytes) and the forecast is that it will reach 1 Zetta-byte (10^{21} bytes) per year in 2015 [4].

Even more impressive is that the number of Internet users reached 2.26 Billion on December 2011 with more than one billion concentrated in Asia [6]. Also, in 2011, the number of networked devices has equalled the world population (7 Billion) and it is estimated to reach more that 14 Billion in 2015 [4].

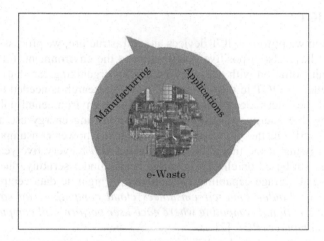

Fig. 2. The ICT life cycle

These billions of networked devices pose enormous questions along their life cycle: where does the material needed for their manufacturing come from? How will we produce the power needed to feed them when in use? How will the growing mountain of electronic waste (e-waste) be managed? How can we design usable and reliable ICTs? In what way should we use ICTs to sustain our interests as human beings?

2.1   Manufacturing ICT

The industrial process for producing microprocessors and chips has one of the highest "material intensities" in the industry [21] and also has an impact on the health of workers [17]. On the other side the dynamic of the so called "Moore's law" is exponential: every eighteen months the chips are more powerful [14] but at the same time they consume a growing quantity of "rare earths" [19]. Nowadays this is starting also to have serious social and political consequences. One example is the "coltan" used for producing many of the electronic devices, from laptops to smart-phones and tablets. Its name comes from the combination of names of two minerals: Columbite and

Tantalite. From them are extracted two elements: Columbium (now called Niobium, Nb) and Tantalum (Ta), fundamental for producing capacitors in the electronic industry. But these special minerals are coming from countries like Congo, where the mining activity is performed in illegal conditions for workers and have also a decisive role in the military conflicts in the area [24].

We need to start an ethical reflection about the sustainability of pursuing this direction, probably it is time to slow-down the speed of electronic market cycles and to re-state the well-known Soesterberg principle about sustainability: "*Each new generation of technical improvements in electronic products should include parallel and proportional improvements in environmental, health and safety, as well as social justice attributes*" [20].

2.2   Using ICT

Of course, when we power on ICT devices and infrastructure, we process information, and this could have also a positive contribution to the environment, for example by reducing the air pollution with tele-working and by organizing car-sharing. Probably we need to better use ICT in this direction: "Further research is needed to understand how ICTs and the Internet can contribute to reaching environmental policy goals by fostering renewable energy, reducing transport, optimising energy use and reducing material use" [15]. On the other side, we see that the power consumption of these machines is growing at the incredible rate of about 100% every five years [11]. The new ICT paradigm based on cloud computing is also under scrutiny, due to the computing power and storage capability concentrated in gigantic data centres located in remote locations: "*under some circumstances cloud computing can consume more energy than conventional computing where each user performs all computing on their own personal computer (PC)*" [2].

In conclusion, we realize that ICT requires more and more energy and many researches now estimate that its contribution to greenhouse gases (such as CO_2) is close to that of airlines.

2.3   Managing e-Waste

It is estimated that, in 2020, Europe will produce more than 12 million tons of e-waste and that the mountain of this electronic waste is growing at 4% per year [8]. Only a small percentage of these devices are recycled in some way and if we have a look at its destinations we will see many poor countries like: Haiti, Kenya, and Nigeria [21]. We now recognize also the importance of introducing new design principles like design-for-recycle and minimizing the power consumption of ICT. Also a promising sign is the new field of "open hardware", where thousands of experts exchange ideas and innovative proposals for improving hardware.

2.4   Social Issues of Post-Turing ICT

The post-Turing ICT scenario poses also new questions about social issues, as discussed in the following paragraphs.

Accessibility and Digital Divide. In the post-Turing ICT scenario, having the network accessibility, the economic conditions and the digital competence for being on-line is becoming more and more a "new human right": Finland, for example, has become the first country in the world to make broadband a legal right for every citizen; since July 2010 every Finnish will have the right to access to a 1Mbps broadband connection. Finland has vowed to connect everyone to a 100Mbps connection by 2015 [3]. So the "digital divide" will risk excluding more seriously those who are still disconnected.

Network Neutrality. The connectivity providers (mainly telecommunication companies) are questioning the business model based on "network neutrality," which is that the Internet works end-to-end and the network is acting as a "pipeline" that is "neutral" in that it does not open the data-packets. This "network neutrality" principle that is at the base of the Internet is also the great enabler of innovations: many start-ups and new companies were able to experiment new services because of this characteristic of the network. But the telcos are willing to introduce new business models where the network will be no more neutral, and the data-packets will not be treated at the same level.

This will risk introducing a kind of first-class and second-class services based on the price you are willing to pay. This could also mine the great opportunity of the post-Turing scenario, since small and innovative companies will have to leave network bandwidth to big companies.

Knowledge as a Commons. The new currency in the post-Turing era will be information (and knowledge). For this reason around knowledge is open a hot debate regarding its openness as "*commons*" or if it should be regarded as any other good subject to restrictions of use and distribution.

This debate is very open now but the main researches around innovation are now demonstrating that intellectual property legislations, born centuries ago, are no more fitting with the new knowledge-based society [12]. Even the 2009 Nobel Prize in Economic Sciences, Elinor Ostrom, underlined the growing importance of understanding knowledge as a shared social-ecological system [16].

The application of this framework is now moving from free and open source software, to open hardware and to scientific knowledge.

Internet Censorship and Control. The knowledge networks of the post-Turing era are, by definition, free and open. At the same time this new scenario, where information and knowledge are becoming strong liberation tools in many cultures, there are a growing number of governments around the world that are trying to stop this "freedom wave."

For example the 2011 Report from Reporters Without Borders, highlighted the fact that "*the Internet and social networks have been conclusively established as tools for protest, campaigning and circulating information, and as vehicles for freedom*" but that at the same time "*repressive regimes responded with tougher measures to what they regarded as unacceptable attempts to 'destabilize' their authority"* [18]. They can also use the information accessible on the Internet to persecute dissidents.

Indeed this new scenario is outside any previous communication schema: it is without a "single point of control" and it is based on a global collaboration between networks based on open standards. It is difficult to control, even if few new titans are emerging and collecting the vast amount of search engines traffic and data about everything, included ourselves [23]. Strong players have always more resources to spread certain information in sophisticated ways in order to manipulate people they target.

Remote Working. The impact of computers into the workplace have been investigated since the 1960's but now, for understanding what does it mean to work in global knowledge networks, we need a leap into a new scenario. In particular for knowledge workers, working in a "virtual workplace for a virtual enterprise" is becoming a daily experience.

The XXI century's enterprise is (symmetrically) becoming, a "workplace without workers." We have more and more knowledge workers hired "on demand" by global job brokers: brains stay in their (poor) countries, but minds cross the oceans. As a consequence, the "social" context of the traditional workers is completely disappearing.

Now we have global job broker agencies like: teamlease.com from India that is providing well-educated workers all over the world; odesk.com that provides all kind of contractors; getacoder.com that helps in finding freelance programmers; and, elance.com that "helps businesses hire and manage in the cloud." Young programmers hired on-demand and with a good knowledge of English can make up to $300 per month [10], [5]. These deep social issues in this post-Turing era restate very old questions: are we going towards a utopian participation of (knowledge) workers in the new enterprises or are we going towards a dystopian new kind of cyber-slavery?

Privacy. Probably privacy is the oldest social and ethical issue related to computing. What is new in our global knowledge networks scenario? From one side the inclusion of our physical body into the network via RFID tags is turning our bodies into nodes at the edge of the network. From the other side we have the gigantic amount of collected data (so called Big Data) that will enable very few powerful organizations to analyse and extract new information through special data mining technologies.

They will be able also to find "*non-obvious relationships*" (also known as the "mosaic" effect) by collecting information about us from different sources. A good example of this advanced use of data mining and Big Data is the "Narwhal Project," a project that could change the results of the 2012 U.S. President elections [9].

Cloud Computing. The vast amount of computing and storage resources available in big data centres, convinced large corporations to start making them available to customers. They can provide on-demand and in a flexible way: software as a service (SaaS), where users can just use sophisticated software applications by paying a fee for each user; platform as a service (PaaS), where users can have access to large processing power and development environments for testing their applications; and infrastructure as a service (IaaS), where users can buy storage and processing capability readily available in the cloud provider's data centre.

This big shift in computing paradigms will enable decision makers to move ICT from capex (capital expenditure, money spent to acquire physical assets, machinery) to opex (operating expense, ongoing cost for running a system). At the same time, this development is opening a long list of issues: strong authentication will become a requirement, using a resource will be completely separated from ownership, cloud brokers will be new intermediaries that complicate the picture, we will have a kind of *de-perimeterization* (disappearing of boundaries between systems and organizations), it will be possible to clone data at a negligible cost, cloud traceability will be necessary in case of disasters, the risk of monopoly and lock-in will increase, and the actual data location must be disclosed for some legal compliance requirements.

Also, information could be downloaded not (necessarily) only by the up-loader, creating an issue of intellectual property: sensitive personal and corporate information risk to be out of the control of the owners.

Internet Governance. The global infrastructure is open and without a center, nevertheless there are few "core" systems that have become very critical for the entire infrastructure, such as the Domain Name System.

The very critical collection of systems and applications that allow the use of symbolic names over the Internet and the Web has to be unique by definition. This uniqueness introduces one of the few "central" resources of the network: the need for an authority that will release unique names and will take care of the management of this gigantic "table."

This authority is now the famous ICANN (Internet Corporation for Assigned Names and Numbers), based in the U.S. This authority is one of the many controversies that have been discussed for several years in the Internet Governance Forum, the last of which was in Nairobi in 2011.

In these yearly forums, several global issues related to the global Internet governance are addressed: security, accessibility, critical infrastructures, and many others. The post-Turing ICT scenario poses huge questions to international bodies like the UN and the ITU (International Telecommunication Union) but it is difficult to find global agreements related to a commons like the Internet.

Information Overload. Once we are globally interconnected and *"always on,"* we recognize also that our minds have a limited bandwidth and have limits in "absorbing" messages. We need time for thinking and questioning, we cannot simply stay always online and receiving millions of inputs. Somewhere we need to stop those inputs and have a little of silence. We need this for avoiding "information overload" and also for building our autonomy, our interpreting codes, and our histories. Otherwise the risk is that we will be totally manipulated. Slowing down the pace of incoming messages will become a strategic resource in a post-Turing scenario.

A New World. A post-Turing scenario implies the creation of a new social world. Its novelty and its difference are of course important aspects but the way it comes to the fore is also significant because it is out of our control. The state of interconnections, communications and collaborations emerges by itself and by chance depending on previous or prevalent conditions at a certain time and place. What is there has not been explicitly designed for any particular reason by anybody. Thus the questions are: Is it sustainable in itself? And where does it lead us?

3   Concluding Discussion

Taking into the account the issues above, what are the implications for society? What are the key aspects we need to change in our paradigms? How could we do that?

The post-Turing scenario will introduce humanity into an interconnected world with global knowledge networks, with the promising "collective intelligence" opportunity. But at the same time, this poses to humanity a collection of sustainability issues on the environmental, personal, biological and social sides.

On the environmental side we will need to slow down the consumption of natural resources for building electronic devices and improve the re-use and re-cycling of hardware. We need to start thinking ourselves as (responsible) "digital citizens" and not just "digital consumers." We need to question the market pressure of consuming new electronic gadgets at a growing speed. Also, in order to have really recyclable hardware, we need to introduce recyclable-by-design devices. This can be optimised by leveraging the collective intelligence enabled by a post-Turing scenario. So we need to introduce an "open hardware" approach [1], where all specifications and documentation are available to experts.

Smart software applications could be also useful in supporting us in decreasing our environmental impact, reaching our main goals and satisfying our significant values.

In the "remote working" area we need to start a new way of thinking that questions the exploitation of knowledge workers: they are the best candidates to become independent workers instead of "employees" of some intermediate obscure job brokers. On the social side of post-Turing ICT the long list of issues in front of us will require a new interdisciplinary approach that will enable the collaboration of many disciplines like: computing and networking, sociology, psychology, anthropology, and philosophy. It is the first time in our history that we have this opportunity at global scale; let us stay humans.

References

1. Arduino, http://www.arduino.cc (accessed March 2012)
2. Baliga, J., Ayre, R.W.A., Hinton, K., Tucker, R.S.: Green Cloud Computing: Balancing Energy in Processing, Storage, and Transport. Proceedings of the IEEE 99(1), 149–167 (2011), Issue Date: January
3. BBC: Finland makes broadband a 'legal right', BBC news (July 1, 2010)
4. Cisco: Cisco Visual Networking Index: Global Mobile Data Traffic Forecast Update (2011–2016),
   http://www.cisco.com/en/US/solutions/collateral/ns341/ns525/ns537/ns705/ns827/white_paper_c11-520862.html
   (accessed February 2012)

5. Codrington, G.: Freelancers, eLancers and Cloud workers, TomorrowToday (July 6, 2010)
6. Internetworldstats: Internet Usage Statistics, The Internet Big Picture, World Internet Users and Population Stats (2012), http://www.internetworldstats.com/stats.htm (accessed February 2012)
7. ISC: Internet Software Consortium, Domain Survey last update (2012), http://www.isc.org/solutions/surveym (accessed February 2012)
8. ISPRA (Istituto Superiore per la Protezione e la Ricerca Ambientale): Rapporto Rifiuti, Rome (2007), http://www.ispra.gov.it (accessed June 2011)
9. Issenberg S.: Obama's White Whale. How the campaign's top-secret project Narwhal could change this race, and many to come (February 15, 2012), slate.com
10. Kock, N.: Encyclopedia of E-collaboration. Information Science Reference (2007)
11. Koomey, J.G.: Estimating total power consumption by servers in the US and the world. Lawrence Berkeley National Laboratory, Stanford University, Stanford CA (2007)
12. Lessig, L.: Free Culture, The Nature and Future of Creativity. Penguin Books (2005)
13. Licklider, J.C.R.: Man-Computer Symbiosis. IRE Transactions on Human Factors in Electronics HFE-1, 4–11 (1960)
14. Moore, G.E.: Cramming more components onto integrated circuits. Electronics Magazine (April 19, 1965)
15. OECD (Organization for Economic Cooperation and Development): Information Technology Outlook, OECD, Paris (2010), http://www.oecd.org (accessed June 2011)
16. Ostrom, E., Hess, C. (eds.): Understanding Knowledge as a Commons: From Theory to Practice. The MIT Press, Cambridge (2006)
17. Patrignani, N., Laaksoharju, M., Kavathatzopoulos, I.: Challenging the Pursuit of Moore's Law: ICT Sustainability in the Cloud Computing Era. In: Whitehouse, D., Hilty, L., Patrignani, N., VanLieshout, M. (eds.) Notizie di Politeia - Rivista di Etica e Scelte Pubbliche, Anno XXVII, Milano, Italy, vol. (104) (2011)
18. RSF: Enemies of the Internet, http://www.rsf.org (released March 2011)
19. Schmitz, O.J., Graedel, T.E.: The Consumption Conundrum: Driving the Destruction Abroad, e360.yale.edu (April 2010)
20. Soesterberg: Trans-Atlantic Network for Clean Production Meeting. Soesterberg, The Netherlands (May 1999), http://icspac.net/anpedwg/publications.aspx (accessed June 2011)
21. SVTC (Silicon Valley Toxics Coalition) (2007), http://svtc.org (accessed June 2011)
22. Turing, A.: On computable numbers, with an application to the Entscheidungsproblem. In: Proceedings of the London Mathematical Society, Ser. 2, vol. 42 (1937)
23. Vaidhyanathan, S.: The Googlization of Everything: And Why We Should Worry. University of California Press (2011)
24. Vazquez-Figueroa, A. Coltan. Ediciones B (2010)
25. W3C: Linking Open Data, W3C SWEO Community Project (2012), http://www.w3.org/wiki/SweoIG/TaskForces/CommunityProjects/LinkingOpenData (accessed February 14, 2012)

ITGS – A Blueprint for a Social Informatics Course in Pre-university Education

Richard Taylor

International Baccalaureate, Cardiff, United Kingdom
richard.taylor@ibo.org

Abstract. The continual development of information and communication technologies in contemporary society has led to a constantly evolving inter-relationship between human beings and these technologies. Within the university sector there is a wide range of courses which examine this inter-relationship, but such courses are largely absent from the pre-university sector. One pre-university course that attempts to examine this inter-relationship is the Information Technology in a Global Society (ITGS) course which is part of the International Baccalaureate (IB) Diploma Programme. This position paper examines whether this course may be seen as a blueprint for the development of other similar courses in the pre-university sector, and how such courses will be able to accurately reflect the constantly evolving inter-relationship between human beings and information and communication technologies.

Keywords: digital capability, digital literacy, digital wisdom[1], Information Communication Technology (ICT[2]), Information Technology in a Global Society (ITGS), International Baccalaureate (IB) Diploma Programme[3], stakeholder analysis, social informatics.

1 Introduction

The introduction of information and communication technologies into schools in the 1980s was followed by the development of related courses. One area of curriculum development was in Computer Science, which was, and still is to a great extent, largely based on programming; a second was linked to the application of new software packages such as Microsoft Office™ and became known as ICT. Over the subsequent two decades the development of information and communication technologies has occurred at a much faster rate than the curriculum development of both ICT

---

[1] Digital wisdom and digital capability in this paper may be viewed as synonyms. Both relate to an interpretation of the term "media wisdom" that encompasses; technical competence, creativity, analysis and reflection (Martens 2011).

[2] Information and Communication Technology is a subject in secondary education. This is different to information and communication technologies, the use of digital devices to store, send and receive information, which is not abbreviated throughout the paper.

[3] International Baccalaureate Diploma Program is a pre-university course for 16-19 year old students. More information can be obtained from www.ibo.org

M.D. Hercheui et al. (Eds.): HCC10 2012, IFIP AICT 386, pp. 192–201, 2012.
© IFIP International Federation for Information Processing 2012

and Computer Science, thus leading to courses that may be seen as anachronistic and largely irrelevant in today's technological landscape. This is illustrated in the decline in the numbers of students that follow these courses, see Table 1.

Table 1. Candidate registrations of UK ICT related pre-university courses (2007 – 2011)

ICT related Course	Registered candidates (2007)	Registered candidates (2011)	Change 2007 - 2011
GCE in ICT	10968	9133	-17%
GCE in Computing	4683	3606	-23%

Source: Shut down and restart [8].

Seminal papers by Wing (Computational Thinking, 2006) and McBride (Death of Computing, 2007) questioned the nature of Computer Science resulting in the revision of the International Baccalaureate Computer Science course and the development of the United States Advanced Placement (AP) Computer Science Principles course. In these courses computational thinking is placed at the heart rather than programming. As the assessment of students[4] in either course will not take place until at least May 2014, the effects of this paradigm shift have yet to be seen.

In ICT the decline in student numbers has continued unabated. However, in contrast to Computer Science, there not been a similar discussion questioning the nature of the subject. This has resulted in the absence of a coherent strategy to provide a subject that is appropriate in the current technological landscape. Changes to technology have occurred far more rapidly than the ability of exam boards[5] to keep pace and have resulted in ICT lagging behind the technologies it studies (or effectively playing 'catch-up'), something that is similar to what occurs in legal and regulatory fields. ICT has also struggled due to a lack of a clear identity and, indeed, many policy makers and school managers regularly use Computer Science and ICT as synonyms.

2   The International Baccalaureate ITGS Course

In the early 1990s a group of teachers and the IB Subject Manager, Ruth Baber, realised that in addition to the Computer Science course there was demand for a course that focussed on the inter-relationship between human beings and the emerging information and communication technologies. As a result, the ITGS course was "born". Since these early days, the course has undergone three curriculum reviews[6] but

---

[4] Assessment refers to the first year that students are examined in these courses. The IB Computer Science course will be taught from August 2012. Pilot studies for the new AP course started in 2011.Registration for the assessment does not need to be completed until November 2013, so the effects on student uptake will not be apparent until then.

[5] Exam boards are responsible for the development and assessment of courses for public examinations.

[6] The IB Curriculum Review is carried out over a 7 year cycle. This leads to the development and implementation of a new course.

struggled to find an appropriate position within the IB Diploma Hexagon[7]. The current version of the course is within Group 3 (Individuals and Societies) and has been taught in schools worldwide since August 2010.

ITGS focuses on stakeholder analysis. The 'ITGS triangle' (see figure 1) is at the heart of the course. Within this framework, scenarios based on the inter-relationship between human beings and information and communication technologies are based on three strands; social/ethical significance, application to specified scenarios, and IT systems. They are taught in an integrated and iterative manner.

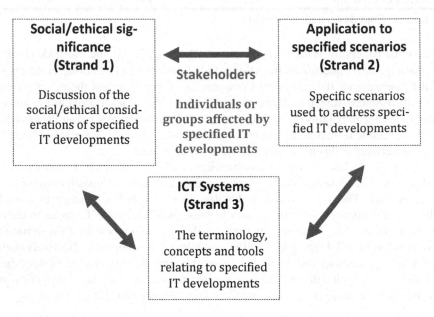

Fig. 1. The integrated stakeholder focussed approach outlined in the ITGS Guide[8] [7]

Teachers may choose any of the three strands as a starting point.

The level of technical knowledge required by students of the course is confined to the general principles that underpin the technology. In summative assessment[9] only lower order command terms[10] such as describe, identify, state and outline are used.

---

[7] Subjects are categorised into six groups (Studies in language and literature, Language acquisition, Individuals and Societies, Experimental sciences (including Computer Science), Mathematics, The arts), see http://www.ibo.org/diploma/curriculum/ and must take a subject from each.

[8] ITGS Guide (Specification), a document that indicates the scope of the ITGS course for teachers.

[9] Summative assessment is assessment that takes place at a given time, for example, at the end of a course.

[10] Command terms provide an indication of the depth of response required and are based on Bloom's Taxonomy.

Therefore a student should be able demonstrate knowledge of a specified technology or provide an overview of a process by identifying the key steps. For example, an ITGS student would be able to identify the steps that a biometric authorisation device would use in the authorisation of an employee to enter a building. In a Computer Science curriculum, instead, it may be necessary to suggest possible algorithms that could be used to determine whether the image captured matches the image in the database.

An equivalent course does not exist in programmes such as the AP Program, Victoria Certificate of Education (VCE) and French Baccalaureate, and the course is significantly different to other IT related courses, such as United Kingdom (UK) A-Levels. In ITGS students are required to apply their knowledge to a wide range of scenarios leading to substantiated opinions being developed that are underpinned by the proficient use of both technical and social/ethical vocabulary whereas in other IT related courses the discussion of social/ethical issues is usually more superficial.

As ITGS may be considered as "low content, high context[11]" compared to other subjects, many senior managers in school and external organisations have not appreciated the transferable and higher order skills such as application, formulation, synthesis and evaluation that are required to successfully follow this course. This is not just an issue for ITGS, both in terms of its perceived rigour, as it is one of the few IB subjects that the Russell Group[12] does not recognise as being sufficiently academic or acting as a facilitating subject, but also for other ICT related courses.

3   Reflections of the Current ITGS Course

There is a widespread belief that once students opt for ITGS they find it a relevant, stimulating and challenging course. Many past students have referred to it as the subject that was the least use for university entrance, but the one that had the most relevance in later life. However, getting this message across to school senior managers, potential students and their parents has proved problematic.

As part of the ongoing curriculum review process for ITGS, which will result in a new course being introduced for the May 2019 examination session, a prototype questionnaire was tested using 64 students from a Florida High School in the US. This school was chosen as the ITGS teacher had been involved in the previous curriculum review and because it provided easy access to a large number of students, something that is not always possible as, in many schools, ITGS classes may have fewer than 10 students.

The main findings from the research indicated in Table 2 below, were most positive. There was a general satisfaction with the nature of the course with none of the 13 questions producing an average response below the no opinion score (3). The students

---

[11] "low content, high context" refers to courses that rely on the application of a smaller body of knowledge to a wide range of scenarios or contexts – an applied course. This is in contrast to a "high content, low context" course where a narrow in-depth field of study occurs based on specified content – a theoretical course.

[12] The Russell Group represents 20 leading UK universities.

felt most strongly that there was an appropriate balance between the three strands of the subject, a mean response of 4.47 (individual responses ranged from 1 to 5). The feedback obtained about each of the strands indicated a reasonable level of satisfaction, although not as much as the overall structure of the course. Comments such as" I feel like there is too much content in the course. I think it is slightly unreasonable to expect students to remember and understand such an extensive list of vocabulary, and then be able to apply them to such a large range of IT subjects and problems" suggest that an appropriate balance between the content and scenarios has yet to be reached.

Table 2. Summary of findings of questionnaire completed by St Petersburg High School

Question	Ave response[13]	Standard error
The ITGS course provides sufficient opportunities to address the attributes of the Learner Profile[14]	4.11	0.09
There is a correct balance between Social/ethical significance, application to specified scenarios and IT systems	4.47	0.08
The range of social/ethical considerations (Strand 1) is appropriate	4.19	0.07
The range of specified scenarios (Strand 2) is appropriate	3.90	0.08
The range or depth of technical knowledge required for IT systems (Strand 3) is appropriate	4.08	0.09
The Project[15] has the right amount of technical difficulty for the subject	4.17	0.09

Sample size = 64

These findings suggest there is a need to amend the nature and/or content of each of the strands. As part of the current curriculum review in 2011 preliminary feedback was obtained from Bradshaw who commented "IT Systems is presented only as an ever increasingly long list of hardware and software that is only ever partially complete, impossible to keep up to date and, of most concern, of variable levels of 'difficulty' for the students" as well as McBride who noted "change is inevitable and the subject matter is volatile. Who can know what the world will be like in 2017? How will technology change? What will be the issues faced in terms of society and ethics? And there is a dynamic population of stakeholders".

---

[13] The questionnaire was based on a 5 point Likert scale (1 – Strongly disagree, 5 – strongly agree).

[14] Learner profile – a set of attributes such as inquirers, thinkers, principled that provide the basis of an IB student.

[15] Project – the internally assessed work (coursework) that is created by students in consultation with a named client. This provides the opportunity for a student to showcase their practical skills.

The Project, an activity that requires students to develop an original product in consultation with a specified client using a simplified project management approach, forms the internal assessment[16] (coursework). The students feel it is appropriate for the course as well as being a part of the course that teachers and students enjoyed. It also allows them to demonstrate their practical IT skills (digital literacy). Currently it is the only place within the IB Diploma, as the existing Computer Science course concentrates on programming, where students could carry out this type of activity.

In the medium term it is highly likely that this component of the ITGS course will need to undergo significant change to a more in-depth evaluation of the socio-technical systems that emerge. The development of the Web as a social machine will require a reduction in emphasis on the skills required to develop products and a more in-depth understanding of the inter-relationship between human beings and information and communication technologies. With the more explicit focus on stakeholder analysis and the ITGS student acting in the role of an intermediary between policy makers and developers within a project management framework, a new internal assessment will need to be developed. This change will also be possible as the assessment of student work may include the students completing their examinations in a digital environment which will allow digital literacy to be assessed through this medium. Furthermore, developments in software allowing students to be able to create highly complex products simply by following on screen menus and the internal assessment of the Computer Science course which is similar to the current Project will render the Project redundant.

4 Possible Constraints in Introducing a Pre-university Social Informatics Course

There are a number of major obstacles that may exist to the development a new ICT course based on Social Informatics. The stigma of ICT, whereby many universities are unwilling to accept students from a course that is ICT related is particularly problematic. One method of resolving this may be to replace ICT as the name of the subject with Social Informatics. However, Social Informatics is a term that has not been used and is likely to not be understood by senior managers and teachers in secondary education or by parents so may simply be a case of replacing a 'tarnished' subject with an unknown one.

Currently, ICT does not have the support of high profile backers, in a way that Computer Science does. Eric Schmidt, the Chairman of Google, commented that the "IT curriculum focuses on teaching how to use software, but it doesn't teach people how it's made" [4]. This could result in the 'technology related' part of the curriculum becoming based on the assumption of the student as a potential developer of information and communication technologies rather than as a user. The potential risks that are associated with an overemphasis of the opinions of special interest groups "they give

---

[16] Internally assessed work – the student completes the work under the supervision of the ITGS which then marks it. The work is then externally moderated.

too much emphasis to the special pleading of particular institutions and industries (universities and software companies, for example), or frame the need for better teaching in purely economic terms as being good for "UK plc" [6] should also be recognised.

Senior managers in schools still view ICT, Computer Science and Digital Literacy as synonyms. Therefore, before the introduction of any Social Informatics course, these distinctions need to be made explicit. Furthermore, the provision of appropriate professional development for teachers who may lack the confidence to be able to teach the subject will be necessary.

5   Leading the Way in Social Informatics

Despite the number of obstacles facing the subject of ICT, the continued emergence of new information and communication technologies makes a case for an appropriate secondary education course more and more compelling [1].

The methodology described previously is similar to that outlined by Duquenoy et al in the paper presented at the 2010 Ethicomp conference. In this paper, the integrated stakeholder focussed approach developed in ITGS is likened to climbing stairs with the students starting with the context and progressing to recommendations for modification to the proposed IT system or alternative solutions. The diagram below shows a revised version of the linear approach proposed (context – stakeholders – ethics – reflexivity[3]) with an iterative approach.

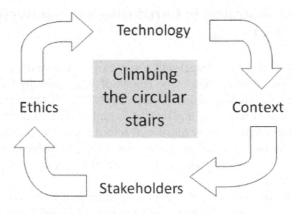

Fig. 2. A model for climbing circular stairs

The role of stakeholder analysis in a Social Informatics course is critical to the development of the student understanding the social/ethical issues that lie beyond the technologies themselves. It was noted that "many students have had no exposure to the ethical issues that are associated with information and communication technologies, so a bottom up approach is required" [3]. Furthermore Gotterbarn and Clear comment that, "many IT related courses which tend to be high-content, low context"

[5] which has led to IT tools being developed at the expense of an understanding of the effects of their use.

The development of Social Informatics courses would place digital wisdom[17], or "digital capability" [1] at the heart of the course. This would require the student to be able to appreciate the implications of the introduction of new technologies and clearly goes beyond digital literacy, a concept championed by the Royal Society[18] and the state of California[19], which may be defined as the ability to use IT tools appropriately. The 2012 ITTE position paper, "the future of ICT in education", argues that "whilst 'Digital Literacy' is well established, it is a broad and often ill-defined concept incorporating a range of associated literacies (media literacy, information literacy, visual literacy, etc.). In addition, as has been highlighted by The Royal Society (2012), Digital Literacy does not readily lend itself to being taught – it constitutes a passive state, rather than the application of digital technologies"[1].

Any Social Informatics course would also need to ensure it addresses the new disciplines that are associated with the emerging technologies. "The movement towards ubiquitous computing is based on interaction and convergence. Here, convergence means a move towards a common content. Interaction means that technology interacts with the social world with values and beliefs" [2].

In recent years, the growth of ubiquitous computing and 'the Cloud' where information is constantly available has led to the most significant changes in the nature of human existence since the Industrial Revolution. The understanding of the constantly ever evolving inter-relationship between human beings and information and communication technologies may be seen as a new discipline that future citizens should have at least an awareness of.

In this 'new world' home and work will become increasingly blurred and the ability to successfully exist in the digital world will rely less on the 'traditional skills' associated with digital literacy and more on those associated with digital wisdom. A parallel may be drawn between the changes that took place in employment where traditional skills developed in primary and secondary industries were replaced by those in tertiary and quaternary industries. Therefore if schools are to provide students with the skills to exist in the emerging technical environments, the study of these skills needs to be far more prominent than they currently are. The issue may fundamentally be about where within the secondary school curriculum this wisdom can be developed, rather than whether it should.

It is critical, therefore, that any course that attempts to reflect these changes is able to adapt at the same speed. This will need a significant rewriting of ICT courses to provide a programme of study that can be as 'future proof' as possible. This would include the re-organisation of subject matter, through curriculum development, to fit into new categories that allow the course to evolve with the technology. The scenarios for discussion that emerge could be supported by teacher resources through wikis,

---

[17] The Association for IT in Teacher Education (ITTE) uses the term digital capability in a similar context

[18] Shut down or restart (Royal Society 2012).

[19] Digital Literacy pathways (2010),
www.ictliteracy.info/rf.pdf/Digital%20LiteracyMaster_July_2010.pdf

such as ITGSopedia[20]. This collective intelligence of teachers and students would ensure the provision of contemporary and appropriate resources that does not have the lag time associated with textbooks.

The study of ethics needs far greater emphasis with an explicit framework, as well as providing a level of recognised academic content that may occur implicitly at present. The uses of models such as the culturally negotiated ethical triangle by authors such as Orams provide a basis for the consideration of ethical decisions within the cycles of stakeholder analysis. With more and more resources being put into 'the Cloud', the ethical issues associated with the remote management of individuals' data will increase in importance. One suggestion for an ethical framework could be based on the ACTIVE[21] framework being developed by McBride et al.

For the introduction of any new subject, professional development would be necessary for secondary school teachers. The skills required to teach this course are closer to those held by social scientists than those from a traditional IT background. However, many of the values, such as those espoused in the IB Learner Profile (inquirers, open-minded, reflective etc.) are as important as subject knowledge for they provide students with the transferable skills and competencies that characterise this type of course. Many teacher training organisations have developed programmes to enhance the skill of digital literacy of their employees or citizens, yet have not provided the opportunities to enable teachers to develop the discursive skills necessary.

6   Conclusions – ICT the Way Forward

Despite the decline in numbers and the uncertainty about what constitutes ICT, groups such as the ITTE see "that education and training in digital technologies is fundamental to all aspects of education in the 21st century" [1]. The current debate may lead to a revision of the courses that are offered based on body of knowledge is appropriate for ICT/Social Informatics and Computer Science as well as the degree of overlap (as both subjects have the requirement for technical knowledge and the social/ethical issues arise from the development and use of technology). Once students make decisions about which subjects they wish to study, it is both possible and desirable that separate courses in Computer Science and a revised ICT can successfully co-exist, as they will appeal to different students.

One possibility for the new ICT could be modelled on an updated version of ITGS, with the stakeholder at the centre, a strengthened focus on ethics, a refining of the specified scenarios and a redesign of IT systems with the main headings such as Overview of the Web, Web Technologies, Data management, and Socio-technical systems. However the redevelopment of ICT, with a possible renaming, will require creating a new brand that is seen as relevant and academically rigorous to ensure its survival in an increasingly competitive marketplace.

---

[20] http://itgsopedia.wikispaces.com/
[21] ACTIVE - Anonymity, Community, Transparency, Identity, Value, Empathy. A framework being developed by McBride et al.

Acknowledgements. Carol Mathis (ITGS teacher at St Petersburg High School, Florida), Neil McBride (Reader in Information Technology Management, Centre for Computing and Social Responsibility, De Montfort University, Leicester, UK) and Pete Bradshaw (Lecturer in Education, Open University, Milton Keynes, UK).

References

1. Association for IT in Teacher Education (ITTE): Position Paper: The future of ICT in education (2012)
2. Bradley, G.: Social and Community Informatics - Humans on the Net. Routledge, London (2006)
3. Duquenoy, P., Martens, B., Patrignani, N.: Embedding Ethics in European Information & Communication Technology Curricula. In: Ethicomp (2010)
4. Gigaom, Eric Schmidt challenges teachers: get with the program,
   http://gigaom.com/2011/08/29/eric-schmidt-challenges-
   teachers-get-with-the-program/ (accessed March 21, 2012)
5. Gotterbarn, D., Clear, T.: Using SoDIS™ as a Risk Analysis Process: A Teaching Perspective (2003),
   http://www.acs.org.au/documents/public/crpit/CRPITV30Gotterba
   rn.pdf (last accessed on April 29, 2012)
6. Guardian: A manifesto for teaching computer science in the 21st century,
   http://www.guardian.co.uk/education/2012/mar/31/manifesto-
   teaching-ict-education-minister?CMP=twt_fd (accessed April 2, 2012)
7. International Baccalaureate Organisation, http://www.ibo.org
8. Furber, S.: Shut down or restart. The Royal Society (2012),
   http://royalsociety.org/education/policy/
   computing-in-schools/report/ (last accessed on April 29, 2012)

Governance, Risk and Compliance: A Strategic Alignment Perspective Applied to Two Case Studies

Abbas Shahim[1], Ronald Batenburg[2], and Geert Vermunt[3]

[1] VU University Amsterdam, Amsterdam, The Netherlands
and Atos Consulting, Utrecht, The Netherlands
abbas.shahim@atos.net
[2] Utrecht University, Utrecht, The Netherlands
r.s.batenburg@uu.nl
[3] BWise, Rosmalen, The Netherlands
geert.vermunt@bwise.com

Abstract. Governance, Risk and Compliance (GRC) has become critical for organizations and so is the need to support this by ICT. This paper positions GRC into an integrated strategic perspective, providing guidelines to assess maturity and defining paths for achieving strategic alignment. The approach is applied to two case studies, clarifying the organizations' GRC maturity "as is" and "to be". These cases were studied in the utilities and financial sectors, both show that organizations can have similar GRC maturity levels but follow quite different paths to achieve alignment with regard to GRC. While the Dutch utility company stuck to a path where the organizational strategy with respect to GRC was taken as a starting point, the financial institution followed a path in which the IT solution strategy was leading. In interpreting this result, it appears that the existing IT assets are strongly impacting the selection of the alignment path. More case studies are advocated to further validate the approach and contribute to optimize the strategic and integrated perspective on GRC.

Keywords: compliance, governance, risk management, strategic alignment.

1   Introduction

From the turn of the millennium, the trusted face of our global economy familiar to many of us has deeply and rapidly changed. Its irreversible shape represents a strong compliance driven approach to business governance that has dominated the agenda of the board ever since. This fundamental and quick transformation is the result of the most known accounting scandals that occurred shortly after the beginning of this century: the collapse of Enron and the fall of WorldCom. As a response to these corporate failures, the Sarbanes-Oxley Act, often abbreviated to SOX (see [16] for further information), was created and passed by the United States Congress in 2002 to stress the importance of business control and auditing so that the national confidence in the securities markets was restored again. Compliance with this enacted legislation is not only required of organizations that are publicly traded in the United States, but is also

M.D. Hercheui et al. (Eds.): HCC10 2012, IFIP AICT 386, pp. 202–212, 2012.
© IFIP International Federation for Information Processing 2012

mandatory for those outside of the Unites States under certain circumstances (e.g., foreign companies listed on the New York stock exchange). In consequence, organizations have placed a great emphasis on description, design and effectively operating controls with the purpose to adequately govern, mitigate risks and comply with SOX [19] – see also [18]. In general, it can be stated that the tightened regulatory compliance pressure put on organizations especially by SOX has in fact given a boost to the improvement of the existing GRC practices in the business and information technology (IT) sector [7]. Nowadays, organizations are confronted with broader GRC-associated matters that have established a new reality in which traditional strategies and assumptions seem to fail [6] – see also [20].

GRC is not new. Issues and challenges with respect to governance, risk management and compliance have always formed a substantial concern for a majority of organizations. Although the abbreviation of this concept indicates an interrelation between its components, the fact is that these functions are yet executed mostly in a fragmented fashion [15]. What is new about GRC is the awareness of organizations to take a united perspective to this concept for creating added-value and realizing competitive advantage. It is rightfully noted that the need for an integrated approach to this concept should at least be fulfilled by sophisticated risk management frameworks, improved compliance disciplines, revamped structures and modern technologies so that an advanced as well as a sound governance on a corporate level can be practiced more readily. GRC as a set of integrated concepts can thus be of significant value and make a contribution to outpace the competition when applied holistically within organizations [14]. Hence, due to this organizational impact, it is necessary to strategize the interrelated GRC perspective and to ascertain that it will be aligned properly with the business mission. In practice, however, we hardly encounter the full convergence of GRC disciplines in theoretical strategic models. GRC implementations are largely based on pragmatic compliance-related activities, and on reporting about these dominating actions despite the clear need to embrace an incorporated and strategic GRC view across business units, oversight functions and strategies. This is the main driver of the present paper that addresses the research question: *How can an integrated GRC approach be applied in organizations using a strategic alignment perspective?*

The paper is organized as follows. Next, we present a brief overview of definitions of integrated GRC. Thereafter we show how a strategic alignment perspective on GRC results in an approach used to assess the GRC maturity and alignment paths. In the empirical part of the paper, the approach is applied to two different case studies. The results of both case studies are presented, leading to a conclusion that will be discussed in the final part of this contribution.

2   Integrated GRC

2.1   Definitions

Various definitions of GRC are provided in the literature (e.g., [21] – see also [3]). Using different point of views, the definitions mostly describe this concept in terms of controlling and improving processes. A scientific GRC definition indicates the ethics in addition to other pertinent aspects such as risk appetite, internal policies and external regulations [14]. The definition presented by one of the Big Four accountancy firms describes that GRC is not a technology tool, but a model that leaders look at to drive maximum value out of the business model [6]. Throughout the rest of this paper, we refer to the GRC definition provided by the Open Compliance & Ethics Group (OCEG) for two main reasons. First, we notice that it is the one that is most referred to in the literature and in practice (e.g., [2], and [8] – see also [10] and [5]). Second, This global non-profit think tank expounds its view on an integrated approach to create a GRC system by means of four perspectives [33, 34]: 1) integration of GRC disciplines, 2) integration of GRC activities across risk categories and departments, 3) integration of GRC activities with business processes, and 4) integration to provide a single version of the truth. OCEG stresses the synergistic impact of an integrated approach to this concept and explains that it is more than solely the consolidation of three disciplines. It defines GRC as follows [9]: "a system of people, processes and technology that enables an organization to understand and prioritize stakeholder expectations, set business objectives congruent with values and risks, achieve objectives while optimizing risk profile and protecting value, operate within legal, contractual, internal, social and ethical boundaries, provide relevant, reliable and timely information to appropriate stakeholders, and enable the measurement of the performance and effectiveness of the system."

2.2   A Strategic Alignment Perspective

One of the key elements in the OCEG definition of GRC is the notion of alignment to achieve integration – of disciplines, activities and information. As a concept, alignment has a long history in both organization science and information systems research. Scholars in the 1990s already argued that companies fail to realize performance improvements due to the lack of alignment between the business and IT strategies [4]. Results of studies dedicated to measuring the effect of business-IT alignment on performance indicate that there is a positive correlation between business-IT alignment and organizational performance, in which top performers are those companies which effectively align their business with their IT strategies. This outcome comes to vitiate the claim that highly sophisticated IT can solely improve business performance, but what is of greater importance is the alignment between both IT and business strategies [17]. Following this line of argumentation, it can be expected that if an organization integrates GRC it will benefit more from IT if its applications are in conformance with the business processes present in the organization. In this context strategic or business-IT alignment implies the process of finding the right match and the alignment between a GRC solution and the organization. If this alignment perspective is applied to integrated GRC, a model can be defined as in figure 1. This model is based on the strategic alignment model of Henderson and Venkatraman [4] and positions an instance of the integrated GRC approach on both the business and on the IT dimension. The idea is that alignment can be realized by bringing the business and IT strategy together, where strategy is involving formulation and implementation [4].

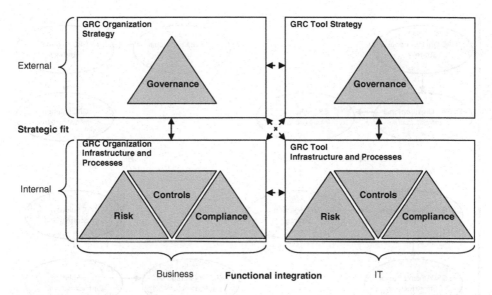

Fig. 1. GRC plotted in the strategic alignment model by [4]; the GRC strategic alignment model

The vision of GRC from a strategic alignment perspective is plotted on the four domains from the strategic alignment model, based on the two building blocks defined by Henderson and Venkatraman: strategic fit and functional integration [4]. The strategic fit dimension represents the integration of the external and internal domain. The external domain, on a business level, addresses the arena in which corporate decisions are made concerning strategy and distinctive strategy attributes which distinguish the firm from competitors. The element 'Governance' is positioned in this domain because it is concerned with the GRC strategy in the organization. The internal domain, on a business level, pertains to the organizational structure and the critical business processes that are available in the organization. The elements of 'Risk', 'Control' and 'Compliance' are positioned in this domain because these elements relate to the structure of GRC and the processes involved with GRC, e.g. the risk-control structure in the organization. The fit between the external and internal domain in the business domain is argued to be critical when maximizing economic performance [1]. This relation can be reflected in the IT domain, resulting in a proposition that in the IT domain a similar separation between the external and internal domains can be made and that a fit between these domains is critical for IT in an organization [4]. Integrating the business and the IT domain is coined by Henderson and Venkatraman as functional integration. In the GRC perspective, the IT domain represents the GRC solution which forms a system of record for GRC in the organization. The strategic alignment model distinguishes two kinds of functional integration between the business and IT domain: strategic integration (i.e. attempts are made to align both business and IT strategy) and integration of organization and processes (i.e. operational integration concerned with aligning infrastructure and processes on both business and IT level) [4]. Following the strategic alignment model of Henderson and Venkatraman, four alignment paths can be applied to the GRC domain illustrated in figure 2:

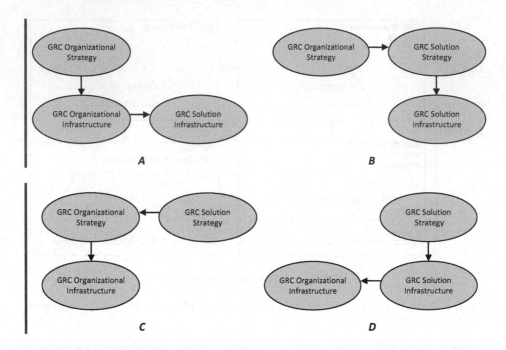

Fig. 2. Four paths to reach strategic alignment in GRC (A: Strategy execution, B: Technology transformation, C: Competitive potential, D: Service level)

1. The "strategy execution" path, translated to a GRC perspective, is displayed as "A". This path indicates that GRC strategy and GRC infrastructure are constructed in the business domain. A GRC solution is selected which could form a fit between the GRC infrastructure on both business and IT domain.
2. The "technology transformation" path for GRC is displayed as "B". In this perspective a GRC strategy is developed in a business domain and a GRC solution is selected which concurs with this strategy. The infrastructure from the GRC solution is embedded in the organization.
3. The "competitive potential" path, translated to a GRC perspective, is displayed as "C". In this path the strategy from the GRC solution is the driver. The GRC strategy and infrastructure in the business domain are geared towards the strategy which is adopted in the GRC solution.
4. The "service level" path for GRC is displayed as "D". In this case the vision of GRC adopted in the GRC solution is integrated in the GRC organizational infrastructure.

3　Methods and Measurements

3.1　A GRC Framework

To operationalize and measure the GRC strategic alignment model as presented in figure 1, the next step needed is a specification of practices related to GRC and a maturity scale to measure these practices. For this aim, practices were distilled from the OCEG maturity models covering GRC. Governance includes 12 practices: code of conduct, strategy, organizational chart, accountabilities, meetings between accountable parties, process integration with business process, KPIs, reporting, budget, cost/benefit monitoring, transparency, and training. Risk holds 7 practices: risk assessment, risk overview, risk overview contains IT risks, risk review, incident reporting, emergency process for gaps and incidents, and root cause analysis for gap or incident. Compliance contains 4 practices: overview of regulatory boundaries, overview of internal and external rules and regulations, compliance review, and processes when confronted with non-compliance [36, 37, 38]. Table 1 provides our measurement framework and shows the proposed five-point scale for maturity levels to measure the three GRC domains.

Table 1. GRC domains and number of practices derived from OCEG [11], [12], [13]

Domain	# Practices	Maturity levels				
		1	2	3	4	5
Governance	12					
Risk	7					
Compliance	4					

The five-level GRC maturity scale is defined as follows:

1. The practice is not available in the organization.
2. The organization is developing the practice.
3. The practice is available in the organization, but fragmented or used inconsistently throughout the organization.
4. The practice is integrated, available in the organization, and used consistently.
5. The practice is consistently measured and undergoing improvements.

We base this scale on the Capability Maturity Model (CMM), which was originally developed by the Software Engineering Institute [22]. The CMM five-level model fits our aim to specifically assess how IT contributes to the maturity of GRC from an alignment perspective. We are aware that there is specific literature describing GRC maturity levels as well such as the model developed by KPMG [6].

4   Analysis of Two Case Studies

In 2008, two case studies of Dutch companies were performed on the role that IT fulfilled in supporting the GRC processes in the organization. The two main goals were (1) to investigate how the organization achieved strategic alignment of IT with the business (applying the four alignment parts as presented in figure 2), and (2) to assess the organization on its GRC maturity (applying the maturity model as presented by Table 1). The approach followed during the two case studies can be described as follows. Firstly, a site visit was planned that included semi-structured interviews with GRC managers. The GRC managers that were invited to the interviews had an in-depth knowledge of the organizations' GRC maturity and deployment of a GRC solution in the organization. The interviews were used to assess the GRC maturity of the organization, by means of a questionnaire based on the measurement framework and practices. This questionnaire covers all three domains, the organization's GRC practices and the accompanying five-point maturity scale. The interview partners were asked to score, for each GRC practice, the "as is" maturity and how the alignment with IT helped to reach a certain "to be" maturity. For each of the three domains (Governance, Risk and Compliance) the scores on the practices were averaged. This processing of the answers resulted in a visualization of the GRC maturity status of the organization, describing the "as is" and "to be" maturity. This visualization was subsequently validated during a site visit. Secondly, the GRC-managers of the organizations were interviewed on the deployment process of IT in their organization, and to document their experiences in aligning IT with the business processes. Based on this interview, the type of alignment path followed by the organization (as defined in figure 2) was reconstructed and likewise validated.

4.1   Case 1: Dutch Utilities Company

Setting & GRC Maturity. This company is a large energy producer and supplier with its customer base located in the Netherlands and Belgium. The company houses approximately 5,500 employees and has a turnover of approximately 9 billion euro. The organization was one of the first companies in the utilities sector to begin with separate compliance activities and integrating these activities with governance and risk management. The GRC maturity questionnaire that was completed by the respondents resulted into the figure 3, indicating the present state of GRC maturity and the maturity level the organization is aiming for within 2-3 years. The company proved to be performing at a maturity level of 3+ for many GRC areas, especially risk management. The lower maturity in the Governance domain can be explained because of the fact that the GRC organization is not yet modelled. The company's ambition is to charter the entire GRC organization with the use of IT and to raise maturity. Also the Compliance domain is lagging behind with respect to Risk management. This can be explained by compliance processes that are not performed as integrated throughout the organization and the use of other, siloed, "home-made", software. Evaluations on the way the software in the company is used should guide the compliance processes to a higher level.

Strategic Alignment. Following our conceptual model as presented in figure 2, the deployment of the GRC IT solution in this case study can be classified as the "Technology transformation" path illustrated in figure 4. The company sensed the need for a specialized solution to support GRC and defined high-level business requirements that should be matched by the GRC solution strategy. The implementation of the GRC solution infrastructure was then done simultaneously and according to the specifications of the GRC solution strategy.

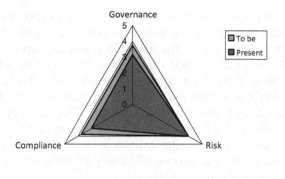

Fig. 3. The present and to be GRC maturity of the Dutch utilities company that was assessed

Fig. 4. Strategic alignment by the Dutch utility company through the "technology transformation" path

The utility company used IT to manage the controls throughout the organization. Future plans consisted of the ambition to evaluate how an improved connection with other IT solutions available in the company (e.g. process modelling software) could be reached, or whether an entirely different solution should be deployed to replace several different solutions. This could bring the alignment between IT and business and the maturity of the GRC processes to yet a higher level.

4.2   Case 2: Dutch Financial Institution

Setting & GRC Maturity. This company is a worldwide financial institution that delivers services in the area of banking, investments, life assurances and pensions. The roots of the institution are present in the Netherlands. The company houses approximately 107,000 employees and has a turnover of approximately 47 billion euro. Besides laws like SOX, the institution has to comply with the Basel II framework (see www.bis.org/publ/bcbsca.htm for further information). This set of international standards and best practices has led to a specific arrangement of the organization into four departments operating as silos. The maturity questionnaire as completed by the respondents results in figure 5. It shows the present state of GRC maturity and the maturity the organization is aiming for within 2-3 years. The institution proves to be at a 3+ maturity for all three areas. The ambition is still to keep on improving the maturity of the GRC practices in their organization, supported by a GRC solution. The institution is quite ambitious in its approach towards GRC. This is, among others, represented by the fact that a chief risk officer is represented on the board. The organization recognizes that a higher maturity concerning GRC can only be obtained by enhancements in the integration between the four departments and to start performing GRC as one integrated activity across the institution. IT needs to play a critical part in this process of integration, but can only be effectively used when it is aligned with the GRC business processes across the organization.

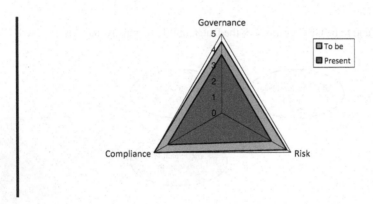

Fig. 5. The present and to be GRC maturity level of the Dutch financial institution that was assessed

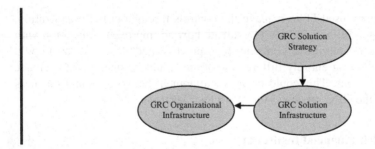

Fig. 6. Strategic alignment of the Dutch financial institution through the "service level" path

Strategic Alignment. As shown in figure 6, the deployment of the IT solution can be characterized by the "service level" perspective, following our conceptual model in figure 2. When aligning IT with the business, the GRC solution strategy of the financial institution was the main driver because the actual GRC solution infrastructure would act as an addition to already available software. Then, the GRC IT solution was adapted the business processes, based on the processes incorporated in the software.

Currently the solution is fully operational within the Operations & IT department, and several other departments have followed this implementation. The institution has the ambition to further deploy the solution throughout the organization, creating one integrated way of handling GRC.

5   Conclusions

This paper was triggered by a need to answer the research question: How can an integrated GRC approach be applied in organizations using a strategic alignment perspective? To achieve an answer to this question, several theoretical definitions of integrated GRC were reviewed, and a strategic alignment perspective was developed for the GRC domain which resulted in an approach to assess the GRC maturity and alignment paths for organizations. The empirical part of the paper then showed how the strategic perspective on GRC and its corresponding assessment framework were applied to two case studies. A large Dutch utility company and a financial institution were studied through a limited number of interviews with responsible managers who also provided feedback on the GRC assessment. Comparing the results of the two case studies showed that organizations have attained similar GRC maturity levels, while they have followed quite different paths to align IT to the business domain. Where the organizational strategy with regard to GRC led at the Dutch utility company, the financial institution selected a path in which the IT solution strategy was taken as starting point. In interpreting this result, it appears that the existing IT assets impact strongly on the selection of the alignment path.

This paper provides new insights but also invites an initiation of new directions for further research. One such direction is to practically support organizations that experience Governance, Risk and Compliance as separate and siloed concepts, and want to develop a holistic and united perspective to these concepts. Obviously, another direction for further research is to further validate and enrich our GRC maturity and alignment approach.

References

1. Chandler, A.D.: Strategy and Structure: Chapters in the history of American Enterprise. The MIT Press, Cambridge (1962)
2. Dupuis, M., Endicott-Popovsky, B., Wang, H., Subramaniam, I., Du, Y.: Top-down mandates and the need for organizational governance, risk management, and compliance in China: A discussion, Asia-Pacific Economic Association (APEA). In: Sixth Annual Conference, Hong Kong (July 2010)
3. Frigo, M.L., Anderson, R.J.: A strategic framework for governance, risk and compliance. Strategic Finance 90(8), 20–61 (2009)
4. Henderson, J.C., Venkatraman, N.: Strategic alignment: Leveraging Information Technology for transforming organizations. IBM Systems Journal 32(1), 472–484 (1999)

5. Koenig, D.R.: Enterprise risk management: A 360 degree review, Ductilibility, LLC, September 11 (2008)
6. KPMG: Survival of the most informed: GRC comes of age – How to envision, strategize, and lead to achieve enterprise resilience. KPMG International Cooperative (2010)
7. Madlener, J.J.: The implications of integrating governance, risk and compliance in business intelligence systems on corporate performance management. Erasmus University Rotterdam (2008)
8. Marks, N.: What is GRC and why does it matter? SAP, London (2010)
9. Mitchell, S.L., Stern Switzer, C.: GRC capability model Red Book 2.0. Open Compliance & Ethics Group, OCEG (April 2009)
10. MHI: Collaborative accountability in governance, risk, & compliance: Creating harmony across business roles, White Paper, MHI (2010)
11. OCEG: OCEG Corporate Compliance and Ethics Maturity Model™ (2007a),
    http://www.oceg.org/Download/OCCEMM
12. OCEG: OCEG Corporate Governance Maturity Model™ (2007b),
    http://www.oceg.org/Download/CGMM
13. OCEG: OCEG Matrix Adapted from RIMS ERM Risk maturity Model (2007c),
    http://www.oceg.org/Download/RIMSERMM
14. Racz, S., Weippl, E., Seufert, A.: A frame of reference for research of integrated governance, risk and compliance (GRC). International Federation for Information Processing (IFIP) (2010)
15. Robb, D.: IT-business alignment takes a step forward with GRC, CIO Update (March 9, 2010)
16. Sarbanes, P., Oxley, M.: Text of the Sarbanes Oxley Act. US Congress, Washington (2002)
17. Scheper, W.: Business IT Alignment: oplossing voor de productiviteitsparadox. Information Science. Utrecht University, Utrecht (2002)
18. Streng, R.J.: Corporate governance, internal control and risk management: The key role of information systems. Bertius Publishers, Moordrecht (2010)
19. Tarantino, A.: Governance, risk and compliance handbook: Technology, finance, environmental, and international guidance and best practices. John Wiley & Sons, Inc., Hoboken (2008)
20. Tiazkun, S., Borovick, L.: Governance, risk and compliance. White Paper. IDC (2007)
21. Vemuri, A.: Strategic themes in risk and compliance. FINSight 2, 2–5 (2008)
22. Venkatraman, N., Henderson, J.C., Oldach, S.: Continuous Strategic Alignment: Exploiting Information Technology Capabilities for Competitive Success. European Management Journal 11(2), 139–149 (1993)

Section 3
ICT for Peace and War

Implementation of a Cyber Security Policy in South Africa: Reflection on Progress and the Way Forward

Marthie Grobler, Joey Jansen van Vuuren, and Louise Leenen

Council for Scientific and Industrial Research, Pretoria, South Africa
{mgrobler1,jjvvuuren,lleenen}@csir.co.za

Abstract. Cyber security is an important aspect of National Security and the safekeeping of a Nation's constituency and resources. In South Africa, the focus on cyber security is especially prominent since many geographical regions are incorporated into the global village in an attempt to bridge the digital divide. This article reflects on current research done in South Africa with regard to a cyber security policy, and proposes the development of methodologies and frameworks that will enable the implementation of such a policy. The focus of this article is the use of an ontology-based methodology to identify and propose a formal, encoded description of the cyber security strategic environment. The aim of the ontology is to identify and represent the multi-layered organisation of players and their associated roles and responsibilities within the cyber security environment. This will contribute largely to the development, implementation and rollout of a national cyber security policy in South Africa.

Keywords: cyber security, ontology, policy, security awareness.

1   Introduction

Information and its related infrastructures are fundamental to cyber security and the implementation of an associated cyber security policy. On the one hand, cyber security pertains to the maintenance of National Security and the interests of citizens; whilst, on the other hand, it can refer to politically motivated hacking to conduct sabotage and espionage against specific nation states. Therefore, the rationale behind national cyber security is to enable the safekeeping of a Nation's constituency and its associated organisational, human, financial, technological and informational resources. This is done to facilitate the achievement of its National objectives [9].

In South Africa, cyber security has been identified as a critical component contributing towards National Security. More geographical regions of South Africa are becoming integrated into the global village, necessitating additional government initiatives aimed at bridging the digital divide and addressing cyber security. One of these initiatives is the development and implementation of a South African specific cyber security policy.

Despite the African continent's recent explosive growth in information and communication technologies, Africa is generally considered as being spared the global high levels of cyber crimes. Although this is often attributed to its traditionally low

M.D. Hercheui et al. (Eds.): HCC10 2012, IFIP AICT 386, pp. 215–225, 2012.

Internet penetration levels with only 139 million Internet users out of a population of more than 2 billion people [16], Africans tend to increasingly fall prey to online predators [14]. In addition, many of the factors that traditionally make African countries more vulnerable (such as increasing bandwidth, use of wireless technologies and infrastructure, high levels of computer illiteracy, ineffective or insufficient legislation to deal with cyber attacks and threats) further expose these countries' crucial infrastructures to cyber risks [12]; hence an effective cyber security policy is urgently needed in order to be able to respond to these risks. A national cyber security policy framework would *"bolster and improve South Africa's cyber security"* [14].

This article will look at the current and future research and development done towards the implementation of a cyber security policy in South Africa. It will present retrospective reflections, as well as proposed future work on selected methodologies and frameworks that will enable the implementation of such a policy. The innovative contribution of this research lies in the argument that an ontology can assist in defining a model that describes the relationships between different cyber security components. Section 2 summarises the development process of a cyber security policy for South Africa. Section 3 gives an overview of cyber security research in South Africa and discusses ways in which the research relates to the development of a cyber security policy. From these two sections it becomes clear that a descriptive model of the cyber security environment in South Africa is required. This leads to a proposal for the development of a cyber security ontology in Section 4. Future research is discussed in Section 5 and the article is concluded in Section 6.

2   Background

South Africa has a huge responsibility to promote cyber security awareness, since the State can be held responsible for wrongful acts committed inside a country, and is obliged to fulfil the interests of the entire international community. As a result, the national cyber security policy framework for South Africa is a long time coming, and initial workshops on the topic were held already in January 2009. Despite the time and effort put into the development of the policy framework, the process of implementation is still not complete.

At the time of writing, the initial published draft version of the policy declared milestones for the imminent establishment of the security CSIRT (Computer Security Incident Response team) and the sector CSERT (Computer Security Emergency Response team) [8]. The decision was made in February 2012 that the Department of State Security should take over responsibility from the Department of Communications (DOC) for drawing the government's policy on cyber crime. In 2010, a similar decision was made to reassign the mandate from the Department of Science and Technology (DST) to the DOC [10].

Given the current status of the policy framework in South Africa, it is agreed that there is not enough emphasis on the national cyber security policy, although reference is made to the policy as the overarching strategy that must guide cyber security. In response, this article proposes five elements as a foundation for the South African cyber security policy requirements: (i) political will; (ii) adapted organisational structures; (iii) identifying accurate proactive and reactive measures; (iv) reducing criminal opportunities; and (iv) education and awareness [9].

It is recommended that these five elements should be present in developing a national strategy for an effective cyber security approach and culture. The next section addresses these elements in more detail, with a preliminary mapping of current South African cyber security research to determine the current state and progress of a cyber security policy implementation. These elements fit with the South African proposed multi-faceted approach to reduce cyber crime [7].

3   Current State of Cyber Security Research in South Africa

The dynamic and volatile nature of the Internet and the cyber domain in general make cyber security research within South Africa an important area to address. Since the cyber domain is inherently globalised, it cannot truly be considered in isolation or on a purely national basis [18]. As such, the South African Justice minister, Jeff Radebe, stated at a parliamentary briefing in February 2012 that finalising specific cyber crime plans would be a priority in 2012 [7]. In addition, the DOC stated that its *"decision to boost cyber security comes in conjunction with the government's plans to battle crime using technology-based solutions and partnerships"* [14]. With this in mind, the five elements identified above as part of the successful development of a national cyber security strategy [9] are discussed next, in relation to current South African research.

3.1   Political Will

To ensure that the cyber security action plan receives government-wide attention, national leadership is imperative both at an individual and organisational level. Furthermore, national cyber security policies as well as national and international strategies should be in place to fight cyber crime. The draft cyber security policy presented by the DOC aims to ensure that organs of state as well as the private sector can cooperate to ensure the security of South Africa's information networks [14].

As mentioned in Section 2, the South African national strategy for cyber security is under development, albeit not yet implemented or enforceable. The draft policy does address some levels of compatibility with international efforts, as proposed by Ghernouti-Hélie [9]. For example, co-operation between police in the Southern African Development Community region and Interpol is a high priority in 2012 to fight cyber criminal syndicates [7].

3.2   Adapted Organisational Structures

It is recommended that adequate national organisational structures should exist to support the deployment of an effective cyber security solution for individuals, organisations and governmental agencies. These organisational structures should be adapted from other national models to take elements such as country-specific culture, economic context and ICT infrastructure development into account [9].

In terms of cyber security, a national CSIRT could be the most appropriate organisational structure for linking communication networks and information systems with economic and social development. Earlier South African research has identified nine steps to ensure that the CSIRT meets the needs of such an organisational structure. The first and most crucial of these steps would be clarifying the mandate and policy related issues involved [10]. At the time of writing, a new move towards the development and establishment of one of the South African CSIRTs is underway by the DOC and joint partners. The necessity of national CSIRTs is underscored in the draft South African cyber security policy [8].

3.3   Identifying Accurate Proactive and Reactive Measures

Since everyday activities have an increasing digital component, it is becoming increasingly urgent to augment and automate cyber security in order to maximise outputs and minimise human error. Both South African individuals and groups are largely dependent on data. This dependence relates not only to physical data, but also to the relationship of this data to specific infrastructures. Accordingly, it is important that these actions can be both proactive and reactive in nature.

Ghernouti-Hélie [9] proposed that cyber security actors can be classified into three roles: the protector; the protected; or the criminal. Once the South African cyber security policy is implemented, it is envisioned that the roles would be addressed appropriately, and South African citizens should have a better understanding of where they fit in terms of, for example, who will play the role of the protector, and what is the punishment for the criminals. Existing South African legislation already addresses criminal punishment for cyber security crimes; this includes: the Electronic Communications and Transactions Act No 25 of 2002; the Regulation of Interception of Communications and Provision of Communication-related information Act No 70 of 2002; and the Protection of Personal Information Bill of 2010 [1].

3.4   Reducing Criminal Opportunities

Due to the international scope of the Internet and wide usage of technology, cyber security intersects largely with the application and implementation of international legislation. Regardless, the foundation for an adequate security strategy is twofold: raise the level of risks taken by the criminal, and raise the level of difficulties faced by the criminal. In all instances, legislative and regulatory measures should concomitantly raise the level of risk perceived by a criminal, and decrease the favourable context to perpetrate an illegal action [9]. Reducing opportunities for crime is one of the ultimate benefits of implementing a cyber security policy framework. As such, South Africa is one of the signatories of the Council of Europe's Convention on Cybercrime [5].

3.5   Education and Awareness

Organisational structures should encourage, lead or coordinate continuing education for professionals in the legal, economical and political fields. In addition, the realisation of a global cyber security awareness culture will contribute to achieving part of the goals of a national cyber security strategy [9]. In South Africa, there are several cyber security awareness programmes aimed at educating user groups in different geographical areas of the country [11], made necessary by the increasing rate of bandwidth consumption or utilisation in South Africa. Already in 2007/2008, South Africa's overall online activity was estimated to be 67% of overall online activity in Africa, whilst its population accounted for only 5% of that of entire continent [19]. This emphasises the importance of proper cyber security awareness and formalised training in this domain.

Research done in the South African provinces of Gauteng, Mpumalanga and Limpopo in general indicates good Internet behaviour on the part of South African citizens. Completed questionnaires were retrieved from different geographical areas and were grouped under urban areas, semi-rural areas and rural areas. The levels of cyber security awareness were calculated as 69% for urban areas, 53% for semi-rural areas, and 40% for rural areas. A cumulative extrapolation of total awareness in South Africa based on the overall awareness of the sample group is estimated at 51% [17]. This aspect still requires a lot of attention in South Africa.

The next section introduces the use of an ontology to assist in the development and implementation of a South African cyber security policy.

4   Using an Ontology to Implement Cyber Security

The mapping of South African research and development activities on the five practical elements as proposed for international cyber security policy implementation (refer to Section 3) shows that some progress has been made. The discussions also highlighted the involvement of a number of entities and functions to ensure the successful implementation of a national cyber security policy. However, since the cyber security environment is not clearly bounded and defined, it is very difficult to put forward an easily understandable and implementable cyber security policy. As such, the authors propose to use an ontological model to formally define and describe the roles of players in this environment together with their functions and responsibilities, as well as the roles of the different stakeholders in the cyber security environment. It is important to realise that there are multiple levels of role players in the cyber security environment and that roles and responsibilities often overlap. It is precisely this layer of complexity that necessitates a structured, formal description of the environment before implementation of the policy can succeed.

This ontology will provide a model of the shared environment (i.e. the cyber security domain), a common vocabulary and formal descriptions of the inter-relationships between the relevant entities and functions as identified in Section 3. Ontologies have been used previously to define policy frameworks and instantiate policies [6]. Although the use of an ontology as proposed here is different to that of Cuppens-Boulahia et al., it is clear that ontologies can be used to assist with the implementation of policy in various ways. Ontologies could therefore be a valuable contribution to the final implementation of a cyber security policy in South Africa.

The methodology of using an ontological model will benefit the communication and sharing of information between role players during the implementation of the policy, the modelling of the implementation phases and functions, and for education and training.

The next sub-section contains an overview of ontologies in general and the subsequent sub-section describes an initial high-level ontology for the cyber security strategic environment.

4.1   What Is an Ontology?

For the purpose of this paper, an ontology is a technology that provides a way to exchange semantic information between people and systems. It consists of an encoded, common domain vocabulary and a description of the meaning of terms in the vocabulary. Grüber [13] defines an ontology as *"formal, explicit specification of a shared conceptualisation"*. A formal ontology specifies a machine-readable domain model depicting entities and their inter-entity relationships. It generally consists of a descriptive part and reasoning technologies. The descriptive part of an ontology captures the domain from the domain experts' point of view, expressing domain information in a way that can be processed by computers and be understood by humans. The use of reasoning technologies enables new information to be derived from the facts contained in an ontology.

The information in an ontology is expressed in an ontology language (logic-based language), and then progressively refined. The construction and maintenance of ontologies greatly depend on the availability of ontology languages equipped with well-defined semantics and powerful reasoning tools. Fortunately, there already exists a class of logics, called description logics (DLs), that provides for both, and are therefore ideal candidates for ontology languages [2]. The Web Ontology Language (OWL) 2.0 was granted the status of a W3C recommendation in 2009, and is the official Semantic Web Ontology language. OWL was designed to provide a common way to process the content of Web information instead of displaying it. It is intended to be interpreted by computer applications and not to be read by people [22]. In this research, OWL was used to interpret the ontological model developed for the cyber security strategic domain.

The use of ontologies is growing rapidly in a variety of application areas, and is the underlying technology driving the Semantic Web initiative [3]. Ontologies vary greatly in their content and intent [4], [25]: upper-level ontologies define general, descriptive terms that are domain independent; core ontologies contain only terms that are domain-neutral, that is, terms that apply to multiple sub-domains; and domain ontologies represent specific terms in a particular domain and are detailed.

4.2   A Domain Ontology for the Cyber Security Environment

There are many benefits to implementing ontologies. As such, the authors used an ontological model to identify and propose a formal, encoded description of the cyber security strategic environment. This will contribute largely to the development, implementation and roll out of a national cyber security policy in South Africa. Benefits include:

- **To enable the re-use of domain knowledge.** There are many role players in South Africa that have performed research and development work on cyber security. Involving these role players as domain experts in the development of the ontology will maximise the utilisation of any existing domain knowledge.
- **To share a common understanding of domain concepts and information among the members of a community.** Due to the dynamic and volatile nature of the cyber security domain, there are often multiple explanations or ambiguous understandings of domain specific concepts. An ontology will assist in standardising these concepts.
- **To facilitate information integration and interoperability between heterogeneous knowledge sources.** As pointed out in Section 3, entities and functions involved in the cyber security domain range from local to international, humans to organisations, and policies to implementation tools. By using an ontology, it would be possible to ensure integration and interoperability between different components of the larger South African cyber domain.
- **To analyse domain knowledge.** Existing domain knowledge, once identified and captured within an ontological model, can be used to finalise the South African cyber security policy, and implement its components to ensure the better protection of National Security and safekeeping [20].

The main benefit of the high-level ontology envisaged here is that a formal, encoded description of the cyber security strategic environment will be created: that is, all the entities, their attributes and their inter-relationships will be defined and represented. There will be a single shareable model of the environment, agreed-upon by subject experts.

This paper presents the upper-level entities of an initial ontology. Subject matter experts have identified these entities. The proposed cyber security strategy environment ontology is implemented in 'Protégé', a free, open-source platform that provides a suite of tools to construct domain models and knowledge-based applications with ontologies [23]. The main entities in the environment are the *Human Domain*, *Information*, *Infrastructure* and *Tools*. Figure 1 illustrates the main entities and their attributes and relationships.

The Human Domain entity consists of either individuals or groups. A group can be public (e.g. a state department) or private (e.g. a company or a terrorist organisation).

A group has the following attributes: size, goal, role, motivation, and it can be regarded as a target.

A goal is an intended outcome whilst a motivation is related to an individual or a group's needs.

An individual shares all of these attributes, but its size is exactly one.

Humans use tools, measures, guidelines, policies, techniques, applications, etc. and infrastructure to protect or attack information security and to manipulate information.

Infrastructure can consist of physical infrastructure, electronic infrastructure, or software. Infrastructure has a location as attribute.

Information has a type and format as attributes. Information and Infrastructure have a security classification, and Information has Infrastructure (e.g. is stored somewhere).

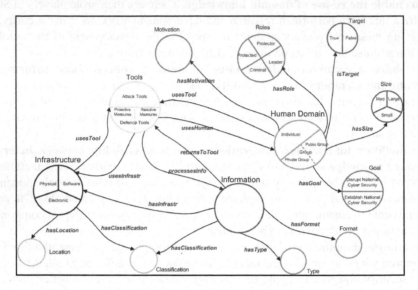

Fig. 1. Illustration of high-level cyber security strategy environment ontology

Cyber security awareness and training are relevant in determining the type of information that must be represented in the ontology, and initial steps have been taken towards the establishment of a Cyber Security Hub in South Africa [19]. This Hub will be responsible for cyber security awareness on a national level. The main role players in terms of cyber security awareness in South Africa are the DOC, the Department of Basic Education, and the South African Police Service (SAPS). A second level of role players includes: Universities and Further Education Training colleges, including the Department of Higher Education and Training; research institutions under the auspices of the DST; non-governmental organisations (NGOs); private organisations; banking sector; mobile sector; MICT SETA (Information Systems, Electronics and Telecommunication Technologies Education and Training Authority); Department of Defence (DOD) and the State Security Agency (SSA); Internet Service Providers; and other government departments.

Most stakeholders have more than one role in the implementation and the application of the policy. For example, DST, the Department of Higher Education and Training and the SSA are jointly responsible for general research on cyber security policy, whilst the SSA takes responsibility for implementing the cyber security policy [15]. Various centres and civil societies in general are responsible for reporting cyber incidents. When a cyber security incident has been reported or a specific instance of the policy has to be implemented, the relevant stakeholders have to be identified and contacted. The initial ontology can be used to support this task.

Fig. 1 only shows the high-level categories of these entities. However, when analysed in more detail, there is a close correlation between the entities identified in Section 3 and the entities in the proposed ontology. For example, the DOC (refer to Section 3.1) can be classified as a public group with the role of leader that uses the cyber security policy as tool (reactive measures) which uses the physical infrastructure of the CSIRT. Citizens (refer to Section 3.3) can be classified as an individual with the role of protected, and an attribute of target. Cyber security awareness programmes (refer to Section 3.5) can be classified as defence tools (proactive measures) that use physical, software and electronic infrastructure in the location of Limpopo.

5   Future Research

The first task in creating the cyber security policy is to set up an implementation framework. The first step must comprise an analysis of the current situation in South Africa. The rationale for this analysis is to break down the implementation into manageable, understandable components, because the role players responsible for the implementation are not necessarily the people who formulated the policy. In addition, the output of the analysis will greatly determine the final organisational structure. It is also necessary to be able to determine the strategies that will achieve the identified objectives of the policy. A final organisational structure needs to be investigated and human, financial, technological and physical resources allocated. A change management plan and commitment plan need to be set up to ensure co-operation between the parties involved. The future research will include:

- Development of the implementation framework;
- Expansion of the analysis of the current structures and role players of cyber security in South Africa. Several other methodologies would be used including Morphological Analysis, a method for systematically structuring and analysing multi-dimensional, non-quantifiable problems [24]. The detailed domain ontologies will be built using all this information;
- Development of organisational structures necessary for implementation of the cyber security policy;
- Extension and implementation of the Cyber Security Awareness Toolkit (Cyber-SAT);
- Development of change management and commitment plans.

Hence, the use of an ontology is initially envisaged to define the role players and their functions. Later on the authors foresee other uses for an extended ontology. Since the cyber domain environment is vast, a core high-level ontology is proposed to be developed in conjunction with sub-domain ontologies. For example, a sub-domain ontology can be developed for predicting network attacks as a sub-component of the proposed cyber security policy implementation. All the sub-domain ontologies which have been developed can be merged once completed with existing techniques, to provide a combined ontological system that can be further extended.

6   Conclusion

This article describes the implementation of a cyber security policy in South Africa, summarises progress made so far of the research and development performed, and proposes the way forward. The authors discuss the requirements that will enable the implementation of the cyber security policy and reflect on research that is currently being done on the use of an ontology in this regard. The aim of the ontology is initially to provide a formal description of role players and their function in the cyber security environment.

Although several research articles and projects have been undertaken during the last three years, only limited research has been done on the implementation of the cyber security policy in South Africa. The article by Phahlamohlaka [21] discussed the CyberSAT as an implementation strategy. This lack of research could be attributed to the delay in the promulgation of the cyber security policy in South Africa. Cyber security awareness is the only research aspect of the cyber security implementation that has been covered in some detail since 2009, with several players starting to implement some awareness training in South Africa.

References

1. Acts: Acts Online (2012), http://www.acts.co.za/ (accessed March 28, 2012)
2. Baader, F., Calvenese, D., McGuinness, D., Nardi, D., Patel-Schneider, P.: The Description Logic Handbook: Theory, Implementation, and Applications. Cambridge University Press, Cambridge (2003)
3. Berners-Lee, T., Hendler, J., Lassila, O.: The Semantic Web. Scientific American 284(5), 33–43 (2001)
4. Boury-Brisset, A.: Ontological Approach to Military Knowledge Modeling and Management. In: Symposium on Military Data and Information Fusion, Czech Republic, Prague (2003)
5. Council of Europe: Convention on Cybercrime. CETS No.: 185 (2010), http://conventions.coe.int/Treaty/Commun/ChercheSig.asp?NT=1 85&CM=8&DF=28/10/2010&CL=ENG (accessed March 28, 2012)
6. Cuppens-Boulahia, N., Cuppens, F., de Vergara, L., Vázquez, E., Guerra, J., Debar, H.: An Ontology-based Approach to React to Network Attacks. International Journal of Information and Computer Security 3(4), 280–305 (2009)
7. Davis, G.: State Security in Charge of Cybercrime Plans (2012), http://www.iol.co.za/dailynews/news/state-security-in-charge-of-cybercrime-plans-1.1238243 (accessed February 21, 2012)
8. Department of Communications: National Cybersecurity Policy Framework for South Africa – Draft. Unpublished document (2011)
9. Ghernouti-Hélie, S.: A National Strategy for an Effective Cybersecurity Approach and Culture. In: ARES 2010 International Conference on Availability, Reliability and Security, Krakow, pp. 370–373 (2010)
10. Grobler, M., Bryk, H.: Common Challenges Faced During the Establishment of a CSIRT. Presented at the ISSA Conference 2010, Sandton, South Africa (2010)

11. Grobler, M., Flowerday, S., Von Solms, R., Venter, H.: Cyber Awareness Initiatives in South Africa: A National Perspective. In: Proceedings of Southern African Cyber Security Awareness Workshop (SACSAW 2011), pp. 32–41 (2011)
12. Grobler, M., Dlamini, Z.: Global Cyber Trends a South African Reality. In: Proceedings of IST-Africa Conference (IST-Africa 2012) (2012)
13. Grüber, T.: A translation approach to portable ontology specifications. Knowledge Acquisition 5, 191–220 (1993)
14. Guy: Cyber Security Policy Will Go Before Cabinet For Approval This Year (2011), http://www.defenceweb.co.za/index.php?option=com_content&view=article&id=13783:cyber-security-policy-will-go-before-cabinet-for-approval-this-year&catid=48:Information%20%20Communication%20Technologies&Itemid=109 (accessed February 24, 2012)
15. ICT Procurement: Cyber Security Mandate Transferred (2012), http://ictprocurement.com/security/cyber-security-mandate-transferred.html (Accessed May 3, 2012)
16. Internetworldstats: Internet Usage Statistics for Africa (2012), http://www.internetworldstats.com/stats1.htm (accessed February 27, 2012)
17. Jansen van Vuuren, J.C., Grobler, M.M., Zaaiman, J.: The Influence of Cyber Security Levels of South African Citizens on National Security. In: Proceedings of ICIW 2012, Seattle, USA, pp. 138–147 (2012)
18. Kramer, F.D.: Cyberpower and National Security: Policy Recommendations for a Strategic Framework. In: Kramer, F.D., Star, S.H., Wentz, L.K. (eds.) Cyberpower and National Security, pp. 3–23. Centre for Technical and National Security Policy, Washington (2009)
19. Moyo, A. , Kayle, A.: DOC Calls for Collaboration, Security Innovation (2012), http://www.itweb.co.za/index.php?option=Com_content&view=article&id=54874 (accessed August 8, 2012)
20. Noy, N.F., McGuiness, D.L.: Ontology Development 101: A Guide to Creating Your First Ontology. Technical Report KSL-01-05. Stanford Knowledge Systems Laboratory (2001)
21. Phahlamohlaka, L.J., Jansen van Vuuren, J.C., Radebe, J.: Cyber Security Awareness Toolkit for National Security: an Approach to South Africa's Cyber Security Policy Implementation. In: Proceedings of the First IFIP TC9/ TC11 Southern African Cyber Security Awareness Workshop 2011 (SACSAW 2011), Gaborone, Botswana, pp. 1–14 (2011)
22. OWL 2 Web Ontology Language (2012), http://www.w3.org/TR/owl-overview (accessed March 27, 2012)
23. Protégé ontology editor (2012), http://protege.stanford.edu/ (accessed February 7, 2012)
24. Ritchey, T.: Wicked Problems. Structuring Social Messes with Morphological Analysis. Adapted from a lecture given at the Royal Institute of Technology in Stockholm (2004), http://www.swemorph.com/downloads.html (2005)
25. Smith, B., Miettinen, K., Mandrivk, W.: The Ontology of Command and Control. In: Proceedings of the 14th International Command and Control Research and Technology Symposium, Buffalo, National Centre for Ontological Research, New York (2009)

Mapping the Most Significant Computer Hacking Events to a Temporal Computer Attack Model

Renier van Heerden[1,2], Heloise Pieterse[1], and Barry Irwin[2]

[1] Council for Scientific and Industrial Research, Pretoria, South Africa
{rvheerden,hpieterse}@csir.co.za
[2] Rhodes University, Grahamstown, South Africa
b.irwin@ru.ac.za

Abstract. This paper presents eight of the most significant computer hacking events (also known as computer attacks). These events were selected because of their unique impact, methodology, or other properties. A temporal computer attack model is presented that can be used to model computer based attacks. This model consists of the following stages: Target Identification, Reconnaissance, Attack, and Post-Attack Reconnaissance stages. The Attack stage is separated into: Ramp-up, Damage and Residue. This paper demonstrates how our eight significant hacking events are mapped to the temporal computer attack model. The temporal computer attack model becomes a valuable asset in the protection of critical infrastructure by being able to detect similar attacks earlier.

Keywords: computer attack model, ontology, network attack prediction.

1 Introduction

Computer hacking (also referred as computer cracking) developed in conjunction with the normal usage of computer systems. This paper discusses some of the most significant hacking events and the features that made them unique. The events listed are considered to be significant because of their unique impact, methodology or other properties. The level of significance is an abstract and relative measure. Other attempts to judge the importance of hacking events have been made by Heater [1], Hall [2] and Julian [3].

Research in computer network attack prediction at the Counsel for Scientific and Industrial Research (CSIR) in South Africa has resulted in the development of a Taxonomy and Ontology of computer network attacks. A temporal attack model was developed with the goal of separating the different stages of a computer network attack. The model consists of the following basic stages: Target Identification; Reconnaissance; Attack; and Post Attack. The Attack stage has the following sub-stages: Ramp-up; Damage; and Residue. Research was also organized into strategies for identifying the Reconnaissance and Ramp-up stages. The attack model is a valuable asset in the protection of critical infrastructure as it has the ability to identify attacks at an earlier stage and so improve the responsiveness to incidents.

M.D. Hercheui et al. (Eds.): HCC10 2012, IFIP AICT 386, pp. 226–236, 2012.

This paper presents the authors' view on the most important hacking events, and cannot in itself be considered absolute. We chose events based on either the uniqueness of the technique used or their unique impact. The attack model is presented in more detail in Section 2. Section 3 describes the most significant hacking events and their characteristics. Section 4 identifies trends in hacking development. Section 5 maps the hacking events to our temporal attack model. Section 6 focuses on the protection of critical infrastructure. Section 7 discusses mayor future hacking events.

2   Attack Model

2.1   Computer Attack Taxonomy and Ontology

A detailed taxonomy that describes computer based attacks has the following classes [4]: actor; actor location; aggressor; attack goal; attack mechanism; automation level; effects; motivation; phase; scope; target; and vulnerability. The taxonomy was then used to describe the following scenarios [4]: denial of service (DoS); industrial espionage; web deface; spear phishing; password harvesting; snooping for secrets; financial theft; amassing computer resources; industrial sabotage; and cyber warfare.

2.2   Temporal Attack Model

The Phase class in Section 2.1 was used to build the Temporal Attack Model. The Target Identification stage represents actions undertaken by an attacker in choosing his/her target. Identification of these actions falls outside the scope of the network attack prediction project, but forms part of the overall attack model. The Reconnaissance stage represents actions undertaken by an attacker to identify potential weak spots. These actions are the earliest indicators of an impending network attack, and occur before any real damage has occurred. Popular reconnaissance actions include network mapping and scanning with tools such as Nmap and Nessus. Google and other search engines can also be used to identify potential weak spots. The Attack stage represents modification of the target system by an attacker. The system can be modified in the following aspects: Confidentiality; Integrity; and Availability.

These aspects are also known as the CIA principles. Confidentiality refers to prevention of disclosure of information to unauthorized individuals or systems. Integrity means that data in a system cannot be modified undetectably. Availability refers to the availability of information when required by the system to serve its purpose. In computing, e-Business and information security, it is necessary to ensure that data, transactions, communications and documents are genuine. It is also important that authentication validates the identities of both parties involved.

In figure 1 the Temporal Attack Model is represented. The Attack stage is subdivided into sub-stages. The first sub-stage is the Ramp-up stage. This sub-stage refers to the preparatory actions performed by an attacker before his/her final goal can be attained. The targeted computer network is modified in this stage, but only in preparation for some other goal. This stage typically includes the installation of backdoors and other malware.

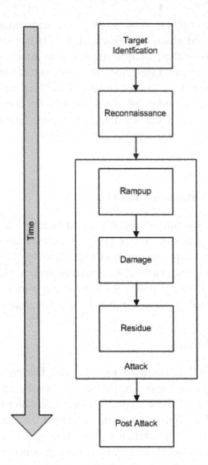

Fig. 1. Temporal Network Attack Model

The Damage sub-stage refers to actions undertaken by an attacker during the achievement of his/her final goal. In this sub-stage the network is damaged according to the Information Security CIA principles. For example when an attacker launches a Distributed Denial of Service (DDoS) attack on a network, the Damage sub-stage is entered as soon as the attack is launched. The action of installing DDoS attack software falls under the Ramp-up stage.

The Residue sub-stage refers to unintended communications and actions by malware after an attack has been completed. For example, computers that have incorrect time settings may attack their target at a later date and/or time than when the original coordinated attack was planned. This is also noticed in DDoS attacks.

The Post-Attack Reconnaissance stage refers to scouting and other similar reconnaissance actions performed by an attacker after completion of the Attack stage. The attacker's goal in this stage is to verify the effects of his/her attack and to assess whether the same methodology can be used again in the future.

3 Significant Hacking Events

We consider the following to be the most significant hacking events.

Brain Virus: The world's first computer virus was created by two brothers, Basit and AmjadFarooqAlvi, in Lahore, Pakistan [5]. This was a boot sector virus since it only affected boot records [6]. The Brain virus marked the area where the virus code was hidden as having bad sectors [7]. It occupied a part of the computer memory and infected any floppy disk that was accessed. It hid itself from detection by hooking into the INT13. When an attempt was made to read the infected sector, the virus simply showed the original sector. This resulted in a change to the volume label.

Morris Worm: On 2nd November 1988 a Cornell graduate student, Robert Tappan Morris, unleashed the first computer worm [8]. It started as a benign experiment with a simple bug in a program, but the worm replicated much faster than anticipated [9]. By the following morning it had infected over 6000 hosts [10]. The worm could not determine whether a host had already been infected or not and as a result distributed multiple copies of itself on a single host. The exponential increase in data load eventually tipped off the system administrators and the worm was discovered.

CIH Virus: The CIH virus, also referred to as the Chernobyl or E95.CIH virus, first appeared in June 1998 [7]. It was created by a Taiwanese college student called Chen Ing-Hau [11]. It possessed a destructive payload with the purpose to destroy data. On release, the virus attempted to override a portion of the hard disk as well as the flash ROM of the PC. It infected over a million computers in Korea at the time [7].

I-LOVE-YOU Worm: The I-LOVE-YOU worm first appeared on May 4, 2000 in the form of an e-mail with the subject: I-LOVE-YOU [7]. It was created by a student named Onel de Guzman, and originated from Manila, Philippines. The worm code was written using Visual Basic and processed by the WScript engine [12]. It targeted computers using Internet Explorer and Microsoft's Outlook. Within a few hours it had spread worldwide via e-mail by making use of Outlook addresses of infected users. It exploited human curiosity, enticing people into opening an untrusted email.

Code Red Worm: The Code Red worm appeared on July 12, 2001. It exploited a buffer-overflow vulnerability in Microsoft's IIS web servers [13]. Upon infection of a machine, it checked whether the date was between the first and the nineteenth of the month. If so, a random list of IP addresses was generated and each machine on the list was probed to infect as many other machines as possible. Proper propagation of the worm failed due to a code error in the random number generator [14]. On 19 July a second version of the Code Red worm appeared that infected computers at a rate of 200 hosts per minute [9].

Estonia Hack Attack: Early in 2007, a series of politically motivated cyber-attacks struck Estonia [16]. The attacks included web defacements and DDoS attacks on Estonia government agencies, banks and Internet Service Providers. The attacks followed the removal of a bronze statue in Tallinn, which commemorated the dead from the Second World War [17]. At the time of the attacks, Estonia was one of the leading nations in Europe with regards to information and communication technologies [16]. This can be considered an example of cyber warfare and its potential effects.

Conficker Worm: The Conficker was the first worm to penetrate cloud technology [15], [18]. It first appeared in November 2008 and quickly became one of the most infamous worms to date. The Conficker worm controlled over 6.4 million computer systems and also owned the world's largest cloud network at the time. As a result of the infrastructure of a cloud, the worm could propagate much faster, infect a broader range of hosts and cause greater damage. Conficker has not been used as an attack weapon since, and it is speculated that it might have been a precursor to Stuxnet.

Stuxnet Worm: Stuxnet was one of the most complex threats ever analysed [19]. The primary purpose of Stuxnet was to target industrial control systems such as gas pipelines and power plants with the goal of reprogramming the programmable logic controls (PLCs) of the systems to enable an attacker to control them. Stuxnet was also the first to exploit four zero-day vulnerabilities as well as compromise two digital certificates. As of September 29, 2010, Iran had the greatest number of infected computer systems. Stuxnet has shown that direct-attack attempts on critical infrastructures are no longer a myth but a definite possibility. Stuxnet actions can be considered an act of war, but no one has officially claimed responsibility for it.

4   Trends

Although our selection of significant hacking events is subjective and does not represent a comprehensive list, some interesting trends can be identified. Firstly, the monetary impact of each event is shown in figure 2. The vertical scale represents an estimation of the effect. Effects are classified as follows: 5 – severe financial impact; 4 – significant financial impact; 3 – major financial impact; 2 – minor financial impact; and 1 – negligible financial impact. On the horizontal scale, the attacks are listed in chronological order.

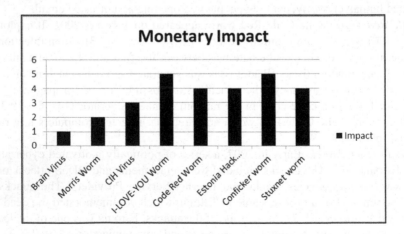

Fig. 2. Monetary impact of hacking events

Figure 3 lists the most common countries of origin of hacking events. Most events surprisingly originate from the Philippines. Figure 4 illustrates the number of events per continent, with Europe and Asia at the top of the list.

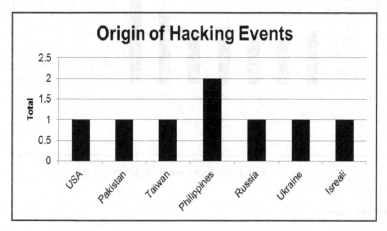

Fig. 3. Countries of origin of hacking events

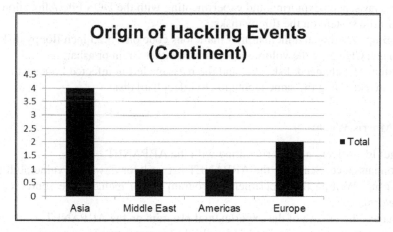

Fig. 4. Hacking events per continent

In most hacking events, small malware of between 1,000 and 100,000 bytes were utilized. The significant exception is Stuxnet, with a size of over 1.5 megabytes. The progressive increase in bandwidth and computer memory size will likely lend itself to the use of bigger malware (figure 5).

5   Attack Model Map

The following sections describe how the most significant hacking events map to the Attack Model in Section 3.

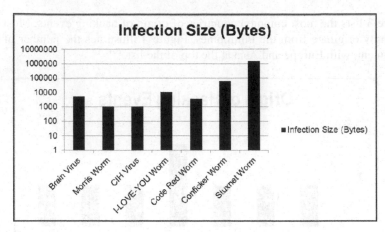

Fig. 5. Infection size in bytes

5.1 Brain Virus

— Target Identification: Experimentation with 5.25 inch floppy disks.
— Reconnaissance: Exploring and experimenting with the DOS File Allocation Table (FAT) file system on the floppy disks.
— Ramp-up: Writing and inclusion of malicious code on a 5.25 inch floppy disk.
— Damage: Changing the volume label to read either Brain or ashar.
— Residue: The changed disk label and the message left in infected boot sectors.
— Post attack: Using the same technique to infect hard disks.

5.2 Morris Worm

— Target Identification: Experimenting with the ARPANET.
— Reconnaissance: Scanning the ARPANET network for flaws and vulnerabilities.
— Ramp-up: Writing the experimental program which includes the source code for the worm.
— Damage: The release of the experimental program on the ARPANET.
— Residue: A machine being infected multiple times rather than only once.
— Post attack: Experimenting with the possibility of a worm in different environments.

5.3 CIH Virus

— Target Identification: Exploring the gaps left in PE (Portable Executable) files.
— Reconnaissance: Experimenting with PE file formats under Windows 95, 98 and ME for potential vulnerabilities.
— Ramp-up: Writing the CIH virus code.
— Damage: Spreading of the CIH virus on computers, and destroying certain PC's BIOS, thus disabling PC use.

- Residue: No unintended attacks caused by the virus in this case.
- Post attack: Verifying the effects of the virus by means of scouting.

5.4   I-LOVE-YOU Worm

- Target Identification: Exploring and experimenting with the Windows operating system and Microsoft Outlook.
- Reconnaissance: Using well-known search engines to search for potential weaknesses in the Windows operating system and Microsoft Outlook.
- Ramp-up: Writing the I-LOVE-YOU worm code.
- Damage: The worm led to an effective DoS attack.
- Residue: Only hidden files with .mp2 and .mp3 extensions.
- Post attack: Searching for other additional weaknesses in the Windows operating system and Microsoft Outlook.

5.5   Code Red Worm

- Target Identification: Exploring the Microsoft IIS server configurations.
- Reconnaissance: Using well-known search engines to search for potential vulnerabilities in the IIS server software.
- Ramp-up: Writing the Code Red worm code and identifying a buffer overflow vulnerability in the software.
- Damage: Launching a DoS attack against randomly selected server IP addresses.
- Residue: The worm used a static seed as its random number generator and so generated identical lists of IP addresses that caused computers to be infected multiple times.
- Post attack: Searching for additional weaknesses in Microsoft's IIS servers.

5.6   Estonia Hack Attack

- Target Identification: The relocation of the Bronze Soldier in Tallinn.
- Reconnaissance: Using well-known search engines to identify possible weaknesses in the websites of well-known Estonian organizations.
- Ramp-up: Installation of malware on targeted computer systems.
- Damage: Government and commercial services (such as banks) became unavailable during the attack.
- Residue: Russian-language bulletin boards and one defaced website with the phrase: "Hacked from Russian hackers".
- Post attack: Scanning of the infected computer networks to determine the effects of the attacks.

5.7   Conficker Worm

- Target Identification: Exploring cloud computing.
- Reconnaissance: Using well-known search engines to identify possible vulnerabilities in a cloud computing system.

— Ramp-up: Writing the code for the Conficker worm.
— Damage: Launching the Conficker worm in the cloud, thus making its target resources available to the attacker.
— Residue: No unintended attacks caused by the worm in this case.
— Post attack: Releasing additional versions of the worm to verify the effects.

5.8   Stuxnet Worm

— Target Identification: Uranium enrichment infrastructure in Iran.
— Reconnaissance: Using well-known search engines to identify possible vulnerabilities in industrial software and equipment developed by Siemens.
— Ramp-up: Writing the code for the Stuxnet worm and installing additional malware on targeted computer networks.
— Damage: It physically damaged the Iranian Nuclear enrichment systems.
— Residue: Infiltration of computer systems other than those in Iran.
— Post attack: Verifying the effects on Iran's industrial software systems.

6   Protection of Critical Infrastructure

The protection of critical infrastructure involves the readiness to act against serious incidents threatening the critical infrastructure of a nation. Recently there is an increasing need to protect critical infrastructure from terrorist or other physical attacks, including cyber-attacks [20]. The previous sections emphasized this need by reviewing eight of the most significant computer network attacks. Apart from Stuxnet, there have been other instances of infrastructure attacks through computer networks [21]:

— Maroochy Shire Council's sewage control system in Queensland, Australia was attacked.
— A teenager in Worcester, Massachusetts broke into the Bell Atlantic computer system and disabled part of the public switched telephone network using a dial-up modem connected to the system. This attack disabled phone services at the control tower, airport security, the airport fire department, the weather service, and carriers that use the airport.
— In 2000, the Interior Ministry of Russia reported that hackers seized temporary control of the system regulating gas flows in natural gas pipelines.
— In August 2005, Zotob worm crashed thirteen of DaimlerChrysler's U.S. automobile manufacturing plants forcing them to remain offline for almost an hour. Plants in Illinois, Indiana, Wisconsin, Ohio, Delaware, and Michigan were also forced down.
— The Sobig virus was blamed for shutting down train signaling systems throughout the east coast of the U.S. The virus infected the computer system at CSX Corp.'s Jacksonville, Florida headquarters, shutting down signaling, dispatching, and other systems.

— The Nuclear Regulatory Commission confirmed that in January 2003, the Microsoft SQL Server worm known as the Slammer worm infected a private computer network at the idled Davis-Besse nuclear power plant in Oak Harbor, Ohio, disabling a safety monitoring system for nearly five hours.

The Attack Model of Section 2.2 is able to map these Infrastructure computer based attacks. The ultimate goal of this research is to prevent such attacks by identifying the initial stages early enough for preventative actions. The model is able to present any type of computer network based attack, since computer based attacks on Infrastructure uses the same techniques and methodologies as traditional computer network attacks. The Reconnaissance and Ramp-up stages for attacking Infrastructure are similar for attacking computer networks.

7   Conclusion and Future Work

The goal of the network attack model was to represent the majority of network based attacks. This temporal model was verified by mapping eight significant computer network attacks. The attacks were chosen to represent the most significant computer attacks (hacks) in the authors view. The mapping of these attacks shows the usability of the temporal model in aiding critical infrastructure protection.

To prevent or protect against computer attacks, the CSIR are investigating methods to detect the Reconnaissance and Ramp-up stages of an attack. If these stages can be detected, mitigating action can be taken against computer attacks. The attack model is under development and will evolve as the research progress. Future work includes adding new dimensions to the classification of attacks, namely origin and motivation of the attack. Reviewing the reasons of why a network was easily penetrated and focusing on the commonalities of learnt lessons will also be explored.

References

1. Heater, B.: Male: A Brief Timeline (2011),
   http://www.pcmag.com/slideshow/story/261678/malware-a-
   brief-timeline/
2. Hall, K.: The 7 worstcyberattacks in history (that we know about) (2012),
   http://dvice.com/archives/2010/09/7-of-the-most-d.php
3. Julian: 10 Most Costly Cyber Attacks in History (2011),
   http://www.businesspundit.com/10-most-costly-cyber-
   attacks-in-history/
4. van Heerden, R.P., Irwin, B., Burke, I.D.: Classifying Network Attack Scenarios using an Ontology. In: Proceedings of the 7th International Conference on Information Warfare and Security, pp. 331–324 (2012)
5. Desai, P.: Towards an undetectable computer virus. Master's thesis, San Jose State University (2008),
   http://www.cs.sjsu.edu/faculty/stamp/students/
   Desai_Priti.pdf

6. Subramanya, S.R., Lakshminarasimhan, N.: Computer viruses. IEEE Potential 20(4), 16–19 (2001)
7. Blümler, P.: I-LOVE-YOU: Viruses. Trojan Horses and Worms,
   http://www.econmr.org/datapool/page/30/virus.pdf
8. Orman, H.: The Morris worm: a fifteen-year perspective. IEEE Security & Privacy 1(5), 35–43 (2003)
9. Chen, T.M., Robert, J.M.: Worm epidemics in high-speed networks. Computer 37(6), 48–53 (2004)
10. Cass, S.: Anatomy of malice (computer viruses). IEEE Spectrum 38(11), 56–60 (2004)
11. Bosworth, S., Kabay, M.E.: Computer security handbook. John Wiley & Sons Inc., New York (2002)
12. Bishop, M.: Analysis of the I LOVE YOU Worm (2000),
    http://nob.cs.ucdavis.edu/classes/ecs155-2005-04/handouts/iloveyou.pdf
13. Moore, D., Shannon, C.: Code-Red: a case study on the spread and victims of an Internet worm. In: Proceedings of the 2nd ACMSIGCOMM Workshop on Internet Measurement, pp. 273–284. ACM (2002)
14. Zou, C.C., Gong, W., Towsley, D.: Code red worm propagation modeling and analysis. In: Proceedings of the 9th ACM Conference on Computer and Communications Security, pp. 138–147. ACM (2002)
15. Sarwar, U., Ramadass, S., Budiarto, R.: Dawn Of The Mobile Malware: Reviewing Mobile Worms. In: Proceedings of the 4th International Conference on Sciences of Electronic, Technologies of Information and Telecommunications (SETIT 2007), pp. 35–39 (2007)
16. Czosseck, C., Ottis, R., Taliharm, A.M.: Estonia after the 2007 Cyber Attacks: Legal, Strategic and Organisational Changes in Cyber Security. International Journal of Cyber Warfare and Terrorism (IJCWT) 1(1), 24–34 (2011)
17. Davis, J.: Hackers Take Down the Most Wired Country in Europe. Wired Magazine 9(15) (2007)
18. Sharma, V.: An Analytical Survey of Recent Worm Attacks. IJCSNS 11(11), 99–103 (2011)
19. Falliere, N., Murchu, L.O., Chien, E.: W32.stuxnet dossier: version 1.4, White paper, Symantec Corp. Security Response (2011),
    http://www.wired.com/images_blogs/threatlevel/2011/02/Symantec-Stuxnet-Update-Feb-2011.pdf
20. Bradley, F.: Critical infrastructure protection. Electric Energy T and D 7(2), 4–6 (2003)
21. Tsang, S.: Cyberthreats, Vulnerabilities and Attacks on SCADA Networks (2009),
    http://gspp.berkeley.edu/iths/TsangSCADA20Attacks.pdf

The Dark Side of Web 2.0

Aubrey Labuschagne[1,2], Mariki Eloff[2], and Namosha Veerasamy[1]

[1] CSIR, Pretoria, South Africa
{wlabuschagne,nveerasamy}@csir.co.za
[2] School of Computing, Unisa, South Africa
eloffmm@unisa.ac.za

Abstract. Social networking sites have increased in popularity and are utilized for many purposes which include connecting with other people, sharing information and creating content. Many people on social networking sites use these platforms to express opinions relating to current affairs within society. People do not realize the value of their data divulged on these platforms and the tactics implemented by social engineers to harvest the seemingly worthless data. An attack vector is created when a user can be profiled using responses from one of these platforms and the data combined with leaked information from another platform. This paper discusses methods for how this data, with no significant value to the users, can become a commodity to social engineers. This paper addresses what information can be deducted from responses on social news sites, as well as investigating how this information can be useful to social engineers.

Keywords: digital footprint, Facebook, information gathering, Internet, LIWC, social engineering, social media, profiling, Web 2.0.

1   Introduction

Social engineering is the process of manipulating people into performing actions or divulging confidential information that they would not have done under ordinary circumstances. This statement is supported by Mann, author of "Hacking the Human," who defines social engineering as means to manipulate people by deception resulting in them giving out information or performing an action [1].

Numerous studies have indicated that the human element is the weakest link in information security, and cyber criminals have adapted attacks to include this human element [2][3]. Most of the security tools deployed to protect assets within the corporate environment have made it more challenging for attackers to gain access to the corporate network infrastructure. Cyber criminals have adapted to these changes and are adopting social engineering as part of their cyber attacks. The success of social engineering attacks relies on the accuracy of the data collected allowing the attacker to profile the target.

Profiling allows the attackers to predict the behavior of the victims and this is made possible by recording and analyzing the psychological and behavioral characteristics of the target [4]. A social engineer prefers anonymity which results in the search for a

M.D. Hercheui et al. (Eds.): HCC10 2012, IFIP AICT 386, pp. 237–249, 2012.

platform which stores valuable and collectable data while protecting the attacker's anonymity. Anonymity defends the attackers from any form of network surveillance which could be used to track the location and identity of the perpetrator. Web 2.0 provides such a platform.

In this paper we investigate how cyber criminals could aggregate the posts and comments on a web platform for malicious intent as part of information gathering used during a social engineering attack. In our investigation we test our approach with a proof-of-concept to determine the adverse effects of participation on Web 2.0 platforms like online news websites and social networking sites. Online news websites allow users to express their opinions on news articles, through posts and comments. In addition, users are permitted to participate on news websites using other social networking sites' login credentials which could be used in harvesting additional data about the user.

The remainder of this paper is structured as follows: Section 2 summarizes other research related to profiling and underlying concepts. Our contribution to the research field is discussed in Section 3. Users on social networking sites are not aware of the value of the data they divulge unknowingly. The work in this paper demonstrates how the user's digital footprint could be used for nefarious purposes. User awareness of techniques used by cyber criminals is essential in the protection against threats from cyber space. The findings add to the body of knowledge in the security awareness domain. The implementation follows in Section 4. The findings are discussed in Section 5 and in Section 6 we discuss an example of how the data could be used. Future work is explained in Section 7. We conclude the paper in Section 8.

2   Related Research and Underlying Concepts

This section describes how social engineers could use the digital environment to harvest valuable data as part of an attack. Thereafter a description is given on how the textual data was analyzed before concluding with the potentially nefarious uses of social networking sites using social engineering.

2.1   Digital Environment

Social engineers require information to initiate a social engineering attack. Social networking sites provide a digital platform to harvest and collect data. Social media sites like news websites allow users to post opinions on published articles and comment on posts created by other users. Evans, Gosling and Carroll suggested an individual's personality could be effectively communicated to other users using social networking sites [5]. One of their findings concluded that men are more likely to disclose political views than women. Social engineers could use this information to either build trust with the target or as an emotional trigger. The use of function words within sentences offers insight into the honesty, stability, and self-image of the person [6]. Furthermore the language use in self-narratives could be used to determine personalities [7]. An investigation by Ryan and Xenos summarized the Big Five and the usage of Facebook [8]. The Big Five are defined as five broad domains of personality used to describe the human personality. The Big Five traits are openness, conscientiousness, extraversion, agreeableness, and neuroticism. For example, neurotic people are easily stressed and upset [9]. This trait can be easily exploited by social engineers.

This iterates the point on gathering reliable and valid information about the target improves the success rate of a social engineering attack. Similarly, the Department of Homeland Security in the United States investigated the possibility to predict when terrorist might launch an attack. The predictions were deducted from 320 translations of Arabic of documents released by the terror groups: al-Qaeda, al Qa'ida, Hizb ut-Tahrir, and the Movement for Islamic Reform in Arabia (MIRA) [10]. Social media have been identified as one of the sources from which data can be collected. The following section describes the application used to analyze the data collected.

2.2 Linguistic Inquiry and Word Count

This section provides a brief overview of linguistic analysis and how writing styles can be analyzed. It also describes how terrorists could use social networking sites and how critical infrastructures could be infiltrated using social engineering techniques.

Linguistic Inquiry and Word Count (LIWC) is a probabilistic text analysis program that counts words in psychological meaningful categories. These categories include but are not limited to positive emotions, negative emotions, social words, anger [11]. Consequently LIWC could be used to identify social relationships, emotions and thinking styles from textual data representing human communication. The clarification is made possible by the design of LIWC which consists of two components: the processing components and the dictionaries. The processing component opens a file containing the text and compares each word within the file with the dictionary file subsequently classifying each word to a corresponding category. Next LIWC calculates the percentage for each category. For example consider the following sentence: *"Today is a beautiful day"*. LIWC would first take the word *"Today"* and determines if it belongs to one or more categories. The program would increment each of the categories the word is associated. If a word belongs to more than one category then all the relevant categories will be incremented. Consequently LIWC would calculate the percentages for each category for example positive (5%) which implies that the text contains 5% of positive words. The percentage is calculated by dividing the sum of a category by the word count resulting in the following output: function (40%), article (20%), verb (20%), auxiliary verb (20%), present tense (20%), affection (20%), positive (20%), perception (20%), visual (20%), relative (40%), and time words (40%). LIWC has been used in numerous studies, covering a wide range of topics which included predicting deception from textual words [12], identifying gender differences in language use [13] and the use of language to identify personality styles [14]. It was also used to reveal the psychological changes in response to an attack, for example, the terrorist attack on 9 September 2001 in the United States [15].

Style features can also be used to identify writing style. The four major categories of style features are: lexical, syntactic, structural, and content-specific [16]. Lexical features include total number of words, words per sentence, and word length distribution. Syntax refers to the patterns used for the formation of sentences, such as punctuation and function/stop words. Structural features deal with the organization and layout of the text, such as the use of greetings and signatures, the number of paragraphs, and average paragraph length. Content-specific features are keywords that are important within a specific topic domain.

2.3   Terrorists Uses

Terrorists also use social networking sites. At the University of Arizona Dark Web Terrorism Research Centre, complex models have been built to study extremist-group web forums and construct social network maps and organization structures. Research has been carried out to analyze social networking sites but terrorists could also use networking sites to their advantage [17]. Work conducted by Veerasamy and Grobler [18] discussed the different methods used by these organizations for recruitment.

Social networking analysis enables multi-variant analysis which is important for terrorism as the combination of multiple factors: for example, poverty and type of government, combined with the link to a terrorist, may cause a person to participate in a terrorist activity [17]. Thus, using linguistic analysis to gauge these various factors can be beneficial into determining a person's potential to be recruited into a terrorist organization. Furthermore, Ressler says that social network analysis should try to understand the underlying root of terrorism and therefore it is useful to understand how terrorist networks recruit participants and why people join terrorist organizations [17]. By studying the social engineering approaches based on linguistic analysis, insight can be gained on terrorist recruitment practices.

Recruitment could further be extended to include insiders, who are people within companies whom are trusted and have authorized access to valuable resources [19]. The recruitment of insiders employed at critical infrastructure [1] establishments could have devastating effects on the services required to operate a country and could constitute a national security risk.

2.4   Method of Data Collection

This study only collected data to demonstrate a possible information gathering phase of a social engineering attack. The only contact made with users was the use of the 'friend request' from Facebook to determine the rate of accepting requests without verifying the true identity and purpose of the request. The friendship was terminated once a request was accepted. Also the data analysis was used to determine potential victims based on emotional response to content; no mechanisms were used to test the findings. No automated tools were used in the data collection as this would transgress the social networking sites the terms of use.

---

[1]   The facilities which are essential for the functioning of a society and economy for example financial services, transportation systems, water supply, public health, etc.

3   Proof-of-Concepts

This section describes the proof-of-concept to determine what data could be gathered from responses on social news sites and how it could be used to conduct a social engineering attack. The process of a social engineering attack consists of three phases: identify a potential target, data collection to understand and find weaknesses within the target and finally exploit the vulnerabilities identified [20]. This experiment followed the same phases. The design of the experiment involved the manual collection of data from a social media news site, which will not be identified in this paper. The web articles published on this site were selected with the criteria of most responses in the form of posts and comments. Users who would like to create responses are required to login using Facebook credentials or can create an account on the site.

The user's response in the form of a post or comment can be extracted including the user name and a URL link to their personal profile. The collection process involved the manual capturing of comments and posts from articles published on the site. The collected information does not consist of any personal information except for the URL of the profile which is not revealed in this paper. The collected data were used in two experiments. The first experiment determines what information can be collected using the profile data collected and the second experiment what information can be deducted from the responses created by the users. These two experiments are explained in the following sections.

3.1   Data Collected on Profile Information

A list of all the unique users with their URLs who created responses were compiled from the data collected. Each of the user's profiles was visited to determine how much data was available. A summary was created to illustrate the following categories: visibility of the activities and interests, listing of friends and contact information. The activities and interests could help social engineers in creating a profile about the user. The summary lists the availability of each of these categories from the public domain (not logged in) and when authenticated (logged in).

The process involved using two web browsers. Facebook was opened in both browsers. In the one browser, which a Facebook user was not logged into, the URL of the collected profile was opened in the browser and subsequently the availability of the required categories was captured. The other browser used the same process except that it used a valid Facebook account and logged into Facebook before opening the collected profile URL. In brief, data was collected about availability of information on a Facebook profile when logged in and not logged in. Next a friend request was send to the collected profiles. The status of the friend request was also recorded. The status conditions are defined as requested, accepted, not enabled and message. There are no responses sent to the requestor if the friendship request is declined, hence no state is created to indicate declined friendship requests.

The different conditions were explained in Table 1. The friend requests are used to determine the current susceptibility of users to accept friend requests without verifying the trustworthiness of the user who sent the friend request.

Table 1. Status description

State	Description
Requested	A friend request has been sent and is pending
Accepted	The friend request has been accepted
Not enabled	Friend request feature disabled by user
Message	Friend request was not accepted but message was sent from user

3.2   Data Regarding Users Responses

The captured responses from the users on the social news website were captured in a database. Some information could be inferred by visiting the profile associated with each user. This experiment analyzes and investigates how the textual responses could be used for profiling as part of a social engineering attack. The data within the database is converted into a text file which is used by LIWC to determine the different emotional dimensions including anger, positive, negative. All of these could be used to determine personality traits. A results file is created once the text files have been processed. The content of the resulting file is extracted and stored in a database which correlates with the previous collected data. This allows the research team to have access to the collected and analyzed data.

Social engineers could use the same process after the collection phase is completed to determine gender. Males have been shown to use more articles (a, the), nouns, prepositions, numbers, words per sentence and use more swear words than females [21]. In this paper we identify negativity and anger as these two emotional states could be employed during a social engineering attack. The use of words could provoke anger in a person which subsequently would prevent the user from making logical decisions [22]. The analyzed data could identify users on social networking sites who are prone to anger; as the high use of negative and anger words could leak this information unknowingly to cyber criminals.

4   Findings

In this section we describe the results from the experiments conducted. This includes information about the data collection method, the findings from the friendship requests and the analysis of the responses collected.

4.1   Data Collection

The following section describes the finding of the two experiments described in Section 3. A total of 353 unique profiles were listed from the sample collected which consisted of 791 comments and 728 posts from nine articles published on the news website. Data was collected and subsequent friend requests were sent to each user. No additional interactions were conducted after the friend request was sent. A total of 130 requests were sent to users over a period of three days. However, Facebook issued a warning after some users reported the friend requests as suspicious behavior. Consequently, we ceased the friendship requests action.

The high acceptance rate was noticed within the first week and then declined after the second week. The collection period spanned over four weeks to ensure that most users had the opportunity to accept the friendship requests sent to them. Security measures implemented by Facebook delayed the collection process using the web browser without having logged into Facebook. Facebook uses mechanisms to identify automated tools and forces the users to prove human behavior with a text challenge e.g. Captcha, before allowing the user to continue. Thus Facebook presents a question and the user must provide a valid answer to be proceed.

4.2   Analysis of Profile Information

This section describes the findings from the information gathered using only the profile URL collected. Findings specifically addressing the friendship requested are depicted in figure 1. At the time of writing the following statistics are available from the data collected. A 35% success rate of friendship requests accepted was obtained from the 130 friend requests sent to the users. Only 4% of users did not enable the "Send Friend Request" feature thus preventing other users from requesting a friendship. An interesting observation is that no users who accepted friendship requests sent messages to request additional information from the unknown user to establish trustworthiness.

Findings on the data leaked from the profiles are depicted in figure 2. Analysis of the data gleaned from the profiles indicates 59% of profiles leak information about interests and activities without the need to log into Facebook. In addition, logging into Facebook and then viewing the profile reveals 79% of interests and activities, an increase of about 20%, compared to the public view of a profile. Equally important is

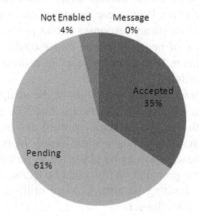

Fig. 1. Facebook friend requests

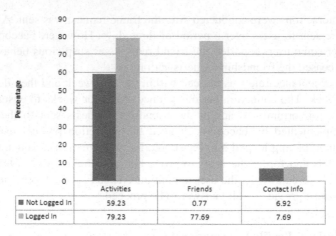

Fig. 2. Data leakage

the availability of the user's friends listing which indicates an increase of about 70% of visibility when using a logged in Facebook session. The availability of contact information does indicate a slight increase when accessed through a logged in account.

4.3   Analysis of Users Responses

The following section discusses the findings to determine if any users have leaked information which would profile them as prone to a social engineering attack using an emotional trigger. Thus, a form of content-specific writing style analysis was carried out. All the posts and comments were processed to determine the overall average negativity. These include but are not limited to the following negative emotion words: arrogant, ineffective, cheating, outrage and shock. The average negativity of the posts was calculated as 2.9% whereas the average negativity of the comments was calculated as 3.03%. This could be due to human nature where people are more reactive to what other people say or write. Posts were responses on an article which was written impartially. However, comments are responses to bias posts. According to research by Pennebaker, the mean use of negative words in personal text, written to express an opinion, is 2.6% [23]. This indicates the existence of posts and comments with a high frequency of negative words.

Figure 3 provides a graphical representation of the analyzed posts with the mean included. One outlier was identified in the results. The 50% post, upon inspection was a two word sentence with one word a negative word and is subsequently not used in the findings. In addition, numerous posts are clearly more negative than the mean average. The writer of these posts can be classified as potential victims by social engineers. The identity of the potential victim could be extracted from the collected data to initiate an attack. No limiting parameters were utilized during the search hence producing a large potential victim set.

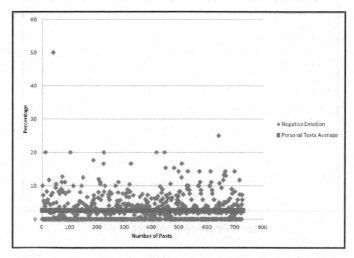

Fig. 3. Negative emotions for posts

In addition, the anger dimension was analyzed from the 728 posts collected. The analysis parameters were set to only include posts with a higher percentage than 10%, thus producing a smaller victim pool which will be more susceptible to a social engineering attack (see figure 4).

5   Discussion of the Experiment

In this section we discuss the results found in Section 4 and how the information could be used for malicious intent. Access to users' information could potentially allow attackers to utilize a wide range of methods for nefarious use. Also the collection and analysis of responses could assist in a successful social engineering attack.

5.1   Using Profile Information to Access Additional Data

The information inferred from using only the URL of the user's profile, found users do not understand the mechanisms provided by Facebook to prevent the leaking of personal data. The privacy control settings are continuously updated by Facebook, adapting both to new features developed by Facebook and to the ever changing threat in the environment. However, according to a study by ProtectMyID it was found that only 18% of users implement privacy setting controls [24]. This implies that attackers could easily harvest personal data about users without the need to bypass security measures implemented by social networks.

The results of this study found that more is available when accessing a profile that has once logged onto Facebook. Also most users make public their friend lists which could be used by social engineers to conduct an attack using an evil twin attack. An

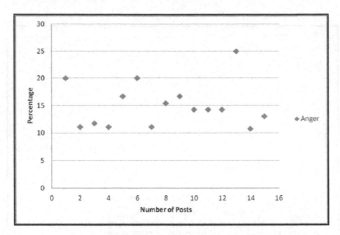

Fig. 4. Anger emotions above 10%

evil twin attack is defined as using a rogue profile [2] to impersonate a legitimate profile [25]. The attacker could use data collected from a friend of a Facebook user to create a similar profile to that of the actual friend and subsequently make a friend request. The victim could implicitly trust the source based on the familiarity of the "friend" making the request and information provided with the request which could include a picture and the name of a trusted friend. Another concern raised by the results of this study is the friend request acceptance rate. The study showed that users accept 30% of friend request without asking for additional information.

5.2   Profiling Users

Responses created by users to raise their opinions on current news events could also be used by social engineers. Some of users' personal traits are leaked by expressing an opinion on a specific topic. The use of tools which conduct linguistic analysis could be used to profile a user. Profiling takes two approaches: prospective and retrospective [26]. Prospective profiling involves the development of a template from previous data. The developed template is then applied to future data to identify individuals whom resemble the characteristics defined within the template. Retrospective profiling uses data left behind to develop a description of the user. In this study retrospective profiling using the data created by the users on the social networking site was used. Such profiling could be used by social engineers to design an attack with elements that improve the probability of success. The results from the data collected in this study demonstrated how anger and negative emotions could be determined from the responses collected. From this data the attacker could extract the original post that would determine the content which provoked the emotion. This could be then used in designing a customized social engineering attack such as a spear-phishing attack. This attack is targeted towards a specific person or group. The use of this information in a possible social engineering attack is describes in the next section.

---

[2]   Profiles with information which creates a false sense of trustworthiness.

6   Application of Data Collected to Conduct a Social Engineering Attack

An attacker could inspect a social news website for controversial articles which have the most responses. Next the attacker collects the data in the form of responses and analyzes these to determine which users have demonstrated the most positive or negative emotions towards an article. These users are classified as victims. The attacker has implicit access to the Facebook profiles of the victims. The attacker uses a fake profile to access data on the individual victim's profile. The attacker next uses an evil twin attack and creates a Facebook profile to impersonate one of the friends from the victim's friend list. Next the attacker creates a malicious PDF, naming the file to correlate with the topic which generated the emotion. The attacker then uses the mail functionality of Facebook to attach the malicious PDF to a Facebook message. The attacker next creates an enticing message using the topic. For example: "Shocking information leaked about the controversial tax". The victim will receive the message with the malicious PDF from the fake profile which has the same profile picture as a trusted friend. The victim could implicitly trust the source and then due to the emotional trigger be influenced to open the malicious PDF and infect their systems.

7   Conclusions

This paper addressed how users' digital footprints in the form of responses on social news website can be used to create additional attack vectors that could be used to target them. Two experiments were carried out to determine whether a user could be profiled from their posts on social news sites and also to investigate users' awareness of privacy control settings on social networks. The results show that users can be naive and have a false sense of security which encourages behavior that exposes them to threats. This could be mitigated with security awareness training which allows users to understand the purpose of privacy setting controls and how to implement these to protect personal information on social networking sites. The training could also include other threats that could be encountered on social networking sites for example the evil twin, social engineering and phishing[3] attacks. Furthermore this study showed how emotional triggers that influence users could be determined from responses collected within the public domain. The users should implement strategies to protect their identities on social networking sites which promote freedom of expression. For example, the user could create an alternative profile specifically used to participate on forums which allow users to raise their opinions. These profiles should contain no information which could be used identify the identity of the user.

Both the methods used in this study could be used by social engineers as part of the information gathering phase. The research revealed that information exposed in social networking platforms could be used for nefarious purposes like retrieving personal information, as well as profiling. Furthermore, the personal information that is obtained

---

[3]   To try to obtain financial or other confidential information from Internet users [27].

through the social engineering techniques could be used in an advanced attack vector which combines multiple attack mechanisms to circumvent protective measures implemented to secure a system. In addition, the work has shown that the profiling techniques could be used for malicious purposes like terrorist recruitment and the identification of insiders within critical infrastructure which poses a significant threat to national security. For example, these attackers could target critical infrastructure by identifying possible individuals to infect with malware which targets the critical infrastructure systems or recruit the individuals to join terrorist groups. These new infected systems or the recruitments could be dormant until action is required by the terrorist group. The access to personal information in the public domain enables these groups to devise strategies to identify and recruit members. These members could be recruited during the planning phase of a possible attack against a country and subsequently become active participants during the execution of the planned attack. Individuals in positions which can cause catastrophic damage to the national security of a country should be cautious of information posted in the public domain. The use of security awareness training that focus on the dangers of personal information in the public domain could provide these individuals with mechanisms to protect themselves against the threats identified. This paper thus aims to create awareness about the dangers of the inference of personal data in the public domain.

References

1. Mann, I.: Hacking the Human. Gower Publishing, Aldershot (2008)
2. Carl, C.: Human factors in information security: The insider threat – Who can you trust these days? Information Security Technical Report 14, 186–196 (2009)
3. Hadnagy, C.: Social Engineering: The Art of Human Hacking. Wiley, Indianopolis (2010)
4. Shinder, D.: Profiling and categorizing cybercriminals (2010)
5. Evans, D.C., Gosling, S.D., Carroll, A.: What elements of an online social networking profile predict target-rater agreement in personality impressions. In: Proceedings of the International Conference on Weblogs and Social Media, pp. 1–6 (2008)
6. Chung, C.K., Pennebaker, J.W.: The psychological function of function words. Social Communication: Frontiers of Social Psychology, 343–359 (2007)
7. Hirsh, J.B., Peterson, J.B.: Personality and language use in self-narratives. Journal of Research in Personality 43, 524–527 (2009)
8. Ryan, T., Xenos, S.: Who uses Facebook? An investigation into the relationship between the Big Five, shyness, narcissism, loneliness, and Facebook usage. Journal of Computer Human Behavior 17, 1–7 (2011)
9. Vollrath, M., Torgersen, S.: Personality types and coping. Personality and Individual Differences 29, 367–378 (2000)
10. Vergano, D.: Terrorists taunts may tell attack (2011),
    http://www.usatoday.com/tech/science/columnist/vergano/
    2011-02-27-terrorist-words_N.htm, (last accessed February 27, 2012)
11. Pennebaker, J.W., Booth, R.J., Booth, M.E.: Linqguistic inquiry and word count (LIWC 2001): A computer-based text analysis program (2001)
12. Newman, M.L., Pennebaker, J.W., Berry, D.S., Richards, J.M.: Lying words: Predicting deception from linguistic styles. Person. Soc. Psychol. Bull. 29, 665–675 (2003)

13. Newman, M.L., Groom, C.J., Handelman, L.D., Pennebaker, J.W.: Gender differences in language use: An analysis of 14,000 text samples. Discourse Processes 45, 211–236 (2008)
14. Pennebaker, J.W., King, L.A.: Linguistic styles: Language use as an individual difference. Journal of Personality and Social Psychology 77, 1296–1312 (1999)
15. Cohn, M.A., Mehl, M.R., Pennebaker, J.W.: Linguistic markers of psychological change surrounding September 11, 2001. Psychological Science 15, 687–693 (2004)
16. Chen, Y.D., Abbasi, A., Chen, H.: Framing Social Movement Identity with Cyber-Artifacts: A Case Study of the International Falun Gong Movement. Security Informatics, 1–23 (2010)
17. Ressler, S.: Social network analysis as an approach to combat terrorism: Past, present, and future research. Homeland Security Affairs 2, 1–10 (2006)
18. Veerasamy, N., Grobler, M.: Terrorist Use of the Internet: Exploitation and Support through ICT infrastructure. Leading Issues in Information Warfare & Security Research, 172–187 (2011)
19. Goodman, S.E., Kirk, J.C., Kirk, M.H.: Cyberspace as a medium for terrorists. Technological Forecasting and Social Change 74, 193–210 (2007)
20. Barrett, N.: Penetration testing and social engineering: Hacking the weakest link. Information Security Technical Report 8, 56–64 (2003)
21. Pennebaker, J.W.: The Secret Life of Pronouns: What Our Words Say About Us. Bloomsbury Press (2011)
22. Brodie, R.: Virus of the Mind: The New Science of the Meme. Hay House Publisher (2011)
23. Pennebaker, J.W., Chung, C.K., Ireland, M., Gonzales, A., Booth, R.J.: The development and psychometric properties of LIWC 2007. Austin, TX (2007), LIWC. Net
24. Whitlock, C.: New survey data from Experian's ProtectMyID™ reveals people are making it easy for cybercriminals to steal their identity (2011),
    http://www.prnewswire.com/news-releases/new-survey-data-
    from-experians-protectmyid-reveals-people-are-making-it-
    easy-for-cybercriminals-to-steal-their-identity-
    131441283.html (last accessed October 10, 2011)
25. Timm, C.: Evil Twin Attacks. Seven Deadliest Social Network Attacks, Syngress, pp. 63–82 (2010)
26. Nykodym, N., Taylor, R., Vilela, J.: Criminal profiling and insider cybercrime. Digital Investigation 2, 261–267 (2005)
27. Anonymous: The Free On-line Dictionary of Computing (2012)

Towards a Social Media-Based Model of Trust and Its Application

Erik Boertjes, Bas Gerrits, Robert Kooij, Peter-Paul van Maanen,
Stephan Raaijmakers, and Joost de Wit

Netherlands Organisation for Applied Scientific Research (TNO)
{erik.boertjes,bas.gerrits,robert.kooij,
peter-paul.vanmaanen,stephan.raaijmakers,joost.dewit}@tno.nl

Abstract. In this paper we describe the development of a model for measuring consumer trust in certain topics on the basis of social media. Specifically, we propose a model for trust that takes into account both textually expressed sentiment and source authority, and illustrate it on a specific case: the iCloud cloud computing service of Apple and its reception on Twitter. We demonstrate that it is possible to parameterize a trust function with weights that interpolate between the contribution of sentiment and the authority of the tweet senders. Feedback data containing perceived trust in the iCloud service was gathered from a community of users. On this data, our model was fitted and evaluated. Finally, we show how such a fitted model can be used as a basis for a visualization tool aimed at supporting professionals monitoring trust, or to simulate implications of interventions. Our approach is a first step towards a dynamic trust monitor that is a viable alternative to more rigid, survey-based approaches to measuring trust.

Keywords: consumer trust, modelling, social media.

1   Introduction

The Internet is developing increasingly into a vital infrastructure that constitutes the foundation of economic and social processes within our society. This development is unstoppable and will in the coming years bring about changes that go beyond information and data exchange. Development of facilities like "Internet of Things", the semantic web and cloud computing all contribute to an increased digitization of society. The role of ICT as the foundation for the acceleration of the information society, is clearly expressed in the "Digital Agenda for Europe (2010-2020)", which was presented by the European Commission early 2010[1]. The success of the digital agenda is largely tied to the trust that society puts in the same developments in the digital plane. In the absence of trust, the essential condition for further dissemination and adoption of ICT services and facilities is lacking. For example, in 2008, the global consulting firm Booz & Company estimated for the European digital economy in 2012 the economic difference between a scenario with high trust in ICT and one with low trust in

---

[1] See http://ec.europa.eu/information_society/
digital-agenda/index_en.htm.

M.D. Hercheui et al. (Eds.): HCC10 2012, IFIP AICT 386, pp. 250–263, 2012.

ICT to consist of an enormous €124 billion. In this estimate of the economic asset of trust, the digital economy is assumed to consist of advertisements, content, e-commerce and access to ICT. Obviously, with the economical and societal increasing dependence on ICT, also the potential for abuse of this medium increases. Cyber criminals are actively exploiting the vulnerabilities of networks, and terrorist organizations use the internet to exchange information. Personal and sensitive data, profiles and digital identities of organizations and end users are stolen and resold. The consequences are both financial and emotional. It is clear from the discussion above that there is a need for increasing trust in ICT. To achieve this, we need to know what factors determine trust in ICT. It is also necessary to examine the relationship between trust and the adoption of ICT services further. It is important to notice that the actual trust organizations or end users have in ICT may be not in line with the actual risks at hand. This may be causing two types of problems. If there is high trust but the risk is actually high, then the user runs the risk of experiencing damage due to unjustified confidence. If the trust is low but the risk is actually low, then the user will tend not to use the service, hence the adoption of the service falls behind for unfounded reasons.

The aim of this paper is twofold. The first aim is to discuss the dimensions on which trust in ICT depends. This discussion will be mainly based upon the work of Kim et al. ([3])) and Corbitt et al. ([1]), in addition to trend reports that appear on an annual basis[2] or on a (bi-)quarterly basis[3]. The second aim this paper is to outline an approach that can be used to assess trust in ICT in near real-time, based on sentiment mining of social media. This approach opens up possibilities for monitoring communities, by either individuals, companies or institutions, in order to assess the current level of trust in certain topics, form or adjust opinions, and to undertake subsequent action, such as active participation in discussions.

2 Dimensions Determining Trust in ICT

According to Kim et al. ([3]) and Corbitt et al. ([1]), six dimensions determine trust in ICT, namely social, institutional, content, product, transactional and technological dimensions. The table below shows the dimensions of trust explained and elaborated into indicators. The indicators in this table affect the trust dimension they belong to, and thus the overall trust in a product or service.

When considering the dimensions in Table 1, one has to bear in mind that several actors influence trust in an ICT service. Although the actors for each service or product may differ, the following general groups can be distinguished:

- Service Providers: The provider of the service used.
- Users: The recipient of a service, this can be both a consumer and another company.
- Technology Providers: All parties who provide the technology needed for the service, such as telecom operators, computer vendors, network infrastructure providers, phone manufacturers, etc.

---

[2] For instance Eurostat data, Ernst & Young Global Information Security Survey (GTISC).
[3] For instance reports on phishing by the Anti-Phishing Working Group (APWG; http://www.antiphishing.org/) or by McAfee.

- Third Parties: All other parties who have a facilitating role in providing a particular service, for instance a payment provider.

Depending on which service is used, various actors play a role. In addition, some players are involved in different roles. This makes the role of the actor in the security and trust in the product not always clear.

Table 1. Six dimensions determining trust in ICT

Trust dimension	Explanation	Indicators
Social	Social factors affecting trust	Experience, reputation, peer pressure, culture, norms and values
Institutional	"Third parties" and institutional context affecting trust	Reputation, accreditation (trust marks), regulations, legal obligations
Content	(External) characteristics of the product or content	Design, customization (personification), brand visibility
Product	Product features that influence purchase/use decisions	Availability, quality, durability, price
Transaction	Characteristics for trust in transactions involved	Transparency, payment options, cost model, discounts
Technology	Characteristics of infrastructure and software related to security and effectiveness	Availability, integrity, authenticity, confidentiality, reliability

The conceptual framework to assess trust according to the above model is first to monitor the various indicators involved, then to map these, for each dimension, to a certain value. Finally, the six individual values are weighted in order to obtain trust in ICT. Obviously, many obstacles still exist in making such a framework operational. First of all, not all indicators are easily assessable, if at all. Even if data is available, data formats will often differ and originate from different sources. Secondly, the translation from indicators to the actual trust dimension is also far from trivial. Finally, to our knowledge, there is no agreement on how to combine the six dimensions by weighing them, to arrive at the final assessment of trust in ICT. All three issues are items for further research, but we will address a possible integration method in Section 3.

Even though the framework may not be fully applicable yet, there are some data sources available that provide useful input for it. As an example we will consider the dimension 'technology'. Most indicators under this dimension fall under the issue of information security. Security generally consists of the following three categories: availability (the information is available when needed), confidentiality (information is not disclosed to unauthorized individuals or systems) and integrity (data cannot be modified undetectably).

Data on these indicators is available through statistics agencies, such as the European Eurostat, who obtain their data through extensive surveys[4]. In addition vendors (such as Microsoft with their Intelligence Report) and security companies (such as McAfee with their Threats Report) report statistics on an annual or (bi-) quarterly basis. For example, according to Eurostat, the percentage of companies in the European Union (EU) that had their ICT service disrupted due to external attacks, was 4% in 2010. According to the Microsoft Security Intelligence Report 2011, 0.1% of all computers worldwide were part of a botnet.

Mainly through Eurostat, there are also statistics available about the perceived trust in ICT. As examples we mention (for end users in the European Union in 2010): 25% is very worried about viruses in the Internet, 16% does not purchase goods or services through the Internet, for security reasons and 15% does not use on-line banking for the same reason. Unfortunately, for the end users that refrain from purchasing goods and using on-line banking, the surveys do not give insight in what this lack of trust is built upon. In summary, our conceptual framework of trust in ICT is hard to apply in practice for several reasons.

In the next section, we propose a way of assessing trust in ICT in an alternative way, i.e. by using sentiment mining of social media. One of the advantages of such a dynamic, non-survey-based method is that it can be applied in near real-time, while the framework above heavily relies on data that only becomes available on an annual or (bi-)quarterly basis.

3   A Social Media-Based Model of Trust

In this section a formal model of trust, measured in social media on the basis of sentiment, is described. With tools based on such models, one can inspect the current level of trust in a certain topic and for a certain (online) community, or assess the impact of certain simulated interventions on trust scores. While a social media-based model of trust may be only partially representing the trust of a larger, *offline* community, information from social media can be relevant here: social media are commonly accessible to large proportions of the community, have large degrees of participation, and are quite dynamic, allowing for the monitoring of rapid changes in online expressed mood. Sentiment analysis is one of the themes of text analytics, and it is highly ranked on the research agenda of academia and industry, as exemplified by thriving, industry-sponsored scientific conferences such as ICWSM[5]. Roughly speaking, sentiment analysis attempts to detect opinions and subjective utterances, labelling subjective, opinion-bearing utterances with polarity scores such as 'negative', 'positive', or points on a metric scale. For an extensive overview, see Pang and Lee ([5]).

In our trust model, we attempt to model the trust of an audience in a certain ICT service as a function of the exposure to social media (i.c. Twitter messages about the service), in combination with information about the authority of the source of the messages. Our hypothesis is that there is a correlation between trust of a population and the exposure of that population to highly polarized (overtly positive or negative) information expressed by people with high authority. In this work, we simplistically

---

[4] For instance the annual reports of the Organisation for Economic Co-operation and Development (OECD; http://www.oecd.org/).

[5] The International Conference of Weblogs and Social Media, http://www.icwsm.org

equate 'authority' with a large number of followers but our approach is open to more advanced measures of authority. Figure 1 shows a formal model for combining sentiment information with authority estimates into a trust score, where the top "trust value" is calculated by $T(t)$, the top "input" of the model combined with its "sentiment" is calculated by $\sigma(t)$, and the bottom "input" combined with its "sentiment" is calculated by $\beta(t)$.

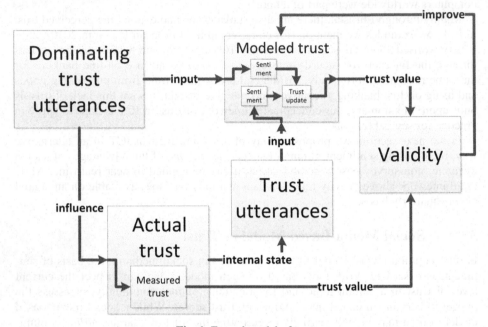

Fig. 1. Formal model of trust

The trust value (or the degree of trust) is a number between 0 and 1 that is an estimate of the tendency of the general public to accept and use a certain ICT service. This estimate is important when one wants to predict future use of the service given the current situation (monitoring and extrapolation), or when one is interested in a possible future introduction of a service (simulation).

3.1   Degree of Trust

The following basic formula is used in order to compute the degree of trust at a certain time point t:

$$T(t) = w_T \cdot \sigma(t) + (1 - w_T) \cdot \beta(t)$$

where $T(t)$ is the degree of trust, $\sigma(t)$ the degree of situational trust, and $\beta(t)$ the degree of behavioural trust, at time point t. The weight w_T regulates the balance between the situational and behavioural trust. We will explain these notions now in further detail.

3.2   Situational Trust

The degree of situational trust is the degree of trust that is deducible from the situation. The situation is determined by the opinions of, and the resulting trust utterances by, people with higher authority. The opinion of people with higher authority is more often taken over by the general public than of people with lower authority. Therefore utterances are weighed according to the degree of authority of the utterances' owners. The above can be formalized as follows:

$$\sigma(t) = \begin{cases} \dfrac{1}{n(t)} \cdot \left(\displaystyle\sum_{i=1}^{n(t)} \dfrac{\left((1-w_a) \cdot \lambda_\sigma + w_a \cdot \left(1 - a_i(t)\right)\right) \cdot \sigma(t-1) +}{\left(1 - \left((1-w_a) \cdot \lambda_\sigma + w_a \cdot \left(1 - a_i(t)\right)\right)\right) \cdot e_i(t)} \right) & \text{if } n(t) > 0 \\[2em] \left((1-w_a) \cdot \lambda_\sigma + w_a\right) \cdot \sigma(t-1) + & \\ \left(1 - \left((1-w_a) \cdot \lambda_\sigma + w_a\right)\right) \cdot e_d & \text{if } n(t) = 0 \end{cases}$$

where n(t) is the total number of trust utterances from time point t-1 until t, and the decay λ_σ regulates the amount of past situational trust that is included when calculating the current situational trust. The weight ω_a regulates the effect of momentary authority. Furthermore, $e_i(t)$ and $a_i(t)$ are the momentary sentiment and authority of utterance I from time point t-1 until t. And finally, e_d is the default momentary sentiment when no utterances are within the time interval t-1 and t (i.e., n(t) = 0), which should be put to 0.5 when regression zero sentiment is assumed. The second case of the above equation is equal to the first case when n(t) = 1, $e_1(t) = e_d$, and $a_1(t) = 0$ is taken in the first case.

3.3   Behavioral Trust

The degree of behavioural trust is the degree of trust that is deducible from behavior. Behavior is observable via trust utterances of people in general. This can be formalized as follows:

$$\beta(t) = \begin{cases} \lambda_\beta \cdot \beta(t-1) + (1 - \lambda_\beta) \cdot \dfrac{1}{n(t)} \cdot \displaystyle\sum_{i=1}^{n(t)} e_i(t) & \text{if } n(t) > 0 \\[2em] \lambda_\beta \cdot \beta(t-1) + \left(1 - \lambda_\beta\right) \cdot e_d & \text{if } n(t) = 0 \end{cases}$$

where decay λ_β regulates the amount of past behavioral trust that is included when calculating the current behavioral trust. For the initial values of $\sigma(t)$ and $\beta(t)$ the following holds:

$$\sigma(0) = \sigma_0$$
$$\beta(0) = \beta_0$$

where initial values σ_0 and β_0 are equal to 0.5 when indifferent trust (neither high nor low trust) is assumed in the case when there are no trust utterances yet.

3.4   Momentary Sentiment and Authority

The momentary sentiment and authority are defined as follows:

$$e_i(t) = w_e + (1 - w_e) \cdot \texttt{sentiment}_i(t)$$

$$a_i(t) = \frac{\texttt{followers}_i(t)}{\frac{1}{t_{end}} \Sigma_{t_j=1}^{t_{end}} \left(\frac{1}{n(t_j)} \Sigma_{p=1}^{n(t_j)} \texttt{followers}_p(t_j) \right)}$$

where weight ω_e regulates the effect of the momentary sentiment. It furthermore holds that $\texttt{sentiment}_i(t) \in \{0,1\}$ and $\texttt{followers}_i(t) \in \mathbb{N}$, for all utterances i and time points t.

In the next section we will apply this model to a use case: the trust in Apple's newly launched cloud service *iCloud*, and describe our experiments.

4   Model Tuning and Validation

This section describes the efforts to tune and validate the model of trust, specifically for trust in Apple's *iCloud*, our use case.

4.1   Gathering Model Input Data

In order to capture a sufficient amount of data as input for the model described in the previous section, we implemented a procedure for harvesting the streaming timeline of Twitter, on the basis of search keys consisting of tags and keywords. Our data collection was created during a time span of three months (from August 25, 2011 to October 13, 2011), based on the keyword icloud and consists of 193,469 tweets of 195,556 different users. For every tweet containing the keyword icloud, the following information was stored in a PostgreSQL database:

- the screen name of the sender
- the personal name of the sender
- the creation date of the tweet
- the tweet text
- the number of followers of the sender at the time the tweet was published
- the tags added by the sender to the tweet
- the number of friends the sender had at the time of the tweet
- the geo-location from which the tweet was sent out (if present)
- the number of retweets of the tweet (measured by the Twitter API in a certain interval starting with the broadcast time of the tweet).

In addition, we trained and applied three *text classifiers* to the tweet text:

- a subjectivity classifier that detects whether the tweet contains an opinion or, on the contrary, consists of factural information only;
- a binary sentiment polarity classifier that estimates the polarity of the sentiment (if present) in the tweet text: either positive or negative.
- a binary topic classifier that estimates whether the tweet is about cloud computing or not.

These classifiers consist of *support vector machines* applied to bag-of-word representations (frequency counts, unnormalized) with *radial basis function (RBF) kernels* Their output was stored in the database as well.

4.2   Gathering Validation Data

As shown in figure 1 the data for validating the trust model are gathered by sampling from the people whose trust is being estimated by the trust model. This was done by questionnaires. For two timestamped events, the official introduction of iCloud, and the death of Steve Jobs, the first twenty tweets were selected, both directly preceding and following these events. These twitter stimuli were sent out through an automated mail procedure to a total number of 61 participants, with two tasks:

- to annotate the sentiment polarity in these tweets on a three-point scale (negative, neutral, positive). This entails a form of affective exposure to the content of these tweets that - to a very limited extent- mimics real-life exposure to this type of information. In addition, the number of followers for every tweet sender at the time of publishing the tweet was listed, with the intent of illustrating somehow the 'authority' of the tweet sender.
- to answer a number of questions in a questionnaire, implemented as a separate (and personal) web page.

So, in total, every participant received 8 questionnaires. In the questionnaires, five questions were posed:

1. Do you know what Apple's iCloud service is? (1=not at all, 5=perfectly)
2. When did you start using iCloud? (1=never used it, 5=from the beginning)
3. Do you think personal files are safe in iCloud? (1=not at all, 5=very safe)
4. Are you enthusiastic about iCloud as a service? (1=not at all, 5=very enthusiastic)
5. How certain are you about the answers above? (1=not at all, 5=very certain)

In order to synthesize a trust value from the answers, we applied the following heuristic. First of all, when the answer to the first or fifth question was 1, the returned answers were excluded. In all other cases, the answers to questions three and four were used to produce a trust value, with the answer to question four serving as a weight factor to the answer of question three.

4.3   Parameter Tuning

The tuning of the five parameters of the trust model was done by means of an exhaustive search with a granularity of 26 (a step size of 0.04 on an interval of 0 to 1 for each of the five parameters). The problem space therefore consisted of $26^5 = 11,881,376$ different parameter settings which needed to be compared to each other. Given that the calculation of the validity of the model for one parameter setting on a regular PC costs roughly one second of time, this would result in a tuning period of 138 days. Instead of going for a heuristic search algorithm to search through the problem space, we chose to implement the problem as a parallel procedure. For larger parameter spaces, this would be a less suitable solution and one could opt for heuristic search algorithms. For instance, an alternative way of parameter estimation could consist of either a stochastic, sampling-based approach (such as a genetic algorithm), or a learning approach with gradient descent and back propagation. For the latter, given a (differentiable) trust function *T(t)*, denoted with τ, we can implement a gradient descent method as follows:

$$\omega^{t+1} = \omega^t - \eta \frac{\partial \tau}{\partial \omega^t}$$

with η a parameter controlling the *learning rate* of the algorithm and

$$\frac{\partial \tau}{\partial \omega^t} = \frac{\partial \tau(\omega)}{\partial \omega}$$

with ω^t the five-dimensional weight vector for the parameters of our model at time *t*. This implements parameter estimation as a form of supervised learning (regression).

The current parallel search was run on a computer cluster using 2048 different cores in total, which would theoretically reduce the tuning period to two hours. But due to other jobs running on the cluster, the task scheduler allowed the script to run in roughly ten hours, which is still a considerable reduction of computing time.

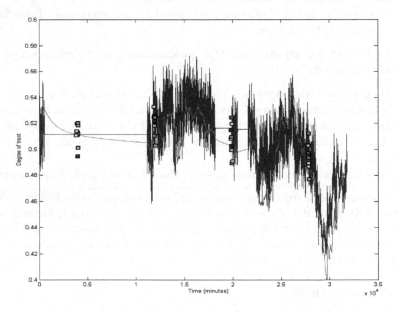

Fig. 2. Trust model output after tuning (line) based on normally randomized validation data (squares) using the output of the trust model with predefined parameter settings

As a first attempt to see if validation data consisting of four data sets of participants estimating their trust in iCloud is sufficient for tuning the trust model, we first tested whether the found optimal parameter settings were satisfactory using artificially generated validation data. These validation data were generated by normally randomizing the output of the model using predefined parameter settings within four different short time intervals. The predefined parameter settings were $(\omega_a, \omega_e, \omega_T, \lambda_\sigma, \lambda_\beta)_p$

= (.9,.95,.5,.999,.999). The normal randomization was carried out ten times (for ten non-existing participants) using the output of the model as mean and 0.01 as standard deviation. The results of the parameter tuning are shown in figure 2.

The used validation data are indicated by black squares. The found parameters after tuning are were $(\omega_a,\omega_e,\omega_T,\lambda_\sigma,\lambda_\beta)_t$ = (.44,.96,.12,1,.84). The mean absolute difference between the tuned output of the model (blue line) and the validation data (squares) is 0.00859. The absolute difference between the tuned (dark line) and the artificially generated output of the model (light grey line) is 0.0114. There is no baseline to compare this result against, but it seems satisfactory enough for using the type of validation data that was proposed in the previous section to get a good result in the case when the validation data is not artificially generated (and no artificially generated output of the model is present (i.e., the light grey line in figure 2).

In order to prevent overfitting on the validation data, 2-fold cross validation has been used. This means that we have randomly split the validation data into two sets and the eventual found optimal model parameters are the average between the two found solutions after tuning on the basis of the two different sets. The estimated error of the model for unseen data is calculated by averaging between the mean squared error (MSE) of the model given the found parameters tuning on the first set and testing on the other and the MSE of the model given the found parameters the other way around.

4.4   Results

The results are shown in figure 3. The gathered validation data are depicted as numbers, where each digit is the number of participants indicating his trust in iCloud.

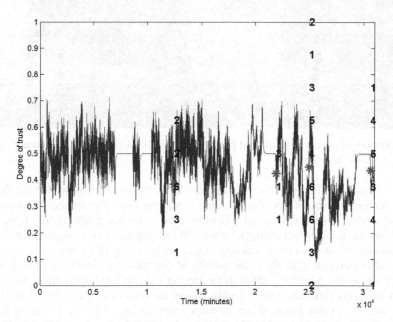

Fig. 3. Trust model output after 2-fold cross validation (line) based on the gathered validation data. The black numbers are the number of participants that indicated the respective trust values in iCloud. The stars are the means of those trust values for each of the four questionnaires.

Based on this gathered validation data, parameter tuning led to the trust model output as indicated by the line. The shown means per questionnaire (stars) are just for illustration purposes, since tuning was done using each individual data point. The found parameters after 2-fold cross validation are $(\omega_a,\omega_e,\omega_T,\lambda_\sigma,\lambda_\beta)_t = (0.92,1,0.3,0.62,0.75)$. The average of the MSEs for these parameters is 0.0439.

5   Visualization

Our proposed model of trust was used as a basis for a visualization tool aimed at supporting professionals in their effort to monitor trust in ICT services or to simulate certain implications given different interventions. Below a first version of this tool is described.

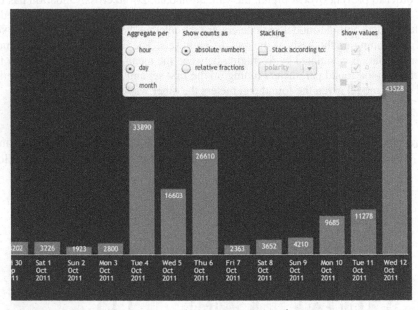

Fig. 4. Number of tweets about iCloud per day. On October 4th iCloud is announced; on October 12th iCloud is launched.

The visualization tool serves two purposes. First, it provides insight into the data that we are scraping from Twitter, through simple statistics like the number of tweets over time and sentiment scores. The tool allows to inspect absolute numbers (see figure 4), to break down the numbers according to sentiment (see figure 5), or to see relative fractions (see figure 6). All this can be shown aggregated per hour, day or month.

The other purpose is to show the results of the trust calculations from the model. The tool shows the trust in a certain topic (in our case: iCloud) over time. This can be done in near real time: the tool not only shows the history of trust, but also what the current trust is. In that sense, it has monitor functionality. The bright line in figure 6 illustrates how the trust value over time, as predicted by our model, could be combined with the distribution of sentiment over time. The starting point for the monitor tool is the data scraped from Twitter, which has been automatically annotated

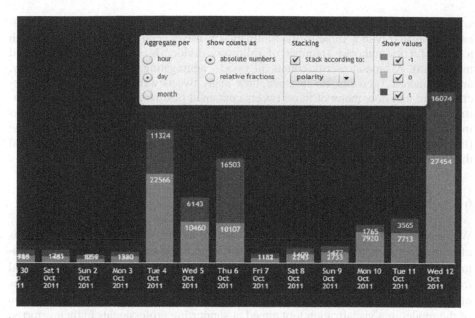

Fig. 5. Number of tweets about iCloud per day, broken down in positive (light colored) and negative (dark colored) tweets. Notice the increase in negative tweets right after the announcement of Jobs' death on October 6th.

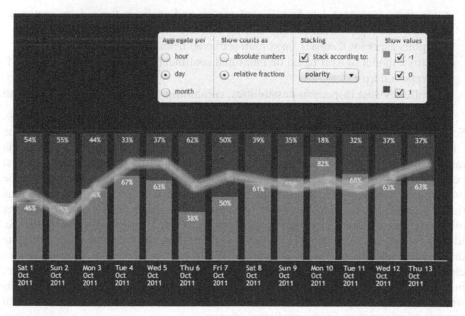

Fig. 6. Percentage of positive tweets and negative tweets about iCloud per day. The bright line is a fictive plot of the calculated trust (not based on the actual model).

with sentiment and authority values. This means that each tweet has been automatically annotated with a value for its sentiment (positive, neutral, or negative) and with a value for its authority (number of followers divided by a certain predetermined maximum). A separate script counts all tweets, aggregating them per hour, per day, and per month. It counts, for instance, how many tweets were about iCloud at a specific hour, and how many of those tweets contained positive, neutral or negative sentiment. The resulting table can directly be visualized by a simple bar chart. The tool is interactive; each time the user selects or deselects an option from the interaction pane (the white pane in the figures), the corresponding data is read from the database and the view is refreshed.

6   Discussion and Conclusions

We presented a social media-based, parameterized model of trust based on the notions of sentiment and authority, as an alternative for report-based, static models for assessing trust. We demonstrated that this model can be fitted to feedback data gathered from participants in an experiment. In addition, we tested the prognostic capabilities of the model when applied to evaluation data. We have also presented an application of the model in a visualization tool aimed at supporting professionals in their effort to monitor trust or to simulate certain implications of interventions.

From a procedural point of view, we have devised and implemented a fully working automated system that:

- gathers (scrapes) data from social media, and analyzes these data (sentiment analysis, topic classification), storing data and analysis results in a database;
- polls users for feedback on stimuli retrieved from the database;
- fits a model of trust based on measured sentiment, observed authority and self-reported trust;
- offers visual inspection possibilities, combining views on the stored data with model predictions.

Several aspects of our approach are open to improvement or further exploration. The current experimental setup suffers from several drawbacks. Specifically, a 'tabula rasa' exposure of participants was not guaranteed. The tweets presented to the test persons were historical, and chances are that they had already been observed by the participants. Furthermore, the current setup does not take into account exogenous (hidden, external) variables to which the participants have been exposed, such as other sources of information (newspapers, blogs, TV), or forms of social influence. Ideally, we would have test persons being exposed to a fixed number of controllable information sources and social influences. While such a laboratory setup is hard to envisage, monitoring devices handed out to test persons, for instance with deep packet inspection and key loggers, would probably yield more reliable information. This would open up the possibility of estimation of a model that weights these several sources of information for the prediction of trust.

Our parameter fitting approach, while powerful, is computationally expensive and required the use of a large computer cluster. Well-known and more practical solutions to finding accurate and robust parameter settings are available, for instance sampling methods (such as genetic algorithms) or learning approaches, such as gradient descent methods. We also suggest the use of many more questionnaires for different time intervals that will also improve the parameter fitting approach. All this emphasizes the need for other parameter fitting methods, which will be addressed in a follow-up of this research.

References

1. Corbitt, B.J., Thanasankit, T., Yi, H.: Trust and e-commerce: a study of consumer perceptions. Electronic Commerce Research and Applications 2(3), 203–215 (2003)
2. Keymolen, E., van den Berg, B., Prins, C., Frissen, V.: Vertrouwen in hybride ketens. Onderzoeksrapport in het kader van Alliantie Vitaal Bestuur, Den Haag (2010)
3. Kim, D.J., Song, Y.I., Braynov, S.B., Rao, H.R.: A multidimensional trust formation model in b-to-c e-commerce: a conceptual framework and content analyses of academia/practitioner perspectives. Decision Support Systems 40(2), 143–165 (2005)
4. Kim, Y.A., Song, H.S.: Strategies for predicting local trust based on trust propagation in social networks. Knowledge-Based Systems 24(8), 1360–1371 (2011)
5. Pang, B., Lee, L.: Opinion mining and sentiment analysis. Foundations and Trends in Information Retrieval 2(1-2), 1–135 (2008)
6. Utz, S.: Rebuilding trust after negative feedback: the role of communication. In: Cook, K., Snyders, C., Buskens, V., Cheshire, C. (eds.) eTrust: Forming Relationships in the Online World, pp. 215–237. Russell Sage Foundation, New York (2009)

Video Games and the Militarisation of Society: Towards a Theoretical and Conceptual Framework

John Martino

The Victoria Institute, Victoria University, Australia
john.martino@vu.edu.au

Abstract. This paper outlines the relationship between military themed or oriented video and computer games and the process of *militarisation*. A theoretical and analytical framework which draws on elements of sociology, cultural studies and media analysis is required to help to understand the complex interplay between entertainment in the form of playable media, the military and the maintenance of *Empire*. At one level games can be described as simple forms of entertainment designed to engage players in a pleasurable fun activity. However, any form of media, whether playable or not, contains within it a set of ideological and political structures, meanings and ways of depicting the world. For the purpose of this paper playable media with a military theme or orientation will be described as political tools helping to shape the mental framework of players through the extension of a form of *"military habitus"*. Playable media with a military theme or orientation such as the *Call of Duty* series promote and facilitate the extension of the process of *militarisation* and impact on how players view the world. This worldview can have consequences for national security in promoting pro-war sentiments.

Keywords: empire, militarisation, video game.

1   Introduction

> *"This game actually makes me flash back and think about the war and the aftermath.... But that's not necessarily bad. Being that I will be going back to Iraq for a 3rd tour, I'll say that it's much better fighting from my PC behind a desk then actually slinging lead at each other."* SGT from HHC 1/64 Armor, 3rd Infantry Division(M). [36]

The relationship between entertainment and war has been the subject of much research, analysis and critique. So too has the emerging nexus between the military and what authors such as Der Derian [1] and others [2-4] have described as the *Media-Entertainment-Industrial complex*. This relationship has been given added influence by the popularity of video and computer games, which contain military themes and content such as the *Call of Duty* series or *Halo*. Military themed video and computer games serve a particular ideological and cultural function within Western societies. These forms of playable media have been harnessed in support of the *"militarisation"*

M.D. Hercheui et al. (Eds.): HCC10 2012, IFIP AICT 386, pp. 264–273, 2012.

of society [5-7] and the maintenance and extension of what Hardt and Negri have described as the "Empire" [8].

Within this paper a number of theoretical constructs will be examined in order to highlight the socio-cultural and political role that war themed computer and video games play in the process of *militarisation*. Reference will be made to the fields of sociology and politics in order to comprehend the complex interaction between video and computer games, the military and war. A broad approach to the theme of information and communicaton technology (ICT) and critical infrastructures will be adopted within this paper. The extent to which military themed video and computer games influence how players view the world will be examined.

2   War, Entertainment and the Ideology of "Empire"

The image of President Obama (figure 1) and his war cabinet huddled around a monitor and laptops' observing in real-time the attack on the Bin Laden compound is reminiscent of a group of teenagers playing *Call of Duty* or *Halo* in their lounge room. The image below of the "War Cabinet" is emblematic of the blurring that has occurred in advanced societies between gaming, simulation and the conduct of war. The growing reliance on remote, and or "drone' technologies to engage in intelligence gathering, target acquisition and combat has become a distinguishing feature of the current era [9-11]. So too is the image of a civilian operator controlling a remote drone from a trailer in the American south-west as if he or she were playing a computer game whilst the drone under their control is engaged in the deadly business of modern warfare [11]. We are witnessing a blurring between the boundaries of war, entertainment and the ideology of "Empire" – as an outcome of a powerful sociopolitical process we can refer to as the *"militarisation of society"* [5], [12].

Fig. 1. Target Bin Laden: President Obama watches images from the raid on the Bin Laden compound in Pakistan, May 1, 2011 [37]

The concept of *"Empire"* used in this paper is drawn in part from the work of Antonio Negri and Michael Hardt in the book published in 2000, *Empire* [8]. According to Negri and Hardt, we are witness to the birth of a planetary wide political, economic, communicative and military structure. This form of *Empire* differs from other historical imperial structures such as that of Ancient Rome or the British empire in that there is "no outside" – the entire planet is part of this imperial system [8]. The modern form of empire as described by Hardt and Negri is governed by a "world market" – dominated by a number of global corporations (Apple, Microsoft, and Nike etc.) and supra-state agencies (the International Monetary Fund, World Bank, and the United Nations). The individual is drawn into the orbit of *Empire* at a range of levels, as a consumer (through marketing), as a labourer (through the exploitation of labour power) and as a learner (through the education system) [8].

3   The Militarisation Thesis

Militarism is a political form which has as its central characteristic the privileging of the military within society and the political dominance of a military caste or clique [6]. Militarism is also characterised by the existence within certain societies of what Gillis has described as 'warlike values' [6]. Militarism in the twentieth century was at the core of particular state formations and political ideologies, such as National Socialism in Germany and Italian Fascism [13]. John Gillis in his book *The Militarisation of the Western World* distinguishes between the terms *militarism* and *militarisation* in the following manner:

> "...(m)ilitarism is the older concept, usually defined as either the dominance of the military over civilian authority, or, more generally, as the prevalence of warlike values in a society" [5].

"*Militarisation*" refers to a more complex and subtle phenomenon than militarism and does not require formal control or dominance by the military. The American historian Michael Geyer has argued that *militarisation* can be understood as "the contradictory and tense social process in which civil society organises itself for the production of violence" [6]. This process does not require the outward signs of military control or dominance one could identify in the military dictatorships of twentieth century Latin America or the Fascist regime of the Spanish dictator Franco. In contrast to the overt and often openly brutal nature of militarist societies, *militarisation* is a social and political process which operates more subtly and at a number of levels within advanced society [12-14].

The feminist writer Cynthia Enloe [15] has defined *militarisation* as:

> "... a step-by-step process by which a person or a thing gradually comes to be controlled by the military or comes to depend for its well-being on militaristic ideas" [15].

3.1   The Garrison State

Underpinning the process of *militarisation* has been a phenomenon that emerged in the mid-twentieth century, which the political scientist Lasswell [16] has described as the 'garrison state'. According to Lasswell from the mid-twentieth century the world has steadily moved:

"... toward ...(the creation)... of "garrison states" – a world in which the specialists on violence are the most powerful group in society" [16].

The social and political importance placed on the specialist in violence that Lasswell first identified last century has not abated. It could be argued that the heightened level of security that has been in place since 9/11 has helped to elevate the role of the specialist in violence through an era of almost continuous war. The twenty-first century has been characterised by Paul Virilio [17] in *Pure War* as representing the emergence of "asymmetrical and *trans-political war*". According to Virilio:

"... (w)hen you've called a war asymmetrical and trans-political, it means that there's a total imbalance between national armies, international armies, world-war armies, and militias of all sorts that practice asymmetrical war. These could be little groups, neighborhood or city gangs, or "paramilitaries", as they're called; Mafioso of all types, without meaning Al Qaeda terrorists, or others. This is what happened in Africa, with countries that have fallen apart" [17].

It is in the context of the emergence of continuous asymmetrical and *trans-political war* that the process of militarisation has emerged as a defining characteristic of modern society. In the remainder of this paper we will examine the complex interplay between video games and the ongoing process of militarisation.

4   Video Games and the Militarisation of Society

The process of *militarisation* reflects a weakening of the boundaries "between military and civilian institutions, activities and aims" [12]. Computer and video games with a military theme act in a manner which extends the process of boundary weakening [12] between military and civilian institutions and activities. Military themed computer and video games such as the first person "Military Shooter" (for example *Doom* or the *Call of Duty: Modern Warfare* game series) enhance the already potent cultural tools that modern political regimes have at their disposal for propaganda purposes through the mass mediums of print, television, film and radio. Video games and their online support communities and websites add another layer of political enculturation to the needs and interests of what Negri and Hardt have described as the "Empire" [8, 18]. In the twenty-first century *militarisation* as a socio-cultural force has at its disposal the product of over four decades of close alignment between the military and the *media-entertainment industries* – the video game.

4.1   Playable Media

The importance of the military in American culture as portrayed in literature, films, television, comics, the press and news media for over a century has been pivotal in this process of boundary weakening. Recent developments in the media and entertainment field – advances in computer and video games, as well as the growth of new forms of the Internet and social media – have meant that the existing conduits for *militarisation* through traditional media and cultural channels have been amplified.

The emergence of powerful new forms of media and the growing sophistication of playable media technologies such as computer and video games has added to the existing array of mechanisms that facilitate the process of *militarisation*. Social media and applications have been harnessed to promote United States (US) values and objectives through the shaping of public opinion [19].

4.2   The "Military Shooter"

Modern computer and video console games with a military theme or with military content use software that has its origins in, or is convertible to, a battle simulator. The inventor of an early arcade video game *Battlezone* describes the process of adapting his game to the requirements of the US military as follows:

> "... we were not modeling some fantasy tank, we were modeling an infantry-fighting vehicle that had a turret that could rotate independently of the tank. It had a choice of guns to use. Instead of a gravity-free cannon, you had ballistics to configure. You had to have identifiable targets because they wanted to train gunners to recognise the difference between friendly and enemy vehicles" [20].

The use of games for training and simulation purposes has extended beyond the tank warfare simulation of *Battlezone* to the more complex infantry focused Military Shooter. A Military Shooter is a military themed variant of the First Person Shooter (FPS) style of computer gaming. A FPS game is " played in the subjective, or first person, perspective and therefore...(is)...the visual progeny of subjective camera techniques in the cinema. But perhaps equally essential to the FPS genre is the players *weapon*, which generally appears in the right foreground of the frame" [21].

This genre of gaming gained a wide audience in the early 1990s with the release of the World War II based *Wolfenstein* (1992) and the science fiction inspired *Doom* (1993) [4]. FPS games such as these have as their defining characteristic a lone hero armed to the teeth and up against hordes of Nazis in *Wolfenstein*, or trans-dimensional demons in *Doom*. *Doom* underwent a military make-over in the 1990s when the US military modified it to become *Marine Doom* which has since been used as an official military training tool [22]. Military Shooters differ from these early games in that they are often realistic in their use of plot, location and weaponry. Military Shooters can also incorporate squad-based tactics as in *Full Spectrum Warrior*.

What distinguishes the modern Military Shooter from early examples of the FPS genre is the attention to realism in the content, the authenticity of weapons, the realistic application of physics and the adherence to narrative and interactivity. The technology behind today's Military Shooters enables program designers to reproduce realistic war settings complete with sights and sounds and the ability to interact with others in an accurate, though virtual war zone. Using today's high capacity computing technology, gamers are able to immerse themselves within a synthetic war zone and use a range of accurate representations of weaponry in settings where the atmospherics of war, wind, light, and terrain etc., are as important within the game as they would be in the real world. This in many ways lifts the modern Military Shooter out of the world of gaming and into the world of simulation and training.

The Military Shooter relies on technology that creates an authentic simulation within which the player is able to interact with autonomous and realistic synthetic agents (humans) within a dynamic narrative framework. The technology underpinning this capacity is the product of a close working relationship between technologists and the military and the goal of enhancing the training effectiveness of simulation technology [1], [23], [24]. One of the key institutions driving the design of the technologies at the core of the modern FPS is the Institute of Creative Technologies located at the University of California. The Institute was funded by the US Army as part of its program to apply new digital technologies to its array of training and simulation tools. The Institute combined the technology of the emergent gaming and simulation fields with the narrative skills of "Hollywood" to produce accurate and engaging simulation and gaming technologies [25].

According to the Institute of Creative Technologies web page, the organisation leads "an international effort to develop virtual humans who think and behave like real people. We create tools and immersive environments to experientially transport participants to other places." [25]. The technology developed by the Institute of Creative Technologies has helped enhance the realism now possible within the Military Shooter genre of gaming. Technologies developed in places such as the Institute of Creative Technologies to help prepare soldiers for the complex task of navigating the modern battle space have been augmented by game designers into a fun activity – complete with "leader-boards" and "kill/death" ratio statistics.

The impact of these games on young people is open to debate, and no clear evidence exists that playing these games turns someone into a killer or the perfect soldier. The issue requires a more nuanced approach than that often engaged in by the mass media, academic critics and supporters. Military themed or oriented games such as *Call of Duty Modern Warfare 3* amplify the already powerful process of *militarisation*. Games desensitise the player to the use and consequences of violence. It is enough that the player becomes habituated to the idea that the use of violence should not be questioned and follows the model of classical conditioning. As the imagery of the television advertisement (Fig. 2) for *Call of Duty Modern Warfare 3* attests anyone (the "Noob" or the novice player) can, through playing the game, bring out the soldier within.

Further, the socio-cultural process of *militarisation* has been enhanced through the materialisation of technological capacity and the popularity of Military Shooter games and other forms of military themed gaming. This coalescence has meant that the increased availability of advanced consumer technology (hardware and software) has provided a mechanism through which the mental framework of young people – "the players" has been shaped by what has been referred to earlier as a military habitus – militarist language, values and practices. This is due in no small part to the level of engagement possible when playing these games. Their scenarios and supporting infrastructure (tally-boards, websites, online forums, and books etc.) enable players to envelope themselves within a world in which they are significant actors amongst a global community of like-minded individuals and "clans".

Fig. 2. "The Vet and the Noob". Image from a Television Advertisement for Call of Duty: Modern Warfare 3 [38].

5   Video Games and the Habitus

In the sections below, the sociological tools needed to help us make sense of how video and computer games and, in particular, the Military Shooter function as mechanisms for the extension of the *militarisation* process will be examined.

5.1   Habitus

The concept of *habitus* is derived from the work of the French sociologist Pierre Bourdieu [26], who describes *habitus* as representing "systems of durable, transposable *dispositions*, structured structures predisposed to function as structuring structures' that is, as principles of the generation...and structuring of practices and representations which can be objectively 'regulated' and 'regular' without any way being the product of obedience to rules, objectively adapted to their goals without presupposing a conscious aiming at ends or an express mastery of the operations necessary to attain them" [26]. In educational settings *habitus* helps reinforce the social and cultural capital that the middle-class arriving at school already possesses. For the middle-class, educational institutions from the architecture, to the curriculum, the staff and the resources at their disposal reinforce and help strengthen a middle-class disposition and way of being in the world.

The application of our understanding of *habitus* is not restricted to analysing institutions such as schools or other educational settings. The concept of *habitus* has been deployed to help understand a range of settings or fields as Bourdieu describes them; in particular sports and sports training have been the focus of significant work [27]. For example the work of one of Bourdieu's students Loïc Wacquant [27], [28] on boxing and the *pugilistic habitus* highlights the significance of this idea for our understanding of how power and culture become embodied. The analysis of sport and the sporting *habitus* [27] can help us to make sense of an evolving ludic based *military habitus*.

5.2   Military Habitus

Preparation for war has traditionally involved soldiers engaging in endless drill, marching in formation, following commands, target practice and the completion of obstacle courses. Modern warfare requires a different set of skills and characteristics. On the modern battlefield the soldier needs to be a thinker, a problem solver and a specialist in applying the necessary level of violence [29]. The Military Shooter has found a niche as a "training" tool for the military, enabling military personnel to realistically simulate complex battle scenarios in order to rehearse the intricacies of modern combat in diverse settings [30-32]. The language, game play (multi-player, head shots and kill points), high-tech weapons and gear (armour, uniforms and insignia) and other military elements of this form of gaming extend and amplify the process of militarisation and helps constitute a ludic based *military habitus.*

This emergent *military habitus* coupled with the immersive and realistic war simulation at the heart of the Military Shooter helps construct a foundation upon which entry into and effective participation within military organisations becomes easier to facilitate. We can begin to understand how this process takes shape by referring to the concept of 'anticipatory socialisation'. Neil Stott describes 'anticipatory socialisation' [33] as a process through which young people are able to rehearse and test future roles and occupations. In this context, playable media such as the *Call of Duty* series become more of a simulation than a form of entertainment and assist in the extension of the process of *militarisation.*

The concept of *habitus* enables us to understand how games help to shape or pattern the mental framework of young people in order to create particular dispositions or ways of looking at and interacting with the world. These dispositions and ways of interacting with, and looking at, the world are neither benign nor value free. Military Shooter and other military themed or oriented video and computer games are ideological tools and artefacts. The Military Shooter and other military themed or oriented video and computer games have political and cultural meaning, and significance [4], [34], [35]. They can be interpreted as more than simple entertainment and, when examined from the position of what Hardt and Negri have described as the "Empire" [8], [18], they can be interpreted as serving a powerful ideological function.

6   "Empire" at War

Gaming has been harnessed in the post-9/11 era to promote a set of values, practices and dispositions which support the ideological and political framework described by Negri and Hardt as "Empire" [8], [18]. Entertainment with a military theme complements the already powerful social, political and cultural forces at work in American society, as well as in other Western societies which position and privilege the military as one of, if not the most influential institutions within those societies. This process has been identified as representing the *militarisation* of society. In Western societies *militarisation* has led to the creation and maintenance of a strong military establishment – which has the ability to engage in continuous geographically dispersed asymmetrical warfare, in support of the politics of Empire [8], [18].

7   Conclusion

The role played by new media such as video and computer gaming in the process of *militarisation* warrants further detailed study and critique. The argument that these forms of playable media are simply harmless diversions ignores the role played by the military in facilitating the development of technology and content, which make these games both realistic and entertaining. Computer and video games such as the *Call of Duty* series have the effect of reinforcing a particular view of the world amongst players. This is a view, which encourages both war as a political tool but also as a form of entertainment. Computer and video games such as the Military Shooters have in effect become part of the fabric of military ICT infrastructure.

References

1. Der Derian, J.: Virtuous war: mapping the military-industrial-media-entertainment network. Routledge, New York (2009)
2. Lenoir, T.: All but war is simulation: The military-entertainment complex. Configurations 8(3), 289–335 (2000)
3. Leonard, D.: Unsettling the military entertainment complex: Video games and a pedagogy of peace. SIMILE: Studies In Media & Information Literacy Education 4(4), 1–8 (2004)
4. Thomson, M.: Military computer games and the new American militarism: What computer games teach us about war, p. 317. University of Nottingham, Nottingham (2009)
5. Gillis, J.R.: The militarization of the western world. Rutgers University Press, New Brunswick (1989)
6. Geyer, M.: The Militarization of Europe, 1914-1945. In: Gillis, J.R. (ed.) The Militarization of the Western World. Rutgers University Press, New Brunswick (1989)
7. Kohn, R.H.: The Danger of Militarization in an Endless" War" on Terrorism. The Journal of Military History 73(1), 177–208 (2009)
8. Hardt, M., Negri, A.: Empire. Harvard University Press, Boston (2000)
9. Graham, S.: Robowar dreams. City 12(1), 25–49 (2008)
10. Martin, M.J., Sasser, C.W.: Predator: The Remote-Control Air War over Iraq and Afghanistan: A Pilot's Story. Zenith Press, Minneapolis (2010)
11. Rodrigues, M.R.A.: Wired for war: The robotics revolution and conflict in the 21st century. Naval Law Review 60, 223–223 (2010)
12. Orr, J.: The militarization of inner space. Critical Sociology 30(2), 451 (2004)
13. Thomas, T.: Banal Militarism: Zur Veralltglichung des Militrischen im Zivilen. Transcript Verlag, Bielefeld (2006)
14. Saltman, K.J.: Education as enforcement: The militarization and corporatization of schools. Routledge, New York (2011)
15. Enloe, C.H.: Maneuvers: the international politics of militarizing women's lives. University of California Press, Los Angeles (2000)
16. Lasswell, H.D.: The garrison state. American Journal of Sociology, 455–468 (1941)
17. Virilio, P., Lotringer, S.: Pure war.semiotext(e), Los Angeles, CA (2008)
18. Hardt, M., Negri, A.: Multitude. Penguin Books, London (2006)
19. Shachtman, N.: Special Forces Get Social in New Psychological Operation Plan, in Danger Room, Wired.com, http://www.wired.com/dangerroom/2012/01/social-network-psyop/ (first accessed January 22, 2012)

20. Kent, S.L.: The ultimate history of video games: from Pong to Pokemon and beyond: the story behind the craze that touched our lives and changed the world. Three Rivers Press, Roseville (2001)
21. Galloway, A.R.: Gaming: essays on algorithmic culture. Electronic Mediations. University of Minnesota Press, Minneapolis (2006)
22. Hoeglund, J.: Electronic Empire: Orientalism Revisited in the Military Shooter. Game Studies 8(1) (2008)
23. Hill Jr., R.W., et al.: Pedagogically structured game-based training: Development of the ELECT BiLAT simulation. DTIC Document (2006)
24. Gagnon, F.: Invading Your Hearts and Minds: Call of Duty and the (Re) Writing of Militarism in US Digital Games and Popular Culture. European Journal of American studies (2) (November 2010)
25. Institute for Creative Technologies. Background (cited March 21, 2012, 9:04:51 AM) (2012), http://ict.usc.edu/background
26. Bourdieu, P.: Outline of a theory of practice (Esquisse d'une theorie de la pratique). Transl. by Richard Nice.(Repr.). In: Gellner, E. (ed.) Cambridge Studies in Social and Cultural Anthropology, vol. 16. Cambridge University Press, New York (1977)
27. Noble, G., Watkins, M.: So, how did Bourdieu learn to play tennis? Habitus, consciousness and habituation. Cultural studies 17(3-4), 520–539 (2003)
28. Wacquant, L.J.D.: Body & Soul. Oxford University Press, New York (2004)
29. McFarland, K.A.: A performance map framework for maximizing soldier performance, p. 408. Doctoral dissertation in Faculty of the Graduate School, University of Texas at Austin, Austin (2011)
30. Smith, R.: The long history of gaming in military training. Simulation & Gaming 41(1), 6 (2010)
31. Nieborg, D.: Training recruits and conditioning youth: the soft power of military games. In: Bogost, I., Huntemann, N.B., Payne, M.T. (eds.) Joystick Soldiers: the Politics of Play in Military Video Games, Taylor & Francis, New York (2009)
32. Mitchell, M., Brown, K.: Development of Simulation Software in Military Training and Gaming Systems (2009), Online version published, http://citeseerx.ist.psu.edu/viewdoc/summary?, doi:10.1.1.134.8352
33. Stott, N.: Anticipating military work; digital games as a source of anticipatory socialization? Paper presented at the British International Studies Association American Foreign Policy Conference, University of Leeds, UK, September 15 (2010)
34. Stahl, R.: Militainment, inc: war, media, and popular culture. Routledge, New York (2010)
35. Masters, C.: Cyborg Soldiers and Militarised Masculinities. In: Shepherd, L. (ed.) Gender Matters, in Global Politics: A Feminist Introduction to International Relations. Routledge, New York (2010)
36. http://www.kumawar.com
37. US Embassy New Zealand Photo stream. Creative Commons license some rights reserved, http://www.flickr.com/photos/us_embassy_newzealand/5681578435/sizes/o/in/set-72157626502891531/
38. http://www.callofduty.com/mw3/videos/vet_n00b

Challenges to Peace in the 21st Century: Working towards a Good Information and Communication Society

Gunilla Bradley[1] and Diane Whitehouse[2]

[1] Royal Institute of Technology (KTH),
School of Information and Communication Technology, Stockholm, Sweden
gbradley@ug.kth.se
[2] The Castlegate Consultancy, Malton, United Kingdom
diane.whitehouse@thecastlegateconsultancy.com

Abstract. This short *reflection paper* emphasises the need for contemporary society to focus on the positive, the beneficial and the humane. There are considerable challenges to peace in the 21st century. People are increasingly concentrating on war and violence. To counter this preoccupation with the negative, the authors explore a number of avenues that may – from a psycho- logical, sociological or societal perspective – help human beings to think and act in a more peaceful, non-violent manner. The ideas covered are contained within an overall framework that focuses on the need to work together towards a Good Information and Communication Society. The focus is on action, education and study that have an international orientation rather than simply being undertaken on the local or national levels.

Keywords: action, education, good information and communication society, electronic violent games, information and communication technologies, international, peace.

1   Introduction

Conference panels often provide opportunities to explore difficult and sensitive subjects in much more open and flexible ways than do standard conferences tracks and themes. Hence, they often contain not only academic papers but also reflection and position papers. This panel on information and communication technologies (ICT) for peace and war, and the imperatives of achieving cyber peace, to which this paper is a contribution, is no exception.

Opportunities and threats related to ICT have been classic themes of many ICT gatherings, conferences and workshops over the past decades. This reflection paper – on issues pertaining to war, ICT, cyber warfare and infrastructure – may well provide a contrast in its freedom of thought and approach to other more academic pieces. It proposes a deliberate focus on the study of ICT and its constructive use in the fields

M.D. Hercheui et al. (Eds.): HCC10 2012, IFIP AICT 386, pp. 274–284, 2012.

of democracy, education, effective organisation, equity, enhancement, human development, justice, learning, and sound policy development. Overall, ICT can help to reduce risks by enhancing discussion between people. The ultimate goal is to build a Good Information and Communication Society. As this conference panel intends, it can do so by "taking into consideration [people's] mutual interests in living a peaceful life".[1]

This paper is structured in the following way. It introduces the background to ICT use in peace and war in a very general way (Section 2). It covers the relationship of ICT with vulnerable ICT critical infrastructures, and it emphasises the way in which ICT can be used in terms of aggression, violence and war whether directly as an instrument or as a support structure. It introduces (in Section 3) the growth in institutions, investigation, and studies relating to violence and war and their links with ICT: for this, it draws especially on the European and Scandinavian contexts. It also highlights current trends in the investigation of the relationship between the use of violent electronic games and behaviour. As a result, several potential possibilities for areas of study are listed (Section 3.4). A plea is then made for alternative thinking and acting in many more positive directions (Section 4). The authors have brainstormed a list of issues that researchers who seek to examine the positive dimensions of ICT might wish to explore (Section 5): the four principal domains are those of awareness-building, education and development, software and games, and adopting an international perspective. Some emerging conclusions are highlighted (Section 6).

This approach does not yet constitute an agenda for a programme of action. Nevertheless, it is hoped that it may provide a helpful set of possibilities to those networks, organisations and institutions that are already working in this field of activity or may go on to do so in the future.

2   Some Observations on War, ICT, Cyber Warfare and Infrastructure

War is scarcely a new phenomenon although, in its early stages, it has been associated more simply with tribal raids. Yet many of the most destructive wars in human history took place in the last century. This growth in destructiveness is assumed to be due directly to the expansion and the efficiency of the technologies used, including – at the end of the Second World War – the use of the atomic bomb.[2]

Two approaches appear to have become necessary. It is now imperative to study not only how war takes place, and with what methods, but also how to resolve war and grow beyond its basis in conflict: nations can thereby be restored to conditions under which they respect and honour peace [11].

Even if war is state-based organised violence, there are many other examples of potential and actual violence that are coming to the fore today. Many *ad hoc* groups

---

[1] Text of Human Choice and Computers 10 (HCC10) Conference Call.

[2] These reflections were concluded after a reading of texts located in Wikipedia on, for example, peace-building, pre-requisites for peace, and war.

are involved in the use of violence whether for "need, greed or creed" [21]³. While violent actions may come from individuals, loosely-organised groups or organised crime, they can also emerge from autocratic – and other types of – states. There will always be countries and regimes interested in exploring the fragilities of other nations.⁴

2.1   ICT and Infrastructure

Critical information infrastructures can be used to avoid engagement in war, but are also implicit in supporting involvement in warfare. Security aspects that support this infrastructure, which can be called "cyber security", can help to maintain national and international security. However, cyber security can also be used to effect in both espionage and sabotage.

Some uses of ICT pose threats of quite new dimensions whether as a result of conscious intent, error or ultimately through the very vulnerability of ICT [2]. It is all too horribly easy to imagine an extreme, and potentially final, catastrophe that could result, for example – whether deliberately or *ad hoc* – from today's combination of ICT and nuclear power. Indeed, while it can be said that nuclear power is only usable and controllable through the use of ICT, ICT's shortcomings can lead to errors, failures and disasters not only in the nuclear domain but also in many other fields [12]. Of course, atomic – and other – crises may occur as a result of natural and unanticipated phenomena: environmental disasters can happen as a result of solar flares, earthquakes or *tsunami*. In contemporary society, particularly in developed countries but also increasingly in emerging economies, critical infrastructures based on ICT can be conceived as being fundamental to the capacity to live in peace and prosperity. Society is so reliant on the use of ICT and its critical infrastructures that the collapse of these systems could leave whole populations without structures, services and applications. Sheer demand, resulting from the expected growth in consumption, may have dire consequences for the capacity to continue to provide energy supplies [19]. Almost all domains of people's lives are dependent on ICT: a situation that we may wish to avoid or at least to counterbalance [6], [7].

This generalised movement towards complete ICT dependency is perceived as meaning that entire societies and nations could collapse with great speed if there were ever to be a massive failure in their ICT infrastructures. Whole societies and civilisations and their infrastructures could quickly be destroyed or rendered inoperable. Societies, communications and people could be left without sustenance and support. Such a crisis could affect the capacity to use any form of ICT, and thereby compromise the financial, business, and public sectors as well as people's working lives (for example, in the fields of health services and public health [20]). It could inhibit the ability to communicate among family members, friends and acquaintances. It could

---

³ This expression was first used by Professor William Zartmann, Jacob Blaustein Professor of International Organizations and Conflict Resolution, Paul H. Nitze School of Advanced International Studies, Johns Hopkins University. It was the title of a public event entitled Civil War: Need, Creed and Greed which took place on October 21, 2004.

⁴ Text of Human Choice and Computers 10 (HCC10) Conference Call.

also impair the continuity of human existence in those communities that are located in either very hot or very cold climates or countries that experience both extreme heat and cold. The implications for peace and harmony, in general, are considerable, since many of these threats could lead to complete societal breakdown.

ICT is directly implicit in these risks. This challenge is perhaps particularly hard for people and politicians to envisage.

3   A Growth in ICT and War Research, Study and Action

At some level, it is to be acknowledged that developments in ICT-related research, study and action around warfare, and cyber warfare particularly, are occurring both quantitatively and qualitatively.

There are more and more institutions dealing with combating warfare and building peace. The trend is very much also to an international and national focus on cyber warfare. However, various broadcasting and other media are also playing a role in this domain in terms of the ways in which they present developments to the public. More than that, they are influential in the manner in which they encourage children, young people and adults to view – and even potentially get involved in – violence, aggression, and even war.

These developments are reviewed before a set of potential research questions is laid out for possible investigation by traditional peace institutes.

3.1   Contemporary Developments in Peace and War Research

To take the Scandinavian countries as just one example, they now have a variety of peace research institutes: a few are mentioned here. On the global level, it can be assumed that each nation has its own similar institutions that research these challenges on some level or in some aspect, and that the United Nations are working on such tasks [8].

In Norway, there is the Peace Research Institute Oslo; Sweden has the Stockholm International Peace Research Institute and, in Uppsala, there is the Uppsala University Department of Peace and Conflict Research, and its Peace Research Programme. The first is known for both its basic research and its policy-relevant research and the way in which it has engaged itself in promoting peace through the resolution of conflict by means of dialogue, reconciliation, public information and policy-making. The second is an internationally-renowned think-tank. As an independent international institute dedicated to research into conflict, armaments, arms control and disarmament, it bases its work on openly-available data sources. The third has a research programme on governance, conflict and peace-building. It concentrates on internal, state-based peace-building in weaker regions and countries around the globe, with a focus on Africa, and the relationship between governance and resources.

The daily press shows that new collaborations are being initiated with the purpose of defending nation states and preventing new potential catastrophes. In the *Svenska Dagbladet*, a major Swedish broadsheet newspaper, headlines announced that Sweden and the United States of America (US) are collaborating on strategies related to cyber warfare [16]. These kinds of efforts are also being pursued at European and international levels.

3.2   Expansion of European and International Focus on Cyber Crime

Peace depends at least to some extent on investing in cyber security.

On the very day of finalisation of this reflection paper, the European Commission launched a proposal for a European Cyber Crime Centre to tackle cyber crime [10]. Cyber crime is essentially seamless or borderless. Its perpetrators prefer to ignore deliberately the locations and countries of the victims of their crimes. This centre will gather together some of Europe's brightest minds in cyber security. Its task will be to warn the Member States of the European Union about any major cyber threats on the horizon and any weaknesses in their online performance. It will identify crime through discerning patterns, for example, in virus attacks. The centre will be located in The Hague in the Netherlands, and will be run by Europol. In the Swedish broadsheet newspaper, the *Svenska Dagbladet*, European Commissioner Cecilia Malmström stated that knowledge about cyber crime is fragmented throughout the authorities of the Member States of the Union, and – to this time at least – co-operation across borders to fight this crime is infrequent [16].

Groups of Scandinavian (and other) investigators have also explored, for example, the growth in profiling by corporations, tracking of suspects, electronic tagging of prisoners at work, and the monitoring of paedophilia, money-laundering, information warfare, and cyber crime as well as assessed the benefits and costs of surveillance, and its future developments [1].

3.3   A Growth in Research on Aggression and Violence in Childhood

Research developments are always in process, and benefit from dynamic discussion in order to progress [14].

A Swedish Media Council report [17] examines decade-long work on the part of several international expert bodies (including the US Department of Health and Human Services and children's medical associations in Australia, Canada and the US). Collectively, these take the position that very violent games increase the likelihood of aggressive behaviour.

In a recent article in the *Dagens Nyheter* [15], three researchers further debate these issues. They agree that it is not easy to distinguish violent games as the unique factor that generates violence and aggressiveness in young people. Among the stronger predictors of violence are family relationships, genetic disposition, personality, and socialisation. For children who grow up in an environment where inter-personal violence is normal, violent games are yet another source of learning aggressive behaviours and stifling empathic development.

The notion of "game dependency" has to be considered in depth through research, study and discussion on the relationship between violent computer games and aggressive behaviour.

Similarly, research indicates a gradual loss of empathy alongside extreme use of mobile phones [13], [22]. It too is a subject deserving of in-depth investigation.

3.4   Proposals for a First set of Questions to Be Explored

Work to reach peace is now increasingly institutionalised. There are surely plenty of theoretical questions that can be studied in the fields of research on war, peace, and violence. Many of the issues raised and questions posed in these fields, and their institutes, are based on experiences with conflicts involving weapons that have either occurred or are on-going.

Based on discussions first initiated in July 2011 in Rome, Italy at the International Association for the Development of the Information Society (IADIS) ICT, Society and Human Beings conference [5], we propose a first set of questions to experts who work within the field of study on ICT and warfare. An attempt has been made to formulate a number of questions that can help analyse issues that are threatening peace in the "here and now". The topics listed strike us as ones that are already deserving of intellectual coverage. The extent to which these issues are currently under investigation in actuality is, however, unknown to us.

It is our hope that these kinds of ideas can help to strengthen the many commendable efforts that are already taking place throughout the globe (not simply in the US, Europe or the other countries of the Organisation of Economic Co-operation and Development), an example of which is under the leadership of the International Telecommunications Union [18].

- **Same or different:** Is cyber warfare different from orthodox or classic warfare? Or is it – even if apparently "non-violent" – just a form of war, adapted to the conditions of contemporary society? Does it require special actions to combat it? What are the "small" or "limited" experiences of cyber attacks that have taken place, for example, in Estonia [9]?
- **Traditional concerns transposed into modern society:** What kind of relationship exists between "attack" and "defence" in various political systems? How do the hierarchies that exist in traditional military domains correspond to the relative lack of hierarchy that exists in cyber warfare? How much does the variability in control of the Internet influence the networks that operate across national borders (i.e., its apparent lack of centralised control or its relative freedom from control)? How do traditional hierarchies complicate these matters?
- **New fields of warfare:** Are there any comparisons to be made between country-based attacks and attacks on global financial systems? What parallels are there between cyber warfare and attacks on international trade? What about attacks that can be made on specific infrastructures such as utilities or energy systems? How similar to each other are threats connected to nuclear power and those associated with cyber warfare?
- **Play versus actuality:** What degree of influence is there on developments in aggression and violence through playing electronic war games and electronic games of extreme violence?

These are, we assume, somewhat classic questions that enable an analysis of the field. However, concern and consideration for these issues can become the starting-point for alternatives in terms of both thinking and acting. From the perspective of the authors, it is a major challenge *not* to restrict such questioning purely to the military domain.

4   A Need for Growth in Alternative Thinking and Acting

A "nonviolence movement" against non-violent cyber warfare is needed: this would be a form of grass roots movement – or network of networks – that shares the same vision of reaching the Good Information and Communication Society.

Historically, advocates of activist philosophies of nonviolence have used a range of methods in their campaigns for social change. These have included critical forms of education and persuasion, civil disobedience and nonviolent direct action, and social, political, cultural and economic forms of intervention. In recent centuries, and also within the first decade of the twenty-first century, nonviolent methods of action have acted as powerful tools for social protest and revolutionary social and political change.

For example, people today need to know how to be resilient even in the most dire of tragic circumstances [7]. Alongside personal, organisational, and national resilience, we need, as a counter-movement, to start a new phase for ICT that is used for peace, harmony and collaboration. The passive acceptance of inappropriate and ill-considered – some might even say, "evil" – use of ICT has to be prevented. If and when secure and sustainable, ICT may actually help to reduce risks.

ICT can and should be used to narrow the gap between subcultures, and to bridge the differences between different religious systems. It could, instead, show their similarities, emphasise the synergies among the various cultural and faith-based blocks, and bring us all into a thrilling, fruitful dialogue with each other. We need quite a different approach which would be based on the achievement of a future "unity and diversity" in the world [5].

This would be a much more cross-disciplinary approach based on broader theoretical perspectives than in times past. It should, first, be feasible to be put into practice and, second, help *all* people to work on preventive action strategies.

5   Constructive Considerations (for a Positive Turnaround?)

People in general, together with academics, need to start a new movement for ICT that is used for peace, harmony and collaboration. The latest forms of ICT can be used for constructive interaction, dialogue and the enrichment of human feelings and thinking. Here, therefore, are some initial thoughts on "tools" that can be used, in particular, to prevent and fight cyber warfare.

A mutual brainstorming, another of the outcomes of the IADIS July 2011 conference [5], highlighted the formulation of an initial set of possible positive positions and tools. These tools relate principally to four domains. They are awareness-building; education and development; software and games; and seeing the issues from an international perspective. These four sets of proposals are laid out here: there is no particular prioritisation to the issues. All are important, and would benefit from further investigation and, moreover, action.

In terms of *awareness-building*, it is important not just to increase the consciousness of the threats of cyber warfare, but also to:

- Create an understanding of how contemporary society is built and its underpinning, invisible infrastructures (for example, based on the economy, electricity, transportation and water). From this understanding, build an awareness of the vulnerability of society.
- Create the potential for positive, new uses of ICT. The 2011 International Association for the Development of the Information Society (IADIS) ICT, Society and Human Beings conference [5], for example, dealt with many examples of ICT use that can help to make people aware of what could be done to combat global warming; what can be done ecologically and environmentally in a positive way; helping people at the bottom of the pyramid; enhancing the lives of the very young and especially the very elderly; and using ICT in health, welfare and well-being.
- Work together to create space and time for constructive discussion and debate in forums and *agora*, as much physically and in real-time as in cyberspace and on the Internet.
- Use cyberspace for dialogue and for the search for the common essence of all faiths, religions and philosophical and spiritual endeavours.
- Hold dialogues about common value systems. Again, for example, the 2011 IADIS ICT, Society and Human Beings conference held inspirational panels on human rights and on "unity and diversity" [5].

In terms of *education and development*, employ ICT directly and indirectly to:

- Examine the experience of early childhood in relation to ICT and its influence on childhood and adult development.[5]
- Explore strategies to encourage human and humane roles instead of further strengthening traditional "male" and "female" roles. Emancipation is needed for men and women, boys and girls. Until now, emancipation has focused largely on what it means for women.
- Emphasise an assessment of ICT's influence on boys and men because it is so much more often the male gender that wages war. While all of us are the victims of warfare, war often particularly affects women and children.
- Consider education more and more in the context of global learning.

---

[5] In this respect, the pedagogical work of Maria Montessori, and schools which follow in the tradition of her thinking, is of especial importance. The celebrated Italian physician and educator devoted her life to developing a learning philosophy for children that has become widespread internationally. Debate about the approach became a hot issue before, during and after World War II. Indeed, she was nominated several times for the Nobel Peace Prize. One of her books dealt with education and peace.

- Ensure that global and international trade shifts instead towards a "Global and International Educational System".
- Explore the potential for "commoning" (sharing) in the ICT society.

In terms of *software and electronic games*, to:

- Begin to use multimedia products in a positive peace-oriented way.
- Focus on developing "peace games" across cultures and religions.
- Develop a role and purpose for anti-war games.
- Stop developing games based on extreme violence.

From an *international perspective*, to:

- Explore the power of good examples.[6]
- Explore what kinds of wise, preventative actions formal international bodies, could take, and compare these with disarmament campaigns.
- Re-think the basis of formal international bodies based on the character of to-day's and tomorrow's threats.
- Explore the collaboration potential between formal bodies and the informal organisations, bodies and networks. Examine how the work and relationships between the non-governmental organisations, bodies and informal networks operating in the field of peace-building could be co-ordinated and strengthened.
- Stop the "robotisation" of international, economic transactions that involve an increase in the risk of conflict development.
- Explore specifically what an organisation like the International Federation for Information Processing could begin to do about these challenges.

6   Emerging Conclusions

In the authors' opinion, there are some phenomenal tools available to help build a Good Information and Communication Society. That society starts within ourselves and with ourselves, and in the networks of which we are members. It also relates to civil society as a whole, and the formal organisations that function in society.

We all have a responsibility in our roles as researchers, policy-makers, citizens and human beings to consider how we can leave after us a society where human rights and peace form its essential elements. Stakeholders, along with ICT experts, can help society to start to answer a vast number of important questions pertaining to the potential turnaround of contemporary society.

---

[6] In 2011, the Nobel Peace Prize was given to three African woman, Ellen Johnson Sirleaf, Leynah Gbowee, and Tanakkol Karman who have applied innovative strategies to strive for democracy and to reach peace. Over the more than one hundred years that the prize has been awarded, there have been fewer than ten women who have received it. Many more have been nominated. http://www.nobelprize.org/nobel_prizes/peace/articles/heroines/html. Accessed 28 March, 2012.

A set of fundamental points, and a number of possible actions are immediately evident:

- Never before in history has there been such a great opportunity for peace. Let us build on that opportunity.
- Rethinking is required to deal with today's global problems, and transparent, rapid action too is needed.
- Visionary strategic tools are needed to help transform dictatorships into democracies, to overcome not only present conflicts but also future risks.

ICT should help people to appreciate diversity. To capture an old saying of Gunilla Bradley's: when we design, work with and use these technologies the focus should be on "ICT for deepening human and societal qualities" [3], [4].

A major re-thinking is needed to deal with today's problems. Transparent, rapid action is needed. Let us act on it!

Acknowledgements. The authors are especially grateful to Mr. Jackie Phahlamohlaka, Chair of the International Federation for Information Processing (IFIP)'s Technical Committee 9 on ICT and Society. He chaired a panel on peace and war at the 2011 IADIS ICT, Society and Human Beings conference in Rome, Italy in July 2011 at which a very preliminary version of this reflection paper was first presented. We also wish to thank Mr. Willny Bradley who has assisted us with background desk research, and Mr. Marc Griffiths and several anonymous reviewers for their careful, constructive criticism and commentary.

References

1. Ball, K., Webster, F. (eds.): The Intensification of Surveillance: Crime, Terrorism and Warfare in the Information Era. Pluto Press, London (2003)
2. Berleur, J., Beardon, C., Laufer, R. (eds.): Facing the Challenge of Risk and Vulnerability in an Information Society. Proceedings of the IFIP WG9.2 Working Conference on Facing the Challenge of Risk and Vulnerability in an Information Society, Namur, Belgium, May 20-22 (1993)
3. Bradley, G. (ed.): Humans on the Net. Information and Communication Technology (ICT) Work Organization and Human Beings. Prevent, Stockholm (2001)
4. Bradley, G.: Social and Community Informatics - Humans on the Net. Routledge, London (2006)
5. Bradley, G., Whitehouse, D., Singh, G.: Proceedings of the IADIS International Conferences ICT, Society and Human Beings 2011 and e-Democracy, Equity and Social Justice 2011. In: Part of the IADIS Multi-Conference on Computer Science and Information Systems 2011. IADIS Press (2011)
6. Bradley, K.: Från fildelning till sakdelning (From sharing files to sharing things). Cogito. Own translation from the Swedish (February 23, 2012)
7. Cameron, J.: A Survival Kit for Resilient Citizens in the Information Society. Presentation made at the IFIP WG9.2 & WG 9.9 Joint Workshop, Milan, Social Accountability & Sustainability in the Information Society: Perspectives on Long-Term Responsibility, June 4-5 (2011)

8. Doyle, M.W., Sambrinis, N.: Making War and Building Peace: United Nations Peace Operations. Princeton University Press, Princeton (2006)
9. Economist, The. War in the Fifth Domain. Are the Mouse and the Keyboard the New Weapons of Conflict? July 1 (2010),
   http://www.economist.com/node/16478792 (accessed March 28, 2012)
10. Commission. Tackling Crime in our Digital Age: Establishing a European Cybercrime Centre. Brussels, European Commission. COM (2012) (140 final),
    http://ec.europa.eu/home-affairs/
    doc_centre/crime/docs/Communication%20-
    %20European%20Cybercrime%20Centre.pdf (accessed March 28, 2012)
11. Höglund, K., Fjelde, H. (eds.): Building Peace, Creating Conflict. Conflictual Dimensions of Local and International Peacebuilding. Nordic Academic Press, Lund (2011)
12. Kajtazi, M.: An Exploration of Information Inadequacy: the Lack of Needed Information in Human, Social and Industrial Affairs. In: Hercheui, M.D. et al. (eds.) HCC10 2012. IFIP AICT 386, IFIP International Federation for Information Processing (2012)
13. Konrath, S.H., O'Brien, E.H., Hsing, C.: Changes in Dispositional Empathy in American College Students over Time. A Meta-Analysis. Personality and Social Psychology 15(2), 80–198 (2011)
14. Kuhn, T.S.: The Structure of Scientific Revolutions. University of Chicago Press, Chicago (1962)
15. Olsson, A., Petrovic, P., Ingvar, M.: Sä ska EU stoppa cyberbrotten. DN Debate (2012)
16. SvD Opinion. Sä ska EU stoppa cyberbrotten, March 28 (2012),
    http://www.svd.se/opinion/brannpunkt/sa-ska-eu-stoppa-
    cyberbrotten_6957681.svd (accessed March 2012 28, 2012)
17. Swedish Media Council. Violent computer games and aggression - an overview of the research 2000-2011. Swedish Media Council (2011),
    http://www.statensmedierad.se (accessed March 28, 2012)
18. Touré, H.I.: The Quest for Cyber Peace, International Telecommunications Union, Geneva (2011)
19. Whitehouse, D., Hilty, L., Patrignani, N., van Lieshout, M.: Introduction. In: Whitehouse, D., Hilty, L., Patrignani, N., van Lieshout, M. (eds.) Social Accountability and Sustainability in the Information Society: Perspectives in Long-term Responsibility, Notizie di Politeia, Rome, pp. 3–12 (2011)
20. Whitehouse, D.: Benchmarking eHealth in the European Union. Presentation made at the IFIP WG9.2 Workshop, London, ICT Critical Infrastructure and Social Accountability: Methods, Tools and Techniques, February 4 (2012)
21. Zartmann, W.: Pronouncement at event entitled Civil War: Need, Creed and Greed, October 21 (2004), http://www.cgdev.org/content/calendar/detail/3019/ (accessed March 28, 2012)
22. Zaki, J.: What, Me Care? Young are less Empathetic. A recent study finds a decline in empathy among young people in the U.S. Scientific American, January 19 (2011)

Section 4

Citizens' Involvement, Citizens' Rights and ICT

Implementing Ethics in Information Systems, Presuppositions and Consequences in Ethics and Information Systems

Laurence Masclet[1] and Philippe Goujon[2]

[1] Facultés Notre Dame de la Paix, FUNDP, Belgium.
laurence.masclet@fundp.ac.be
[2] Facultés Notre Dame de la Paix, FUNDP, Belgium
pgo@info.fundp.ac.be

Abstract. This paper focuses on the relationship between information systems and ethics, and in particular, on the complexity of implementing ethics in information systems. Both fields are subject to various presuppositions that have consequences for how they manage the relationship of ethics implementation. Those presuppositions are related to the problem of "the construction of the norm" and the relationship – or absence of it in most governance theories – between norms and context. Ethicists seem to be reluctant to take into account the field of application of the norms created by the procedure it constructs. This is due mainly to a certain closure to elements other than rational argumentation in procedural ethics. Information systems' professionals, as we have seen in a study undertaken for the IDEGOV[1] project, also have a narrow vision of what is ethics. They often reduce ethics to a constraint that has to be fulfilled. They also have a very stereotypical vision of what are the issues present in the field of information systems – privacy, surveillance, and security – and how to answer these questions, mainly through more information. We will show that these presuppositions on both sides have a huge impact on the manner in which ethics is "done" in technical projects, and more importantly, we will give hints on how to improve the relationship. The term implementation is itself inappropriate, because it supposes that ethics is something external to information systems. This presupposition is shared to some extent by both fields i.e., ethics and information systems: it is the central point where we see the problem, but also the solution. Working on the framings of both ethical and technical communities is for us the way to overcome ethical problems in information system, and to reach appropriate ethical technology development.

Keywords: comprehensive proceduralism, ethics, governance, information systems, technology assessment.

---

[1] IDEGOV "IDEntification and GOVernance of ethical issues in information systems" is a project funded by the Club Informatique des Grandes Entreprises Françaises (CIGREF) foundation. It aims at giving ethical governance recommendations to information systems' professionals and organisations. It does on the grounds of theoretical background development (a grid of analysis, and determination of parameters) and an empirical study, based on interviews and questionnaires made among information systems' professionals around the world on the basis of the grid of analysis.

M.D. Hercheui et al. (Eds.): HCC10 2012, IFIP AICT 386, pp. 287–298, 2012.
© IFIP International Federation for Information Processing 2012

1   Introduction

Ethics is increasingly being recognized as a necessity in the field of information systems and in every technological project. There are some common features to every project involving technological development. Every project has to be ethically developed. This means that a project cannot just be submitted for ethical assessment when it has been completely developed.

Indeed, the very existence of a technology has an ethical impact, whether or not the technology is accepted by an ethical committee to be implemented in society. Nuclear power, for example, has an impact, whether it is used or not. The existence of a virus so powerful that it can kill half the population of the earth is of ethical preoccupation, no matter how secure and well protected it is. It is the virus's development and very existence itself that has to be evaluated. The conception that a piece of research is just research, that a technology is itself neutral before being used and, therefore, that it is the implementation that matters and has to be ethical, has caused a lot of misconceptions about the role of ethics. This is still a view that is prevalent in the technological and scientific world, even though it is starting to change at the political level. Projects are beginning to be stopped for ethical reasons, but this event is still very rare.

Ethical reflection has to play a part in every technology development project. In this paper, we will see what that means for technologies and for ethics, and how ethics has to change itself to take into account more parameters in its conceptions of itself and its procedure. However, first, we have to understand the specificities of the field of information systems.

2   Ethical Specificities of Information Systems

Information systems are well implemented in society. Its area of technological development does not seem to raise the problem of acceptance. As stated by Van den Hoven [24], information technologies have the particularity of being ubiquitous and persuasive. The main specificity of information systems is their links with information. Because information is such a positive value nowadays, information systems (which are comprised by information technology (IT)), seem to carry a positive bias by association. Indeed, with the development of cybernetics through the work of Wiener, Von Neumann, and Turing, information started to replace other values in the public sphere. Information seemed to be the best way to forget those morals and ideals that had been devaluated by the barbarism of two world wars. From its start as a strictly mathematical concept, information has invaded step by step every sphere of society, and become an ideology – a development that we can see in the work of Wiener [27]. Information and communication became the prevalent values of post-war society, and are still largely unquestioned.

This is partly why information systems seem so harmless in society. Nobody will ever say that they need less information, because information and communication are associated with the morally "good". Information and communication carry positive moral values. Actually, they *became* moral values. As a consequence, they are a very convenient instrument of persuasion and manipulation.

To explore the field of information systems and ethics in information systems, in the IDEGOV project, we questioned information systems professionals on the ethical issues of information systems [14]. We found two main invading types of ethical worries: the first ethical worry was privacy, and the second was security, but these two concerns are usually linked together. Surveillance was also mentioned a lot, and can be considered a middle term between the two types of ethical worries. Not surprisingly, the solutions that are raised by almost everyone to these three concerns involve more information: for example, "raise awareness of the issue", "inform people", and "educate users and professionals".

Such a consensual way of thinking has, however, some background difficulties. One of the problems with offering information on ethical issues as an answer is that it does not address the existence of the ethical issue itself, in the sense that information on its own does not involve a reflection on the *legitimacy* of the technology. The technology itself is not questioned when someone offers the answer of awareness. Information is an *a posteriori* response to a technology that is already judged as inevitable. The ethical issues are therefore seen as inevitable, and the only strategy left is to "take [the technology] into account", and to "be aware" of its possible impacts. If the only solution to ethical problems in information systems is more information, then the system is in a loop. The system tries to heal itself by implementing education and ethical awareness, in order to get rid of ethical worries, but not every ethical issue can be solved by more information.

This focus on information is also partly due to the migration of the bioethical grid of analysis to the problem of governance [23]. Because bioethics is more developed than governance or at least has managed a better implementation, the bioethical way to deal with issues – awareness, informed consent, and so on – became the only way to judge ethical issues. However, some ethical issues are embedded in the information system itself, and can only be resolved by deeply changing the system or even withdrawing from a specific technological development. Ethics needs an engagement that cannot be reduced to awareness. Reducing ethics to a manageable scheme is very tempting, but it can make problems worse. To avoid paying the price of living in an unethical society, we should be ready to pay the price of ethics.

The development of a particular technology *can* and *should* be questioned[2]. Norms exist to regulate technological development and applications and, in the absence of

---

[2] Technology is already increasingly being questioned. The European Commission seems to care more and more about ethical problems and the shortcomings of the approach to ethics in research projects that it uses (such as an ethics check-list). On the academic side, a lot of studies have been conducted on this issue in recent years (see, for example [25]). We can also refer to the various publications of the International Federation of Information Processing's special interest group on the framework of the ethics of computing on this subject. Philosophers, scientists, developers and politicians appear to care increasingly about these issues. This can provide a good field for change if they think carefully about the presuppositions embedded in their respective approaches. In that sense, we see this IDEGOV-related work as a step *before* the elaboration of strategies to deal with the obligation to create guidelines and develop methods or meta-methods to implement reflexivity in technology assessment. This step aims at pointing out the common presuppositions and considerations that are not always taken into account by researchers in ethics and in technology.

such norms, they can be constructed. The ways to construct ethical norms and to reach governance is one of the main questions of ethics. However, by taking only the problem of the construction of norms into account, ethics seems to have missed the opportunity to rally together technology developers and scientists. This is why ethical issues in information systems, as in any technological field, are not solely a matter of presupposition on the part of the technology developers. We cannot only blame misconceptions and prejudices from the field. We have to think about ethics and ethical theories and the way they address the issue of implementation of their own theories. Ethics can be a field for preconceptions and presuppositions. We have to take a critical stand on ethics and ethical theories themselves, in order to fully understand the problem of implementation of ethics in information systems.

3   Ethics as a Question

Many ethical theories focus on the procedures of the construction of norms. The philosophical trend that has the task of creating such procedures is called proceduralism. Proceduralism has taken various forms throughout history. The most famous sets of procedures have been written by Habermas and Rawls. But the proceduralism trend cannot be reduced to the work of these two philosophers.

> *"Proceduralism as a general idea encompasses any sort of procedural device for making a decision or resolving a dispute. It takes different forms[3]. In democratic polities, procedures can specify everything from the forms of participation and adjudication to the forms of implementation. These democratic preoccupations drive the current literature[4]. Joshua Cohen sees democracy as a "procedure that institutionalizes an idea of citizens as equals."[5] For John Rawls, the only political consensus we can reasonably hope for is confined to democratic political procedures," such as the "right to vote and freedom of political speech and association, and whatever else is required for the electoral and legislative procedures of democracy."[6] Jürgen*

---

[3] As a procedure by which conflicts may be settled, Brian Barry, Political Argument (London: Routledge and Kegan Paul, 1970) p. 85-91, distinguishes combat, bargaining, discussion on merits, voting, context, and authoritative determination.

[4] David Estlund, "Beyond Fairness and Deliberation: The Epistemic Dimension of Democratic Authority" in James Bohman and William Rehg, (ed.), *Deliberative Democracy: Essay on Reason and Politics* (Cambridge MIT Press, 1997); Allan Gibbard, "Morality as Consistency in Living: Korsgaard's Kantian Lectures" *Ethics* 110 (1999); Axel Honneth "Democracy as Reflexive Cooperation: John Dewey and the Theory of Democracy Today" *Political Theory* 26 (1998); Lenore Langsdorf and Darrin Hicks, "Regulating Disagreement, Constituting Participants: A Critique of Proceduralist Theories of Democracy" *Argumentation* 13 (1999); Michel Rosenfeld, "A Pluralist Critique of Contractarian Proceduralism", *Ratio Juris* 11 (1998).

[5] Joshua Cohen, "Pluralism and Proceduralism", *Chicago-Kent Law Review,* 69, (1994), p. 610.

[6] John Rawls, *Political Liberalism* (New York: Columbia University Press, 1993), p. 159.

> *Habermas claims that the "central element of the democratic process resides in the procedure of deliberative politics."[7] [4]*

Proceduralism is the product of our societies' pluralism (in particular the passage to multiple sources of normativity[8]). It was initially developed to resolve value conflicts by taking formal, "procedural" steps, and restricting debates to the level of rational argumentation. This trend has been very active in the field of ethics and governance, and has been very influential both with regard to the construction of procedures to assess technologies and political systems.

However, proceduralism has a blind spot that has had major consequences for the relationship between ethics and technologies [10]. Proceduralism focuses on norm construction but has, as a secondary task, the step of application. This is due to the presupposition that this step of application, or implementation, will necessarily follow if the norm is valid.

> *"Procedural ethical theories, in particular, first set themselves the task of indicating a procedure through which norms and modes of action can be rationally grounded or criticized, as the case may be. Because they must deal with this task separately, the impartial application of valid principles and rules arises only as a subsequent problem." [7]*

It is clear in this quotation that procedural ethical theories make a distinction between the task of norm construction or norm criticism, which has to be rationally grounded, and the "impartial application" of the norm that has *previously* been constructed. This means that the demands of the problem of application are not taken into account in the theory that frames the norm construction process. The blind spot of procedural theories is the actual effect that the context of application has on the norm construction.

Procedural ethical theories have determined that the best way to ensure fair and "right" norms, that exclude bias and unresolved conflict, is through rational consensus on the part of every stakeholder. There are various examples of such rational consensus. They include the law of the better argument[9] from Habermas' discourse ethics [5], the overlapping consensus[10] from Rawls' political liberalism [17], and the

---

[7] Jürgen Habermas, *Between Facts and Norms: Contribution to a Discourse Theory of Law and Democracy* Cambridge, MIT Press, 1996, p. 296.

[8] Normativity is a property of norms. It is what gives the prescriptive impact to the norms. A normative statement is a statement regarding how things should or ought to be. The normative level is a level that is not attached to what things are, but how they should be.

[9] The law of the best argument implies that there is/will be an argument in the discussion, which will be the object of consensus and that is the most rational argument, which is to say, in that type of theory, the best one.

[10] Overlapping consensus involves that citizens accept and support the same basic rules, even if for different reasons. The overlapping consensus does not include reasons why someone agrees to a norm, but only the norm itself that everybody accepts whatever the reasons why they do so.

problem of how to shape the discussion to validate and legitimate the norms that emerge. The theories cited are reluctant to include application in their construction and, more generally, to integrate the problem of context, because this would once again open the door to value conflicts. That door was closed so as to exclude values and beliefs as a source of legitimate norms in a rational debate.

However, a number of philosophers nowadays are criticising the reduction of ethics to rationality. The criticisms started with Simon and his theory of bounded rationality [20], and have not stopped since. Such thinkers as Lenoble and Maeschalck [10], [12], Sabel [19], Schön [21], Ferry [5], Sen [22], Von Schomberg [25], and many others, are now addressing the conditions and consequences of a re-inclusion of values, beliefs, context, narrative, interpretation, life experience, and everything that was left to one side as a result of the procedural turn in ethics that led to procedural theories of norm construction. Most philosophers remain within the broad trend of proceduralism, but want to open up its framing[11] so as to open it up to more complexity[12].

Lenoble and Maesschalck have criticised the development of this growing critique of the procedural approach [12]. They emphasize three presuppositions that are implied in a lot of ethical theories: the mentalist, intentionalist, and schematising presuppositions. These presuppositions are linked to their critique of the separation made by Habermas of the context of application from the context of justification.

In the *intentionalist presupposition*, the effects of norms are supposed to be deducible from the simple intention to adopt the norm. Additionally, there is the presupposition that the actors in a participatory approach will have the capacity and intention to contribute to the participatory discussion. The *schematising presupposition* involves Kantian schemes (i.e., rules developed by the philosopher, Immanuel Kant), in which the operation of the application of a norm is a simple formal deductive reasoning on the basis of the rule itself. The determination of the norm is linked to these rules, that include examples such as ethical guidelines, laws, or other external sets of rules. The *mentalist presupposition* is so named because it relies on the mind having a set of rules (or schemes, in Kant's words), that predetermines the effect of a norm and does not depend on any context exterior to that of the thinker. This is commonly seen

---

[11] The notion of framing covers everything that informs and conditions an action, an opinion or a research. It includes context, presuppositions, things that are considered normal in a society and everything that determines the shape and/or the content of a decision. There is no action and *a fortiori* no research without its own framing. Every epistemological choice frames a piece of research. A reflexive framing is necessary for good research (good research has to narrow the subject, define how it will be using concepts, methods, explain its objective, its starting hypothesis, the process of thought and experiment or tests that will come to test those hypotheses, and so on). The issue with framing is not its existence, it is whether people are conscious of it or not. That is where reflexivity has its part to play. Making people aware of their own framing, making people realize the presuppositions that are at stake when they act and think, is the first step in a process of changing behaviours to reach more ethical behaviours.

[12] The same movement can be seen in the field of economics. There has been a shift from the paradigm of the "rational agent" to the acceptance of more and more complex models that include irrational behaviour.

when participants in a participatory approach come to the setting with their own particular ethical framing, or with preconceptions as to what ethical issues might arise. As noted by the analysis of Lenoble and Maesschalck regarding governance and norms [12], it is the failure to account for the epistemological position of the social actors that leads to those presuppositions.

The position of the normative device (experts, guidelines, etc.) as a judging entity (exerting top-down pressure) does not permit the adequate elaboration of a governance approach. These presuppositions facilitate failure insofar as they underwrite inattention to the material that informs the perspective of any given social actor. Thus, they facilitate the elaboration of governance that has a built-in "gap" between governing and the governed. Another presupposition, identified by Ferry, is that most ethical theories and governance arrangements ignore that the conditions why we accept a norm are not equal to the condition of its justification [5]. This means that we can both accept a norm for reasons other than its rational justification, and without agreeing with its justification.

We have seen that there are many presuppositions on both sides. Ethical theories are failing to pay enough attention to their application in the field, and developers are failing to consider ethics as a complex task that cannot be reduced to some obvious issues and some convenient answers. Now we have to determine how we could overcome those presuppositions. However, as we will see, this is not a simple question, because we have to understand what our own presuppositions are whenever we are talking about the implementation of ethics in information systems.

Indeed, this way of talking about the problem of implementation raises a huge problem. Talking about implementation would mean that there is something to be implemented. But ethics is not a product. Ethics, as we have said, has to be a question. We cannot "sell" ethics as if it were a medicine to be taken, as if the only issue were to write and explain the instructions well enough to be understood entirely.

If ethicists, over the years, did try to influence ethics to become an instruction book to be applied by developers, technicians and scientists, by writing codes of conduct, checklists of ethical issues and assessment procedures, this method does not seem to work. This is because, by using that kind of approach, the philosophers who write the instructions do not offer the key to its understanding to the reader, so that the reader can understand the true meaning of the instructions on his/her own and, hence, learn to act ethically in an independent way.

Talking about implementation seems improper, because it does not involve the implications for and the engagement of developers. So, what could ethicists and technology developers together actually do to create technologies that are ethical, and to make the process of the development of a technology or an information system ethical?

4 Hints Towards a Solution

Two important hints are offered that could lead to eventual solutions. They include adapting ethical theories to their context of application, and reaching a form of ethical development for information systems. Each is explored in somewhat more detail below.

4.1   Adaptation of Ethical Theories to their Context of Application

The identification of ethical issues is not sufficient to resolve the issues. The presupposition that identification was actually sufficient has been a brake to both ethical theories and ethical technological development.

In our research, we have found various forms of closure and presuppositions on the part of both the communities of "ethical people" and "technology people". There is also a gap between the two communities. The reasons for this include differences in "jargon", disinterest in implementation from the philosophers, disinterest in both ethics and its assimilation in laws from information systems' professionals, the separation between "human" sciences and "pure" sciences, notably in education, and so on. The role of ethics in recent years seems to be to open up framings and allow full reflexivity [21] for everybody, in order to create bonds between ethics and technology.

This approach involves reflexivity on the trends of ethical and governance research. This first is a task that has always been prevalent in the work of philosophers. Reflection on its own activity lies at the heart of philosophy. Putting that task back into the centre of the research in ethics is a good first step. However, the presuppositions in ethics are not really about reflexivity *per se*. The challenge might be that ethics researchers are too focused on the theories they are elaborating. The presupposition that a theory will answer all problems without being sensitive to the context of its application is still prevalent.

A good balance between reflexivity in ethics and a renewed interest in the context of the application of the theories has to be found. Our diagnosis, after research undertaken for three projects, EGAIS[13], ETICA[14] and IDEGOV, is that ethical theories have to take into account the context of application of their own theories, within the theory itself. That is to say that the theories must include an "opening" to challenges coming from the field to which they want to apply their theories, and to society in general.

The validity of the theories, ensured by ethical procedures, does not necessarily mean that the theories will actually be applicable. There is more to take into account than the legitimacy of the procedure to create norms. In the procedure, it should be acknowledged that the validity of a norm is not always sufficient to ensure its acceptance. Furthermore, somebody who can accept rationally a norm, and even help to create it within a discussion framed by ethical procedure (taking into account every argument, the law of the best argument, and so on), will not necessarily take that norm as a maxim for action [5].

4.2   How to Reach Ethical Development of Information Systems

We have said that information system is a particular field of application for ethics. We have also seen that the context of application has to be taken into account in the the-

---

[13] The EGAIS project was co-funded under the FP7 framework. See http://www.egais-project.eu/

[14] The ETICA project was co-funded under the FP7 framework. See http://ethics.ccsr.cse.dmu.ac.uk/etica/

ory. So how could we possibly take into account the context of information systems' development?

There are many presuppositions coming from the technical community about ethics. Ethics is generally seen as a constraint to be dealt with, more than an opportunity to "think outside the box" or even to improve the products under development. However, what is relevant for ethical theories seems to be also relevant to information systems' development. The context of the application of the product developed (here, an information system device) has to be taken into account as well as the acceptance of this technology by the public. The fact that information has such a positive value to society makes it easily accepted. However, there are a lot of issues, made stronger by the lack of wariness on the part of civil society. There are some ethical issues that are commonly admitted: privacy, security and surveillance. There are, however, issues that are more hidden, and that may depend on a particular situation. The question of trust, for example, cannot be reduced simply to privacy or security. Information systems touch questions of changes in time and space, changes in human interaction, the status of the person and a lot of other huge questions, which cannot be reduced to concepts that are on the edge of being deprived of meaning, due to their over-utilisation[15].

Creating a list of issues is irrelevant. We have to think ethically all the time, and assess technologies as we develop them. It is not a matter of changing professional rules and code of conducts; it is a matter of changing professionals' thinking about ethics. There is no ethical thinking "to be implemented"; there is rather ethical thinking to be thought.

Taking part in the process of norm construction is a good first step for information systems' professionals, to open up their framing and gain awareness of their own presuppositions and of others' points of view. It is not because we agree with the norms that we comply with them. There is a need for constant reflexive thinking about the technologies developed and the systems created. Ethical thinking cannot be assumed to be something in the minds of the people, coming from general principle they agreed on explicitly or implicitly. That is why the gap between the ethical community and the scientific community is so tragic. As a society, we need to reduce that gap; we need to find common ground on which to collaborate.

In that process, both disciplines have to reassess their own positions, rethink their own presuppositions and discuss them. There is a need in both disciplines for second-level reflexivity, which is different from just thinking about its immediate action [1]. Reflexivity at a second level is much deeper. It involves questioning the maxim of its action *and* the presuppositions that are at its very basis. Those presuppositions can come from various sources: they can come from the structure of the society, the field in which one is working, or one's personal history, beliefs, and so on.

This is why one of the solutions we have to think about in ethics is narration in the process of norm construction. Not everything can be transformed into a rational

---

[15] The same is true of the term "ethics", which seems to have lost a lot of its meaning to become either a derogatory term or a category into which every non-technical aspect of technology development that nobody knows how to address is put.

argument. A life story is very often more powerful and convincing than a rational argument, and this fact has to be taken into account.

As for the assessment process of a technology, there is a need for a shift in the assessment procedure from an ethical analysis of the issues to a meta-ethical analysis of the governance process. This need has been discussed in both the EGAIS and IDEGOV projects, but is also the subject of lots of publications in the area of information systems. Harris et al. for example are developing a tool called DIODE [9], which is a meta-methodology aimed at offering guidance to professionals while avoiding reduction to a check-list or expert-driven assessments, by bringing together top-down and bottom-up approaches, and broadly by combining teleological and deontological ethical principles. These kinds of tools are a good step, especially when, like in DIODE, they include ethical training for the persons who would assess the technology. However, they are also often on the edge of falling into the presuppositions discussed earlier – reliance on procedures, not taking into account the acceptance of norms, the gap between rational acceptance and application, and so on.

A completely inclusive way to incorporate multiple sources of information within discussions about norms, in order not to reject them in the unthought-of area of presuppositions and prejudices, has still to be found. The way forward is to explore more carefully the relationship between ethics and technology. This means to try to overcome the presuppositions that undermine this relationship and construct a method that is fully aware of its own limitations, the limitation of the persons involved and yet which also takes into account every aspect of the context (in the broadest sense of the term, which includes the context of the persons involved: values, life experiences, and so on).

This solution involves being ready, as a society, to invest time into ethics. For both ethical and technological communities, it means to be ready to work together, with their differences but also without too neat a border, since ethics is something that anybody could think about, no matter what its speciality. Ethical responsibilities have to be shared but they have also to be *taken* by people in the creation and development process (and not only at the ethical assessment step).

5   Conclusion

The problem of implementation may appear as a "subsequent" problem in ethical theories. However, it is actually at the heart of the governance. In the last analysis, it touches the challenge of ethical norms construction, and the ethicity of norms. As we have seen, implementing ethics in information systems raises a lot of issues, both theoretical and practical.

The first reason is that the term "implementation" is already wrong. It is not really a matter of implementing ethical rules and codes of conduct for information systems' professionals, and technology developers in general. The way to overcome presuppositions in ethics and technology seems to be by trying to reach reflexivity by opening the framing of every stakeholder (by showing them the presuppositions they are working under). The first step towards this seems to be by finding ways to encourage ethics researchers and technology developers to work together.

Because reflexivity at a second level is impossible to implement from an external point of view, we have to rely on what has already been developed in philosophy: discussion and procedures of norms construction. These procedures, however, are themselves subject to presuppositions, notably the fact that they are closed to the context of their own application, and that they deny legitimacy to a part of reality. (Indeed, irrationality exists, and people act as a result of other means and reasons than reason itself; they do not necessarily obey the best – the most rational – argument.)

So we have to create a proceduralism that would take into account more complexity than the current version of proceduralism that we have. Researchers in governance and ethics – including the authors – are currently in the process of systematising this approach in a theory which is called "comprehensive proceduralism". Comprehensive proceduralism goes a step further into the questions and explores the hints towards various answers given in this paper.

By exploring the presuppositions that lie in the background of the theories of ethical technology assessment, we give some keys to understand further the failures and successes of the current ways of undertaking ethical assessment. We also offer a more comprehensive framework in which it would be easier to collaborate, take on board others' perspectives, and find solutions that will already be "implemented" from the ground upwards at the very beginning of their conception because they will have taken into account the context of the application in their own construction.

References

1. Argyris, C., Schön, D.A.: Organisational Learning. A Theory of Action Perspective, vol. 1. Addison Wesley, Reading (1978)
2. Brey, P.: Method in Computer Ethics: Towards a Multi-Level Interdisciplinary Approach. Ethics and Information Technology 2(3), 1–5 (1999)
3. Duquenoy, P.: Ethics of Computing. Perspectives and Policies on ICT in Society. Springer & SBS Media, Heidelberg (2005)
4. Gregg, B.: Proceduralism reconceived: Political conflict resolution under condition of moral pluralism. Theory and Society 31, 741–776 (2002)
5. Ferry, J.-M.: Valeurs et Normes, La question de l'éthique. Edition de l'université de Bruxelles, Bruxelles (2002)
6. Habermas, J.: The Theory of Communicative Action. English translation by Thomas McCarthy. Beacon Press, Boston (1981)
7. Habermas, J.: Erläuterungen zur Diskursethik. Frankfurt am Main, Suhrkamp (1991)
8. Habermas, J.: Between Facts and Norms: Contribution to a Discourse Theory of Law and Democracy. MIT Press, Cambridge (1996)
9. Harris, I., Jennings, R.C., Pullinger, D., Rogerson, S., Duquenoy, P.: Ethical assessment of new technologies: a meta-methodology. Journal of Information, Communication and Ethics in Society 9(1), 49–64 (2011)
10. Laudon, K., Laudon, J.: Management des systèmes d'information, 11th edn. Pearson Education, London (2011)
11. Lenoble, J., Maesschalck, M.: Toward a Theory of Governance, the Action of Norms (trad. Paterson, J.). Kluwer Law International, The Hague (2003)

12. Lenoble, J., Maesschalck, M.: Beyond Neo-institutionalist and Pragmatic Approaches to Governance. Carnets du centre de philosophie du droit, Louvain-la-Neuve, no 130 (2007)
13. Masclet, L., Goujon, P.: IDEGOV D.1.1. Grid of Analysis, CIGREF Foundation (2011)
14. Masclet, L., Goujon, P.: IDEGOV D.3.2. Model of current and emerging governance strategies, Map of governance and ethics, CIGREF Foundation (2012)
15. Pearson, J.M., Crosby, L., Shim, J.P.: Modeling the relative importance of ethical behaviour criteria: A simulation of information systems professionals' ethical decisions. Journal Strategic Information Systems 5(4), 275–291 (1996)
16. Rainey, S., Goujon, P.: EGAIS 4.1 Existing Solutions to the Ethical Governance Problem and Characterisation of their Limitations (2009)
17. Rainey et al.: EGAIS 4.3 New Guidelines Addressing the Problem of Integrating Ethics into Technical Development Projects (2012)
18. Rawls, J.: A Theory of Justice. Harvard University Press, Cambridge (1971)
19. Sabel, C., Zeitlin, J.: Learning from Difference, The New Architecture of Experimentalist Governance in EU, European Governance Papers, Eurogov, C-07-02 (2008)
20. Simon, H.A.: Theories of bounded rationality. In: McGuire, C.B., Radned, R. (eds.) Decision and Organization, North-Holland Publishing Company, Amsterdam (1972)
21. Schön, D.: The Reflective Practitioner. How professionals think in action. Temple Smith, London (1983)
22. Sen, A.: The Idea of Justice. Harvard University Press, Boston (2009)
23. Stahl, B.C.: Ethical Issues of Information and Business. In: Himma, K., Tavani, H. (eds.) The Handbook of Information and Computer Ethics, pp. 311–337. Wiley, Hoboken (2008)
24. Van den Hoven, J.: Moral Methodology and Information Technology. In: Himma, K., Tavani, H. (eds.) The Handbook of Information and Computer Ethics, pp. 49–68. Wiley, Hoboken (2008)
25. Von Schomberg, R.: Discourse and Democracy: Essays on Habermas's Between Facts and Norms. State University of New York Press, New York (2002)
26. Webley, S.: Making Business Ethics Work: the foundations of effective embedding. The Institute of Business Ethics, London (2006)
27. Wiener, N.: The Human Use of Human Beings: cybernetics and society. The Riverside Press (Houghton Mifflin Co.), Chicago (1950)

Redesigning the Relationship between Government and Civil Society: An Investigation of Emerging Models of Networked Democracy in Brazil

Eduardo Henrique Diniz and Manuella Maia Ribeiro

Escola de Administração de Empresas de São Paulo, Fundação Getulio Vargas
São Paulo, Brazil
eduardo.diniz@fgv.br, maiamanuella@gmail.com

Abstract. The concept of networked public sphere [3] modifies the original Habermasian definition of public sphere by considering the dissemination of new interactive technologies that potentially allow new relations between civil society and government. The objective of this paper is to investigate the emergence of the networked public sphere based on the in-depth study of two Brazilian cities that have created conditions for their citizens to influence public policies through the use of Internet-based virtual platforms. To develop our study we adapt the method for analyzing political participation called democracy cube [13] that considers mechanisms of participation along three dimensions: a) who participates, b) how participants communicate with each other and make decisions, and c) how these decisions relate to political action and public policies. Our investigation shows that citizens of the two cities presented in this study use the virtual platform to engage in lively discussions and exchange of information as a way to propose and implement new public policies that are eventually adopted by their city governments. We conclude that, albeit at an early stage, the use of virtual platforms to share opinions on topics that citizens want to be recognized helps to mobilize public opinion and participation and influence the opinion of local public officials on policy implementations.

Keywords: city government, e-democracy, networked civil sphere, public participation, virtual platform.

1   Introduction

More than 1,000 reports of irregularities were submitted by citizens in a platform created by volunteers to monitor the Brazilian elections of October 2010. Since the Chinese government refused to disclose the names of the victims of an earthquake in 2008, citizens struggle to ensure transparency through a website created to investigate the identity of killed students. In Jundiaí, Brazil, a city of 370,000 inhabitants 60 km from São Paulo, a social network discussed and approved citizen initiatives to guarantee funding for the municipal government to build 25 km of bike lanes in the city. In India, a collaborative website was created to receive complaints of bribing to public officials.

M.D. Hercheui et al. (Eds.): HCC10 2012, IFIP AICT 386, pp. 299–309, 2012.

These are four examples of Internet use by civil society available on the Technology for Transparency Network website, an initiative created by the non-governmental organization (NGO) Global Voices to map experiences of how information and communication technologies (ICTs) are being used by citizens around the world to promote transparency, accountability and civic engagement.

The potential of the Internet to impact the relationship between government and civil society is also being highlighted since several demonstrations in several Arab countries were driven by the innovative use of social network technologies, some with the power to overthrow governments. The force of this media was recognized by Hosni Mubarak's dictatorial government that blocked access to the Internet for five days, showing the importance of Internet in the Egyptian conflict [15].

On the one hand, despite the massive use of the Internet in those conflicts, sometimes presented as the "Twitter Revolution" or the "Facebook Revolution", there is still no consensus on the technology's role as a democratization tool, since it also can be used as a mechanism for monitoring citizens, spreading propaganda and sustaining authoritarian regimes [20]. On the other hand, if the Internet could not be promoted as a tool for revolution, tools for decentralized distribution of messages, such as "tweets", have clearly helped to mobilize protesters and attract more people to the streets [4].

As pointed by Foth et al. [11, p. x], "over the past decade, ubiquitous computing, social media, and mobile technologies have become integral parts of our social lives and work practices, as well as shaping the way we make sense of our cultures and engage as citizens". In whatever way they are used, ubiquitous ICTs redefine citizens' social network activities [18] and are among the challenges surrounding contemporary democracies, in particular the relationship between civil society and governments.

To explain the role of these new technologies for social activism, Benkler [3] extends the Habermasian definition of public sphere into a concept of networked public sphere. Originally defined as the space in which civil society asserts that public authorities will act in accordance with its expectations, for Habermas [14] the public sphere was dominated by mass media. In a networked society, the virtual space created by the dissemination of new interactive technologies potentially allows new relations between civil society and government.

This paper investigates ways that civil society through virtual platforms has influenced local governments. Based on the study of two cases in Brazilian municipalities, the paper addresses the following research question: How do virtual platforms supported by ICTs provide coordination and collaboration in order to make civil participation effective in influencing government policies?

2   Theoretical Framework

2.1   Networked Public Sphere

Since the emergence of the Internet and universal access to information, the idea of the free flow of information has led to a series of economic, political and cultural changes, with clear impacts for governments and civil society. In his concept of net-worked society, Castells [8] states that the more technology is being incorporated into society, the more a dependency on knowledge and information generated and en-hanced by ICTs becomes part of the overall structure. As a corollary, the networked society changes crucial sources of domination and transformation of our society.

The networked and information-based society would foster the emergence of a par-ticipatory culture capable of accepting and maintaining multiple points of view. The promise of this networked democracy lies in encouraging broader participation and taking advantage of the collective wisdom and the perspectives of crowds [19].

The concept of web 2.0 emphasizes the development of a networked world through interactive platforms where users create content individually and collectively, sharing and updating information and knowledge using sophisticated, diverse devices and sharing tools, remixing and improving content created by each other [24]. In the same way, crowdsourcing government is a concept related to the networked society that focuses on impacts on government actions created by citizens' input generated from small individual contributions made by a large number of people [7].

ICTs' potential for provoking substantial changes in democracy and the public sphere is also highlighted by Benkler [3] with the concept of the networked public sphere. Benkler emphasizes the possibilities of citizens redesigning their relations with public administration by using new technology platforms, thereby making civil society more engaged and participative in its relationship with government as interac-tions and communication between them become more electronic and virtually-based.

Benkler's networked public sphere is based on the cooperative production that emerges with individual freedom and made feasible by the digital environment. The success of such cooperative production will rely both on the design of the digitally networked environment and the participatory involvement of the public. Considering design, Benkler states that being modular and maintaining the capacity to integrate fine-grained contributions must be part of the technical and organizational character-istics in virtual platforms for social participation. As the networked public sphere enables individuals and groups to play a role traditionally assigned to the mass-media-dominated public sphere, Benkler stresses its connections with the idea of public par-ticipation in the democratic process.

2.2 e-Democracy

For the concept of e-democracy, the part concerning the use of technology is some-how the easiest to understand. Just as there are different views on the meaning of democracy [27], [16], [10], there are many different understandings about what e-democracy could be. Definitions also vary, and include: electronic democracy [9], [17], [23], cyberdemocracy [25], [21], digital democracy [12] and virtual democracy [27], among others. Sometimes different terms are used simultaneously as synonyms.

For advocates of participatory democracy, e-democracy would be an attempt to practice democracy without limits of time, place or other physical conditions, using ICTs or other kinds of computer-mediated communication [27]. Nevertheless, to achieve democracy as "a system for making decisions about public affairs in which citizens are directly involved" ([16], p. 4) would necessitate transformations of representation and the role of actors and civil society organization [6]. However, since political dialogue aimed at solving collective problems will require a plurality of perspectives together with styles of speech and ways to express the particularity of social situations, the implementation of a technology platform for a constant decision-making process with citizens is still virtually impossible. Thus, the Internet has not changed representative structures to revolutionize political processes [9], [12].

Given the limits for implementing such a deliberative democracy model, the more inclusive concept of communicative democracy could be considered as an alternative [28]. In other words, "virtual public sphere as a civil conversation seems to be more feasible [...] than implementation of decision mechanisms about policies through the exercise of institutional power" ([22], p. 181) considered by the direct democracy.

Regardless of the different concepts of democracy, all of them include public participation and social control over government actions [5]. According to Fung [13], public participation must work in synergy with representation processes. This author presents a model known as democracy cube, and considers that mechanisms of participation vary along three dimensions: a) those who participate, b) how participants communicate with each other and make decisions, and c) how these decisions relate to political action and public policy.

Combined with the networked civil society as defined by Benkler, the democracy cube of Fung provides us with a useful framework to capture the perspective of civil society influencing government actions through the active use of a virtual platform. Benkler's model of networked civil society is divided into two levels, platform organization and public participation. In this study, we subdivide each of these levels: we deal with two dimensions for the platform organization – modularity and granularity – as defined by Benkler, and three dimensions of public participation – the democracy cube – as defined by Fung.

3   Research Methods

Our main goal is to understand how civil society could influence local governments through virtual platforms in Brazil.

The case studies presented in this paper are both intrinsic and instrumental [26]. They are intrinsic because the cases themselves are of interest, in all their particularity and ordinariness. They also are instrumental because we seek to advance the understanding of those particular cases to produce relevant and actionable knowledge that could be transferable to other similar contexts.

We defined two stages of research:

1. Investigation of the main characteristics of a Brazilian virtual platform created to provide a mechanism for the civil society to influence public policies, in line with the networked public sphere proposed by Benkler;

2. Investigation of two cases of that use of the virtual platform by civil society discussed in the previous stage, adapting the democracy cube proposed by Fung to analyze political participation.

Thus, to answer the question of the paper, we use Benkler's concept of virtual platform for a networked public sphere combined with the democracy cube proposed by Fung.

3.1   Understanding the Virtual Platform

According to Benkler [3], collaborative production on the web is one of the most significant attributes allowed by new technologies. This collaborative or peer-production process has been enabled through Internet-based coordination, where decisions arise from the free engagement and cooperation of the people who coalesce to create common value [19].

For Benkler, the success of the peer-production processes has been the adoption of architectures that have allowed people to pool such diverse efforts effectively. The core characteristics underlying the success of these enterprises are their modularity and their capacity to integrate many fine-grained contributions.

The platform to be investigated is Cidade Democrática, which has been chosen because of its representativeness for civil society to discuss causes, solutions and problems in different Brazilian cities. Cidade Democrática is constantly open to receive contributions from society, and has the explicit intention to influence government actions based on the requests and demands raised on its platform. It is also open to any citizen. Therefore, this initiative is related to the networked public sphere by allowing a space for the dissemination, debate, and expression of public opinion.

3.2   Applying the Democracy Cube

The three dimensions of participation from the democracy cube were investigated in two selected case studies, both using the same platform, Cidade Democrática, as the virtual infrastructure for citizens and organizations from the civil society to influence local government actions. The two cases are projects in cities located in São Paulo state: Jundiaí and Várzea Paulista. Both initiatives are being used by their respective local governments to define their public policies.

To develop the in-depth case of the two cities using the Cidade Democrática platform, data collection was performed through:

a) Structured observation of project websites of the two cities inside the platform;
b) Document analysis of civil society organizations available on the web, blogs posted by citizens in the platforms, media news and city administration documents related to the two projects;
c) Semi-structured interviews in person or through questionnaires via e-mail with two founders and managers of the Cidade Democrática platform, three citizens users of the platform, three members of civil society and eight city officials of the two cities investigated. All interviews were done between December 2011 and January 2012.

4   Cidade Democrática Platform

Cidade Democrática was launched to the public in October 2009 and works as a social network platform designed for the discussion of city problems. Any citizen can post problems or solutions that matter to a specific region and can also comment on, support or discuss ideas posted by other citizens. Thus, this platform is a space on the Internet where Brazilians can publish and discuss problems and solutions for municipalities. Registered users can create different types of profiles that range from citizens to entities such as nongovernmental organizations and public officials. In February 2012, there were 11,135 registered users, approximately 97% of whom are citizens.

The Digital Cities Program was created by Cidade Democrática in 2011 as an experiment aiming to create public agendas through collaboration between local governments and society. The two cases studied in this paper are part of Digital Cities program. The first case is a pilot project called "Cidadonos" ("City owners") and was held in the city of Jundiaí. The second was a competition called "Digital Várzea 2022" held by the city of Várzea Paulista.

4.1   Cidadonos Project in Jundiaí

The Cidadonos project emerged in 2011 from a competition created by the informal group named "Movimento Voto Consciente Jundiaí" (Conscientious Vote Jundiaí). It was created to encourage citizens to publish proposals and raise issues for the construction of a civic agenda in order to foster involvement in public policy issues and other matters of public interest.

The project was a competition which took place through a customized portal of the Cidade Democrática platform developed to reward the 12 best ideas and proposals that would make true the dreams of the population of the city of Jundiaí. Citizens, NGOs, schools, businesses and government stakeholders could participate by presenting their own ideas and voting on others' proposals, supporting the implementation of a better Jundiaí. The competition was open from April 15 to August 8, 2011.

Although the word "reward" was contained in the description of the competition, the winners did not win any cash or other kind of prize, but would have their proposals included in the agenda of the Movimento Voto Consciente Jundiaí and receive a certificate of participation. About 3,500 citizens took part in the contest and 12 proposals were chosen based on the list of supporters, and the number of comments and followers.

After the competition, in December 2011, the Movimento Voto Consciente Jundiaí started a new stage of engagement which was directed to announce the awarded proposals to local government, NGOs and local businesses in order to discuss ways to implement the successful ideas. Among the actions in this stage are: forwarding proposals to government officials, such as secretaries, mayors and state and federal deputies of the region and to civil society organizations and businesses, then inviting them to talk about how they could put these ideas into effect.

4.2   Várzea Digital 2022 Competition

The Várzea Digital 2022 competition was held by the City Hall of Várzea Paulista and was one of the actions of the Plan 2022 launched in early 2011 by the city government. Organized by the Secretary of Social Development of the city, the competition is considered to be an instrument of participatory planning of the city government. The goal of the competition was to stimulate the digital participation of citizens, especially the young people, in public policy issues. It was a strategy of participation that complemented the traditional practices of government.

The competition lasted two months, from September 19 to November 20, 2011 and citizens, NGOs, local business, city officers, and politicians from Varzea Paulista could participate by presenting proposals and making comments. By registering on the Cidade Democrática platform, the eight proposals and issues with the most votes were selected to be presented at the City Conference, and were included in the Developing Plan of the city to be implemented by 2022. Close to 600 citizens enrolled in the competition.

5   Analysis of the Cases

The analysis of the cases was divided in two parts:

• The structured observation of the Portal Cidade Democrática to analyze its type of relationship model in the networked public sphere;
• Two in-depth case studies (the municipalities of Jundiaí and Várzea Paulista in the State of São Paulo). The case studies helped to understand the institutional design of participation through the Internet using an adapted model of the democracy cube.

5.1   Type of Relationship Model in the Networked Public Sphere

Cidade Democrática is a platform for content creation by either the owners of the initiative or any other participant in the project, who are free to post comments, vote or follow any posted issue or proposal. This type of platform allows and encourages discussion and collaborative production between users. Its initiatives include the collaborative construction of bills and public policies, mashups or crowdsourcing, for example. The content of this kind of initiative depends on public participation. Examples of technological tools available are:

• Wiki: it allows the construction of collaborative texts. Its main feature is that anyone can easily add, delete or change any part of a published text [1];
• Social Networking: it allows people connected to these networks to interact with friends and contacts through sharing and discussing interests, ideas, events, activities and media [2].

At Cidade Democrática, the contributors point out problems or solutions to problems in their cities and / or regions. Citizens can also comment on, support and follow the contributions made by other users. It features profiles on social networks and allows sharing of content across these.

Considering the characteristics of the virtual platform as described by Benkler that are necessary to create an environment for the networked civil sphere, Cidade Democrática presents both the granularity and modularity capabilities. The granularity is expressed by the possibility of collecting contributions from the public as small as it is possible, allowing them to post new proposals, comment on those already available, or even just supporting (similar to the "like" tool in Facebook) or voting for proposals already posted by other participating citizens. The modularity feature is also very important and has allowed different projects in different cities to re-use the same capabilities developed for previous initiatives. This improves the platform power as it helps to create distributed knowledge about the platform usage that is very important to disseminate, and to consolidate the platform as a robust and easy-to-use environment. The very situation we are investigating here with two different initiatives in two different cities using the same platform, each for its own purposes, is a clear demonstration of the modularity capability of Cidade Democrática.

5.2 Classification of Jundiaí and Várzea Paulista Initiatives in the Democracy Cube

To better understand the democracy cube for the two investigated initiatives, we are going to analyze them answering the main questions proposed by Fung to frame the public participation process.

Who Participates? Initially, competitions were open to all residents in Jundiaí and Várzea Paulista, i.e., everyone could participate in offering proposals or issues, posting comments, or registering their support by following a proposal or issue.

However, as stated by Fung [13], to be open to the whole of society does not mean that everyone will participate and that all groups called to participate will be represented. Therefore these initiatives would be classified in the self-selection category, defined as one in which the selection process is open to the whole population, although only the people concerned with the debate will effectively participate.

In addition to online participation, mobilization workshops were provided to publicize the capabilities of Cidade Democrática's web tools in order to mobilize citizens and help them to post, comment on or support proposals or issues. Some actions taken to publicize Cidade Democrática's capabilities were lectures and workshops in private and public schools as well as in some civil society organizations and companies. The general public was also encouraged to participate through partnerships with radio stations, newspapers and local television. These actions were fruitful especially among young people, who were usually more familiar with new technologies although, in general, less close to the more traditional ways of participation.

Thus, among the categories presented by Fung, the selection of participants in the case studies could be considered as selective recruitment, i.e., despite participation being open to everyone, tools have been created to reach certain groups and stimulate them to participate.

How Do Participants Communicate and Make Decisions Together? In both cases, participants had to mobilize other users as much as possible, making them comment on or support their proposals, so the winning proposals would depend on the level of mobilization provoked by the group that presented them. Interviews with the winners showed that they employed the most diverse modes of communication with others about their proposals, varying from online to face-to-face.

To gather support, users could also expose their proposals through social networks, blogs, videos, and photos. Although there was intense use of a variety of strategies, the Cidade Democrática platform was a space of constant interaction and exchange of views. It consolidated discussion about the projects in the competition. Among the categories presented by Fung [13], we identify the mode of communication of the projects studied as those related to the development of citizen preferences.

On the one hand, as a collaboration and interaction platform, Cidade Democrática ensured that citizen users of the platform may disagree, exchange information, and propose new ways to implement their proposals, among others. On the other hand, that does not mean necessarily that potential participants use the discussion capability of the platform during the competitions. For instance, support which depended only on a single click by the citizen received more than twice as many comments. In those cases, there was no discussion. The citizen's preference was captured only by a single-click interaction with that specific proposal.

How Discussions Are Linked with Policy or Public Action? First of all, we need to point out the differences between the initiatives taking place in Jundiaí and in Várzea Paulista. While in Jundiaí the initiative was conducted by a civil society organization that had been operating since 2006 in the municipality, in Varzea Paulista the initiative was led by the city government. This difference is crucial in understanding the political actions subsequent to the digital debate in the virtual environment.

In Jundiaí, the category defined as communicative influence prevailed. In this type of participatory mechanism, influencing the state is related to the ability to change or mobilize public opinion. The Voto Consciente Movement had this role to exert pressure on the city government to implement policies in accordance with the proposed agenda that emerged from the citizen participation in the digital environment. In addition, the authors of the winning proposals stated that they plan to continue mobilizing public opinion to make the city government pay attention to their demands.

In the case of Várzea Paulista, since the initiative was conducted by the city government, winning proposals presented by the citizens became part of the municipal plan goals for the medium and long term. City Hall created a commission composed of representatives of civil society and government to monitor the implementation of the proposals, either in person or through the city web site. In this sense, this particular experience approaches the category of co-governance in which there is a partnership between citizens and government to develop strategies for public action.

6   Conclusions

As a theoretical contribution, this article intends to test the concept of networked public sphere in relation to the use of new technologies that allow citizens to participate actively in the public sphere and thereby generate some kind of impact on society. Proposed by Benkler [3], the concept of networked public sphere modifies the original definition of public sphere developed by Habermas, and seeks new understandings about it from the possibilities presented by new Internet-related interactive technologies such as blogs, websites, and Twitter.

As a contribution to the practice of management, the article analyzes, through the study of two particular cases in Brazil, how citizens are engaging in the use of virtual platforms, how effective those platforms are in achieving their purposes, what are the main characteristics of those platforms, what are the main difficulties faced by citizens and managers to operate and use such platforms, and how government officials incorporate contributions coming from those platforms. Understanding the operations of those platforms, their main challenges and the effectiveness of each of the tools used, would be helpful to improve the platforms themselves and will provide additional knowledge to those interested in creating similar platforms in Brazil and possibly in other countries and contexts.

We conclude that, albeit in an early stage, the use of virtual platforms to share opinions on topics that citizens want government to recognize helps with mobilization and influences local public officials on policy implementations. Our investigation shows that citizens of the two Brazilian cities studied use the virtual platform to engage in lively discussion and exchange information as a way to propose and implement new public policies that are eventually adopted by their city governments.

References

1. Baltzersen, R.K.: Radical transparency: open access as a key in wiki pedagogy. Australasian Journal of Educational Technology 26(6), 791–809 (2010)
2. Bekri, D., Dunn, B., Oguzertem, I., Su, Y., Upret, S.: Harnessing Social Media Tools to Fight Corruption. Final project for degree at LSE Department of International Development, London (2011)
3. Benkler, Y.: The Wealth of Networks: How Social Production Transforms Markets and Freedom. Yale University Press, New Haven (2006)
4. Bertot, J.C., Jaeger, P.T., Grimes, J.M.: Using ICTs to create a culture of transparency: E-government and social media as openness and anti-corruption tools for societies. Government Information Quarterly 27(3), 264–271 (2010)
5. Bobbio, N.: O futuro da democracia; uma defesa das regras do jogo. Paz e Terra, Rio de Janeiro (1986)
6. Brelàz, G.: de: Advocacy das organizações da sociedade civil: um estudo comparativo entre Brasil e Estados Unidos. Masters dissertation, FGV (2007)
7. Brito, J.: Hack, Mash and Peer: crowdsourcing government transparency. Science and Technology Law Review 9, 119–157 (2008)
8. Castells, M.: A Sociedade em Rede. Paz e Terra, São Paulo (2008)

9. Chadwick, A.: Bringing E-Democracy Back In. Social Science Computer Review 21(4), 443–455 (2003)
10. Dahlberg, L., Siapera, E.: Radical democracy and the Internet: Interrogating Theory and Practice. Palgrave Macmillan, London (2007)
11. Foth, M., Forlano, L., Satchell, C., Gibbs, M. (eds.): From social butterfly to engaged citizen: urban informatics, social media, ubiquitous computing, and mobile technology to support citizen engagement. MIT Press, Cambridge (2011)
12. Fuchs, C.: Internet and Society: social theory in the information age. Routledge, New York (2008)
13. Fung, A.: Varieties of participation in a complex governance. Public Administration Review (Special Issue), 66-75 (December 2006)
14. Habermas, J.: Mudança estrutural da esfera pública. Tempo Brasileiro, Rio de Janeiro (2003)
15. Harb, Z.: Arab revolutions and the social media effect. M/C Journal, 14(2) (2011), http://journal.media-culture.org.au/index.php/mcjournal/article/viewArticle/364
16. Held, D.: Models of Democracy. Polity Press, Cambridge (2006)
17. Keskinen, A.M.: Models for Interactive Decision Making. Electronic Journal of e-Government 2(1), 55–64 (2004)
18. Kim, B.J., Adam, F.: Social Media, Social Design and Social Construction: Dialectic Approach for the Use of Social Media in the Public Sector. The International Journal of Technology, Knowledge and Society 7(3), 65–78 (2011)
19. Kostakis, V.: The Advent of Open Source Democracy and Wikipolitics. Human Technology 7(1), 9–29 (2011)
20. Kyriakopoulou, K.: Authoritarian states and internet social media: instruments of democratization or instruments of control? Human Affairs 21, 18–26 (2011)
21. Lévy, P.: Pela ciberdemocracia. In: Moraes, D. (org.) Por uma outra comunicação, pp. 367–384. Record, Rio de Janeiro (2003)
22. Marques, F.P.J.A.: Dimensões da ciberdemocracia: conceitos e experiências fundamentais. Master Dissertation, UFBA, Bahia (2004)
23. Peixoto, T., Wegenast, T.A.: Democracia eletrônica no Brasil e no mundo. Revista do Legislativo (2010)
24. Petrik, K.: Deliberation and Collaboration in the Policy Process: A Web 2.0 approach. Journal of E-democracy 2(1) (2010)
25. Poster, M.: Cyber Democracy: Internet and the Public Sphere. In: Porter, D. (ed.) Internet Culture. Routledge, New York (1995)
26. Stake, R.E.: Qualitative Case studies. In: Denzin, N.K., Lincoln, Y.S. (eds.) Handbook of Qualitative Research, pp. 435–466. Sage Publications, Thousand Oaks (2005)
27. Van Dijk, J.A.G.M.: Digital democracy: issues of theory and practice. Sage Publications (2000)
28. Young, I.: Comunicação e o outro, além da democracia deliberativa. In: Souza, J. (org.) Democracia Hoje. Editora da UnB, Brasília (2001)

Cyberactivism and Collective Agency: Cases from China

Yingqin Zheng[1] and Cheng Zhang[2]

[1] School of Management, Royal Holloway, University of London, United Kingdom
yingqin.zheng@rhul.ac.uk
[2] School of Management, Fudan University, China
zhangche@fudan.edu.cn

Abstract. It has been observed that global cyberactivism has challenged the limits of conventional social movement thinking which focuses on shared identity and strategic intention. The objective of this paper is to propose a conceptualisation of 'collective agency,' underlined by an ontology of 'becoming,' which seeks to expand the conceptual space that accounts for the heterogeneity and complexity of online practices in China that are increasingly mediated by the Internet. The conceptualisation of collection agency serves as a theoretical basis for the analysis of China's cyberactivism, which has become increasingly significant in its impact on public life over the last two decades.

Keywords: cyberactivism, collective action, collective agency, social movements, rhizome.

1 Introduction: Cyberactivism in China

The so-called "new media power" [1] has never been more manifested than the current global social movements mediated by a growing array of Internet affiliated technologies, including mobile and smart phones, cameras and video cameras, Personal Digital Assistants and Global Positioning System. Compared to democratic countries, China embraces the Internet in a distinct manner in that it is largely disconnected from the global movements yet full of vigor on its own playing ground. The Chinese cyberspace has been found to give rise to alternative communication practices, supporting an emerging public space and facilitating collective action [2], [3].

Cyberactivism started soon after the Internet was brought to China in the late 1990s and has gone through three different technological platforms as central players: Bulletin Board Systems (BBS) entering China in 1998, blogs in 2002, and *weibo* (Chinese microblog platform, similar to Twitter) in 2010. The latter two are connected to, but have not replaced, previous platforms. In 2010, there are over 148 million BBS users, 294.5 million blog users, and over 63 million microblog users [4] – with overlaps among the three groups. It is reported that 54.5% of Chinese bloggers prefer to express their views about social affairs in their blogs [5]. While blogs have played a leading role in cyberactivism since their birth, they have been overtaken by *weibo* as the leader in promoting public participation. For example, in 2011 representatives attending the People's Congress publicized their policy proposals on *weibo*,

M.D. Hercheui et al. (Eds.): HCC10 2012, IFIP AICT 386, pp. 310–319, 2012.
© IFIP International Federation for Information Processing 2012

which were open for public comments and discussions -- a preliminary type of political participation that never existed before.

Cyberactivism in China is embedded in a social institutional context with the following characteristics: there is a persistent hegemony of state media, which no longer inspires trust from the people; an emerging middle class is increasingly discontent with the lack of public space and political participation; and, more importantly, the perceived deficiency of social justice under the current regime combined with a sense of powerlessness. Cyberactivism, thus, arises as a partial pursuit for freedom of speech and democratic debates. Despite the panopticon of state and commercial censorship, the Chinese cyberspace has over recent years expanded the boundaries of public expression, public debates, as well as explicit criticism on government.

2   Conceptualization of Collective Agency

Rodríguez-Giralt [6] argues that collective action should be considered results, effects, generative consequences of heterogeneous networks of action and interaction, and collective action that is performed: "rather than seeing the 'social movement' as a 'centre of calculation' that successfully coordinates and manages a series of networked organizations, resources and materials, we actually have a series of operators (both human and nonhuman) that create a network and relate to each other, and that, through their interaction, perform a movement" (p. 19). The paper extends from this conception and seeks to move beyond seeing cyberactivism as series of technology-mediated collective actions. Instead, it is considered a form of empowerment, a construction of "collective agency" of which collective actions are instantiations. Collective agency is emergent, dynamic and irreducible to the success and failure of specific actions. It is rather a disposition, property, or propensity of the sociomaterial configuration of the information society in contemporary China.

To develop a conceptualization of "collective agency," we need to draw upon the posthumanist school of thought. The traditional concept of agency attaches exclusively to human, starting from Kant's vision of moral autonomy to Giddens' image of voluntary and knowledgeable actors [7]. On this basis collective agency is normally viewed as human agency expressed through collectivities, or a collectivity that exerts human-like agency, with intentionality, directionality, and causality, such as a government. The posthumanist school of thought rejects such an asymmetrical account of agency and argues that even "human agency" is bound with and exercised through materiality. This not only includes material that humans live and act with, such as clothing, building, tools, but also components inside the human body that are not susceptible to human intentionality. The posthumanist stream of research presents a broad philosophical movement in social science that seeks to challenge the modern dualistic perception of reality.

French philosopher Gilles Deleuze and Felix Guattari, put forward an *ontology of becoming* [8-11]. Similarly, Andrew Pickering has been discussing the double dance of human and nonhuman agency, the "politics of becoming", and the need to recognize phenomena of temporal emergence [12], [13]. A key concept from Deleuze is *assemblage*. What is an assemblage? As Bennett [14] explicates:

"An assemblage is, first, an ad hoc grouping, a collectivity whose origins are historical and circumstantial, though its contingent status says nothing about its efficacy, which can be quite strong. An assemblage is, second, a living, throbbing grouping whose coherence coexists with energies and countercultures that exceed and confound it. An assemblage is, third, a web with an uneven topography: some of the points at which the trajectories of actants cross each other are more heavily trafficked than others, and thus power is not equally distributed across the assemblage. An assemblage is, fourth, not governed by a central power: no one member has sufficient competence to fully determine the consequences of the activities of the assemblage. An assemblage, finally, is made up of many types of actants: humans and nonhumans; animals, vegetables, and minerals; nature, culture, and technology" (p.445).

Another metaphor developed by Deleuze and Guattari [8] is *rhizome*. In botany, rhizome refers to horizontal, underground plant stem capable of producing the shoot and root systems of a new plant, ranging from potato, ginger to weed. As a metaphor, Deleuze and Guattari contrast it to the image of a tree, and characterize it with the following principles:

- Connection and heterogeneity: "any point of a rhizome can be connected to anything other, and must be. [...] A rhizome ceaselessly establishes connections between semiotic chains, organizations of power, and circumstances relative to the arts, sciences, and social struggles"[8].
- Multiplicity: "reflects the multidimensionality of a rhizome and its process character. This principle acknowledges the variety of horizontal, vertical and lateral relations within a network, as well as its alterability over time [15].
- A signifying rupture: "a rhizome may be broken, shattered at a given spot, but it will start up again on one of its old lines, or on new lines. [...] Every rhizome contains lines of segmentation according to which it is stratified, territorialized, organized, signified, attributed, etc., as well as lines of deterritorialization down which it constantly flees" [8].
- Cartography and decalcomania: 'The rhizome is altogether different, a map and not a tracing. [. . .] The map is open and connectable in all of its dimensions; it is detachable, reversible, and susceptible to constant modification. It can be torn, reversed, adapted to any kind of mounting, reworked by any individual group, or social formation" [8].

Collective agency is thus conceptualized as the *agency of assemblages* [14], not possessed by any member of the collective, although it certainly does not deny the agentic performativity of each member as an actant. Instead, it is distributed and emerges temporally from the interactions among actants, constantly influx. The inclusion and exclusion of actants in the assemblage are often *ad hoc* and unpredictable, as the image of rhizome implies, so a clear boundary is difficult to define. Collective agency is rhizomatic in the sense that it "operates by variation, expansion, conquest, capture, offshoots" [8]. It thrives in multiplicity by forming connections in all dimensions without the coordination from a central power.   Collective agency could grow rapidly by coalescing into a great number of participants over expansive spatiality. It could also be broken, subdued, "shattered" at one point, yet emerge again at another time and place, extending the previous connections or starting new ones.

Bennett [14] links the notion of agency of assemblages to the Chinese character *shi*, which implicates the level of energy in a force field and serves to "illuminate something that is usually difficult to capture in discourse: namely, the kind of potential that originates not in human initiative but instead results from the very disposition of things [16]." The character of *shi*, 𝌆 𝌆 , is constructed by two characters piled together – hold and force. However, rather than referring to the possession of power by individuals, it depicts the position or shape of a "spatiotemporal configuration" and the potential force to which that the configuration gives rise. Power and status result from being attached to a strong or well positioned *shi*. So state of affairs is *xing* (shape)-*shi*, advantage is *you* (better)-*shi*, aggression is *qiang* (strong)-*shi*.

Shi is dynamic and always flows. It is possible to build up *shi*, for example via publicity campaign, to ride *shi* to a more advantageous position, and to lose *shi*, usually due to broken connections to powerful networks. Extensively used in ancient military strategy, *shi* is typically assessed by taking into account material elements like geographical conditions (e.g., mountain and river), weather (e.g., such as wind direction, armaments, food supply, as well as social elements like soldiers' morale), and capability (e.g., are they used to fighting on boats?). A Chinese idiom says "times and *shi* create heroes," in contrast to the individualistic and self-made image of heroes in Western mass culture. The Chinese culture, thus, sees heroes, or individuals, as the effect or outcome of a particular configuration of time, space and the energy that flows through. In this sense, it endorses a decentered ontology of becoming.

3   The Collective Agency of Cyberactivism in China

There has been a wide range of cyberactivism since the late 1990s mediated by BBSs, blogs, and *weibo*. They are mostly self-organized, unplanned and rhizomatic, namely, decentered. In this section, we will examine different types of online activism on the Chinese Internet in terms of the effect they produce, especially in relation to public events which trigger online contention. The Internet projects "the gaze" from netizens to authority, a leveling effect of rhizomatic assemblage, and at times leads to direct impact on government behavior (i.e., instantiations of *shi*). Cyberactivism is found to be "fluid, episodic, and emergent", engaging in "informational politics" which asserts widespread influence and public pressure on the authority, and in some cases, result in changes in governmental behavior or even institutional and regulatory changes [17].

With rapid economic progress and a rising middleclass, the Chinese people are increasingly frustrated with the lack of access to public information, or truthful information, given the low credibility of state-owned media sources and the Great China Firewall. New media technologies have become the most important source of information in the Chinese society mostly gathered and communicated by netizens themselves, namely online citizen journalists [17]. For example, a famous blogger Qu Minglei runs a blog called "One Man's Newspaper", which includes real time photos and reports sent by villagers defending their land from being enlisted by local government, as well as in-depth investigation on the silence of earthquake warning in the

2008 Sichuan earthquake with 85,000 dead or missing [18]. His blog is pushing the limits of critical journalism in China where traditional media are still handicapped.

The challenge to traditional media is even more obvious with *weibo*, where users can follow a large number of microbloggers, ranging from celebrities and media to public intellectuals and opinion leaders. *Weibo* provides faster, wider, more diverse, more direct, and less censored information. News agents often release firsthand news briefs on *weibo* before broadcasting them through their formal channels. The press actively follows and responds to emerging public issues and sentiments on *weibo*. Some *weibo* accounts owned by international or Diaspora users serve as bridges across the two sides of the Great Fire Wall. One prominent example is Lao Rong, a Muslim businessman devoted to broadcasting news from foreign media, covering the Libyan civil war by transmitting information from the Al-Jazeera and Western news programs. Publicly opposing to state-led public opinion that initially perceived Gaddafi as an anti-American hero, Rong supported the revolution, attracting hundreds of thousands of followers on *weibo*.

The most critical agentic performativity emerging from cyberactivism is sustaining the virtual "Gaze", referring to focused public attention on specific public events. One of the earliest and most cited examples is the famous case of Sun Zhigang in 2003 [17], whose death in a custody and repatriation centre led to public outrage on BBSs and blogs, and consequently the repeal of a state regulation aimed to control mobility of population. In the years that followed this even, slow and painstaking changes were seen, which indicated that some of those in government are reluctantly learning to respond to an unprecedented level of bottom-up attention and criticism, as opposed to being solely accountable to superior authority as in the pre-Internet era.

The gaze on the cyberspace has a Chinese term *weiguan,* the surrounding gaze [19] which literally means "crowds of people gathering around some kind of public spectacle." On the cyberspace, *weiguan* constitutes a collective gaze from numerous people on public events, mediated by posts, blogs, and *weibo* on the topic. Some believe that the power of the *weiguan* can "transform" China. One of the recent examples is the Yihuang public incident [20]. A couple of Zhong sisters escaped abduction from local government rescued by real time *weibo* broadcast by a journalist Deng Fei who was connected to them by mobile phone. The two young women were cornered in an airport toilet by local government agents blocking them from flying to Beijing to report the dismantling of their house by local authority, which led to the self-immolation of three members of the family in protest. Within hours of the incident, the tweets on *weibo* were followed and re-tweeted by tens of thousands of netizens and brought local journalists to the live scene. With the event publicized, the Zhong sisters and their family members were released after brief detainment, and a number of local government officials were disciplined afterwards.

In 2009, the Propaganda Department of Yuannan Provincial Committee invited ten netizens to participate in the investigation of the death of a man Li who died in prison[1]. The cause of death given by the local police was that Li accidentally hit his head on the wall while playing "duomaomao" (hide and seek) with his eyes covered. The

---

[1] http://news.sina.com.cn/z/ynduomaomao/

incredulous excuse sparked discussion among netizens. While those who participated in the investigation complained that they were unable to reach the core of the issue, the police eventually admitted that Li died of violent abuse from fellow inmates. Some argue that the participation of citizens in a criminal investigation was not necessarily beneficial to the rule of law, yet it clearly indicates the intensification of the public gaze on the authority.

"Duomaomao" subsequently became a popular Internet catchphrase as a mockery on the corruption and absurdity of authority. Other similar phrases include "push up" (referring to a suspected case of rape murder that led to a local riot) and "to buy soy sauce" (referring to apathy to public events). The cyberspace in China, albeit censored, seems to produce a type of public discourse characterized by subdued satire, dark humor underlined by suppressed discontent. This online discourse is an extension of the "nonofficial discourse universe" carried on short messaging services (SMS) [21]. Similar to SMS practices that are disorderly, disposable, and ephemeral [22], public discourses constitute an alternative form of media to the top-down, durable and purposeful traditional Chinese media. In face of the abuse of power, social inequality and institutionalized injustice, many people express their discontent through satire and subtle critique. The remarks are often not directly subversive to the political regime, but constitute a moderate form of cultural and ideological challenge to existing social conditions, contributing to increasingly pluralistic political undercurrents that defy the discursive hegemony of the Communist Party [21].

The creativity and versatility of the Chinese language is fantastically demonstrated in new media discourses. A rich and innovative vocabulary has evolved from new media and spread on the Chinese Internet. New characters, words, phrases, and expressions have been created (or modified from the original to bypass censorship) that can be easily grasped by anybody immersed in the new media habitats. For example, the verb "harmonize" has been used to mean state censorship or crackdown, a sarcastic reference to the state slogan of "a harmonious society". A person could be "harmonized," meaning excluded or disappeared; a "harmonized" public scandal means it was covered up or censored. Later the phrase evolves to "river crab," a synonym of "harmony" (he-xie), to avoid censorship.

Weibo discourses often reveal people's emotions which reflect social sentiments in that period. For example, the majority of netizens showed sympathy towards a young man who killed six police officers at a police station as revenge for the abuse and humiliation he received from the police when he was accused of bicycle theft. While he readily pleaded guilty to manslaughter, many viewed him as a victim. This sentiment of netizens clearly pointed to the tension between citizens and the police representing the authority with unrestrained power and minimal accountability. In contrast, many netizens were elated at the death penalty of another young man Yao Jiaxin who stabbed a middle age woman eight times to death when she tried to write down his car plate number after being run over. A well-behaved university student with elitist parents, Yao repeatedly apologized and shed tears on TV yet failed to receive public sympathy, especially from those who perceived him symbolic of the dehumanizing effect of social inequality. Rational or not, public emotions related to social justice could be expressed and debated via new media and traditional media.

Various voices can be heard and different perspectives are allowed to interact publicly. Even though radical comments are likely to be "harmonized", the virtual civil space is closer to the Habermasian "public sphere" than what was ever conceivable before the Internet era.

4   The Case of South China Tiger

Described above are aspects of collective agency performed and enacted by cyberactivism, what Yang [2], [17] calls "information politics," which are bottom-up and highly inclusive. It should be noted that the assemblages of cyberactivism are deeply intertwined with the lifeworlds of actors; hence, there is the possibility of practical social changes. Cyberactivism rhizomatically extends to, and becomes intertwined with offline activities, through mobilization of individual or collective action. The following case of the South China Tiger serves as one such example[2].

The South China Tiger is believed to have been extinct for half a century. In 2007, a villager Zhou Zhenglong in Shaan'xi province reported that he spotted one in the local woods with a number of photos he claimed to have taken within a short distance from the tiger. Zhou was given financial rewards and praised as a "hero," and the provincial Forest Bureau set up a natural reservation park in the area. One week after the news appeared in press, a researcher from the Chinese Academy of Science commented in his blog that the photo could be a forgery, while others disputed such accusation and the provincial Forestry Administration dismissed any unofficial challenge. With growing public attention, the State Forestry Bureau (SFB) subsequently decided to start an investigation to verify the claim but did not reach any conclusion.

In November, a legal scholar Hao Jingsong appealed to the SFB to investigate the case further. His request was denied. A few days later, on a photography BBS, it was pointed out that the tiger in the photos resembled a painting on a Chinese calendar. A lawyer filed a formal complaint to a local police station, which turned the case into criminal investigation. In December, Netese (www.163.com), organized a collaborative analysis of the case among a group of experts including a biologist, forensic experts, a criminal detective, a digital image analyst and a telecommunication professor, who concluded that the photos were fabricated. Later, legal scholar Hao Jingsong filed a lawsuit at the Beijing Intermediate People's Court against the SFB's decision to deny his request. Again losing the case, he appealed at the Beijing High People's Court. Meanwhile, more academic publications disputed the authenticity of the photos. In May 2008, Dr. Li Changyu, a famous American Chinese detective, discredited the tiger photos. Drawing upon the Act of Government Information Openness that took effect on 1st May 2008, Hao requested the State Forestry Bureau and Shaan'xi Forestry Administration to release information on the case. Under relentless public pressure, at the end of June 2008, the Shaan'xi government admitted that the South China Tiger was a "paper tiger". Zhou was arrested, the award withdrawn, and a number of government officials penalized.

---

[2] http://news.sina.com.cn/z/hnhzhpyy/

5   Analysis

This case shows that heterogeneous actors and actants form connections that constitute a socio-material assemblage. While the assemblage was decentralized, networked and fluid, strategic actors play critical roles in translating and mobilizing the network. For example, the legal scholar Hao perseveres in enacting legal procedures to hold the authority accountable. However, his agency would be unproductive without the support of *weiguan* and participation from netizens, which builds up the *shi* of the assemblage and changes the power dynamic between the state and citizens. Artifacts also serve as important actants in the assemblage, which demonstrate significant performativity in the mobilization processes. While the new media tools, the Internet, computers and smart phones, and the *weibo* platform provide infrastructural support to cyberactivism, the tiger photos serve as "boundary objects" [23] of the networks which link participants, while legal procedures have agency strong enough to change the momentum of the mobilization of the assemblage.

In our case, it is easy to observe the rhizomatic and temporal emergent character of the movement. Unexpected connections are forged contingently, for example, a blog post, a publication, an individual, or an organization, could join the assemblage without centralized, and pre-conceived design. Linkages could be broken, dissipated, modified, resumed or reinforced. With cyberactivism, participation is usually voluntary and ties tend to be loose among actors, so it is normal for people or things to come in and out of the network at any point. The outcome of the movements is contingent upon the rhizomatic movement, and "things can always be otherwise".

While the case reported here has produced visible institutional result (whether the result has any sustaining effect is another point), there are numerous cases where the assemblage is not sufficiently mobilized to mount to any significant public event, or are simply suppressed by the regime, as in the China Red Cross scandal in 2011[3]. From the perspective of collective action, they may be considered failures. If, however, we take the perspective of collective agency with a rhizomatic ontology, the failures should not be dismissed as insignificant, because they are deeply connected to collective agency emerging from cyberactivism.

If cyberactivism can be said to be contributing to an emerging civil society, it is through the reconfiguration of relative *shi* of social actors, thereby partially and gradually transforming power relations under the current institutional and political settings. *Shi* is defined by the temporal, spatial and resourceful position of an actant. The collective agency of the assemblage of citizens, technologies, and relevant social and civil groups can be perceived as the *shi* of this collective as opposed to the authoritative actors. A formerly powerless individual becomes empowered when connected to the sociomaterial assemblages in cyberspace and in real life, as shown in the examples presented in this paper. While *shi* is fluid and constantly changing, it depicts dynamics of the field of civil society with potentially institutional consequences.

---

[3] http://news.hexun.com/2011/gmm/

6   Conclusion

The traditional concept of collective action is not sufficient to account for new forms of social movements in the cyberspace. This paper suggests that collective actions are instantiations of collective agency, which does not necessarily feature pre-defined identities, groups or organizational strategies. The conceptualization of collective agency is based on a decentered ontology of becoming, constantly in flux and flows and its instantiations are often episodic, improvised, and ephemeral. The performance of collective agency of Chinese netizens is deeply entangled in the tension and power dynamics between authority and citizens. While far from deliberating democratic processes, collective agency has opened up a public sphere as an important pre-cursor to a civil society. This expanding capability of public participation and civic engagement constitutes a type of collective agency that is not reducible to individual agency, although individual agency is very important and can be well exercised if enacted.

It is not the intention of this paper to paint a rosy picture of cyberactivism in China as democratic vehicle. It is clear that the majority of Internet users show little interest in public affairs and political issues. Cyberactivism are often perceived as chaotic, destructive and irrational. Faced with waves of public discontent, State censorship on the Internet has strengthened in recent years rather than loosened. The authority has greatly increased its effort in deploying technological and political strategies to divert, dissipate, or suppress online contention. Nevertheless, this paper attempts to move beyond a deterministic view of cyberactivism. What distinguishes online activism from conventional collective action lies with, at one level, structural manifestation as decentered networks and diversified identities, and at another level, temporal and situational fluidity. A more long-term perspective that accommodates rhizomatic dynamics may be more suitable for us to understand cyberactivism.

If we consider cyberactivism a type of social movement, it is perhaps short-sighted to focus solely on success and failure or particular episodes of collective actions. Rather, the ontology of becoming with rhizomatic dynamism allows us to move away from a perception of social progress as a linear process to that of temporal emergence that entails both "successes" and "failures", uncertainty and spontaneity, improvisation and struggles, growth and disruption, and progress and regress. The collective agency emerging from cyberactivism can be compared to tides with ebbs and flows, and moments that are high or low. As indicated by recent global movements and societal changes transitions, the power of tides is too easily predictable.

References

1. Bennett, W.L.: New Media Power: The Internet and Global Activism. In: Couldry, Curran (eds.) Contesting Media Power. Rowman & Littlefield (2003)
2. Yang, G.: The co-evolution of the Internet and civil society in China. Asian Survey 43, 405–422 (2003)
3. Zheng, Y., Wu, G.: Information Technology, Public Space, and Collective Action in China. Comparative Political Studies 38, 507–536 (2005)

4. CNNIC China Internet Development Report 27th edition. China Internet Network Information Center (2011),
http://www.cnnic.cn/xzzx/tjbgxz/201010/t20101020_16004.html
5. CNNIC Market and Blogger Report 2008-2009. China Internet Network Information Center (2009),
http://www.cnnic.cn/xzzx/tjbgxz/201010/t20101020_16004.html
6. Rodríguez-Giralt, I.: Social Movements as Actor-Networks: Prospects for a Symmetrical Approach to Doñana's Environmentalist Protests. Convergencia. Revista de Ciencias Sociales 18, 13–35 (2011)
7. Giddens, A.: The Constitution of Society, Outline of the Theory of Structuration. Polity Press, Cambridge (1984)
8. Deleuze, G., Guattari, F.: A Thousand Plateaus: Capitalism and Schizophrenia. University of Minnesota Press (1987)
9. Chia, R.: A 'Rhizomic' Model of Organizational Change and Transformation: Perspective from a Metaphysics of Change. British Journal of Management 10, 209–227 (1999)
10. Sørensen, B.: M. Gilles Deleuze and the intensification of social theory. Ephemera: Theory & Politics in Organization 3, 50–58 (2003)
11. Williams, J.: Deleuze's Ontology and Creativity: Becoming in Architecture (2000)
12. Pickering, A.: The Mangle of Practice: Time, Agency and Science. University of Chicago Press (1995)
13. Pickering, A.: The Mangle of Practice: Agency and Emergence in the Sociology of Science. American Journal of Sociology 99, 559–589 (1993)
14. Bennett, J.: The agency of Assemblages and the North American Blackout. Public Culture 17, 445–465 (2005)
15. Hess, M.: 'Spatial' Relationships? Towards a Reconceptualization of Embeddedness. Progress in Human Geography 28, 165–186 (2004)
16. Jullien, F.: The Propensity of Things: Toward a History of Efficacy in China. Zone Books. Distributed by MIT Press, New York (1995)
17. Yang, G.: Activists beyond Virtual Borders: Internet-Mediated Networks and Information Politics in China. First Monday (September 2006)
18. Zhai, M., Chen, W., Qian, G.: China's Bold Bloggers: The Power of Civil Discourses in the New Media Era (Zhongguo meng bo: xin mei ti shi dai de min jian hua yu li liang), Cosmos Books, Hong Kong (2009)
19. The Surrounding Gaze 围观. China Media Project Hong Kong University (2011),
http://cmp.hku.hk/2011/01/04/9399/
20. Microblogs reshape news in China. China Media Project, Hong Kong University (2010),
http://cmp.hku.hk/2010/10/12/8021/
21. He, Z.: SMS in China: A Major Carrier of the Nonofficial Discourse Universe. The Information Society: An International Journal 24, 182–190 (2008)
22. Latham, K.: Sms, Communication, And Citizenship in China's Information Society. Critical Asian Studies 39, 295–314 (2007)
23. Star, S.L., Griesemer, J.R.: Institutional Ecology, 'Translations' and Boundary Objects: Amateurs and Professionals in Berkeley's Museum of Vertebrate Zoology, 1907-39. Social Studies of Science 19, 387–420 (1989)

Information Inadequacy:
The Lack of Needed Information in Human,
Social and Industrial Affairs

Miranda Kajtazi

Linnaeus University, School of Computer Science, Physics and Mathematics, Växjö, Sweden
miranda.kajtazi@lnu.se

Abstract. This study investigates the phenomenon of the lack of needed information, predominantly experienced through difficulties in human, social and industrial affairs. The key concern is, thus, to understand what really causes the lack of needed information. Answers to this concern have been provided from an array of studies mostly focused in the area of information management. However, the literature shows that there is no comprehensive a priori theory to guide an empirical investigation on this matter. Thus, the empirical investigation conducted here is based on grounded theory approach that investigates fifty cases, where the lack of needed information is clearly manifested. The empirical investigation suggests that the phenomenon of the lack of needed information seems to emerge because of diverse factors, ranging from political and cultural structures, through human individual capabilities, and ending with procedural and technological artefacts. The results present an initial outline for a possible future theory of information inadequacy.

Keywords: information inadequacy, information management, information needs, information retrieval.

1   Introduction

Some fundamental questions in contemporary debates about the information society are concerned with phenomena that relate to information problems, predominantly experienced through difficulties in human, social and industrial affairs. Examples include the dramatic situations of the release of the atomic bomb in 1945, the Space Shuttle Challenger destruction in 1986, the tsunami in Indonesia in 2004, and the Lehman Brothers bankruptcy in 2008.

These dramatic situations, hereafter situations, show that human beings experience situations that are diverse in nature and context, yet they feature one key phenomenon: the lack of needed information. The central challenge in this research is to understand why such situations emerge. The discussion of this challenge is carried on by exploring the role of information in dramatic situations as a source of unwanted consequences, along with its importance in human life.

Situations like these are concerned with decision-making processes and require a rational behaviour to process information related to them [1]. Philosophers, scientists

M.D. Hercheui et al. (Eds.): HCC10 2012, IFIP AICT 386, pp. 320–329, 2012.
© IFIP International Federation for Information Processing 2012

and industrialists hypothesize about information problems and intend to develop theories or solutions that are partially helpful [2], [3], [4].

Information has a deep impact on personal well-being, decision-making processes, innovation and production [5], [6]. But, the failure to achieve balance between the surging volumes of information we access (mostly affected by electronic information) and its obverse, information underload [7]. Our everyday experiences manifest numerous instances in which information is the key characteristic that generates various consequences, many of which are experienced as failures or fatalities. Therefore, in this paper a core phenomenon is explored: the lack of needed information in human, social and industrial affairs.

The lack of needed information is understood as a composition of different behavioural aspects on the part of human agents that have implications for the production, the transfer or the use of information in a specific context. Although related topics have tackled similar phenomena for some decades now [5], [6], [7], [8], [9], there is little we understand about it. Indeed, there is no comprehensive understanding that has tackled such a phenomenon at length.

The objective of this paper is to give an understanding of the phenomenon of the lack of needed information by developing a model that intends to explain the causes of the lack of needed information that contribute to unwanted consequences. Empirically, the exploration of this phenomenon is based on the grounded theory approach [10] which has since been further developed [11], [12], [13].

The paper is organized as follows. First, a background and motivation is presented. Then, an overview of grounded theory approach is provided. Furthermore, the application of the grounded theory approach (based on a coding process) and a model derived from data analysis are presented. Finally, the paper describes some practical and theoretical implications that may advance studies with a focus on the lack of needed information and its impact on organizations and societies.

2   Background and Motivation

Situations, such as a global financial crisis or a tsunami catastrophe, are the focus of this research. Hence, the intention is to explore and understand the phenomenon of the lack of needed information. Such situations present various experiences that are dependent on information practices. These practices are understood as processes that govern decision-making, which mainly developed during the information revolution [5], [6], [7], [14]. The information revolution can be understood as an era in which technological breakthroughs have profoundly transformed human behaviour and cultures, and which provided the foundations for the establishment and development of the information society [15], [16]. In practical terms, scholars call for joint efforts to try to resolve the dark side of the information revolution [6], mainly represented by information overflow, which is affected by electronic information that negatively affects productivity and creativity [5].

The information society that developed through the information revolution seems to have no safeguards [17]. It concerns information that offers to human beings "*new and unparalleled opportunities to create novel social networks, new cultural configu-rations with innovative ideas, commitments and aspirations, and also new political structures"* [17]. Apart from this, the information revolution implies reshaping the material basis of the information society [16]. It is suggested that this is a movement that has been enormously visible during the post-industrial society, in which it is said that humans receive more information than ever before [18]. There are many unre-solved issues that still question what an information revolution implies for our as-sumed information society. Are we really getting enough information? If so, what kind of information is it? Also, how is it possible that there are still many restricted channels of communication, which may hold some of the most important informa-tion? Consider the two following situations, which have been selected for the purpose of explicating typical situations where the lack of needed information has occurred, and where ICT infrastructures have failed to spread information to the public at the needed time.

The tsunami natural disaster in Indonesia occurred in December 2004 and claimed thousands of lives around the Indian Ocean. Activated by a 7.7 Richter scale undersea earthquake with its epicentre in the Indian Ocean, the tsunami was a tremendous natu-ral disaster that happened unexpectedly and without any warnings being sent to civi-lians. In fact, the United Nations Education, Scientific and Cultural Organization (UNESCO) has declared that the Pacific Tsunami Warning Centre (PTWC) in Hawaii did detect the Java region tsunami. But, due to gaps in broadcasting critical informa-tion to the public, no warnings were sent on time, which otherwise could have saved thousands of lives. Seismological centres worldwide usually spread rapid information to the public about any earthquake detection, but failed to reach citizens in this situa-tion. The signs of the Indian Ocean tsunami were first picked up by the PTWC in Hawaii, 17 minutes after the earthquake but before the tsunami hit the coast of Java. Its immediate response was a warning message transmitted to its Jakartan colleagues, who also informed 400 Indonesian authorities. However, there was little they could do. Sadly, they claimed that there were no alarms, no emergency broadcasts or break-ing news information transmitted through radio or television; and there was just no way to reach the public on the coast. The Hawaiian PTWC argued that it was the In-donesians' responsibility to inform the public. So what went wrong in this situation? Why did all the possible communication channels fail to deliver information on time?

History then repeated itself. Indonesia was struck again by a powerful tsunami in October 2010. Witnesses have described this tsunami as being like a "runaway train". The only thing they could do was to run as far away from the shore as they could. Unfortunately, many people did not escape and, as a result, perished. This tsunami was registered for the first time by the PTWC in Hawaii, and the official tsunami warnings that went out after the quake either arrived too late or not at all in those communities that were most at risk. Many survivors have said that they were totally unprepared when the three metre high wall of water swept in over land. But why did information fail to inform the public a second time? Was the region not prepared for this situation as a result of the detecting system established after the tsunami catastro-phe in December 2004?

The key concern in such situations is to understand what really causes the lack of needed information. Answers to this concern have been investigated from an array of studies mostly concentrated on the area of information management. Theoretical fields of information logistics [19], information literacy [20] and information behaviour theories [21] show that their theories, concepts and aspirations focus on problems generated by the lack of needed information. However, these theoretical fields that claim to successfully explain or solve information-related problems show that their ambitions can only provide a partial understanding of what causes the lack of needed information. These theories indicate that they cannot truly account for the phenomenon of the lack of needed information. The implications of such theories have led to the understanding that the phenomenon of the lack of needed information remains unexplored and requires thorough investigation. Thus, there is no comprehensive a priori theory to be used for the design of an empirical investigation. In this study, therefore, it was necessary to continue with an analytical approach – empirically oriented – that is presented in the next section.

3   Empirical Investigation: A Grounded Theory Approach

A number of authors have developed theories that postulate how problems connected with information in human affairs arise in different circumstances [2], [5], [14], [22]. These problems may be caused by different factors, among which are the management factor, the political factor or the ethical factor, e.g. [5], [7]. In practice, information is considered as an invaluable asset in three core organizational processes engaged in communication: (a) information production; (b) information exchange; and (c) information receipt [23].

Communication in organizational processes is often followed by unprecedented difficulties that result in the failure of successful management of information-related practices [7], [24]. Recent investigations, especially those of the last two decades, have documented different information-related problems that occur in an unexpected fashion [9].

By systematically applying a grounded theory approach, this study finds an explanation for how the phenomenon of the lack of needed information arises in human, social and industrial affairs. Details related to the empirical findings are presented below.

3.1   A Summary of Selected Empirical Cases

In this study, data collection and analysis are based on secondary sources. All the data have been collected from news reports that were carefully reviewed in order to derive an understanding of why the lack of needed information emerged in these cases. The collection resulted in fifty empirical cases (see [26] for more details on case description and news sources). The vast majority of the empirical cases selected have occurred during the last two decades. However, this selection is driven by the accessibility of data on the Internet, which covers the selected cases much more comprehensively compared to cases that emerged before the Internet existed. The data analysis was conducted using open coding, axial coding and selective coding, which were adapted for the purpose of this research according to procedural aspects illustrated by [27], and enhanced by [11], [12], [13].

The fifty empirical cases comprise different situations that are selected for the purpose of emphasizing the phenomenon of the lack of needed information. More concretely, the selected situations are grouped as follows: Natural Disasters (9); Environmental Disasters (6); Financial Failures (7); Health Failures (6); Political Scandals (6); Conflict Situations (3); Engineering and Technological Failures (8); Nuclear and Chemical Disasters (5). The fifty cases identified are analyzed using a grounded theory approach. They are categorized in an a priori manner, solely for the purpose of facilitating the reader's understanding of what situations have been taken into consideration. However, this categorization does not have any influence on the empirical analysis.

3.2   Research Approach: Analysis and Results

Data analysis emerged iteratively, starting with early open-ended research, primarily line-by-line text analysis, and continued with more strategic selection of emerging concepts and categories [11]. The benefit of the iterative process is that the initial phase of exploration followed a flexible path in terms of understanding and collecting data, while the later phase of conceptualization followed a more strictly organized path based on the strategic planning of analysis.

The coding process as formulated by the grounded theory approach is employed more formally in data analysis after all the data have been collected, selected and refined. The analyses were based on three types of coding presented by [27], which are: open coding, axial coding, and selective coding.

The actual conceptualization and interpretation of the phenomenon of the lack of needed information became clear in the early phase of data analysis. The conceptualization of fifty cases developed on the basis of analyzing each case to derive characteristics that could show the causes of the lack of needed information. The results of such a conceptualization were mainly dependent on several codes that were identified as recurring in many situations. For instance, codes such as "did not alert" or "warning system(s)" were crucial for interpreting the phenomenon in context. The use of the majority of codes clearly presented significant similarities in all the situations, resulting in an early, yet crucial, interpretation of the phenomenon in context.

Axial coding continued with constant comparative analysis of the data. Codes found in the data became more meaningful when they continued to be merged, changed, and even eliminated. The codes that were merged represented a type of code used to show a key input for the purpose of generating categories. The codes that were changed were adapted to other similar codes, which may have reduced redundancy. The eliminated codes were primarily redundant. With axial coding, the analysis process led, firstly, to a refinement of the identified codes and induction of concepts.

The axial coding analysis was based on classifications, and comparative analysis resulted in the identification of eight sub-categories. As a result, the comparative analysis showed two main differences between the eight identified sub-categories. The differences resulted in grouping the sub-categories by introducing two main axial categories, i.e. information lack and information overflow, based on the following definitions:

Information Lack

1. *Information is non-existent* – is characterized by failure to communicate information in situations when actions are unforeseen and the responsible body for transmitting information is unaware of such a need, usually due to mismanagement.
2. *Information is insufficient* – is characterized by failure to communicate on-time information as a result of pre-planning of circumstances that may cause unwanted results in a specific situation. Lack of awareness, mismanagement and difficulty in understanding represent failure to act in a timely fashion.
3. *Information is censored* – is characterized by serious violation of information. Such information is usually hindered intentionally, secretly and illegally for the purpose of suppressing original information that is intended for the people and that may be significant for people's needs. Fraud is one of the key acts that reflect the censoring of information.
4. *Information is undelivered* – is characterized by incompetent acts of humans, with a dual outcome. The act is either undertaken intentionally by prohibiting the use of information or the undelivered information is caused by lack of awareness.

Information Overflow

5. *Information is ambiguous* – is characterized by lack of control of information. It is usually accompanied by miscalculations and lack of accurate evidence that misleads important decision-making processes.
6. *Information is redundant* – is characterized by duplication or even multiplication of the same information (repetition of information's message in synonyms or with the same excessive expression) due to lack of control or lack of awareness.
7. *Information is irrelevant* – is characterized by types of information that have no validity and are shared by unknown sources. Such information holds misinterpretations.
8. *Information is undervalued* – is characterized by mismanagement that may cause misinterpretation of information, possibly by lack of awareness or lack of awareness.

A significant number of codes, both substantive and theoretical, that are ultimately used in generating the eight sub-categories have been recurrent in one or more of the sub-categories, as presented in figure 1.

Selective coding is employed as the final step required to generate the core category, ultimately to generate a middle-range theory, which represents an initial outline for a possible future theory [13]. The data analysis has developed the core category by verifying that the phenomenon of the lack of needed information is evident in practical senses. Thus, the core category as a result of analysis is named in this study "information inadequacy". With the core category at hand, the aim is to integrate all the analysis into one formulated comprehensive outline that could portray the phenomenon of the lack of needed information.

Analyses generated new and interesting results that are used to formulate an explicit meaning of what is characterized as "information inadequacy," and which is defined as follows: *"dramatic situations (many of which happen on a daily basis) that encounter information as the key resource in different situations and circumstances, manifest various consequences, many of which are experienced as failures and fatalities in human, social and industrial affairs."*

Figure 1 illustrates the process of developing substantive and theoretical codes that lead to the creation of concepts. The concepts consist of various sub-categories that can be classified into two main categories that, in turn, can be brought together in a single category.

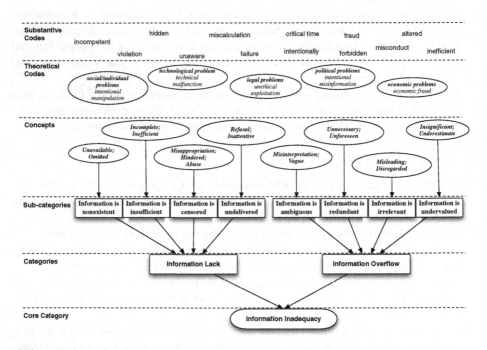

Fig. 1. Results from the Coding Process (Open Coding, Axial Coding, Selective Coding) leading to the development of the core category "Information Inadequacy"

4   Discussion and Conclusion

This study has proposed an initial outline of information inadequacy that resulted from the need to understand the phenomenon of the lack of needed information.

Initially, this study found that theoretical fields that claim to handle the phenomenon of the lack of needed information cannot account for, explain, or suggest a remedy for the dramatic situations where there is a lack of needed information. They can only account for a partial and, hence, a limited understanding of the phenomenon in context.

A need for empirical investigations thus became crucial. It triggered new explorations in interpreting what is changing about today's information access and what remains critical in global information landscapes (these may vary from social, political, economic or environmental contexts). The empirical investigation was based on a grounded theory approach applied to a collection of fifty empirical cases. This investigation resulted in the identification of characteristics, patterns and causes of how the needed information fails to reach the intended person at the right time and place, causing unwanted and even disastrous consequences. The analysis suggested that information-related problems of this nature appear mainly due to difficulties that are caused by the information source (sender) and information mediator – whether human or machine. The results of this investigation have developed an initial outline of information inadequacy that could guide the development of a future theory of information inadequacy.

The grounded theory approach became instrumental in this study. The development of an understanding of the phenomenon in context is achieved by suggesting that a number of characteristics (information is ambiguous, information is non-existent, information is redundant, and the like) and their interrelationships present various patterns (described as information inadequacies) that emerge in a communication process. These are followed by a number of diverse factors, ranging from political and cultural structures, through human individual capabilities, that culminate with procedural and technological artefacts and that influence the increase in consequences.

In practice, the proposed concept of information inadequacy addresses all human beings who are concerned with information in their everyday practices and intend to enhance their time by carefully managing information. More importantly, information inadequacy can act as a diagnosis tool that allows industrialists, technology developers, environmentalists and others to consider how to enhance information communication in the future. It is justifiable, as well as moderate, to state that information inadequacy as such is not taken as seriously as a problem in our current information society, and that it is usually accompanied by unwanted consequences.

Given the results of the empirical investigation conducted here, the identified factors indicate how hindrances to information provision may be used as guidelines for the diagnosis and re-design of information provision processes. In short, this would imply that each pattern of information inadequacy identified might be used to direct new and innovative diagnostic and re-design teams that focus on information management and on the more careful planning of information flows that are present and important in dramatic situations. Such an understanding may possibly guide further development of a future theory of information inadequacy that can be instrumental in developing more efficient information systems for organizations and societies and for an operational use of information.

Apart from realizing that a digital future may seem promising, information inadequacy remains a challenging dilemma that will continue to rely on human or machine-based communication. The current results that present an initial outline of information inadequacy can be developed in at least three dimensions: (i) further development of the content that represents information inadequacy, i.e. factors and their interrelations; (ii) the empirical validity of the current elaboration, based on a very large number of cases (e.g. 1,000); (iii) the research object, i.e. not only "dramatic situations" but also the "everyday situations". These can be studied by looking more concretely at socio-psychological factors and technological factors that today are regarded as crucial aspects that affect information inadequacy.

References

1. Newell, A., Simon, H.A.: Human problem solving. Prentice-Hall, Englewood Cliffs (1972)
2. Akerlof, G.: The market for 'Lemons': quality uncertainty and the market mechanism. Quart. J. Econ. 84, 488–500 (1970)
3. Bandura, A.: Self-efficacy: toward a unifying theory of behavioral change. J. Psych. Rev. 84, 191–215 (1977)
4. Ennals, R., Stratton, L., Moujahid, N., Kovela, S.: Global information technology and global citizenship education. AI & Soc. 23, 61–68 (2009)
5. Dean, D., Webb, C.: Recovering from information overload. McKinsey Q (2011)
6. Hemp, P.: Death by information overload. Harvard Bus. Rev. (2009)
7. O'Reilly, C.A.: Individuals and information overload in organizations: is more necessarily better? The Acad. Manag. J. 23, 684–696 (1980)
8. Creese, G.: Information scarcity to information overload. Info., Manag., Magaz, 20–22 (2007)
9. Ojala, M.: Transforming information quality 33 (2009) Online
10. Glaser, B., Strauss, A.L.: The discovery of grounded theory: strategies for qualitative research. Aldine, Chicago (1967)
11. Orlikowski, W.J.: CASE tools as organizational change: investigating incremental and radical changes in systems development. MISQ 17, 309–340 (1993)
12. Sarker, S., Lau, F., Sahay, S.: Using an adapted grounded theory approach for inductive theory building about virtual team development. The Database for Adv. IS 32, 38–56 (2001)
13. Charmaz, K.: Constructing Grounded Theory: A Practical Guide Through Qualitative Analysis. Sage Publications, Thousand Oaks (2006)
14. Eppler, M.J., Mengis, J.: The concept of information overload: a review of literature from organization science, Accounting, Marketing, MIS, and Related Disciplines. Info Soc. 20, 325–344 (2004)
15. Boyd, D.: Taken Out of Context: American Teen Sociality in Networked Publics (Doctoral Dissertation). University of California- Berkley Press (2008)
16. Castells, M.: The Power of Identity: The Information Age: Economy, Society and Culture, 2nd edn. Wiley-Blackwell, Chichester (2010)
17. Haftor, D.M., Mirijamdotter, A., Kajtazi, M.: In search for unity within the diversity of information societies. In: Haftor, D.M., Mirijamdotter, A. (eds.) Information and Communication Technologies, Society and Human Beings: Theory and Framework, pp. 540–546. IGI Publishing, New York (2010)

18. Lonsdale, J.D.: The nature of war in the information age. Routledge, New York (2004)
19. Haftor, D.M., Kajtazi, M., Mirijamdotter, A.: A Review of Information Logistics Research Publications. In: Abramowicz, W., Maciaszek, L., Węcel, K. (eds.) BIS Workshops 2011 and BIS 2011. LNBIP, vol. 97, pp. 244–255. Springer, Heidelberg (2011)
20. Bruce, C.: Informed Learning. Association of College and Research Libraries (2008)
21. Fisher, E.K., Erdelez, S., McKechnie, L. (eds.): Theories of Information Behavior, 2nd edn. American Society for Information Science and Technology, New Jersey (2006)
22. Mingers, J.C.: Information and meaning: foundations for an intersubjective account. J. IS 5, 285–306 (1995)
23. Mortensen, C.D. (ed.): Communication theory, 2nd edn. Transaction Publishers, New Jersey (2009)
24. Hwang, M.I., Lin, J.W.: Information dimension, information overload and decision quality. J. IS 25, 213–219 (1999)
25. Bawden, D., Robinson, L.: Training for information literacy: diverse approaches. In: Proceedings of the International Online Information Meeting, London (UK), pp. 87–90. Learned Information Europe Ltd., Oxford (2001)
26. Kajtazi, M.: An exploration of Information Inadequacy: Instances that cause the lack of needed information. Licentiate Thesis, School of Computer Science, Physics and Mathematics, Linnaeus University, Växjö, Sweden (2011)
27. Strauss, A., Corbin, J.: Basics of qualitative research. Sage Publications, Newbury Park (1990)

Social Games: Privacy and Security

Mathias Fuchs

Leuphana University, Lüneburg Centre for Digital Cultures
School of Art & Design, Manchester, United Kingdom
mathias.fuchs@creativegames.org.uk

Abstract. Recent online gaming developments and para-gaming environments, i.e., the social software tools to communicate with fellow gamers, report, discuss and disseminate assets and experience, strongly resemble social media like Facebook or Twitter. It has therefore been suggested that games like World of Warcraft, Little Big Planet, The Godfather, or The Secret World should be called "social games." Privacy and security is an issue in these social games, as the players of these games do often not realize that they inhabit environments that have real estate outside the safe borders of the Magic Circle. The games companies harvest information about the players in ways that are far from transparent. The author will present examples of data mining and harvesting of data within a playful environment, analyze code segments that implement data collection, and suggest methods of refusal, sabotage, or disclosure of breeches of contract.

Keywords: social games, magic circle, scripting languages, digital footprint, computer forensics.

1 Digital Surveillance

Surveillance has been associated with punishment, with the notion of crime, and with torture or imprisonment. It has been described as adding to a disciplinary technique that penetrated modern society and became apparent in the structure of prisons, hospitals, schools and military organizations [1], [2]. Authors like Michel Foucault have focused on the institutional backbone of the modern national states to describe how discipline emerged as a new technological power [1]. In his analysis leisure, entertainment or games play hardly more than a minor role. It seems that the "*Magic Circle*" that used to have ring-fenced play from all of society's evil [3], has also kept surveillance out. There is of course and has always been cheating, hiding and penalties in games, but those were not considered criminal acts, camouflage or punishment in a Foucauldian sense. Recent developments in games technology, but also the social changes that stem from the phenomenal success of computer games challenge the concept of the magic circle [4], [5] and ask for an answer to the question of whether gaming can be seen as ordinary social practice that is influenced by power structure, economic system, mediatic transformations, and real world relevance in general [6].

It has been suggested that computer games that build upon a large number of online players and in particular games that are embedded in a framework of para-ludic

M.D. Hercheui et al. (Eds.): HCC10 2012, IFIP AICT 386, pp. 330–337, 2012.

activities like chats, memorabilia exchange, fanzines, gadget shops, and the like should be called "social games." Such are World of Warcraft, Little Big Planet, Unreal Tournament, The Godfather, or The Secret World.

Privacy and security is an issue in these social games, as the players of these games often do not realize that they inhabit environments that have real estate outside the safe borders of the Magic Circle. The games companies harvest information about the players in ways that are far from transparent. Data harvesting tools and technologies include the following: path tracking, eye tracking, heat maps, activity monitoring, non-game user information retrieval, and digital forensics.

Data visualization toolkits like the one offered by *Epic Megagames* and less well-documented surveillanceware allows for the recording of location, time and speed of movement, appearance and dress code, aggressiveness, solidarity, social behaviour, anti-social behaviour, and many other session attributes.

2   Social Games Data Harvesting Technology

When playing online games the players leave traces on the terrain they wander about that are more accurate than footprints in the snow and certainly much longer lasting. It is of importance to game developers to track down where players used to walk. It is also important for game developers to know which possible paths are highly frequented and which ones are rarely used. Almost every modern game engine has built-in functions to record, store and transfer these paths to the central server, that have been taken by a player at a given time. Many game engines also offer tools to analyse huge sets of paths and to visualize the statistical data generated from these data sets. Alastair Hebson's *Unreal Visualisation Toolkit* (UVT) allows users to record the paths that players make on a given *Unreal* map. The programmer's company that aptly calls themselves *Digital Footprints* offers a data log mutator and a screen capture mutator. Mutators are add-ons to the game engine that perform special operations enhancing standard gameplay. If the implementation of the mutator is not transparent to the user and if the programmer does not announce those special operations, no gamer would suspect that anything unusual takes place during gameplay. Whilst this is not a problem when used by games developers to create more interesting games, to optimize gameplay balance or to design terrain of high unpredictability, it poses a problem when used by parties with other interests. A marketing and advertising company can read whether in-game ads have been visited, it can observe whether certain content has been approached or what the mobility patterns of the players are. Players can therefore easily be classified as following certain consumer patterns, mobility modes or types of behaviour. The observation becomes even more useful when in-game eye tracking technology is used. Eye tracking is not at all easy in physical situations, but when the virtual eye is tracked in a computer game the accuracy of measurement is at a maximum. The data log mutator can record how long a player has been looking at an in-game ad, how often and how long he or she was focusing on an object or a detail belonging to that object. Games become a digital panopticon that outperform Bentham's invention: The ones that are under surveillance are not only deprived of facing their wardens, they do not even know that the wardens are looking at them.

Surveillance algorithms become more powerful when they collect not only individual user data, but create complex statistical data. The location of an individual user is not of high interest for market analysis, a heatmap generated from the locations where millions of users walk through is of great interest. A heatmap can as a 2D graphical representation indicate behavioural patterns, preferences, gaps in the attention or knowledge of the user.

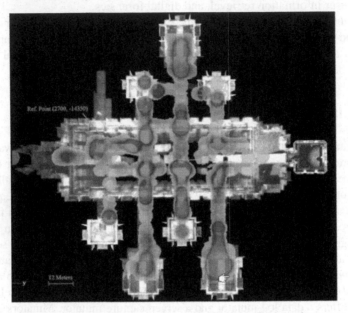

Fig. 1. Automatically generated heatmap of a Unity3D level. Frequently accessed areas are colour-coded in purple, rarely visited areas are in light blue.

At first sight one might think that the purpose of this is to track user experience throughout the world in order to assess which areas the gamers find interesting and which areas they are avoiding. This is often said to be used for debugging purposes or to improve gameplay for future updates. *Epic Megagames* states: "The purpose of this is to track user experience throughout the world in order to assess which areas the gamers find interesting and which areas they are avoiding" [7]. It is however quite obvious that the same map could easily be enhanced with information that goes beyond in-game information and contains user information or private data.

Code Example 1: Code sequence for the Unity3D player class to store player positions and to add personal user data to the generated log file that is contained in the file devlist.txt

```
var positionTrackingFrequency : int = 2; //How often to
store player position
private var timer : float = 0;            //The timer
```

```
static var posArray : Vector2[]; //Local array storing
player position
private var arrayIterator : int = -1;
function Update(){
    timer += 1 * Time.deltaTime;
        if(timer >= positionTrackingFrequency){
            storePos()}}
function storePos(){
    timer = 0;
    var localArray : Array = new Array();
    if(posArray != null)
        localArray = new Array(posArray);
    localArray.Push(Vector2(transform.position.x,
transform.position.z) )
    posArray = localArray.ToBuiltin(Vector2);
    arrayIterator++;
    Debug.Log(" " + posArray[arrayIterator] + "
Iteration =  " + arrayIterator);}
import System.IO;
var fileName = "devlist.txt";


function ReadPersonalData () {
    var sr = new StreamReader("C:" + "/" + fileName);
    var fileContents = sr.ReadToEnd();
    sr.Close();
    var lines = fileContents.Split("\n"[0]);
for (line in lines) {
    Debug.Log (line);}}
```

The information saved by the function storePos() saves the player's position at a certain interval, and the function ReadPersonalData() in the code example above contains information about the graphics card, processor, WiFi equipment and other devices that are installed on the player's PC, in the case of the author's PC a total of 168 devices. It is beyond the knowledge of most Unity users that such detailed information is polled and can easily be transferred to a company server via TCP/IP protocol. In this regard the algorithms providing the surveillance possibilities implement what Foucault called an "unequal gaze" [1], the constant possibility of observation, a one-directional view of the observer upon the information the user holds.

It does not happen very often that gamers become aware of path tracking, eye tracking or other surveillance techniques, and even less often do users complain about it. A recent protest about data harvesting in games took place, when German *Battlefield 3* players sued the company *Electronic Arts (EA)* to stop spying on data that leaked to them whenever their game *Battlefield* was played. The online software component *Origin*, which was originally declared to spy on license fraud and to illegally install software from *EA*, seems to have the potential to send non-authorized user data to the company's server. The German television news programme "die Tagesschau" reported on the 8th of May 2012 that Thomas Schwenke, the lawyer of the plaintiffs in the Battlefield lawsuit, declared that "what looks like a copy protection mechanism, actually works like spyware" [8]. Evidence has been presented in this case that private data has been transferred to a server of *Amazon* company. As a partial success German gamers are now allowed to return copies of *Battlefield 3* to stores. The German retailers *Media Markt* and *Saturn* have given refunds to customers for used editions of Battlefield 3, even after their PC keys had been redeemed. But even so, *Electronic Arts* did not concede to having violated user rights. "We have updated the End User License Agreement of Origin, in the interests of our players to create more clarity. Origin is not spyware. Neither do we use nor install spyware on the PCs of users." The updated End User License now contains a line that states: "We have taken every precaution to protect the personal and anonymous user data collected." This seems to say that there is still user data being collected and that *Electronic Arts* keeps the right to do with it whatever they want. This is not a unique case; other companies operate in a similar way.

Linden Labs, for example, has stated: "Our Privacy Policy sets forth the conditions under which you provide personal and other information to us. You understand and agree that through your use of the Service you consent to the collection and use of your information in accordance with our Privacy Policy. If you object to your information being used in this way, please do not use the Service."

3   Digital Panopticon

If social games companies have the possibility of establishing a system of surveillance, and if they do so sometimes in individual cases, or even regularly on a large scale, then one could rightly ask how far the encompassing surveillance system within social games resembles Bentham's Panopticon - and in what respect it differs from the latter. There is no doubt that digital surveillance has a greater ability to surveil subjects than the brick-and-mortar structures Foucault was worried about. The computer game *Battlefield 3* that has recently been accused of spying on its users, sold 5 million copies in its first week of sales and, thereby, beat *Gears of War 3* and *FIFA 12*, each of which sold 3 million copies. Digital surveillance resembles the processes that lead to discipline in a Foucauldian sense [1], [2] by replacing arbitrary actions of those who hold power with a systematic and anonymous system of surveillance. Foucault points out that the opacity of the system of surveillance contributes considerably to its success. In digital online environments an end-user agreement usually empowers the provider of the environment to investigate secretly, to pronounce judgment without the right of appeal, and to punish users by banning them from their online environment.

In *Linden Lab's Second Life* the end-user agreement demands that [9]: " …you agree that you shall not:

(i) take any action or upload, post, e-mail or otherwise transmit Content that infringes or violates any third party rights;

(ii) impersonate any person or entity without their consent, including, but not limited to, a Linden Lab employee, or falsely state or otherwise misrepresent your affiliation with a person or entity;

(iii) take any action or upload content that is harmful, threatening, abusive, harassing, causes tort, defamatory, vulgar, obscene, libelous, invasive of another's privacy, hateful, or racially, ethnically or otherwise objectionable."

In case of an infringement of these conditions, users will, without having seen any evidence of the criminal procedure, be banned from *Second Life*. That any action of the criminal that is "otherwise objectionable" can lead to punishment evokes in a cynical manner what prisoners in the Gulag or in torture camps like camp Guantanamo experience. Foucault's description of discipline and the procedure of investigation fits well with the procedures *Linden Lab* executes, when banning inhabitants. These procedures do not relate to transparent codes of law, but to the symbolic affirmation of sovereign power. This sovereign power once was the king, the army, the national state, and is nowadays *Linden Lab*, *Electronic Arts* or *SONY*. These new sovereign powers can even override federal law or state law. As *Linden Lab* put it: "As a condition of access to the Service, you release Linden Lab (and its officers, directors, shareholders, agents, subsidiaries, and employees) from claims, demands, losses, liabilities and damages (actual and consequential) of every kind and nature, known and unknown (...) If you are a California resident, you waive California Civil Code Section 1542, which says: 'general release does not extend to claims which the creditor does not know or suspect to exist in his favor at the time of executing the release, which if known by him must have materially affected his settlement with the debtor.' If you are a resident of another jurisdiction, you waive any comparable statute or doctrine" [9].

There are similarities of the digital Panopticon, but there are also differences. For Foucault it was the body that worked as the physical centre and constituting factor for discipline and punishment. In the digital realm bodies are replaced by locations of actors. IP addresses or GPS-coordinates replace what the physical body once has been for surveillance. That is why Metadata is so important for a system of control. Once every image is time-stamped and location-stamped, the process of monitoring the generation and dissemination of information can be optimized. Software can be identified as legally copied or illegally cloned; emails can be assigned to paths; mail servers and client IDs images can be tracked down for the real physical location at which they were taken. The system of micro-power has no longer to refer to the body of the individual, but to the location of the actors in the system. In the age of disembodiment "disciplinary power" is no longer – as Foucault had it – coinciding with the birth of "an art of the human body," but with the emergence and success of location-based media and the importance of the politics of space. Indeed, when Foucault spoke of the four characteristics of individuality that discipline constructs as cellular, organic, genetic, and combinatory, I would suggest that digital discipline replaces the organic with the location-based whereas cellular, genetic and combinatory characteristics remain essential for digital discipline. Cellular aspects guarantee that the identity of the units is not corrupted by clones, copies or replicated assets. Genetic consistency is essential for tracking down generations of code, programme versions and the whole process of inheritance in object-oriented systems. Finally the combinatory serves to enhance the power of individual actors, to form clouds and distributed computing, and to establish discipline not only in the individual units, but in large systems as well.

4   Counter-Strike

Is there a chance to escape digital surveillance, if it is as powerful as the technical system suggests? Three suggestions should sketch alternative routes to escaping, playing with, and fighting digital surveillance.

4.1   Camouflage

This is probably the least delightful alternative, but still a chance to escape surveillance. The possibility of setting up firewalls, playing games secretly and in solitude without using the multiplayer mode clearly exists. One might choose to not connect to the Internet, and send emails anonymously from hotmail accounts at Internet cafes, but what life is that? Remaining completely invisible will turn the social gaming experience into a digital hermitage.

4.2   Manipulation of Data

Users with programming skills and with a profound knowledge of the systems they use can write software that filters the information they provide to the outside world or they can alter information that social games transmit to the game companies and the providers. The functions in programme example.1 would only require minor amendments to avoid the leak that prepares the device information for transmission. Change

```
var fileName = "devlist.txt";
```

into

```
var fileName = "noinformation.txt";
```

Then put a text file on your C: drive that contains any message to the games company and it will be sent there. This process of course, is very time consuming and one would enter a rat race of finding out where the next data leaks are in the programmes one has bought can be found.

4.3   Cloning and Multiple Identities

There have been successful attempts to escape control mechanisms by disclosing or confusing the personalization of actors in social games. In *Second Life,* there have been protests that gathered identical clones of avatars to show up at places and to demonstrate against constraints of *Second Life* civilian rights. By sharing an identical appearance, such interventions make a strong statement against the pseudo-individualism that is promoted by the company. The creation of self-spawning clones is subverting the possibilities of tracking down individuals and punishing them for breeches of the End User License Agreement. "Every Resident has a right to live their Second Life. Disrupting scheduled events, … following or self-spawning items" are forbidden in Second Life as are demonstrations in real life authoritarian regimes. And in the digital world as well as in modern national states it is up to the sovereign, of course, to decide what a "disrupting event" is.

5   Conclusion

Social Games provide possibilities for monitoring user behaviour that other electronic media lack. In such games, it is not only possible to count how often a user visits a place where an advert is located; such games can also measure and document the duration of the eye contact with the object in question, to describe watching patterns (or listening patterns) in detail, and to relate this to game states, movement patterns, private information and any other conceivable information that can be retrieved from the gamer's computer. The surveillance mechanisms that have been proven to have been installed in modern social games resemble the "unequal gaze" that Michel Foucault found characteristic for the technology of discipline and for the setting of Bentham's Panopticon. There are, however, differences in the way modern surveillance works and how digital surveillance in social games works. The body as the centre of modern pre-digital surveillance has been replace by location as the main instrument of surveillance and a new micro-politics of power emerges that causes new threads but also new hopes for resistance.

References

1. Foucault, M.: Discipline and Punish. Vintage Books (1995) (orig. in French 1975)
2. Foucault, M.: Birth of the Clinic. Vintage Books (1973) (orig. in French 1963)
3. Huizinga, J.: Homo ludens. Vom Ursprung der Kultur im Spiel. Reinbek bei Hamburg (1987) (orig. in Dutch 1938)
4. Liebe, M.: There is no Magic Circle. On the Difference between Computer Games and Traditional Games. In: Stephan, G., Dieter, M. (eds.) Conference Proceedings of The Philosophy of Computer Games 2008, Potsdam, pp. 324–341 (2008)
5. Günzel, S.: Der reine Raum des Spiels – Zur Kritik des Magic Circle. In: Fuchs, M., Strouhal, E. (eds.) Passagen der Spiele II, pp. 189–202. Springer, Vienna (2010)
6. Montola, M.: Exploring the Edge of the Magic Circle. Defining Pervasive Games. In: Proceedings of the 6th DAC Conference. IT University of Copenhagen, Copenhagen (2005)
7. Unreal Developer Network webpages, by Epic Games,
   http://udn.epicgames.com/Three/
   GameStatsVisualizerReference.html
8. German ARD Broadcasting Network reports on its webpages on (May 8, 2012),
   http://www.tagesschau.de/inland/battlefield100.html
9. Second Life EULA, http://secondlife.com/corporate/tos.php

Is Privacy Dead? – An Inquiry into GPS-Based Geolocation and Facial Recognition Systems

Jens-Martin Loebel

Humboldt-Universität zu Berlin, Department of Computer Science, Berlin, Germany
`loebel@informatik.hu-berlin.de`

Abstract. This paper discusses, conceptually and empirically, the proliferation of geolocation and face recognition systems embodied in modern smartphones and social media networks, which presents a growing concern for a user's rights to privacy. This increase in data sharing brings about the very real threat of misuse, as most users are not aware that their geolocation data can easily be assembled into complete profiles of their everyday activities and movements, their habits and social life. Paired with facial recognition capabilities already present in current social media services, this allows for an unprecedented tracking of users, even those "tagged" through photo uploads by other people. To illustrate this, the author analyzes his own profile, which was created by recording GPS data over a time span of five years. A critical discussion of the results follows.

Keywords: GPS, geolocation, social networks, tagging, privacy, facial recognition, locational privacy.

1 Introduction

Ubiquitous energy-self-sufficient devices like smartphones and mobile navigation systems allow the user to easily track his or her position using GPS and cell tower triangulation. This in turn enables new kinds of useful applications, especially in the realm of social media. However, these applications and systems create and digitally store a plethora of user information including movements through the public space. In the coming years these systems will become more entrenched in the everyday life of Internet users but their impact is already noticeable today. Services like Foursquare, Gowalla or Apple's Find my Friends App allow the user to "check-in" and share their physical location with friends, collect virtual badges and get coupons by visiting restaurants or shops using their GPS-enabled smartphones in real time.

Social media giants like Facebook or Twitter have followed suit, enabling users to enrich their posts with GPS coordinates. This increase in data sharing brings about the very real threat of misuse, as most users are not aware that their geolocation data can easily be assembled into complete profiles of their everyday activities and movements, their habits and social life. Paired with facial recognition capabilities already present in current social media services, this allows for an unprecedented tracking of users, even those "tagged" through photo uploads by other people.

M.D. Hercheui et al. (Eds.): HCC10 2012, IFIP AICT 386, pp. 338–348, 2012.

The problem lies in the aggregation and mixing of different data sets, creating new contexts in which user data may be misused, leading to a loss of control on the part of the user. In this paper the technical details of geolocation and facial recognition systems are discussed, common applications are presented and threats to privacy and data protection are identified. To illustrate this I will create my own movement profile from meticulously recorded location data over a time period of five years. Using data mining techniques, I will present my aggregated profile to visualize what information can be derived simply from using geolocation data, facilitating a discussion about privacy.

2   GPS and Assistive Technologies

The satellite-based NAVSTAR Global Positioning System (GPS) consists of 24 active satellites on different paths in an orbit of 20183 km, completing two revolutions in a sidereal day (about 23 hours and 56 minutes). Originally developed in 1973 by the U.S. Department of Defense to provide precise guidance and navigation for missiles and soldiers in armed conflicts, the system has been fully operational since 1994. The conception as a war material manifested itself in certain design choices notably a high navigational accuracy, high resistance against signal jamming and – most importantly – the ability to passively calculate one's position using only the received GPS satellite data. Furthermore satellite distribution is not equal but higher over inhabited areas (possible conflict zones) [1].

After the deactivation of the signal degrading "Selective Availability" feature by President Clinton in 2000 the systems now allows for a high degree of accuracy (less than five meters) in civilian application. This in turn enabled civilian users to fully utilize the system, leading to a wide range of applications including electronic sea/land/air navigation systems, progress analysis and tracking in running sports and even new leisure sports like "geocaching" (a GPS driven outdoor treasure hunt) or the enrichment of holiday photos with GPS coordinates of their location. Affordable hardware GPS receivers in mobile phones or dedicated car navigation systems have made the GPS system the predominant method for position tracking, navigation and meeting friends in the real world using location-based social networks.

However, a large user base also raises the potential for abuse. Gathered location data may be used to create detailed movement profiles from which daily routines, lifestyle habits or social contacts of a user can be inferred. In order to better assess the possibilities and limits of these systems, a brief description of the technical process follows.

2.1   Reception and Mobile Phones

GPS relies on the principle of indirectly measuring the distance between simultaneously observed (received) satellites and the antenna of the GPS receiver. Using an atomic clock, each satellite continuously calculates its orbital position and broadcasts a message containing the current time and an ephemeris (a table of values which help provide the precise orbit for the satellite) wirelessly with the GPS signal.

A GPS receiver on earth – also containing a clock – then simultaneously receives the signals of all satellites above the horizon. The receiver will then calculate a pseudo distance (called pseudorange) to the respective satellite's orbital position (as received with the ephemeris) using the time difference between the received timestamp and the current time. This approximation however does not represent the actual geographical distance as the radio waves from the satellite get distorted, deflected and even slowed down on their way to earth, affecting their transit time.

The biggest source of measuring error is the complex dispersive interactions of the radio waves with the ionosphere (the so called ionospheric effect) that heavily distorts the signal and for which there is no good mathematical approximation model. However the amount of distortion is the same across all frequencies. The system therefore broadcasts two sets of data on two different frequencies.

One is the C/A-Code (Coarse/Acquisition), part of the civilian Standard Positioning Service, which is transmitted on the frequency L1 (1,57542 GHz). The other is the secret encrypted P(Y)-Code, part of the military Precise Positioning Service, which is transmitted both on L1 and on a secondary frequency L2 (1,2276 GHz), which allows the ionospheric effect to be factored out. Since the mathematical function for decoding the Y-Code is unknown, only the U.S. military and allied government forces can use it. Civilian GPS receivers do not have this advantage, which leads to a severely reduced accuracy of the calculated position to a range of about 20-50 m [1]. To compensate for this and keep the deviation less than 10 meters, a range of assistive technologies utilizing satellite and ground radio stations as well as internet-based extensions, that deliver correcting data, are being used. Satellite based systems use evenly distributed fixed reference ground stations to cover a wide area. These stations receive the GPS signal, compare the calculated location with their own known location and subsequently use this information to create a map of the ionospheric distortions. This information in turn is then sent to a satellite, which rebroadcasts the signal to GPS receivers. This technique is called differential GPS (DGPS). There are several compatible DGPS-Systems in different geographic regions of the world. In widespread use are the Wide Area Augmentation System (WAAS) in North America, the European Geostationary Navigation Overlay Service (EGNOS) in Europe, the Multifunctional Satellite Augmentation System (MSAS) in Japan and the Globalnaja Nawigazionnaja Sputnikowaja Sistema (GLONASS) in Russia. A respective system for India (GAGAN) is currently being deployed [2].

The GPS signal itself is encoded using code division multiple access (CDMA, spread spectrum around a carrier frequency) allowing for a high resistance against signal jamming. A sequence of pseudo random numbers (created with a mathematical function) is being used to synchronize the signal between the satellite and the receiver by encoding the GPS message data with it. The initialization vector of this function is the time measured by the atomic clock on the respective satellite. The GPS receiver on the ground calculates the same values using its built-in clock and then tries to find a maximum correlation with the received numbers. This process leads to an initial startup delay as the GPS receiver tries to synchronize with all satellites and build an almanac from the received ephemerides.

The calculated pseudoranges span a spherical surface around each satellite and the GPS receiver. The intersection of two spheres is a circle. The intersection of three spheres represents the GPS receiver's position on earth (and another point inside the plasmasphere which is discarded). In the real world however, a forth sphere/satellite is needed because the clock in a GPS receiver is not precise enough to sync exactly with the atomic clock aboard the satellite. The forth sphere is used to determine the time drift between the clocks. This allows the receiver to derive the correct geographical distance from the calculated pseudorange. Therefore to calculate a GPS position at least four satellites need to be observed at the same time with each additional satellite enhancing the position accuracy.

Smartphones and other mobile devices are nowadays usually equipped with a GPS receiver chip and have access to the Internet. These devices employ a different technology to combat the aforementioned shortcomings (long initial startup time and poor accuracy without correction data). They utilize additional information like the ID number of connected nearby mobile GSM cell towers or the MAC-address of visible WiFi networks [2]. This data is sent via the phone's Internet connection to special information services (operated by commercial enterprises) and/or the user's cell phone carrier. The inquired services maintain a database with the geographical location of every cell phone tower as well as commercial and private user WiFi networks (if recorded). The gathered locations can then be used to triangulate the phone's location within a radius of about 50 to 500 meters. This rough location can then be used to narrow the search within the calculated satellite spheres leading to a significantly shorter startup time. In addition GPS almanac data may be received over the Internet. This technique is called assisted GPS (AGPS). Also DGPS data may be received from a server on the Internet instead of a satellite.

2.2 Geodetic Datum and Address Resolution

The thus derived GPS map datum consists of latitude, longitude, height above sea level and a (system-inherent) current timestamp. A GPS datum is therefore always a 4-dimensional vector. Latitude and longitude are represented as degrees and arc minutes after the World Geodetic System of 1984 (WGS-84). This geodetic reference system defines a reference ellipsoid (segmented in degrees of latitude and longitude) around the earth and its atmosphere that is the basis for all position information.

To be useful for the user the map datum (e.g. "52° 22.711' N, 4° 54.020' E") needs to be augmented with a meaningful semantic connotation (like "Centraal Station, Entrance, Amsterdam, Netherlands"). On mobile phones this is accomplished by querying an online semantic map database with the user's location. With few exceptions these databases are again operated by commercial enterprises (see chapter 4). In any case a digital map is needed to show the user's position in a geographical context.

Most importantly the usage of such assistive technologies and online map databases add an active return channel to the otherwise passive GPS system that needs to be examined further.

3   Facial Recognition Systems

In addition to GPS chipsets practically all modern smartphones are equipped with a digital camera. In recent years advances in image and face recognition algorithms have led to a number of online applications that could potentially affect a user's right to privacy.

Traditionally facial recognition/identification has been employed in a security context, particularly in the realm of government (e.g. biometric passports) and law enforcement applications. However face detection and recognition systems are increasingly being used in consumer products and social network software. One has to differentiate between full-fledged face recognition and simple face detection algorithms, which are built-in to digital cameras, smartphones and webcams, tracking user movement and helping to adjust lens/focus settings. These systems while able to detect a human face cannot differentiate between two or more faces. For this purpose face recognition systems are employed that have the ability to match human faces in images or video frames. Utilizing feature detection algorithms the geometry of a detected face is analyzed and distilled as a unique hash value / feature set for a particular person.

3.1   Common Uses and Privacy Concerns

Such technology is ubiquitously being used in consumer photo manipulation and/or digital media management applications – offline as well as online.

Programs like Apple's iPhoto automatically detect faces in all imported photos and can match faces with the user's address book contacts after an initial pairing. While iPhoto works "offline", online photo albums like the Windows Live Photo Gallery and Google's Picasa have the ability to automatically detect faces in all uploaded photos. These services are popular and commonly used to share photos with family and friends. Moreover the images may be enriched with GPS location data.

Social media giant Facebook adds another dimension by employing face recognition on all stored photos as well as the ability for users to manually "tag" photos with the person's name in any public photo and identify the faces of users, helping to organize and easily find photos of friends and family.

The main privacy issue affected by face recognition technology is the ability to covertly and more or less reliably identify persons using only the facial features extracted from a photograph. It therefore becomes possible to do this on a large scale and match faces in newly uploaded photographs with previously extracted facial features. This makes it possible to attribute online behavior and posts to specific users and infer more information like visited places or travel patterns.

If deployed widely enough or given a big enough database these systems can reliably track users online and offline movements (if used in CCTV systems), which could fundamentally change expectations of privacy, as it becomes possible for commercial enterprises to covertly track users and use the gathered information for advertising and other purposes. As it is undesirable or even impossible to constantly cover one's face when moving through the public sphere there is little a user can do to protect him or herself. However privacy-preserving facial algorithms do exist and are currently being researched which could help mitigate this problem [3].

4   Location-Based Applications and Dangers

While the use of GPS and facial recognition systems yields many benefits for users, the potential for misuse is high. Complications may arise from concatenating or merging separate data sets (thereby creating a complete profile of the user's social activities), using the acquired information in a new and unwanted context or even deriving new data from gathered profiles. Since most of this information is gathered by or stored at private companies, commercial interests play an important part.

As security expert Bruce Schneier recently pointed out, private companies are on the verge of becoming huge data collectors of personal information. With their business interests in marketing and profiling, this creates new kinds of threats that as of yet are not always fully governed by current laws. Schneier calls this new model "feudal security", whereby users have to place their trust with companies like Apple or Facebook [4].

Also, since most online map databases are operated by commercial enterprises, the aggregation of (new) location information is very valuable. Besides fee-based services from companies like Navteq or Tele-Atlas one of the biggest players is Google, which offers its "Google Maps" service and accompanied digital maps free of charge for end users. Users with smartphones running the Google-owned Android operating system (but also those using Apple's iOS devices) compulsorily transmit their phone's current location to Google each time the service is queried as these systems utilize the Google's database and maps.

If AGPS is being used, data identifying a user's location is also transmitted to either the cell phone carrier or – in the case of using WiFi data – to other companies like Skyhook Wireless[1]. Beyond that Google and Apple actively build up and maintain their own respective location databases utilizing the user's phone to (in the background) constantly transmit anonymized information about observed WiFi networks paired with a GPS location. Apple grants itself and its partners and licensees extensive rights to "collect, use, and share precise location data, including the real-time geographic location of your Apple computer or device" [5]. Accepting these terms of service is mandatory if a user wants to use the GPS features and "Location-Based Services" provided by Apple.

Even though clearly stated in the terms of service's privacy policy, concerns about the possibility of abuse led to outrage and criticism in 2010 in U.S. specialized and daily press as well as online publications [6-8]. In Germany federal commissioner for data protection (Bundesbeauftragter für den Datenschutz) Peter Schaar and federal consumer affairs minister (Bundesverbraucherschutzministerin) Ilse Aigner voiced concerns and condemned the hidden transmission of location data when using geolocation applications [9].

---

[1] Skyhook (http://www.skyhookwireless.com/) is one of the biggest companies offering MAC address to geographical location translation services.

Another example of hidden data transmission is online navigation systems for cars. These systems (available either as dedicated hardware or in the form of a mobile phone app) – while in navigation mode – transmit the car's exact position, speed and heading in regular intervals to the navigation system's manufacturer. The collected movement data is then used by the manufacturer to create traffic profiles and identify areas of traffic congestion. This information in turn is transmitted back to every connected navigation device, helping users of the system to avoid congested areas. The upside of this is highly accurate and up to date traffic information, the downside being that the manufacturer gains a complete movement profile of the user [10].

There is a strong imbalance between the commercial value of a complete movement profile and (in this case) the user's ability to better avoid traffic jams. It is technically easy to (covertly) collect and transmit GPS data. The associated monetary value makes this a desirable enterprise in the private sector with the main focus being the usage of a user's location especially for location-based ads (mobile ad targeting)[2]. The Trojan "AndroidOS.Tapsnake" for Android phones, which was discovered in 2010 by Symantec, exemplifies the value of location data. Disguised as a simple game, this program sends the user's location to a remote server that can be freely configured by the attacker.

The movement data of its citizens may also be of interest to the government as shown by the recent call for a GPS-based car toll system for German highways [11].

4.1   Location-Based Social Networks

The transmission of location data is not always hidden from the user. In fact in the majority of cases the user consciously and willingly initiates the transfer to gain some form of added value.

For example Apple's "Find my Friends" app – built into iOS version 5 – is based on this concept[3]. Users can allow their friends to track their location to arrange a meeting or quickly find one another in crowed public places. As long as the user does not block a "friend" again, he or she may constantly monitor the user's whereabouts. For this to work the device periodically send the user's location to Apple's servers which in turn theoretically allows Apple to create complete movement profiles of all participants.

Furthermore Internet enabled smartphones allow the user to participate in so-called location-based social networks. These networks make it possible (like "Find my Friends") to share the user's location in real-time with friends or others. Moreover they offer new forms of interaction like the possibility to collect "virtual badges" or get coupons by visiting certain hotels, restaurants or clubs. Known representatives of this genre are networks like Foursquare (http://www.foursquare.com), Gowalla (http://www.gowalla.com) and Google Latitude (http://www.google.com/latitude),

---

[2]   In fact Google owns a Patent concerning location-based advertising. See U.S. Patent number 8,138,930 "Advertising based on environmental conditions".

[3]   See "Find my Friends" and "Find my iPhone" at
http://www.apple.com/icloud/features/find-my.html

which enjoy increasing popularity. The allure of combining the virtual world of the Internet with the real world using location data hasn't passed social media giants like Facebook or Twitter. Both have for some time now offered the ability to enrich user posts with location data. The use cases for location enabled social networks are predominantly to make contact with other persons in the vicinity, play location-based games (with either virtual or real rewards) and to automatically record one's daily routing in a virtual diary [12].

Location data may also be used associate digital photos with the photograph's location (called Geotagging). Paired with Facebook's facial recognition and tagging ability this allows to identify a user at a given location even if the photo was taken by someone else. What all these services have in common is the concatenation of location data with personal information or posts, which can become a sort of "currency" within these services [13].

As is the case with any economic system, the increased availability of this type of data brings with it (besides benefits) an increased potential for commercial exploitation and misuse like identity theft. It is possible for these companies to generate detailed movement profiles from the aggregated data with insights into a user's daily routine, lifestyle and social contacts. This carries broad implications for user privacy rights and is in direct contrast to their expectation when using these services or networks. A user generally does not assume that his or her every step will be recorded, kept indefinitely and mined at any point in the future for alienated purposes.

The hazard potential is best made clear by the 2010 project "Please Rob Me" [14]. The algorithm on the associated website raided social networks for private information like home address, first and last name and the current location that users had posted publically. If distance between the home address and the current location stayed above a certain value for several days, the collected information was published on the site as an "opportunity" for theft. The authors wanted to raise awareness about the inherent dangers of location sharing in social networks.

The Electronic Frontier Foundation (EFF), a U.S.-based non-profit digital rights group, summarized this problem in 2009 and coined the term Locational Privacy as "the ability of an individual to move in public space with the expectation that under normal circumstances their location will not be systematically and secretly recorded for later use" [15]. Locational Privacy is a property worthy of protection, as it cannot be regained once the data has been shared.

5   Self Experiment

To bring this unperceived data to the surface and generate my own extensive movement profile to see what data can be inferred, I started my own experiment. For the past five years I have recorded all of my movements in the public sphere using several GPS receivers. With the collected data I was able to create and analyze a comprehensive movement profile. Of particular concern were questions about what conclusions about my social contacts and personal lifestyle could be drawn from my profile, and how much data over what time period was necessary to answer the first question to a high degree of accuracy.

The data was stored in the form of waypoints, which were arranged logically as tracks by my GPS receivers. Each time satellite reception was lost for more than 30 seconds or the device was turned on (usually when entering or leaving a building) a new track was created. If the device could determine my location, a waypoint was automatically recorded once every second if it was at least 5 meters apart from the last waypoint or a maximum of 5 seconds had passed.

The collected data was extracted from the devices using the open source software GPS-Babel (http://www.gpsbabel.org) and subsequently stored in a SQL database.

5.1   Data Analysis and Combination

Only two consecutive waypoints are needed to infer my current speed (using the difference between timestamps) and heading (creating a vector from the coordinates). Combining speed information with digital maps that show roads and train tracks, it was possible to reliably infer my mode of transportation, whether I was walking, riding a bike, driving a car or boat or even being a passenger in an airplane.

More importantly the accumulation of several consecutive waypoints around an area or a speed of 0 km/h would indicate that I stayed at a certain place for longer periods of time. If the time difference between the first and last recorded waypoint in this area was greater than 15 minutes this usually indicated that the place was somehow significant. It could be my residence, my place of work, hotel, restaurant or a doctor's office that I visited. To identify such significant places in the database I used time-based cluster analysis algorithms [16], which interpret the waypoint data as a directed graph (waypoints being the knots, the vector of two adjacent waypoints being an edge). The computed clusters represent waypoints of proximity in time and space. The time-based approach also eliminates intermittent measuring errors due bad GPS reception [17]. In this case all clusters represent significant places.

My next step was to attach a semantic meaning (like "Fernsehturm, Alexanderplatz, Panoramastraße 1a, Berlin, Germany") to every cluster using the Google's as well as the OpenStreetMap project's map databases. This information was stored again in my SQL database. Using the timestamps of each cluster I was able to construct a graph with chronologically sorted transitions between clusters representing my complete movement profile.

This profile showed every place I had visited and I could easily infer a lot of my lifestyle choices (e.g. what food I prefer based on the restaurants I had visited).

I was also able to construct a probability model by analyzing the frequency of transitions between two places in the graph. This allowed me to make educated guesses with a high degree of accuracy about my future movements, especially if they were part of my daily routine [18]. If I had the movement profile of other people (like social network operators do) I could have inferred all my social contacts using profile correlation.

Generally only 3 to 4 weeks worth of data was needed to create a 90% accurate probability model of future movements, the worst-case being 3 months worth of data.

5.2   Technical, Lawful, Social Restrictions/Limits

My experiment faced pragmatic and technical limits that prevented a complete capture in certain situations. Sometimes it was not possible to wait for a satellite fix after turning on the receiver (as not all receivers I used had AGPS) due to time constraints or pressure from colleagues to start walking. Due to the low power nature and chosen frequency of the GPS signal the radio waves can only penetrate bodies of water up to a depth of about 2 meters. This meant that I could not record any of my scuba dives. When travelling in an airplane all electronic devices must be switched off during taxiing, takeoff and landing, which prevented me from recording a complete flight. Reception was generally only possible in a window seat given the shielded nature of airplanes. Lastly certain countries like Egypt prohibit the use and possession of civilian GPS receivers. Despite these constraints I was able to construct a complete movement profile. For further details on how the conscious process of recording affected my behavior in the public space and data visualization techniques see [19].

6   Conclusion

Portable GPS receivers like mobile phones or navigation systems have permeated our daily life and allow for new and interesting usage scenarios and applications. The (unwanted) continuous transmission of location data via a return channel as well as the enrichment of personal information or photos with location data in social networks, however, have a high potential for misuse with concrete ramifications for a user's privacy and data protection. Combined with facial recognition technology and the ability to tag persons in photos on social media networks this allows for an even higher degree of surveillance and yields the ability to connect location data with the identity of a user. In addition face recognitions systems are covert by nature and do not require any action or presence on part of the user.

The experiment shows how easy it is to collect and process GPS data. Users are generally unaware of the extent to which their data are transmitted, processed and used, which creates a gap between what is technically possible and a user's assessment of the situation. Using cluster analysis I was able to determine all significant places in my daily routine, create a detailed movement profile and make highly accurate predictions about my lifestyle choices and future movements. On the one hand the wealth of information that can be deducted is frightening. On the other hand the conclusion should not be to avoid geolocation services and applications, as they offer many benefits. Rather one should take the EFF's position and educate users about the process, clearly explain benefits and possible dangers, and teach a principle of data economy.

This could help users to critically reflect on the services they use. In addition many services have data protection and privacy settings that can be enabled by the user. Smartphones using Android or iOS, for example, have the ability to disable location sharing on a per-app basis. Additionally it is the job of regulators to augment current privacy laws to better reflect current use cases and to set up barriers for companies and government bodies on what information may be recorded and in what context it may be processed and used. These new systems need to have locational privacy built-in.

References

1. Xu, G.: GPS – Theory, Algorithms and Applications, 2nd edn. Springer, Berlin (2007)
2. Dodel, H., Häupler, D.: Satellitennavigation, 2. korrigierte und erweiterte Auflage. Springer, Berlin (2010)
3. Sadeghi, A.-R., Schneider, T., Wehrenberg, I.: Efficient Privacy-Preserving Face Recognition. In: Lee, D., Hong, S. (eds.) ICISC 2009. LNCS, vol. 5984, pp. 229–244. Springer, Heidelberg (2010)
4. Goodin, D.: Schneier: government, big data pose bigger 'Net threat than criminals. In: ars technica, blog article (February 23, 2012),
   http://arstechnica.com/business/news/2012/02/schneier-gov-big-data-pose-bigger-net-threat-than-criminals.ars
5. Apple: Privacy Policy, http://www.apple.com/privacy/ (last revised October 2011)
6. Sarno, D.: Apple Collecting, Sharing iPhone Users' Precise Locations, Los Angeles Times Online, http://latimesblogs.latimes.com/technology/2010/06/apple-location-privacy-iphone-ipad.html
7. Allan, A., Warden, P.: Got an iPhone or 3G iPad? Apple is recording your moves, O'Reilly radar (April 20, 2010), http://radar.oreilly.com/2011/04/apple-location-tracking.html
8. Johnson, B.: Researcher: iPhone Location Data Already Used By Cops, GigaOM Blog (April 21, 2011), http://gigaom.com/2011/04/21/researcher-iphone-location-data-already-used-by-cops/
9. Meyer, C.: Datenschutzbeauftragter warnt vor Missbrauch bei Handy-Ortung, Heise-Newsticker (May 30, 2010), http://heise.de/-1010712
10. Greene, K.: Staumeldung gegen Bewegungsprofil, Technology Review Online (November 25, 2008), http://www.heise.de/tr/artikel/Staumeldung-gegen-Bewegungsprofil-275834.html
11. Barczok, A.: Kretschmann will satellitengestützte PKW-Maut, Heise-Newsticker (October 16, 2011), http://heise.de/-1361871
12. Kirkpatrick, M.: Why We Check In. The Reasons People Use Location-Based Social Networks, ReadWriteWeb, http://www.readwriteweb.com/archives/why_use_location_checkin_apps.php
13. Heuer, S.: Sag mir, wo Du bist! – Geodaten werden zur neuen Währung im Web – mit zwiespältigen Folgen für Anbieter und Nutzer. Technology Review, 07, 44–49 (2010)
14. Borsboom, B., van Amstel, B., Groeneveld, F.: Please Rob Me – Raising Awareness about Over-Sharing, http://pleaserobme.com/
15. EFF – Electronic Frontier Foundation (ed.): On Locational Privacy, and How to Avoid Losing it Forever, Whitepaper, San Francisco, CA (2009),
    http://www.eff.org/wp/locational-privacy
16. Cao, X., et al.: Mining Significant Semantic Locations from GPS Data. Proceedings of the VLDB Endowment 3, 1009–1020 (2010)
17. Kang, J.H., et al.: Extracting Places from Traces of Locations. ACM SIGMOBILE Mobile Computing and Communications Review 9(3), 58–68 (2005)
18. Gutjahr, A.: Bewegungsprofile und -vorhersage, LBS/Location Awareness - Technische Hintergründe und juristische Implikationen, http://www.ks.uni-freiburg.de/download/papers/interdiszWS08/Alexander_Gutjahr.pdf
19. Loebel, J.-M.: Aus dem Tagebuch eines Selbstaufzeichners. Laborgespräch mit Ute Holl und Claus Pias. In: Zeitschrift für Medienwissenschaft, Volume 4 – Menschen & Andere, pp. 115–125. Akademie Verlag, Berlin (2011)

Theorising Open Development through an Institutional Lens: A Study of Iranian Online Interactions

Magda David Hercheui[1], Brian Nicholson[2], and Aghil Ameripour[2]

[1] Westminster Business School, London, United Kingdom
m.hercheui@westminster.ac.uk
[2] Manchester Business School, Manchester, United Kingdom
brian.nicholson@manchester.ac.uk, ameripour@googlemail.com

Abstract. Open development has been conceptualised as initiatives that use information technology to foster citizen participation and freedom of debate in development projects. The Internet has brought hope that citizens would have an opportunity to organise campaigns, thus fostering democracy. These possibilities face a number of obstacles. Analysing case evidence from Iran, this study explores how institutions have influenced the forms of appropriation of Internet tools in initiatives intended to enable open development. The paper contributes to our understanding of institutional mechanisms for controlling and constraining open development initiatives, and the relevance of institutional environments when planning open development projects.

Keywords: democracy, institutional theory, Internet, Iran, open development.

1   Introduction

The idea that openness is an important step towards development has been explored by academic research. In the field of development studies (social science studies on developing countries), it is proposed that democracy and political freedom are important fundamental elements for development [26]. The emergence of the Internet and other computer networks has brought a new perspective on openness. Some scholars posit that information technology may foster freedom of expression, enabling citizens to have more participation in political processes [5].

Some authors have related open development to the possibilities that emerge when open information networked activities are fostered in particular environments and societies [27]. The idea of openness in development studies is broadly related to many aspects of adopting and appropriating information technology, from having access to technology and its use to being able to reach relevant content and to participate in the creation of content. Open development refers to a set of possibilities to catalyse positive change through open information networked activities. Openness that serves the purpose of development implies that positive outcomes are expected when societies engage in a participatory way, e.g. when people have access to network technologies enabling democracy, freedom of expression, inclusion, and participation in decision

M.D. Hercheui et al. (Eds.): HCC10 2012, IFIP AICT 386, pp. 349–359, 2012.

making on matters which are relevant for them [27]. However, it is also expected that such citizen participation would impact power structures in society, fostering institutional change [2]. In such a situation, attempts to foster open development may face opposition from particular social actors who fear losing power, especially in countries in which citizen engagement and freedom of expression are suppressed.

Prior research has considered whether the Internet may foster more democratic institutions, permitting citizens to share opinions and information, and offer tools for political mobilisation [5], [8], [12], [23]. On the one hand, in some contexts, the Internet opens up spaces for public debates and citizen empowerment [10], [13], [14], [23], [29]; on the other hand, states also have instruments to control Internet interactions and to use Internet tools to increase citizen surveillance, especially in environments which do not have functional democratic institutions [1], [15], [19], [20].

State institutions influence the way Internet tools are appropriated. This has been seen when access to the Internet was curtailed to prevent the use of social media (such as YouTube, Facebook, Twitter, and Blogs) during turbulent political manifestations in Egypt and Libya in 2011, as broadly discussed by news media[1] and some academic papers[2]. Another example is the prosecution of activists who use the Internet to oppose political power in China[3] and Iran[4]. This study proposes to investigate how state institutions influence the forms of appropriation of Internet tools in open development initiatives.

This research focuses on two case studies in Iran, in which citizens have used Internet tools to manifest their opinions in political debates. The first case describes the story of an Iranian news website (Alef) which questioned the nomination of a Minister of Interior in 2008. The second case explores two Iranian activist movements which rely on the Internet (websites, blogs and forums) to organise and communicate with citizens. One fights for women's equal rights (1 Million Signature Campaign), and another focuses on stopping stoning, the punishment reserved for those who are condemned to execution for adultery (Stop Stoning Forever Campaign). Both movements, studied in 2007, challenge established institutions in Iranian society.

This study reveals that there is evidence that Internet tools enable citizen empowerment; however, the Iranian state possesses legitimating and sanction mechanisms to

---

[1] http://www.guardian.co.uk/world/2011/dec/29/arab-spring-captured-on-cameraphones?INTCMP=SRCH;
http://www.guardian.co.uk/technology/2011/jul/07/telecomix-arab-spring?INTCMP=SRCH;
http://www.guardian.co.uk/world/2011/dec/25/egyptian-judge-frees-blogger?INTCMP=SRCH

[2] http://www.caida.org/publications/papers/2011/outages_censorship/outages_censorship.pdf

[3] http://cyber.law.harvard.edu/filtering/china/;
http://en.wikipedia.org/wiki/Internet_censorship_in_the_People%27s_Republic_of_China

[4] http://www.guardian.co.uk/world/2012/jan/05/iran-clamps-down-internet-use;
http://en.wikipedia.org/wiki/Internet_censorship_in_Iran

constrain this empowerment. The paper is organised as follows: the next section introduces an operational summary of institutional theory. Subsequently, the methodology used to collect data is explained. This is followed by the case description, and analysis of cases. In the final section are the conclusions.

2   Institutional Theory

Institutions are understood as resilient social structures that are reproduced in society. In other words, institutions may be defined as social behaviour that follows defined patterns and is diffused through settings and times [3], [25].

Supported by rules, norms, and cultural-cognitive systems, institutions are resilient: it is difficult to change established social structures [6], [25]. However, society also has a degree of freedom to change institutions, either because there are conflicts of interest between social actors or because new contexts and situations emerge [11], [16]. In any society, there are institutions which are in conflict with each other [16]. Thus, institutions may be changed at any time, when social actors act in the direction of fostering new social structures [16].

In addition to rules, norms and cultural-cognitive systems, sanction mechanisms of reward and punishment support the reproduction of institutions [11], [25]. When behaviour is institutionalised, it implies that society has the means to control it [3]. For instance, judicial systems apply judgment based on rules and control mechanisms of punishment; society disapproves and ostracises people who do not comply with norms [21]. Powerful actors keep the control of resources, which are fundamental for applying sanction mechanisms, either rewarding those who comply with the institutions or imposing punishment on those who not [18], [21].

Legitimacy is also a relevant pillar of institutions. Within a social system, when a pattern of behaviour is understood as appropriate in a given situation, society attributes legitimacy to actors that repeat such behaviour [21], [28]. Legitimacy depends on conformity to rules, norms and cognitive frames of reference [18], [21]. Social actors may comply with institutions as a way of obtaining social legitimacy, thus increasing their chances of receiving resources from society [18]. However, legitimacy is not without ambiguity: actions may be interpreted as legitimate, or not, according to different perspectives and contexts [3], [16].

3   Methodology

This research follows an interpretive approach to explore the meanings social actors give to their actions in particular situations [3], [9]. The approach is particularly interesting to understand the how institutions influence behaviour, and how behaviour reinforce and challenge institution. The data collection is based on semi-structured interviews (nine related to the case of activist movements) (table 1) and content analysis of the material published on the websites and blogs studied (Alef's website and 30 blogs related to both activist movements) [7], [17].

Interviews were limited in number because of the sensitivity of the theme: activists feared to be identified. Interviews were conducted by phone or the Internet, to protect the identity of interviewees. Because of the limited number of interviews, this research focuses mainly on incorporating content analysis of published material. The interviews have aimed to confirm details observed on websites and to explore topics that were not present in the published content.

Table 1. Details of the interviews

Role	Gender	Communication Channel	Date	Duration
Feminist activist	Female (assumed)	Email	23/04/2007	Not applicable
Feminist activist	Female (assumed)	Email	14/07/2007	Not applicable
Feminist activist	Female (assumed)	Email	29/07/2007	Not applicable
Blogger 1	Unknown	Email	12/06/2007	Not applicable
Blogger 2	Unknown	Email	01/07/2007	Not applicable
An academic involved in the developments of the Iranian Internet	Male	Email	05/04/2007	Not applicable
Mayoral candidate	Female	Telephone interview	20/07/2007	Approximately 40 minutes
Senior official from the Ministry of ICT, Iran	Male	Telephone interview	11/04/2007	Approximately 40 minutes
Previously jailed blogger (Journalist)	Male	Telephone interview	02/07/2007	Approximately 40 minutes

From these primary data (available in Farsi), the research has built constructs (in English), which in this paper are presented below as case descriptions. The descriptions are narratives (second-level constructs) which summarise both cases. They take into consideration first-level constructs from interviews and content analysis (expressions also come from contributions to websites and blogs) [24]. All second-level constructs have been confirmed from more than one source (triangulation of sources) [4]. The final descriptions have been verified against the original data, confirming that the narratives are coherent and logically consistent with both sets of data, in such a way that the parts and the whole are meaningfully connected [9], [17].

This research has confirmed the symmetry between the case and the analysis, and the theoretical coherence between the case description, the analysis and institutional theory [9], [17]. The research is limited, however, in the number of cases and the timeframe of the investigation. Longitudinal analysis and a bigger number of cases could bring light to other aspects relevant to understanding the studied cases.

4   Case Description

This research is based on two case studies that show forms of Internet tools that have been appropriated by different segments of Iranian citizens towards open development. It includes people who are resident inside and outside the country, during the studied timeframe (2007-2008). The cases illustrate two sets of findings, bringing examples of open development that respect and challenge institutions.

4.1   Open Development Respecting State Institutions

The first case involves an Iranian news website that involved its readership in online questioning of the forged qualifications of a Minister leading eventually to his impeachment. In August 2008, the validity of the Honorary Doctorate of Law degree from Oxford University held by Ali Kordan was disputed during his confirmation hearings as the Minister of Interior. The news agency Alef (http://www.alef.ir), headed by Ahmad Tavakkoli questioned the validity of the degree and published information that the University has no record of Kordan as a PhD student.

In spite of the state having issued warnings to Iranian media that recommended against the reporting of this topic, Alef began a campaign by asking readers to bring evidence on the certificate's authenticity. Alef readers, mainly through anonymous contributions (the website does not ask participants to use their real names), provided evidence that refuted the legitimacy of the degree. The mobilisation against the minister then spread to wider groups of citizens (not only those related to Alef), including university student groups which demanded the removal of Kordan.

Alef's campaign encountered state countermeasures when the Prosecutor General of Tehran imposed the filtering of the website (12th August 2008), alleging there were multiple legal actions filed against Alef. Iranian Internet Service Providers (ISPs) complied, but not all providers were able to implement the filtering immediately. Alef responded by continuing to publish content related to Kordan and permitting members to access the website through other proxies (mirror websites such as alef.com and alef-1.ir), thus avoiding the censorship imposed. Subsequently Alef complied with the recommendation to stop publishing (19th August 2008) until clearance was given for the website to resume without filtering by the head of the Judiciary.

In spite of suffering sanctions on website access, Alef continued to lead the action which generated protests and petitions all around the country against Kordan and which focused on the evidence of a forged degree certificate. The campaign against Kordan gained momentum until, finally, the Iranian parliament dismissed Kordan. Table 2 summarises the development of the case.

The dismissal of Kordan appears to present a significant victory for the proponents of open development as citizens used Internet channels to share knowledge that led to the eventual removal the official. However, Alef used the Internet to challenge the nomination of an individual to an official post without challenging state institutions. The campaign was conducted against Kordan although, in challenging him, Alef risked opposing the Iranian state which had nominated and defended Kordan until his impeachment.

Alef required legal authorisation to operate under State monitoring. It did not have the goal of confronting the state. Alef moderated all readership contributions on the Kordan issue. Each message has been approved by editors before being published online in accordance with their political perspective on appropriateness. Many of the published contributions reiterated trust in the Iranian state, and questioned Kordan instead as an individual. Thus, the campaign was not associated clearly to the opposition to the State institutions.

The Alef case is promising for the practice of open development in developing countries, but the challenge was personally focused on an individual rather than on institutions. Anonymous contributions interrogated the authenticity of the degree document, and Alef overcame filtering during the period of the campaign against Kordan. However, the website also self-censored its own content, and complied with the confirmation of its legal status in the Iranian judiciary system.

Table 2. Development of Kordan's case

Event	Date (2008)
Parliament gives vote of confidence to Kordan	5th August
Oxford denies any record of Ali Kordan's degree	6th August
Media warned not to speculate on the case	9th August
The degree certificate published and refuted by Alef's readers	10th August
Oxford refutes the published certificate	11th August
Investigation group assigned by the Parliament	11th August
Alef is filtered	12th August
Alef imposes self-censure	19th August
Filter is removed	6th September
Kordan admits that the degree is fake	30th September
Parliament removes the minister from his role	6th November

4.2   Open Development Challenging State Institutions

The second case explores more radical approaches to open development. The cases of two Iranian activist movements with the express aim of mobilising support to confront the state and changing aspects of the legal framework are presented. The two campaigns rely on Internet tools to organise campaigns to fight for women's equal rights (1 Million Signature Campaign), and to stop stoning (Stop Stoning Forever Campaign). Both activist movements, studied in 2007, use Internet tools (websites, blogs and forums) to organise the campaign.

The 1 Million Signature Campaign depends mainly on Internet tools to mobilise citizens' action and distribute educational information to women. For instance, PayPal was used to raise money to finance the legal costs of a woman facing the death penalty for having killed a man who allegedly was trying to rape her. The feminist websites also publishes photos, news and content that are banned from Iranian media for being considered by the state as threats to the Islamic Republic.

The Stop Stoning campaign challenges the legislation which allows the death penalty for stoning for those who are condemned of adultery, a punishment prescribed by the Iranian constitution and based on Sharia Law. The campaigners do not challenge Sharia Law, but that its rules have not been followed by judges. The movement aims to ban stoning from the constitution; in the short term, the objective is stopping those convicted of adultery from being stoned. The feminist and stop stoning movements confront Iranian institutions, thereby challenging the state. Both movements oppose institutions that are pervasive and resilient in Iranian society: the discrimination of women and the punishment of adultery by stoning.

Both movements depend mainly on anonymous contributions, as contributors risk punishment. Websites and blogs linked to these campaigns are registered in other countries (they are illegal in Iran), and their content is censured in Iran.

Both movements use Internet tools to overcome the filtering imposed by the Iranian state, by using proxies (URLs that are not in the list of filtered sites, which redirect communications to correct addresses) and gateways (addresses that disguise censors, presenting content within a URL that is not filtered) to permit access to content. Furthermore, both movements observe a high degree of support among similar websites and blogs to overcome state censorship. When the state censures a URL that is related to the movements, another URL or proxy is created. The network of supporters informs others how to access the censured page, overcoming the blockage.

In spite of their efforts, both movements have had limited success in changing the Iranian institutions. Stoning is still legal, although stoning has been stopped on isolated occasions. Campaigners publish the contact details of officials and details of execution arrangements, thus activists can gather to protest and impede the stoning in the locale. The 1 Million Signature Campaign attracted only a few thousand signatures. The campaign experienced some success, however, in changes to the law on the right to maternal citizenship of children born from non-Iranian fathers.

5   Analysis

Drawing on institutional theory, this section analyses how state institutions influence the forms of appropriation of Internet tools in open development initiatives.

5.1   Institutional Legitimacy

The legitimacy of open development initiatives is an important precursor to the success of the campaigns. The Alef website is legally registered in Iran, recognised by the Iranian state. In the campaign against Kordan, Alef framed its action in accordance with the state institutional legal system. Although it published content during the initial stage of filtering, it did so understanding that no judicial order has been issued against the agency. Alef applied self-censure, interrupting activities until confirming its legal status. In addition, Alef was owned by a member of the parliament, Ahmad Tavakkoli, who had the political support of peers to question the validity of the degree and the appropriateness of having a minister who has allegedly faked documents.

In contrast, the campaigners in activist movements do not register their websites and blogs in the Iranian legal system, and thus do not having legal legitimacy in the country. The lack of institutional legitimacy implies access to websites and blogs requires knowledge of tactics on how to find the actual material, and many citizens avoid engaging with the websites for fear of being punished.

5.2   Punishment Mechanisms

The cases demonstrate how punishment mechanisms act to impede open development in numerous ways. In spite of not having a formal court order, the Iranian state filtered Alef, blocking access to its content. In the first days of the filtering, Alef maintained its activities by using proxies to reach readers. Subsequently, it stopped publishing until legal compliance was established, avoiding prosecution. ISPs could also be prosecuted if they did not comply with the legal order of filtering Alef.

In contrast, feminist and stop stoning activists maintain their anonymity and operate through URLs that were not registered in Iran. If activists in Iran are discovered, they are prosecuted and imprisoned, and run the risk of torture and even death in the country's prisons. Citizens may be punished if they are discovered reading or contributing to illegal websites and blogs. Finally, ISP owners and professionals face risks of prosecution and imprisonment if they do not comply with the filtering orders.

5.3   Fostering Institutional Change

Alef has been successful in proving the disputed degree was fake. The minister lost his position, which may seem like a success story for open development. However, formal institutions have not changed: the episode finished with the punishment of an individual. For instance, there are no new institutional mechanisms that request more transparency and accountability from the state on the qualifications of ministers. However, the impeachment may have influence in the future questioning of decisions regarding ministerial appointments.

The activist movements have also not been able to change the legal system during the period of analysis in 2007. However, the stop stoning campaign has been successful in creating actual obstacles to stoning. Activists announce the details of planned execution, mobilising action which has resulted in cancellations. Calling attention to specific causes emphasises voices in society with different perspectives on particular institutions which may over time support activist movements both inside and outside Iran. Even though this does not represent institutional change per se, showing that institutions are contested may be an important step for fostering change [22].

5.4   The Role of the Internet

Alef is a registered website that depends on having a formal URL, which is controlled by the Iranian state. Alef may publish contributions from anonymous citizens but the agency is responsible for the published content. Indeed, Alef is the gatekeeper of contributions that are published on the website. The readers do not have access to what people post before moderation, but to what Alef permits the audience to know about what people have posted.

For instance, during the campaign against Kordan, 25% of the contributions were not published. The diversity of opinions presented, with some readers supporting and some opposing Alef's questioning of the document, may not represent the whole spectrum of contributions. The centralised approach adopted by Alef, through moderation of contributions, permits the organisation to select the spectrum and frequency of opinions in its website. Alef depends on this centralised model to have a legal URL. The chosen centralised technological infrastructure is thus coherent with the institutional status of the news agency.

The activist movements use technology differently to build a decentralised collaborative network. Internet interfaces may be set up by many providers, mainly in other countries, to direct content to Iran. The state may force Iranian ISPs to filter specific Internet addresses and key words. However, because of the decentralised nature of activist networks, there is a cat and mouse game between state censorship and activists which are able to change URLs, use proxies and gateways to circumvent the filtering of their web interfaces, and operate in other countries. This decentralised technological infrastructure allows diverse content on activist websites. Activists are anonymous, which permits them to be stronger in their criticisms. Also activists support each other by giving links to filtered URLs. This network of bloggers keeps censured websites accessible, even when their perspectives are not the same.

There is the possibility of moderation in these platforms (each blog may have moderation). However, if one blog excludes a particular opinion, the censured person may send the same content to another network node. The fragmented design of these networks (with their decentralised content production) makes it impossible for one node to control what is available in the whole network of activists.

6   Concluding Discussion

This paper brings two theoretical contributions to the discussion on open development. Firstly, it shows how institutions may affect open development projects. It identifies the relevance of considering the institutional context when planning open development initiatives, since powerful social actors are able to mobilise against institutional changes which challenge social structures from which they benefit. Secondly, it illustrates different models of technology appropriation when facing state constraints to open development projects, and it contrasts centralised and decentralised structures in using technology and producing content. These arguments are explained below.

This paper shows the complex interaction between forms of appropriation of technology and the institutional environment. Internet tools per se do not define whether the appropriation fosters more democratic social structures. Internet tools offer an opportunity for intensifying citizen participation and freedom of debate. However, the state has mechanisms to limit and frame this expression of dissent through filtering and censuring Internet spaces, in association with legal and illegal punishment mechanisms (from prosecution and imprisonment, to torture and execution).

Activist movements show that it is possible to overcome state censure through the use of technical tactics (for example, changing URLs, creating proxies, using portals, and linking decentralised groups of blogs). However this implies that activists need to have substantial technical knowledge to operate in this environment. Even more difficult, readers and contributors also need to have considerable technical knowledge to find related websites and blogs. In addition, citizens in Iran may avoid reading activist content, fearing punishment. In such a repressive institutional environment, the availability of tools and contents are not enough to engage citizens in open development initiatives, especially when they do not have knowledge of the use of Internet tools and do not understand the actual risks of engagement.

The cases also point out that a decentralised strategy of content production, and loosely coupled networks of websites and blogs, may be an interesting tactic to overcome state censure. This model is more democratic in allowing the emergence of a broader range of opinions. However, states may be efficient in generating filters and in identifying contributors and supporters. The more efficient the mechanisms for identifying users, the more difficult it is to use Internet-mediated communication as a means to organise democratic debate in non-democratic environments.

The relevance of the institutional environment can be expected to be present in other initiatives that use information technology for fostering open development. This study focuses on only two cases that explore the interaction as means of fostering freedom of expression. Other studies would be necessary to understand how the appropriation of information technology for open development is affected by institutional environments in other contexts.

This study has results which indicate the limitations of Internet tools as instruments for fostering open development. Although a certain level of freedom of debate has been reached through virtual interactions, the mobilisation of citizens through the Internet has not yet been able to change Iranian institutions substantially. This paper points out thus that the resilience of institutions should be taken into account when practitioners are planning for open development. Understanding institutions, and their related legitimating and sanction mechanisms, may help to foresee obstacles to the changing of power structures brought by open development initiatives.

References

1. Alavi, N.: We are Iran. Portobello, London (2006)
2. Avgerou, C.: Discourses on ICT and development. Information Technologies and International Development 6(3), 1–18 (2010)
3. Berger, P., Luckmann, T.: The Social Construction of Reality. Allen Lane The Penguin Press, London (1966-1967)
4. Bryman, A.: Social Research Methods, 3rd edn. Oxford University Press, Oxford (2008)
5. Castells, M.: The Internet Galaxy. Oxford University Press, Oxford (2001)
6. DiMaggio, P.J., Powell, W.W.: The Iron Cage Revisited: Institutional Isomorphism and Collective Rationality in Organizational Fields. In: Powell, W.W., DiMaggio, P.J. (eds.) The New Institutionalism in Organizational Analysis, pp. 63–82. The University of Chicago Press, Chicago (1991 (1983))
7. Esterberg, K.G.: Qualitative Methods in Social Research. McGraw-Hill, Boston (2002)

8. Feenberg, A.: Critical Theory of Communication Technology: Introduction to the Special Section. The Information Society 25(2), 77–83 (2009)

9. Gadamer, H.: Truth and Method, 2nd edn. Sheed and Ward, London (1975 (1989))

10. Grant, W.J., Moon, B., Grant, J.B.: Digital Dialogue? Australian Politicians' use of the Social Network Tool Twitter. Australian Journal of Political Science 45(4), 579–604 (2010)

11. Jepperson, R.L.: Institutions, institutional effects and institutionalism. In: Powell, W.W., DiMaggio, P.J. (eds.) The New Institutionalism in Organizational Analysis, pp. 143–163. The University of Chicago Press, Chicago (1991)

12. Jones, S.G.: Understanding community in the information age. In: Jones, S.G. (ed.) Cybersociety: Computer-mediated Communication and Community, pp. 10–35. Sage Publications, London (1995)

13. Kahn, R., Kellner, D.: New media and internet activism: From the 'Battle of Seattle' to blogging. New Media and Society 6, 87–95 (2004)

14. Kim, Y.: The contribution of social network sites to exposure to political difference: The relationships among SNSs, online political messaging, and exposure to cross-cutting perspectives. Computers in Human Behavior 27, 971–977 (2011)

15. Klang, M.: Virtual censorship: controlling the public sphere. In: Berleur, J., Numinen, M.I., Impagliazzo, J. (eds.) Social Informatics: An Information Society for All? In Remembrance of Rob Kling. IFIP, vol. 223, pp. 185–194. Springer, Boston (2006)

16. March, J.G., Olsen, J.P.: Rediscovering Institutions: the Organizational Basis of Politics. Free Press, New York (1989)

17. Mason, J.: Qualitative Researching, 2nd edn. Sage Publications, London (2002)

18. Meyer, J.W., Rowan, B.: Institutionalised Organizations: Formal Structures and Myth and Ceremony. The American Journal of Sociology 83(2), 340–363 (1977)

19. Morozov, E.: The Net Delusion: How Not to Liberate the World. Allen Lane, London (2011)

20. Norris, P.: Digital Divide: Civic Engagement, Information Poverty, and the Internet Worldwide. Cambridge University Press, Cambridge (2001)

21. North, D.C.: Institutions, Institutional Change and Economic Performance. Cambridge University Press, Cambridge (1990)

22. Oliver, C.: The antecedents of desinstitutionalization. Organisation Studies 13(4), 563–588 (1992)

23. Rheingold, H.: The Virtual Community: Homesteading on the Electronic Frontier, rev. edn. MIT Press, Cambridge (1993 (2000))

24. Schutz, A.: Collected Papers: The Problem of Social Reality. M. Nijhoff, The Hague (1962)

25. Scott, W.R.: Institutions and Organizations, 2nd edn. Sage Publications, London (2001)

26. Sen, A.: Development as Freedom. Alfred A. Knopf, New York (1999)

27. Smith, M.L., Elder, L., Emdon, H.: Open Development: A new theory for ICT4D. Information Technology and International Development 7(1), iii–ix (2011)

28. Suchman, M.C.: Managing legitimacy: strategic and institutional approaches. Academy of Management Review 20(3), 571–610 (1995)

29. Wheeler, D.L.: Working around the state: internet use and political identity in the Arab world. In: Chadwick, A., Howard, P.N. (eds.) Routledge Handbook of Internet Politics, pp. 305–320. Routledge, London (2009)

Packet Inspection — Shifting the Paradigm of Fundamental Rights

Agata Królikowski

Humboldt-Universität zu Berlin, Department of Computer Science, Berlin, Germany
krolikow@informatik.hu-berlin.de

Abstract. In recent years deep packet inspection (DPI) has often been cited as a major factor in the debate concerning net neutrality. Packet inspection (PI) enables a profound analysis of the contents of IP-packets, especially with respect to the application layer and private data. To protect against this sort of privacy invading attack users are usually advised to encrypt as much of their data as possible in an online transaction. However, current PI-engines not only use plain text analysis but also employ a variety of statistical methods. This in turn allows the analysis and classification of packets even if encryption or obfuscation methods have been applied. It is possible to monitor and shape packet flows in real time and on a large scale. These PI-engines are deeply embedded in the current network infrastructure due to the requirements of lawful interception. This brings about a huge potential for misuse, because the engine's operation is not 'visible' to the end-user.

Keywords: packet inspection, fundamental rights.

1   Introduction

The following paper reflects a recurring debate concerning how far technology may push the legal envelope. This aspect is particularly noticeable in technologies such as nuclear power plants, where the question arises: to what extent is the state under obligation to protect the rights of its citizens [1], [2]? In this example, the fundamental rights involved are the right to life or environmental protection — which for example in Germany is a constitutional principle, pursuant to Article 2 and 20 a Grundgesetz (GG) — and shows impressively the tension between a technological advance and legal boundaries. Technological developments may lead into a legal grey area where fundamental rights still apply but the lack of regulations makes it likely that these rights will not be enforced. This aspect also occurs in packet inspection (PI) since analyses in telecommunication systems also affect fundamental rights such as the protection of private data, the privacy of correspondence, posts and telecommunications,[1] freedom of expression and

---

[1] Article 8 of the Charter of Fundamental Rights of the European Union, the German Bundesdatenschutzgesetz (BDSG) or § 88 and Section 2 of the Telekommunikationsgesetz (TKG).

M.D. Hercheui et al. (Eds.): HCC10 2012, IFIP AICT 386, pp. 360–368, 2012.

information,[2] freedom of the arts and science,[3] freedom to conduct a business,[4] freedom of thought, conscience and religion,[5] or freedom of assembly and of association.[6]

The question at hand is not the use of PI in the way it is used in non-democratic countries, e.g., to censor information [3], [4], but how PI may affect fundamental rights when it is used according to its purposes: to secure networks, to shape traffic, or to allow new pricing models.

Another concern is that in contrast to civil law, which regulates the matter between private persons, fundamental rights may only be enforceable against the state. Since networks are operated by private corporations this raises the question of how and with whom should protections of fundamental rights that may be affected by PI be enforced. This implies also both the questions of how to regulate the use of PI and how to implement regulations regarding the technology as a regulatory subject.

This paper addresses different aspects of packet inspection. Starting with general concepts such as the development and challenges of packet inspection it is shown that for Internet users it is virtually impossible to protect themselves against packet inspection in a technical manner. Section 3 describes the use cases of packet inspection. Section 4 describes why as a result from section 2 and 3 fundamental civil rights cannot be enforced by or guaranteed to the Internet users.

2   Technical Aspects of PI

Network packets are pieces of information that consist of a header and the payload. Packet inspection first emerged in the 1980s [5]. While early firewall systems performed analyses on the network layer, better hardware and new approaches lead to firewalls that were both able to examine packets on different OSI layers and to keep track of sessions and connections (thus, called stateful PI). These different concepts are unified in current PI systems that combine firewalls, stateful PI, and intrusion detection systems (IDS) [6].

An analysis consists of two phases. In the first phase, patterns (signatures) of packets or flows are examined. In the second phase, packets are classified based upon these signatures and – depending on their class – forwarded, delayed or dropped.

These signatures can be determined in different ways. Regarding the OSI model, PI performed on different layers it is called shallow, medium, or deep packet inspection (DPI). DPI therefore denotes the analysis of every bit of a packet including every header and personal data like emails, chat messages, pictures or passwords [6], [7].

However, generating signatures by analyzing data streams bit by bit involves many difficulties. String matching algorithms require a lot of storage and processing power.

---

[2] Article 11 of the Charter of Fundamental Rights of the European Union, Article 5 GG.
[3] Article 13 of the Charter of Fundamental Rights of the European Union, Article 5 GG.
[4] Article 16 of the Charter of Fundamental Rights of the European Union, Article 12 GG.
[5] Article 1 of the Charter of Fundamental Rights of the European Union, Article 4 GG.
[6] For example in Germany Article 12 of the Charter of Fundamental Rights of the European Union, Article 9 GG.

In addition to this, the analyses have to be performed at wire speed since packet delays may cause a network bottleneck. Common throughput rates in networks now are 10 Gbit per second, a newer standard called 100 GbE (with a throughput up to 100 Gbit per second) is on the horizon [6], [9].

Therefore, on the one hand, existing string matching algorithms have been evolved, while on the other hand special purpose hardware has been developed. String matching algorithms accomplish classification by either comparing predefined (exact) strings, regular expressions, or calculating hash values [6]. New hardware systems like the Advanced Telecommunications Computing Architecture or new processor designs like hybrid multi-core architectures are highly specialized and therefore able to meet the demands of real time and accurate (i.e., false positive rates are below 1%) analysis [10], [12].

But DPI fails as soon as the data are encrypted or obfuscated. Encryption not only replaces plain text with cipher text but also changes the distribution of occurring characters and thus removes links between the plain and the cipher text. Methods based on string matching algorithms or hash values are not able to reliably classify signatures anymore.

This is a significant drawback since encryption is used in standard protocols such as SSH, SSL/TLS, IPSec or in implementations like PGP, just to name a few. Therefore, numerous research projects have addressed this issue and developed new approaches to overcome DPI's deficiencies.

Instead of analyzing plain text, statistical packet inspection methods (SPI) exploit the fact that even if data are encrypted or obfuscated there is enough information left that can be classified without breaking the encryption. Signatures are then generated by analyzing patterns (in this context commonly referred to as fingerprints), that emerge within single packets, fragments, or packet flows. The patterns depend on the underlying protocol, the applied encryption algorithm, or the transmitted personal data.

Such patterns include different features and there are various ways to define and calculate them. Common features, for example, are the packet size or interarrival times between packets [13], [14]. As described in [15], the range of features is broad and all of them may be combined in a fingerprint if necessary. The more features are used to generate a pattern the more robust it is against network influences or user protection such as padding or traffic obfuscation.

Generally pattern recognition is implemented in machine learning algorithms such as clustering, Bayesian filters (as is the case with spam filters), and support vector machines, just to mention a few. These algorithms have been tried and tested for a long time in classification research and are, therefore, ideal as a basis for further developments [16].

By now these methods are able to calculate patterns and apply them as signatures to classify data in real-time as described in [17].

Usually traffic classification is performed on distinct application layer protocols such as BitTorrent or Skype, which also use strong encryption algorithms and obfuscation. But classification may also be applied to web sites, downloaded films or spoken language even if the packet flow is encrypted. The use of encryption or obfuscation itself may even be utilized as information to pre-sort data into classes of encrypted and non-encrypted data and from there perform either DPI or SPI. It is also applicable in cases where any kind of data protection is prohibited or raises suspicion of malicious behavior to block this traffic. Thus, common protection such as tunnel software or encryption does not prevent traffic analysis. In combination with DPI PI-engines currently permit throughput rates of several hundreds of Gbit per second [18]. In comparison, the greatest Internet exchange point of the world (Deutscher Commercial Internet Exchange DE-CIX) has a throughput of 1.85 Tbit per second [19].

In conclusion, PI inspection may be performed either in unencrypted or encrypted data in real time at any place and any time on any user [20].

3   Use Cases

As stated above, PI can be used to secure networks. But the development of elaborate algorithms and highly specialized high-end hardware has led to a further possibility of applications such as traffic shaping, new pricing models or personalized advertisements.

In all these cases the basic technology is the same allowing different system extensions [21].

Traffic shaping includes both quality of service (QoS) and specific content filtering. It is used to control the efficiency of a network that is to delay packets to avoid congestion and thus improve latency.

While QoS is a technical term and refers to packet handling depending on whether it is a real-time/non-real-time application (e. g. post office protocol (POP) vs. real-time transport protocol (RTP)), specific content filtering refers to blocking or delaying packets depending on the content of packets such as P2P-traffic, certain websites or VoIP [6], [22].

By analyzing the amount of data a user has downloaded or applications he or she may have used it is possible for ISPs to charge every service separately. For example, the company Plusnet uses different pricing depending on volume, amount of emails, or hours of game playing [23].

Another application of PI is the identification of users' interests to be able to customize advertisements. The perhaps most prominent company in this context is Phorm, which delivered personalizes ads to users depending on the data delivered by British Telecom (BT), TalkTalk and Virgin Media and thus triggered a popular outrage [24]. The company Kindsight on the other hand uses these kinds of ads in a no-cost version of their security services. While Kindsight analyzes a user's traffic by applying DPI to detect attacks on his or her network, at the same time this data is used to personalize ads. The user may prevent this by paying a monthly fee [25]. Furthermore, there is lawful interception that refers to surveillance of private communication pursuant to lawful authority by government agencies.

As a general rule, network operators are legally bound to provide a surveillance infrastructure in order to be granted permission to exploit their network commercially.[7] According to the European Council Resolution on the lawful interception of telecommunications, "Law enforcement agencies require a real-time, fulltime monitoring capability for the interception of telecommunications" [26]. Because the technology

---

[7] Pursuant to § 110 TKG.

in lawful interception engines is basically the same as in traffic shaping machines, there is no possibility to distinguish if PI is performed for legal or commercial reasons. Thus the paradigm of fundamental rights may be shifted.

4   Impact on Fundamental Rights

4.1   Analyses and Storage of Data

To determine the legal implications of PI it is necessary to distinguish between the analysis of encrypted and unencrypted data.

While the analysis of unencrypted data may result in the examination of private data, in those cases where data is encrypted the examination of private data depends on the OSI-layer the encryption is applied to. For example, suppose that the entire payload of a packet is encrypted and only the IP-addresses are visible (as it is in the IPSec tunnel mode using Encapsulating Security Payload (ESP)) [27]. Then it might appear that a statistical analysis of the payload would not imply an examination of private data since the plain text is not visible. Thus the right of protection of private data would not be affected. But statistical analyses are specifically designed to overcome this obstacle and to derive the content from encrypted data.

As described above, it is possible to derive information from spoken words, downloaded movies or visited websites even if encryption or tunneling is applied. It is then possible to link the gathered information and to create a new context out of it. This picture can be so accurate that it profiles users even if this data is 'anonymized'. However, it is not anonymous, because it is possible to distinguish every single user [28].

With this in mind it can reasonably be assumed that the analysis of encrypted and unencrypted data may result in similar legal consequences regarding the invasion of privacy. The following discussion is based on this assumption.

4.2   Lawful Analyses

As stated above, law enforcement authorities are empowered to intercept communications based on different laws. Lawful interception is strictly regulated regarding the legal requirements involved in the application to monitor the communication of persons. In Germany only judges may order an interception and only in cases of serious offenses such as high treason or murder.[8] Furthermore, the core area of the private conduct of life must be granted.[9]

A critical point concerning which data may be monitored is so-called traffic data. This data includes all information regarding a telecommunication transaction, "indicating the communication's origin, destination, route, time, date, size, duration, or type of underlying service" [29]. Traffic data is very sensitive information, since it

---

[8] For example, in Germany pursuant to § 3 Gesetz zur Beschränkung des Brief-, Post- und Fernmeldegeheimnisses (Artikel 10-Gesetz - G10), § 20l Bundeskriminalamtgesetz (BKAG) or § 100 a Strafprozessordnung (StPO).
[9] For example, example pursuant to European Council Resolution on the lawful interception of telecommunications (96/C 329/01) or § 3 a G10.

might provide a detailed knowledge about a user's habits, friends, lifestyle etc. For this reason, Germany's highest Constitutional Court (Bundesverfassungsgericht – BVerfG) decided to annul the implementation of the European directive regarding data retention [30].

On the other side, ISPs are allowed to collect traffic data for billing purposes. If this data is encrypted they have to distinguish different services by applying SPI methods. So traffic data may be collected in real time regarding every user at any point in time, though it may only be used for billing purposes. The resulting question therefore is whether it is possible to know which data is analyzed and for whatever reason. The answer is: We cannot know. Furthermore, in cases of traffic analyses for billing purposes this data has to be stored to issue the invoice. This information is then available and may be used for further analyses. Similar to data retention, this mirrors certain characteristics of preventive surveillance.

4.3   Commercial Analyses

Besides the right to privacy there are other fundamental rights that may be affected. Delaying or blocking packets may affect the right to freedom of expression and information.

One peril is that network operators discriminate against packets of competitors thus causing economic damage [31].

It is also worrying, however, when packets are discriminated against on the basis of their content or because of monetary reasons.

On the one hand there is political, religious and other information available on the Internet that determines freedom of information, when a person wants to form an opinion based on this information and there is the freedom of expression on the other hand when the same person wants to voice his or her opinion. Blocking or delaying packets within this process would affect fundamental rights regarding freedom of expression, thought, religion, art etc.

Besides, the Internet not only provides a platform for communication or downloading media, but is also a platform for concluding contracts or forming associations of any type. Interferences with this kind of use of the Internet may affect the right regarding the freedom to conduct a business or freedom of assembly and of association.

But it is a technical challenge to detect traffic discrimination. There are different projects concerning this issue, but they take standard protocols such as peer-to-peer, POP or video downloads into account, but not other benchmarks [32-34].

These projects may help us to understand if and how traffic shaping may be applied. Therefore it is necessary to raise awareness and to educate users to use software that may help detect packet discrimination.

5   Shifting the Paradigm of Fundamental Rights

Taking all this into consideration, the paradigm of the fundamental right regarding the protection of private data is shifting in many different ways:

Firstly, network operators are legally bound to provide surveillance infrastructure, which they in turn may use for their own interests.

Secondly, in order to meet their economic interests, private corporations such as ISPs are allowed to collect data that normally is restricted and may only be collected within the scope of lawful interception. In contrast to enforcement authorities, companies do not have to meet the high legal requirements regarding the cause of the collection and the extent of the collected data. Finally, the storage of such data corresponds to data retention, which may undermine the principle of presumption of innocence and right of defense.

Furthermore, due to the fact that corporations may collect data or shape traffic because of their economic interests, there is a shift in weighting particular rights because these interests appear to weigh more than the right to privacy, freedom of expression and information and the other rights that were mentioned above.

Finally, another shift should be noted. Fundamental rights apply in the relation between citizen and state. They serve the purpose to restrict the power of a state. However, companies are private institutions. This therefore raises the question of how to enforce fundamental rights against them, which is beyond the scope of this paper. But it should be noted that PI increases the number of fundamental rights affected by private companies.

6   Conclusion

PI-engines serve different purposes. On the one hand they have been designed to secure networks, help to avoid congestion and increase bandwidth efficiency. On the other hand PI may be used to deliver personalized ads, shape traffic or to monitor communication on behalf of law enforcement authorities. Due to the fact that network operators are obliged by law to provide a surveillance infrastructure, which in the case of PI may also be used to meet business interests, these operators are offered a loophole for misuse.

Thus, the essence of several fundamental rights is affected. It is necessary to draw the attention of politicians and legislators to these shifts and to close the gap between the technology and the law.

References

1. Boehme-Neßler, V.: Unscharfes Grundgesetz — Anmerkungen zum Verfassungsrecht in der digitalisierten Welt. In: Institut für Wirtschaftsrecht, 60 Jahre Grundgesetz, pp. 155–188. Kassel University Press (2010)
2. Roßnagel, A., Mayer-Tasch, P. C., Saladin, P. V.: Radioaktiver Zerfall der Grundrechte: Zur Verfassungsvertraglichkeit der Kernenergie. Beck, München (1984)
3. Champagne, A.: Watching over you. In: Le Monde diplomatique (January 2012), http://mondediplo.com/2012/03/16internet

4. Brodkin, J.: Iran reportedly blocking encrypted Internet traffic (February 2012),
   http://arstechnica.com/tech-policy/news/2012/02/iran-reportedly-blocking-encrypted-internet-traffic.ars
5. Ingham, K., Forrest, S.: A History and Survey of Network Firewalls, A history and survey of network firewalls. Tech. Rep. TR-CS-2002-37, University of New Mexico Computer Science Department (2002)
6. Serpanos, D.N., Wolf, T.: Architecture of network systems. Morgan Kaufmann, Burlington (2011)
7. Anderson, N.: Deep packet inspection meets 'Net neutrality, CALEA, vom 25 July (2007),
   http://arstechnica.com/hardware/news/2007/07/Deep-packet-inspection-meets-net-neutrality.ars/2
8. IEEE 802.3 Ethernet,
   http://standards.ieee.org/about/get/802/802.3.html
9. IEEE P802.3ba 40Gb/s and 100Gb/s Ethernet Task Force Public Area,
   http://www.ieee802.org/3/ba/public/index.html
10. Ipoque, Deep packet inspection solutions for network operators,
   http://ipoque.com/en/products/pace-network-analysis-with-deep-packet-inspection
11. Netronome,
   http://www.netronome.com/pages/heterogeneous-architecture
12. AdvancedTCA Specifications for Next Generation Telecommunications Equipment,
   http://www.picmg.org/v2internal/resourcepage2.cfm?id=2
13. Liberatore, M., Levine, B.N.: Inferring the Source of Encrypted HTTP Connections. In: CCS 2006: Proceedings of the 13th ACM Conference on Computer and Communications Security, pp. 255–263. ACM Press, New York (2006)
14. Alshammari, R., Nur Zincir-Heywood, A.: Can encrypted traffic be identified without port number, IP addresses and payload inspection? Computer Networks 55, 1326–1350 (2010)
15. Hjelmvik, E., John, W.: Breaking and Improving Protocol Obfuscation, Dep. of Computer Science and Engineering, Chalmers University of Technology, Technical Report No. 2010-05 (2010) ISSN 1652- 926X,
   http://publications.lib.chalmers.se/cpl/record/index.xsql?pubid=123751
16. Webb, A.: Statistical Pattern Recognition. Wiley, Chichester (2003)
17. Ipoque, Net Reporter, http://ipoque.com/en/products/net-reporter
18. Procera, Products,
   http://www.proceranetworks.com/pdf/products/overview/Procera_Overview_Brochure_mech_2012-4-8.pdf
19. Packet Clearing House, Internet Exchange Directory,
   https://prefix.pch.net/applications/ixpdir/?show_active_only=0&sort=traffic&order=desc
20. Nguyen, T.T.T., Armitage, G.: A survey of techniques for internet traffic classification using machine learning. IEEE Communications Surveys and Tutorials 10(4), 56–76 (2008)
21. Ipoque, Products, http://ipoque.com/en/products
22. Bendrath, R.: Global technology trends and national regulation: Explaining Variation in the Governance of Deep Packet Inspection (2009),
   http://userpage.fu-berlin.de/bendrath/ISA09_Paper_Ralf%20Bendrath_DPI.pdf
23. Plusnet, http://www.plus.net/broadband/?source=subBox

24. Pfanner, E.: 3 Internet Providers in Deal for Tailored Ads,
    http://www.nytimes.com/2008/02/18/technology/
    18target.html?_r=1&oref=slogin
25. Kindsight: Subscription options,
    http://www.kindsight.net/en/solution/subscription
26. European Council Resolution on the lawful interception of telecommunications (96/C 329/01),
    http://eur-lex.europa.eu/LexUriServ/
    LexUriServ.do?uri=CELEX:31996G1104:EN:HTML
27. Kent, S., Seo, K.: Security Architecture for the Internet Protocol, RFC 4301 (2005),
    http://tools.ietf.org/html/rfc4301
28. Hoeren, T.: Google Analytics — datenschutzrechtlich unbedenklich? Zeitschrift für Datenschutz (ZD) 1/2001, 3–6 (2011)
29. Convention Committee on Cybercrime, Convention on Cybercrime,
    http://conventions.coe.int/Treaty/EN/Treaties/html/185.htm
30. Decision of the German Federal Constitutional Court, BVerfG, 1 BvR 256/08 vom 2.3 (March 2, 2010),
    http://www.bverfg.de/entscheidungen/
    rs20100302_1bvr025608.html
31. Gilroy, A.A.: Access to Broadband Networks: The Net Neutrality Debate. CRS Report for Congress (2011)
32. Dischinger, M., Marcon, M., Guha, S., Gummadi, K.P., Mahajan, R., Saroiu, S.: Glasnost: Enabling End Users to Detect Traffic Differentiation. In: Proceedings of the 7th USENIX Conference on Networked Systems Design and Implementation (2010)
33. Kanuparthy, P., Dovrolis, C.: Diffprobe: Detecting ISP service discrimination. In: 2010 Proceedings IEEE INFOCOM, pp. 1–9 (2010)
34. Basso, S., Servetti, A., De Martin, J.C.: The network neutrality bot architecture: a preliminary approach for self-monitoring of Internet access QoS. In: Proceedings of ISCC 2011, pp. 1131–1136 (2011)

Civic Intelligence and CSCW

Douglas Schuler

The Evergreen State College, The Public Sphere Project, Seattle, USA
douglas@publicsphereproject.org

Abstract. Civic intelligence is a form of existing — and potential — collective intelligence that is dedicated towards the reconciliation of problems that affect society collectively. The civic intelligence perspective has helped spawn various frameworks and models that can be used to inform CSCW analysis and design. This paper examines the particular relevance of civic intelligence to CSCW and discusses the implications and utility of its employment.

Keywords: civic intelligence, CSCW, social learning, social issues.

1   Current Circumstances

Words often fail to adequately portray the massive changes, both quantitative and qualitative, that have been made (and are continuing to be made) in humankind's vast and still-evolving information and communication complex over the past few decades. Historically cumbersome, rare, under-powered, and over-specialized, computers and other smart devices are now indispensable and are now more-or-less ordinary aspects of everyday life. Although the world has become increasingly globalized and interconnected, many problems still plague humankind. Additionally, new vexing problems have arisen in these new circumstances. In the face of these rapid changes that have brought us into unfamiliar territory, where opportunities and challenges are both abundant, we must continue to examine the perspectives and frameworks that we use to envision our work and carry it forward.

Civic intelligence is a concept that focuses attention on those issues. Civic intelligence is the form of collective intelligence that is operating when civic ends are pursued through civic means [15]. Without an explicit name, the phenomenon is less likely to receive the attention and other resources that it needs. John Dewey described the need for civic intelligence in 1927 [8, p. 143] when he stated that: "The idea of democracy is a wider and fuller idea than can be exemplified in the state even at its best. To be realized, it must affect all modes of human association, the family, the school, industry, religion." Although Dewey probably did not have a sense for the global ICT complex that would soon exist, his insights have particular relevance for today's CSCW researchers. And if we accept his implicit challenge, one of the specific questions we should address is: What perspectives do we as CSCW workers need to effectively think about (and even help imagine and realize) this "wider and fuller idea"?

M.D. Hercheui et al. (Eds.): HCC10 2012, IFIP AICT 386, pp. 369–375, 2012.

2   The Civic Intelligence Perspective

Civic intelligence is the name of an existing yet generally unexamined social pheno-menon. Civic intelligence refers to any manifestation of collective intelligence (see e.g. [10]) that specifically addresses civic ends using civic means. The expression refers to a group's capacity to perceive existing and future social problems and to address them effectively and equitably [15]. And since CSCW is interested in under-standing and developing systems that support cooperative work and employs an interdisciplinary and research-action perspective, it is one particularly appropriate intellectual "home" for an exploration of civic intelligence.

While not being labeled as "civic intelligence" explicitly, the topic is increasingly common as awareness that new, generally interdisciplinary, approaches will be neces-sary if our unprecedented opportunities will be used appropriately in addressing our unprecedented challenges. These ideas are being discussed in various forms including addressing global environmental problem-solving [18], new, more action-oriented mod-els of democracy (e.g. [4]), and many others. "Civic agency" [3], "strong democracy" [2], "civilizational competency" [6], "democratic reason" [13], and "civic capacity" [4] have been advanced in recent years. The term "civic intelligence" has also been invoked intermittently over the last century (see [14] for example). Since social progress (wom-en's' suffrage, environmentalism, abolition of slavery, etc.) has typically been attained as the result of citizen mobilization, this is an important expression of civic intelligence.

Civic intelligence captures a wide range of ideas in a conceptualization that strong-ly complement the ideas above. The concept of intelligence in a general way provides a variety of useful orienting features for an exploration of civic intelligence:

1. Captures the dense, dynamic, and omnipresent interplay between thinking and doing that is in constant interaction with the environment;
2. Captures the integration of disparate capabilities;
3. Learning is an essential capability;
4. Capabilities of intelligence (perception, for example) take on new important meanings;
5. Implications of being "tested" for adequacy or inadequacy in given situations.

Finally, although intelligence can be a useful metaphor, there are caveats regarding its use. Intelligence is not the only frame to use nor one that ought to be taken too literal-ly; while we can get value from comparisons with other types of intelligences we should not assume a strong, enduring, one-to-one relationship between intelligence in individuals and intelligence in groups. So, while we rely on our brain's amygdala for emotional cues and, apparently our sense of justice, there is no reason to assume that society ought to have a precise analogue. Also although a vast part of the brain is devoted to processing visual information, we on a societal level probably need to spend more of our attention on symbolic information processing.

3   Recognizing Civic Intelligence

Schuler [15] has developed a descriptive framework for naturalistic descriptions of civic intelligence examples and a more detailed functional or relational approach using the graphical modeling language SeeMe [12]. These approaches were used to derive the examples and traits listed below. Briefly, an organization or other group that manifests civic intelligence will demonstrate all or most of the following characteristics:

1. It has a civic orientation and works in civic ways mobilizing around shared challenges;
2. It does things effectively and in novel ways when appropriate;
3. It thinks, learns, and acts;
4. It performs metacognition; in other words, it thinks about its thinking;
5. It promotes civic intelligence in others.

Below is a list of examples of applied civic intelligence which, although generic, each has broad, direct implications for CSCW work.

1. Transforming schools and other institutions devoted to public problem solving — or, even, starting new ones;
2. Developing policy that promotes civic intelligence;
3. Organizing workshops or conferences where people develop skills or learn new knowledge;
4. Developing software that improves civic engagement (e.g. collaboration, information sharing, deliberation);
5. Developing new incentives and making resources (such as information) available for people who are doing this work;
6. Increasing public consciousness about public problems;
7. Developing new ways to think about public problems or to address new challenges;
8. Hosting public demonstrations or otherwise making public statements on these topics;
9. Using collaborative and other participatory techniques to create actionable knowledge.

4   Arenas for CSCW and Civic Intelligence

The classic paper by Heath and Luff [11] that analyzes the work of controllers in the London Underground is an early study of coordinated and distributed work that is supported by computers and other ICT. It is interesting to note that by extending that basic paradigm to its logical limit arrives at something like civic intelligence: we are all "controllers" to some extent, we monitor the environment and, after consulting with others, make adjustments. The world's environment, of course, dwarfs the environment that the tube controllers must consider and contend with.

In a comment about their work Heath and Luff [11, p. 143] also claim that "Despite technical advances over the past few years in the area of systems support for cooperative work there is still relatively little understanding of the organization of collaborative activity in real world, technologically supported, work environments." Now, nearly 20 years later, with the arena magnified by several orders of magnitude and the "work" far less clearly delineated, their original question takes on added significance.

The remaining part of this section briefly discusses a variety of new arenas that have emerged recently including deliberation, disaster remediation, social movements, and hybrid sensor/human based networks. The sketches below are intended only to provide some insight into how a civic intelligence perspective could play valuable roles in these arenas, through identifying and motivating new classes of tools, new partners, etc.

4.1   Deliberation (and Other Collaborative Tools)

Deliberation is essential to democratic societies and is increasingly being adopted in non-democratic societies as well [1]. It is the quintessential cooperative "work" of citizens and civil society. In 2006 an estimated 1,300,000 organizations used Roberts Rules of Order as their formal guideline for conducting meetings. Currently, however, there is little in the way of computer support for distributed meetings using these protocols (see [16] for one exception). While progress is being made [7], important and interesting projects involving a variety of "border crossing" deliberative approaches between people in a variety of countries and between people and their governments are still in their infancy. Additionally since deliberation is a type of collaboration it should be possible to transform these systems to include domain specific knowledge and practice.

4.2   Social Change

The recent Tunisian, Egyptian and other Arab Spring movements help highlight the new varieties of computer supported cooperative work we are seeing. And while people are still debating the relative importance of Twitter and other social media, the fact that they were used is indisputable. The new reality of oppressive governments seeking to neutralize these movements by adopting a social media strategy [17] as a way to counteract these liberating movements is also a part of the new reality. Although their work may arguably be called computer supported oppressive work, it is, in any case, an expression of the new realities which need to be considered as key contextual elements in the competing CSCW efforts.

The use of communication facilities to promote social change in oppressive countries can be extremely dangerous, of course, which prompts privacy requirements that are stronger than with other forms of CSCW. Also, it should be noted that activism for social change, a critical type of cooperative work, can also be met with resistance — even in democratic societies — at various levels. At any rate, professional interest in supporting change may be limited by a number of structural factors including funding.

4.3   Disaster Remediation

Disasters such as the recent earthquake and tsunami in Japan provide a useful, focused arena for civic intelligence approaches. For one thing, disasters help to focus attention on shared civic problems. They also supply a "testing" situation that is more readily examined than slower-moving, distributed, and more complex situations such as adaption to climate change. Also due to the immediacy of life-threatening circumstances it is easier to determine what is needed at any given time. Finally, there is growing evidence of "emergence intelligence" that arises on the part of the citizenry to deal quickly with specific situations on an "as-needed" basis often aided with social media and other new ICT. It is not obvious in advance who the new actors will be in such situations. This emergent intelligence is developed by latent, often un- or under-recognized civic capacity, that is often working in conjunction with established more "official" agencies. Bruns [5] does a good job of illustrating this in his study of the online response to the massive flooding of 2011 in eastern Australia.

Ideally a civic intelligence perspective on the disaster would necessarily move beyond the immediacy of the disaster as it was unfolding into a study of the indicators that preceded the disaster and the steps that are (or could be) followed afterwards. Civic intelligence establishes an expectation that we can devise systems that help prevent or at least mitigate the damage of future disasters and make recovery efforts of these future disasters more effective and efficient.

4.4   Hybrid Sensor/Human Based Networks

The distribution of sensors around the world extends humankind's perception and helps to create new hybrid socio-technological networks. For example, the new Pacific Northwest Geodetic Array (PANGA) that tracks small motions of the earth enables researchers to "see" almost instantaneously whether the Pacific Coast or Mount Rainier moves a few centimeters, thus enabling researches and officials to discover earthquakes more quickly and with greater precision than mainstream seismometers [9]. This results in earlier warnings, with benefits for the affects areas. This new field is poised to grow tremendously and with it a variety of collaborative challenges.

4.5   Other Arenas

Other new arenas including new media and open government tools, as well as any number of tools to support local (and extended) community work. The new field of serious games could also integrate and focus on civic intelligence in many ways, perhaps by explicitly linking the "games" to "real world" data and actions.

5   Civic Intelligence Perspective: Implications

Integrating a civic intelligence perspective into CSCW has a variety of implications, some quite large. After all, it is intended to help nudge the CSCW community (at least part of it) to modify its practice to some degree. This section discusses these implications.

Integrating civic intelligence into CSCW work could assume at least five forms, each of which has important implications:

— Adopting civic intelligence as the research or development orientation. Explicitly naming the phenomenon will help orient design activities through the use of civic intelligence as a conceptual frame.
— Designing systems based on civic intelligence principles and models. These principles and models were derived from successful examples and are likely to promote success. Hence, the evaluation of systems is also likely to help refine the models further.
— Promoting civic intelligence in users. This includes people who are involved in its design, development, and maintenance of the system, as well as casual or infrequent users, and indirect users. This includes awareness and motivation as well as the ultimate effectiveness of users in the use and promotion of civic intelligence.
— Creating socio-technological systems that demonstrate and manifest civic intelligence. The realization that our information and communication needs evolve as our understanding increases assists us in our design of technology that is designed with evolution in mind.
— Cultivating and engaging in deep and extended conversations with people and organizations about the future and its relation to information and communication technologies, especially with those who are generally not part of the discussion.

Adopting a strong civic intelligence orientation would certainly call into question how do we conduct our work and who is a worker anyway? We would also need to ask whom would we work and what roles would the various partners assume? What would the goals be and how would they be determined. It also, I believe, ultimately would force us to ask the questions regarding the support structure for this work. Does funding come from national science foundations or other government agencies? Does it come from corporations? Unfortunately the availability of funding — not need — can determine what tasks are undertaken and for what purpose.

Finally, of course, we believe that this work could be useful in helping to ameliorate some of society's problems. With involvement from the CSCW community, we can foresee refined and improved concepts and methodological approaches as well as new CSCW applications that promoted social learning and civic intelligence.

6   Conclusions

Civic intelligence informally describes how "smart" a society is and it's tested when societies confront shared challenges. It integrates social imagination, memory, cognition, learning, and engagement. Exploring civic intelligence is important as societies attempt to find solutions to shared problems — both large and small. The civic intelligence perspective integrates theory and practice by bringing diverse perspectives together into a common "real world" focus.

Civic intelligence, at least potentially, can inform the CSCW community by helping to:

1.   Establish broader problem domains;
2.   Establish normative and other orienting frameworks;

3. Provide a rich metaphorical orientation;
4. Embed the work in a broader context;
5. Provide a common link — or at least opportunities for articulation — between disciplines and sectors;
6. Link research and action;
7. Identify new roles and participants;
8. Inform methodology;
9. Consider our own civic intelligence.

References

1. Baogang, H., Warren, M.: Authoritarian Deliberation: The Deliberative Turn in Chinese Political Development. American Political Science Association Annual Meeting, August 28-31 (2008)
2. Barber, B.: Strong Democracy. Univ. of CA. Press, California (1984)
3. Boyte, H.: Reframing Democracy: Governance, Civic Agency, and Politics. Public Administration Review 65(5), 536–546 (2005)
4. Briggs, X.: Democracy as Problem Solving. MIT Press, Cambridge (2008)
5. Bruns, A.: Towards Distributed Citizen Participation. In: Conference for E-Democracy and Open Government, May 5-6 (2011)
6. Caidi, N.: Building "Civilizational Competence": a new role for libraries? Journal of Documentation 62(2), 194–212 (2006)
7. Davies, T., Gangadharan, S.: Online Deliberation: Design, Research, and Practice. University of Chicago Press, Chicago (2009)
8. Dewey, J.: The Public and Its Problems. Ohio University Press, Athens (1927 (1954))
9. Doughton, S.: GPS network may give us jump on trouble underfoot. Seattle Times, May 30 (2011)
10. Handbook of Collective Intelligence. MIT Center for Collective Intelligence, http://scripts.mit.edu/~cci/HCI/
11. Heath, C., Luff, P.: Collaboration and control: Crisis Management and Multimedia Technology in London Underground Line Control Rooms. CSCW Journal 1(1-2), 69–94 (1992)
12. Herrman, T.: SeeMe in a Nutshell (2002), https://web-imtm.iaw.ruhr-uni-bochum.de/pub/bscw.cgi/0/208299/30621/30621.pdf
13. Landemore, H.: Democratic Reason: the Mechanisms of Collective Intelligence in Politics. Collective Wisdom. In: Principles and Mechanisms Conference, Collège de France, Paris (2008)
14. Mathews, D.: Civic Intelligence. Social Education (November-December 1985)
15. Schuler, D.: Cultivating Society's Civic Intelligence. Information, Communication & Society 4(2), 157–181 (2001)
16. Schuler, D.: Online Civic Deliberation Using E- Liberate. In: Davies, T., Gangadharan, S. (eds.) Online Deliberation: Design, Research, and Practice. CSLI Publications, pp. 293–302. University of Chicago Press, Chicago (2009)
17. Sheridan, M.: Autocratic Regimes Fight Web-savvy Opponents with Their Own Tools. Washington Post, May 22 (2011)
18. Social Learning Group. Learning to Manage Global Environmental Risks. MIT Press, Cambridge (2001)

Informed Strategies of Political Action in IP-Based Social Media

Andrea Knaut

Informatik in Bildung und Gesellschaft, Humboldt University, Berlin, Germany
knaut@informatik.hu-berlin.de

Abstract. Political campaigning involves the intense usage of all possible media that the campaigners can afford to reach as many potential supporters as possible. Networked information technologies provide an endless source of applications and means of communication. When using computer technologies as a campaigning medium, it is essential to carefully assess the efforts concerning infrastructural and social requirements in consideration of the benefits gained. Therefore, the intertwined dimensions of political campaigning – content, infrastructure, community, protection of activists, planning, and archiving – are discussed as related to the involvement of IP-based media.

Keywords: computerized activism, electronic civil disobedience, political Internet campaign, participatory campaign, social movement, IP-based social media.

1   Introduction

In the late 1990s, Stefan Wray, member of The Electronic Disturbance Theater, divided Internet usage by extra-parliamentary grassroots social movements into five categories of "direct action Net politics": Computerized Activism, Grassroots Infowar, Electronic Civil Disobedience (ECD), Politicized Hacking (Hacktivism) and Resistance to Future War [1]. Networking technologies prior to the Internet Protocol, for example the Unix-to-Unix Copy Protocol (UUCP) or various bulletin-board systems, were already being used for political campaigns in the 1980s, yet it was the Internet Protocol (IP) that inspired the name Internet and which is now known for providing solutions to almost any problem. For example, concerning its capacities to be used as a political activist's medium, the "Internet allows for the convergence of meetings, debates, and research in one convenient and fast medium that greatly enhances not only activists' organizational capabilities but also the ability of activists to react to a constantly changing world in a timely manner" as the author metac0m states in the text 'What is Hacktivism? 2.0' [2].

In this article I will take a closer look at the basic structural requirements for integrating *IP-based social media* or the *Internet* into political campaigns.

Speaking of IP-based social media instead of the Internet in the title of this text is an attempt to explicitly connect *media* and *social* to *Internet* while still relating the

M.D. Hercheui et al. (Eds.): HCC10 2012, IFIP AICT 386, pp. 376–386, 2012.

technology and its history: *Internet* represents – as a historical name – the central idea of the implementation of an open architecture, all of which could globally network any computers regardless of their being parts of different networks. It was meant as an "Internetworking Architecture" [3]. Technically, IP is only one possible implementation of a certain part of this idea, which breaks down into several sub-concepts such as the layer model of data transmission, packet switching, or end-to-end principle. The IP is herein the technical realization of packet switching, and has established itself as the World Wide Web's underlying technology along with the Transport Control Protocol (TCP). *IP-based social media* are an implementation-independent computer network which underlies the constantly expanding plethora of media applications that allow for social interactions. Considering this, one could briefly pause to reflect on the triple tautology of *IP-based social media* and afterwards continue using the synonyms *Internet, Net, Web*.

The concept of *political campaigning* is understood according to Ulrike Röttger's definition: "Campaigns are dramaturgically constructed, thematically limited, terminable communication strategies to generate public attention using a set of different communicative tools and techniques [...]. Targets of campaigns are: raising awareness, building confidence in their own credibility and generating support for their own intentions and/or subsequent action" (my translation, [4]). Based on the idea of grassroots campaigning, according to Lohmeier, the actors of a campaign are to be included in the term: "A political campaign can be described as participatory if it can be influenced by everybody who should and wants to participate in it [...]" (my translation, [5]).

The structural problem areas of *Internet-based participatory campaign politics*, described below, are exemplified in the campaigns 'Initiative in Memory of Oury Jalloh' and 'Deportation.Class'. These are/were mainly German based extra-parliamentary initiatives in the field of human rights policy that gained a lot of attention. Both involved the Web "in a timely manner," but quite differently. These grassroots movements are described briefly as follows.

1.1   'Initiative in Memory of Oury Jalloh'

"Break the Silence" is the motto of the 'Initiative in Memory of Oury Jalloh' [6]. It was founded as a consequence of asylum seeker Oury Jalloh being burnt to death on January 7, 2005 while in Dessau police custody. Oury Jalloh's parents joined the prosecution in a lawsuit against two police officers for grievous bodily harm with fatal consequences and involuntary manslaughter. An entry on the website of the organization 'Caravan for the Rights of Refugees and Migrants' keeps a reader available on the Net, explaining to "all clubs, organizations, groups and individuals [how] to commit [...] publicly to the demands of the 'Initiative in Memory of Oury Jalloh' and to actively support it [...]". They propose, amongst other things, "making the demands of the initiative publicly known in your community (e.g., Internet, newspapers, magazines, mailing lists, etc.) [... and] sending your own experiences with police brutality and judicial arbitrariness to our contact address. We want to collect and document the cases to show that the case of Oury Jalloh is not an isolated one and that structural racism and police brutality exist" (my translation, [7]).

Accordingly, activists of different groups and individuals persistently arranged memorial rallies, demonstrations and an intensive monitoring of the judicial proceeding [8]. The case has received quite a lot of attention in the conventional mass media: there are numerous film, radio and press contributions.[1]

The initiative's website is hosted by the blog-publishing service Wordpress.com and there are relatively well maintained records of Oury Jalloh in the German [10] and English Wikipedia [11].

1.2   'Deportation. Class Campaign'

Since 2000 the Deportation.Class Campaign [12] has been supported by a broad anti-racist, decentralized Europe-wide alliance "against the deportation business" [13]. It aimed at making it widely known that airlines earn money with forced deportations. The violent death of refugee Aamir Ageeb during deportation was the campaign's motive [14]. A spectacular online protest explicitly based on the concept of *Electronic Civil Disobedience* was part of the campaign. On June 20, 2001 thousands of people paralyzed Lufthansa's servers for almost two hours with a distributed denial of service (DDoS) attack [15]. Their calculation of attracting a lot of public attention eventually reached the mass media.[2]

The campaign never ended officially but its online content is archived on [12] and has not been extended since 2003. The goal of stopping the deportation business was only partially achieved. I will return to both campaigns again in the following text which analyzes the cornerstones of an Internet-based campaign, the most important element of which concerns:

2   Content First

A problem and *political demands* connected to it need to be written out in full on many levels. It is necessary to address people with similar problems, to win supporters, to persuade others and to lead discussions with reproducible, solid arguments. These are usually published in brochures, leaflets, posters, press releases, and other publications with differing complexities of textual content. Additionally, there could be movies, sound files, perhaps even tactile elements, whole performances, in short: a campaign usually talks to all the human senses, its activists are looking for a broad multimedia implementation.

Initiators and supporters, however, should be encouraged to discuss *principal aims*, underpinning them with arguments. The reasons for participation and support – the analysis, interpretation and implementation of ideas – ideally constitute a truly

---

[1] The outstanding include the ARD documentary "Tod in der Zelle – Warum starb Oury Jalloh?", the Human Rights Film Award-winning movie "Oury Jalloh" [9] and many press reports, partly documented in [8] and [9].

[2] Some reactions of the press have been documented at [16].

participatory campaign. "In the ideal case, the difference between the initiators of a campaign and dialogue groups dissolves in a process of mutual influence and involvement; the *objects* of a campaign become themselves the *subject* of the campaign and thus experience themselves as politically decisive persons" (my translation, [5]). In conventional models of political interaction – without the Internet – this is achieved through workshops or alliance meetings.

The Internet can now broaden this discussion and strongly modify spatial and temporal constraints. In part, this initially can be done as unidirectional content provision using communication channels such as blog entries, postings on mailing lists, forums, in social networks, newsletters, film or image hosting, or by creating one's own campaign website. Furthermore, research opportunities are linked to for background information. Most of the chosen content provided on the Net can easily become bidirectional if people use the functions to comment and reply.[3] The range of ways to present and discuss content on the Net is versatile, as still newer tools evolve and commercial content providers change. It needs to be structured beyond specific software labels, structured according to the *degree of content processing on the Net;* to *the number of presentation channels being used,* to the *degree of the campaigner's creation of their own design;* according to the *accessibility by potential recipients* including, of course, barriers of language, writing, reading, and physical access (see also the following section on 'infrastructure'); according *to respectability of the resource being used; and* according to *the echo in those media not controlled by the campaigners.* This echo might be influenced in an advantageous way, but to some extent negative dynamics may also develop because a campaign is always a part of a complex discourse.[4] The degree of influence on the shape and durability of Internet-supplied content is strongly linked to the infrastructure requirements described later. Smaller initiatives often rely on the many existing commercial and semi-commercial specific application providers, where content can be freely designed only in moderation, yet in most cases relatively intuitively. Especially popular are blog and wiki hosts, video and photo portals, social networks, and online petitions. The administrative structures of these providers are often opaque and impersonal. So too is the administration of the content, the servers, databases, and backups used. Usually one is required to register before being able to communicate and/or provide content. Preferably very creative information should be used as personal data to this end (see section 'protection of individual activists'). Moreover no one is liable for the great risk of sudden data loss or spying on surfers' behavior via cookies or static IP addresses. Posting and retrieval of content such as streaming media or images almost always requires modern browsers and either large bandwidth or a lot of patience and

---

[3] There is also software like LiquidFeedback or Adhocracy that enhances political discussions by computer-based consultation and intervention processes. There is petition, bookmarking, calendar software and so forth.

[4] Discourses are interpreted here in the Foucauldian sense as "systems of knowledge formation, that control the conditions for exclusion and production of statements. They manifest as ensembles of statements, in which a subject is negotiated on a societal level." They always "depend [...] on platforms of social exchange, i.e. media" (my translation, [17]).

the graphical complexity or inefficient programming of hosting systems can also lead to too much traffic.

If I consider the two example campaigns given above: there has been a huge dynamic in the content production accompanying the Oury Jalloh campaign. The 'Initiative in Memory of Oury Jalloh' provides its press releases and reports in an online blog. The movies, radio broadcasts, and the many press reports are an echo of good public relations through a diverse and widely-dispersed community. The actual website is kept minimal, probably maintained by very few people. The contents are easily accessible for everyone with Internet access. There are some multilingual presentations and moderated comments.

Ultimately, the campaign depends mainly on the on-site presence in real life, the commemoration marches, and the anti-racist lobbying. The blog entries are used by activists especially for getting information about where and when the next direct on-site actions will occur, besides the painstaking trial reports and the links to other reports.

The web content of the Deportation.Class campaign distinguished itself by the fact that the campaigners created a very professional specifically elaborate design and launched it on a domain labeled with the campaign's name. In keeping with the guerilla communication-like character of the campaign [18], the design of the website and any printed materials strongly echoed the former Corporate Design of Lufthansa's advertising materials. One could order the printed materials through the online shop. Partial successes, reporting and links to reports have been documented in the campaign's log. The broad, pan-European network and the many decentralized activities of the alliance have been documented on the multilingual site http://www.deportation-alliance.com. Altogether the campaign thrived on the enormous ingenuity of the activists in how to circulate the central objectives. This included the purchase of Lufthansa' shares to facilitate protests at shareholder meetings against forced deportations tolerated by Lufthansa. Other activists regularly dressed in flight attendants' uniforms and distributed campaign materials at airports or tourism fairs. The online demonstration in the form of a DDoS attack against the Lufthansa website on June 20, 2001 was another central form of action. According to the district court of Cologne, the protest software was launched from 13,614 different IP addresses. Lastly, Lufthansa filed a complaint claiming to have suffered economic damage from the attacks [19]. The actual prior mobilization for the online demonstration had mainly been run off-line. The campaign Deportation.Class and its well-designed paper materials were extremely professional considering that it was a matter of autonomous extra-parliamentary activism.

3   Infrastructure

Both the creators of campaign content and the potential recipients most notably need access to a sufficiently *modern computer* with sufficiently *fast network access* and *enough time online*. If any of these core infrastructural components are not available for the initiators or the central target group, the use of the Internet medium is not a priority to take into consideration. Furthermore at this point, the *accessibility of a website in terms of poor environmental conditions*, including non-existent computer and/or network access or extremely outdated, slow, or unaffordable technology, rank among the main structural marginal conditions as well. Finally, *the accessibility in accordance with the "Web Content Accessibility Guidelines 2.0"* is also concerned. "Following these guidelines will make content accessible to a wider range of people with disabilities, including blindness and low vision, deafness and hearing loss, learning disabilities, cognitive limitations, limited movement, speech disabilities, photosensitivity and combinations of these. Following these guidelines will also often make your Web content more usable to users in general" [20].

The core infrastructure components of computerized activism thus correspond with the problem of the so-called *digital divide*, that spells out the Net's accessibility as a social privilege. Relating to above mentioned criteria Kling's two-level-model of the *digital divide* fits best: a computerized political campaign needs *technological access*: "the physical ability of suitable equipment, including computers that are of adequate speed and equipped with appropriate software for a given activity" as well as *social access*: "know-how – a mix of professional knowledge, economic resources, and technical skills – for using technologies in ways that enhance professional practices and social life" (as cited in [21, p. 96]). This view is appropriate here, though the term *digital inequality* is preferred and Zillien developed a more differentiated definition that resolves the inherent dichotomy of *digital divide* [p. 93]. *Digital inequality* includes the "technological, socio-economic and political realities of Internet use" (my translation, [21, p. 90]).

With regard to technological access, in the worst case there is neither a computer nor access to a network with high bandwidth availability. Confronted with that situation an activist can still use – if available – public institutions, call shops, and asynchronous communication such as mail. On the basis of the given financially affordable and professionally usable time, time-consuming items in highly interactive, real time applications are rather discarded. Ultimately, even small, seemingly static and unidirectional communication draws further reactions: These may be requests for interviews, comments in forums, emails or calls. Some of it might already be anticipated in advance (e.g., text blocks or fact sheets could be prepared). Any communication tasks on the campaign should be delegated to as many supporters as possible. Everyone is also encouraged to take over responsibility in designing the campaign in regard to the participatory factor.

At best, it is possible to fall back on a volunteer provider with dedicated servers in a trusted environment connected to broadband access. The campaigners acquire their own domain names and possess full right of access to the web servers. This would allow for a lot of room to maneuver, but can cause delays with unnecessary tasks as well.

The aforementioned campaigning examples already necessitated various degrees of technical and social conditions on both the initiating side and the side addressed by activists. In particular, the Deportation.Class campaign required people with expertise in professional web design, programming the online-demonstration software, and in hosting everything. Especially for such a campaign, the use of a "friendly" host is recommended. A host like that offers reasonably protected areas if it comes to the interests of powerful institutions. *Providing alternative medial infrastructure* for non-commercial, self-organized extra-parliamentary grassroots movements is an old strategy comparable to the creation of free radios, small nonprofit printing shops and the like. This could be seen as politically conscious technological access provision. Examples in Germany are antira.info [22] and so36.net [23] that offer Internet services such as mailing lists, email, web space, online project management software for developers, or chat clients. Sometimes small companies also support such initiatives – for example, the Chaos Computer Club seeing themselves as "Europe's largest hacker association and for over 25 years mediators in the stress field of technical and social developments" (my translation, [24]) lists sponsorship by medium-sized ISPs like HostEurope GmbH, Speedbone, Nessus GmbH, Inter.net Germany GmbH, and nonprofit associations like Individual Network Berlin e.V. [25]. The voluntary association Individual Network Berlin e.V. offers modem or ISDN dial-up, leased lines, DSL connections, and Internet services [26].

4   Community

A supportive community is part of the *social infrastructure*. In the development of a community, perhaps even with organized allies, it is essential to the scope of a campaign to have people who support and disseminate information about the cause, who solve many of the issues mentioned above concerning physical infrastructure, and who discuss the topics and campaigning strategies. The community is made up of activists who join the activities, who raise money, who allocate offices, and who act protectively in cases of repression. They also use their online time to pass the concern to others. Word of mouth is very important whether online or offline. Talking about the campaign, linking it on and to the right spots is essential. In a truly participatory campaign, every contributor acts in an emancipated manner and the initiators of a campaign merge into the community.

5   Protection of Individual Activists

The Deportation.Class shows quite clearly the boundary between Computerized Activism and Electronic Civil Disobedience. As in the offline world, both of which can already have threatening consequences for the protesters. ECD is more likely to end up in small complaints – depending on the legal status of a person or of the country even in big complaints, imprisonment, or deportation. As a consequence of the Deportation.Class online demonstration, for example, the offices of the organizing group Libertad! have been searched, and computers and volumes were seized. The domain holder of www.libertad.de was accused in a lawsuit [19]. The Federal Crime Police Office tried to pursue all IP addresses back to their users as part of their investigations. The programmers of the protest software were not implementing proxy usage by intention to underscore the legality of the venture. In addition, plans to conduct the online demonstration were announced to the regulatory authority in

Cologne [27]. Fortunately, the publication of the personal data behind the IP addresses failed at the time due to the refusal of the Internet service providers (ISP) [18]. Attempts by the authorities to acquire such IP addresses are less likely to fail now given the new telecommunications monitoring and surveillance regulation of 2002 in Germany and the consequent provision of the necessary interfaces to law enforcement authorities. However, the Federal Crime Police Office even then visited several institutions from which attacks were launched to try to get information about the users.

Anonymity as a means of protecting protesters is almost impossible to fully realize in the Net, especially if Internet services require mandatory registration and lots of social linking. A high degree of invisibility on the Net requires media literacy to ensure proper private browsing settings, usage of anonymizing services, and data-economical surfing. In addition, parts of the infrastructure would have to be housed by trusted providers who cannot be directly associated with initiators of ECD actions. Anonymous political action should be seen as impossible within the scope of the Internet. The protection provided for activists tends to come from the community acting in solidarity with activists facing repression. In every campaign, a real existing trust structure is essential for effective protection of endangered persons, and can probably not be fully built online.

Certainly, there may be a central disputable question, to what extent should communities account for political attitudes. Courageous people have to represent themselves as individuals, so that they display a level of persuasiveness. But ideas of justice, equality, or freedom from domination are universal and not tied to individuals. However, leaders, protagonists, or authors of important texts of a movement always play a key role. From religion to political ideologies to mass media discourses, both the author and the fictitious protagonist are important for the protest narratives. Thus, actors are formed with whom protesters would identify. An anarchistic approach to solving this problem results in the use of *collective pseudonyms* as Luther Blisset[5] or Guy Fawkes[6].

Overall, the role in which individuals perform should always be balanced based on political goals and the circumstances. There are also intermediate solutions. Responsible persons and participants of an activity do not always need to stand behind it with their name. At certain levels, pseudonyms, fictitious personal data can be useful; however, when it comes to the personal involvement of individuals, for

---

[5] "'Luther Blissett' is a multi-use name, an 'open reputation' informally adopted and shared by hundreds of artists and social activists all over Europe since Summer 1994. For reasons that remain unknown, the name was borrowed from a 1980's British soccer player of Afro-Caribbean origins" [28].

[6] In 2008, 7,000 people protested against Scientology worldwide synchronously forming a "global protest movement known as Project Chanology, a concept devised by a leaderless, decentralised group calling itself Anonymous" [p. 96]. They wore masks – "Mirroring *V For Vendetta*, the Guy Fawkes masks are provided to the public by rebels in a dystopian fascist state, in order to enable the public to organise mass protests" [29, p. 102]. The Anonymous movement itself is, by the way, a very interesting object of study of current hacktivism or ECD.

example, who bring charges of injustice against someone who is representative of many other persons concerned, an individualized trial can encourage a huge amount of solidarity for protestors, which is possibly an effective form of protection for them.

6   Planning

Right from the start, it should be clear how long a political campaign should last and what its different milestones will be. Of course, this can be changed later on, but a timeline helps in assessing the effort that can and should be spent on online communication. The capacities of an alliance cannot be bound for many years to one special topic. The Deportation.Class campaign gives a good example on this – it clearly focused on core events such as the shareholders' general meeting in 2001. The memorial movement for the death of Oury Jalloh is strongly oriented to the course of the lawsuit as well as to the continuous goal of keeping awake the memory of this peak of racist violence by state organs. But the character of a commemoration is not the same as a campaign's. Campaigning is not thought to be that open-ended.

7   Archiving

Documenting the history of a campaign is, therefore, implicitly or explicitly part of the same. Daily newspaper articles; radio and television broadcasts; and a campaign's own text documents such as reports and logs, photos, interviews, books, and all of its virtual and material scraps have to be collected and structured. That makes a lot of work and the new media makes the matter a little more confusing. Once the campaign has stopped, the feeds, tweets, and comments, briefly, the whole attention subsides and many sites become orphaned.

The problem of the transience of Web content is on the one hand a major challenge for libraries [30]. But, on the other hand, the uncontrollability of what remains and what disappears and of how non-vanishing is related to other data are precisely the challenges for new media in relation to privacy [31].

The non-profit organization Internet Archive, for example, crawls the web regularly automatically like a search engine for archiving purposes. The reliability of such services for documenting a campaign is questionable [30]. The collection and archiving of remotely scattered reactions, and the various copies and comments in different contexts can only be partially automated. One who wants to be the historian of her campaign and the reactions to it, has to write her own story. The 'Initiative in Memory of Oury Jalloh' is an example of this; it is to some extent a documentation campaign, whose own changes would in turn only be documented by Internet Archive with a few snapshots. The Deportation. Class campaign, however, has been partly swallowed as a primary source already as the domain was put out of use. Instead, the 'No Border network' has archived the websites of the deportation-class domain.

To this meta-level archiving many archaeological problems are connected (e.g., the illegibility of website artifacts if the formats on the Web are changing).

8   Conclusion

A network-based, participatory campaign presupposes a freely usable Internet. So will the hacktivists be able to keep their self-set role as guards of a free network world?

"Hacktivism is a form of electronic direct action in which creative and critical thinking is fused with programming skill and code creating a new mechanism to achieve social and political change. Hacktivists are committed to securing the Internet as a platform for free speech and expression. This ensures that the Internet remains a medium for activism and an environment that facilitates the free flow of information" [2].

The Internet is seen as an open space permanently threatened and monitored. A high level of expertise, such as programming skills, is needed for its preservation. The use of the Internet is to that effect and concerning the discussed infrastructural provisions a social privilege. In the quote above, creative and critical thinking was not forgotten – for all the knowledge of the technology may not help anyone if the Internet is not understood as social and as medium. IP is, as said before, a basically interchangeable technology and does not make THE mythical difference, as the title suggests, for the offline world [32]. The Internet is, on the contrary, in many respects similar to the offline world in its social complexity, regardless of the technology: "The forms of control the Internet enables are not complete, and the freedom we experience stems from these controls; the forms of freedom the Internet enables stem from our vulnerabilities, from the fact that we do not entirely control our own actions" [33, p. 3].

References

1. Wray, S.: Electronic Civil Disobedience and the World Wide Web of Hacktivism. SWITCH New Media Journal 9 (1998),
   http://switch.sjsu.edu/web/v4n2/stefan/index.html
2. metacOm: What is Hacktivism? 2.0 (2003),
   http://www.thehacktivist.com/whatishacktivism.pdf
3. Leiner, B.M., Cerf, V.G., Clark, D.D., Kahn, R.E., Kleinrock, L., Lynch, D.C., Postel, J., Roberst, L.G., Wolff, S.: Brief History of the Internet,
   http://www.internetsociety.org/internet/internet-51/
   history-internet/brief-history-internet
4. Röttger, U.: Kampagnen. In: Jaren, O., Sarcinelli, U., Saxer, U. (Hg.) Politische Kommunikation in der demokratischen Gesellschaft. Ein Handbuch mit Lexikonteil, S. 667. Opladen, Wiesbaden (1998)
5. Lohmeier, T.: Inhalt braucht Form. Partizipatorische Kampagnenführung für eine emanzipatorische Linke – eine Einführung. rls standpunkte 1 (2009)
6. Break the Silence, Initiative in Gedenken an Oury Jalloh e. V.,
   http://initiativeouryjalloh.wordpress.com/
7. Break The Silence, Inforeader Initiative in Gedenken an Oury Jalloh,
   http://thecaravan.org/node/702
8. Warum starb Oury Jalloh? Der Prozess, http://www.prozessouryjalloh.de/
9. Oury Jalloh, http://www.ouryjalloh-derfilm.de
10. Oury Jalloh,
    http://de.wikipedia.org/w/index.php?title=
    Oury_Jalloh&oldid=100873633#Einzelnachweise

11. Oury Jalloh, http://en.wikipedia.org/w/index.php?title=
    Death_of_Oury_Jalloh&oldid=471656087
12. deportation-class.com,
    http://www.noborder.org/archive/www.deportation-class.com/
13. deportation-class.com | campaign log,
    http://www.noborder.org/archive/www.deportation-
    class.com/log/index.html
14. Dokumentationsseite Aamir Ageeb, http://www.aamirageeb.de
15. Kampagne Libertad! – Projekte: Online-Demo gegen Lufthansa (2001),
    http://www.libertad.de/inhalt/projekte/
    depclass/onlinedemo/index.shtml
16. Index of archive, http://www.deportation-class.com/lh/presse
    http://www.noborder.org/archive/www.deportation-
    class.com/lh/presse/
17. Fraas, C., Klemm, M.: Diskurse – Medien – Mediendiskurse. Begriffsklärungen und
    Ausgangsfragen. In: Dies (Hg.): Mediendiskurse. Bestandsaufnahme und Perspektiven, S.
    1-8. Lang, Frankfurt am Main u.a (2005)
18. autonome a.f.r.i.k.a. Gruppe, Luther Blissett, Sonja Brünzels: Handbuch der
    Kommunikationsguerilla. Assoziation A, Berlin (2001)
19. Infomappe zum Prozess Online-Demo 2001, gegen Lufthansa (2001),
    http://www.scribd.com/doc/45267095/2001-Online-
    Demonstration-gegen-Deportation-Asylsuchender
20. Web Content Accessibility Guidelines (WCAG) 2.0,
    http://www.w3.org/TR/WCAG/
21. Zillien, N.: Digitale Ungleichheit. Neue Technologien und alte Ungleichheiten in der
    Informations- und Wissensgesellschaft. VS Verlag für Sozialwissenschaften, Wiesbaden
    (2009)
22. about antira.info, http://antira.info/about-antira-info/
23. so36.net e. V, http://so36.net/
24. CCC, http://www.ccc.de/
25. CCC | Sponsoren, http://www.ccc.de/de/sponsors
26. IN-Berlin im Web: Darstellung IN-Berlin,
    http://www.in-berlin.de/about/darstellung.html
27. Libertad!: Online-Demo vor Gericht. Ziviler elektronischer Widerstand oder
    Computersabotage? ak – analyse & kritik – zeitung für linke Debatte und Praxis 492
    (2005), http://www.akweb.de/ak_s/ak492/19.htm
28. Luther Blisset, http://www.lutherblissett.net/
29. Elliot, D.C.: Anonymous Rising. LINQ 36, 96–111 (2009)
30. Rauber, A., Kaiser, M.: Web Archivierung und Web Archive Mining: Notwendigkeit,
    Probleme und Lösungsansätze. HMD – Praxis der Wirtschaftsinformatik 268, S.35–S.43
    (2009)
31. Schaar, P.: Der digitale Radiergummi und das Recht, vergessen zu werden (2010),
    https://www.bfdi.bund.de/bfdi_forum/showthread.php?1697-Der-
    digitale-Radiergummi-und-das-Recht-vergessen-zu-werden
32. Cannon, R.: Will the Real Internet Please Stand Up: An Attorney's Quest to Define the
    Internet. In: Telecommunications Policy Research Conference 2002. Social Science
    Research Network (2004)
33. Chun, W.H.K.: Control and Freedom. Power and Paranoia in the Age of Fiber Optics. MIT
    Press, Cambridge u.a. (2006)

Corporate Social Media Use Policy: Meeting Business and Ethical Responsibilities

Don Gotterbarn

Centre for Computing and Social Responsibility, De Montfort University, Leicester, England
don@gotterbarn.com

Abstract. Rapidly developing social media technology has made obsolete many corporate computer use policies. New types of policies need to be developed which address the blurring of the distinction between corporate and personal computing. The gradual change in whose smart technology is used, and how it is used in the service of employers needs to be controlled to promote possible positive effects for the employer and reduce potential negative issues. The development of these policies raises significant ethical tensions in potentially controlling and limiting employee rights. These changes in technological convergence add new ethical requirements for an adequate policy. The lines between "business ethics" and "personal ethics" intersect here, and the ethical foundations of these need to be articulated in developing and/or promoting these policies. A technique is suggested as a starting point for companies to use in addressing these new ethics requirements for adequate social media policies.

Keywords: ethics, moral responsibility, social media policy, socio-technical isues.

1 Introduction to ICT Governance

The rapid changes in information and communication technology (ICT) have always presented a problem for industry in determining how to use and manage the new technology in achieving its goals. Attempts to do this have led to the development of ICT governance. ICT governance is an attempt on the part of business to deal with the impacts of major software system failures on business. ICT governance is both proactive and reactive. It is proactive in providing the structure for determining organizational objectives and monitoring performance to ensure that objectives are attained, and it is reactive in providing a standard approach to computing accountability in industry. The increase in the speed and types of technological convergence makes it especially difficult to specify a single framework to help with decisions, articulate rights, and specify accountability. ICT governance requires a specific strategy providing direction, policies setting boundaries, and writing procedures and guidelines providing clear details of accountability clarifying roles and responsibilities.

1.1 Early Corporate Computer Use Policies

Prior to the current technology shift, computing devices were corporate assets and employees used those assets. Those assets' communication capabilities and external networking infrastructure were paid for by the corporation.

M.D. Hercheui et al. (Eds.): HCC10 2012, IFIP AICT 386, pp. 387–398, 2012.

Policy Justifications: Ownership and Employment. A corporation's computer use policies were justified by simple principles about business requirements and the financial relationship between employer and employee. The physical computing hardware was a corporate asset which operated on a network paid for by the employer. Following these policies, employees should not attend to personal tasks during working hours. The organization owns the computers and the data on them, and these devices should not be used for personal communications. These claims were used to justify Internet and corporate IT policies such as restricting employee computer use only to business functions, and corporations' monitoring email on the corporate computer for legal compliance. Because all email was of a business nature, employees were aware of the normal business protocol of polite speech.

Social Media Policy and the Law. Laws eventually supported these claims based on the ownership of assets by industry. Some of these claims have been upheld in United States (US) court cases and also used to justify inspection and restriction/censorship of employee email on corporate machines. One problem with using laws to judge the use of computers at work is that technology moves faster than the law. This means that laws appropriate to an earlier generation of technology are used to adjudicate current technology issues, in effect, trying to apply policy designed for one technology to new technologies and to social changes. Inappropriate employee communication was easily controlled both by employer computer use policy and mechanical restrictions on the employer's computers. These computer use policies were about the use of computers at work and were based on at least two presumptions: the financial/work agreement between employer and employee, and the computers in question were corporate assets. The ICT equipment was the corporation's, and the company supplied staff to maintain it.

Negative Impacts of Social Media on Corporate Survival. The relation between the employer and the employee was an implicit contract that the corporation provides fair pay for a focused fair amount of work to support the corporation. Companies needed to control the amount of time devoted to work to meet project plans. The company's survival also depended on protecting trade secrets and business plans, and complying with financial regulations and environmental controls.

1.2   Mediamorphosis: Blurring the Lines between Home and Work

Improvements in technology (such as wireless communication and miniaturization), and the change in the ways we communicate (generally referred to as 'social media'), have caused many new and significant problems for employers. The boundaries between computing and communication have been blurring and raise questions such as: Is an Internet search on the phone while at work business or personal use of a computer? These changes blur the lines between personal and corporate computer use. Our concepts are further muddied by employees bringing their own computers, in the form of smart phones and other devices, into the work place.

Acceptability of Disruptions and Distractions. These technological changes have also facilitated radical changes in the acceptable use patterns of technology outside of the work place. Individuals are now in almost continuous contact through social media. Both the technology and its usage patterns in social media require careful ethical evaluation. Among the problems generated by social media are: a failure to see that the nature of the medium sometimes significantly distorts the messages; not realizing that built-in phone tracking may make it wrong to transmit messages from some locations: equating the degree of repetition with truth; the failure to understand the impact of messages beyond their video screen representation; and the career impacts of widespread digital information.

Prior to the development of digital media, in many cases work was partially defined geographically; people went to work, left one place for another where they worked. This difference in place made it easy to distinguish acceptable behaviors in work places and home. In the work place the employer's restrictions on computer use applied, and at home they did not. The information was also geographically distinct. Work-related information was stored at work on the corporate machine.

The convergence of technologies, such as the use of smart phones at home or work, for personal or work-related activities, has added to the difficulties of using geographical and ownership criteria to help employer management of employee computer use. Some have tried to maintain this simple physical separation model by having employees only use corporate supplied devices for their work activities just like the ones their employees own. Now employees are tethered to two separate, sometimes identical devices, one that they use for work and one that they use for personal activity. But both devices can be brought to work or home and used at either place. This weakens the geographical basis for distinguishing between personal and business computing. The clear geographical distinction was reduced to a distinction between the ownership of the tools. This was later replaced by the use of the employee personal smart device but with corporate software and an electronic partition of corporate data on the employee device. This physical blurring of the distinction between home and work tools is also the beginning of the blurring of when one is 'at work' and is 'doing work'.

Mediamorphosis. The blurring of distinctions within and across technologies is called "converging technology". Different technologies were enhanced and made more marketable by also performing tasks from other technologies. Computers were tools to do spreadsheets while telephones were used for verbal communications. These separate technologies now share resources and interact. It is now commonplace for individuals and organizations to deliver all forms of material over both wired and wireless communications. This has been called "mediamorphosis" [1].

2   Consequences of Convergence

The convergence affecting work, and the relationship of employers to their employees, is due to the connection of computing with other information technologies, media content, and communication networks. They form the activities, products and services that have emerged in the digital media space on information and communication technology devices (ICTDs).

There are numerous examples of the impact of the proliferation of ICTDs. Many employees own their own smart ICTDs using the associated social media. The introduction of smart technologies – such as iPods, iPads, and iPhones – has permeated society. The technology encourages and legitimizes their communicating on the Internet as soon as they are thinking it. These devices have introduced broad social changes. The impact of some of these changes has been addressed in legislation.

The systems developed for these technologies, such as aggregated searches, Facebook, LinkedIn, and Twitter have complicated the question of how to manage social media and maintain a necessary distinction between business and personal activities. Both businesses and individuals have accounts on Facebook. Individuals' LinkedIn connections can be used to make business contacts or to look for another job.

2.1   Social Media Policy: Requirements

Employers need to change the model of ICT governance, its justifications and its focus on internal corporate issues to address the changes in business context caused by converging technology. The new model of governance in its simplest form is a corporate social media policy. An effective policy must maximize the positive possibilities for the corporation to take advantage of social media and minimize its negative impact while, having a consistent ethically responsible policy for its employees.

Employer Benefits. Employers need to consider what this change means for them. This change seems to introduce possibilities of employees using their own ICTDs to accomplish employer tasks while 'at work' reducing corporate IT expenses for new equipment and the upgrade of devices and ICTD support staff. The phrase 'at work' begins to lose its geographical connotation and just describes the relation of the activity to the interest of the employer. Convergence opens up the possibility of a 24/7 work week. Since devices belong to the individual, it will be less likely that they will be subject to negligent wear and tear. From an employer perspective these possibilities are positive; however, there are also negative issues.

Need to Address Unintentional Harm. Employees using their own devices open up the whole question of how to monitor and control the work-related activity on these devices and whether activity on these devices can be monitored without negatively impacting employee privacy. In some contexts personal interactions assume a much less structured, and casual, form than business communications. Companies are finding it necessary to remind employees about proper business protocols when talking to a client. A policy needs to fulfil this reminder function because some employees are not mindful of these communications breaches but, once reminded, an employee cannot engage in unregulated, unmanaged use of social media.

A social media policy is an attempt to deal with the impacts of unregulated use of social media on business and it must include in its scope a broader context than is circumscribed by the physical work place. Sometimes, the problems are simply that employees have operated in a normal mode of sharing information but in an unthinking way. For example, a waiter used his cell phone to post a picture of a credit card receipt showing a very large tip from an American footballer. The waiter was elated at the extent of the tip and wanted to share the information with his friends; an almost 50% tip on a several hundred dollar bill. The picture went viral [2]. This waiter perhaps did not intend anything negative, but it would seem that he broke the trust between the establishment and the clientele, and this had consequences.

The waiter was fired for several reasons. The waiter violated company policy; the restaurant which often serves celebrities has a strict policy that their private dining experiences stay private. The picture he posted shows the footballer's signature used on licensed merchandise, and shows the last four digits of a credit card number, which in some circles are used for identity verification purposes. The footballer makes part of his living doing advertisements for a particular credit card company, had the footballer used a different credit card from the one he advertised then the footballer's livelihood could have been impacted by the waiter's posting the picture. The waiter does not own the credit card receipt, the company does and it is part of its confidential business information. The negative impact on the restaurant probably was not intentional. There are however uses of social media that can intentionally harm companies.

Need to Address Intentional Harm. The Internet has been used to record consumer complaints and record likes or dislikes, so some people have used it to develop corporation-critical websites such as www.walmartsucks.org/, IHateBarclaysBank, Starbucked, AOLsucks, and Noamazon.com. Some websites are designed to facilitate corporate criticism. Sucks.com is a micro-review site that does not require a name, email or a registration to express an opinion. Policies have to address these risks to corporate reputation. They need to address these attacks as well as employees' use of their own machine at home or at work, and employees' activities at home and work which might get then in trouble at work. One of the difficulties for a social media policy is that many employees consider social media use to be a purely personal behavior and reject as improper corporations' attempts to control it.

2.2   Inadequate Policies

Earlier employee computer use policies are inadequate and inappropriate for convergent social media. The basis for managing working time now has to include reference to usage of personal computing devices and social media accounts inside and outside of the workplace, and to corporate brand and image protection. Such policies can no longer simply rely on claims about corporate ownership of the computer and communications being done during working hours. Some problems for social media policies arise in part because an individual's use of social media blurs the distinction between public and private information, and between work information and personal information. Notes on LinkedIn, MySpace and Facebook are a blend of private and public information. These social media can be used to promote, criticize, or not mention a corporation. There is a need to balance the positive and negative effects of the policy.

Sample Policy Problem. In 2010 a company, American Medical Response of Connecticut (AMRC), fired an employee who had made untoward remarks about her manager on her personal Facebook account from her home computer. AMRC's policy stated that "Employees are prohibited from making disparaging, discriminatory or defamatory comments when discussing the Company or the employee's superiors, co-workers and/or competitors." In the United States of America (USA), the National Labor Relations Board (NLRB) brought a suit for the employee against AMRC to see if this policy violated employee rights and free speech standards.

The AMRC policy included the following restrictions: "Employees are prohibited from posting pictures of themselves in any media, including but not limited to the Internet, which depicts the Company in any way, including but not limited to a Company uniform, corporate logo or an ambulance, unless the employee receives written approval ... in advance of the posting;" and "Employees are prohibited from making disparaging, discriminatory or defamatory comments when discussing the Company or the employee's superiors, co-workers and/or competitors."

The NLRB settlement required AMRC to: (1) revise its overly broad rules; (2) ensure that its rules do not improperly restrict employees from discussing their wages, hours and working conditions; and (3) not discipline or discharge employees for engaging in such discussions. The NLRB concluded that such provisions interfere with an employee's right to engage in protected activity but it is reasonable to prohibit employees from revealing confidential, proprietary or trade secret information about the company. Employers may also incorporate anti-harassment and discrimination policies into social media policies and otherwise legitimately curtail employees' use of social media as it relates to the workplace.

3   Business Use of Employee Devices: New Requirements for Social Media Policies

The potential savings of having employees do additional work at home, be available outside of the normal work day, and use their own devices to do business has appealed to organizations. However, there are significant issues that a social media policy must address to facilitate a "Bring Your Own Device" (BYOD) environment.

Manage the Data on Employee Devices. The first puzzle is how to manage these devices. As in any work situation, the organization must be observed to direct and allocate rewards and encourage improvement of the work. Work must also be monitored so as to detect non-work activity. There are also security requirements that must be met, and the use of personal devices must meet the same standards as those of corporate devices. These standards include client confidentiality, protection of data, financial security protection, and legal notification. The policy must provide for ways to remove confidential data from employee devices and procedures to safeguard the data when and if it leaves the premises with the employee.

Manage the Software on Employee Devices. There is a need to control the types of software used on these systems. For example, some document-reading software has known but not fixed weak spots [3]. There are legal issues for a company if the employee device has and uses pirated software. Because of compatibility issues, once acceptable software has been tested and approved by the organization, the types of devices that can be used/owned by the employees will be limited.

In the USA more than half of the federal agencies encourage staff to bring their own devices. More than 50% of federal employees do this. The major puzzle for any social media policy which incorporates a BYOD option is "How do you control someone else's device?" This has been answered on a technical level using mobile device management (MDM) software, which enables corporate IT departments to manage the many mobile devices used throughout the enterprise.

Software is placed on employee devices. Policy enforcement typically calls for a small client to be installed on the device, and managed from a central server using over-the-air management. Functions such as policy enforcement and remote wipe are now standard. If a phone is lost or stolen, and this is discovered in time, confidential data can be wiped off the device. To protect the data they use a "sandbox approach" – they store enterprise data, including email and applications, in a distinct area of the device, and encrypt and password protect only that data. All other files including personal data are available to the employee.

These solutions are not available to smaller companies even though they are increasingly compelled to support mobile devices with fewer resources for managing all of them. A technical solution addresses some of the issues raised by social media in the workplace; restricting the applications that can be used in a sandbox (located on an employee's smart device) does not address how they use those systems and what they do when outside their smart device sandbox while at work. A corporate trade secret could be photographed and posted to "friends" using other applications on a phone. MDM software does not address the employee's relation to and comments about the company on social media. What is needed in a social media policy? The technical solutions and the justifications used to control employee computing are no longer adequate. A social media policy requires something more.

4   Social Media Policy

The basic positive goals of the policy should be to promote the business, maintain a positive social media presence, and promote the brand. The defensive functions of such a policy should be to reduce the impact of social media attacks on the Internet. An overriding goal of all corporate policies is to be fair and supportive to an employee's productivity in an ethically and legally responsible way. MDM, and similar technological solutions, do not accomplish this. A specific policy is required to help employers and employees make good, ethical decisions. The differences among cultures make it difficult to see common ethical principles that would cover the handling of social media. Some policies in fact render the lines between home and work less distinct because corporations have their own social media accounts on Facebook or LinkedIn. Corporations want to promote company-supportive use of social media, but the same channels can be used to corporate disadvantage.

4.1   The Goals of a Policy

Social media policy for organizations (a policy which has broad application to public, private and governmental sectors) should be easy for employees to agree to and understand why following it is important and reasonable; so giving (light) philosophical and practical justification for the policy is useful. The goal is to develop a policy that organizations can use, starting with behavioral regulations that is justified by high-level ethical/normative standards that address (i.e., include) business ethics issues.

Include Business Goals. A possible strategy to develop such a policy is to start by identifying the business principles that need to be protected, encouraged, and enforced by the policy guidelines/rules. The policy needs to cover both positive and negative elements, for example, "don't say bad things about your company on social media" or "without revealing corporate secrets indicate the virtues of working for the company and the joys of using corporate media to communicate on social media."

Consider Ethical Issues. After this we need to identify the categories and ethical principles that the policy must address. There needs to be an identification of the ethical principles that a corporate social media policy may be in tension with, for example, "free speech" and restricting employees from mentioning their work on social media, "the right to form a union", and "trade secrets". Some companies, like Telstra [5], limit the scope of its policy to the work environment. The policy developers need to identify what should be contained in the policy statement. It is imperative that they then do a preliminary ranking of the principles by significance (to an organization) including why it would value these principles, because it may not be possible to advocate all of these principles in a single consistent policy.

With these preliminaries out of the way, developers then need to address the internal consistency of the different social media guidelines/rules and conformance with basic ethical principles. Such issues might include how to articulate and address tensions between the control desired by business and freedom desired by individuals.

Given a general satisfactory set of initial principles, we may try to move from general rules to rules for several business models such as public, private and non-profit, and then examine sector-specific rules. Areas such as the law need to include rules to restrain staff from giving legal advice. Sectors like health care and insurance need to have specific rules about privacy and confidentiality. Be sure to identify and include other elements needed in other cultures. What parts of the policy will only require a minor change to make it relevant as it moves to different cultures? We should test what we do by asking how it would change when it is embedded in other cultures.

4.2   Requirements of a Policy

A social media policy has both business and ethical requirements, discussed below.

Business Requirements for a Social Media Policy. There are a number of employee rights which should not be restricted including: the right to organize and discuss working conditions, the freedom to depict the company in any way without permission and from making disparaging remarks when discussing the company or supervisors, and the terms and conditions of their employment. As a practical matter, the policy should define its scope to include all sorts of social media in any sort of devices. In the USA, under Federal Trade Commission (FTC) requirements, the policy should require employees to communicate that they are an employee of their employer when communicating information about the employer and make it clear that the comments reflect their own opinions and not those of their employer. The policy should make clear what information is restricted including employer's and customer's information but they may discuss their terms and conditions of employment.

Policy Examples. Many companies have started to rewrite their social media policies [6]. Policies vary from encouraging web participation to helping a company to promote its image to developing more restrictive policies, in CISCO, for example. IBM [7] emphasizes that companies should develop supportive social media policies, and it used a blog to develop its own policy. Kodak's [8] policy includes training in all forms of social media. Several of the more inviting policies still require permission and do not conform to the National Labor Relations Board (NLRB) recommendations above. Most of the policies predate the NLRB decisions of early 2011.

None of the policies speaks of the above-identified problems with social media. The convergence of communications and computers and social media systems has combined to modify the socio-technical context of work. This revised context requires attention to be focused on explicit ethical issues; yet the closest that existing policies come to address ethical issues is to say "be polite" and "use common sense". Intel's policy talks of "respect" [9]. Its primary focus seems to be on protecting and supporting the company. These policies could be significantly improved with some discussion of ethics and the moral responsibility of the user.

Ethical Requirements for a Social Media Policy. Social media policies tend to have a narrow scope that focuses on the relation between employees and corporations. Policy makers focus on how to reduce problems for industry caused by its use. They tend to focus on a limited set of stakeholders, and pay limited attention to those others who will be impacted. Stakeholders who are addressed in social media policies are the user and the company or, at most, those who have a financial interest in the company. Best Buy, for instance, has a clear social media policy [10], but with a limited view of who the stakeholders are. If you violate the Best Buy policy you could: "Get fired (and it's embarrassing to lose your job for something that's so easily avoided); Get Best Buy in legal trouble with customers or investors; Cost us the ability to get and keep customers. Remember: protect the brand, protect yourself."

Corporations tend to have a narrow a view of the stakeholders as being those with a financial interest in the system – the company and its customers. Corporations need to address a broader range of stakeholders impacted by their employees' social media use. The extended stakeholders are all those who are affected by the use of social media. In addition, a wider range of risks – social, political, and ethical – have to be addressed by any social media policy. Unfortunately, international standards are making the same mistake of focusing just on "evaluating and directing the plans for usage of [SM][1] within the organization and monitoring this use to achieve those plans" [11].

5   Concluding Discussion

As technology has converged there has been a gradual blurring of the distinction between working life and private life. Traditionally, the computer-use policy generally only needed to address managing employee use of computing while on employer premises. With the development of telecommuting, the policies were redefined in terms of ownership of the computing and networking equipment and of the data. Policies could be adequate if they focused primarily on the interaction and impacts of the relation between employer and employee. The current degree of technological convergence has introduced new requirements for any computer-use/social media policy. The whole range of social media is used by employees and the impacts of all of these social media need to be addressed.

Overly constraining policies tends to violate employee rights and causes resentment by employees. Such constraining policies also limit potential employer benefits from positive social media use of their employees. Technical management of social media used by employees is limited in scope to those employee personal devices that are known about by the employer. One of the critical weaknesses in many current policies is the limited view of who is impacted by employee computer use; also lacking is an attempt to develop buy-in by employees as responsible computer users.

5.1   Addressing the Ethical Responsibility of Social Media

In 2010 an Ad Hoc Committee for Responsible Computing was formed to develop a set of rules describing the Moral Responsibility for Computing Artifacts [12]. The rules currently consist of five rules as a normative guide for people who design, develop, deploy, evaluate or use computing artifacts. The document focuses on "the importance of moral responsibility for these artifacts" and encourages "individuals and institutions to carefully examine their own responsibilities with respect to computing artifacts." The document includes a preliminary definition of "moral responsibility" as indicating "that people are answerable for their behavior when they produce or use computing artifacts, and that their actions reflect on their character... 'Moral responsibility' includes an obligation to adhere to reasonable standards of behavior and to respect others who could be affected by the behavior" [13].

---

[1] Social media.

These rules capture some significant common elements of ethical action in different business sectors and across divergent cultures. Although they were not developed to explicitly address the specific problems identified above, they have identified some essential elements of moral responsibility that could help address some of the issues about social media. This can be seen by some minor modifications of these rules so as to show their relevance to the development of an effective social media policy.

Rule 1: The people who communicate via social media are morally responsible for that communication and for the foreseeable effects of it. This responsibility is shared with other people who have affected and contributed to that communication as part of a sociotechnical system.

This identifies moral responsibility both for those who create the message for its unintended but foreseeable effects, and for those who use a system to wrongfully harm others.

Rule 2: The shared responsibility of a social media communication is not a zero-sum game. The responsibility of an individual is not reduced simply because more people become involved in designing, developing, deploying or using the artifact. Instead, a person's responsibility includes being answerable for the behaviors of the artifact and for the artifact's effects after deployment, to the degree to which these effects are reasonably foreseeable by that person.

This emphasizes the relevance of all participants – tweeters, followers, re-tweeters, mis-tweeters, bloggers, and subscribers for the effects of a message. The one who unthinkingly re-tweets every message is responsible for its increased credibility. The one who designs or modifies the Page Rank algorithm is responsible for the censorship and impressions it produces. The use of the word 'foreseeable' indicates that a morally responsible person should pause and think about the consequences of each use of social media.

Rule 3: People who knowingly use a particular computing artifact are morally responsible for that use.

The moral responsibility of a user includes an obligation to learn enough about the social media and its effect to make an informed judgment. Claims about others on Facebook have had notorious consequences. The seemingly mundane playing of a video game at work may delay the delivery of a safety-critical product.

Rule 4: People who knowingly design, develop, deploy, or use a computing artifact can do so responsibly only when they make a reasonable effort to take into account the sociotechnical systems in which the artifact is embedded.

This requires that a person tries to understand the relevant system and how the nature of the system and its context will impact others.

Rule 5: People who design, develop, deploy, promote, or evaluate a computing artifact should not explicitly or implicitly deceive users about the artifact or its foreseeable effects, or about the sociotechnical systems in which the artifact is embedded.

Incorporating the sense of these rules in a social media policy would help address the socio-technical problems of social media identified above, and an awareness of these rules would help provide a reason to adhere to a social media policy which is not primarily based on corporate self-interest[2]. No corporate social media policy will be effective without the moral support of those whose actions are within the scope of the policy. This will be possible by using and promoting these rules as part of that policy or part of the education in support of the policy.

References

1. Fidler, R.: Mediamorphosis: Understanding New Media. Pine Forge Press, Thousand Oaks (1997)
2. Gibson, D.: Angus Barn's Eure: Peyton Manning check posting 'horrible'. Triangle Business Journal (March 7, 2012),
   http://www.bizjournals.com/triangle/blog/2012/03/peyton-leaves-whopper-tip-at-angus-barn.html
3. Lemos, R.: Espionage network exploiting Adobe Reader flaw. Infoworld (December 9, 2011)
4. http://www.informationweek.com/news/government/mobile/232600428
5. http://www.telstra.com.au/abouttelstra/download/document/social-media-company-policy-final-150409.pdf?red=/at/m/d/smcpf150409pdf
6. Boudreaux, C.: Social Media Governance, Policy database 2009-2011 (2011),
   http://socialmediagovernance.com/policies.php,
   (last accessed on June 10, 2011)
7. IBM, http://www.ibm.com/blogs/zz/en/guidelines.html
8. Kodak, http://www.kodak.com/US/images/en/corp/aboutKodak/onlineToday/Social_Media_10_7aSP.pdf
9. Intel, http://www.intel.com/content/www/us/en/legal/intel-social-media-guidelines.html
10. Best Buy, http://forums.bestbuy.com/t5/Welcome-News/Best-Buy-Social-Media-Policy/td-p/20492
11. ISO 38500, 2008, AS8015 (2005),
    http://www.iso.org/iso/catalogue_detail?csnumber=51639
12. Miller, K.: Ad Hoc Committee for Responsible Computing. Moral Responsibility for Computing Artifacts: Five Rules. Version 27 (2010),
    https://edocs.uis.edu/kmill2/www/TheRules/moralResponsibilityForComputerArtifactsV27.pdf, (last accessed on June 10, 2011)
13. Davis, M.: 'Ain't no one here but us social forces:' Constructing the professional responsibility of engineers. Science and Engineering Ethics (2011),
    http://ethics.iit.edu/publication/E-0077
    (last accessed on May 24, 2012)
14. Gotterbarn, D.: Tweeting is a beautiful sound, but not in my backyard: Employer Rights and the ethical issues of a tweet free environment for business. In: Bissett, A., et al. (eds.) Conference Proceedings of the Ethicomp 2011, Sheffield Hallam University Press, Sheffield (2011)

---

[2] This use of moral rules was first addressed in an earlier work, see reference [14].

Author Index

Alghatam, Noora H.   11
Ameripour, Aghil   349
Amrit, Chintan   134

Batenburg, Ronald   202
Boertjes, Erik   250
Bohas, Amélie   143
Bonina, Carla M.   22
Bouzidi, Laïd   143
Bradley, Gunilla   274

Cardoso, Ana   69
Carvalho, João   69
Cornford, Tony   100
Cukier, Wendy   156

de Wit, Joost   250
Dietz, Pim   134
Diniz, Eduardo Henrique   299

Eloff, Mariki   237

Fox, Valerie   156
Fuchs, Mathias   330

Gerrits, Bas   250
Gotterbarn, Don   387
Goujon, Philippe   287
Grobler, Marthie   215
Guldemond, Nick   123

Hercheui, Magda David   1, 123, 349
Herzog, Christina   79
Höjer, Mattias   170

Irwin, Barry   226

Jansen van Vuuren, Joey   215

Kajtazi, Miranda   320
Kavathatzopoulos, Iordanis   183
Knaut, Andrea   376
Kooij, Robert   250
Królikowski, Agata   360

Labuschagne, Aubrey   237
Larsen, Katarina   170

Leenen, Louise   215
Lefèvre, Laurent   79
Lichtner, Valentina   100
Loebel, Jens-Martin   338

Martin, Aaron K.   44
Martino, John   264
Masclet, Laurence   287
Masiero, Silvia   34
McIver Jr., William J.   1

Nicholson, Brian   349

Padovani, Claudia   56
Patrignani, Norberto   183
Pavan, Elena   56
Petković, Milan   111
Phahlamohlaka, Jackie   1
Pierson, Jean-Marc   79
Pieterse, Heloise   226

Raaijmakers, Stephan   250
Rahnama, Hossein   156
Ribeiro, Manuella Maia   299

Schuler, Douglas   369
Shahim, Abbas   202

Taylor, Richard   192
Twinomurinzi, Hossana   90

van Heerden, Renier   226
van Maanen, Peter-Paul   250
Vavilis, Sokratis   111
Veerasamy, Namosha   237
Vermunt, Geert   202

Whitehouse, Diane   1, 274
Wijnhoven, Fons   134
Wintzell, Helene   170

Zannone, Nicola   111
Zhang, Cheng   310
Zheng, Yingqin   310

Printed in the United States
by Baker & Taylor Publisher Services

Printed in the United States
by Baker & Taylor Publisher Services